Programming .NET
Components

Other Microsoft .NET resources from O'Reilly

SECOND EDITION

Programming .NET
Components

Juval Löwy

O'REILLY®

Beijing · Cambridge · Farnham · Köln · Paris · Sebastopol · Taipei · Tokyo

Programming .NET Components, Second Edition
by Juval Löwy

Copyright © 2005, 2003 O'Reilly Media, Inc. All rights reserved.
Printed in the United States of America.

Published by O'Reilly Media, Inc., 1005 Gravenstein Highway North, Sebastopol, CA 95472.

O'Reilly Media, Inc. books may be purchased for educational, business, or sales promotional use. Online editions are also available for most titles (*safari.oreilly.com*). For more information, contact our corporate/institutional sales department: (800) 998-9938 or *corporate@oreilly.com*.

Editor:	John Osborn
Development Editor:	Brian MacDonald
Production Editor:	Sarah Sherman
Cover Designer:	Ellie Volckhausen
Interior Designer:	David Futato

Printing History:

April 2003:	First Edition.
July 2005:	Second Edition.

 This book uses RepKover,™ a durable and flexible lay-flat binding.

ISBN-10: 0-596-10207-0
ISBN-13: 978-0-596-10207-4
[M]

To my daughter, Abigail

Table of Contents

Preface

I've been fortunate in my career to have lived through most generations of Microsoft component technologies. In the mid-1990s, I developed dynamic link libraries and exported their functions, and I used Microsoft Foundation Class (MFC) extension DLLs to expose classes. I experienced firsthand the enormous complexity involved in managing a set of interacting applications comprised of 156 DLLs and deployed as a single unit, as well as the maintenance and versioning issues raised by their use of ordinal numbers. I helped design COM-like solutions to those problems, and I remember when I first heard about COM and when I generated my first GUID using a command-line utility.

I learned how to write class factories and IDL interfaces long before the release of ATL, and I tried to use RPC before DCOM abstracted it away. I designed component-based applications using COM and experienced what it takes to share design ideas with other developers who aren't familiar with its requirements. I programmed with MTS and learned the workarounds involved in its use, and I marveled at the elegance and usefulness of COM+ when it came to architecting large-scale enterprise frameworks.

My understanding of component-oriented programming has evolved and grown over that time, just as the component-based technologies themselves have done. I have often asked myself what the fundamental principles of using components are, and in what ways they differ from traditional object-oriented programming. I have tried to learn from my mistakes and to abstract and generalize the good ideas and techniques I have encountered or developed on my own. I believe that I have identified some core principles of component-oriented design that transcend any technologies available today and that result in components that are easier to reuse, extend, and maintain over the long term.

With the advent of the .NET Framework, Windows developers finally have at their disposal a first-class technology that aims at simplifying the task of developing and deploying component-based applications. .NET is the result of much soul-searching by Microsoft, and in my view it improves on the deficiencies of previous technologies—especially COM. It incorporates and enforces a variety of proven methodologies and approaches, while retaining their core benefits.

To me, .NET is fundamentally a component technology that provides an easy and clean way to generate binary components, in compliance with what I regard as sound design principles. .NET is engineered from the ground up to simplify component development and deployment, and to support interoperability between programming languages. It is highly versatile, and .NET components are used for building a wide range of component-based applications, from standalone desktop applications to web-based applications and services.

Of course, .NET is more than just a component technology; it's actually a blanket name for a set of technologies.

In the context of this book, whenever I use the term ".NET," I'm referring to the .NET Framework in general and the component technology it embodies in particular.

.NET provides several specialized application frameworks, including Windows Forms for rich Windows clients, ADO.NET for data access, ASP.NET for web applications, and web services for exposing and consuming remote services that use the SOAP and other XML-based protocols. Visual Studio 2005 supports the development of .NET applications in C#, Visual Basic, Managed C++, and J#, but you can use more than a dozen other languages as well. You can host .NET applications in Windows or in SQL Server 2005. Microsoft server products will increasingly support .NET-connected applications in the coming years, and future versions of Windows will be heavily based on .NET.

Scope of This Book

This book covers the topics and teaches you the skills you need to design and develop component-based .NET applications. However, to make the most of .NET, it helps to know its origins and how it improves on the shortcomings of past technologies. In addition to showing you how to perform certain tasks, the book often explains the rationale behind them in terms of the principles of component-oriented programming. Armed with such insights, you can optimize your application design for maintainability, extensibility, reusability, and productivity. While the book can be read without prior knowledge of COM, I occasionally use COM as a point of reference when it helps explain why .NET operates the way it does.

In this book, you'll learn not only about .NET component programming and the related system issues, but also about relevant design options, tips, best practices, and pitfalls. The book avoids many implementation details of .NET and largely confines its coverage to the possibilities and the practical aspects of using .NET as a component technology: how to apply the technology and how to choose among the available design and programming models. In addition, the book contains many useful utilities, tools, and helper classes I've developed since .NET was introduced five years ago.

These are aimed at increasing your productivity and the quality of your .NET components. After reading this book, you will be able to start developing .NET components immediately, taking full advantage of the .NET development infrastructure and application frameworks. The book makes the most of what both .NET 1.1 and .NET 2.0 have to offer.

Here is a brief summary of the chapters and appendixes in this book:

Chapter 1, *Introducing Component-Oriented Programming*
> Provides the basic terminology used throughout the book. This chapter contrasts object-oriented programming with component-oriented programming and then enumerates the principles of component-oriented programming. These principles are the "why" behind the "how" of .NET, and understanding them is a prerequisite to correctly building component-based applications.

Chapter 2, *.NET Component-Oriented Programming Essentials*
> Describes the elements of .NET, such as the Common Language Runtime (CLR), .NET programming languages, the code-generation process, assemblies, and building and composing those assemblies. This chapter ends by explaining how .NET maintains binary compatibility between clients and components and discussing the implications of this solution for the programming model. If you are already familiar with the fundamentals of the .NET Framework, both in version 1.1 and version 2.0, feel free to skim over or entirely skip this chapter.

Chapter 3, *Interface-Based Programming*
> Examines working with interfaces. This chapter explains how to separate an interface from its implementation in .NET, how to implement interfaces, and how to design and factor interfaces that cater to reusability, maintainability, and extensibility.

Chapter 4, *Lifecycle Management*
> Deals with the way .NET manages objects, and the good and bad implications this has for the overall .NET programming model. This chapter explains the underlying .NET garbage-collection mechanism and shows component developers how to dispose of resources held by instances of a component.

Chapter 5, *Versioning*
> Begins by describing the .NET version-control policy and the ways you can deploy and share its components. After dealing with the default policy, this chapter shows how to provide custom version binding and resolution policies to address application- or even machine-specific needs. The chapter also discusses how to develop applications that support multiple versions of .NET itself.

Chapter 6, *Events*
> Shows how to publish and subscribe to events in a component-based application. After discussing the built-in support provided by .NET, this chapter presents a number of best practices and utilities that are designed to make the most of the basic event support and to improve it.

Chapter 7, *Asynchronous Calls*

Describes .NET's built-in support for invoking asynchronous calls on components, the available programming models, their trade-offs, when to use them, and their pitfalls.

Chapter 8, *Multithreading and Concurrency Management*

Explains in depth how to build multithreaded components. No modern application is complete without multiple threads, but multithreading comes with a hefty price—the need to synchronize access to your components. This chapter shows how to create and manage threads and how to synchronize access to objects, using both the little-known synchronization domains and the manual synchronization locks. The chapter ends with a rundown of various multithreading services in .NET, such as the thread pool and timers.

Chapter 9, *Serialization and Persistence*

Shows how to persist and serialize an object's state. Serialization is useful when saving the state of an application to a file and in remote calls. This chapter demonstrates the use of automatic and custom serialization and shows how to combine serialization with a class hierarchy. You will also see how to improve on the basic serialization offering using generics.

Chapter 10, *Remoting*

Demystifies .NET support for remote calls. This chapter starts by explaining application domains and the available remote object types and activation modes. After a discussion of the remoting architecture, it shows how to set up a distributed component-based .NET application, both programmatically and administratively. The chapter concludes by explaining how to manage the lifecycle of remote objects using leasing and sponsorship. Even if you do not intend to use remoting, this chapter provides a lot of details on the inner workings of .NET and its object activation mechanism, as well as scalability strategies.

Chapter 11, *Context and Interception*

Describes a powerful and useful (but undocumented) facet of .NET: its ability to provide ways to define custom services via contexts and call interception. This chapter explains contexts and how they are used to implement component services, as well as the interception architecture and how to extend it. It ends with a walk-through of two real-life productivity-oriented custom services.

Chapter 12, *Security*

Addresses the rich topic of .NET code-access security. Unlike Windows security, .NET security is component-based, not user-based. As such, it opens new possibilities for component developers. This chapter shows how to administer security using the .NET configuration tool and how to provide additional security programmatically. It also covers how to use .NET role-based security and how to install a custom authorization mechanism.

Appendix A, *Interface-Based Web Services*

Shows how to enforce a core principle of component-oriented programming—separation of interface from implementation—when using .NET web services, both on the service side and the client side.

Appendix B, *Unifying Windows Forms and ASP.NET Security*

Presents a set of interacting helper classes and controls that enable a Windows Forms application to use the ASP.NET 2.0 credential-management infrastructure with the same ease as if it were an ASP.NET application. This provides the productivity benefits of ASP.NET as well as a unified credentials store, regardless of the application user interface.

Appendix C, *Reflection and Attributes*

Explains .NET reflection and how to develop and reflect custom attributes. If you aren't familiar with reflection, I recommend reading this appendix before the rest of the chapters.

Appendix D, *Generics*

Briefly explains generics, which are some of the most powerful and useful features of .NET 2.0. This book makes extensive use of generics in almost every chapter. If you are unfamiliar with generics, I recommend that you read this appendix before the rest of the chapters. More advanced aspects of generics are covered in the chapters themselves.

Appendix E, *C# Coding Standard*

Presents a consolidated list of all the best practices and dos and don'ts mentioned thought the book. The standard is all about the "how" and the "what," not the "why"; the rationale behind it is found in the rest of the book. The standard is based on the IDesign Coding Standard, which has become the de facto industry coding standard for .NET development. The IDesign standard in turn was based on the first edition of this book.

Some Assumptions About the Reader

I assume that you, the reader, are an experienced developer and that you feel comfortable with object-oriented concepts such as encapsulation and inheritance. I also assume that you have basic familiarity with either C# or Visual Basic, both in versions 1.1 and 2.0 of the languages. Although the book uses C# for the most part, it's just as pertinent to Visual Basic 2005 developers. In cases in which the translation from C# to Visual Basic 2005 isn't straightforward or when the two languages differ significantly, I've provided either matching Visual Basic 2005 sample code or an explicit note.

If you're experienced with COM, this book will port your COM understanding to .NET. If you've never used COM before, you'll find the coverage of the principles of component-oriented programming especially useful.

Conventions Used in This Book

The following typographic conventions are used in this book:

- *Italic* is used for definitions of technical terms, URLs, filenames, directory names, and pathnames.
- `Constant width` is used for code samples, statements, namespaces, classes, assemblies, interface directives, operators, attributes, and reserved words.
- **`Bold constant width`** is used for emphasis in code samples.

 This icon designates a note that is an important aside to the nearby text.

 This icon designates a warning relating to the nearby text.

Whenever I wish to make a point in a code sample, I do so with the static `Assert` method of the `Debug` class:

```
int number = 1+2;
Debug.Assert(number == 3);
```

The `Assert` method accepts a Boolean statement and throws an exception when the statement is false.

This book follows the recommended naming guidelines and coding style presented in Appendix E. Whenever it deviates from that standard, it is likely the result of space or line-length constraints. With respect to naming conventions, I use "Pascal casing" for public member methods and properties; this means the first letter of each word in the name is capitalized. For local variables and method parameters I use "Camel casing," in which the first letter of the first word of the name is not capitalized. I prefix private member variables with an `m_`:

```
public class SomeClass
{
  private int m_Number;

  public int Number
  {get;set};
}
```

I use ellipses between curly braces to indicate the presence of code that is necessary but unspecified:

```
public class SomeClass
{...}
```

In the interests of clarity and space conservation, code examples often don't contain all the using statements needed to specify all the namespaces the examples require; instead, such examples include only the new namespaces introduced in the preceding text.

Comments and Questions

Please address comments and questions concerning this book to the publisher:

O'Reilly Media, Inc.
1005 Gravenstein Highway North
Sebastopol, CA 95472
(800) 998-9938 (in the United States or Canada)
(707) 829-0515 (international/local)
(707) 829-0104 (fax)

There is a web page for this book, which lists errata, examples, and any additional information. You can access this page at:

http://www.oreilly.com/catalog/pnetcomp2

To comment or ask technical questions about this book, send email to:

bookquestions@oreilly.com

You can also contact the me at:

http://www.idesign.net

For more information about books, conferences, Resource Centers, and the O'Reilly Network, see the O'Reilly web site at:

http://www.oreilly.com

Safari Enabled

 When you see a Safari® Enabled icon on the cover of your favorite technology book, that means the book is available online through the O'Reilly Network Safari Bookshelf.

Safari offers a solution that's better than e-books. It's a virtual library that lets you easily search thousands of top tech books, cut and paste code samples, download chapters, and find quick answers when you need the most accurate, current information. Try it free for at *http://safari.oreilly.com*.

Acknowledgments

Shortly after the unveiling of .NET in the summer of 2000, John Osborn from O'Reilly and I started discussing a book that would explore the uses of .NET as a component-based application development platform. The first edition of the book was the result of John's sponsorship and support. Over the last three years I have worked closely with Microsoft as part of the Strategic Design Review process for .NET 2.0, which has provided me with experience and insight into the making of .NET 2.0. I am grateful to the following product and project managers: Dan Fernandez and Eric Gunnerson from the C# team, Amanda Silver from the Visual Basic team, John Rivard from the CLR team, and Matt Tavis and Yasser Shohoud from the Indigo team. Special thanks to Anson Horton, a C# program manager, for his insight, amazing expertise, and guidance.

The following friends and colleagues helped with the first edition of the book: Chris W. Rea, Billy Hollis, Jimmy Nilsson, Nicholas Paldino, Ingo Rammer, and Pradeep Tapadiya. The following provided valuable feedback for the second edition: Sam Gentile, Richard Grimes, Norman Headlam, Benjamin Mitchell, and Brian Noyes. All of them gave generously of their time. In particular, I am grateful to Nicholas Paldino for his help with the second edition. Nick's knowledge of the framework is unsurpassed, and his meticulous attention to details contributed greatly to the quality and cohesiveness of this book.

Finally, my family. Many thanks to my wife Dana, who knows all too well that writing a book entails time away from the family but still encourages me to write. I dedicate this book to my five-year-old daughter Abigail. She has her own computer now, where she enthusiastically plays her Princesses games. I am waiting for the day I can talk with her about the principles of building systems and services out of components. I think I am going to start with interfaces.

CHAPTER 1

Introducing Component-Oriented Programming

Over the last decade, component-oriented programming has established itself as the predominant software development methodology. The software industry is moving away from giant, monolithic, hard-to-maintain code bases. Practitioners have discovered that by breaking down a system into binary components, they can attain much greater reusability, extensibility, and maintainability. These benefits can, in turn, lead to faster time to market, more robust and highly scalable applications, and lower development and long-term maintenance costs. Consequently, it's no coincidence that component-oriented programming has caught on in a big way.

Several component technologies, such as DCOM, CORBA, and JavaBeans™ give programmers the means to implement component-oriented applications. However, each technology has its drawbacks; for example, DCOM is too difficult to master, and the Java™ Virtual Machine (JVM) doesn't support interoperation with other languages.

.NET is the latest entrant to the field, and as you will see later in this chapter and in the rest of this book, it addresses the requirements of component-oriented programming in a way that is both unique and vastly easier to use. These improvements are of little surprise, because the .NET architects were able to learn from both the mistakes and successes of previous technologies.

In this chapter, I'll define the basic terms of component-oriented programming and summarize its core principles and their corresponding benefits. These principles apply throughout the book, and I'll refer to them in later chapters when describing the motivations for particular .NET design patterns.

Component-oriented programming is different from object-oriented programming, although the two methodologies do have things in common. You could say that component-oriented programming sprouted from the well of object-oriented programming methodologies. Therefore, this chapter also contrasts component-oriented programming and object-oriented programming, while briefly discussing .NET as a component technology.

Basic Terminology

The term *component* is probably one of the most overloaded and therefore most confusing terms in modern software engineering, and the .NET documentation has its fair share of inconsistency in its handling of this concept. The confusion arises in deciding where to draw the line between a class that implements some logic, the physical entity that contains it (typically a dynamic link library, or DLL), and the associated logic used to deploy and use it, including type information, security policy, and versioning information (called an *assembly* in .NET). In this book, a component is a .NET class. For example, this is a .NET component:

```
public class MyClass
{
    public string GetMessage( )
    {
        return "Hello";
    }
}
```

Chapter 2 discusses DLLs and assemblies and explains the rationale behind physical and logical packaging. It also discusses why it is that every .NET class, unlike traditional object-oriented classes, is a binary component.

A component is responsible for exposing business logic to clients. A *client* is any entity that uses the component, although typically, clients are simply other classes. The client's code can be packaged in the same physical unit as the component, in the same logical unit but in a separate physical unit, or in separate physical and logical units altogether. The client code should not have to make any assumptions about such details. An *object* is an instance of a component, a definition that is similar to the classic object-oriented definition of an object as an instance of a class. The object is also sometimes referred to as the *server*, because the relationship between client and object is often called the *client/server* model. In this model, the client creates an object and accesses its functionality via a publicly available entry point, traditionally a public method but preferably an interface, as illustrated by Figure 1-1. Note that in the figure an object is an instance of a component; the "lollipop" denotes an interface.

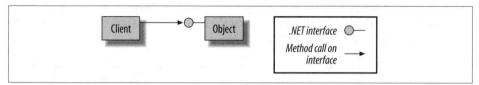

Figure 1-1. A client accessing an object

I'll discuss .NET interface-based programming in detail in Chapter 3. For now, it's important to emphasize that while .NET doesn't force you to do interface-based programming, as you will see shortly, you should strive to do so whenever possible. To emphasize this practice, I represent the entry points of the components that appear in my design diagrams as interfaces rather than mere public methods.

Although the object depicted in Figure 1-1 is drawn like a COM object, with its characteristic lollipop icon, use of this icon isn't restricted to COM—it is accepted as the standard UML symbol for an interface, regardless of the component technology and development platform that implement it.

Interface-based programming promotes *encapsulation*, or the hiding of information from the client. The less a client knows about the way an object is implemented, the better. The more the details of an implementation are encapsulated, the greater is the likelihood that you can change a method or property without affecting the client code. Interfaces maximize encapsulation because the client interacts with an abstract service definition instead of an actual object. Encapsulation is key to successfully applying both object-oriented and component-oriented methodologies.

Another important concept that originated with object-oriented programming is *polymorphism*. Two objects are said to be polymorphic with respect to each other when both derive from a common base type (such as an interface) and implement the exact set of operations defined by that base type. If a client is written to use the operations of a base type, the same client code can interact with any object that is polymorphic with that base type. When polymorphism is used properly, changing from one object to another has no effect on the client; it simplifies maintenance of the application to which the client and object belong.

Component-Oriented Versus Object-Oriented Programming

If every .NET class is a component, and if classes and components share so many qualities, then what is the difference between traditional object-oriented programming and component-oriented programming? In a nutshell, object-oriented programming focuses on the relationships between classes that are combined into one large binary executable, while component-oriented programming focuses on interchangeable code modules that work independently and don't require you to be familiar with their inner workings to use them.

Building Blocks Versus Monolithic Applications

The fundamental difference between the two methodologies is the way in which they view the final application. In the traditional object-oriented world, even though you may factor the business logic into many fine-grained classes, once those classes are compiled, the result is monolithic binary code. All the classes share the same physical deployment unit (typically an EXE), process, address space, security privileges, and so on. If multiple developers work on the same code base, they have to share source files.

In such an application, a change made to one class can trigger a massive re-linking of the entire application and necessitate retesting and redeployment of all the other classes.

On the other hand, a component-oriented application comprises a collection of interacting binary application modules—that is, its components and the calls that bind them (see Figure 1-2).

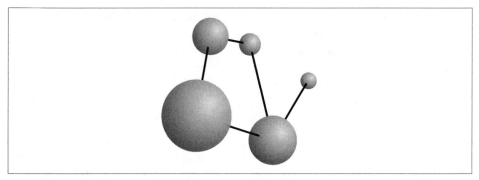

Figure 1-2. A component-oriented application

A particular binary component may not do much on its own. Some may be general-purpose components, such as communication wrappers or file-access components. Others may be highly specialized and developed specifically for the application. An application implements and executes its required business logic by gluing together the functionality offered by the individual components. Component-enabling technologies such as COM, J2EE, CORBA, and .NET provide the "plumbing" or infrastructure needed to connect binary components in a seamless manner, and the main distinction between these technologies is the ease with which they allow you to connect those components.

The motivation for breaking down a monolithic application into multiple binary components is analogous to that for placing the code for different classes into different files. By placing the code for each class in an application into its own file, you loosen the coupling between the classes and the developers responsible for them. If you make a change to one class, although you'll have to re-link the entire application, you'll only need to recompile the source file for that class.

However, there is more to component-oriented programming than simple software project management. Because a component-based application is a collection of binary building blocks, you can treat its components like LEGO bricks, adding and removing them as you see fit. If you need to modify a component implementation, changes are contained to that component only. No existing client of the component requires recompilation or redeployment. Components can even be updated while a client application is running, as long as the components aren't currently being used. Improvements, enhancements, and fixes made to a component will immediately be available to all applications that use that component, whether on the same machine or across a network.

A component-oriented application is easier to extend, as well. When you have new requirements to implement, you can provide them in new components, without having to touch existing components not affected by the new requirements.

These factors enable component-oriented programming to reduce the cost of long-term maintenance, a factor essential to almost any business, which helps explain the widespread adoption of component technologies.

Component-oriented applications usually have a faster time to market, because you can select from a range of available components, either from in-house collections or from third-party component vendors, and thus avoid repeatedly reinventing the wheel. For example, consider the rapid development enjoyed by many Visual Basic projects, which rely on libraries of ActiveX controls for almost every aspect of the application.

Interfaces Versus Inheritance

Another important difference between object-oriented and component-oriented applications is the emphasis the two models place on inheritance and reuse models.

In object-oriented analysis and design, applications are often modeled as complex hierarchies of classes, which are designed to approximate as closely as possible the business problem being solved. You reuse existing code by inheriting it from an existing base class and specializing its behavior. The problem is that inheritance is a poor way to achieve reuse. When you derive a subclass from a base class, you must be intimately aware of the implementation details of the base class. For example, what is the side effect of changing the value of a member variable? How does it affect the code in the base class? Will overriding a base class method and providing a different behavior break the code of clients that expect the base behavior?

This form of reuse is commonly known as *white-box reuse*, because you are required to be familiar with the details of the base class implementation. White-box reuse simply doesn't allow for economy of scale in large organizations' reuse programs or easy adoption of third-party frameworks.

Component-oriented programming promotes *black-box reuse* instead, which allows you to use an existing component without caring about its internals, as long as the component complies with some predefined set of operations or interfaces. Instead of investing in designing complex class hierarchies, component-oriented developers spend most of their time factoring out the interfaces used as contracts between components and clients.

 .NET does allow components to use inheritance of implementation, and you can certainly use this technique to develop complex class hierarchies. However, you should keep your class hierarchies as simple and as flat as possible, and focus instead on factoring interfaces. Doing so promotes black-box reuse of your component instead of white-box reuse via inheritance.

Finally, object-oriented programming provides few tools or design patterns for dealing with the runtime aspects of the application, such as multithreading and concurrency management, security, distributed applications, deployment, or version control. Object-oriented developers are more or less left to their own devices when it comes to providing infrastructure for handling these common requirements. As you will see throughout this book, .NET supports you by providing a superb component-development infrastructure. Using .NET, you can focus on the business problem at hand instead of the software infrastructure needed to build the solution.

Principles of Component-Oriented Programming

Component-oriented programming requires both systems that support the approach and programmers that adhere to its discipline and its core principles. However, it's often hard to tell the difference between a true principle and a mere feature of the component technology being used. As the supporting technologies become more powerful, no doubt software engineering will extend its understanding of what constitutes component-oriented programming and embrace new ideas, and the core principles will continue to evolve. The most important principles of component-oriented programming include:

- Separation of interface and implementation
- Binary compatibility
- Language independence
- Location transparency
- Concurrency management
- Version control
- Component-based security

The following subsections discuss these seven important principles. As discussed in the next section, .NET enables complying with all of the core principles, but it does not necessarily enforces these principles.

Separation of Interface from Implementation

The fundamental principle of component-oriented programming is that the basic unit in an application is a binary-compatible interface. The interface provides an abstract service definition between a client and the object. This principle contrasts with the object-oriented view of the world, which places the object, rather than its interface, at the center. An *interface* is a logical grouping of method definitions that acts as the *contract* between the client and the service provider. Each provider is free to provide its own interpretation of the interface—that is, its own implementation.

The interface is implemented by a black-box binary component that completely encapsulates its interior. This principle is known as *separation of interface from implementation.*

To use a component, the client needs only to know the interface definition (i.e., the service contract) and to be able to access a binary component that implements that interface. This extra level of indirection between the client and the object allows one implementation of an interface to be replaced by another without affecting the client code. The client doesn't need to be recompiled to use a new version. Sometimes the client doesn't even need to be shut down to do the upgrade. Provided the interface is immutable, objects implementing the interface are free to evolve, and new versions can be introduced smoothly and easily. To implement the functionality promised by an interface inside a component, you use traditional object-oriented methodologies, but the resulting class hierarchies are usually simpler and easier to manage.

Interfaces also facilitate reuse. In object-oriented programming, the basic unit of reuse is the object. In theory, different clients should be able to use the same object. Each reuse instance saves the reusing party the amount of time and effort that would have been spent implementing the object. Reuse initiatives have the potential for significant cost reductions and reduced product-development cycle time. One reason why the industry adopted object-oriented programming so avidly was its desire to reap the benefits of reuse.

In reality, however, objects are rarely reusable. They are often specific to the problems and particular contexts for which they were developed, and unless the objects are "nuts and bolts"—that is, simple and generic—they can't be reused even in very similar contexts. This is also true in many engineering disciplines, including mechanical and electrical engineering. For example, consider the computer mouse you use with your workstation. Each part of this mouse is designed and manufactured specifically for your make and model. For reasons of branding and electronics specifics, parts such as the body case can't be used in the manufacturing of any other type of mouse (even very similar ones), whether made by the same manufacturer or others. However, the interface between mouse and human hand is well defined, and any human (not just yourself) can use the mouse. Similarly, the typical USB interface between mouse and computer is well defined, and your mouse can plug into almost any computer adhering to that interface. The basic units of reuse in the computer mouse are the interfaces with which the mouse complies, not the mouse parts themselves.

In component-oriented programming, the basic unit of reuse is the interface, not a particular component. By separating interfaces from implementation in your application, and using predefined interfaces or defining new interfaces, you enable that application to reuse existing components and enable reuse of your new components in other applications.

Binary Compatibility Between Client and Server

Another core principle of component-oriented programming is *binary compatibility* between client and server. Traditional object-oriented programming requires all the parties involved—clients and servers—to be part of one monolithic application. During compilation, the compiler inserts the addresses of the server entry points into the client code. Component-oriented programming, in contrast, revolves around packaging code into components (i.e., binary building blocks). Changes to the component code are contained in the binary unit hosting the component; you don't need to recompile and redeploy the clients. However, the ability to replace and plug in new binary versions of the server implies binary compatibility between the client and the server, meaning that the client's code must interact at runtime with exactly what it expects as far as the binary layout in memory of the component entry points. This binary compatibility is the basis for the contract between the component and the client. As long as the new version of the component abides by this contract, the client isn't affected. In Chapter 2, you will see how .NET provides binary compatibility.

Language Independence

Unlike in traditional object-oriented programming, in component-oriented programming, the server is developed independently of the client. Because the client interacts with the server only at runtime, the only thing that binds the two is binary compatibility. A corollary is that the programming languages that implement the client and server should not affect their ability to interact at runtime. *Language independence* means exactly that: when you develop and deploy components, your choice of programming language should be irrelevant. Language independence promotes the interchangeability of components, and their adoption and reuse. .NET achieves language independence through an architecture and implementation called the Common Language Runtime (CLR), which is discussed further in Chapter 2.

Location Transparency

A component-based application contains multiple binary components. These components can all exist in the same process, in different processes on the same machine, or on different machines on a network. With the advent of web services, components can also now be distributed across the Internet.

The underlying component technology is required to provide a client with *location transparency*, which allows the client code to be oblivious to the actual locations of the objects it uses. Location transparency means there is nothing in the client's code pertaining to where the objects execute. The same client code must be able to handle all cases of object location (see Figure 1-3), although the client should be able to insist on a specific location as well. Note that in the figure, the object can be in the same process (e.g., Process 1 on Machine A), in different processes on the same machine (e.g., Process 1 and Process 2 on Machine A), on different machines in the same local network (e.g. Machine B), or even on different machines across the Internet (e.g., Machine C).

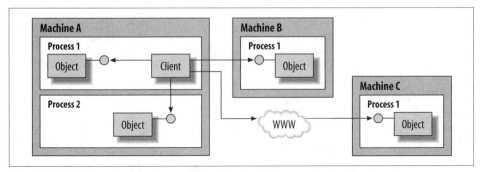

Figure 1-3. With location transparency, the client is oblivious to the actual object location

Location transparency is crucial to component-oriented programming for a number of reasons. First, it lets you develop the client and components locally (which leads to easier and more productive debugging), yet deploy the same code base in distributed scenarios. Second, the choice of whether to use the same process for all components or multiple processes for multiple machines has a significant impact on performance and ease of management versus scalability, availability, robustness, throughput, and security. Organizations have different priorities and preferences for these trade-offs, yet the same set of components from a particular vendor or team should be able to handle all scenarios. Third, the locations of the components tend to change as an application's requirements evolve over time. If the locations are transparent to the client, this movement does not cause problems.

To minimize the cost of long-term maintenance and extensibility, you should avoid having client code make any assumptions regarding the locations of the objects it uses and avoid making explicit calls across processes or across machines. *.NET remoting* is the name of the technology that enables remote calls in .NET. Chapter 10 is dedicated to .NET remoting and discusses .NET support for location transparency.

Concurrency Management

A component developer can't possibly know in advance all the possible ways in which a component will be used, and particularly whether multiple threads will access it concurrently. The safest course is to assume that the component will be used in concurrent situations and to prepare for this eventuality. One option is to provide some mechanism inside the component for synchronizing access. However, this approach has two flaws. First, it may lead to deadlocks; if every component in the application has its own synchronization lock, a deadlock can occur if two components on different threads try to access each other. Second, it's an inefficient use of system resources for all components in the application to be accessed by the same thread.

To get around these problems, the underlying component technology must provide a *concurrency management* service—that is, a way for components to participate in some application-wide synchronization mechanism, even when the components are developed separately. In addition, the underlying component technology should allow components and clients to provide their own synchronization solutions for fine-grained control and optimized performance. .NET concurrency management support is discussed in Chapter 8 as part of developing multithreaded .NET applications.

Versioning Support

Component-oriented programming must allow clients and components to evolve separately. Component developers should be able to deploy new versions (or just fixes) of existing components without affecting existing client applications. Client developers should be able to deploy new versions of the client application and expect them to work with older versions of components. The underlying component technology should support *versioning*, which allows a component to evolve along different paths and allows different versions of the same component to be deployed on the same machine, or even in the same client process, *side by side*. The component technology should also detect incompatibility as soon as possible and alert the client. .NET's solution to version control is discussed in Chapter 5.

Component-Based Security

In component-oriented programming, components are developed separately from the client applications that use them. Component developers have no way of knowing how a client application or end user will try to use their work, so a benign component could well be used maliciously to corrupt data or transfer funds between accounts without proper authorization or authentication. Similarly, a client application has no way to know whether it's interacting with a malicious component that will abuse the credentials the client provides. In addition, even if both the client and the component have no ill intent, the end application user can still try to hack into the system or do some other damage (even by mistake).

To lessen the danger, a component technology must provide a security infrastructure to deal with these scenarios, without coupling components and client applications to each other. Security requirements, policies, and events (such as new users) are among the most volatile aspects of the application lifecycle, and security policies vary between applications and customers. A productive component technology should allow for the components to have as few security policies as possible and for there to be as little security awareness as possible in the code itself. It should also allow system administrators to customize and manage the application security policy without requiring changes to the code. .NET's rich security infrastructure is the subject of Chapter 12.

Version Control and DLL Hell

Historically, the versioning problem has been the source of much aggravation. Early attempts at component technology using DLL and DLL-exported functions created the predicament known as *DLL Hell*. A typical DLL Hell scenario involves two client applications, say A1.0 and B1.0, each using version C1.0 of a component in the *mydll.dll* file. Both A1.0 and B1.0 install a copy of *mydll.dll* in some global location, such as the *System* directory. When version A1.1 is installed, it also installs version C1.1 of the component, providing new functionality in addition to the functionality defined in C1.0. Note that *mydll.dll* can contain C1.1 and still serve both old and new client application versions, because the old clients aren't aware of the new functionality, and the old functionality is still supported. Binary compatibility is maintained via strict management of ordinal numbers for the exported functions (a source for another set of problems associated with DLL Hell). The problem starts when Application B1.0 is reinstalled. As part of installing B1.0, version C1.0 is reinstalled, overriding C1.1. As a result, A1.1 can't execute.

Interestingly enough, addressing the issue of DLL Hell was one of the driving forces behind COM. Even though COM makes wide use of objects in DLLs, COM can completely eliminate DLL Hell. However, COM is difficult to learn and apply and consequently can be misused or abused, resulting in problems similar to DLL Hell.

Like COM, .NET was designed with DLL Hell in mind. .NET doesn't eliminate all chances of DLL Hell, but does reduce its likelihood substantially. While it's true that the default versioning and deployment policies of .NET don't allow for DLL Hell, .NET is, after all, an extensible platform. You can choose to override its default behavior to meet some advanced need or to provide your own custom version control policy, but in doing so you risk creating DLL Hell.

.NET Adherence to Component Principles

One challenge facing the software industry today is the skill gap between what developers should know and what they do know. Even if you have formal training in computer science, you may lack effective component-oriented design skills, which are primarily acquired through experience. Today's aggressive deadlines, tight budgets, and a continuing shortage of developers precludes, for many, the opportunity to attend formal training sessions or to receive effective on-the-job training. Nowhere is the skill gap more apparent than among developers at companies who attempt to adhere to component development principles. In contrast, object-oriented concepts are easier to understand and apply, partly because they have been around much longer (and hence a larger number of developers are familiar with them) and partly because of the added degree of complexity involved with component development as compared to development of monolithic applications.

.NET Versus COM

If you're a seasoned COM developer, .NET might seem to be missing many of the elements you have taken for granted as part of your component development environment. If you have no COM background, you can skip this sidebar. If you are still reading, you should know that the seemingly missing elements remain in .NET, although they are expressed differently:

- There is no base interface, such as IUnknown, from which all components derive. Instead, all components derive from the class System.Object. Every .NET object is therefore polymorphic with System.Object.

- There are no class factories. In .NET, the runtime resolves a type declaration to the assembly containing it and the exact class or struct within the assembly. Chapter 2 discusses this mechanism.

- There are no Interface Definition Language (IDL) files or type libraries to describe your interfaces and custom types. Instead, you put those definitions in your source code. The compiler is responsible for embedding the type definitions in a special format in your assembly, called *metadata*. Metadata is described in Chapter 2.

- Component dependencies are captured by the compiler during compilation and persisted in a special format in your assembly, called a *manifest*. The manifest is described in Chapter 2.

- There is no reference counting of objects. .NET has a sophisticated garbage-collection mechanism that detects when an object is no longer being used by clients and then destroys it. Chapter 4 describes the .NET garbage-collection mechanism and the various ways you can manage resources held by objects.

- Identification isn't based on globally unique identifiers (GUIDs). Uniqueness of type (class or interface) is provided by scoping the types with the namespace and assembly name. When an assembly is shared between clients, the assembly must contain a *strong name*—i.e., a unique digital signature generated by using an encryption key. The strong name also guarantees component authenticity, and .NET refuses to execute a mismatch. In essence, these are GUIDs, but you don't have to manage them any more. Chapter 5 discusses shared assemblies and strong names.

- There are no apartments. By default, every .NET component executes in a free-threaded environment, and it's up to you to synchronize access. Synchronization can be done either by using manual synchronization locks or by relying on automatic .NET synchronization domains. .NET multithreading and synchronization are discussed in Chapter 8.

A primary goal of the .NET platform is to simplify the development and use of binary components and to make component-oriented programming more accessible. As a result, .NET doesn't enforce some core principles of component-oriented programming, such as separation of interface from implementation, and unlike COM, .NET allows binary inheritance of implementation. .NET enforces a few of the core concepts and merely enables the rest. Doing so caters to both ends of the skill spectrum. If you understand only object-oriented concepts, you will develop .NET "objects," but because every .NET class is consumed as a binary component by its clients, you can still gain many of the benefits of component-oriented programming. If, on the other hand, you understand and master how to apply component-oriented principles, you can fully maximize the benefits of .NET as a powerful component-development technology.

This duality can be confusing. Throughout the book, whenever applicable, I will point out the places where .NET doesn't enforce a core principle and suggest methods to stick with it nonetheless.

Developing .NET Components

A component technology is more than just a set of rules and guidelines for how to build components. A successful component technology must provide a development environment and tools that will allow you to rapidly develop components. .NET offers a superb development environment and semantics that are the product of years of observing the way developers use COM and the hurdles they face. .NET 2.0 also includes innovative solutions to problems faced by developers using previous versions. All .NET programming languages are component-oriented in their very nature, and the primary development environment (Visual Studio 2005) provides views, wizards, and tools that are oriented toward developing components. .NET shields you from the underlying raw operating services and instead provides operating-system-like services (such as filesystem access or threading) in a component-oriented manner. The services are factored into various components in a logical and consistent fashion, resulting in a uniform programming model. You will see numerous examples of these services throughout this book. The following subsections detail key factors that enable .NET to significantly simplify component development.

The .NET Base Classes

When you develop .NET components, there is no need to master a hard-to-learn component development framework such as the Active Template Library (ATL), which was used to develop COM components in C++. .NET takes care of all the underlying plumbing. In addition, to help you develop your business logic faster, .NET provides you with thousands of classes and types (from message boxes to security permissions), accessible through a common library available to all .NET languages. The base classes are easy to learn and apply, and you can use them as they are or derive from them to extend and specialize their behavior. You will see examples of how to use these base classes throughout this book.

Declarative Programming

When developing components, you can use attributes to declare their special runtime and other needs, rather than coding them. This is analogous to the way COM developers declare the threading model attribute of their components. .NET offers numerous attributes, allowing you to focus on the domain problem at hand. You can also define your own attributes or extend existing ones. This book makes extensive use of .NET attributes and declarative programming. Appendix C discusses reflection and custom attributes.

Component-Oriented Security

The classic Windows NT security model is based on what a given user is allowed to do. This model emerged at a time when COM was in its infancy and applications were usually standalone and monolithic. In a modern, highly distributed, component-oriented environment, you need a security model based on what a component is allowed to do, not just on what its caller is allowed to do.

.NET allows you to configure permissions for a piece of code and to provide evidence proving the code has the right credentials to access a resource or perform sensitive work. System administrators can decide that they trust all code that came from a particular vendor but distrust everything else, from downloaded components to malicious attacks. A component can also demand that a permission check be performed to verify that all callers in its call chain have the right permissions before it proceeds to do its work. Chapter 12 is dedicated to .NET's rich security infrastructure.

Simplified Deployment

Installing a .NET component can be as simple as copying it to the directory of the application using it. This is in contrast to COM, which relies on the Registry for component deployment to let it know where to look for the component file and how to treat it. .NET maintains tight version control, enabling side-by-side execution of new and old versions of a shared component on the same machine. The net result is a zero-impact install; by default, you can't harm another application by installing yours, thus ending the problem of DLL Hell.

If you want to install components to be shared by multiple applications, you can install them in a storage area called the *global assembly cache* (GAC). If the GAC already contains a previous version of your assembly, it keeps it for use by clients that were built against the old version. You can purge old versions as well, but that isn't the default behavior. .NET shared deployment and version control are discussed in Chapter 5.

.NET Component-Oriented Programming Essentials

Regardless of what you use .NET components for, you need to be familiar with the essentials of .NET as a component technology and deployment platform. This chapter introduces basic concepts such as the assembly, metadata, and the Common Language Runtime (CLR). You will see how to compose client and class library assemblies and how to consume a binary component in one assembly by a client in another. The chapter then discusses how .NET achieves binary compatibility, demonstrating how .NET supports this important component-oriented principle presented in the previous chapter. Although I use C# to demonstrate the key points in this chapter and elsewhere in this book, the discussion (unless explicitly stated otherwise) is always from a language-agnostic perspective. The information is applicable to every .NET language, so the focus is on the concept, not the syntax. If you are already familiar with .NET essentials both in .NET 1.1 and 2.0, feel free to skip this chapter and move on to Chapter 3.

Language Independence: The CLR

The .NET CLR provides a common context within which all .NET components execute, regardless of the language in which they are written. The CLR manages every runtime aspect of the code, providing it with memory management, a secure environment to run in, and access to the underlying operating system services. Because the CLR manages these aspects of the code's behavior, code that targets the CLR is called *managed code*. The CLR provides adequate language interoperability, allowing a high degree of component interaction during development and at runtime. This is possible because the CLR is based on a strict type system to which all .NET languages must adhere—all constructs (such as classes, interfaces, structures, and primitive types) in every .NET language must compile to CLR-compatible types. This gain in language interoperability, however, comes at the expense of the ability to use languages and compilers that Windows and COM developers have been using for years. The problem is that pre-existing compilers produce code that doesn't target the CLR, doesn't comply with the CLR type system, and therefore can't be managed by the CLR.

To program .NET components, you must use one of the .NET language compilers available with the .NET Framework and Visual Studio. The first release of Visual Studio (version 1.0, called Visual Studio .NET 2002) shipped with three new CLR-compliant languages: C#, Visual Basic .NET, and Managed C++. The second version (version 1.1, called Visual Studio .NET 2003) contained J# (Java for .NET). The third release of Visual Studio (version 2.0, called Visual Studio 2005) provided extensive language extensions, such as generics, supported by both C# 2005 and Visual Basic 2005. Third-party compiler vendors are also targeting the CLR, with more than 20 additional languages, from COBOL to Eiffel.

Intermediate Language and the JIT Compiler

One detail that often confuses .NET novices is how transformations are made from high-level languages (such as C# or Visual Basic) to managed code to machine code. Understanding this process is key to understanding how .NET provides support for language interoperability (that is, the core principle of language independence), and it has implications for binary compatibility. Although this book tries to steer away from most underlying implementation details and instead focus on how to best apply .NET, a brief overview of the CLR code-generation process goes a long way toward demystifying it all. In addition, understanding the .NET code-generation process is key to dealing with some specific security issues (discussed further in Chapter 12).

Compiling .NET managed code is a two-phase process. First, the high-level code is compiled into a language called *intermediate language* (IL). The IL constructs look more like machine code than a high-level language, but the IL does contain some abstract concepts (such as base classes and exception handling), which is why the language is called intermediate. The IL is packaged in either a DLL or an EXE. The main difference between an EXE and a DLL assembly in .NET is that only an EXE can be launched directly, while both DLLs and EXEs can be loaded into an already running process (more on that later). Because the machine's CPU can execute only native machine code, not IL, further compilation into actual machine code (the second phase) is required at runtime. *Just-in-Time* (JIT) compiler handles this compilation.

When the high-level code is first compiled, the high-level language compiler does two things: first it stores the IL in the EXE or the DLL, and then it creates a machine-code stub for every class method. The stub calls into the JIT compiler, passing its own method address as a parameter. The JIT compiler retrieves the corresponding IL from the DLL or EXE, compiles it into machine code, and replaces the stub in memory with the newly generated machine code. The idea is that when a method that is already compiled calls into a method that isn't yet compiled, it actually calls the stub. The stub calls the JIT compiler, which compiles the IL code into native machine code. .NET then repeats the method call to actually execute the method. Subsequent calls into that method execute as native code, and the application pays the compilation penalty only once per method actually used. Methods that are never called are never compiled.

When the compiler generates an EXE file, its entry point is the Main( ) method. When the loader loads the EXE, it detects that it is a managed EXE. The loader loads the .NET runtime libraries (including the JIT compiler) and then calls into the EXE's Main( ) IL method. This triggers compilation of the IL in the Main( ) method into native code in memory, and the .NET application starts running. Once compiled into native code, it can call other native code freely. When the program terminates, the native code is discarded, and the IL will need to be recompiled into native machine code by the JIT compiler the next time the application runs.

JIT compilation provides a number of important benefits. As you will see later in this chapter, JIT compilation offers .NET developers late-binding flexibility combined with compile-time type safety. JIT compilation is also key to .NET component binary compatibility. In addition, if all the implementations of the .NET runtime on different platforms (such as Windows XP and Linux) expose exactly the same standard set of services, then at least in theory, .NET applications can be ported between different platforms.

You might be concerned with the JIT compilation performance penalty. However, this concern should be mitigated by the fact that the JIT compiler can generate code that runs faster than code generated by traditional static source code compilers. For example, the JIT compiler looks at the exact CPU type (such as Pentium III or Pentium IV) and takes advantage of the added instruction sets offered by each CPU type. In contrast, traditional compilers have to generate code that targets the lowest common denominator, such as the 386-instruction set, and therefore can't take advantage of newer CPU features. Future versions of the JIT compiler may be written to keep track of the way an application uses the code (frequency of branch instructions used, forward-looking branches, etc.) and then to recompile in order to optimize the way the particular application (or even a particular user!) is using the components. The JIT compiler can also optimize the machine code it generates based on actual available machine resources, such as memory or CPU speed. Note that these advanced options aren't yet being implemented, but the mechanism has the potential of providing all of them. In general, JIT compiler optimization is a trade-off between the additional compilation time required and the increased application performance that results, and its effectiveness depends on the application calling patterns and usage. In the future, this cost can be measured during application installation or looked up in a user preferences repository.

.NET Programming Languages

The IL is the common denominator for all .NET programming languages. At least in theory, equivalent constructs in two different languages should produce identical IL. As a result, the traditional performance and capability attributes that previously distinguished between programming languages don't apply when comparing .NET languages. However, that doesn't imply that it doesn't matter which language you choose (as discussed later).

Native Image Compilation

As an alternative to JIT compilation, developers can compile their IL code into native code using a utility called the *Native Image Generator* (*Ngen.exe*). For example, the Windows Forms framework is installed in native image form. Native images are stored automatically in a special global location called the *native image cache*, a dedicated per-machine global storage. When searching for an assembly to load, the assembly resolver first checks the native image cache for a compatible version, and if one is found, the native image version is used. You can use *Ngen.exe* to generate native images during deployment and installation, to take advantage of potential optimizations done on a per-machine basis. The primary motivation for using *Ngen.exe* is to avoid the JIT compiler's performance penalty, which may be a reason for concern in a client application. You don't want a user-interface application to take more than a second or two to load, nor do you want the end user to wait after selecting a menu item or clicking a button for the first time. The downside is that using native images voids most of the benefits of JIT compilation.

Another *Ngen.exe* liability is that it adds a step to your installation program. Deploying .NET applications can be as easy as copying the EXEs and DLLs to the customer's machine, but you lose that simplicity with *Ngen.exe*. I recommend using *Ngen.exe* only after careful examination of your case and when you are convinced that there is a performance bottleneck in your application specifically caused by the JIT compiler. The easiest way to verify that is to run your profiling and test suite against both a JIT-compiled version and a native image version of the application, and compare the measurements.

The fact that all .NET components, regardless of language, execute in the same managed environment, and the fact that all constructs, in every language, must compile to a predefined CLR-compatible type, allows a high degree of language interoperability. Types defined in one language have equivalent native representation in all others. You can use the existing set of CLR types that are supported by all languages, or define new custom types. The CLR also provides a uniform exception-based error-handling model: an exception thrown in one language can be caught and handled in another, and you can either use the predefined set of CLR exception classes or derive and extend them for a specific use. You can also fire events from one language and catch them in another. Furthermore, because the CLR knows only about IL, security permissions and security demands travel across language barriers. The CLR has no problem, for example, verifying that the calling client has the right permissions to use an object even if they were developed in different languages.

.NET Components Are Language-Independent

As explained in Chapter 1, a core principle of component-oriented programming is language independence. When a client calls methods on an object, the programming language that was used to develop the client or the object should not be taken into account and should not affect the client's ability to interact with the object. Because all .NET components are compiled to IL before runtime, regardless of the higher-level language, the result is language-independent by definition. At runtime, the JIT compiler links the client calls to the component entry points. This sort of language independence is similar to the language independence supported by COM. Because the .NET development tools can read the metadata accompanying the IL, .NET also provides development-time language independence, which allows you to interact with or even derive from components written in other languages. For example, all the .NET Framework base classes were written in C# but are used by both C# and Visual Basic developers.

Choosing a .NET Language

Visual Studio 2005 ships with four CLR-compliant languages: Visual C# 2005 (C# for short), Visual Basic 2005 (Visual Basic for short), J#, and Managed C++. Managed C++ is mostly for interoperability, porting, and migration purposes, as well as advanced cases; the majority of .NET developers choose to disregard it as a mainstream language. J# is for maintaining and porting of former J++ applications. Thus, the real question is: as a .NET developer, should you choose C# or Visual Basic 2005? The official Microsoft answer is that all .NET languages are equal in performance and ease of use, and therefore choosing a language should be based on personal preference. According to this philosophy, if you come from a C++ background, you will naturally pick up C#, and if you come from a Visual Basic 6 (VB6) background, you will select Visual Basic 2005. However, I believe that basing the decision merely on your past language experience is not the best approach, and that you have to look not only at where you are coming from, but also at where you are heading.

Although C# and VB.NET and their respective development environments were practically identical in the first release of .NET, the third release of .NET (version 2. 0) and Visual Studio 2005 introduced major differences between the environments, the programming models, and the programming experiences. C# introduced out-of-the-box code refactoring, code expansions, iterators, code formatting options, and numerous handy language features such as delegate inference. Visual Basic 2005 introduced the My object (in essence, a collection of global variables), VB6-like hiding of the Main( ) method, innovative project options and built-in implementation of many features, and task automation tools, all geared at enhancing developer productivity. The goal for Visual Basic 2005 was to approximate VB6 in its ease of use while allowing developers to generate applications as fast as possible. While both languages introduced generics support, it was the prime feature for the C# team and only a later addition to the Visual Basic 2005 product. Conversely, while both languages introduced edit-and-continue, it was the prime feature for the Visual Basic 2005 product and only a last-minute addition to C#.

I believe this trend will continue as the two languages continue to evolve to better serve their different markets and needs, and will only intensify in future releases of .NET. This is because the development community today is roughly divided into two types of development-tools users: the rapid application developers and the enterprise (or system) developers. The two communities are distinct not only because of the different languages they use, but primarily because of the different types of applications they develop and methodologies they employ.

Being first to market and developing the application as rapidly as possible often comes at the expense of long-term maintainability. In addition, these goals require different sets of skills, quality control practices, and management mentality. Traditionally, the rapid application development (RAD) market was ruled by VB6 and its predecessors. With relatively low skills, developers could produce applications quickly and effectively. VB6 did a great job of encapsulating the underlying Windows programming model and the interaction with COM. The problem with VB6 was that at a certain functional point of the application, you hit the VB6 glass ceiling—there were things you simply could not do in VB6 without either resorting to tools outside the environment or having extraordinary knowledge of the internal workings of VB6. This skill curve is shown in Figure 2-1.

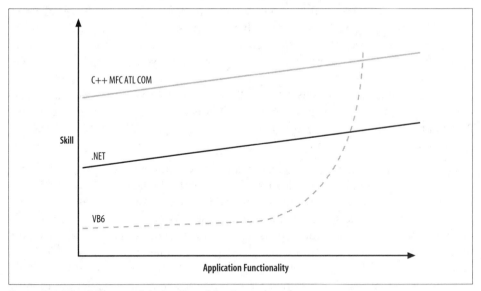

Figure 2-1. The skill versus functionality of development tools

Languages such as C++ and technologies such as MFC and COM were unlimited in their capabilities, from multithreading to object-oriented modeling to Windows message hooking, and new functionality was usually gained at an incremental cost in skill. However, even the most trivial MFC application required a considerable amount of skill, and more complex applications were often beyond the reach of most developers. .NET offered a clean slate, substantially lowering the entry barrier compared with C++, and there was no glass ceiling in .NET: .NET's advantages and programming models are analogous to those of COM and MFC. C++ and COM developers love .NET because it makes everything so much easier. Advanced VB6 developers like .NET because instead of needing to go through the roof skill-wise to develop the required advanced functionality, they can linearly acquire new skills to add functionality. The question that arises is how to address the area exemplified in Figure 2-1 between the .NET curve and the VB6 curve. Unfortunately, most VB6 developers are in that area of the chart. .NET currently has little to offer to them, because for RAD purposes they are better off with VB6, rather than .NET with its higher skill and capability requirements.

I believe Microsoft is well aware of this situation, and that to better serve its target audience, future versions of Visual Basic will evolve to cover this missing area in the skill/functionality curve. The other side of the coin is that amortized over five or seven years of an enterprise application's lifecycle, the time saved using a RAD tool is insignificant—the real question is the cost of long-term maintenance. Applying component-oriented analysis and design methodologies in a large application requires great deal of skill and time and will result in unmaintainable code if done poorly. Moreover, the larger the application, the more likely you are to wish to maintain it for longer period of time, in order to maximize the return on the investment of development. Maintenance and extensibility have much to do with proper design, architecture, and abstractions, as well as component and interface factoring. Enterprise developers tend to spend the bulk of their time focusing on the code itself, rather than on the wizards and the surrounding tools. For enterprise developers, Microsoft designates C#, with its focus on code structure and constructs. Since a typical enterprise application debug session involves contemplative, time-consuming analysis of the problem, it's no wonder that the C# team had little regard for edit-and-continue capabilities.

I believe that if you are a RAD developer, Visual Basic 2005 is the tool for you, even if you're coming from a C++/MFC background. If you are an enterprise developer, where the cost of long-term maintenance is the overwhelming factor, you should choose C# even if you have a VB6 background.

Packaging and Deployment: Assemblies

.NET assemblies were developed to try to improve the ways previous technologies packaged and deployed components. To make the most of .NET assemblies, it's best to first understand the rationale behind them. Understanding the "why" will make the "how" a lot easier.

DLLs and COM Components

Microsoft's first two attempts at component technologies (first, raw DLLs exporting functions, and then later, COM components) used raw executable files for storing binary code. In COM, component developers compiled their source code, usually into a DLL or sometimes into an EXE, and then installed these executables on the customer's machine. Higher-level abstractions or logical attributes shared by all the DLLs had to be managed manually by both the component vendor and the client-side administrator. For example, even though all DLLs in a component-oriented application should be installed and uninstalled as one logical operation, developers had to either write installation programs to repeat the same registration code for every DLL used, or copy them one by one. Most companies didn't invest enough time in developing robust installation programs and procedures, and this in turn resulted in orphaned DLLs bloating the clients' machines after uninstallation. Even worse, after a new version was installed, the application might still try to use the older versions of the DLLs.

Another attribute that should have applied logically to all DLLs that were part of the same application was a version number. Imagine a particular vendor providing a set of interacting components in two DLLs, both labeled version 1.0. When a new version (1.1) of these components became available, the vendor had to manually update the version number of both DLLs to 1.1. A change to the version number of one DLL didn't trigger an automatic change in the other DLL, even though logically both were part of the same deployment unit.

A third logical attribute typically associated with a set of DLLs from the same vendor was their security credentials—what the DLLs were allowed to access, what the DLLs were allowed to do share with other applications, and so on. The client application administrator needed to manage the way he trusted these components and had to repeat this process for all the DLLs, even though they shared the same security origin. Client-side developers and system administrators used clumsy tools such as DCOMCFG to manage these attributes in a fragile and error-prone manner.

Why not simply put all the components that logically comprise a single deployment unit into the same DLL? The answer is simple: doing so would result in monolithic applications, sacrificing many of the benefits of component-oriented programming. In contrast, when components are deployed in separate DLLs, the client application has to pay the time penalty for loading a DLL only when it requires its component. Moreover, the memory footprint of the components of an application is kept to a minimum, because only the DLLs actually used are kept in memory. If the client application needs to download the DLLs dynamically, it pays the download latency penalty only for those it requires.

.NET Assemblies

Clearly there's a need to separate the logical attributes shared by a set of components (such as version, security, and deployment) from their physical packaging (the file that actually contains each component), while avoiding the problems of traditional DLLs. The solution is the .NET concept of the *assembly*: a single deployment, versioning, and security unit. The assembly is the basic packaging unit in .NET. It's called an assembly because it assembles multiple physical files into a single logical unit. An assembly can be a class library (DLL) or a standalone application (EXE) and can contain multiple physical modules, each with multiple components. An assembly usually contains just one file (a single DLL or a single EXE), but it still offers the component developer significant versioning, sharing, and security advantages. These are described later in this book.

Think of an assembly as a logical library: a metafile that can contain more than one physical file (see Figure 2-2).

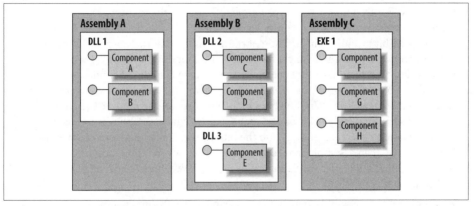

Figure 2-2. Assemblies as logical packaging units

The physical DLLs in an assembly are also referred to as *modules*. For example, in Figure 2-2, Assembly A contains a single module, while Assembly B contains two. The multi-module assembly option exists to support two scenarios. The first is a pay-as-you-go approach for assembly download, so that when a client downloads an assembly it can download only the required code modules, in a trickle-down fashion. The second scenario enables multi-language, multi-file assemblies: you can develop each module in a different language and simply link them together. As it turns out, these two scenarios are fairly rare. Assemblies are relatively small, and bandwidth today is cheap and readily available. Also, most teams are homogenous when it comes to their programming language, and for many other practical reasons (such as accountability and management), the team boundary is also the assembly boundary. Because of that, .NET doesn't promote the use of multiple modules unnecessarily. In fact, Visual Studio 2005 won't generate multi-module assemblies.

To do that, you have to step outside the visual environment, compile your code using a command-line compiler, and then use the *Assembly Linker* (*AL.exe*) command-line utility or the MSBuild engine. *AL.exe* offers switches you can use to incorporate more than one DLL into your assembly. MSBuild is a rich environment that offers some integration with Visual Studio 2005. See the MSDN Library for more information on using *AL.exe* and MSBuild.

An assembly can contain as many components as required. All code in the assembly is IL code. An assembly can also contain resources such as icons, pictures, or localized strings.

Assemblies and CPU Architectures

In theory, any IL-based assembly can run on any target CPU, because of the two-phase compilation process—if the IL has nothing in it that pertains to specific CPU architecture or machine languages, the JIT compiler will generate the machine instructions for the target CPU at runtime. However, in practice, it is possible to write un-portable assemblies. For example, C# lets you explicitly dictate the memory layout of structures. If you use explicit x86 memory layout, your code will not work on Itanium or any other 64-bit machines. In addition, if the assembly imports legacy COM objects it will not work on 64-bit machines, because 64-bit Windows does not support COM natively. For that, your assembly will have to execute in the Win32 emulation environment (known as the WOW, or *Windows-on-Windows*). However, if you simply load that assembly on a 64-bit Windows machine, it will run in the native 64 environment, not the WOW. The only solution for such CPU-specific assemblies is to incorporate the information on the target CPU into the binary executable that contains the assembly. That way, if an assembly that requires the 32-bit WOW emulation is loaded on a 64-bit machine, the loader will launch it in the WOW, where the 32-bit JIT compiler will compile it correctly.

If you develop an assembly that requires a particular CPU architecture, you need to inform Visual Studio 2005 about that CPU so that it can incorporate the information into the binary. In every project in Visual Studio 2005, in the Build tab under the project properties is the Platform Target drop-down list. The default is AnyCPU, but you can select x86, x64, or Itanium. When you specify a particular CPU, you are guaranteed that the assembly will always execute on that CPU architecture (or an emulation of it).

 Applications that display a user interface shouldn't store their resources in the same assembly as the code using those resources. For localization, it's better to generate a separate satellite assembly that contains only resources. You can then generate one such satellite resource assembly per locale (culture) and load the resources from the assembly corresponding to the locale of the specific customer site. Visual Studio 2005 automates most of this process when localizing applications.

Assemblies and Visual Studio 2005

.NET components can reside in either EXE- or DLL-based assemblies. An EXE assembly is called an *application assembly*, and a DLL assembly is called a *library assembly*. As a component developer, you will usually develop components that reside in library assemblies. Visual Studio 2005 has a dedicated project template called Class Library that you should use as a starting point for a server-side assembly. A Visual Studio 2005 Class Library project generates a single DLL class library assembly.

 All the .NET Framework base classes are available in the form of class libraries, and they can be used by component and client application developers.

To add a binary component to a class library, all you have to do is declare a class in one of the project source files using a .NET-compliant language. For existing Class Library projects, Visual Studio provides an Add Class option and an Add New Item dialog window.

To create a new C# library assembly in Visual Studio 2005, select the File → New → Project... menu item. When the New Project dialog window appears, select Visual C# under "Project types," then select Windows. Under Windows, select the Class Library template, as shown in Figure 2-3. Name the library MyClassLibrary in the Name box, and specify a location for the project files in the Location box. If you want the solution files to be in a root directory with the project files underneath it, make sure to check the "Create directory for solution" checkbox, name the solution, and click OK.

These actions create a project named *MyClassLibrary*, which should be visible in the Solution Explorer window along with a number of files, including one named *Class1.cs*. *Class1.cs* defines a single class named `Class1` in the default `MyClassLibrary` namespace. There is no connection between namespaces and assemblies: a single assembly can define multiple namespaces, and multiple assemblies can all contribute components to the same namespace.

To prepare for Example 2-1, rename *Class1.cs* to *MyClass.cs* in the Solution Explorer window and modify the code in the *MyClass.cs* file (comments excluded) to:

```
namespace AssemblyDemo
{
   public class MyClass
   {
      public MyClass()
      {}
      public string GetMessage()
      {
         return "Hello";
      }
   }
}
```

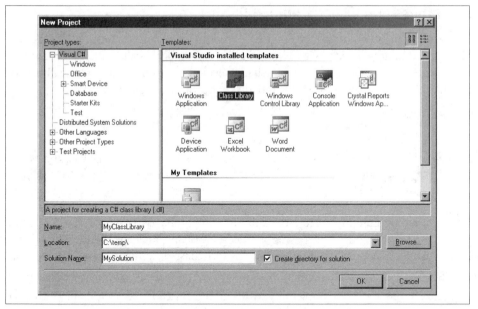

Figure 2-3. A Visual Studio 2005 Class Library project

Partial types

C# 1.1 requires you to put all the code of a type (a class or a structure) in a single file. C# 2.0 allows you to split the definition and implementation of a class or a struct across multiple files—that is, you can put one part of a class in one file and another part of the class in a different file. To do so, use the reserved word partial. For example, you can put this code in the file *MyClassMethods.cs*:

```
public partial class MyClass
{
   public void Method1( )
   {...}
}
```

and this code in the file *MyClassFields.cs*:

```
public partial class MyClass
{
   public int Number;
}
```

In fact, you can have as many parts as you like to any given class. Partial types are a very handy feature. It allows segmenting machine-generated code and user-edited code, placing them in separate files. For example, Windows Forms 2.0 uses partial classes for separating the machine-generated code from the developer's part of the form code. ASP.NET 2.0 also uses partial classes, but the machine-generated code is only generated at compile time. A class (or a struct) can have two kinds of aspects or qualities: accumulative and non-accumulative. The accumulative aspects are things that each part of the class can choose to add, such as interface derivations, properties, indexers, methods, and member variables. The non-accumulative aspects are things that all the parts of a type must agree upon, such as whether the type is a class or a struct, type accessibility (`public` or `internal`, discussed later), and the base class. For example, the following code does not compile because not all the parts of `MyClass` concur on the base class:

```
public class MyBase
{}
public class SomeOtherClass
{}
public partial class MyClass : MyBase
{}
//Does not compile
public partial class MyClass : SomeOtherClass
{}
```

When the compiler builds the assembly, it combines the parts of a type from the various files and compiles them into a single type in the IL. The generated IL has no recollection of which part came from which file, just as the IL contains no trace of which file was used to define which type. Also worth noting is that partial types cannot span assemblies, and that a type can refuse to have other parts by omitting the `partial` qualifier at its definition. Because all the compiler is doing is accumulating parts, a single file can contain multiple parts, even of the same type (although the usefulness of that is somewhat questionable).

Adding a reference

Any client, regardless of the assembly in which it resides (be it a class library or an application assembly), can use the `MyClass` component, but first the client developer needs to import the definitions of the types and components in the server assembly to the client assembly. This import process is called *adding a reference* to the server assembly. In the client project, select Project → Add Reference... to bring up the Add Reference dialog box (see Figure 2-4).

The Add Reference dialog allows client developers to add references to assemblies from five sources. The .NET tab lists predefined .NET class library assemblies. The COM tab lists all the registered COM objects on the machine (each COM component can be treated as a .NET component). The Projects tab lets you add a reference to a library or application project already defined in the client solution. The Browse tab lets you browse to a specified location and select the assembly to add. The Recent tab lists the assemblies that have most recently been browsed to and added, accumulated across all solutions. References made via the Projects tab are not listed on the Recent tab.

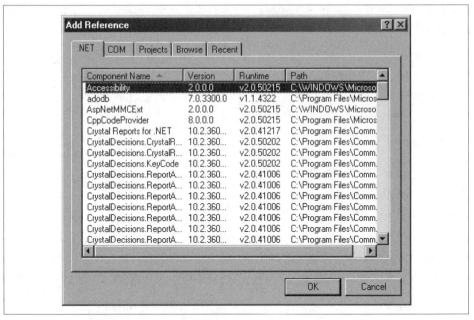

Figure 2-4. The Add Reference dialog

The Add Reference dialog is misleading. The dialog allows you to add references only to other assemblies, yet it refers to assemblies as components (under the Component Name column). There is no way in .NET to add a reference to an individual component inside an assembly. Adding a reference is strictly an assembly-level operation.

To demonstrate how you can add a reference and use a component in a class library, follow these steps:

1. Create a new C# Windows Application project.

2. Add a reference to the *MyClassLibrary* assembly.

3. Add a using statement for the AssemblyDemo namespace.

4. Add a button to the form.

5. Add an event handler to the button's Click event.

6. Use the component in the referenced assembly as if it's defined in the client assembly.

The resulting client-side code should look similar to Example 2-1. Notice that although the MyClass component resides in another assembly, it can be referenced as if it were local to the client code.

Example 2-1. Using a component defined in another assembly

```
using System;
using System.Windows.Forms;
using AssemblyDemo;

partial class ClientForm : Form
{
    void OnClicked(object sender,EventArgs e)
    {
        MyClass obj = new MyClass();
        string nessage = obj.GetMessage();
        MessageBox.Show(nessage);
    }
    /* Rest of the client code  */
}
```

The `ClientForm` client creates an object of type `MyClass` using the new operator and retrieves the message string. The client then uses the static method `Show()` of the class `MessageBox` to display a message box with the message. The `MessageBox` class is part of the .NET Framework and is defined in the `System.Windows.Forms` namespace, in the `System.Windows.Forms` assembly. Note that Example 2-1 includes the `using System.Windows.Forms` and `using AssemblyDemo` statements at the beginning of the file. Without these statements, you need to use *fully qualified type names* (names that include the containing namespace as part of the type declaration).

The important thing about Example 2-1 is the fact that nothing in the client's code indicates that the components it uses come from other assemblies. Once you've added the references, it's as if these components were defined in the client's assembly. As C/C++ programmers will notice, no header, *.def*, or *.lib* files are required.

The reference path

When you add a reference to an assembly, Visual Studio 2005 remembers that assembly name and location. During compilation, Visual Studio 2005 will use that path to look for an assembly with a matching name and import the type definitions. However, you can override that behavior and provide Visual Studio 2005 with alternative reference locations. To do so, open the project properties and select the Reference Paths pane (see Figure 2-5).

You can add as many folders as needed as additional reference paths. The pane also lets you change the order of the references and update (or edit) a reference. The reference path is an ordered list. Visual Studio 2005 will use the first referenced folder to try to locate as many of the referenced assemblies as possible. If some of the assemblies are not found in the first folder, it will move to the second path and try to locate the missing assemblies, and so on down the list. If an assembly is present in multiple folders, only its first occurrence will be used. If an assembly is not found in any of the referenced folders, Visual Studio 2005 will use the original location specified when the reference was added.

The global Namespace

By default, all C# 2.0 namespaces nest in a root namespace called `global`. For example, this definition of the class `MyClass`:

```
class MyClass
{}
```

is identical to this one:

```
namespace global
{
    class MyClass
    {}
}
```

because both define the class `MyClass` in the `global` namespace.

Whenever you reference a type, either using a fully qualified name or via a using statement, C# 2.0 implicitly starts the name-resolution search at the current enclosing namespace. You can explicitly instruct C# 2.0 to start resolving at the `global` root by using the `::` operator. For example, when referencing the type `MyClass` in the namespace `MyNamespace`:

```
namespace MyNamespace
{
    class MyClass
    {}
}
global::MyNamespace.MyClass obj;
```

The global namespace qualifier is instrumental in resolving nested namespaces conflicts. It is possible to have a nested namespace that has the same name as some other global namespace. In such cases, the compiler will have trouble resolving the namespace reference unless you explicitly instruct it to start resolving at the global root.

Consider the following example:

```
namespace MyNamespace
{
    namespace System
    {
        class MyClass
        {
            public void MyMethod( )
            {
                global::System.Diagnostics.Trace.WriteLine("It
                                                Works!");
            }
        }
    }
}
```

—continued—

Without the `global` qualifier, the call to the `Trace` class would produce a compilation error—when the compiler tries to resolve the reference to the `System` namespace it would use the immediate containing scope, which, although it contains a `System` namespace, does not contain the `Diagnostics` namespace. The `global` qualifier instructs the compiler how to correctly resolve the conflict.

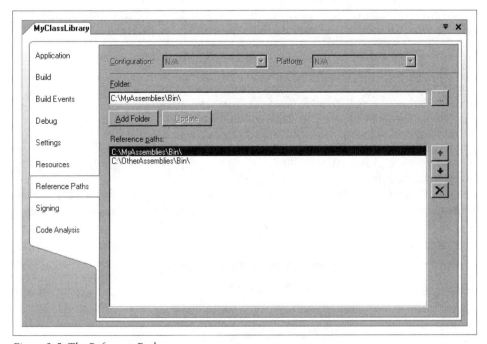

Figure 2-5. The Reference Paths pane

 The reference path is strictly a build-time entity and has no bearing whatsoever on where the assembly will be loaded from at runtime. Runtime assembly resolution is covered in Chapter 5.

Aliasing a reference

When adding an assembly reference, it is possible to create a conflict with another type already defined by your application in another assembly it references. For example, consider the assemblies *MyApplication.exe* and *MyLibrary.dll*, both defining the class `MyClass` in the namespace `MyNamespace`:

```
//In MyApplication.exe
namespace MyNamespace
{
   public class MyClass
   {...}
```

```
}

//In MyLibrary.dll
namespace MyNamespace
{
   public class MyClass
   {...}
}
```

Each definition of MyClass is completely distinct, providing different methods and behaviors. If you add a reference to *MyLibrary.dll* from within *MyApplication.exe*, when you try to use the type MyClass like so:

```
using MyNamespace;
MyClass obj = new MyClass();
```

the compiler will issue an error, because it does not know how to resolve it—that is, it does not know which definition of MyClass is referenced.

C# 2.0 allows you to resolve the conflict by *aliasing* the assembly reference. By default, all namespaces are rooted in the global namespace (see the sidebar "The global Namespace" if you are not familiar with this term). When you alias an assembly, the namespaces used in that assembly will be resolved under the alias, not under global. To alias an assembly, first add a reference to it in Visual Studio 2005. Next, expand the *Reference* folder in the Solution Explorer, and display the properties of the referenced assembly (see Figure 2-6).

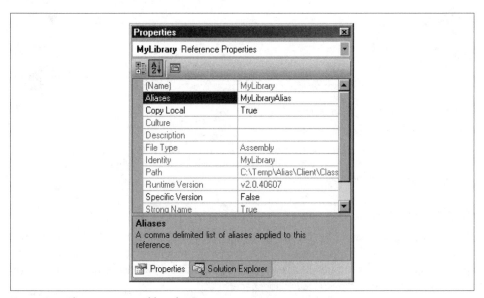

Figure 2-6. Aliasing an assembly reference

If you added the reference by browsing to the assembly, the Aliases property will be set explicitly to global. If you added the reference by selecting the assembly from the

Projects tab, the Aliases value will be empty (but implicitly global). You can specify multiple aliases, but for addressing most conflicts a single alias will do (unless you also have conflicts with other aliases).

Next, add as the first line of the file the extern alias directive, instructing the compiler to include the types from the alias in the search path. You can now refer to the class MyClass from *MyLibrary.dll*:

```
extern alias MyLibraryAlias;

MyLibraryAlias::MyNamespace.MyClass obj;
obj = new MyLibraryAlias::MyNamespace.MyClass();
```

Note that the extern alias directive must appear before any using directives, and that all types in *MyLibrary.dll* can only be referred to via the alias, because these types are not imported to the global scope.

Use of aliases and fully qualified namespaces may result in exceedingly long lines. As shorthand, you can also alias the fully qualified name:

```
using MyLibrary = MyLibraryAlias::MyNamespace;
MyLibrary.MyClass obj;
obj = new MyLibrary.MyClass();
```

The Visual Studio 2005 assembly host

When building an application assembly (either a Windows Forms or a Console application), in addition to the application EXE assembly, Visual Studio 2005 creates an application assembly called *<application name>.vshost.exe*. That assembly is found in the same folder as your application assembly, both in the *Debug* and *Release* folders.

Whenever you're working in a debug session, *<application name>.vshost.exe* is the process being launched, not your original *<application name>.exe*. For debugging purposes, Visual Studio 2005 loads your own *<application name>.exe* into *<application name>.vshost.exe* and debugs it (hence the name *vshost*—the process that hosts your application).

<application name>.vshost.exe is in fact an identical copy of the *vshost.exe* file found under *<Program Files>\Microsoft Visual Studio 8\Common7\IDE*. All Visual Studio 2005 does is copy that file to your *Debug* and *Release* folders and rename it. *vshost. exe* is a simple application assembly with only a Main() method. The Main() method interacts with a set of .NET hosting management classes that facilitate debugging capabilities not available when simply launching your application assembly directly and attaching the debugger to it. These features are:

Partial-trust debugging
This enables you to test how your application behaves under reduced security permissions. Partial-trust debugging is covered in Chapter 12.

Shorter startup time

Each time you launched your application in Visual Studio 2003, it had to create a new process and attach the debugger to that process before starting the application. This introduced a noticeable delay. In Visual Studio 2005 the hosting process is kept running between debug sessions, significantly shortening startup time.

Design-time expression evaluation

The Intermediate Window lets you test code from your application without launching it. This is done by running the code in the readily available, already running *<application name>.vshost.exe* file.

Note that you can only run *<application name>.vshost.exe* from within the debugger, and it only works when placed in the same folder as the application it hosts.

You can also turn off the use of the Visual Studio host process by going to the Debug pane of the project properties and unchecking the "Enable the Visual Studio hosting process" checkbox.

Client and Server Assemblies

Visual Studio 2003 only allowed developers to add references to library assemblies. The client of a component in a class library assembly could reside in the same assembly as the component, in a separate class library assembly, or in a separate application assembly. The client of a component in an application assembly, however, could only reside in the same application assembly as the component. This was analogous to the use of classic Windows DLLs, though there was nothing specific in .NET itself that precluded clients from using components in other application assemblies.

Visual Studio 2005 allows developers to add references to both library and application assemblies. This enables you to treat an EXE application assembly as if it were a DLL library assembly. There is no longer the strict distinction between DLL and EXE assemblies, and the lines between them are very much blurred.

Anything you can do with a DLL library assembly, you can do with an EXE application assembly. For example, nothing prevents you from having a logical application comprised of one EXE application assembly with the user interface in it and several other EXE application assemblies referenced by the user-interface assembly, all loaded in the same process (as well as the same app domain, as explained in Chapter 10).

However, the reverse is not true—there are four things that are specific to EXE application assemblies:

- You can only directly launch an application assembly (be it a Windows or a Console application). You cannot launch a class library.

- Only an application assembly used to launch the process has a say which CLR version is used. This is discussed at length in Chapter 5.

- Partial-trust debugging in Visual Studio 2005 is available only for application assemblies.
- ClickOnce publishing and deployment in Visual Studio 2005 is available only for application assemblies.

That said, I still recommend that you put components in library assemblies whenever possible. This will enable the components to be used by different applications with different CLR versioning policies. It will also enable bundling the components with different ClickOnce applications and deploying the components with different security and trust policies (as discussed in Chapter 12).

Figure 2-7 shows one typical topology of a client application assembly using class libraries. If the client is in the same assembly as the component, the client developer can simply declare an instance of the component and use it. However, if the component is in one class library and the client is in another assembly (be it another library assembly or an application assembly), the client developer first needs to add a reference to the assembly library. Once you've added references to them, the client assembly can use as many class libraries as required.

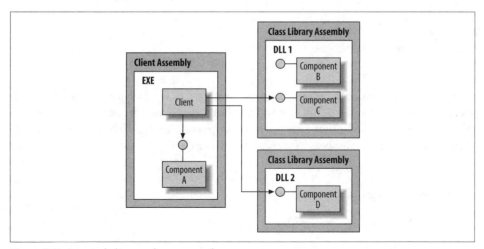

Figure 2-7. A typical client and server topology

Managing Component Visibility in Assemblies

A set of interoperating components often includes components that are intended only for private, internal use by other components in the same assembly. These components aren't intended for outside use and should not be shared with your clients.

In .NET there are two kinds of components: internal and public. An *internal* component can be accessed only by clients inside its own assembly. If client code in one assembly tries to use an internal component from a different assembly, it will not compile. In the case of a multi-module class library, any client in any module can still access the internal component, because both reside in the same assembly. A *public* component is accessible to clients from inside and outside its assembly.

.NET supports special component-oriented access modifiers. To mark a component as internal, use the C# `internal` access modifier (`Friend` in Visual Basic 2005):

```
internal class MyClass
{
   public MyClass()
   {}
   public string GetMessage()
   {
      return "Hello";
   }
}
```

If you wish to make the component available to outside clients, use the `public` access modifier:

```
public class MyClass
{
   public MyClass()
   {}
   public string GetMessage()
   {
      return "Hello";
   }
}
```

.NET makes exposing components explicit: if you don't provide any access modifier, the default modifier is `internal`. The `public` and `internal` access modifiers can also be applied to any other types defined in the assembly, such as interfaces. You can mark individual members of a class or a structure as internal, too:

```
public class MyClass
{
   public MyClass()
   {}
   internal string GetMessage()
   {
      return "Hello";
   }
}
```

Internal members (even on public types) are accessible only inside the assembly. To outside clients, internal members appear as private members.

Another form of component usage by outside entities other than object instantiation and method calls is inheritance. Developers may want to allow access to class members to internal clients and external subclasses only. To support this need, .NET adds the `protected internal` access modifier. For example, consider this class definition:

```
public class MyClass
{
```

```
    public MyClass()
    {}
    public string GetMessage()
    {
        return DoWork();
    }
    protected internal string DoWork()
    {
        return "Hello";
    }
}
```

To subclasses outside the assembly, the DoWork( ) method appears as a protected method, yet inside the assembly the DoWork( ) method behaves as an internal method.

Assembly Metadata

Given that client assemblies add references to component assemblies, and that no source-file-sharing (such as C++ header files) is involved, how does the client-side compiler know what types are in the assembly? How does the compiler know which types are public and which are internal? How does it know what the method signatures are? This classic component-oriented programming problem—the problem of *type discovery*—is raised by the fact that the client application is trying to use a binary component. The solution .NET introduces is called *metadata*.

Metadata is a comprehensive, standard, mandatory, and complete way of describing what is in an assembly. Metadata describes what types are available in the assembly (classes, interfaces, enums, structs, etc.) and their containing namespaces, the name of each type, its visibility, its base class, which interfaces it supports, its methods, each method's parameters, and so on. The assembly metadata is generated automatically by the high-level compiler directly from the source files. The compiler embeds the metadata in the physical file containing the IL (either a DLL or an EXE). In the case of a multi-file assembly, every module with IL must contain metadata describing the types in that module. In fact, a CLR-compatible compiler is required to generate metadata, and the metadata must be in a standard format.

Metadata isn't just for compilers, though. .NET makes it possible to read metadata programmatically, using a mechanism called *reflection*. Reflection is particularity useful from a software-engineering standpoint when used in conjunction with *attributes*, which provide you a way to add your own information to the metadata describing the types used to build your application. Both reflection and attributes are addressed in Appendix C.

Metadata is pivotal for .NET both as a component technology and as a development platform. For example, .NET uses metadata for remote-call marshaling across execution boundaries. *Marshaling* involves forwarding calls made by a client in one execution context (such as a process or machine) to another where the objects reside, invoking the calls in the other execution context, and sending the responses back to

COM Type Libraries Versus Metadata

COM developers usually provided *type libraries* to address the type-discovery problem. The COM type library included the definitions of the interfaces the components implemented and a list of the components themselves. Type libraries had many problems, but foremost among them was the low affinity between what type libraries described and what the binaries actually contained. The binaries could contain types not listed in the type libraries, and the type libraries could list components not present in the binaries. The type library was limited in its description of the actual method signatures and often presented a dumbed-down version of the actual interfaces and method parameter semantics. Type libraries could be used to marshal method calls across context and process boundaries, but that in turn imposed some restrictions on the method parameters. For unusual custom types, type-library marshaling was powerless, and developers had to build custom proxy/stub pairs. Finally, type libraries could be embedded in the binaries or handed to the client separately, creating a development and deployment pitfall.

Even with all these shortcomings, though, type libraries provided client developers for the first time with a way to interact with binary components without involving source files. .NET takes the type library concept to a whole new level, because metadata provides all the information that type libraries do with precise type affinity, as well as additional type information, from base classes to custom attributes. Fundamentally, however, they serve the same purpose.

the client. Marshaling typically uses a *proxy*—an entity that exposes the same entry points as the object. The proxy is the entity responsible for marshaling the call to the actual object. Because of the metadata's exact and formal description of the object's types and methods, .NET is able to construct proxies automatically to forward the calls. Chapter 10 discusses the link between remoting and metadata.

Visual Studio 2005 uses metadata, too. IntelliSense is implemented using reflection. The code editor simply accesses the metadata associated with the type the developer uses and displays the content for autocompletion or type information. Another nifty metadata-based feature in Visual Studio 2005 is Go to Definition, which allows you to get the definition of any type—even those for which you do not have the source files. Right-click on a type name and select Go to Definition from the pop-up context menu. Visual Studio 2005 will create a new file and dump in it the definition of the type (public and protected members only), including XML comments and attributes. This often saves you the trouble of sifting through the help files looking for type information.

You can view the metadata of your assembly with the *ILDASM* utility.

The Assembly Manifest

Just as metadata describes the types in an assembly, the *manifest* describes the assembly itself, providing the logical attributes shared by all the modules and all components in the assembly. The manifest contains the assembly name, the version number, the locale, and an optional strong name uniquely identifying the assembly (discussed in Chapter 5). It also contains the security demands to verify for the assembly (discussed in Chapter 12), as well as the names and hashes of all the files that make up the assembly. Under COM, a malicious party (or even a benevolent party, by mistake) could swap an original DLL or EXE file with another and cause damage. In .NET, every manifest contains a cryptographic hash of the different modules in the assembly. When the assembly is loaded, the .NET runtime recalculates the cryptographic hash of the modules at hand. If the hash generated at runtime is different from that found in the manifest, .NET assumes foul play, refuses to load the assembly, and throws an exception.

Like the metadata, the manifest is generated automatically by the high-level compiler directly from the source files of all the modules in the assembly. Unlike metadata, there is no need to duplicate and embed the manifest for every module in the assembly; only one copy of it is embedded in one of the assembly's physical files. Any CLR-compatible compiler must generate a manifest, and the manifest has to be in a standard format.

The manifest is also the way .NET captures information about other referenced assemblies. This information is crucial to ensure version compatibility and to ensure that the assembly gets to interact with the exact trusted set of other assemblies it expects. For every other assembly referenced by this assembly, the manifest contains the name, the public key (if a strong name is available), the version number, and the locale. At runtime, .NET guarantees that only the referenced assemblies are used and that only compatible versions are loaded (Chapter 5 discusses .NET's versioning policy in depth). When strong names are used, the manifest maintains trust between the component vendor and its clients, because only the original vendor could have signed the referenced assembly with that strong name. You can view the manifest of your assembly with the *ILDASM* utility.

You can provide the compiler with information to add to the assembly manifest using special *assembly attributes*, defined in the System.Runtime.CompilerServices and System.Reflection namespaces. Typically, you provide identity information and security permissions, as explained in the subsequent chapters. Although you can sprinkle these attributes all over the assembly source files, a more structured and maintainable approach is to have a dedicated source file containing only these attributes. The convention is to name this file *AssemblyInfo.cs* in a C# project, or *AssemblyInfo.vb* in a Visual Basic 2005 project. In fact, Visual Studio 2005 generates an assembly information file for every new project under the *Properties* folder in the Solution Explorer. The Visual Studio 2005–generated assembly information file contains an initial set of assembly attributes with default values. Example 2-2 shows a typical set of assembly attributes.

Example 2-2. The assembly information file

```
using System.Reflection;
using System.Runtime.CompilerServices;

[assembly: AssemblyTitle("MyAssembly")]
[assembly: AssemblyDescription("Assembly containing my .NET components")]
[assembly: AssemblyCompany("My Company")]
[assembly: AssemblyCopyright("Copyright © My Company 2005")]
[assembly: AssemblyTrademark("MyTrademark")]
[assembly: AssemblyVersion("1.2.3.4")]
```

Friend Assemblies

An interesting assembly-level attribute introduced by .NET 2.0 is the `InternalsVisibleTo` attribute, defined in the `System.Runtime.CompilerServices` namespace. This attribute allows you to expose internal types and methods to clients from another specified assembly. This is also known as declaring a *friend assembly*. For example, suppose the server assembly *MyClassLibrary.dll* defines the internal class `MyInternalClass` as:

```
internal class MyInternalClass
{
    public void MyPublicMethod( )
    {...}
    internal void MyInternalMethod( )
    {...}
}
```

If you add this line to the *AssemblyInfo.cs* file of *MyClassLibrary.dll*:

```
[assembly: InternalsVisibleTo("MyClient")]
```

any client in the assemblies *MyClient.dll* and *MyClient.exe* will be able to use `MyInternalClass` and call its public or internal members. In addition, any subclass in the *MyClient* assembly will be able to access members marked as `protected internal`.

Declaring an assembly as a friend could easily be abused, violating the essential encapsulation of the internals of the assembly and tightly coupling the client to the internals of the server assembly. Declaring a friend assembly is available for when you break an existing assembly into one or more assemblies by moving some of the types to new assemblies. If the relocated types still rely on internal types in the original assembly, declaring a friend assembly is a quick (albeit potentially dirty) way of enabling the move. Another case where a friend assembly is handy is when you want to test internal components but the test client resides in a different assembly.

Composing Assemblies

There are many ways to compose an assembly. The only two rules are:

- Every assembly must contain a manifest.
- Every assembly module that contains IL must embed in it the corresponding metadata for that IL.

Assemblies can optionally contain resources such as strings or images. Of course, a single class library or application assembly contains all these items in one file. A multi-module assembly, on the other hand, has much more latitude in how it is composed. Figure 2-8 shows a few possibilities for composing assemblies.

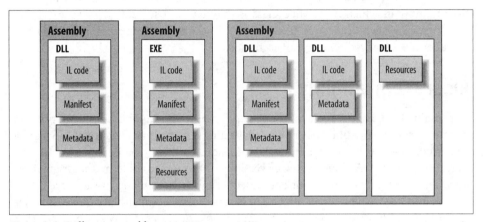

Figure 2-8. Different assembly compositions

As you can see, you can compose multi-module assemblies in almost any way and use compiler switches to bind all your files together. In practice, I recommend abiding by the following composition rules:

- Always store locale-specific resources in a separate satellite assembly, rather than as an embedded resource in the assembly using them. Doing so will greatly simplify localization issues. This is, by the way, the default behavior of Windows Forms.
- Avoid multi-file class library assemblies with modules that don't contain IL.
- Minimize the code in an application assembly. Focus instead on visual layout, and encapsulate business logic in separate class library assemblies.
- Make sure all the components in a class library have the same lifecycle and will always have the same version number and security credentials. If you anticipate the possibility of divergence, split the assembly into two class libraries.

The Assembly Type

.NET provides a class for programmatic representation of an assembly. This is the `Assembly` class, defined in the `System.Reflection` namespace. `Assembly` provides numerous methods for retrieving detailed information about the assembly (location, files, etc.) and the types it contains, as well as methods for creating new instances of types defined in the assembly. You typically access an assembly object using a static method of `Assembly`. For example, to get the assembly from which the current code is running, use the static `GetExecutingAssembly( )` method:

```
Assembly assembly = Assembly.GetExecutingAssembly( );
```

Using other static methods, you can access the assembly that called your assembly, the assembly in which a specified class is defined, and so on. The `Assembly` type is most often used with reflection to obtain information about an assembly or to implement certain advanced remote-call scenarios.

Binary Compatibility

As explained in Chapter 1, one of the core principles of component-oriented programming is binary compatibility between client and server. Binary compatibility enables binary components because it enforces both sides to abide by a binary contract (typically, an interface). As long as newer versions of the server abide by the original contract between the two, the client isn't affected by changes made to the server. COM was the first component technology to offer true binary compatibility free of DLL Hell (described in the previous chapter), and many developers have come to equate COM's implementation of binary compatibility (and the resulting restrictions, such as immutable COM interfaces) with the principle itself. The .NET approach to binary compatibility is different from that of COM, though, and so are the implications of the programming model. To understand these implications and why they differ from COM's, this section first briefly describes COM's binary-compatibility implementation and then discusses .NET's way of supporting binary compatibility.

COM Binary Compatibility

COM provides binary compatibility by using interface pointers and virtual tables. In COM, the client interacts with the object indirectly via an interface pointer. The interface pointer actually points to another pointer called the *virtual table pointer*. The virtual table pointer points to a table of function pointers. Each slot in the table points to the location where the corresponding interface's method code resides (see Figure 2-9).

When the client uses the interface pointer to call a method (such as the second method of the interface), all the compiler builds into the client's code is an instruction to jump to the address pointed to by the second entry in the virtual table. In

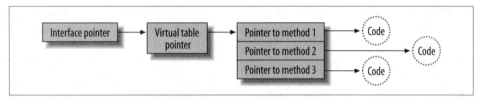

Figure 2-9. COM binary compatibility

effect, this address is given as an offset from the table's starting point. At runtime, the loader patches this jump command to the actual address, because it already knows the table memory location. All the COM client records in its code is the offset from the virtual table start address. At runtime, any server that provides the same in-memory table layout (in which the table entries point to methods with exactly the same signatures) is considered binary-compatible. This is, by the way, exactly the definition of implementing a COM interface. This model yields the famous COM prime directive: *Thou Shalt Not Change a Published Interface.* Any change to the virtual table layout will break the existing client's code. The virtual table layout is isomorphic to the interface definition—for example, the second method in the interface is the second entry in the virtual table. The virtual table must have the exact same number of entries as the interface has methods. Any change to the interface's definition must result in the recompiling and redeploying of all clients as well; otherwise, the clients are no longer binary-compatible with the server.

.NET Binary Compatibility

.NET provides binary compatibility using metadata. The high-level client code (such as C# or Visual Basic 2005) is compiled to IL. The client code can't contain any offsets from memory addresses, because those offsets depend on the way the JIT compiler structures the native code. At runtime, the JIT compiler compiles and links the IL to native machine code. The original IL contains only requests to invoke methods or access fields of an object, based on that type's metadata—it's as if instead of a traditional method call in native code, the IL contains only a token identifying the method to invoke. Any type that provides these methods or fields in its metadata is binary-compatible, because the actual binary layout in memory of the type is decided at runtime by the JIT compiler, and there is nothing pertaining to this layout in the client's IL.

The main benefit of .NET metadata-based binary compatibility is that every class is a binary component. This, in turn, simplifies developing components tremendously compared with COM. There's no need for complex frameworks such as ATL, because .NET supports components natively. .NET can bridge the skill gap (mentioned in Chapter 1) between what most developers can do and what traditional component technologies demand. If you understand only object-oriented programming, you can do that and still gain some component-oriented programming benefits, relying on .NET to manage binary compatibility and versioning. If you understand the core issues of component-oriented programming, you can maximize your productivity and potential while gaining the full benefits of component-oriented applications. Unlike with COM, with .NET binary compatibility isn't limited to interface-based programming. Any .NET type, be it a class or a struct, is compatible with its clients. Any entry point, be it an instance method, object field, static method, or static field, is binary-compatible. The other main benefit of metadata-based binary compatibility is that it gives you the flexibility of late binding with the safety of early binding—the code never jumps to the wrong address, and yet you don't bake actual entry-point addresses or offsets into the client's code. For example, consider the following .NET interface:

```
public interface IMyInterface
{
   void Method1( );
   void Method2( );
}
```

The interface is defined and implemented in a server assembly, and its client resides in a separate assembly. The client is compiled against the interface definition, and the compiler provides type safety by enforcing correct parameter types and return values. However, the same client will function just fine (without recompiling) if you change the order of the methods in the interface:

```
public interface IMyInterface
{
   void Method2( );
   void Method1( );
}
```

or if you add a new method:

```
public interface IMyInterface
{
   void Method3( );
   void Method1( );
   void Method2( );
}
```

If the client doesn't use one of the methods, you can remove it, and the client will be unaffected. In the past, this level of flexibility was available only with late-binding scripting languages, which interpreted the code instead of compiling it. All these changes are forbidden in COM interfaces, because they contradict the prime directive of not changing published interfaces. Adding new methods was the main reason for defining new interfaces in COM (which in turn complicated the COM programming model). However, .NET lets you remove unused methods, add new methods (or fields), and change the order of methods (although you can't change method parameters or remove methods that clients expect to use).

Binary Inheritance

An interesting side effect of metadata-based binary compatibility is that it allows binary inheritance of implementation. In traditional object-oriented programming, the subclass developer had to have access to a source file describing the base class in order to derive her class from it. In .NET, types are described using metadata, so the subclass developer needs to access the metadata only of the base class. The compiler reads the metadata from the binary file and knows which methods and fields are available in the base type. In fact, even when both the base class and the subclass are defined in the same project, the compiler still uses the metadata in the project to compile the subclass. This is why in .NET the order in which classes are defined doesn't matter (unlike in C++, which often requires forward type declarations or a particular order of listing the included header files). All the non-sealed .NET Framework base classes are available to you to derive and extend using binary inheritance. Note that inheritance is a double-edged sword, though. Inheritance is a form of white-box reuse: it tends to couple the subclass to the base class, and it requires intimate knowledge of the base class's functionality. Part of the reason why COM didn't allow binary inheritance of implementation (only of interfaces) was because the COM architects were aware of these liabilities. The .NET architects wanted to support inheritance as part of bridging the skill gap. However, I strongly advise against abusing inheritance. Try to keep your class hierarchies as simple and as flat as possible, and use interface-based programming as much as possible.

CHAPTER 3

Interface-Based Programming

As explained in Chapter 1, separation of interface from implementation is a core principle of component-oriented programming. When you separate interface from implementation, the client is coded against an abstraction of a service (the interface), not a particular implementation of it (the object). As a result, changing an implementation detail on the server side (or even switching to a different service provider altogether) doesn't affect the client. This chapter starts by presenting .NET interfaces and describing what options are available to .NET developers when it comes to enforcing the separation of interface from implementation. It then addresses a set of practical issues involving the definition and use of interfaces, such as how to implement multiple interfaces and how to combine interfaces and class hierarchies. After a detailed look at generic interfaces, the chapter ends with a discussion of interface design and factoring guidelines.

Separating Interface from Implementation

In both C# and Visual Basic 2005, the reserved word `interface` defines a CLR reference type that can't have any implementation, can't be instantiated, and has only public members. Saying that an interface can't have implementation means that it's as if all the interface's methods and properties were abstract. Saying it can't be instantiated means the same as if the interface were an abstract class (or `MustInherit` in Visual Basic 2005). For example, this interface definition:

```
public interface IMyInterface
{
   void Method1( );
   void Method2( );
   void Method3( );
}
```

is almost equivalent to this class definition:

```
public abstract class MyInterface
{
    public abstract void Method1();
    public abstract void Method2();
    public abstract void Method3();
}
```

In traditional object-oriented programming, you typically use an abstract class to define a service abstraction. The abstract class serves to define a set of signatures that multiple classes will implement after deriving from the abstract class. When different service providers share a common base class, they all become polymorphic with that service abstraction, and the client can potentially switch between providers with minimum changes. There are a few important differences between an abstract class and an interface:

- An abstract class can still have implementation: it can have member variables or non-abstract methods or properties. An interface can't have implementation or member variables.

- A .NET class can derive from only one base class, even if that base class is abstract. However, a .NET class can implement as many interfaces as required.

- An abstract class can derive from any other class or from one or more interfaces. An interface can derive only from other interfaces.

- An abstract class can have nonpublic (protected or private) methods and properties, even if they are all abstract. In an interface, by definition, all members are public.

- An abstract class can have static methods and static members and can define constants. An interface can have none of those.

- An abstract class can have constructors. An interface can't.

These differences are deliberately in place, not to restrict interfaces, but rather to provide for a formal public contract between a service provider (the classes implementing the interface) and the service consumer (the client of the classes). Disallowing any kind of implementation details in interfaces (such as method implementations, constants, static members, and constructors) enables .NET to promote loose coupling between the service providers and the client. Because there is nothing in the contract that even hints at implementation, by definition the implementation is well encapsulated behind the interface, and service providers are free to change their implementations without affecting the client. You can even say that the interface acts like a binary shield, isolating each party from the other.

Because interfaces can't be instantiated, .NET forces clients to choose a particular implementation to instantiate. Having only public members in an interface complements the contract semantics nicely: you would not want a contract with hidden clauses or "fine print." Everything the contract implies should be public and well defined. The more explicit and well defined a contract is, the less likely it is that there will be conflicts down the road regarding exactly what the class providing the service is required to do. The class implementing the interface must implement all the interface members without exception, because it has committed to providing this exact service definition. An interface can extend only other interfaces, not classes. By deriving a new interface from an existing interface, you define a new and specialized contract, and any class that implements that interface must implement all members of the base interface(s). A class can choose to implement multiple interfaces, just as a person can choose to commit to multiple contracts.

Interface Implementation

To implement an interface, all a class has to do is derive from it. Example 3-1 shows the class MyClass implementing the interface IMyInterface.

Example 3-1. Defining and implementing an interface

```
public interface IMyInterface
{
   void Method1( );
   void Method2( );
   void Method3( );
}

public class MyClass : IMyInterface
{
   public void Method1( )
   {...}
   public void Method2( )
   {...}
   public void Method3( )
   {...}
   //other class members
}
```

As trivial as Example 3-1 is, it does demonstrate a number of important points. First, interfaces have visibility—an interface can be private to its assembly (using the internal access modifier) or it can be used from outside the assembly (with the public access modifier), as in Example 3-1. Second, even though the methods the interface defines have no access modifiers, they are by definition public, and the implementing class has to declare its interface methods as public. Third, there is no need to use new or override to qualify the method redefinition in the subclass, because an interface method by its very nature can't have any implementation and therefore has nothing to override. (If you aren't familiar with the new or override keywords, see the sidebar "C# Inheritance Directives" later in this chapter.) Finally, the class must implement all the methods the interface defines, without exception. If the class is an abstract class, it can redefine the methods without providing concrete implementation.

Example 3-2 shows how to define and implement an interface in Visual Basic 2005. In Visual Basic 2005, you need to state which interface method a class method corresponds to. As long as the signature (i.e., the parameters and return value) matches, you can even use a different name for the method. In addition, because the default accessibility in Visual Basic 2005 is public, unlike in C#, adding the Public qualifier is optional.

Example 3-2. Defining and implementing an interface in Visual Basic 2005

```
Public Interface IMyInterface
    Sub Method1()
    Sub Method2()
    Sub Method3()
End Interface

Public Class SomeClass
    Implements IMyInterface

    Public Sub Method1() Implements IMyInterface.Method1
    ...
    End Sub

    Public Sub Method2() Implements IMyInterface.Method2
    ...
    End Sub

    Public Sub Method3() Implements IMyInterface.Method3
    ...
    End Sub
End Class
```

To interact with an object using an interface, all a client has to do is instantiate a concrete class that supports the interface and assign that object to an interface variable, similar to using any other base type. Using the same definitions as in Example 3-1, the client code might be:

```
IMyInterface obj;
obj = new MyClass();
obj.Method1();
```

Interfaces promote loose coupling between clients and objects. When you use interfaces, there's a level of indirection between the client's code and the object implementing the interface. If the client wasn't responsible for instantiating the object, there is nothing in the client code that pertains to the object hidden behind the interface shield. There can be many possible implementations of the same interface, such as:

```
public interface IMyInterface
{...}
public class MyClass : IMyInterface
{...}
public class MyOtherClass : IMyInterface
{...}
```

When a client obtains an interface reference by creating an object of type MyClass, the client is actually saying to .NET "give me MyClass's *interpretation* of the way IMyInterface should be implemented."

Treating interfaces as binary contracts, which shields clients from changes made to the service providers, is exactly the idea behind COM interfaces, and logically, .NET interfaces have the same semantics as COM interfaces. If you are an experienced COM developer or architect, working with interfaces is probably second nature to you, and you will feel right at home with .NET interfaces.

However, unlike COM, .NET doesn't enforce separation of the interface from the implementation. For example, using the definitions in Example 3-1, the client's code can also be:

```
MyClass obj;
obj = new MyClass( );
obj.Method1( );
```

Because of the way the server in Example 3-1 implements the interface (as public members), nothing prevents the client from programming directly against the object providing the service, instead of the interface. I believe this is because .NET tries to make component-oriented programming accessible to all developers, including those who have trouble with the more abstract concepts of interface-based programming (see the section ".NET Adherence to Component Principles" in Chapter 1). The fact that something is possible, of course, doesn't mean you should go ahead and do it. Disciplined .NET developers should always enforce the separation, to retain the benefits of interface-based programming.

Explicit Interface Implementation

The way of implementing an interface shown in the previous section is called *implicit interface implementation*, because a public method with a name and signature that match those of an interface method is implicitly assumed to be an implementation of that interface method.

Example 3-3 demonstrates a simple technique that allows server developers to enforce the separation of the interface from the implementation. The server implementing the interface can actually prevent clients from accessing the interface methods directly by using *explicit interface implementation*. Implementing an interface explicitly means qualifying each interface member name with the name of the interface that defines it.

Example 3-3. Explicitly implementing an interface

```
public interface IMyInterface
{
   void Method1( );
   void Method2( );
}
public class MyClass : IMyInterface
{
   void IMyInterface.Method1( )
   {...}
   void IMyInterface.Method2( )
   {...}
   //Other methods and members
}
```

Note that the interface members must be implicitly defined as private at the class's scope; you can't use any explicit access modifiers on them, including private. The only way clients can invoke the methods of explicitly implemented interfaces is by accessing them via the interface:

```
IMyInterface obj;
obj = new MyClass( );
obj.Method1( );
```

To explicitly implement an interface in Visual Basic 2005, you need to explicitly set the method access to Private, as in Example 3-4.

Example 3-4. Explicitly implementing an interface in Visual Basic 2005

```
Public Interface IMyInterface
   Sub Method1( )
   Sub Method2( )
End Interface

Public Class SomeClass
   Implements IMyInterface

   Private Sub Method1( ) Implements IMyInterface.Method1
   ...
   End Sub

   Private Sub Method2( ) Implements IMyInterface.Method2
   ...
   End Sub
End Class
```

You should avoid mixing and matching explicit and implicit interface implementations, as in the following fragment:

```
//Avoid mixing and matching:
public interface IMyInterface
{
   void Method1( );
```

```
    void Method2( );
}
public class MyClass : IMyInterface
{
    void IMyInterface.Method1( )
    {...}
    public void Method2( )
    {...}
    //Other methods and members
}
```

Although .NET lets you mix and match implementation methods, for consistency, you should avoid it. Such mix and match forces the client to adjust its references depending on whether a particular method is accessible via an interface or directly via the object.

Assemblies with Interfaces Only

Because interfaces can be implemented by multiple components, it's good practice to put them in a separate assembly from that of the implementing components. Maintaining a separate assembly that contains only interfaces allows concurrent development of the server and the client, once the two parties have agreed on the interfaces. Such assemblies also extend the separation of interface from implementation to the code-packaging units.

Working with Interfaces

Now that you have learned the importance of using interfaces in your component-based application, it's time to examine a number of practical issues regarding working with interfaces and tying them to the rest of your application. Later in this chapter, you will also see the support Visual Studio 2005 offers component developers when it comes to adding implementation to your classes for predefined interfaces.

 When you name a new interface type, you should prefix it with a capital I and capitalize the first letter of the domain term, as in IAccount, IController, ICalculator, and so on. Use the I prefix even if the domain term itself starts with an I (such as in IIDentity or IImage). .NET tries to do away with the old Windows and C++ Hungarian naming notations (that is, prefixing a variable name with its type), but the I prefix is a direct legacy from COM, and that tradition is maintained in .NET.

Interfaces and Type Safety

Interfaces are abstract types and, as such, can't be used directly. To use an interface, you need to cast into an interface reference an object that supports it. There are two types of casting—implicit and explicit—and which type you use has an impact on type safety.

Assigning a class instance to an interface variable directly is called an *implicit cast*, because the compiler is required to figure out which type to cast the class to:

```
IMyInterface obj;
obj = new MyClass();
obj.Method1();
```

When you use implicit casts, the compiler enforces type safety. If the class MyClass doesn't implement the IMyInterface interface, the compiler refuses to generate the code and produces a compilation error. The compiler can do that because it can read the class's metadata and can tell in advance that the class doesn't derive from the interface. However, there are a number of cases where you cannot use implicit casting. In such cases, you can use *explicit cast* instead. Explicit casting means casting one type to another type:

```
IMyInterface obj;
/* Some code here */
obj = (IMyInterface)new MyClass();
obj.Method1();
```

However, bear in mind that explicit casts to an interface are made at the expense of type safety. Even if the class doesn't support the interface, the compiler will compile the client's code, and .NET will throw an exception at runtime when the cast fails.

An example where implicit cast is unavailable is when dealing with non-generic class factories. In object-oriented programming, clients often don't create objects directly, but rather get their instances from a *class factory*—a known object in the system that clients ask to create objects they require, instead of creating them directly.[*] The advantage of using a class factory is that only the factory is coupled to the actual component types that provide the interfaces. The clients only know about the interfaces. When you need to switch from one service provider to another you only need to modify the factory (actually, instantiate a different type of a factory); the clients aren't affected. When using a class factory that returns some common base type (usually object), you can use an explicit cast from the returned object to the interface type:

```
public interface IClassFactory
{
    object GetObject();
```

---

[*] See the Abstract Factory design pattern in *Design Patterns*, by Erich Gamma, Richard Helm, Ralph Johnson, and John Vlissides (Addison-Wesley).

```
}
IClassFactory factory;
/* Some code to initialize the class factory */
IMyInterface obj;
obj = (IMyInterface)factory.GetObject( );
obj.Method1( );
```

 When using generics (where the type parameter is defined at the factory or the method level), there is no need for the cast:

```
public interface IClassFactory<T>
{
    T GetObject( );
}
IClassFactory<IMyInterface> factory;
/* Some code to initialize the class factory */
IMyInterface obj;
obj = factory.GetObject( );
obj.Method1( );
```

Generic interfaces are discussed in more detail later in this chapter.

Another example where implicit cast is impossible is when you want to use one interface that the class implements to get a reference to another interface that the class
also supports. Consider the code in Example 3-5. Even when the client uses an
implicit cast to get hold of the first interface, it needs an explicit cast to obtain the
second.

Example 3-5. Defining and using multiple interfaces

```
public interface IMyInterface
{
    void Method1( );
    void Method2( );
}
public interface IMyOtherInterface
{
    void Method3( );
}

public class MyClass : IMyInterface,IMyOtherInterface
{
    public void Method1( )
    {...}
    public void Method2( )
    {...}
    public void Method3( )
    {...}
}
//Client-side code:
IMyInterface obj1;
IMyOtherInterface obj2;
```

Example 3-5. Defining and using multiple interfaces (continued)

```
obj1 = new MyClass( );
obj1.Method1( );

obj2 = (IMyOtherInterface)obj1;
obj2.Method3( );
```

In all these examples that use explicit casts, you must incorporate error handling, in case the type you are trying to cast from doesn't support the interface, and use try and catch statements to handle any exceptions.

There is, however, a safer, defensive approach to explicit casting-the as operator. The as operator performs the cast if it's legal and assigns a value to the variable. If a cast isn't possible, instead of throwing an exception, the as operator assigns null to the interface variable. Example 3-6 shows how to use the as operator to perform a safe cast that doesn't result in an exception in case of an error.

Example 3-6. Using the as operator to cast safely to the desired interface

```
SomeType obj1;
IMyInterface obj2;

/* Some code to initialize obj1 */

obj2 = obj1 as IMyInterface;
if(obj2 != null)
{
    obj.Method1( );
}
else
{
    //Handle error in expected interface
}
```

> Interestingly enough, using the as operator to find out whether a particular object supports a given interface is semantically identical to COM's QueryInterface( ) method. Both mechanisms allow clients to defensively obtain an interface from an object and handle the situation where the interface isn't supported.

In general, you should always program defensively on the client side, using the as operator as shown in Example 3-6, instead of explicit casting. Never assume an object supports an interface—that leads both to robust error handling and to separation of the interface from the implementation, regardless of whether or not the server is using explicit interface implementation. Make it a habit on the client side to use the server via an interface and thus enforce the separation manually.

Interface Methods, Properties, and Events

An interface isn't limited only to defining methods. An interface can also define properties, indexers, and events. Example 3-7 shows the syntax for defining all of these in an interface and the corresponding implementation.

Example 3-7. An interface can define methods, properties, indexers, and events

```
public delegate void NumberChangedEventHandler(int number);

public interface IMyInterface
{
   void Method1( ); //A method
   int  SomeProperty{ get; set; }//A property
   int  this[int index]{ get; set;}//An indexer
   event NumberChangedEventHandler NumberChanged;//An event
 }

public class MyClass : IMyInterface
{
   public event NumberChangedEventHandler NumberChanged;

   public void Method1( )
   {...}
   public int  SomeProperty
   {
      get
      {...}
      set
      {...}
   }
   public int  this[int index]
   {
      get
      {...}
      set
      {...}
   }
}
```

Interfaces and Structs

An interesting use of interfaces with properties involves structs. In .NET, a struct (a Structure in Visual Basic 2005) can't have a base struct or a base class, because it's a value type. However, .NET does permit structs to implement one or more interfaces. The reason for this is that sometimes you want to define abstract data storage, and there are a number of possible implementations for the actual structure. By defining an interface (preferably with properties only, but it can have methods as well), you can pass around the interface instead of the actual struct and gain the benefits of polymorphism, even though structs aren't allowed to derive from a common base struct. Example 3-8 demonstrates the use of an interface (with properties only) as a base type for structs.

Example 3-8. Using an interface as a base type for structs

```
public interface IMyBaseStruct
{
   int    SomeNumber{ get; set; }
   string SomeString{ get; set; }
}

struct MyStruct : IMyBaseStruct
{
   public int SomeNumber
   { get{...} set{...} }
   public string  SomeString
   { get{...} set{...} }
   //Rest of the implementation
}
struct MyOtherStruct : IMyBaseStruct
{
   public int SomeNumber
   { get{...} set{...} }
   public string  SomeString
   { get{...} set{...} }
   //Rest of the implementation
}
//A method that accepts a struct, without knowing exactly the type
public void DoWork(IMyBaseStruct storage)
{...}
```

Interfaces and Partial Types

Partial types allow the component architect to define interface derivation for a class but have another developer implement it (similar to the old C++ distinction between header files and CPP files):

```
//In App.cs
public interface IMyInterface
{
   void Method1( );
   void Method2( );
}

public partial class MyClass : IMyInterface
{}

//In MyClass.cs

public partial class MyClass
{
   public void Method1( )
   {...}
   public void Method2( )
   {...}
}
```

With a partial class, each part of the class can choose to add interface derivation, or interface derivation and implementation:

```
public partial class MyClass
{}

public partial class MyClass : IMyInterface
{
   public void Method1( )
   {...}
   public void Method2( )
   {...}
}
```

However, only a single part can implement an interface member.

Implementing Multiple Interfaces

A class can derive from as many interfaces as required (see Example 3-5), but from at most one base class. When a class derives from a base class and from one or more interfaces, the base class must be listed first in the derivation chain (a requirement the compiler enforces):

```
public interface IMyInterface
{}
public interface IMyOtherInterface
{}
public class MyBaseClass
{}
public class MySubClass : MyBaseClass,IMyInterface,IMyOtherInterface
{}
```

Even such a trivial example raises a number of questions. What if both interfaces define identical methods? What are the available ways to resolve such collisions? What if the base class already derives from one or more of the interfaces?

When a class derives from two or more interfaces that define an identical method, you have two options: the first is to channel both interface methods to the same actual method implementation, and the second is to provide separate method implementations. For example, consider two interfaces that define the identical method Method1( ):

```
public interface IMyInterface
{
   void Method1( );
}
public interface IMyOtherInterface
{
   void Method1( );
}
```

If you want to channel both interface methods to the same method implementation, all you have to do is derive from the interfaces and implement the method once:

```
public class MyClass : IMyInterface,IMyOtherInterface
{
   public void Method1()
   {...}
   //Other methods and members
}
```

Regardless of which interface the client of MyClass chooses to use, calls to Method1() will be channeled to that single implementation:

```
IMyInterface obj1;
IMyOtherInterface obj2;

obj1 = new MyClass();
obj1.Method1();

obj2 = obj1 as IMyOtherInterface;
Debug.Assert(obj2 != null);
obj2.Method1();
```

To provide separate implementations, use explicit interface implementation by qualifying the method implementation with the name of the interface that defines it:

```
public class MyClass : IMyInterface,IMyOtherInterface
{
   void IMyInterface.Method1()
   {...}
   void IMyOtherInterface.Method1()
   {...}
   //Other methods and members
}
```

Now, when the client calls an interface method, that interface-specific method is called. You can even have separate explicit implementations for some of the common methods and channel the others to the same implementation. However, as mentioned before, for the sake of consistency it's better to avoid mixing and matching.

If you want to both use explicit interface implementation and channel the implementation from one interface to the other, you will need to use the this reference to query for the desired interface and delegate the call:

```
public class MyClass : IMyInterface, IMOtherInterface
{
  void IMyInterface.Method1 ( )
  {...}
  void IMyOtherInterface.Method1 ( )
  {
    IMyInterface myInterface = this;
    myInterface.Method ( );
  }
  //Other methods and members
}
```

Using the this reference this way is the only way to call an explicit interface method by its own implementing class.

Interfaces and Class Hierarchies

In component-oriented programming, you focus on defining and implementing interfaces. In object-oriented programming, you model your solution by using class hierarchies. How do the two concepts interact? The answer depends on the way you override or redefine the interface methods at the different levels of the class hierarchy. Consider the code in Example 3-9, which illustrates that when defining an interface only at the root of a class hierarchy, each level must override its base-class declarations to preserve semantics.

Example 3-9. Overriding an interface in a class hierarchy

```
using System.Diagnostics;//For the Trace class

public interface ITrace
{
   void TraceSelf();
}
public class A : ITrace
{
   public virtual void TraceSelf()
   {
      Trace.WriteLine("A");
   }
}
public class B : A
{
   public override void TraceSelf()
   {
      Trace.WriteLine("B");
   }
}
public class C : B
{
   public override void TraceSelf()
   {
      Trace.WriteLine("C");
   }
}
```

In a typical class hierarchy, the topmost base class should derive from the interface, providing polymorphism with the interface to all subclasses. The topmost base class must also define all the interface members as virtual, so that subclasses can override them. Each level of the class hierarchy can override its preceding level (using the override inheritance qualifier), as shown in Example 3-9. When the client uses the interface, it then gets the desired interpretation of the interface. For example, if the client code is:

```csharp
ITrace obj = new B();
obj.TraceSelf();
```

the object traces "B" to the output window, as expected.

Things are less obvious if the subclasses use the new inheritance qualifier. The new modifier gives subclass behavior only when dealing with an explicit reference to a subclass, such as:

```csharp
B obj = new B();
```

In all other cases, the base class implementation is used. If the code in Example 3-9 was written as:

```
public class A : ITrace
{
    public virtual void TraceSelf( )//virtual is optional
    {
        Trace.WriteLine("A");
    }
}
public class B : A
{
    public new void TraceSelf( )
    {
        Trace.WriteLine("B");
    }
}
public class C : B
{
    public new void TraceSelf( )
    {
        Trace.WriteLine("C");
    }
}
```

then this client code:

```
ITrace obj  = new B( );
obj.TraceSelf( );
```

would now trace "A" to the output window instead of "B." Note that this is exactly why the new inheritance modifier is available. Imagine a client that somehow depends on the base class's particular implementation. If a new subclass is used instead of the base class, the new modifier ensures that the client will get the implementation it expects. However, this nuance makes sense only when you're dealing with clients that don't use interface-based programming but rather program directly against the objects:

```
A obj = new B( );
obj.TraceSelf( );//Traces "A"
```

You can support such clients and still provide interface-based services to the rest of the clients. To achieve that, each class in the hierarchy can reiterate its polymorphism with the interface by explicitly deriving from the interface (in addition to having the base class derive from the interface). Doing so (as shown in Example 3-10) makes the new modifier yield the same results as the override modifier for the interface-based clients:

```
ITrace obj  = new B( );
obj.TraceSelf( );//Traces "B"
```

Note that using virtual at the base-class level is optional.

In general, you should use the override modifier, as in Example 3-9, with virtual interface members at the topmost base class. Such code is readable and straightforward. Code such as that in Example 3-10 makes for an interesting exercise but is rarely of practical use.

Example 3-10. Deriving from the interface explicitly at each level of the class hierarchy

```
using System.Diagnostics;//For the Trace class

public interface ITrace
{
   void TraceSelf();
}
public class A : ITrace
{
   public virtual void TraceSelf()//virtual is optional
   {
      Trace.WriteLine("A");
   }
}
public class B : A,ITrace
{
   public new void TraceSelf()
   {
      Trace.WriteLine("B");
   }
}
public class C : B,ITrace
{
   public new void TraceSelf()
   {
      Trace.WriteLine("C");
   }
}
```

If you want to combine explicit interface implementation and class hierarchy, you should do so in a way that allows a subclass to call its base-class implementation. Because with explicit interface implementation, the implementation is private, you will need to add at the topmost base class a protected virtual method for each interface method. Only the topmost base class should explicitly implement the interface, and its implementation should call the protected virtual methods. All the subclasses should override the protected virtual methods:

```
public class A : ITrace
{
   protected virtual void TraceSelf()
   {
      Trace.WriteLine("A");
   }
   void ITrace.TraceSelf()
   {
      TraceSelf();
```

```
        }
    }
    public class B : A
    {
        protected override void TraceSelf()
        {
            Trace.WriteLine("B");
            base.TraceSelf();
        }
    }
```

Interfaces and Generics

Like classes or structures, interfaces too can be defined in terms of generic type parameters.* Generic interfaces provide all the benefits of interface-based programming without compromising type safety, performance, or productivity. All of what you have seen so far with normal interfaces you can also do with generic interfaces. The main difference is that when deriving from a generic interface, you must provide a specific type parameter to use instead of the generic type parameter. For example, given this definition of the generic IList<T> interface:

```
    public interface IList<T>
    {
        void AddHead(T item);
        void RemoveHead(T item);
        void RemoveAll();
    }
```

you can implement the interface implicitly and substitute an integer for the generic type parameter:

```
    public class NumberList : IList<int>
    {
        public void AddHead(int item)
        {...}
        public void RemoveHead(int item)
        {...}
        public void RemoveAll()
        {...}
        //Rest of the implementation
    }
```

When the client uses IList<T>, it must choose an implementation of the interface with a specific type parameter:

```
    IList<int> list = new NumberList();
    list.AddHead(3);
```

* If you are not familiar with generics, Appendix D provides a concise overview.

Generic interfaces allow you to define an abstract service definition (the generic interface) once, yet use it on multiple components with multiple type parameters. For example, an integer-based list can implement the interface:

```
public class NumberList : IList<int>
{...}
```

And so can a string-based list:

```
public class NameList : IList<string>
{...}
```

Once a generic interface is *bounded* (i.e., once you've specified types for it) it is considered a distinct type. Consequently, two generic interface definitions with different generic type parameters are no longer polymorphic with each other. This means that a variable of the type IList<int> cannot be assigned to a variable or passed to a method that expects an IList<string>:

```
void ProcessList(IList<string> names)
{...}

IList<int> numbers = new NumberList();
ProcessList(numbers);//Does not compile
```

You can maintain the polymorphism with generic interfaces if you keep the use of the interface in generic type parameter terms:

```
public class ListClient<T>
{
    public void ProcessList(IList<T> list)
    {...}
}
IList<int>    numbers = new NumberList();
IList<string> names   = new NameList();

ListClient<int>    numbersClient = new ListClient<int>();
ListClient<string> namesClient   = new ListClient<string>();

//Reuse of the code and algorithms of ProcessList():
numbersClient.ProcessList(numbers);
namesClient.ProcessList(names);
```

Deriving from a Generic Interface

When you derive an interface from a generic interface, you have a number of options as to how to define the sub-interface. Usually, you will prefer to have the sub-interface be a generic interface and provide the sub-interface's generic type parameters as type parameters to the base interface:

```
public interface IBaseInterface<T>
{
    void SomeMethod(T t);
}
public interface ISubInterface<T> : IBaseInterface<T>
{...}
```

However, you can also specify a particular type to the base interface, thus making the sub-interface non-generic:

```
public interface ISubInterface : IBaseInterface<string>
{...}
```

Typically, when you derive from a generic interface you will do so in a generic sub-class and let the client decide on the particular type parameters to use. This is an alternative to defining type-specific subclasses, and it does not limit the subclasses to the use of a particular type parameter:

```
public class List<T> : IList<T>
{
    public void AddHead(T item)
    {...}
    //Rest of the implementation
}
IList<int> numbers  = new List<int>();
IList<string> names = new List<string>();
```

When a generic class or a generic interface derives from a generic interface, it cannot specify multiple naked generic types to the interface:

```
//Does not compile:
public class List<T,U> : IList<T>,IList<U>
{...}
```

Doing so unifies the interfaces when the same type is specified, which violates the uniqueness of interfaces. If that were allowed, the compiler would not know how to resolve a definition such as this:

```
List<int,int> list;
```

Explicit Generic Interface Implementation

Just as with regular interfaces, you can implement a generic interface explicitly:

```
public class NumberList : IList<int>
{
    void IList<int>.AddHead(int item)
    {...}
    void IList<int>.RemoveHead(int item)
    {...}
    void IList<int>.RemoveAll()
    {...}
    //Rest of the implementation
}
```

Note the specification of the type parameter in the explicit implementation:

```
void IList<int>.AddHead(int item);
```

This is required because the AddHead() method is not just a method of the generic interface IList<T>; rather, it is a method of the generic interface IList<T> with an

---

integer as a type parameter. The same would be true if the implementing list were itself a generic class:

```
public class List<T> : IList<T>
{
    void IList<T>.AddHead(T item)
    {...}
    //Rest of the implementation
}
```

Explicit generic interface implementation is especially handy when the same type implements multiple versions of the generic interface, each with a different concrete type parameter. Although you can use implicit interface implementation, like this:

```
public class List : IList<int>,IList<string>
{
    public void AddHead(int item)
    {...}
    public void AddHead(string item)
    {...}
    public void RemoveAll()
    {...}
    //Rest of the implementation
}
```

it is preferable in such cases to use explicit interface implementation. The reason is that in methods such as RemoveAll( ), you channel the implementation of both IList<int> and IList<string> to the same method. The client can use either IList<int> or IList<string>:

```
IList<int> list = new List();
list.RemoveAll();
```

Yet you have no way of knowing in the implementation of RemoveAll( ) which internal data structure you should clear when the client calls it. In addition, when you implement the same generic interface multiple times with different type parameters, you often have to use explicit implementation when the compiler cannot resolve the ambiguity. For example, if IList<T> has a method called GetHead( ), defined as:

```
public interface IList<T>
{
    void AddHead(T item);
    void RemoveHead(T item);
    void RemoveAll();
    T GetHead();
}
```

you must use explicit interface implementation, because in C# you cannot overload methods only by a different returned type:

```
public class List : IList<int>,IList<string>
{
    int IList<int>.GetHead()
    {...}
```

```
string IList<string>.GetHead( )
{...}
//Rest of the implementation
}
```

Generic Interfaces as Operators

C# 2.0 has an additional interesting use for generic interfaces. In C# 2.0, it is impossible to use operators such as + or += on generic type parameters. For example, the following code does not compile because C# 2.0 does not have operator constraints:

```
public class Calculator<T>
{
   public T Add(T argument1,T argument2)
   {
      return argument1 + argument2;//Does not compile
   }
   //Rest of the methods
}
```

The compiler does not know whether the type parameter the client will specify supports the + operator, so it will refuse to compile that code.

Nonetheless, you can compensate by using interfaces that define generic operations. Since an interface method cannot have any code in it, you can specify the generic operations at the interface level and provide a concrete type and implementation at the subclass level:

```
public interface ICalculator<T>
{
   T Add(T argument1,T argument2);
   T Subtract(T argument1,T argument2);
   T Divide(T argument1,T argument2);
   T Multiply(T argument1,T argument2);
}
public class Calculator : ICalculator<int>
{
   public int Add(int argument1, int argument2)
   {
      return argument1 + argument2;
   }
   //Rest of the methods
}
```

Interface-Level Constraints

An interface can define constraints for the generic types it uses. For example:

```
public interface IList<T> where T : IComparable<T>
{...}
```

However, you should be very mindful about the implications of defining constraints at the scope of an interface. An interface should not have any shred of implementation details, to reinforce the notion of separation of interface from implementation. There are many ways to implement the generic interface, and the specific type parameters used are, after all, an implementation detail. Constraining them commonly couples the interface to specific implementation options.

For example, constraining a type parameter on an interface to derive from a particular class, like this, is a bad idea:

```
public class Customer
{...}
public interface IList<T> where T : Customer
{...}
```

This, in effect, makes the generic IList<T> useful only for managing lists of customers. If you want this level of strong typing with polymorphism, define a new interface dedicated to managing customers, instead of skewing the general-purpose definition of the generic IList<T>:

```
public interface ICustomerList : IList<Customer>
{...}
```

Constraining a default constructor, as follows, is also something to avoid:

```
public interface IList<T> where T : new( )
{...}
```

Not all types have default public constructors, and the interface doesn't really care that they do not; the interface cannot contain any implementation code that uses such constructors anyway.

Even constraining an interface's generic type parameter to derive from another interface should be viewed with extreme caution. For example, you may think you should add a constraint for IComparable<T> to the list interface definition if you add a method that removes a specified item from the list:

```
public interface IList<T> where T : IComparable<T>
{
    void Remove(T item);
    //Rest of the interface
}
```

While implementing this method will often involve comparing the specified item to items in the list, which will in turn necessitate having the type parameter support IComparable<T>, this is still an implementation detail. Perhaps the implementing data structure has other ways of comparing the type parameters it uses, or perhaps it does not implement the method at all. All of that is irrelevant to the pure interface definition. Let the class implementing the generic interface add the constraint, and keep the interface itself constraint-free:

```
public class List<T> : IList<T> where T : IComparable<T>
{
    public void Remove(T item)
```

```
    {...}
    //Rest of the implementation
}
```

Generic Derivation Constraints

When a generic class constrains one of its type parameters to derive from an interface, the client may provide as a specific type parameter a particular implementation
of the interface:

```
public class ListClient<L,T> where L : IList<T>
{
    public void ProcessList(L list)
    {...}
}
public class NumberList : IList<int>
{...}

ListClient<NumberList,int> client = new ListClient<NumberList,int>();
NumberList numbers = new NumberList();
client.ProcessList(numbers);
```

However, you can also satisfy the constraint by specifying as a type parameter the
very interface the type parameter is constrained against, not a particular implementation of it:

```
public class ListClient<L,T> where L : IList<T>
{
    public void ProcessList(L list)
    {...}
}
public class List<T> : IList<T>
{...}

ListClient<IList<int>,int> client = new ListClient<IList<int>,int>();
IList<int> numbers = new List<int>();
client.ProcessList(numbers);
```

or even:

```
public class AnotherClient<U>
{
    ListClient<IList<U>,U> m_ListClient;
}
```

This helps to separate the client code from particular interface implementations.

Generics, Interfaces, and Casting

The C# compiler will only let you implicitly cast generic type parameters to object,
or to constraint-specified types, as shown in Example 3-11. Such implicit casting is of
course type-safe, because any incompatibility is discovered at compile time.

Example 3-11. Implicit casting of generic type parameters

```
public interface ISomeInterface
{...}
public class BaseClass
{...}
public class MyClass<T> where T : BaseClass,ISomeInterface
{
   void SomeMethod(T t)
   {
      ISomeInterface obj1 = t;
      BaseClass      obj2 = t;
      object         obj3 = t;
   }
}
```

The compiler will let you explicitly cast generic type parameters to any other interface, but not to a class:

```
public interface ISomeInterface
{...}
public class SomeClass
{...}
public class MyClass<T>
{
   void SomeMethod(T t)
   {
      ISomeInterface obj1 = (ISomeInterface)t;//Compiles
      SomeClass      obj2 = (SomeClass)t;     //Does not compile
   }
}
```

Such explicit casting is dangerous, because it may throw an exception at runtime if the specific type parameter used does not support the interface to which you explicitly cast. Instead of risking a casting exception, a better approach is to use the is and as operators, as shown in Example 3-12. You can use is and as both on naked generic type parameters and on generic classes with specific parameters.

Example 3-12. Using is and as operators on generic type parameters

```
public interface IMyInterface
{...}
public interface ISomeInterface<T>
{...}
public class MyClass<T>
{
   public void MyMethod(T t)
   {
      if(t is IMyInterface)
      {...}

      if(t is ISomeInterface<T>)
      {...}
```

```
      IMyInterface obj1 = t as IMyInterface;
      if(obj1 != null)
      {...}

      ISomeInterface<T> obj2 = t as ISomeInterface<T>;
      if(obj2 != null)
      {...}
   }
}
```

Generic Interface Methods

In C# 2.0, an interface method can define generic type parameters, specific to its execution scope:

```
public interface IMyInterface<T>
{
   void MyMethod<X>(T t,X x);
}
```

This is an important capability, because it allows you to call the method with a different type every time, which is often very handy for utility classes.

You can define method-specific generic type parameters even if the containing interface does not use generics at all:

```
public interface IMyInterface
{
   void MyMethod<T>(T t);
}
```

This ability is for methods only. Properties or indexers can use only generic type parameters defined at the scope of the interface.

When you call an interface method that defines generic type parameters, you can provide the type to use at the call site:

```
public class MyClass : IMyInterface
{
   public void MyMethod<T>(T t)
   {...}
}
IMyInterface obj = new MyClass();
obj.MyMethod<int>(3);
```

That said, when the method is invoked, the C# compiler is smart enough to infer the correct type based on the type of parameter passed in, and it allows you to omit the type specification altogether:

```
IMyInterface obj = new MyClass();
obj.MyMethod(3);
```

This ability is called *generic type inference*. Note that the compiler cannot infer the type based on the type of the returned value alone:

```
public interface IMyInterface
{
    T MyMethod<T>();
}
public class MyClass : IMyInterface
{
    public T MyMethod<T>()
    {...}
}
IMyInterface obj = new MyClass();
int number = obj.MyMethod();//Does not compile
```

When an interface method defines its own generic type parameters, it can also define constraints for these types:

```
public interface IMyInterface
{
    void MyMethod<T>(T t) where T : IComparable<T>;
}
```

However, my recommendation to avoid constraints at the interface level extends to method-level generic type parameters as well.

Designing and Factoring Interfaces

Syntax aside, how do you go about designing interfaces? How do you know which methods to allocate to which interface? How many members should each interface have? Answering these questions has little to do with .NET and a lot to do with abstract component-oriented analysis and design. An in-depth discussion of how to decompose a system into components and how to discover interface methods and properties is beyond the scope of this book. Nonetheless, this section offers a few pieces of advice to guide you in your interface-design effort.

Interface Factoring

An interface is a grouping of logically related methods and properties. What constitutes "logically related" is usually domain-specific. You can think of interfaces as different facets of the same entity. Once you have identified (after a requirements analysis) all the operations and properties the entity supports, you need to allocate them to interfaces. This is called *interface factoring*. When you factor an interface, always think in terms of reusable elements. In a component-oriented application, the basic unit of reuse is the interface. Would this particular interface factoring yield interfaces that other entities in the system can reuse? What facets of the entity can logically be factored out and used by other entities?

Suppose you wish to model a dog. The requirements are that the dog be able to bark and fetch and that it have a veterinary clinic registration number and a property for having received shots. You can define the IDog interface and have different kinds of dogs, such as Poodle and GermanShepherd, implement the IDog interface:

```
public interface IDog
{
    void  Fetch();
    void  Bark();
    long  VetClinicNumber{get;set;}
    bool  HasShots{get;set;}
}
public class Poodle : IDog
{...}

public class GermanShepherd : IDog
{...}
```

However, such a composition of the IDog interface isn't well-factored. Even though all the interface members are things a dog should support, Fetch and Bark are more logically related to each other than to VetClinicNumber and HasShots. Fetch() and Bark() involve one facet of the dog, as a living, active entity, while VetClinicNumber and HasShots involve a different facet, one that relates it as a record of a pet in a veterinary clinic. A better approach is to factor out the VetClinicNumber and HasShots properties to a separate interface called IPet:

```
public interface IPet
{
    long  VetClinicNumber{ get; set; }
    bool  HasShots{ get; set; }
}
public interface IDog
{
    void  Fetch();
    void  Bark();
}
```

Because the pet facet is independent of the canine facet, other entities (such as cats) can reuse the IPet interface and support it:

```
public interface IPet
{
    long  VetClinicNumber{ get; set; }
    bool  HasShots{ get; set; }
}
public interface IDog
{
    void  Fetch();
    void  Bark();
}
public interface ICat
{
    void  Purr();
```

```
      void  CatchMouse( );
}

public class Poodle : IDog,IPet
{...}
public class Siamese : ICat,IPet
{...}
```

This factoring, in turn, allows you to decouple the clinic-management aspect of the application from the actual pet type (be it dogs or cats). Factoring operations and properties into separate interfaces is usually done when there is a weak logical relation between methods. However, identical operations are sometimes found in several unrelated interfaces, and these operations are logically related to their respective interfaces. For example, both cats and dogs need to shed fur and feed their offspring. Logically, shedding is just a dog operation, as is barking, and is also just a cat operation, as is purring. In such cases, you can factor the interfaces into a hierarchy of interfaces instead of separate interfaces:

```
public interface IMammal
{
   void ShedFur( );
   void Lactate( );
}
public interface IDog : IMammal
{
   void  Fetch( );
   void  Bark( );
}
public interface ICat : IMammal
{
   void  Purr( );
   void  CatchMouse( );
}
```

Factoring Metrics

As you can see, proper interface-factoring results in more specialized, loosely coupled, fine-tuned, and reusable interfaces, and subsequently, those benefits apply to the system as well. In general, interface factoring results in interfaces with fewer members. When you design a component-based system, however, you need to balance out two countering forces (see Figure 3-1).

If you have too many granular interfaces, it will be easy to implement each interface, but the overall cost of interacting with all those interfaces will be prohibitive. On the other hand, if you have only a few complex, large, poorly factored interfaces, the cost of implementing those interfaces will be a prohibitive factor, even though the cost of interacting with them might be low. In any given system, the total effort involved in designing and maintaining the components that implement the interfaces is the sum of those two factors. As you can see from Figure 3-1, there is an area of minimum

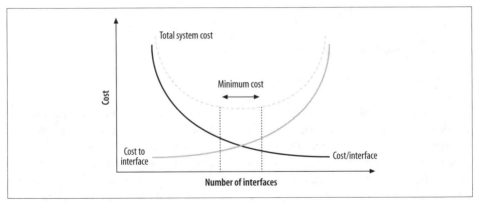

Figure 3-1. Balancing the number of components and their size

cost or effort in relation to the size and number of interfaces. Because these interface-factoring issues are independent of the component technology used, I can extrapolate from my own and others' experiences of factoring and architecting large-scale applications and share a few rules of thumb and metrics I have collected about interface factoring.

Interfaces with just one member are possible, but you should avoid them. An interface is a facet of an entity, and that facet must be pretty dull if you can express it with just one method or property. Examine that single method: is it using too many parameters? Is it too coarse, and therefore, should it be factored into several methods? Should you factor this method or property into an already existing interface?

The optimal number of interface members (in my opinion and experience) is between three and five. If you design an interface with more members—say, six to nine—you are still doing relatively well. However, try to look at the members to determine whether any can be collapsed into each other, since it's quite possible to over-factor methods and properties. If you have an interface with 12 or more methods, you should definitely find ways to factor the members into either separate interfaces or a hierarchy of interfaces. Your coding standard should set some upper limit never to be exceeded, regardless of the circumstances (say, 20).

Another rule involves the ratio of methods to properties among interface members. Interfaces allow clients to invoke abstract operations, without caring about actual implementation details. Properties are what is known as *just-enough-encapsulation*. It's much better to expose a member variable as a property than to give direct access to it, because then you can encapsulate the business logic of setting and reading that variable's value in the object, instead of spreading it over the clients. Ideally, you shouldn't bother clients with properties at all. Clients should invoke methods and let the object worry about how to manage its state. Consequently, interfaces should have more methods than properties, by a ratio of at least 2:1. The one exception is interfaces that do nothing except define properties; such interfaces should have properties only, with no methods.

It's best to avoid defining events as interface members, if possible. Leave it up to the object to decide whether it needs an event member variable or not. As you'll see in Chapter 6, there is more than one way to manage events.

Is .NET Well-Factored?

After writing down my rules of thumb and metrics for interface factoring, I was curious to see how the various interfaces defined by the .NET Framework look in light of these points. I examined more than 300 interfaces defined by .NET. I excluded from the survey the COM interoperation interfaces redefined in .NET, because I wanted to look at native .NET interfaces only. I also excluded from the results the outliers—interfaces with 0 members and interfaces with more than 20 members. I consider an interface with more than 20 members to be a poorly factored one, not to be used as an example. On average, a .NET Framework interface has 3.75 members, with a methods-to-properties ratio of 3.5:1. Less than 3% of the members are events. These metrics nicely reaffirm the rules of thumb outlined in this section; you could say that on average, .NET interfaces are well-factored.

A word of caution about factoring metrics: rules of thumb and generic metrics are only tools to help you gauge and evaluate your particular design. There is no substitute for domain expertise and experience. Always be practical, apply judgment, and question what you do in light of the metrics.

Interfaces in Visual Studio 2005

Visual Studio 2005 has excellent support for implementing and refactoring interfaces. As a component developer, your classes will occasionally need to implement an interface defined by another party. Instead of copying and pasting the interface definition, or typing it in, you can use Visual Studio 2005 to generate a *skeletal* implementation of the interface. A skeletal implementation is a do-nothing implementation: all implanted methods or properties throw an exception of type Exception and do not contain any other code. A skeletal implementation is required to at least get the code compiled as a starting point for your implementation of an interface, and it prevents clients from consuming a half-baked implementation. To have Visual Studio 2005 generate a skeletal interface implementation, you first add the interface to the class derivation chain. When you finish typing the interface name (such as IMyInterface), Visual Studio 2005 marks a little underscore tag under the I of the interface name. If you hover over IMyInterface, Visual Studio 2005 pops up a smart tag with a tool tip, "Options to implement interface." If you click the down arrow of the smart tip you can select from two options in the menu, implementing the interface either implicitly or explicitly (see Figure 3-2).

```
    public interface IMyInterface
    {
        void Method1();
        int Method2(int number);
        string Method3();
    }
    public class MyClass : IMyInterface
    {

    }
```

Implement interface 'IMyInterface'

Explicitly implement interface 'IMyInterface'

Figure 3-2. Using Visual Studio 2005 to provide a skeletal interface implementation

Once you select an option, Visual Studio 2005 creates a skeletal implementation of the interface on your class and scopes it with a collapsible #region directive. For example, consider this interface definition:

```
public interface IMyInterface
{
    void Method1( );
    int Method2(int number);
    string Method3( );
}
```

If you select explicit implementation, Visual Studio 2005 generates this skeletal implementation:

```
public class MyClass : IMyInterface
{
    #region IMyInterface Members
    void IMyInterface.Method1( )
    {
        throw new Exception( );
    }
    int IMyInterface.Method2(int number)
    {
        throw new Exception( );
    }
    string IMyInterface.Method3( )
    {
        throw new Exception( );
    }
    #endregion
}
```

Implementing a skeletal interface also works with generic interfaces.

> Visual Basic 2005 has only IntelliSense-level skeletal interface implementation, and it doesn't generate a region around the skeleton.

Interface Refactoring

Code *refactoring* allows you to change the code structure without changing or affecting what the code itself actually does. Changing a variable name or packaging a few lines of code into a method are examples of code refactoring. Visual Studio 2005 contains a simple refactoring engine that enables several actions, including renaming types, variables, methods, or parameters; extracting a method out of a code section (and inserting a method call instead); encapsulating type members as properties; automating many formatting tasks; and auto-expanding common statements. The main difference between C# refactoring and doing a mere edit or find-and-replace is that you can harness the intelligence of the compiler to distinguish between code and comments, and so on.

 In Visual Studio 2005, refactoring changes are limited to a single solution and do not propagate to client assemblies in different solutions.

You can invoke refactoring in two ways: you can select Refactor from the top-level Visual Studio 2005 menu, or you can select it from the pop-up context menu.

Of particular interest in the context of this chapter is the refactoring ability to extract an interface definition out of a set of public methods the type implements. For example, consider the following `Calculator` class:

```
public abstract class Calculator
{
    public int Add(int argument1,int argument2)
    {
       return argument1 + argument2;
    }
    public int Subtract(int argument1,int argument2)
    {
       return argument1 - argument2;
    }
    public virtual int Divide(int argument1,int argument2)
    {
       return argument1 + argument2;
    }
    public abstract int Multiply(int argument1,int argument2);
}
```

To extract an interface out of the `Calculator` class, right-click anywhere inside the class definition and select Extract Interface... from the Refactor menu. This will bring up the Extract Interface dialog box, shown in Figure 3-3.

The dialog box will propose a name for the interface: the type's name, prefixed with an `I`. The refactoring will use the default (also called *root*) namespace of the project, as configured in the project settings.

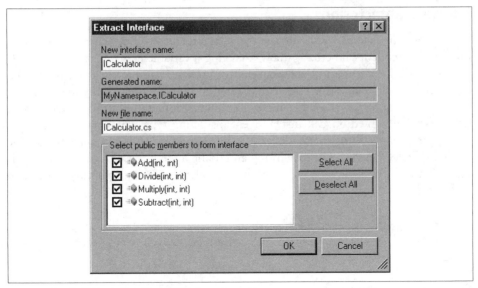

Figure 3-3. The Extract Interface dialog box

The interface will be extracted to a separate file, which will automatically be added to the project. You can provide a filename in the dialog. Finally, all the public methods (or properties) of the type will be listed in the dialog, regardless of whether they are public, virtual, or abstract. Note that when a class hierarchy is involved, the refactoring engine will only include public methods explicitly declared by the class or overridden by it. To include the suggested methods in the new interface definition, you must explicitly check the checkboxes to the left of each method. After you click the OK button, the new interface will be placed in the specified new file, and Visual Studio 2005 will add the interface derivation to the Calculator class, as shown here:

```
//In the file ICalculator.cs
interface ICalculator
{
    int Add(int argument1,int argument2);
    int Divide(int argument1,int argument2);
    int Multiply(int argument1,int argument2);
    int Subtruct(int argument1,int argument2);
}

//In the file Calculator.cs
public abstract class Calculator : ICalculator
{...}
```

Note that the extracted interface is internal, and that you have to explicitly make it public.

You can also extract one interface from the definition of another, in which case the new interface will be placed in a new file, but the original interface definition will not change (i.e., it will not inherit from the new interface). Visual Studio 2005 will not prefix the new interface name with an I, because that would result in a double II. Instead, it will append an ordinal number to the interface name.

Note that if the type already implements an interface implicitly, that interface's members will be included in the list in the Extract Interface dialog. Use explicit interface implementation on existing interfaces to avoid including them in the refactoring.

CHAPTER 4

Lifecycle Management

Traditionally, most defects in implementation that aren't business logic–specific can be traced back to memory management and object lifecycle issues. These defects include memory leaks, cyclic reference counts, the failure to release an object, the failure to free allocated memory, accessing already de-allocated objects, accessing not yet allocated memory or objects, and so on. Writing impeccable code is possible, but it takes years of experience, iron discipline, a mature development process, commitment to quality from management, and strict coding and development standards, such as code reviews and quality control. Most software organizations today lack most of these ingredients. To cope with this reality, .NET aims at simplifying component development to bridge the skill gap and increase the quality of the resulting code. .NET relieves developers of almost all the burden of memory allocation for objects, memory de-allocation, and object lifecycle management. This chapter describes the .NET solution for memory and object lifecycle management and its implications for the programming model, including the pitfalls and workarounds that component developers need to apply.

The Managed Heap

.NET components aren't allocated off the raw memory maintained by the underlying operating system. Instead, in each physical process that hosts .NET, the .NET runtime pre-allocates a special heap called the *managed heap*. This heap is used like traditional operating system heaps: to allocate memory for objects and data storage. Every time a .NET developer uses the new operator on a class:

```
MyClass obj = new MyClass();
```

.NET allocates memory off the managed heap.

The managed heap is just a long strip of memory. .NET maintains a pointer to the next available address in the managed heap. When .NET is asked to create a new object, it allocates the required space for the object and advances the pointer, as you can see in Figure 4-1. (Figure 4-1 is adapted with permission from Figure 1 in

"Garbage Collection: Automatic Memory Management in the Microsoft .NET Framework," by Jeffrey Richter (*MSDN Magazine*, November 2000.)

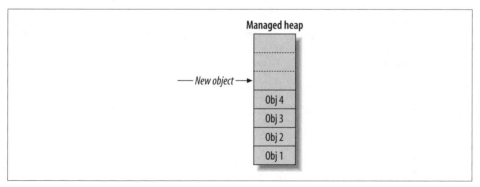

Figure 4-1. The managed heap

This allocation method is orders of magnitude faster than raw memory allocation. In unmanaged environments such as C++, objects are allocated off the native operating system heap. The operating system manages its memory by using a linked list of available blocks of memory. Each time the operating system has to allocate memory, it traverses that list looking for a big enough block. After a while, the memory can get fragmented, and consequently the list of available blocks gets very long. Memory fragmentation is a major source of performance problems because of the time it takes to traverse the list for allocation requests, combined with added memory page faults and disk access penalties.

Traditional Memory De-allocation Schemas

De-allocation of memory and the destruction of objects are also different in .NET, as compared with raw C++ or COM. In C++, the object destructor is called when a stack-based object goes out of scope:

```
{//beginning of a C++ scope
    MyClass object;
    //use object;
}//end of scope, C++ calls the object destructor
```

The object destructor is also called in C++ when the delete operator is used:

```
//in C++:
MyClass* pObject = new MyClass;
//using pObject, then de-allocating it
delete pObject;
```

COM uses reference counting, and it's up to the client to increment and decrement the counter associated with each object. Clients that share an object have to call AddRef( ) to increment the counter. New COM objects are created with a reference count of one. When a client is done with an object, it calls `Release( )` to decrement the counter:

```
//COM pseudo-code:
IMyInterface* pObject = NULL;
::CoCreateInstance(CLSID_MyClass,IID_IMyInterface,&pObject);
//using pObject, then releasing it
pObject->Release( );
```

When the reference count reaches zero, the object destroys itself:

```
//COM implementation of IUnknown::Release( )
ULONG MyClass::Release( )
{
    //m_Counter is this class counter
    m_Counter--;
    if(m_Counter == 0)
    {
        delete this;
        return 0;
    }
    //Should return the counter:
    return m_Counter;
}
```

.NET Garbage Collection

In .NET programming, exiting a scope doesn't destroy an object, and unlike COM, .NET doesn't use reference counting of objects. Instead, .NET has a sophisticated garbage-collection mechanism that detects when an object is no longer being used by clients and then destroys it. To do so, .NET must keep track of accessible paths to objects in the code. In the abstract, when the JIT compiler compiles the IL code, it updates a list of *roots*—top-level primordial application starting points, such as static variables and methods (`Main`, for example), but also internal .NET entities that should be kept alive as long as the application is running. Each root forms the topmost node in a tree-like graph. .NET keeps track of each new object it allocates off the managed heap and of the relationship between this object and its clients. Whenever an object is allocated, .NET updates its graph of objects and adds a reference in the graph to that object from the object that created it. Similarly, .NET updates the graph every time a client receives a reference to an object and when an object saves a reference to another object as a member variable. The JIT compiler also injects code to update the graphs each time the execution path enters or exits a scope.

The entity responsible for releasing unused memory is called the *garbage collector*. When garbage collection is triggered (usually when the managed heap is exhausted, but also when garbage collection is explicitly requested by the code), the garbage collector deems every object in the graphs as garbage. The garbage collector then recursively traverses each graph, going down from the roots, looking for *reachable* objects. Every time the garbage collector visits an object, it tags it as reachable. Because the graphs represent the relationships between clients and objects, when the garbage collector is done traversing the graphs, it knows which objects were reachable and which were not. Reachable objects should be kept alive. Unreachable objects are considered garbage, and therefore destroying them does no harm. This algorithm handles cyclic references between objects as well (i.e., where Object A references Object B, which references Object C, which references back to Object A). When the garbage collector reaches an object already marked as reachable, it doesn't continue to look for other objects reachable from that tagged object.

Next, the garbage collector scans the managed heap and disposes of the unreachable objects by compacting the heap and overwriting the unreachable objects with reachable one (see Figure 4-2). The garbage collector moves reachable objects down the heap, writing over the garbage, and thus frees more space at the end for new object allocations. All unreachable objects are purged from the graphs.

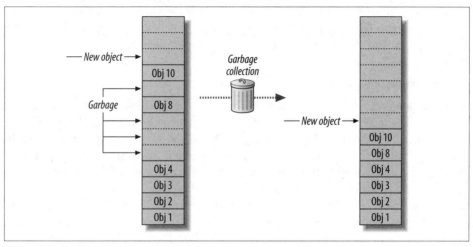

Figure 4-2. Garbage collection results in heap compaction

However, compacting the heap by moving down all the reachable objects means that any client that has a reference to those objects (e.g., Objects 8 and 10 in Figure 4-2) now holds an invalid reference. The garbage collector compensates for that by patching up all the references to the moved objects in the client code.

Another problem faced by the garbage collector is that it must ensure that the application code doesn't change the structure of the object graphs or the state of the heap during the cleanup. The only safe way to cope with that is to suspend all application threads during garbage collection. So how does .NET know when it's safe to suspend a thread? The thread might be in the middle of some allocation or data structure modification, such as adding an element to a linked list. To handle this problem, the JIT compiler inserts *safe points* into the code—that is, points in the execution path (such as those returning from a method call) that are safe for thread suspension.

The garbage collector actually hijacks the thread by inserting a different return address from the safe point: an address that includes a call to suspend that thread. When garbage collection is done, .NET sends the thread back to its original return address to continue normal execution.

 Garbage collection is usually triggered in .NET by heap exhaustion, but application shutdown also triggers garbage collection.

Object Finalization

.NET objects are never told when they become garbage; they are simply overwritten when the managed heap is compacted. This presents you with a problem: if the object holds expensive resources (files, connections, communication ports, data structures, synchronization handles, and so on), how can it dispose of and release these resources? To address this problem, .NET provides *object finalization*. If the object has specific cleanup to do, it should implement a method called Finalize( ), defined as:

```
protected void Finalize( );
```

When the garbage collector decides that an object is garbage, it checks the object metadata. If the object implements the Finalize( ) method, the garbage collector doesn't destroy the object. Instead, the garbage collector marks the object as reachable (so it will not be overwritten by heap compaction), then moves the object from its original graph to a special queue called the *finalization queue*. This queue is essentially just another object graph, and the root of the queue keeps the object reachable. The garbage collector then proceeds with collecting the garbage and compacting the heap. Meanwhile, a separate thread iterates over all the objects in the finalization queue, calling the Finalize( ) method on each and letting the objects do their cleanup. After calling Finalize( ), the garbage collector removes the object from the queue.

Explicit Garbage Collection

You can trigger garbage collection explicitly with the static method Collect( ) of the GC class, defined in the System namespace:

```
public static class GC
{
    public static void Collect( );
    /* Other methods and members */
}
```

However, I recommend avoiding explicit garbage collection of any kind. Garbage collection is an expensive operation, which involves scanning of object graphs, thread context switches, thread suspension and resumption, potential disk access, and extensive use of reflection to read object metadata. The reason to initiate garbage collection is often because you want to have certain objects' Finalize( ) methods called to dispose of resources the objects hold. Instead of initiating garbage collection to achieve this, you can use deterministic finalization, which will be discussed later in this chapter.

Increasing Memory Pressure

Normally, garbage collection is triggered when the managed heap is exhausted—the garbage collector watches the heap, and when the memory usage exceeds a certain threshold, it triggers garbage collection. The GC class provides the AddMemoryPressure( ) method for lowering that threshold, causing more frequent collections:

```
public static class GC
{
    public static void AddMemoryPressure(long pressure);
    public static void RemoveMemoryPressure(long pressure);
    /* Other methods and members */
}
```

You can also remove the added pressure via the RemoveMemoryPressure( ) method, but you can only remove pressure you have explicitly added—you can't lower the threshold below its default setting.

There are two possible uses for adding memory pressure. The first is when dealing with objects that are resource-intensive but memory-cheap. Increasing the memory pressure will result in more collections and will potentially collect the expensive objects, whose Finalize( ) methods will be called to release those resources. The problem is that it is difficult to tell by how much to increase the pressure, and doing so will not always yield deterministic results. I recommend that you avoid adding memory pressure in such cases, and instead use deterministic finalization (discussed later).

The second use for adding memory pressure is during stress testing. If you want to test how your application functions in an environment with intense garbage collection, AddMemoryPressure( ) offers a simple and easy way to find out. Such use of AddMemoryPressure( ) is benign and acceptable.

You can also trigger garbage collection using the HandleCollector helper class, introduced in .NET 2.0 in the System.Runtime.InteropServices namespace:

```
public sealed class HandleCollector
{
    public HandleCollector(string name,int initialThreshold,int maximumThreshold);
    public HandleCollector(string name,int initialThreshold);

    public void Add( );
    public void Remove( );
    public int InitialThreshold{get;}
```

```
    public int MaximumThreshold{get;}
    public int Count{get;}
    public string Name{get;}
}
```

HandleCollector allows you to keep track of allocations of expensive unmanaged resources, such as Windows or file handles. You use a HandleCollector object for each type of resource you manage. HandleCollector is meant to deal with objects that are not expensive in the amount of memory they consume, but that do hold onto expensive unmanaged handles. Whenever you allocate a new unmanaged resource monitored by HandleCollector, you call the Add( ) method. When you de-allocate such a resource in your Finalize( ) method, you call Remove( ). Internally, HandleCollector maintains a counter that it increments or decrements based on the calls to Add( ) or Remove( ). As such, HandleCollector functions as a simplistic reference counter for each handle type. When constructing a new HandleCollector object, you specify *initial* and *maximum thresholds*. As long as the number of resources allocated is under the initial threshold, there are no garbage-collection implications. If you call Add( ) and the resource counter exceeds the initial threshold (but is still under the maximum threshold), garbage collection may or may not take place, based on a self-tuning heuristic. If you call Add( ) and the resource counter exceeds the maximum threshold, garbage collection will always take place.

Using HandleCollector raises several problematic issues:

- What values should you use for the thresholds? These values may change between customer environments and for the same customer over time.
- How will your components know what other applications on the same machine are doing with the same handles?
- If you do trigger collections and the objects maintaining the handles are not garbage, you will end up paying for the collection but not benefit from it at all.

In the final analysis, using HandleCollector is a crude optimization technique, and like most optimizations, you should avoid it. Rely instead on deterministic finalization.

Finalize( ) Method Implementation

There is much more to object finalization than meets the eye. In particular, you should note that calling Finalize( ) is nondeterministic in time. This may postpone the release of resources the object holds and threaten the scalability and performance of the application. There are, however, ways to provide deterministic object finalization, addressed later in this chapter.

To end this section, here are a number of points to be mindful of when implementing the Finalize( ) method:

- When you implement Finalize( ), it's important to call your base class's Finalize( ) method as well, to give the base class a chance to perform its cleanup:

```
protected void Finalize()
{
    /* Object cleanup here */
    base.Finalize();
}
```

  Note that the canonical .NET type System.Object has a do-nothing, protected Finalize( ) method so that you can always call it, regardless of whether your base classes actually provide their own Finalize( ) methods.

- Make sure to define Finalize( ) as a protected method. Avoid defining Finalize( ) as a private method, because that precludes your subclasses from calling your Finalize( ) method. Interestingly enough, .NET uses reflection to invoke the Finalize( ) method and isn't affected by the visibility modifier.

- Avoid making blocking calls, because you'll prevent finalization of all other objects in the queue until your blocking call returns.

- Finalization must not rely on thread affinity to do the cleanup. *Thread affinity* is the assumption by a component designer that an instance of the component will always run on the same thread (although different objects can run on different threads). Finalize( ) will be called on a garbage-collection thread, not on any user thread. Thus, you will be unable to access any of your resources that are thread-specific, such as thread local storage or thread-relative static variables.

- Finalization must not rely on a specific order (e.g., Object A should release its resources only after Object B does). The two objects may be added to the finalization queue in any order.

- It's important to call the base-class implementation of Finalize( ) even in the face of exceptions. You do so by placing the call in a try/finally statement:

```
protected virtual void Finalize()
{
    try
    {
        /* Object cleanup here */
    }
    finally
    {
        base.Finalize();
    }
}
```

Because these points are generic enough to apply to every class, the C# compiler has built-in support for generating template Finalize( ) code. In C#, you don't need to provide a Finalize( ) method; instead, you provide a C# destructor. The compiler converts the destructor definition to a Finalize( ) method, surrounding it in an exception-handling statement and calling your base class's `Finalize( )` method automatically on your behalf. For example, for this C# class definition:

```
public class MyClass
{
   public MyClass( )
   {}
   ~MyClass( )
   {
      //Your destructor code goes here
   }
}
```

here's the code that is actually generated by the compiler:

```
public class MyClass
{
   public MyClass( )
   {}
   protected virtual void Finalize( )
   {
      try
      {
         //Your destructor code goes here
      }
      finally
      {
         base.Finalize( );
      }
   }
}
```

If you try to define both a destructor and a `Finalize( )` method, the compiler generates a compilation error. You will also get an error if you try to explicitly call your base class's `Finalize( )` method. Finally, in the case of a class hierarchy, if all classes have destructors, the compiler-generated code calls every destructor, in order, from that of the lowest subclass to that of the topmost base class.

Deterministic Finalization

.NET tries to simplify the management of object lifecycles by relieving you of the need to explicitly de-allocate the memory occupied by their objects. However, simplifying the object lifecycle comes with potential penalties in terms of system scalability and throughput. If the object holds onto expensive resources such as files or database connections, those resources are released only when `Finalize( )` (or the C# destructor) is called. This is done at an undetermined point in the future, usually when certain memory-exhaustion thresholds are met. In theory, releasing the expensive resources the object holds may never happen, thus severely hampering system scalability and throughput.

There are a few solutions to the problems arising from nondeterministic finalization. These solutions are called *deterministic finalization*, because they take place at a known, determined point in time. In all deterministic finalization techniques, the object has to be explicitly told by the client when it's no longer required. This section describes and contrasts these techniques.

The Open/Close Pattern

In order for deterministic finalization to work, you must first implement methods on your object that allow the client to explicitly order cleanup of expensive resources the object holds. Use this pattern when the resources the object holds onto can be reallocated. If this is the case, the object should expose methods such as Open( ) and Close( ).

An object encapsulating a file is a good example. The client calls Close( ) on the object, allowing the object to release the file. If the client wants to access the file again, it calls Open( ), without re-creating the object. The classic example of classes that implement this pattern are the database connection classes.

The main problem with using Close( ) is that it makes sharing the object between clients a lot more complex than COM's reference counting. The clients have to coordinate which one is responsible for calling Close( ) and when it should be called—that is, when it is safe to call Close( ) without affecting other clients that may still want to use the object. As a result, the clients are coupled to one another. There are additional problems, as well. For example, some clients may interact with the object only using one of the interfaces it supports. In that case, where should you implement Open( ) and Close( )? On every interface the object supports? On the class directly, as public methods? Whatever you decide is bound to couple the clients to your specific object-finalization mechanism. If the mechanism changes, the change triggers a cascade of changes on all the clients.

The Dispose( ) Pattern

The more common case is when disposing of the resources the object holds amounts to destroying the object and rendering it unusable. In that case, the convention is for the object to implement a method called Dispose( ), defined as:

```
void Dispose( );
```

When a client calls Dispose( ), the object should dispose of all its expensive resources, and the disposing client (as well as all other clients) shouldn't try to access the object again. In essence, you put in Dispose( ) the same cleanup code you put in Finalize( ) (or the C# destructor), except you don't wait until garbage-collection time for the cleanup.

If the object's base class has a Dispose( ) method, the object should call its base-class implementation of Dispose( ) to dispose of resources the base class holds.

The problems with Dispose( ) are similar to those with Close( ). Sharing the object between clients couples the clients to one another and to the object-finalization mechanism, and again, it's unclear where should you implement Dispose( ).

The IDisposable Pattern

A better design approach to deciding where and how you should implement Dispose( ) is to factor the method to a separate interface altogether. This special interface (found in the System namespace), called IDisposable, is defined as:

```
public interface IDisposable
{
   void Dispose( );
}
```

In the object's implementation of IDisposable.Dispose( ), the object disposes of all the expensive resources it holds:

```
public interface IMyInterface
{
   void SomeMethod( );
}
public class MyClass : IMyInterface,IDisposable
{
   public void SomeMethod( )
   {...}
   public void Dispose( )
   {
      //Do object cleanup and call base.Dispose( ) if it has one
   }
   //More methods and resources
}
```

Having the Dispose( ) method on a separate interface allows the client to use the object's domain-specific methods and then query for the presence of IDisposable and always call it, independent of the object's actual type and actual finalization mechanism:

```
IMyInterface obj = new MyClass( );
obj.SomeMethod( );

//Client wants to dispose of whatever needs disposing:
IDisposable disposable = obj as IDisposable;
if(disposable != null)
{
   disposable.Dispose( );
}
```

Note the defensive way in which the client calls Dispose( ), using the as operator. The client doesn't know for certain whether the object supports IDisposable. The client finds out in a safe manner, because if the object doesn't support IDisposable, as returns null. However, if the object does support IDisposable, the client would like to expedite disposing of the expensive resources the object holds. The clear advantage of IDisposable is that it further decouples the client from the object-finalization mechanism and provides a standard way to implement Dispose( ). However, the disadvantage is that sharing objects between clients is still complicated, because the clients have to coordinate among themselves who is responsible for calling IDisposable.Dispose( ) and when to call it; thus, the clients remain coupled to each other. In addition, a class hierarchy should implement IDisposable in a consistent manner—that is, implement it at each level of the class hierarchy and have every level call its base level's Dispose( ).

Disposing and Error Handling

Whether the object provides IDisposable or just Dispose( ) as a public method, the client should scope the code using the object and then dispose of the resources it holds in a try/finally block. The client should put the method calls in the try statement and put the call to Dispose( ) in the finally statement, as shown in Example 4-1. The reason is that calling methods on the object may cause an error that throws an exception. Without the try/finally block, if this happens the client's call to dispose of the resources will never be reached.

Example 4-1. Using Dispose( ) with error handling

```
MyClass obj = new MyClass( );
try
{
   obj.SomeMethod( );
}
finally
{
   IDisposable disposable = obj as IDisposable;

   if(disposable != null)
   {
      disposable.Dispose( );
   }
}
```

The problem with this programming model is that the code gets messy if multiple objects are involved, because each one can throw an exception, and you should still clean up after using them. To automate calling Dispose( ) with proper error handling, C# supports the using statement, which automatically generates a try/finally block using the Dispose( ) method. For example, for this class definition:

```
public class MyClass : IDisposable
{
   public void SomeMethod( )
   {...}
```

```
    public void Dispose()
    {...}
    /* Expensive resources here  */
}
```

if the client code is:

```
MyClass obj = new MyClass();

using(obj)
{
    obj.SomeMethod();
}
```

the C# compiler converts that code to code semantically equivalent to:

```
MyClass obj = new MyClass();

try
{
    obj.SomeMethod();
}
finally
{
    if(obj != null)
    {
        IDisposable disposable = obj;
        disposable.Dispose();
    }
}
```

You can even stack multiple using statements to handle multiple objects:

```
MyClass obj1 = new MyClass();
MyClass obj2 = new MyClass();
MyClass obj3 = new MyClass();

using(obj1)
using(obj2)
using(obj3)
{
    obj1.SomeMethod();
    obj2.SomeMethod();
    obj3.SomeMethod();
}
```

The using statement and interfaces

The using statement has one liability: the compiler-generated code either uses a type-safe implicit cast from the object to IDisposable, or it requires that the type passed in provide a Dispose() method. That precludes using the using statement with interfaces in the general case, even if the implementing type supports IDisposable:

```
public interface IMyInterface
{
```

```
    void SomeMethod( );
}
public class MyClass: IMyInterface,IDisposable
{
    public void SomeMethod( )
    {}
    public void Dispose( )
    {}
}

IMyInterface obj = new MyClass( );
using(obj)//This line does not compile now
{
    obj.SomeMethod( );
}
```

Three workarounds allow for combining interfaces with the using statement. The first is to have all interfaces in the application derive from IDisposable:

```
public interface IMyInterface : IDisposable
{
    void SomeMethod( );
}
public class MyClass: IMyInterface
{
    public void SomeMethod( )
    {}
    public void Dispose( )
    {}
}
IMyInterface obj = new MyClass( );
using(obj)
{
    obj.SomeMethod( );
}
```

The disadvantage of this workaround is that the interface is now less factored.

 Having all interfaces derive from IDisposable is analogous to having every COM interface derive from IUnknown so that the interfaces will have the reference-counting methods.

The second workaround is to coerce the type used in IDisposable with an explicit cast to fool the compiler:

```
public interface IMyInterface
{
    void SomeMethod( );
}
public class MyClass: IMyInterface,IDisposable
{
    public void SomeMethod( )
    {}
```

```
    public void Dispose()
    {}
}
IMyInterface obj = new MyClass();
using((IDisposable)obj)
{
    obj.SomeMethod();
}
```

The problem with the explicit cast is that it is made at the expense of type safety, because if the underlying type does not support IDisposable, you will encounter an invalid cast exception at runtime. You can use an explicit cast to IDisposable only if you know for certain that the underlying type will support it. This, of course, negates separation of interface from implementation and introduces coupling between the client and the actual finalization mechanism used by the object that supports the interface.

The third and best workaround is to use the as operator:

```
using(obj as IDisposable)
{
    obj.SomeMethod();
}
```

As shown previously, the code the compiler generates for the using statement checks that the variable passed in is not null before proceeding to implicitly casting it to IDisposable and calling Dispose(). Because the as operator returns null if the underlying type does not support IDisposable, incorporating the as operator into the using statement decouples the client from the underlying server type and actual finalization mechanism used and allows it to defensively dispose of the resources the object holds.

The using statements and generics

When you supply an object of a generic type parameter to the using statement, the compiler has no way of knowing whether the actual type the client will specify supports IDisposable. The compiler will therefore not allow you to specify a naked generic type for the using statement:

```
public class MyClass<T>
{
    public void SomeMethod(T t)
    {
        using(t)//Does not compile
        {...}
    }
}
```

When it comes to generic type parameters, you can actually constrain the type parameter to support IDisposable, using a derivation constraint:

```
public class MyClass<T> where T : IDisposable
{
```

```
public void SomeMethod(T t)
{
    using(t)
    {...}
}
}
```

The constraint ensures that the client specifies only type parameters that support IDisposable. As a result, the compiler will let you use the type parameter directly in the using statement. Even though you can certainly apply this constraint, I recommend against doing so. The problem with the constraint is that now you cannot use interfaces as generic type parameters, even if the underlying type supports IDisposable:

```
public interface IMyInterface
{}
public class SomeClass : IMyInterface,IDisposable
{...}
public class MyClass<T> where T : IDisposable
{
    public void SomeMethod(T t)
    {
        using(t)
        {...}
    }
}
SomeClass someClass = new SomeClass();
MyClass<IMyInterface> obj = new MyClass<IMyInterface>(); //Does not compile
obj.SomeMethod(someClass);
```

Fortunately, you can use the as operator with the using statement on generic type parameters to enable its use when dealing with interfaces:

```
public class MyClass<T>
{
    public void SomeMethod(T t)
    {
        using(t as IDisposable)
        {...}
    }
}
```

Dispose( ) and Finalize( )

Dispose( ) and Finalize( ) (or the C# destructor) aren't mutually exclusive, and in fact, you should actually provide both. The reason is simple: when you have expensive resources to dispose of, even if you provide Dispose( ) there is no guarantee that the client will actually call it, and there is a risk of unhandled exceptions on the client's side. Therefore, if Dispose( ) isn't called, your fallback plan is to use Finalize( ) to do the resource cleanup. On the other hand, if Dispose( ) is called, there is no point in postponing object destruction (that is, the de-allocation of the memory the object itself occupies) until `Finalize()` is called. Recall that the garbage collector detects the presence of `Finalize()` from the metadata. If a `Finalize()` method is detected, the object is added to the finalization queue and destroyed later. To compensate for that, if `Dispose()` is called, the object should suppress finalization by calling the static method `SuppressFinalize()` of the `GC` class, passing itself as a parameter:

```
public static void SuppressFinalize(object obj);
```

This prevents the object from being added to the finalization queue, as if the object's definition didn't contain a `Finalize()` method.

There are other things to pay attention to if you implement both `Dispose()` and `Finalize()`. First, the object should channel the implementation of both `Dispose()` and `Finalize()` to the same helper method, to enforce the fact that it's doing exactly the same thing regardless of which method is used for the cleanup. Second, it should handle multiple `Dispose()` calls, potentially on multiple threads. The object should also detect in every method whether `Dispose()` was already called, and if so refuse to execute the method and throw an exception instead. Finally, the object should handle class hierarchies properly and call its base class's `Dispose()` or `Finalize()`.

Deterministic Finalization Template

Clearly, there are a lot of details involved in implementing a bulletproof `Dispose()` and `Finalize()`, especially when inheritance is involved. The good news is that it's possible to provide a general-purpose template, as shown in Example 4-2.

Example 4-2. Template to implement Dispose() and Finalize() on a class hierarchy

```
public class BaseClass: IDisposable
{
   private bool m_Disposed = false;
   protected bool Disposed
   {
      get
      {
         lock(this)
         {
            return m_Disposed;
         }
      }
   }

   //Do not make Dispose() virtual - you should prevent subclasses from overriding
   public void Dispose()
   {
      lock(this)
      {
         //Check to see if Dispose() has already been called
         if(m_Disposed == false)
```

```csharp
            {
                Cleanup( );
                m_Disposed = true;
                //Take yourself off the finalization queue
                //to prevent finalization from executing a second time.
                GC.SuppressFinalize(this);
            }
        }
    }
    protected virtual void Cleanup( )
    {
        /*Do cleanup here*/
    }
    //Destructor will run only if Dispose( ) is not called.
    //Do not provide destructors in types derived from this class.
    ~BaseClass( )
    {
        Cleanup( );
    }
    public void DoSomething( )
    {
        if(Disposed)//verify in every method
        {
            throw new ObjectDisposedException("Object is already disposed");
        }
    }
}

public class SubClass1 : BaseClass
{
    protected override void Cleanup( )
    {
        try
        {
            /*Do cleanup here*/
        }
        finally
        {
            //Call base class
            base.Cleanup( );
        }
    }
}

public class SubClass2 : SubClass1
{
    protected override void Cleanup( )
    {
        try
        {
            /*Do cleanup here*/
        }
        finally
```

```
    {
        //Call base class
        base.Cleanup();
    }
  }
}
```

Each level in the class hierarchy implements its own resource cleanup code in the `Cleanup()` method. Calls to either `IDisposable.Dispose()` or the destructor (the `Finalize()` method in Visual Basic 2005) are channeled to the `Cleanup()` method. Only the topmost base class in the class hierarchy implements `IDisposable`, making all subclasses polymorphic with `IDisposable`. On the other hand, the topmost base class implements a non-virtual `Dispose()` method, to prevent subclasses from overriding it. The topmost base class's implementation of `IDisposable.Dispose()` calls `Cleanup()`. `Dispose()` can be called by only one thread at a time, because it uses a synchronization lock (discussed in Chapter 8). This prevents a race condition in which two threads try to dispose of the object concurrently. The topmost base class maintains a Boolean flag called m_Disposed, signaling whether or not `Dispose()` has already been called. The first time `Dispose()` is called, it sets m_Disposed to true, which prevents itself from calling `Cleanup()` again. As a result, calling `Dispose()` multiple times is harmless.

The topmost base class provides a thread-safe, read-only property called Disposed that every method in the base class or subclasses should check before executing method bodies and throw an `ObjectDisposedException` if `Dispose()` is called.

Note that `Cleanup()` is both virtual and protected. Making it virtual allows subclasses to override it. Making it protected prevents clients from using it. Every class in the hierarchy should implement its own version of `Cleanup()` if it has cleanup to do. Also note that only the topmost base class should have a destructor. All the destructor does is delegate to the virtual, protected `Cleanup()`. The destructor is never called if `Dispose()` is called first, because `Dispose()` suppresses finalization. The only difference between calling `Cleanup()` via the destructor or via `Dispose()` is the Boolean parameter m_Disposed, which lets `Dispose()` know whether to suppress finalization.

Here is how the mechanism shown in the template works:

1. The client creates and uses an object from the class hierarchy and then calls `Dispose()` on it by using `IDisposable` or `Dispose()` directly.
2. Regardless of which level of the class hierarchy the object is from, the call is served by the topmost base class, which calls the virtual `Cleanup()` method.
3. The call travels to the lowest possible subclass and calls its `Cleanup()` method. Because at each level the `Cleanup()` method calls its base class's `Cleanup()` method, each level gets to perform its own cleanup.
4. If the client never calls `Dispose()`, the destructor calls the `Cleanup()` method.

Note that the template correctly handles all permutations of variable type, actual instantiation type, and casting:

```
SubClass1 a = new SubClass2( );
a.Dispose( );

SubClass1 b = new SubClass2( );
((SubClass2)b).Dispose( );

IDisposable c = new SubClass2( );
c.Dispose( );

SubClass2 d = new SubClass2( );
((SubClass1)d).Dispose( );

SubClass2 e = new SubClass2( );
e.Dispose( );
```

CHAPTER 5

Versioning

As discussed in Chapter 1, a component technology must provide some sort of version-control support, which ensures that client applications have a deterministic way of always interacting with a compatible version of a server component. The component-versioning challenges you face are closely related to the component-sharing mode you choose. *Private* components (components that reside in a location private to the application using them) are far less exposed to versioning issues, because each application comes bundled with its own private set of compatible components—you have to explicitly intervene to cause incompatibilities. *Shared* components, on the other hand, can cause a lot of versioning headaches because they are stored in a globally known location and are used by multiple applications. Nonetheless, a mature component technology must allow multiple applications to share server components. A mature component technology should also allow different client applications to use different versions of the server components. Placing DLLs in global locations such as the system directory, as done in the past, proved fatal in the end, resulting in the devil's choice of either stifling innovation or suffering DLL Hell. Not surprisingly, one of the major goals set for the .NET platform was to simplify component deployment and version control. This chapter starts by presenting the principles behind .NET version control and assembly sharing, then explains how you can provide custom versioning policies for cases in which the .NET default isn't adequate. The chapter ends by describing how you should deal with versioning of .NET itself.

Assembly Version Number

Every assembly has a version number. That number applies to all components (potentially across multiple modules) in the assembly. You typically specify the version number in the Visual Studio 2005 project settings, although you can also assign a version number during the link phase, using command-line utilities and switches or MSBuild.

To specify the version number using Visual Studio 2005, bring up the assembly properties, and open the Application tab. Click the Assembly Information button to display the Assembly Information dialog (see Figure 5-1).

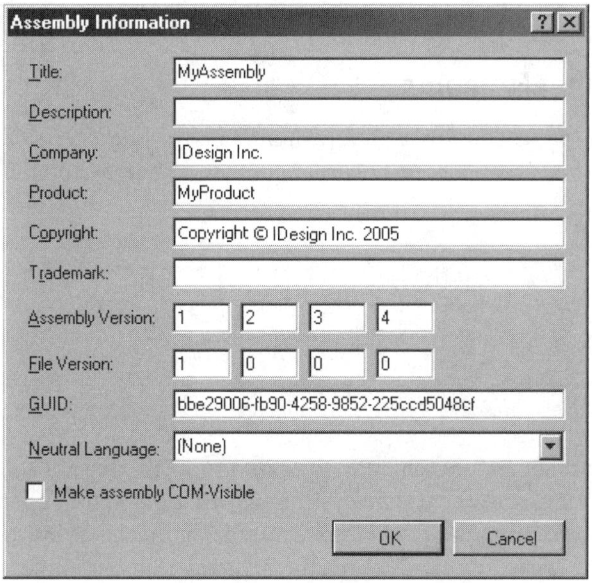

Figure 5-1. Specify the assembly version in the Assembly Information dialog

Next to Assembly Version are four text boxes used to specify the assembly version. The Assembly Information dialog is merely a visual editor for a set of assembly attributes. These attributes are stored in the project's *AssemblyInfo.cs* file. The attribute used for the assembly version is `AssemblyVersion`. For example, the `AssemblyVersion` value corresponding to the settings in is:

```
[assembly: AssemblyVersion("1.2.3.4")]
```

The version number is recorded in the server assembly manifest. When a client developer adds a reference to the server assembly, the client assembly records in its manifest the name and the exact version of the server assembly against which it was compiled. If the client uses the class `MyClass` from version 1.2.3.4 of the assembly `MyAssembly`, the manifest of the client will record that the client requires version 1.2.3.4 of `MyAssembly` to operate and will contain this declaration:

```
.assembly extern MyAssembly
{
  .ver 1:2:3:4
}
```

At runtime, .NET resolves the location of the requested assembly, and the client is guaranteed to get a compatible assembly. If a compatible assembly isn't found, an exception is thrown. The question is, what constitutes a compatible assembly? The rule of compatibility is straightforward: for a strongly named assembly (defined in the section "Strong Assembly Names"), a compatible assembly must have the exact same version number that the client's manifest requests. For a friendly named assembly, any assembly with the same friendly name is considered compatible.

Version Number Elements

The version number is composed of four numbers: the *major version number*, *minor version number*, *build number*, and *revision number*. Figure 5-2 points out these numbers, in order.

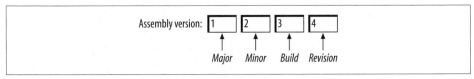

Figure 5-2. Breakdown of the assembly version number

Although you can assign any semantic to these numbers, there is a guideline or convention you should follow that conveys the meaning of version changes to the consumers of your assembly: a greater build number indicates a newer version of the same compatible assembly, and a greater revision number indicates some minor change (perhaps a minor bug fix) or changes made due to localization. As part of the product release procedures, you should verify that you have incremented the appropriate part of the version number, which reflects the nature of the new release.

 The Assembly Information dialog also lets you specify the file version number. The file version number has no bearing whatsoever on .NET versioning; it is simply available for your custom needs if you want to apply proprietary semantics.

Providing the Version Number

The default version number provided by Visual Studio 2005 for new assemblies is 1.0.0.0. However, you can provide parts of the version number explicitly, or let Visual Studio 2005 generate them automatically. If you specify all four numbers explicitly, that will be the version number used. You can also provide * for the build and leave the revision number blank. This instructs the compiler to automatically generate build and revision numbers. For the build number, the compiler uses the number of days since January 1, 2000, local time. For the revision number, the compiler uses the number of seconds since midnight, local time, divided by two (without adjustment for daylight savings). A possible assembly version number generated by the compiler could be:

```
1.2.1642.18000
```

If you have some other schema for generating build numbers, you can use it and choose just to mask out the revision number—simply specify the first three numbers manually and use a * for the revision number. The compiler then generates only the revision number, as just described.

 .NET has an assembly attribute called `AssemblyInformationalVersion`:

```
[assembly: AssemblyInformationalVersion("1.2.3.4")]
```

This attribute is available as a complementary service for you to store a custom version number. It is ignored when .NET is trying to resolve the assembly version.

Obtaining the Assembly Version

You can obtain the assembly version programmatically, using the `GetName()` method of the `Assembly` type. `GetName()` returns an instance of the `AssemblyName` class. The `AssemblyName` class has a public property called `Version`, of the type `Version`:

```
public sealed class Version : ICloneable,IComparable,
                              IComparable<Version>
{
   // Constructors
   public Version();
   public Version(int major, int minor);
   public Version(int major, int minor, int build);
   public Version(int major,int minor,int build,
                                      int revision);
   public Version(string version);

   // Properties
   public int Build{get;}
   public int Major{get;}
   public int Minor{get;}
   public int Revision{get;}
}
```

You can either access individual version numbers or convert it to a string:

```
Assembly assembly = Assembly.GetExecutingAssembly();
Version version = assembly.GetName().Version;
Trace.WriteLine("Version is " + version);
```

Assembly Deployment Models

.NET supports two assembly deployment models: private and shared. With a *private assembly*, each client application maintains its own private local copy of the assembly. Deploying a private assembly is as simple as copying it to the directory of the application using it. Although client applications will typically deploy all their required private assemblies during installation, nothing prevents a new private assembly from being copied over later. This allows for different lifecycles for the client and server and lets both evolve separately. When you copy a new version of a private assembly to the client directory, if the application has a previous copy of the assembly, the new copy overrides the old copy because a file directory can't have multiple files with the same name. Private assemblies are usually backward-compatible, meaning that they must support all the functionality available in the previous version. If that isn't the case, an old client application will break when it tries to access functionality in the new version that differs from the old version.

A *shared assembly* is an assembly that can be used by multiple client applications. You must install shared assemblies in a well-known global location called the *global assembly cache* (GAC). The GAC can support multiple versions of the shared assembly, enabling side-by-side execution of different versions of the assembly. That means that if an older version is still present, a shared assembly doesn't have to be backward-compatible. Shared assemblies simplify complicated deployment situations, especially for framework or third-party component vendors, because when a new version is installed in the GAC it instantly becomes available for all client applications on that machine. This chapter dedicates a separate section to generating and using shared assemblies.

The .NET entity responsible for managing assembly compatibility and for making sure a client application always gets a compatible assembly is called the *assembly resolver*. When a client application declares a type whose assembly isn't yet loaded, .NET looks in the client's assembly manifest to find the exact name and version of the server assembly the client expects and then passes that information to the assembly resolver. The assembly resolver always tries to give the client assembly a version-compatible server assembly. The resolver first looks in the GAC (for strongly named assemblies only, as explained next), and loads the compatible assembly from there if it is found. If no compatible assembly is found in the GAC, the resolver looks in the client application folder. If the client application folder contains a compatible private version of the assembly (it can have only one such assembly file in its folder), the resolver loads and uses that version. .NET throws an exception if no matching private assembly is found. By default, .NET does not let a client application interact with an incompatible assembly.

 Avoid mixing and matching private and shared server assemblies (that is, different versions of the same assembly, one used as private and some as shared). This can lead to conflicts between older and newer versions that are difficult to discern and resolve.

Strong Assembly Names

As discussed in the previous section, an assembly can be either private or shared. A private assembly resides in the client application directory, whereas a shared assembly resides in the GAC. Although private assemblies are straightforward and easy to use, there are two cases in which you should consider using shared assemblies. The first case is to support side-by-side execution of different versions of the same assembly. The second case is to share assemblies between multiple client applications. Sharing allows multiple applications to take advantage of an improved compatible version as soon as it's available, without patching up each application's private assemblies individually. Framework and class library vendors tend to use shared assemblies.

 The client assembly can specify another location where its private assemblies are found using the .NET Configuration tool (presented later in this chapter).

The GAC is likely to contain assemblies from many vendors, so .NET must provide a way to uniquely identify shared assemblies. A *friendly name* such as *MyAssembly* isn't good enough, because multiple vendors might come up with identical friendly names for their assemblies. .NET must have a way to guarantee assembly uniqueness. There are a number of ways to produce uniqueness. COM used *globally unique identifiers* (GUIDs)—unique 128-bit numbers assigned to each component. Using a GUID is simple enough, but it has a fatal flaw: any party can see it, duplicate it, and swap in a new, potentially malicious component that uses the copied GUID. COM GUIDs provided uniqueness, because at any point in time there could be only one registered component with a given GUID on any machine; however, GUIDs don't provide authenticity and integrity.

For both uniqueness and authenticity, .NET shared assemblies must contain unique proof of their creator and original content. Such proof is called a *strong name*. .NET uses a pair of encryption keys to create a strong name. The pair contains two keys, called the public and private keys. There is nothing special about the private key, other than its designation and the way you treat it. What is important about the public and private keys is that anything encrypted with one key can only be decrypted with the other. For example, anything encrypted with the private key can only be decrypted with the public key; the private key cannot decrypt its own encryption.

During compilation, the compiler uses the private key to encrypt the assembly's hash. (Recall that the manifest contains not only the assembly's friendly name and version number but also a hash of all the modules comprising the assembly.) The resulting encrypted blob is therefore a unique digital signature, ensuring both origin and content. The compiler then appends that signature and the public key to the manifest. Every client thus has access to the public key. The private key, on the other hand, should be kept inaccessible, under lock and key (literally). During compilation, a client referencing a strongly named assembly records in its assembly manifest a token representing the public key of the server assembly, in addition to the server assembly version number:

```
.assembly extern MyServerAssembly
{
  .publickeytoken = (22 90 49 07 87 53 81 9B )
  .ver 1:2:3:4
}
```

When the client assembly triggers .NET to try to find the server assembly, .NET starts its search algorithm (first in the GAC, then in the application folder). If an assembly with a matching friendly name is found, .NET reads its public key, computes its token, and compares that with what the client expects. .NET then decrypts the digital signature using the public key and compares the value of the assembly's hash captured in the digital signature with a hash of the assembly found. If the two match, then it has to be the assembly the client expects.

Because the private key is unique and is kept safe by the organization that created it, a strong name ensures that no one can produce an assembly with an identical digital signature. Using the encryption keys, .NET maintains both uniqueness and authenticity.

An assembly with only a friendly name can add a reference to any strongly named assembly. For example, all the .NET Framework classes reside in strongly named assemblies, and every client assembly can use them freely. The reverse, however, isn't true: a strongly named assembly can reference and use only other strongly named assemblies. The compiler refuses to build and assign a strong name to any assembly that uses types defined in assemblies equipped with only friendly names. The reason is clear: a strong name implies that the client can trust the assembly's authenticity and the integrity of the service provider. With a strong name, the client also assumes that it will always get this exact version. This cycle of trust is breached if the strongly named assembly can use other assemblies with potentially dubious origins and unverifiable versions. Therefore, strongly named assemblies can reference only other strongly named assemblies.

Signing Your Assembly

You can instruct Visual Studio 2005 to both create the encryption keys for you and sign the assembly. In the project properties, select the Signing pane (see Figure 5-3).

By checking the "Sign the assembly" checkbox, you instruct the compiler to sign the assembly with the key file specified. You can select to use a key from an existing file, or you can create a new file. The "Choose a strong name key file" combo box allows you to either create a new key or to browse to an existing file.

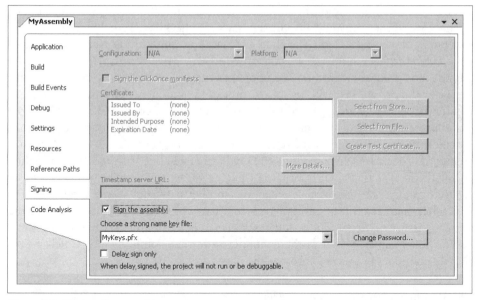

Figure 5-3. Signing the assembly

 The Signing pane also contains the settings used to sign a ClickOnce application manifest using a certificate. Signing a ClickOnce application manifest is discussed in Chapter 12.

Generating a strong name key file

If you choose to create a new key, Visual Studio 2005 will bring up the Create Strong Name Key dialog, shown in Figure 5-4.

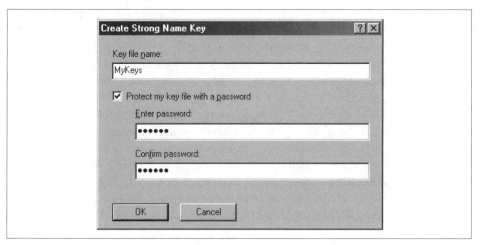

Figure 5-4. Creating a strong name key file

Strong name key files come in two flavors: plain and password-protected. If you uncheck the "Protect my key file with a password" checkbox, Visual Studio 2005 will generate a file with the name specified and with the *.snk* (Strong Name Key) extension. However, keeping the key in this raw format carries a great liability: since the strong name uniquely identifies a component vendor, any malicious party who compromises the private key will be able to produce components and pass them off as coming from that vendor. To reduce the risk, I strongly recommend always choosing to protect the key using a password. Visual Studio 2005 insists that the password specified has six or more characters. If you check the "Protect my key file with a password" checkbox, Visual Studio 2005 will generate a file with the name specified and with the *.pfx* (Personal Information Exchange) extension. The *.pfx* file is more secure than an *.snk* file, because whenever another user tries to use the file for the first time, that user will be prompted for the password. Once the user provides the correct password, Visual Studio 2005 extracts the key from the *.pfx* file, stores it in a certificate container, and uses the container from that point onward, which means that the user does not have to provide the password again.

Selecting an existing strong name key file

When you choose to browse for an existing key, Visual Studio 2005 will bring up a dialog letting you browse for either *.snk* or *.pfx* files. Once you have selected a file, Visual Studio 2005 copies that file to the project folder. There is no way to share an existing file; every project must have its own physical copy of the file.

Handling large organizations' keys

An organization's strong-name private key should be kept under lock and key. If an organization's private key is compromised, less reputable parties can impersonate that organization and distribute their own components as originals. The security and reputation (as well as potential legal liability) implications cannot be underestimated. Therefore, access to the private key of a large organization has to be restricted, preferably to just the build team (with a backup copy in the senior manager's vault). However, this raises a few questions. How can you perform your intermediate internal builds without the private key? And how can the client assembly reference your assembly? To address these issues, .NET provides *delay signing*. When you check the "Delay sign only" checkbox on the Signing pane (see Figure 5-3), the compiler will embed the public key in the assembly's manifest, but will not generate the digital signature. This allows you to install the assembly in the GAC and have client assemblies reference it (which requires only the public key), so you can carry out your internal builds and testing cycles. Merely delay-signing the assembly will allow you to build the assembly and its clients, but not to run it, because the strong name verification process will fail during load time.

For delayed signing, you can use the -p switch of the *SN.exe* utility to extract the public key from a file containing both public and private keys:

```
SN.exe -p MyKeys.pfx MyPublicKey.pfx
```

Solution Info File

Consider a .NET application comprised of multiple projects, all part of a single solution. Often, you want all the projects in the solution to have the same version number. Several of the assembly attributes commonly found in the *AssemblyInfo.cs* file (such as the company name and the copyright statement) are relatively static and are usually identical across projects in the same solution. However, the version number is typically a dynamic value. If you want to enforce a uniform version number, by default you have to update that value in every assembly. This, of course, is tedious, not to mention error-prone.

Fortunately, there is an easy workaround. First, factor the solution-wide attributes into a *SolutionInfo.cs* file:

```
[assembly: AssemblyCompany("MyCompany")]
[assembly: AssemblyProduct("MyProdcut")]
[assembly: AssemblyCopyright("Copyright © MyCompany
                                                2005")]
[assembly: AssemblyTrademark("MyTrademark")]
[assembly: AssemblyVersion("1.2.3.4")]
```

The *SolutionInfo.cs* file contains the solution-wide version number, the company's name and copyright notice, and a trademark (if any). Place that file in the root of the solution. To add it to the solution, right-click on the solution and select Add → Add Existing Item from the pop-up menu. Then select *SolutionInfo.cs* and click Add. Visual Studio 2005 will create a new folder called *Solution Items* in the solution and place the *SolutionInfo.cs* file in it. Next, edit each project's *AssemblyInfo.cs* file so that it contains only project-specific attributes, such as the assembly title, description, and culture:

```
[assembly: AssemblyTitle("MyAssembly")]
[assembly: AssemblyDescription("Some Description")]
[assembly: AssemblyConfiguration("")]
[assembly: AssemblyCulture("")]
```

Finally, you need to link the projects to *SolutionInfo.cs*. In each project, select Add → Add Existing Item... from the project's pop-up context menu. Browse to the root of the solution, and highlight the *SolutionInfo.cs* file. Do not double-click on it, because that will simply make a copy of the file and add it to the project. Instead, click the drop-down arrow to the right of the Add button, and select Add As Link. This will add a link to the *SolutionInfo.cs* file to the project. The code in a linked file is part of the project, while the file itself is not.

Note that when using a *SolutionInfo.cs* file to hold the common attributes, you cannot use the Assembly Information dialog to edit individual projects' assembly information. Doing so will add duplicate assembly attributes to the individual *AssemblyInfo.cs* files.

For consistency's sake, you can move the links to *SolutionInfo.cs* to each project's *Properties* folder. The solution should now look like Figure 5-5. Note the shortcut symbol in the lower-left corner of the linked files' icons.

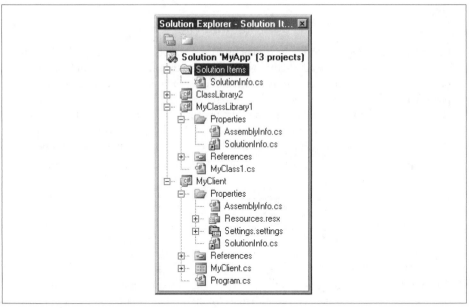

Figure 5-5. Sharing a version number across the solution

You can now freely distribute the public key file within the organization. To run the delay-signed assembly, you will need to turn off the digital signature verification of the assembly, using the –Vr switch:

```
SN.exe -Vr  MyAssembly.dll
```

You still need to sign the assembly with the actual private key before shipping it, though. You can either uncheck the "Delay sign only" checkbox and provide the complete key file, or use the -R switch of the *SN.exe* utility to resign the assembly using both keys:

```
SN.exe -R  MyAssembly.dll MyKeys.pfx
```

Strong Names and Private Assemblies

.NET distinguishes between strongly named private assemblies and private assemblies that have only friendly names. If a private assembly has only a friendly name, .NET records the private assembly version in the client's assembly manifest, as shown earlier:

```
.assembly extern MyServerAssembly
{
  .ver 1:2:3:4
}
```

However, in reality .NET ignores version incompatibility between the client application and the private assembly, even though the version number is available in the client's manifest. If an application references a private assembly with a friendly name only, that private assembly is always the one used, and .NET doesn't look in the GAC at all. For example, imagine a client application that was compiled and deployed with version 1.0.0.0 of a private server assembly that doesn't have a strong name. Later, version 2.0.0.0 (an incompatible version, according to .NET's strict versioning rules) becomes available. If you copy version 2.0.0.0 to the client application directory, it overrides version 1.0.0.0. At runtime, .NET will try to load the new version. If the new version is backward-compatible the client application will work just fine, but if version 2.0.0.0 is incompatible with 1.0.0.0 the client application may crash. However, unlike with DLL Hell, the problem will be confined to just that client application and won't affect other applications with their private copies of other versions of the assembly. .NET behaves this way because it assumes that the client application administrator knows about versions and compatibility and has judged that the flexibility of being able to copy version 2.0.0.0 is worth the risk.

On the other hand, if the private assembly *does* contain a strong name, .NET zealously enforces its version-compatibility policy. .NET records in the client's manifest the token representing the public key of the private assembly and insists on a version match. Going back to the example just discussed, in this case the assembly resolver will attempt to look up a compatible version in the GAC. If no compatible version is found in the GAC, .NET will throw an exception because the private version 2.0.0.0 will be considered incompatible. The important conclusions from this are:

- Private assemblies with only friendly names must be backward-compatible.
- Private assemblies with strong names don't need to be backward-compatible, because the GAC can still contain an older compatible version.
- Even if a private assembly with a strong name is backward-compatible (with respect to content), if the version number isn't compatible, it results in an exception (unless the GAC contains an older compatible version).
- The private assembly deployment model is intended to work with friendly names only.

Friend Assemblies and Strong Names

Chapter 2 introduced the InternalsVisibleTo attribute, used to designate a friend client assembly. A friend assembly can access all internal types and internal members in the server assembly. However, a server assembly without a strong name can only designate as a friend assembly a client assembly that also lacks a strong name, by specifying the name of the assembly in question to the InternalsVisibleTo attribute:

```
[assembly: InternalsVisibleTo("MyClient")]
```

Obviously, this is not a very secure or safe way of exposing your internal types, because all a third-party assembly has to do to access the server assembly internals is change its friendly name. Use of the `InternalsVisibleTo` attribute should be restricted to assemblies developed in conjunction with the server assembly.

To provide an additional degree of security to the `InternalsVisibleTo` attribute, a server assembly with a strong name can only designate as a friend assembly a client assembly that also has a strong name. You must include both the name of the client assembly in question and the token of its strong name to the `InternalsVisibleTo` attribute:

```
[assembly:InternalsVisibleTo("MyClient,PublicKeyToken=745901a54f88909b")]
```

Doing so indicates that the server assembly grants permission to access its internals only to client assemblies with a matching friendly and strong name, and the client-side compiler enforces that restriction.

Installing a Shared Assembly

Once you assign a strong name to an assembly, you can install it in the GAC. The GAC is located in a special folder called *assembly* under the *Windows* folder. There are a number of ways to view and manipulate the GAC. .NET installs a Windows shell extension that displays the assemblies in the GAC using the File Explorer. You can navigate to the GAC and simply drag and drop a shared assembly into the *GAC* folder. You can also use the File Explorer to remove assemblies from the GAC. The second option is to use a command-line utility called *GACUtil* that offers a number of switches. You typically use *GACUtil* in your application's installation program. The third option for managing the GAC is to use a dedicated .NET administration tool called the *.NET Configuration tool*. You will see this tool used later in this chapter to configure custom version-binding policies and in Chapter 12 for specifying security policies. The .NET Configuration tool is a Microsoft Management Console snap-in. After a normal .NET installation, you can find it at *<Windows>\Microsoft. NET\framework\<version>\mscorcfg.msc* or as a Control Panel applet under the *Administrative Tools* folder. Figure 5-6 shows the .NET Configuration tool.

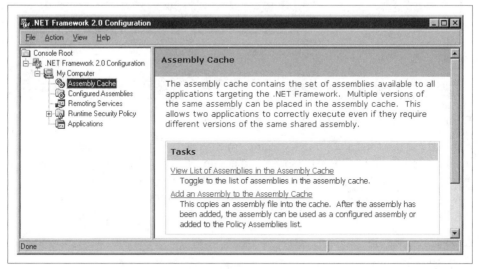

Figure 5-6. The .NET Configuration tool for managing the GAC

After launching the .NET Configuration tool, click on the Assembly Cache item in the lefthand tree pane, and then click on "Add an Assembly to the Assembly Cache" in the righthand pane. This brings up a file locator dialog. Browse to where the assembly is located, and select it. This adds the assembly to the GAC. You can now view the assemblies in the GAC using the .NET Configuration tool. Select "View List of Assemblies in the Assembly Cache" in the righthand pane. Figure 5-7 shows a typical view of the assemblies in the GAC. The view contains each assembly's friendly name, version number, locale, and public-key token. You would typically use this view to look up the version numbers of assemblies in the GAC, to troubleshoot some inconsistency, or just to verify that all is well.

 Only members of the system administrators group can add assemblies to or remove assemblies from the GAC.

Verifying shared assembly mode

For some development and debugging purposes, it's useful to programmatically verify that the server assembly is being used as a shared assembly. You can take advantage of the Assembly type's GlobalAssemblyCache Boolean property to do this. GlobalAssemblyCache is set to true when the assembly is loaded from the GAC. You

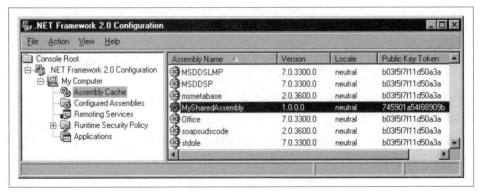

Figure 5-7. The GAC view of the .NET Configuration tool

can also use the Location property to inform the user where the assembly is actually loaded from. Example 5-1 shows the implementation and use of the AssertSharedAssembly( ) helper method, which verifies whether a given assembly is indeed loaded from the GAC. If not, the method alerts the user and specifies where the assembly is actually loaded from.

Example 5-1. The AssertSharedAssembly( ) method

```
using System.Reflection;

static void AssertSharedAssembly(Assembly assembly)
{
   bool shared = assembly.GlobalAssemblyCache;
   Debug.Assert(shared);
   if(shared == false)
   {
      string message = @"The assembly should be used as a shared assembly.
                  It was loaded instead from: ";
      string currentDir  = assembly.Location;
      MessageBox.Show(message + currentDir);
   }
}
Assembly assembly = Assembly.GetExecutingAssembly( );
AssertSharedAssembly(assembly);
```

 Writing code that depends on the assembly's deployment mode or location is wrong. Methods such as AssertSharedAssembly( ) should be used only for troubleshooting during development—that is, when you're trying to analyze what's going on and why the assembly isn't being used as a shared assembly.

Side-by-side execution

The GAC can store multiple versions of an assembly with the same name. This is because although it uses the Windows filesystem, the GAC is not a flat structure. For

---

each assembly added to the GAC, .NET creates a set of folders whose path is comprised of the assembly name, its version number, and a token of the assembly's public key. For example, such a path could be:

```
C:\WINDOWS\assembly\GAC_MSIL\MySharedAssembly\1.0.0.0__745901a54f88909b\
MySharedAssembly.dll
```

As a result, two different versions of the same assembly will be placed in two different folders—two assemblies with the same friendly name and version number but from different vendors will be placed in different folders because the public-key tokens will be different. Since each client manifest contains the referenced assembly's friendly name, its version number, and a token, that information is sufficient for the assembly resolver to locate the correct assembly in the GAC and load it. This enables side-by-side execution: two clients that reference different versions of the same assembly can coexist on the same machine, because each client application will get the assembly it expects out of the GAC.

Visual Studio 2005 and Versioning

The shared assemblies in the GAC are readily available for any client application to use. However, using Visual Studio 2005, there is no easy way to extract the server metadata from a shared assembly in the GAC to compile a client application. To build a client assembly, the client project must be given access to the server metadata. That means that somewhere on the client machine (usually in the server project, if you develop both server and client) there must be a copy of the server assembly.

When you use Visual Studio 2005 to add a reference to a server assembly, Visual Studio 2005 copies the referenced server assembly to the client directory by default. This constitutes a private server assembly for the use of the client assembly. You can, of course, manually remove that private copy of the server assembly, but there is a better way: you can instruct Visual Studio 2005 to only use metadata from the server assembly, and not to copy the assembly to the client directory. This enables compilation on the one hand and loading the shared assembly from the GAC on the other. For example, suppose a client assembly wants to use the shared assembly *MySharedAssembly*. The file *MySharedAssembly.dll* is already installed in the GAC and is available in some other location. First, add a reference to *MySharedAssembly.dll* using the Add Reference dialog box. This copies the assembly locally to the client directory and adds an item called *MySharedAssembly* to the client's *References* folder in the Solution Explorer in Visual Studio 2005. Display the Properties window of the referenced *MySharedAssembly* assembly, and set the Copy Local property to False (see Figure 5-8); this prevents Visual Studio 2005 from generating a private local copy of the server assembly.

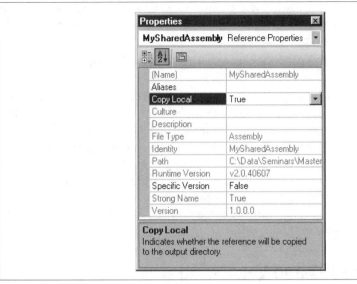

Figure 5-8. Referenced assembly properties

Now you can build the client without using a local copy of the server assembly (when you set Copy Local to False, Visual Studio 2005 actually removes the local copy and avoids copying it again). When you run the client, the assembly resolver will use the shared assembly in the GAC.

 In Visual Studio 2005, when you use the Browse tab of the Add Reference dialog to add a reference to an assembly that's already in the GAC, the Copy Local property of the reference is automatically set to False. However, when you use the Projects tab to add a reference to an assembly in a different project in the solution, Copy Local is always set to True, even when a copy of the referenced assembly is present in the GAC.

Specific Reference Version

By default, Visual Studio 2005 does not keep track of the referenced assembly version. For example, suppose you browse in Visual Studio 2005 and add a reference to version 1.0.0.0 of the assembly *MyAssembly.dll*. The reference properties will reflect the assembly version (see Figure 5-8) but will not have any affinity to it. If you replace the referenced assembly on disk with version 2.0.0.0 (while keeping the same friendly name, or even the same strong name), the next time you build the client, the client-side compiler will use the metadata and type definitions from version 2.0.0.0 of the server assembly. The manifest of the client assembly will record 2.0.0.0 as the server assembly version number, and .NET will try to provide version 2.0.0.0 to the client, not version 1.0.0.0 (the version to which the client developer added a reference). In dynamic build environments, this default behavior will allow the client developer always to be synchronized with the latest server assembly version without doing anything special about it.

The default behavior works well in a client project that adds references to other projects in the same solution—whether you change the referenced assemblies' version explicitly or let the compiler do it for you, you will always get the latest assemblies for your client debug sessions. However, you can easily run into situations where this behavior is not what you want. Imagine developing a client application against a specific version of a control (say, version 1.0.0.0). The control is part of a framework that adds its components to the GAC when it is installed. The framework also provides a folder on the disk for you to add references to. If you install version 2.0.0.0 of the framework, it will add its components to the GAC, but it will also override the disk folder with the newer assemblies. Consequently, your application will not be able to use version 1.0.0.0 of the control, even though it makes specific use of that version.

To address this problem, Visual Studio 2005 provides the Specific version property of the assembly reference. Specific version is set by default to False for all references. When it is set to True, Visual Studio 2005 will build the client only if it has access to the specifically referenced version of the assembly. Setting Specific version to True will have an effect whether the referenced assembly has a strong name or not.

If Copy Local is set to True and the version number does not match, Visual Studio 2005 will not copy the referenced assembly. When trying to build the client assembly, Visual Studio 2005 will look for an assembly with a matching version number, according to the search algorithm described in Chapter 2. If an assembly with a matching version is not found but the assembly has a strong name, Visual Studio 2005 will try to look up the specific assembly version in the GAC. In this respect, the GAC on the development or build machine is actually used as a development resource, hosting side-by-side versions of component frameworks. If Visual Studio 2005 cannot find the specific version of the assembly in the GAC, it will display a warning icon on the reference in the *References* folder and will expect the developer to resolve the problem.

 The Specific version property is only a build-time directive. It has no effect on the runtime version resolution of the referenced assembly.

Custom Version Policies

.NET allows administrators to override the default assembly-resolving policy and provide a custom version-binding policy. Administrators can provide custom policies for individual applications that affect only the way a particular application binds to its private or shared assemblies. They can also provide machine-wide custom policies that affect the way every application on the machine binds to specific shared assemblies in the GAC. Administrators can choose to create custom policies for any reason, but typically they do so when a new and improved version of a server assembly is available and the server assembly vendor guarantees backward compatibility with the older version. The administrator in that case would like to take advantage of the new version; however, .NET's default version-binding and resolving policy always tries to load the exact version with which the client application was compiled. If the new version overrides a strongly named private copy of the older version, the assembly resolver will throw an exception when it fails to find the old version. Even when the new version is installed in the GAC, the resolver will ignore it and continue to load the older version. To deal with these situations, .NET allows administrators to redirect from the requested version to a different version. .NET also allows administrators to specify a particular location to look for a specific version, instead of the default location (first the GAC, then the application directory). This allows administrators to take advantage of private assemblies in other applications, or to redirect assembly loading from the GAC to a different location altogether.

Application Custom Policies

The .NET Configuration tool has a top-level folder called *Applications*. To provide a custom policy to an application, you need to add it to the *Applications* folder. Right-click the *Applications* folder and select Add to bring up a selection dialog showing all the .NET EXE applications previously run on the machine. Select the application from that list, or browse and select the application from a location on disk. Once you've added it, you can configure a custom version policy for that application. The application will have a subfolder called *Configured Assemblies* (see Figure 5-9). Note in the figure that the righthand pane displays the configured assemblies and shows whether custom version-binding or codebase policies have been created for those assemblies.

The *Configured Assemblies* folder contains all the assemblies used by this application that have some custom policy. To provide a custom policy for an assembly, you must add it to the folder. Right-click the *Configured Assemblies* folder and select Add to bring up the Configure an Assembly dialog (see Figure 5-10).

You can select an assembly either from the GAC or from a list of all assemblies used by this application (the list is generated by reading the application manifest). Note that although the list displays all the assemblies used, including private ones with only friendly names, there's no point in selecting those because the resolver ignores version issues when the assembly doesn't have a strong name. You can easily tell which assemblies have strong names: strongly named assemblies have a value in the PublicKeyToken column (see Figure 5-11).

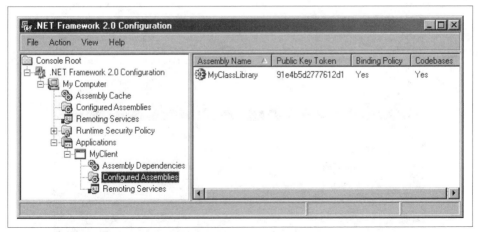

Figure 5-9. The Configured Assemblies folder

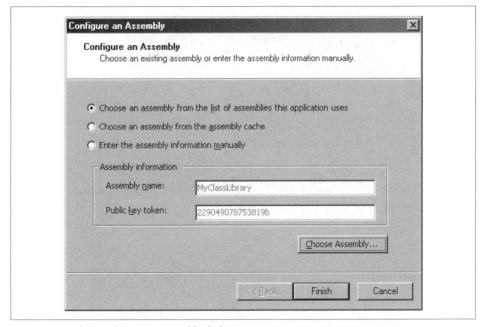

Figure 5-10. The Configure an Assembly dialog

Custom version-binding policies

Once you choose an assembly, the .NET Configuration tool immediately presents you with that assembly's properties. The Binding Policy tab lets you specify a custom version-binding policy (see Figure 5-12).

The tab contains a table listing any version redirections. As the name implies, a *redirection* instructs .NET to look for a different version than the one the application requests.

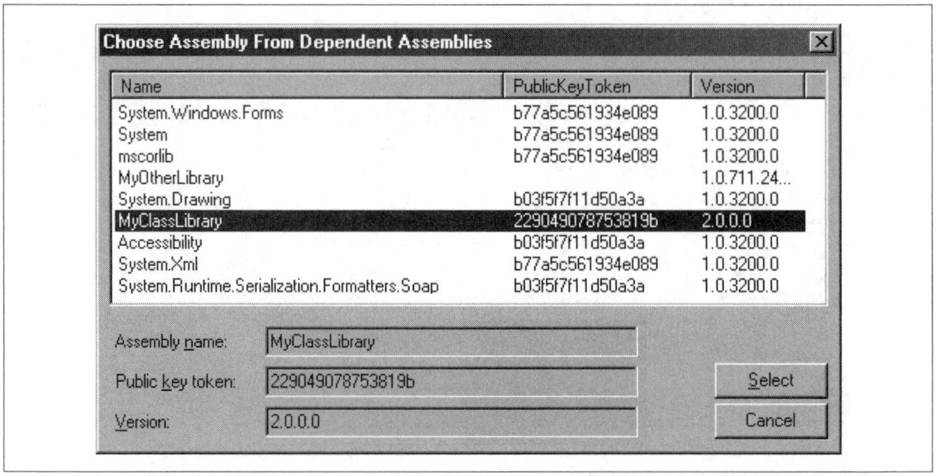

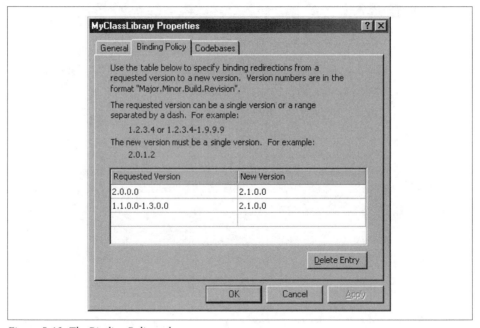

Figure 5-11. The Dependent Assemblies list

Figure 5-12. The Binding Policy tab

Administrators can specify a redirection from a particular version to another particular version (such as from 2.0.0.0 to 2.1.0.0), or they can specify a range of redirections (such as from 1.1.0.0–1.3.0.0 to 2.1.0.0). Redirections can be made from any version to any other version, including from newer versions to older versions (perhaps as a result of discovering a defect in a new version). The only requirement is that the version be specified in the .NET format of *Major.Minor.Build.Revision* number. Administrators can add as many version-redirection requests as needed.

Custom codebase policies

The Codebases tab on the assembly properties page lets administrators dictate where the assembly resolver should look for particular versions of the assembly (see Figure 5-13).

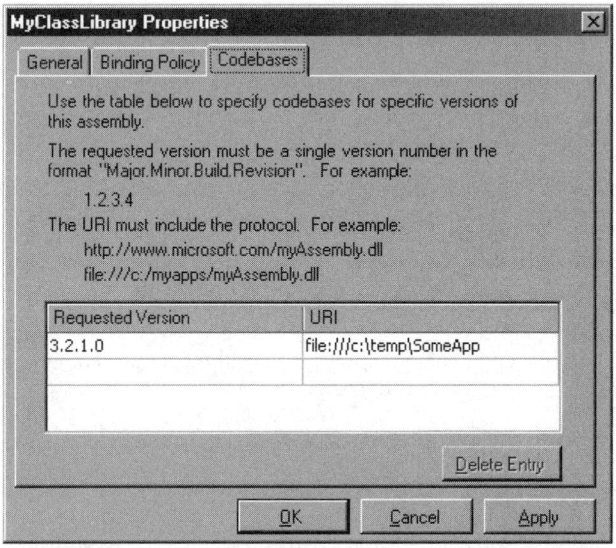

Figure 5-13. The Codebases tab

Administrators can redirect requests for private or shared assemblies to any other location. For example, if the assembly resolver is asked to load version 3.2.1.0 of an assembly and there is a codebase redirection for that version, the resolver will look for that version in the redirected location, even if a suitable version is available privately or in the GAC. The only requirement is that the redirection must be given in the .NET format of *Major.Minor.Build.Revision* number and the location must be in the form of a URL. Administrators can add as many codebase-redirection requests as needed.

Application configuration file

When you provide a custom policy for an application, the configurations you make with the .NET Configuration tool are saved in a special configuration file in the application folder. That file is called *<application name>.config* (e.g., *MyClient.exe. config*). The configuration file contains the custom policy in a simple XML format. For example, here is the configuration file containing the custom version-binding policies and codebase redirection shown in Figures 5-12 and 5-13:

```
<?xml version="1.0"?>
<configuration>
```

```
        <runtime>
            <assemblyBinding xmlns="urn:schemas-microsoft-com:asm.v1">
                <dependentAssembly>
                    <assemblyIdentity name="MyClassLibrary"
                                      publicKeyToken="229049078753819b" />
                    <publisherPolicy apply="yes"/>
                    <bindingRedirect oldVersion="2.0.0.0" newVersion="2.1.0.0" />
                    <bindingRedirect oldVersion="1.1.0.0-1.3.0.0" newVersion="2.1.0.0" />
                    <codeBase version="3.2.1.0" href="file:///c:\temp\SomeApp" />
                </dependentAssembly>
            </assemblyBinding>
        </runtime>
    </configuration>
```

The configuration file allows you to duplicate an application's custom version policies across multiple machines. Normally, you don't need to edit the application configuration file manually—instead, use the .NET Configuration tool to edit that file, and then simply deploy it on every required target machine.

> The application configuration file may also contain remoting configuration settings, described in Chapter 10.

Global Custom Policies

Administrators can also provide global custom policies for assemblies in the GAC—you can add assemblies from the GAC to the .NET Configuration tool's *Configured Assemblies* folder (shown in Figure 5-9) and then specify custom version-binding and codebase policies for those assemblies. Specifying such custom policies is done exactly the same way as specifying custom policies for individual applications. Note that global custom policies affect all applications on the machine. In addition, global custom policies are applied downstream, meaning that the application applies its custom policies first, and then global custom policies are applied. For example, suppose an application was built with version 1.0 of a class library. The application can install a custom version policy that asks to use version 2.0 instead of 1.0. In addition, suppose that on the machine there is a global custom policy that redirects requests for version 2.0 of the class library to version 3.0. When the application runs in the situation just described, it will use version 3.0 of the class library.

When you provide a global custom policy, the configurations made using the .NET Configuration tool are saved in a special configuration file that affects the entire machine. This machine-wide configuration file is called *machine.config*, and it resides in the *<Windows Folder>\Microsoft.NET\Framework\<version number>\CONFIG* folder. The machine-wide configuration file contains the global custom policy in an XML format identical to that of an application configuration file. The *machine.config* file also contains configuration settings for predefined remoting channels and ASP.NET. Normally, you don't need to edit *machine.config* manually. Use the .NET

Configuration tool for editing, and copy the file between machines only if you need to duplicate global custom policies on multiple machines.

CLR Versioning

.NET's rigorous enforcement of version compatibility raises an interesting problem: if an application is built against version 2.0 of .NET, when version 3.0 of .NET becomes available, the application will not be able to take advantage of it. The reason is that the application's manifest contains the version numbers of all the assemblies it relies on, including the CLR and application frameworks. The .NET assemblies are strongly named, and therefore the assembly resolver will insist on a perfect version match.

To overcome the issue of version compatibility with its own assemblies, .NET provides a different set of ground rules. The issues involved are intricate. The exact version of the CLR used by the components in a class library or an EXE may vary, and it depends on what they were compiled with, the available .NET versions, and the application versioning policy.

The .NET architects tried to strike a balance between allowing innovation and new versions on the one hand, and supporting existing applications on the other. Ultimately, it's up to the application vendor to decide whether to support a particular CLR version. This marks a change of philosophy: Microsoft no longer guarantees absolute backward and forward compatibility. Instead, Microsoft pledges to make every effort to be backward-compatible and to point out where there are incompatibilities. That, of course, does not mean that a new .NET version will be fully backward-compatible; all it means is that in the places that it is not backward-compatible, this was not done deliberately. The one exception to that pledge is security—Microsoft will knowingly make breaking changes in newer versions of .NET in order to deal with security breaches.

This section describes the ground rules and the actions component vendors and application developers need to take to maintain compatibility and, if possible, take advantage of new versions.

CLR Side-by-Side Execution

Even though the CLR and the various .NET application frameworks consist of many assemblies, all are treated as a single versioning unit. Multiple versions of these units can coexist on any given machine. This is called CLR *side-by-side execution*. Side-by-side execution is possible because .NET is deployed in the GAC, and the GAC supports side-by-side execution of different versions of the same assembly. As a result, different .NET applications can simultaneously use different versions of .NET. It's also possible to install new versions of .NET or remove existing versions. Side-by-side coexistence reduces the likelihood of impacting one application when installing another, because the old application can still use the older .NET version (provided you take certain steps, as described next). Nonetheless, CLR side-by-side execution allows you to choose when to upgrade to the next version, rather than having it ordained by the installation of the latest CLR version.

 If you choose to take advantage of features available in a newer version of .NET but not in older ones, your components will no longer be compatible with older versions. As a result, you must test and certify your components against each .NET version and state clearly in the product documentation which .NET versions are supported.

Version Unification

All .NET applications are hosted in an unmanaged process, which loads the CLR DLLs. That unmanaged process can use exactly one version of each CLR assembly. In addition, the version number of the CLR dictates which version of the .NET application frameworks you can use, because the CLR and its application frameworks assemblies are treated as a single versioning unit. The fact that .NET always runs a unified stack of framework assemblies is called *version unification*. Unification is required because the CLR and the .NET application frameworks aren't designed for mixing and matching (say, with some assemblies coming from version 1.1 and some from version 2.0 of the .NET Framework).

Typically, a .NET application contains a single EXE application assembly used to launch the process, and potentially multiple other assemblies (class library assemblies or application assemblies) loaded into that process. Unification means that in a process containing a managed application, the EXE application assembly and the assemblies it loads use the same .NET version. It's up to the EXE used to launch the process to select the CLR and application frameworks version; the assemblies it loads have no say in the matter. For example, all of the assemblies in the first release of .NET (.NET 1.0) have the version number 1.0.3300.0. All assemblies in the second release of .NET (.NET 1.1) are numbered 1.1.5000.0. Imagine a machine that has both versions installed. When an EXE assembly uses .NET version 1.1.5000.0, it makes all assemblies it loads use 1.1.5000.0, even if they are compiled with version 1.0.3300.0. This is not a problem, because .NET 1.1 is backward-compatible with .NET 1.0. Conversely, however, if the EXE assembly selects version 1.0.3300.0, all the assemblies it loads will use version 1.0.3300.0, even if they require the newer features of 1.1.5000.0. This may cause your application to malfunction.

The next section describes how to indicate explicitly which CLR versions your application supports. In any case, with unification and side-by-side execution, it's possible at the same time for one application to use version 1.0.3300.0 and another application to use 1.1.5000.0, even if they interact with each other.

Avoid using custom version-binding policies to override unification. It can lead to undetermined results.

Specifying a CLR Version

On a given machine, there can be any combination of CLR versions. Applications can implicitly rely on a default CLR version-resolution policy, or they can provide explicit configuration indicating the supported CLR versions.

Default version binding

If an application doesn't indicate to .NET which CLR versions it requires, the application is actually telling .NET that any compatible CLR version is allowed. In that case, .NET detects the CLR version the application was compiled with and uses the latest compatible CLR version on the machine. To that end, .NET is aware of which CLR versions are backward-compatible with other versions. Presently, Microsoft considers all newer .NET versions to be backward-compatible. Note that CLR backward compatibility is not the same as forward compatibility. Backward compatibility deals with the question of whether an assembly built against an older CLR version can execute on a newer CLR version. Forward compatibility deals with whether an assembly that was built against a newer CLR version can execute on an old CLR version. Backward compatibility is mostly the product of changes to type definition and type behavior. Forward compatibility is governed by the metadata version. .NET 1.0 and .NET 1.1 have the same metadata version, so they are both backward- and forward-compatible with respect to each other. .NET 2.0 has a new metadata version, so it is only considered backward-compatible—.NET 2.0 assemblies require the .NET 2.0 runtime.

Table 5-1 depicts the CLR version-compatibility matrix. The lefthand column lists the CLR version against which an assembly was built, and the rest of the columns list whether those assemblies can run against the other CLR versions.

Table 5-1. CLR version compatibility

Assembly\CLR version	1.0	1.1	2.0
1.0	+	+	+
1.1	+	+	+
2.0	-	-	+

A similar compatibility table is maintained in the Registry. .NET uses that table when deciding which CLR version to provide for an application (the default is to always use the highest available compatible version). Applications that rely on this default policy are typically mainstream applications that use the subset of types and services supported by all the CLR versions. Applications that take advantage of new features or types can't use the default policy, because they may be installed on machines with only older versions of the CLR. Similarly, applications that use features that are no longer supported can't use the default policy.

Specifying supported CLR versions

Using the default version may cause applications to run against CLR versions they were not tested for, resulting in undetermined behavior. If you don't want your application to rely on the default version-binding policy, and you want it to have deterministic behavior, you can provide explicit version configuration. In such cases, the application must indicate in its configuration file which versions of the CLR it supports, using the startup tag with the supportedRuntime attribute:

```xml
<?xml version="1.0"?>
<configuration>
   <startup>
       <supportedRuntime version="v2.0.5500.0"/>
       <supportedRuntime version="v1.1.5000.0"/>
   </startup>
</configuration>
```

Generally speaking, you should not add a CLR version to the list without going through a testing and verification cycle to ensure version compatibility. The order in which the CLR versions are listed indicates priority. .NET will try to provide the first CLR version to the application. If that version isn't available on the machine, .NET tries to use the next version down the list, and so on. If none of the specified versions is available, .NET refuses to load the application and presents a message box asking the user to install at least one of the supported versions specified in the configuration file. Note that the startup directive overrides any default behavior .NET can provide, meaning that even if another compatible version is available on the machine, if it is not listed in the configuration file .NET will refuse to run the application. Consequently, if an application explicitly lists its supported CLR versions, it can't be deployed on a machine with a new version that isn't listed.

Visual Studio 2005 can build only applications targeting CLR version 2.0.

CHAPTER 6

Events

In a component-oriented program, an object provides services to clients by letting clients invoke methods and set properties on the object. But what if a client (or more than one client, as shown in Figure 6-1) wants to be notified about an event that occurs on the object's side? This situation is very common, and almost every application relies on some sort of event subscription and publishing mechanism.

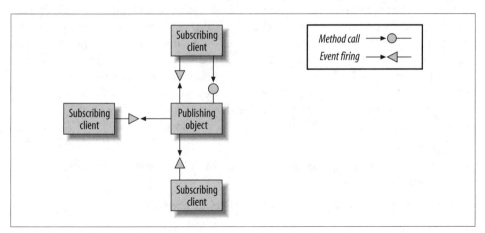

Figure 6-1. A publishing object can fire events at multiple subscribing clients

Because events are actually nothing more than method calls, there is nothing inherently special about firing events, and therefore I have chosen not to consider event support as a core principle of component-oriented programming. However, that doesn't mean that the component technology used should not try to ease the task of subscribing to and publishing events. Not surprisingly, .NET event support automates the process as much as possible. This chapter starts by describing the essential concepts of .NET event support and then provides a set of practical guidelines for effectively managing events and extending the basic event support.

Delegate-Based Events

Before I describe .NET event support, here are a few terms. The object publishing the event is called the *source* or the *publisher*, and any party interested in the event is called a *sink* or a *subscriber*. The event notifications are in the form of the publisher calling methods on the subscribers. Publishing an event is also called *firing* an event. .NET offers native support for events by providing dedicated CLR types and base-class implementations. .NET defines a standard mechanism for source and sink connection setup and tear-down, a standard and concise way of firing events, and a ready-made implementation of the sink list.

.NET event support relies on *delegates*. Conceptually, a delegate is nothing more than a type-safe method reference—you can think of it as a type-safe C function pointer or a function object in C++. As the name implies, a delegate allows you to delegate the act of calling a method to somebody else. The delegate can call static or instance methods. Consider, for example, the delegate NumberChangedEventHandler, defined as:

```
public delegate void NumberChangedEventHandler(int number);
```

This delegate can be used to call any method with a matching signature (a void return type and one int parameter). The name of the delegate, the names of the target methods, and the names of those methods' parameters are of no importance. The only requirement is that the methods being called have the exact signature (i.e., the same types) that the delegate expects. You typically define a delegate with a meaningful name, to convey its purpose to the readers of your code. For example, the name NumberChangedEventHandler indicates that this delegate is used to publish an event notifying subscribers that the value of a certain number they are monitoring has changed.

In the case of the event just described, the event publisher has a public member variable of the delegate type:

```
public delegate void NumberChangedEventHandler(int number);

public class MyPublisher
{
   public NumberChangedEventHandler NumberChanged;
   /* Other methods and members  */
}
```

The event subscriber has to implement a method with the required signature:

```
public class MySubscriber
{
   public void OnNumberChanged(int number)
   {
      string message = "New value is " + number;
      MessageBox.Show(message,"MySubscriber");
   }
}
```

The compiler replaces the delegate type definition with a sophisticated class providing the implementation of the sink list. The generated delegate class derives from the abstract class Delegate, shown in Example 6-1.

Example 6-1. Partial definition of the Delegate class

```
public abstract class Delegate : //Interface list
{
    public static Delegate Combine(Delegate a, Delegate b);
    public static Delegate Remove(Delegate source, Delegate value);
    public object DynamicInvoke(object[] args);
    public virtual Delegate[] GetInvocationList();
    //Other members
}
```

You can use the =, +=, and -= operators to manage the list of target methods. That list is actually a list of delegate objects, each referencing a single target method. The += operator adds a new subscriber (actually, just a new target method wrapped in a delegate) to the end of the list. To add a new target, you need to create a new delegate object wrapped around the target method. The -= operator removes a target method from the list (either by creating a new delegate object wrapped around the target method or using an existing delegate that targets that method). The = operator can initialize the list, typically with a delegate pointing at a single target. The compiler converts the use of the operators to matching calls to the static methods of the Delegate class, such as Combine( ) or Remove( ). When you want to fire the event, simply call the delegate, passing in the parameters. This causes the delegate to iterate over its internal list of targets, calling each target method with those parameters.

Example 6-2 shows how to add two subscribers to the delegate list of sinks, how to fire the event, and how to remove a subscriber from the list.

Example 6-2. Using delegates to manage event subscription and publishing

```
MyPublisher  publisher   = new MyPublisher( );
MySubscriber subscriber1 = new MySubscriber( );
MySubscriber subscriber2 = new MySubscriber( );

//Adding subscriptions:
publisher.NumberChanged += new NumberChangedEventHandler
                                (subscriber1.OnNumberChanged);
publisher.NumberChanged += new NumberChangedEventHandler
                                (subscriber2.OnNumberChanged);

//Firing the event:
publisher.NumberChanged(3);

//Removing a subscription:
publisher.NumberChanged -= new NumberChangedEventHandler
                                (subscriber2.OnNumberChanged);
```

All the code in Example 6-2 does is delegate to the NumberChanged delegate the act of calling the subscribers' methods. Note that you can add the same subscriber's target method multiple times, as in:

```
publisher.NumberChanged += new NumberChangedEventHandler
                                (subscriber1.OnNumberChanged);
publisher.NumberChanged += new NumberChangedEventHandler
                                (subscriber1.OnNumberChanged);
```

or:

```
NumberChangedEventHandler del;
del = new NumberChangedEventHandler(subscriber1.OnNumberChanged);
publisher.NumberChanged += del;
publisher.NumberChanged += del;
```

The delegate then simply calls that subscriber a matching number of times. When you remove a target method from the list, if it has multiple occurrences, the first one found (i.e., the one closest to the list's head) is removed.

 Delegates are widely used in .NET, not just as a consistent way of managing events but also for other tasks, such as asynchronous method invocation (described in Chapter 7) and creating of new threads (described in Chapter 8).

Delegate Inference

In C# 2.0, the compiler can infer the type of delegate to instantiate when adding or removing a target method. Instead of instantiating a new delegate object explicitly, you can make a direct assignment of a method name into a delegate variable, without wrapping it first with a delegate object. I call this feature *delegate inference*. Example 6-3 shows the same code as in Example 6-2, this time using delegate inference.

Example 6-3. Using delegate inference

```
MyPublisher  publisher   = new MyPublisher();
MySubscriber subscriber1 = new MySubscriber();
MySubscriber subscriber2 = new MySubscriber();

//Adding subscriptions:
publisher.NumberChanged += subscriber1.OnNumberChanged;
publisher.NumberChanged += subscriber2.OnNumberChanged;

//Firing the event:
publisher.NumberChanged(3);

//Removing a subscription:
publisher.NumberChanged -= subscriber2.OnNumberChanged;
```

Using delegate inference, you can pass just the method name to any method that expects a delegate. For example:

```
delegate void SomeDelegate( );

class SomeClass
{
    public void SomeMethod( )

    {...}
    public void InvokeDelegate(SomeDelegate del)

    {

        del( );

    }

}
SomeClass obj = new SomeClass( );
obj.InvokeDelegate(obj.SomeMethod);
```

When you assign a method name into a delegate, the compiler first infers the delegate's type, then the compiler verifies that there is a method by that name and that its signature matches that of the inferred delegate type. Finally, the compiler creates a new object of the inferred delegate type wrapping the method, and assigns that to the delegate. The compiler can only infer the delegate type if that type is a specific delegate type—that is, anything other than the abstract type Delegate. Delegate inference makes for readable and concise code, and it is the coding style used throughout this book.

 Delegate inference is supported only by C# 2.0. If your code is required to run on earlier versions of .NET, use explicit delegate instantiation, as in Example 6-2.

Generic Delegates

The introduction of generics in .NET 2.0 opens a new set of possibilities for event definition and management. As you will see later in this chapter, the ability to define generic delegates means that you will rarely have to define any new delegates to handle events. A delegate defined in a class can take advantage of the generic type parameter of that class. For example:

```
public class MyClass<T>
{
    public delegate void GenericEventHandler(T t);
    public void SomeMethod(T t)
    {...}
}
```

When you specify a type parameter for the containing class, it will affect the delegate as well:

```
MyClass<int>.GenericEventHandler del;
MyClass<int> obj = new MyClass<int>();
del = obj.SomeMethod;
del(3);
```

Note that the compiler is capable of inferring the correct delegate type to instantiate, including the use of the correct generic type parameter. Therefore, this assignment:

```
del = obj.SomeMethod;
```

is actually converted at compile time to this assignment:

```
del = new MyClass<int>.GenericEventHandler(obj.SomeMethod);
```

Like classes, interfaces, structs, and methods, delegates too can define generic type parameters:

```
public class MyClass<T>
{
    public delegate void GenericEventHandler<X>(T t,X x);
}
```

Delegates defined outside the scope of a class can also use generic type parameters. In that case, you have to provide the specific types for the delegate when declaring and instantiating it:

```
public delegate void GenericEventHandler<T>(T t);

public class MyClass
{
    public void SomeMethod(int number)
    {...}
}

GenericEventHandler<int> del;

MyClass obj = new MyClass();
del = obj.SomeMethod;
del(3);
```

And, naturally, a delegate can define constraints to accompany its generic type parameters:

```
public delegate void GenericEventHandler<T>(T t) where T : IComparable<T>;
```

The delegate-level constraints are enforced only on the using side, when declaring a delegate variable and instantiating a delegate object, similar to any other constraint at the scope of types or methods.

The event Keyword

Using raw delegates for event management is simple enough, but it has a flaw: the publisher class should expose the delegate member as a public member variable so that any party can add subscribers to that delegate list. Exposing the delegate as a public member allows anyone to access it and publish the event, however, even if no event takes place on the object side. To address this flaw, C# refines the type of delegates used for event subscription and notification, using the reserved word event. When you define a delegate member variable as an event, even if that member is public, only the publisher class (not even a subclass) can fire the event (although anyone can add target methods to the delegate list). It's then up to the discretion of the publisher class's developer whether to provide a public method to fire the event:

```
public delegate void NumberChangedEventHandler(int number);

public class MyPublisher
{
    public event NumberChangedEventHandler NumberChanged;
    public void FireEvent(int number)
    {
        NumberChanged(number);
    }
    /* Other methods and members */
}
```

The code that hooks up subscribers with the publisher remains the same as that shown in Example 6-2 or Example 6-3 (using the += and -= operators). Using events instead of raw delegates also promotes looser coupling between the publisher and the subscribers, because the business logic on the publisher side that triggers firing the event is hidden from the subscribers.

When you type the += operator to add a target method to a delegate in Visual Studio, IntelliSense presents a tool tip offering to add a new delegate of the matching type when you press the Tab key. If you don't like the default target method name, simply type in a different name. If the target method doesn't exist, IntelliSense lets you generate a handling method by that name by pressing Tab once more. This IntelliSense support works only with delegates defined as events (not mere delegates). There is no IntelliSense support for removing a subscription.

Events in Visual Basic 2005

The semantics of the operations for event handling in Visual Basic 2005 are exactly the same as those described for C#. The syntax, however, is sufficiently different to merit a few words and some sample code. Visual Basic 2005 doesn't provide overloaded operators for adding and removing event-handling methods; instead, it uses the reserved words AddHandler and RemoveHandler. The AddressOf operator is used to obtain the address of the event-handling method. To fire the event in Visual Basic 2005, instead of using the delegate directly, as in C#, you need to use the RaiseEvent operator.

Example 6-4 uses Visual Basic 2005 to implement the NumberChanged event. The code is comparable to that in Example 6-2, except it uses an event instead of a raw delegate.

Example 6-4. .NET events using Visual Basic 2005

```
Public Delegate Sub NumberChangedEventHandler(ByVal number As Integer)

Public Class MyPublisher
    Public Event NumberChanged As NumberChangedEventHandler
    Public Sub FireEvent(ByVal number As Integer)
        RaiseEvent NumberChanged(number)
    End Sub
End Class

Public Class MySubscriber
    Public Sub OnNumberChanged(ByVal number As Integer)
        Dim message As String
        message = "New value is " + number.ToString()
        MessageBox.Show(message, "MySubscriber")
    End Sub
End Class

Dim publisher   As MyPublisher  = New MyPublisher()
Dim subscriber1 As MySubscriber = New MySubscriber()
Dim subscriber2 As MySubscriber = New MySubscriber()

'Adding subscriptions:
AddHandler publisher.NumberChanged, AddressOf subscriber1.OnNumberChanged
AddHandler publisher.NumberChanged, AddressOf subscriber2.OnNumberChanged

publisher.FireEvent(3)

'Removing a subscription:
RemoveHandler publisher.NumberChanged, AddressOf subscriber2.OnNumberChanged
```

Working with .NET Events

This section discusses .NET event-design guidelines and development practices that promote loose coupling between publishers and subscribers, improve availability, conform to existing conventions, and generally take advantage of .NET's rich event-support infrastructure. Another event-related technique (publishing events asynchronously) is discussed in Chapter 7.

Defining Delegate Signatures

Although technically a delegate declaration can define any method signature, in practice, event delegates should conform to a few specific guidelines.

First, the target methods should have a void return type. For example, for an event dealing with a new value for a number, such a signature might be:

```
public delegate void NumberChangedEventHandler(int number);
```

.NET Loosely Coupled Events

.NET event support eases the task of managing events, and it relieves you of the burden of providing the mundane code for managing the list of subscribers. However, .NET delegate-based events do suffer from several drawbacks:

- The subscriber (or the client adding the subscription) must repeat the code for adding the subscription for every publisher object from which it wants to receive events. There is no way to subscribe to a type of event and have the event delivered to the subscriber, regardless of who the publisher is.

- The subscriber has no way to filter events that are fired (e.g., to say "Notify me about the event only if a certain condition is met").

- The subscriber must have a way to get hold of the publisher object in order to subscribe to it, which in turn introduces coupling between clients and objects and coupling between individual clients.

- The publisher and the subscribers have coupled lifetimes; both publisher and subscriber have to be running at the same time. There is no way for a subscriber to say to .NET, "If any object fires this particular event, please create an instance of me and let me handle it."

- There is no easy way for doing disconnected work, where the publisher object fires the event from an offline machine and the event is subsequently delivered to subscribing clients once the machine is brought online. The reverse—having a client running on an offline machine and later receiving events fired while the connection was down—is also not possible.

- Setting up connections has to be done programmatically. There is no administrative way to set up connections between publishers and subscribers.

To offset these drawbacks, .NET supports a separate kind of events, called *loosely coupled events* (LCE). LCE support is provided in the System.EnterpriseServices namespace. Even though LCE aren't based on delegates, their use is easy and straightforward and offers additional benefits, such as combining events with transactions and security. .NET Enterprise Services are beyond the scope of this book, but you can read about them in my book, *COM and .NET Component Services* (O'Reilly). Loosely coupled events are described in depth in Chapters 9 and 10 of that book.

The reason you should use a void return type is that it simply doesn't make sense to return a value to the event publisher. What should the event publisher do with those values? The publisher has no idea why an event subscriber wants to subscribe in the first place. In addition, the delegate class hides the actual publishing act from the publisher. The delegate is the one iterating over its internal list of sinks (subscribing objects), calling each corresponding method; the returned values aren't propagated to the publisher's code. The logic for using the void return type also suggests that you should avoid output parameters that use either the ref or out parameter modifiers, because the output parameters of the various subscribers don't propagate to the publisher.

Second, some subscribers will probably want to receive the same event from multiple event-publishing sources. Because there is no flexibility in providing as many methods as publishers, the subscriber will want to provide the same method to multiple publishers. To allow the subscriber to distinguish between events fired by different publishers, the signature should contain the publisher's identity. Without relying on generics (discussed later), the easiest way to do this is to add a parameter of type object, called the *sender* parameter:

```
public delegate void NumberChangedEventHandler(object sender,int number);
```

A publisher then simply passes itself as the sender (using this in C# or Me in Visual Basic 2005).

Finally, defining actual event arguments (such as int number) couples publishers to subscribers, because the subscriber has to expect a particular set of arguments. If you want to change these arguments in the future, such a change affects all subscribers. To contain the impact of an argument change, .NET provides a canonical event arguments container, the EventArgs class, that you can use in place of a specific list of arguments. The EventArgs class definition is as follows:

```
public class EventArgs
{
    public static readonly EventArgs Empty;
    static EventArgs()
    {
        Empty = new EventArgs();
    }
    public EventArgs()
    {}
}
```

Instead of specific event arguments, you can pass in an EventArgs object:

```
public delegate void NumberChangedEventHandler(object sender,EventArgs eventArgs);
```

If the publisher has no need for an argument, simply pass in EventArgs.Empty, taking advantage of the static constructor and the static read-only Empty class member.

If the event requires arguments, derive a class from EventArgs, such as NumberChangedEventArgs; add member variables, methods, or properties as required; and pass in the derived class. The subscriber should downcast EventArgs to the specific argument class associated with this event (NumberChangedEventArgs, in this example) and access the arguments. Example 6-5 demonstrates the use of an EventArgs-derived class.

Example 6-5. Events arguments using an EventArgs-derived class

```
public delegate void NumberChangedEventHandler(object sender,EventArgs eventArgs);

public class NumberChangedEventArgs : EventArgs
{
    public int Number;//This should really be a property
```

Example 6-5. Events arguments using an EventArgs-derived class (continued)

```
}
public class MyPublisher
{
    public event NumberChangedEventHandler NumberChanged;
    public void FireNewNumberEvent(EventArgs eventArgs)
    {
        //Always check delegate for null before invoking
        if(NumberChanged != null)
            NumberChanged(this,eventArgs);
    }
}
public class MySubscriber
{
    public void OnNumberChanged(object sender,EventArgs eventArgs)
    {
        NumberChangedEventArgs numberArg;
        numberArg = eventArgs as NumberChangedEventArgs;
        Debug.Assert(numberArg != null);
        string message = numberArg.Number;
        MessageBox.Show("The new number is "+ message);
    }
}
//Client-side code
MyPublisher publisher = new MyPublisher( );
MySubscriber subscriber = new MySubscriber( );
publisher.NumberChanged += subscriber.OnNumberChanged;

NumberChangedEventArgs numberArg = new NumberChangedEventArgs( );
numberArg.Number = 4;

//Note that the publisher can publish without knowing the argument type
publisher.FireNewNumberEvent(numberArg);
```

Deriving a class from EventArgs to pass specific arguments allows you to add arguments, remove unused arguments, derive yet another class from EventArgs, and so on, without forcing changes on the subscribers that do not care about the new aspects.

Because the resulting delegate definition is now so adaptable, .NET provides the EventHandler delegate:

```
public delegate void EventHandler(object sender,EventArgs eventArgs);
```

EventHandler is used extensively by the .NET application frameworks, such as Windows Forms and ASP.NET. However, the flexibility of an amorphous base class comes at the expense of type safety. To address that problem, .NET provides a generic version of the EventHandler delegate:

```
public delegate void EventHandler<E>(object sender,E e)
                                           where E : EventArgs;
```

If you subscribe to the belief that all your events take the form of a sender object and an `EventArgs`-derived class, then this delegate can suffice for all your needs. In all other cases, you still have to define delegates for the specific signatures you have to deal with.

 The convention for the subscriber's event-handling method name is `On<EventName>`, which makes the code standard and readable.

Defining Custom Event Arguments

As explained in the preceding section, you should provide arguments to an event handler in a class derived from `EventArgs` and have the arguments as class members. The delegate class simply iterates over its list of subscribers, passing the argument objects from one subscriber to the next. However, nothing prevents a particular subscriber from modifying the argument values and thus affecting all successive subscribers that handle the event. Usually, you should prevent subscribers from modifying these members as they are passed from one subscriber to the next. To preclude changing the argument, either provide access to the arguments as read-only properties or expose them as public members and apply the readonly access modifier. In both cases, you should initialize the argument values in the constructor. Example 6-6 shows both techniques.

Example 6-6. Preventing subscribers from modifying parameters in the argument class

```
public class NumberEventArgs1 : EventArgs
{
    public readonly int Number;
    public NumberEventArgs1(int number)
    {
        Number = number;
    }
}
public class NumberEventArgs2 : EventArgs
{
    int m_Number;

    public NumberEventArgs2(int number)
    {
        m_Number = number;
    }
    public int Number
    {
        get
        {
            return m_Number;
        }
    }
}
```

The Generic Event Handler

Generic delegates are especially useful when it comes to events. Assuming that all delegates used for event management should return void and have no outgoing parameters, then the only thing that distinguishes one such delegate from another is the number of arguments and their type. This difference can easily be generalized using generics. Consider this set of delegate definitions:

```
public delegate void GenericEventHandler();
public delegate void GenericEventHandler<T>(T t);
public delegate void GenericEventHandler<T,U>(T t,U u);
public delegate void GenericEventHandler<T,U,V>(T t,U u,V v);
public delegate void GenericEventHandler<T,U,V,W>(T t,U u,V v,W w);
public delegate void GenericEventHandler<T,U,V,W,X>(T t,U u,V v,W w,X x);
public delegate void GenericEventHandler<T,U,V,W,X,Y>(T t,U u,V v,W w,
                                                       X x,Y y);
public delegate void GenericEventHandler<T,U,V,W,X,Y,Z>(T t,U u,V v,W w,
                                                         X x,Y y,Z z);
```

 The technique used in the definition of GenericEventHandler is called *overloading by type parameter arity*. The compiler actually assigns different names to the overloaded delegates, distinguishing them based on the number of arguments or the number of generic type parameters. For example, the following code:

```
Type type = typeof(GenericEventHandler<,>);
Trace.WriteLine(type.ToString());
```

traces:

```
GenericEventHandler`2[T,U]
```

because the compiler appends `2 to the delegate name (2 being the number of generic type parameters used).

The various GenericEventHandler versions can be used to invoke any event-handling method that accepts between zero and seven arguments (more than five or so arguments is a bad practice anyway, and you should use structures, or an EventArgs-derived class, to pass multiple arguments). You can define any combination of types using GenericEventHandler. For example:

```
GenericEventHandler<int> del1;
GenericEventHandler<int,int> del2;
GenericEventHandler<int,string> del3;
GenericEventHandler<int,string,int> del4;
```

or, for passing multiple arguments:

```
struct MyStruct
{...}
public class MyArgs : EventArgs
{...}
GenericEventHandler<MyStruct> del5;
GenericEventHandler<MyArgs> del6;
```

Example 6-7 shows the use of `GenericEventHandler` and a generic event-handling method.

Example 6-7. Generic event handling

```
public class MyArgs : EventArgs
{...}
public class MyPublisher
{
   public event GenericEventHandler<MyPublisher,MyArgs> MyEvent;
   public void FireEvent()
   {
      MyArgs args = new MyArgs(...);
      MyEvent(this,args);
   }
}
public class MySubscriber<A> where A : EventArgs
{
   public void OnEvent(MyPublisher sender,A args)
   {...}
}
MyPublisher publisher = new MyPublisher();
MySubscriber<MyArgs> subscriber = new MySubscriber<MyArgs>();
publisher.MyEvent += subscriber.OnEvent;
```

This example uses `GenericEventHandler` with two type parameters, the sender type and the argument container class, similar to generic and non-generic versions of `EventHandler`. However, unlike `EventHandler`, `GenericEventHandler` is type-safe, because it accepts only objects of the type `MyPublisher` (rather than merely `object`) as senders. Clearly, you can use `GenericEventHandler` with all event signatures, including those that do not comply with the sender object and the `EventArgs` derivation guideline.

For demonstration purposes, Example 6-7 also uses a generic subscriber, which accepts a generic type parameter for the event argument container. You could define the subscriber to use a specific type of argument container instead, without affecting the publisher code at all:

```
public class MySubscriber
{
   public void OnEvent(MyPublisher sender,MyArgs args)
   {...}
}
```

If you want to enforce the use of an `EventArgs`-derived class as an argument, you can put a constraint on `GenericEventHandler`:

```
public delegate void GenericEventHandler<T,U>(T t,U u) where U : EventArgs;
```

However, for the sake of generic use of `GenericEventHandler`, it is better to place the constraint on the subscribing type (or the subscribing method), as shown in Example 6-7.

Sometimes is it useful to alias a particular combination of specific types. You can do that via the using statement:

```
using MyHandler = GenericEventHandler
                              <MyPublisher,MyArgs>;
public class MyPublisher
{
    public event MyHandler MyEvent;
    //Rest of MyPublisher
}
```

Note that the scope of aliasing is the scope of the file, so you have to repeat aliasing across the project files, in the same way you would if you were using namespaces.

Publishing Events Defensively

In .NET, if a delegate has no targets in its internal list, its value will be set to null. A C# publisher should always check a delegate for a null value before attempting to invoke it. If no client has subscribed to the event, the delegate's target list will be empty and the delegate value set to null. When the publisher tries to access a nulled delegate, an exception is thrown. Visual Basic 2005 developers don't need to check the value of the delegate because the RaiseEvent statement can accept an empty delegate. Internally, RaiseEvent checks that the delegate is not null before accessing it.

A separate problem with delegate-based events is exceptions. Any unhandled exception raised by the subscriber will be propagated to the publisher. Some subscribers may encounter an exception in their handling of the event, not handle it, and cause the publisher to crash. For these reasons, you should always publish inside a try/catch block. Example 6-8 demonstrates these points.

Example 6-8. Defensive publishing

```
public class MyPublisher
{
    public event EventHandler MyEvent;
    public void FireEvent()
    {
        try
        {
            if(MyEvent != null)
                MyEvent(this,EventArgs.Empty);
        }
        catch
        {
            //Handle exceptions
        }
    }
}
```

However, the code in Example 6-8 aborts the event publishing in case a subscriber throws an exception. Sometimes you want to continue publishing even if a subscriber throws an exception. To do so, you need to manually iterate over the internal list maintained by the delegate and catch any exceptions thrown by the individual delegates in the list. You access the internal list by using a special method every delegate supports (see Example 6-1), called GetInvocationList( ). The method is defined as:

```
public virtual Delegate[] GetInvocationList();
```

GetInvocationList( ) returns a collection of delegates you can iterate over, as shown in Example 6-9.

Example 6-9. Continuous publishing in the face of exceptions thrown by the subscribers

```
public class MyPublisher
{
   public event EventHandler MyEvent;
   public void FireEvent()
   {
      if(MyEvent == null)
      {
         return;
      }
      Delegate[] delegates = MyEvent.GetInvocationList();
      foreach(Delegate del in delegates)
      {
         EventHandler sink = (EventHandler)del;
         try
         {
            sink(this,EventArgs.Empty);
         }
         catch{}
      }
   }
}
```

The EventsHelper class

The problem with the publishing code in Example 6-9 is that it isn't reusable—you have to duplicate it each time you want fault isolation between the publisher and the subscribers. It's possible, however, to write a helper class that can publish to any delegate, pass any argument collection, and catch potential exceptions. Example 6-10 shows the EventsHelper static class, which provides the static Fire( ) method. The Fire( ) method defensively fires any type of event.

Example 6-10. The EventsHelper class

```
public static class EventsHelper
{
   public static void Fire(Delegate del,params object[] args)
   {
      if(del == null)
```

Example 6-10. The EventsHelper class (continued)

```
      {
         return;
      }
      Delegate[] delegates = del.GetInvocationList( );
      foreach(Delegate sink in delegates)
      {
         try
         {
            sink.DynamicInvoke(args);
         }
         catch{}
      }
   }
}
```

There are two key elements to implementing EventsHelper. The first is its ability to invoke any delegate. This is possible using the DynamicInvoke( ) method, which every delegate provides (see Example 6-1). DynamicInvoke( ) invokes the delegate, passing it a collection of arguments. It is defined as:

```
public object DynamicInvoke(object[] args);
```

The second key in implementing EventsHelper is passing it an open-ended number of objects as arguments for the subscribers. This is done using the C# params parameter modifier (ParamArray in Visual Basic 2005), which allows inlining of objects as parameters. The compiler converts the inlined arguments into an array of objects and passes in that array.

Using EventsHelper is elegant and straightforward: simply pass it the delegate to invoke and the parameters. For example, for the delegate MyEventHandler, defined as:

```
public delegate void MyEventHandler(int number,string str);
```

the following can be the publishing code:

```
public class MyPublisher
{
   public event MyEventHandler MyEvent;
   public void FireEvent(int number, string str)
   {
      EventsHelper.Fire(MyEvent,number,str);
   }
}
```

When using EventsHelper from Visual Basic 2005, you need to access the delegate directly. The Visual Basic 2005 compiler generates a hidden member variable corresponding to the event member. The name of that hidden member is the name of the event, suffixed with Event:

```
Public Delegate Sub MyEventHandler (ByVal number As Integer, ByVal str As String)
Public Class MyPublisher
   Public Event MyEvent As MyEventHandler
```

```
      Public Sub FireEvent (ByVal number As Integer, ByVal str As String)
         EventsHelper.Fire(MyEventEvent, number, str)
      End Sub
   End Class
```

Making EventsHelper type-safe

The problem with EventsHelper as presented in Example 6-10 is that it is not type-safe. The Fire( ) method takes a collection of amorphous objects to allow any combination of parameters, including an incorrect combination. For example, given this delegate definition:

```
public delegate void MyEventHandler(int number,string str);
```

the following publishing code will compile fine but will fail to publish:

```
public class MyPublisher
{
   public event MyEventHandler MyEvent;
   public void FireEvent(int number, string str)
   {
      EventsHelper.Fire(MyEvent,"Not","Type","Safe");
   }
}
```

Any mismatches in the number of arguments or their type will not be detected at compile time. In addition, EventsHelper will snuff out the exceptions, and you will not even be aware of the problem.

However, if you can commit to always using GenericEventHandler instead of defining your own delegates for event handling, there is a way to enforce compile-time type safety. Instead of defining the delegate like so:

```
public delegate void MyEventHandler(int number,string str);
```

use GenericEventHandler directly, or alias it:

```
using MyEventHandler = GenericEventHandler<int,string>;
```

Next, combine EventsHelper with GenericEventHandler, as shown in Example 6-11.

Example 6-11. The type-safe EventsHelper

```
public static class EventsHelper
{
   //Same as Fire( ) in Example 6-10
   public static void UnsafeFire(Delegate del,params object[] args)
   {...}
   public static void Fire(GenericEventHandler del)
   {
      UnsafeFire(del);
   }
   public static void Fire<T>(GenericEventHandler<T> del,T t)
   {
      UnsafeFire(del,t);
```

Example 6-11. The type-safe EventsHelper (continued)

```
    }
    public static void Fire<T,U>(GenericEventHandler<T,U> del,T t,U u)
    {
        UnsafeFire(del,t,u);
    }
    public static void Fire<T,U,V>(GenericEventHandler<T,U,V> del,
                                                        T t,U u,V v)

    {
        UnsafeFire(del,t,u,v);
    }
    public static void Fire<T,U,V,W>(GenericEventHandler<T,U,V,W> del,
                                                        T t,U u,V v,W w)

    {
        UnsafeFire(del,t,u,v,w);
    }
    public static void Fire<T,U,V,W,X>(GenericEventHandler<T,U,V,W,X> del,
                                                  T t,U u,V v,W w,X x)

    {
        UnsafeFire(del,t,u,v,w,x);
    }
    public static void Fire<T,U,V,W,X,Y>(GenericEventHandler<T,U,V,W,X,Y> del,
                                                  T t,U u,V v,W w,X x,Y y)

    {
        UnsafeFire(del,t,u,v,w,x,y);
    }
    public static void Fire<T,U,V,W,X,Y,Z>(GenericEventHandler<T,U,V,W,X,Y,Z> del,
                                              T t,U u,V v,W w,X x,Y y,Z z)

    {
        UnsafeFire(del,t,u,v,w,x,y,z);
    }
}
```

Because the number and type of arguments passed to GenericEventHandler are known to the compiler, you can enforce type safety at compile time. Thanks to the overloading by the number of generic type parameters, you need not even specify any of the generic type parameters passed to the Fire( ) methods. The publishing code remains the same as if you are using the definition of Example 6-10:

```
using MyEventHandler = GenericEventHandler<int,string>;

public class MyPublisher
{
    public event MyEventHandler MyEvent;
    public void FireEvent(int number, string str)
    {
        //This is now type-safe
        EventsHelper.Fire(MyEvent,number,str);
    }
}
```

The compiler infers the type and number of type parameters used and selects the correct overloaded version of Fire( ).

If you can only guarantee the use of EventHandler, rather than GenericEventHandler, you can add these overloaded methods to EventsHelper:

```
public static void Fire(EventHandler del,object sender,EventArgs e)
{
   UnsafeFire(del,sender,e);
}
public static void Fire<E>(EventHandler<E> del,object sender,E e)
                                            where E : EventArgs
{
   UnsafeFire(del,sender,t);
}
```

This will enable you to publish defensively, in a type-safe manner, any EventHandler-based event.

EventsHelper can still offer the non-type-safe UnsafeFire( ) method:

```
public static void UnsafeFire(Delegate del,params object[] args)
{
   if(args.Length > 7)
   {
      Trace.TraceWarning("Too many parameters. Consider a structure
                    to enable the use of the type-safe versions");
   }
   //Rest same as in Example 6-11
}
```

This is required in case you are dealing with delegates that are not based on GenericEventHandler or EventHandler, or when you have more than the number of parameters GenericEventHandler can deal with. Obviously, using more than even five parameters should be avoided for any method by definition, but at least now the developer using EventsHelper is aware of the type-safety pitfall. If you want to always enforce the use of the type-safe Fire( ) methods, simply define UnsafeFire( ) as private:

```
static void UnsafeFire(Delegate del,params object[] args);
```

Event Accessors

To hook up a subscriber to a publisher, you access the publisher's event member variable directly. Exposing class members in public is asking for trouble; it violates the core object-oriented design principle of encapsulation and information hiding, and it couples all subscribers to the exact member variable definition. To mitigate this problem, C# provides a property-like mechanism called an *event accessor*. Accessors provide a benefit similar to that of properties, hiding the actual class member while maintaining the original ease of use. C# uses add and remove—performing the functions of the += and -= operators, respectively—to encapsulate the event member variable. Example 6-12 demonstrates the use of event accessors and the corresponding client code. Note that when you use event accessors, there is no advantage to marking the encapsulated delegate member as an event.

Example 6-12. Using event accessors

```
using MyEventHandler = GenericEventHandler<string>;
public class MyPublisher
{
    MyEventHandler m_MyEvent;
    public event MyEventHandler MyEvent
    {
        add
        {
            m_MyEvent += value;
        }
        remove
        {
            m_MyEvent -= value;
        }
    }
    public void FireEvent()
    {
        EventsHelper.Fire(m_MyEvent,"Hello");
    }
}
public class MySubscriber
{
    public void OnEvent(string message)
    {
        MessageBox.Show(message);
    }
}
//Client code:
MyPublisher publisher = new MyPublisher();
MySubscriber subscriber = new MySubscriber();

//Set up connection:
publisher.MyEvent += subscriber.OnEvent;

publisher.FireEvent();

//Tear down connection:
publisher.MyEvent -= subscriber.OnEvent;
```

Managing Large Numbers of Events

Imagine a class that publishes a very large number of events. This is common when developing frameworks; for example, the class Control in the System.Windows.Forms namespace has dozens of events corresponding to many Windows messages. The problem with handling numerous events is that it's simply impractical to allocate a class member for each event: the class definition, documentation, CASE tool diagrams, and even IntelliSense would be unmanageable. To address this predicament, . NET provides the EventHandlerList class (found in the System.ComponentModel namespace):

```
public sealed class EventHandlerList : IDisposable
{
    public EventHandlerList();
    public Delegate this[object key]{get;set;}
    public void AddHandler(object key, Delegate value);
    public void AddHandlers(EventHandlerList listToAddFrom);
    public void RemoveHandler(object key, Delegate value);
    public virtual void Dispose();
}
```

EventHandlerList is a linear list that stores key/value pairs. The key is an object that identifies the event, and the value is an instance of System.Delegate. Because the index is an object, it can be an integer index, a string, a particular button instance, and so on. You add and remove individual event-handling methods using the AddHandler and RemoveHandler methods, respectively. You can also add the content of an existing EventHandlerList, using the AddHandlers() method. To fire an event, you access the event list using the indexer with the key object, and you get back a System.Delegate object. You then downcast that delegate to the actual event delegate and fire the event.

Example 6-13 demonstrates using the EventHandlerList class when implementing a Windows Forms–like button class called MyButton. The button supports many events, such as mouse click and mouse move, all channeled to the same event list. Using event accessors, this is completely encapsulated from the clients.

Example 6-13. Using the EventHandlerList class to manage a large number of events

```
using System.ComponentModel;

using ClickEventHandler = GenericEventHandler<MyButton,EventArgs>;
using MouseEventHandler = GenericEventHandler<MyButton,MouseEventArgs>;

public class MyButton
{
    EventHandlerList m_EventList;
    public MyButton()
    {
        m_EventList = new EventHandlerList();
        /* Rest of the initialization */
    }
    public event ClickEventHandler Click
    {
        add
        {
            m_EventList.AddHandler("Click",value);
        }
        remove
        {
            m_EventList.RemoveHandler("Click",value);
        }
    }
    public event MouseEventHandler MouseMove
    {
```

```
    add
    {
        m_EventList.AddHandler("MouseMove",value);
    }
    remove
    {
        m_EventList.RemoveHandler("MouseMove",value);
    }
}
void FireClick()
{
    ClickEventHandler handler = m_EventList["Click"] as ClickEventHandler;
    EventsHelper.Fire(handler,this,EventArgs.Empty);
}
void FireMouseMove(MouseButtons button,int clicks,int x,int y,int delta)
{
    MouseEventHandler handler = m_EventList["MouseMove"] as MouseEventHandler;
    MouseEventArgs args = new MouseEventArgs(button,clicks,x,y,delta);
    EventsHelper.Fire(handler,this,args);
}
/* Other methods and events definition */
}
```

The problem with Example 6-13 is that events such as mouse move or even mouse click are raised frequently, and creating a new string as a key for each invocation increases the pressure on the managed heap. A better approach would be to use pre-allocated static keys, shared among all instances:

```
public class MyButton
{
    EventHandlerList m_EventList;
    static object m_MouseMoveEventKey = new object();

    public event MouseEventHandler MouseMove
    {
        add
        {
            m_EventList.AddHandler(m_MouseMoveEventKey,value);
        }
        remove
        {
            m_EventList.RemoveHandler(m_MouseMoveEventKey,value);
        }
    }
    void FireMouseMove(MouseButtons button,int clicks,int x,int y,int delta)
    {
        MouseEventHandler handler;
        handler = m_EventList[m_MouseMoveEventKey] as MouseEventHandler;
        MouseEventArgs args = new MouseEventArgs(button,clicks,x,y,delta);
        EventsHelper.Fire(handler,this,args);
    }
    /* Rest of the implementation   */
}
```

Writing Sink Interfaces

By hiding the actual event members, event accessors provide barely enough encapsulation. However, you can improve on this model. To illustrate, consider the case where a subscriber wishes to subscribe to a set of events. Why should it make multiple potentially expensive calls to set up and tear down the connections? Why does the subscriber need to know about the event accessors in the first place? What if the subscriber wants to receive events on an entire interface, instead of individual methods? The next step is to provide a simple but generic way to manage the connections between the publisher and the subscribers—one that will save the redundant calls, encapsulate the event accessors and members, and allow sinking interfaces. This section describes a technique I have developed to do just that. Consider an interface that defines a set of events, the IMySubscriber interface:

```
public interface IMySubscriber
{
    void OnEvent1(object sender,EventArgs eventArgs);
    void OnEvent2(object sender,EventArgs eventArgs);
    void OnEvent3(object sender,EventArgs eventArgs);
}
```

Anybody can implement this interface, and the interface is really all the publisher should know about:

```
public class MySubscriber : IMySubscriber
{
    public void OnEvent1(object sender,EventArgs eventArgs)
    {...}
    public void OnEvent2(object sender,EventArgs eventArgs)
    {...}
    public void OnEvent3(object sender,EventArgs eventArgs)
    {...}
}
```

Next, define an enumeration of the events and mark the enum with the Flags attribute:

```
[Flags]
public enum EventType
{
    OnEvent1,
    OnEvent2,
    OnEvent3,
    OnAllEvents = OnEvent1|OnEvent2|OnEvent3
}
```

The Flags attribute indicates that the enum values could be used as a bit mask (see the EventType.OnAllEvents definition). This allows you to combine different enum values using the | (OR) bitwise operator or mask them using the & (AND) operator.

The publisher provides two methods, Subscribe( ) and Unsubscribe( ), each of which accepts two parameters: the interface and a bit-mask flag to indicate which events to

---

subscribe the sink interface to. Internally, the publisher can have an event delegate member per method on the sink interface, or just one for all methods (it's an implementation detail, hidden from the subscribers). Example 6-14 uses an event member variable for each method on the sink interface. It shows Subscribe( ) and Un Subscribe( ), as well as the FireEvent( ) method, with error handling removed for clarity. Subscribe( ) checks the flag and subscribes the corresponding interface method:

```
if((eventType & EventType.OnEvent1) == EventType.OnEvent1)
{
    m_Event1 += subscriber.OnEvent1;
}
```

UnSubscribe( ) removes the subscription in a similar fashion.

Example 6-14. Sinking interfaces

```
using MyEventHandler = GenericEventHandler<object,EventArgs>;
public class MyPublisher
{
    MyEventHandler m_Event1;
    MyEventHandler m_Event2;
    MyEventHandler m_Event3;

    public void Subscribe(IMySubscriber subscriber,EventType eventType)
    {
        if((eventType & EventType.OnEvent1) == EventType.OnEvent1)
        {
            m_Event1 += subscriber.OnEvent1;
        }
        if((eventType & EventType.OnEvent2) == EventType.OnEvent2)
        {
            m_Event2 += subscriber.OnEvent2;
        }
        if((eventType & EventType.OnEvent3) == EventType.OnEvent3)
        {
            m_Event3 += subscriber.OnEvent3;
        }
    }
    public void Unsubscribe(IMySubscriber subscriber,EventType eventType)
    {
        if((eventType & EventType.OnEvent1) == EventType.OnEvent1)
        {
            m_Event1 -= subscriber.OnEvent1;
        }
        if((eventType & EventType.OnEvent2) == EventType.OnEvent2)
        {
            m_Event2 -= subscriber.OnEvent2;
        }
        if((eventType & EventType.OnEvent3) == EventType.OnEvent3)
        {
            m_Event3 -= subscriber.OnEvent3;
        }
    }
```

Example 6-14. Sinking interfaces (continued)

```
    public void FireEvent(EventType eventType)
    {
        if((eventType & EventType.OnEvent1) == EventType.OnEvent1)
        {
            EventsHelper.Fire(m_Event1,this,EventArgs.Empty);
        }
        if((eventType & EventType.OnEvent2) == EventType.OnEvent2)
        {
            EventsHelper.Fire(m_Event2,this,EventArgs.Empty);
        }
        if((eventType & EventType.OnEvent3) == EventType.OnEvent3)
        {
            EventsHelper.Fire(m_Event3,this,EventArgs.Empty);
        }
    }
}
```

The code required for subscribing or unsubscribing is equally straightforward:

```
MyPublisher publisher = new MyPublisher();
IMySubscriber subscriber  = new MySubscriber();
//Subscribe to events 1 and 2
publisher.Subscribe(subscriber,EventType.OnEvent1|EventType.OnEvent2);
//Fire just event 1
publisher.FireEvent(EventType.OnEvent1);
```

Still, it shows the elegance of this approach for sinking whole interfaces with one call, and shows how completely encapsulated the actual event class members are.

CHAPTER 7

Asynchronous Calls

When a method call is made on an object, the client is typically blocked while the object executes the call, and control returns to the client only when the method completes execution and returns. However, there are quite a few cases in which you want to call methods asynchronously; that is, you want control to return immediately to the client, while the object executes the called method in the background and then somehow lets the client know that the method has completed execution. Such an execution mode is called *asynchronous method invocation*, and the action is known as an *asynchronous call*. Asynchronous calls allow you to improve availability, increase throughput and performance, and scale up your application.

In the past, developers often had to handcraft proprietary mechanisms for asynchronously invoking calls on their components. One recurring mechanism was to have the object spin off a worker thread to process the client's request and immediately return control to the client. The object would later signal the client somehow when the call completed (if the client wanted to know), and the client had to have some way of distinguishing between multiple method completions. These mechanisms were difficult to develop and test, and they forced developers to spend a disproportionate amount of their time reinventing the wheel instead of adding business value to their applications. In addition, such solutions coupled the clients to the objects and were not consistently designed or implemented. Different vendors provided slightly different solutions, requiring at times different programming models on the client side. This predicament diminished the benefits of component-oriented programming, because the component developers had to make some assumptions about the client's way of using the component, and vice versa.

The .NET mechanism for asynchronous calls is a mainstream facility used consistently and pervasively across the .NET application frameworks and base classes. .NET asynchronous calls are an essential addition to your arsenal as a component developer, because implementing robust asynchronous execution on your own is a demanding task, requiring a lot of effort spent on design, implementation, and testing. By providing support for asynchronous calls, .NET lets you focus on the domain problems at hand, rather than on complicated asynchronous plumbing. First, I'll explain the requirements for any asynchronous system in general. Then, because .NET asynchronous calls are based on delegates (introduced in Chapter 6), this chapter takes a closer look at delegates and then proceeds to describe how best to use .NET asynchronous calls.

Requirements for an Asynchronous Mechanism

To make the most of the various options available with .NET asynchronous calls, you first need to understand the generic requirements set for any modern component-oriented asynchronous calls support. These include the following:

- The same component code should be used for both synchronous and asynchronous invocations. This allows component developers to focus on the business logic and facilitates using a standard mechanism.
- A corollary of the first requirement is that the client should be the one to decide whether to call a component synchronously or asynchronously. This, in turn, implies that the client will have different code for invoking the call synchronously and asynchronously.
- The client should be able to issue multiple asynchronous calls and have multiple asynchronous calls in progress. It should be able to distinguish between multiple method completions.
- By the same token, the component should be able to serve multiple concurrent calls.
- If component methods have output parameters or return values, these parameters or results aren't available when control returns to the client. The client should have a way to access them when the method completes.
- Similarly, errors on the component's side should be propagated to the client side. Any exceptions thrown during the method execution should later be played back to the client.
- The asynchronous-calls mechanism should be straightforward and simple to use (this is more a design guideline than a requirement). For example, the mechanism should hide its implementation details—such as the worker threads used to dispatch the call—as much as possible.

When the client issues an asynchronous method call, it can then choose to:

- Perform some work while the call is in progress, then block until completion.
- Perform some work while the call is in progress, and then poll for completion.

- Perform some work while the call is in progress, wait for a predetermined amount of time, and then stop waiting, even if the method execution has not yet completed.

- Wait simultaneously for completion of multiple methods. The client can choose to wait for all or any of the pending calls to complete.

- Receive notification when the method has completed. The notification will be in the form of a callback on a client-provided method. The callback should contain information identifying which method has just completed and its return values.

.NET offers all these options to clients, which can be confusing when you first start using asynchronous calls. This chapter will demonstrate each option and recommend when to use it. First, though, let's talk a little more about delegates.

Revisiting Delegates

As explained in Chapter 6, to the programmer, a delegate is nothing more than a type-safe method reference. The delegate (as the name implies) is used to delegate the act of calling a method on an object (or a static method on a class) from the client to the delegate class. For example, consider a `Calculator` class:

```
public class Calculator
{
    public int Add(int argument1,int argument2)
    {
        return argument1 + argument2;
    }
    public int Subtract(int argument1,int argument2)
    {
        return argument1 - argument2;
    }
    //Other methods
}
```

Instead of calling the `Add()` method directly, you can define a delegate called `BinaryOperation`:

```
public delegate int BinaryOperation(int argument1,int argument2);
```

and use `BinaryOperation` to invoke the method:

```
Calculator calculator = new Calculator();
BinaryOperation oppDel  = calculator.Add;//Can use += as well
int result = 0;
result = oppDel(2,3);
Debug.Assert(result == 5);
```

By default, when you use a delegate to invoke methods, the delegate blocks the caller until all target methods return. In the example just shown, the caller is blocked until `Add()` returns. However, the delegate can also be used to invoke its target method asynchronously. The truth is that there isn't really anything special about delegates, because delegates are actually compiled to classes. When you define a delegate type, the compiler converts the delegate declaration to a sophisticated, signature-specific class definition and inserts that class instead of the delegate definition. For example, for this delegate definition:

```
public delegate int BinaryOperation(int argument1,int argument2);
```

the compiler generates this class definition:

```
public sealed class BinaryOperation : MulticastDelegate
{
    public BinaryOperation(Object target,int methodPtr)
    {...}
    public virtual int Invoke(int argument1,int argument2)
    {...}
    public virtual IAsyncResult BeginInvoke(int argument1,int argument2,
                                  AsyncCallback callback,object asyncState)
    {...}
    public virtual int EndInvoke(IAsyncResult result)
    {...}
}
```

When you use the delegate simply to invoke a method, such as in this code:

```
Calculator calculator = new Calculator();
BinaryOperation oppDel = calculator.Add;
oppDel(2,3);
```

or, in Visual Basic 2005:

```
Dim calculator As New Calculator()
Dim oppDel As BinaryOperation
oppDel = New BinaryOperation(AddressOf calculator.Add)
oppDel(2, 3)
```

the compiler converts the call to oppDel(2,3) to a call to the Invoke() method. The Invoke() method blocks the caller, executes the method on the caller's thread, and returns control to the caller.

The compiler-generated BinaryOperation class derives from a class called MulticastDelegate, which is defined in the System namespace. MulticastDelegate provides the implementation of the internal list of delegates every delegate has, and it is in turn derived from the abstract class Delegate (described in the previous chapter).

The compiler also declares two methods that manage asynchronous method invocation. These methods are BeginInvoke() and EndInvoke(), and their proper use is the subject of this chapter.

Asynchronous Call Programming Models

To support asynchronous invocation, multiple threads are required. However, it would be a waste of system resources and a performance penalty if .NET spun off a new thread for every asynchronous method invocation. A better approach is to use a pool of already created worker threads. .NET has just such a pool, called the *.NET thread pool.* One of the nice things about the .NET way of supporting asynchronous calls is that it hides this interaction completely. As previously indicated, there are quite a few programming models available for dealing with asynchronous calls. This section examines the various options: blocking, waiting, polling, and completion callbacks. In general, BeginInvoke( ) initiates an asynchronous method invocation. The calling client is blocked for only the briefest moment—the time it takes to queue up a request for a thread from the thread pool to execute the method—and then control returns to the client. EndInvoke( ) manages method completion; specifically, retrieving output parameters and return values, and error handling.

Using BeginInvoke( ) and EndInvoke( )

The compiler-generated BeginInvoke( ) and EndInvoke( ) methods take this form:

```
public virtual IAsyncResult BeginInvoke(<input and input/output parameters>,
                             AsyncCallback callback,
                             object asyncState);
public virtual <return value> EndInvoke(<output and input/output parameters>,
                             IAsyncResult asyncResult);
```

BeginInvoke( ) accepts the input parameters of the original signature the delegate defines. Input parameters include both value types passed by value or by reference (using the out or ref modifiers) and reference types. The original method's return values and any explicit output parameters are part of the EndInvoke( ) method. For example, for this delegate definition:

```
public delegate string MyDelegate(int number1,out int number2,ref int number3,object
obj);
```

the corresponding BeginInvoke( ) and EndInvoke( ) methods look like this:

```
public virtual IAsyncResult BeginInvoke(int number1,out int number2,ref int
                             number3,object obj,
                             AsyncCallback callback,object asyncState);
public virtual string EndInvoke(out int number2,ref int number3,
                             IAsyncResult asyncResult);
```

BeginInvoke( ) accepts two additional input parameters, not present in the original delegate signature: AsyncCallback callback and object asyncState. The callback parameter is actually a delegate object representing a reference to a callback method that receives the method-completed notification event. asyncState is a generic object that passes in whatever state information is needed by the party handling the method completion. These two parameters are optional: the caller can choose to pass in null instead of either one of them. For example, to asynchronously invoke the Add( ) method of the Calculator class, if you have no interest in the result and no interest in a callback method or state information, you would write:

```
Calculator calculator = new Calculator();
BinaryOperation oppDel = calculator.Add;
oppDel.BeginInvoke(2,3,null,null);
```

The object itself is unaware that the client is using a delegate to asynchronously invoke the method. The same object code handles both the synchronous and asynchronous invocation cases. As a result, every .NET class supports asynchronous invocation. Note that the classes should still comply with certain design guidelines described in this chapter, even though the compiler will compile them if they don't.

Because delegates can be used on both instance and static methods, clients can use BeginInvoke( ) to asynchronously call static methods as well. The remaining question is, how would you get the results of the method?

The IAsyncResult interface

Every BeginInvoke( ) method returns an object implementing the IAsyncResult interface, defined as:

```
public interface IAsyncResult
{
    object AsyncState{get;}
    WaitHandle AsyncWaitHandle{get;}
    bool CompletedSynchronously{get;}
    bool IsCompleted{get;}
}
```

You will see a few uses for the properties of IAsyncResult later. For now, it's sufficient to know that the returned IAsyncResult object uniquely identifies the method that was invoked using BeginInvoke( ). You can pass the IAsyncResult object to EndInvoke( ) to identify the specific asynchronous method execution from which you wish to retrieve the results. Example 7-1 shows the entire sequence.

Example 7-1. Simple asynchronous execution sequence

```
Calculator calculator = new Calculator();
BinaryOperation oppDel = calculator.Add;

IAsyncResult asyncResult1 = oppDel.BeginInvoke(2,3,null,null);
IAsyncResult asyncResult2 = oppDel.BeginInvoke(4,5,null,null);

/* Do some work */

int result;

result = oppDel.EndInvoke(asyncResult1);
Debug.Assert(result == 5);
```

Example 7-1. Simple asynchronous execution sequence (continued)

```
result = oppDel.EndInvoke(asyncResult2);
Debug.Assert(result == 9);
```

As simple as Example 7-1 is, it does demonstrate a few key points. The most important of these is that because the primary use of EndInvoke() is to retrieve any output parameters as well as the method's return value, EndInvoke() blocks its caller until the method it's waiting for (identified by the IAsyncResult object passed in) returns. The second point is that the same delegate object (with exactly one target method) can invoke multiple asynchronous calls on the target method. The caller can distinguish between the different pending calls using each unique IAsyncResult object returned from BeginInvoke(). In fact, when the caller makes asynchronous calls, as in Example 7-1, the caller must save the IAsyncResult objects. In addition, the caller should make no assumption about the order in which the pending calls complete. Remember: the asynchronous calls are carried out on threads from the thread pool, and because of thread context switches (as well as internal pool management and bookkeeping), it's quite possible that the second call will complete before the first one.

There are other uses for the IAsyncResult object besides passing it to EndInvoke(): you can use it to get the state object parameter of BeginInvoke(), you can wait for the method completion, and you can get the original delegate used to invoke the call. You will see how to do all that later. Although they aren't evident in Example 7-1, there are three important programming points you must always remember when using delegate-based asynchronous calls:

- EndInvoke() can be called only once for each asynchronous operation. Trying to call it more than once results in an exception of type InvalidOperationException.

- Although in general the compiler-generated delegate class can manage multiple targets, when you use asynchronous calls the delegate is only allowed to have exactly one target method in its internal list. Calling BeginInvoke() when the delegate's list contains more than one target will result in an ArgumentException being thrown, reporting that the delegate must have only one target.

- You can pass the IAsyncResult object to EndInvoke() only on the same delegate object that was used to dispatch the call. Passing the IAsyncResult object to a different delegate results in an exception of type InvalidOperationException, stating "The IAsyncResult object provided doesn't match this delegate." Example 7-2 demonstrates this point. It results in the exception, even though the other delegate targets the same method.

Example 7-2. Pass the IAsyncResult object only to the same delegate that invoked the call

```
Calculator calculator = new Calculator();
BinaryOperation oppDel1 = calculator.Add;
BinaryOperation oppDel2 = calculator.Add;

IAsyncResult asyncResult = oppDel1.BeginInvoke(2,3,null,null);
```

Example 7-2. Pass the IAsyncResult object only to the same delegate that invoked the call (continued)

```
//This will result in an InvalidOperationException
oppDel2.EndInvoke(asyncResult);
```

> To emphasize that the delegate can have only one target method in its list when used to invoke an asynchronous call, I recommend using the = operator to add the target method to the delegate list:
>
> ```
> Binary Operation oppDel;
> oppDel = calculator.Add;
> ```
>
> although the += operator works just as well:
>
> ```
> Binary Operation oppDel = null;
> oppDel += calculator.Add;
> ```
>
> An advantage to using the = operator is that you don't need to initialize the delegate object before assigning it.

The AsyncResult class

Often, one client initiates an asynchronous call, but another calls EndInvoke( ). Even when only one client is involved, it's likely to call BeginInvoke( ) in one code section (or method) and EndInvoke( ) in another. It's bad enough that you have to either save the IAsyncResult object or pass it to another client. It would be even worse if you had to do the same for the delegate object that invokes the asynchronous call, just because you needed that delegate to call EndInvoke( ). Fortunately, an easier solution is available, because the IAsyncResult object itself carries with it the delegate that created it. When BeginInvoke( ) returns the IAsyncResult reference, it's actually an instance of a class called AsyncResult, defined as:

```
public class AsyncResult : IAsyncResult, IMessageSink
{
    //IAsyncResult implementation
    public virtual object AsyncState{get;}
    public virtual WaitHandle AsyncWaitHandle{get;}
    public virtual bool CompletedSynchronously{get;}
    public virtual bool IsCompleted{get;}

    //Other properties
    public bool EndInvokeCalled{get; set;}
    public virtual object AsyncDelegate{get;}

    /* IMessageSink implementation */
}
```

AsyncResult is found in the System.Runtime.Remoting.Messaging namespace. AsyncResult has a property called AsyncDelegate, which, as you might guess, is a reference to the original delegate that dispatches the call. Example 7-3 shows how to use the AsyncDelegate property to call EndInvoke( ) on the original delegate.

Example 7-3. Using the AsyncDelegate property of AsyncResult to access the original delegate

```
using System.Runtime.Remoting.Messaging;

public class CalculatorClient
{
   IAsyncResult m_AsyncResult;

   public void AsyncAdd( )
   {
      Calculator calculator = new Calculator( );
      DispatchAdd(calculator,2,3);
      /* Do some work */
      int result = GetResult( );
      Debug.Assert(result == 5);
   }
   void DispatchAdd(Calculator calculator,int number1,int number2)
   {
      BinaryOperation oppDel = calculator.Add;
      m_AsyncResult = oppDel.BeginInvoke(2,3,null,null);
   }
   int GetResult( )
   {
      int result = 0;

      //Obtain original delegate
      AsyncResult asyncResult = (AsyncResult)m_AsyncResult;
      BinaryOperation oppDel  = (BinaryOperation)asyncResult.AsyncDelegate;

      Debug.Assert(asyncResult.EndInvokeCalled == false);
      result = oppDel.EndInvoke(m_AsyncResult);
      return result;
   }
}
```

Note that because the AsyncDelegate property is of type object, you need to down-cast it to the actual delegate type (BinaryOperation in Example 7-3).

Example 7-3 demonstrates using another useful property of AsyncResult—the Boolean EndInvokeCalled property. You can use it to verify that EndInvoke( ) hasn't been called:

```
Debug.Assert(asyncResult.EndInvokeCalled == false);
```

Polling or waiting for completion

In the programming model described in the previous section, when a client calls EndInvoke( ), the client is blocked until the asynchronous method returns. This may be fine if the client has a finite amount of work to do while the call is in progress, and if, once that work is done, the client can't continue its execution without the returned value or the output parameters of the method (or even just the knowledge that the method call has completed). However, what if the client only wants to

Asynchronous COM

Windows 2000 introduced *asynchronous COM* and the async_uuid IDL interface attribute. This attribute caused the MIDL compiler to generate two interface definitions: one for synchronous calls and one for asynchronous calls. For every method on the normal synchronous interface, the asynchronous interface (named AsyncI<interface name>) had a method called Begin_<method name>, which dispatched the call asynchronously to the corresponding method. The Begin_<method name> method had only the input parameters of the original method. The asynchronous interface also had a matching method called Finish_<method name> for every method on the original interface; this method retrieved the output parameters and blocked the method completion. Asynchronous COM also supported a notification mechanism to signal the client upon method completion, as an alternative to polling with Finish_<method name>.

MIDL implemented asynchronous COM by generating a custom marshaling proxy and stub, which used threads from the RPC thread pool to dispatch the call. The major advantage of asynchronous COM was that the same component code could be used both synchronously and asynchronously, so developers didn't have to waste time developing their own asynchronous method invocation mechanisms. The main disadvantages were that it was an esoteric mechanism (the majority of COM developers were not even aware it existed), it was supported only on Windows 2000 and above, it had limitations on parameter types, and it was difficult to use. However, the abstract principles of the mechanism and its design pattern (i.e., that of using a tool to generate a standard solution for asynchronous support and using the same component code in both cases) were sound, and they might well have been the inspiration for the .NET architects.

check if the method execution is completed? Or what if the client wants to wait for completion for a fixed timeout, do some additional finite processing, and then wait again? .NET supports these alternative programming models.

The IAsyncResult interface returned from BeginInvoke() has the AsyncWaitHandle property, of type WaitHandle. WaitHandle is actually a .NET wrapper around a native Windows waitable event handle. WaitHandle has a few overloaded wait methods. For example, the WaitOne() method returns only when the handle is signaled. Example 7-4 demonstrates using WaitOne().

Example 7-4. Using IAsyncResult.AsyncWaitHandle to block until method completion

```
Calculator calculator = new Calculator();
BinaryOperation oppDel = calculator.Add;

IAsyncResult asyncResult = oppDel.BeginInvoke(2,3,null,null);

/* Do some work */
```

Example 7-4. Using IAsyncResult.AsyncWaitHandle to block until method completion (continued)

```
asyncResult.AsyncWaitHandle.WaitOne( ); //This may block

int result;
result = oppDel.EndInvoke(asyncResult); //This will not block
Debug.Assert(result == 5);
```

Logically, Example 7-4 is identical to Example 7-1, which called only EndInvoke( ). If the method is still executing when WaitOne( ) is called, it will block. If, however, the method execution is complete, WaitOne( ) will not block and the client will proceed to call EndInvoke( ) for the returned value. The important difference between Example 7-4 and Example 7-1 is that the call to EndInvoke( ) in Example 7-4 is guaranteed not to block its caller.

Example 7-5 demonstrates a more practical way of using WaitOne( ), by specifying a timeout (10 milliseconds in this example). When you specify a timeout, WaitOne( ) returns when the method execution is completed or when the timeout has elapsed, whichever condition is met first.

Example 7-5. Using IAsyncResult.AsyncWaitHandle to specify the wait timeout

```
Calculator calculator = new Calculator( );
BinaryOperation oppDel = calculator.Add;

IAsyncResult asyncResult = oppDel.BeginInvoke(2,3,null,null);

while(asyncResult.IsCompleted == false)
{
   asyncResult.AsyncWaitHandle.WaitOne(10,false); //This may block
   /* Do some work */
}

int result;

result = oppDel.EndInvoke(asyncResult); //This will not block
```

 When you specify a timeout, WaitOne( ) also accepts a Boolean flag, whose meaning is discussed in Chapter 8. You can ignore that flag for now, as it bears no relevance to this discussion.

Example 7-5 also uses another handy property of IAsyncResult, called IsCompleted. IsCompleted lets you find the status of the call without waiting or blocking. You can even use IsCompleted in a strict polling mode:

```
while(asyncResult.IsCompleted == false)
{
   /* Do some work */
}
```

This, of course, has all the adverse effects of polling (e.g., consuming CPU power for nothing), so you should generally avoid using IsCompleted this way.

The AsyncWaitHandle property really shines when you use it to manage multiple concurrent asynchronous method calls in progress. You can use the WaitHandle class's static WaitAll() method to wait for completion of multiple asynchronous methods, as shown in Example 7-6.

Example 7-6. Waiting for completion of multiple methods

```
Calculator calculator = new Calculator();
BinaryOperation oppDel1 = calculator.Add;
BinaryOperation oppDel2 = calculator.Add;

IAsyncResult asyncResult1 = oppDel1.BeginInvoke(2,3,null,null);
IAsyncResult asyncResult2 = oppDel2.BeginInvoke(4,5,null,null);

WaitHandle[] handleArray = {asyncResult1.AsyncWaitHandle,asyncResult2.
AsyncWaitHandle};

WaitHandle.WaitAll(handleArray);

int result;
//These calls to EndInvoke() will not block
result = oppDel1.EndInvoke(asyncResult1);
Debug.Assert(result == 5);

result = oppDel2.EndInvoke(asyncResult2);
Debug.Assert(result == 9);
```

To use WaitAll(), you need to construct an array of handles. Note also that you still need to call EndInvoke() to access the returned values.

Instead of waiting for all the methods to return, you can choose to wait for any of them to return. To do so, use the WaitAny() static method of the WaitHandle class:

```
WaitHandle.WaitAny(handleArray);
```

Like WaitOne(), both WaitAll() and WaitAny() have a few overloaded versions that let you specify a timeout period to wait instead of waiting indefinitely.

Using Completion Callback Methods

As an alternative to the previous options for managing asynchronous calls (blocking, waiting, or polling), .NET offers another programming model altogether: *callbacks*. The idea is simple: the client provides .NET with a method and requests that .NET call that method back when the asynchronous method completes. The client can provide a callback instance method or static method and have the same callback method handle completion of multiple asynchronous methods. The only requirement is that the callback method have the following signature:

```
<visibility modifier> void <Name>(IAsyncResult asyncResult);
```

The convention for a callback method name is to prefix it with On<>—for example, OnAsyncCallBack( ), OnMethodCompletion( ), and so on. Here is how the callback mechanism works. As explained previously, .NET uses a thread from the thread pool to execute the method dispatched via BeginInvoke( ). When the asynchronous method execution is completed, instead of quietly returning to the pool, the worker thread calls the callback method.

To use a callback method, the client needs to provide BeginInvoke( ) with a delegate that targets the callback method. That delegate is provided as the penultimate parameter to BeginInvoke( ) and is always of type AsyncCallback. AsyncCallback is a .NET-provided delegate from the System namespace, defined as:

```
public delegate void AsyncCallback(IAsyncResult asyncResult);
```

Example 7-7 demonstrates asynchronous call management using a completion callback method.

Example 7-7. Managing asynchronous completion using a callback method

```
public class CalculatorClient
{
    public void AsyncAdd( )
    {
        Calculator calculator = new Calculator( );
        BinaryOperation oppDel = calculator.Add;
        oppDel.BeginInvoke(2,3,OnMethodCompletion,null);
    }
    void OnMethodCompletion(IAsyncResult asyncResult)
    {
        int result = 0;

        AsyncResult resultObj = (AsyncResult)asyncResult;

        Debug.Assert(resultObj.EndInvokeCalled == false);
        BinaryOperation oppDel  = (BinaryOperation)resultObj.AsyncDelegate;

        result = oppDel.EndInvoke(asyncResult);
        Trace.WriteLine("Operation returned " + result);
    }
}
```

When providing the completion callback method to BeginInvoke( ), you can rely on delegate inference and pass the method name directly, as shown in Example 7-7.

Unlike with the previous programming models described in this chapter, when you use a completion callback method, there's no need to save the IAsyncResult object returned from BeginInvoke( )—when .NET calls the callback method, it provides the IAsyncResult object as a parameter. Note in Example 7-7 the use of a downcast of the IAsyncResult parameter to an AsyncResult class to get the original delegate that dispatched the call. You need that delegate to call EndInvoke( ). Because .NET provides a unique IAsyncResult object for each asynchronous method, you can channel multiple asynchronous method completions to the same callback method:

```
Calculator calculator = new Calculator( );

BinaryOperation oppDel1 = calculator.Add;
BinaryOperation oppDel2 = calculator.Add;

oppDel1.BeginInvoke(2,3,OnMethodCompletion,null);
oppDel2.BeginInvoke(4,5,OnMethodCompletion,null);
```

Completion callback methods are by far the preferred model in any event-driven application. An event-driven application has methods that trigger events (or dispatch requests and post and process messages) and methods that handle these requests and fire their own events as a result. Writing an application as event-driven makes it easier to manage multiple threads, events, and messages and allows for greater scalability, responsiveness, and performance. .NET asynchronous call management using completion callback methods fits into such an architecture like a hand in a glove. The other options (waiting, blocking, and polling) are available for applications that are strict, predictable, and deterministic in their execution flow. I recommend that you use a completion callback method whenever possible.

Callback methods and thread safety

Because the callback method is executed on a thread from the thread pool, you must provide for thread safety in the callback method and in the object that provides it. This means you must use synchronization objects or locks to access the object's member variables. You need to worry about synchronizing between the "normal" thread of the object and the worker thread from the pool, and, potentially, synchronization between multiple worker threads all calling concurrently into the callback method to handle their respective asynchronous method completion. The callback method must be reentrant and thread-safe. Thread safety and synchronization are covered in the next chapter.

Passing state information

I have ignored the last parameter to BeginInvoke( ), object asyncState, up until now, when its use can be best appreciated. The asyncState object, known as a *state object* in .NET, is provided as a generic container for whatever need you deem fit. The party handling the method completion can access such a container object via the object AsyncState property of IAsyncResult. Although you can certainly use state objects with any of the other .NET asynchronous call programming models (blocking, waiting, or polling), they are most useful in conjunction with completion methods. The reason is simple: in all the other programming models, it's up to you to manage the IAsyncResult object, and managing an additional container isn't that much of an added liability. When you are using a completion callback the container object offers the only way to pass in additional parameters to the callback method, whose signature is predetermined by .NET.

Example 7-8 demonstrates how you might use a state object to pass an integer value as an additional parameter to the completion callback method. Note that the callback method must downcast the AsyncState property to the actual type that Debug.Assert( ) expects.

Example 7-8. Passing an additional parameter using a state object

```
public class CalculatorClient
{
   public void AsyncAdd( )
   {
      Calculator calculator = new Calculator( );
      BinaryOperation oppDel = calculator.Add;
      int asyncState = 4;
      oppDel.BeginInvoke(2,3,OnMethodCompletion,asyncState);
   }
   void OnMethodCompletion(IAsyncResult asyncResult)
   {
      int asyncState;
      asyncState = (int)asyncResult.AsyncState;
      Debug.Assert(asyncState == 4);

      /* Rest of the callback */
   }
}
```

Performing Asynchronous Operations Without Delegates

Delegate-based asynchronous calls like those described in the preceding sections let you asynchronously invoke any method, on any class. This technique provides valuable flexibility to a client, but it requires that you define a delegate with a signature that matches the method you want to invoke. Certain operations, such as disk or network accesses, web requests, web service calls, committing transactions or message queuing, may be long in duration or even open-ended in their very nature. In such cases, you will usually opt to invoke the operations asynchronously. The designers of the .NET Framework sought to ease the task of performing such operations by building into the classes that offer them Begin<Operation> and End<Operation> methods. These methods always take a form identical to the BeginInvoke( ) and EndInvoke( ) methods provided by a delegate class:

```
public <return type> <Operation>(<parameters>);
IAsyncResult Begin<Operation>(<input and input/output parameters>,
                                      AsyncCallback callback,
                                            object asyncState);
public <return type> End<Operation>(<output and input/output parameters >
                                          IAsyncResult asyncResult);
```

For example, the abstract class Stream, defined in the System.IO namespace, provides asynchronous Read( ) and Write( ) operations:

```
public abstract class Stream : MarshalByRefObject,IDisposable
{
   public virtual int Read(byte[]buffer,int offset,int count);
```

```
      public virtual IAsyncResult BeginRead(byte[]buffer,int offset,int count,
                                            AsyncCallback callback,object state);
      public virtual int EndRead(IAsyncResult asyncResult);

      public virtual void Write(byte[]buffer,int offset,int count);
      public virtual IAsyncResult BeginWrite(byte[]buffer,int offset,int count,
                                             AsyncCallback callback,object state);
      public virtual void EndWrite(IAsyncResult asyncResult);

      /* Other methods and properties */
   }
```

The Stream class is the base class for all other stream classes, such as FileStream,
MemoryStream, and NetworkStream. All the Stream-derived classes override these methods and provide their own implementations.

Example 7-9 demonstrates an asynchronous read operation on a FileStream object.
Note the passing of the useAsync parameter to the FileStream constructor, indicating
asynchronous operations on the stream.

Example 7-9. Asynchronous stream read with a completion callback

```
public class FileStreamClient
{
   Byte[] m_Array = new Byte[2000];
   public void AsyncRead( )
   {
      bool useAsync = true;
      Stream stream = new FileStream("MyFile.bin",FileMode.Open,FileAccess.Read,
                                            FileShare.None,1000,useAsync);
      using(stream)
      {
         stream.BeginRead(m_Array,0,10,OnMethodCompletion,null);
      }
   }
   void OnMethodCompletion(IAsyncResult asyncResult)
   {
      bool useAsync = true;
      Stream stream = new FileStream("MyFile.bin",FileMode.Open,FileAccess.Read,
                                            FileShare.None,1000,useAsync);
      using(stream)
      {
         int bytesRead = stream.EndRead(asyncResult);
      }
      //Access m_Array
   }
}
```

Another example of a class that provides its own asynchronous methods is the web
service proxy class that you can generate using the *WSDL.exe* comand-line utility.
Imagine that the Calculator class in the following code snippet exposes its methods,
such as Add( ), as web services:

```
using System.Web.Services;

public class Calculator
{
   [WebMethod]
   public int Add(int argument1,int argument2)
   {
      return argument1 + argument2;
   }
   //Other methods
}
```

The proxy class *WSDL.exe* auto-generates for the client will contain BeginAdd( ) and
EndAdd( ) methods that invoke the web service asynchronously:

```
using System.Web.Services.Protocols;

public partial class Calculator : SoapHttpClientProtocol
{
   public int Add(int argument1,int argument2)
   {...}
   public IAsyncResult BeginAdd(int argument1,int argument2
                              AsyncCallback callback,object asyncState)
   {...}
   public int EndAdd(IAsyncResult asyncResult)
   {...}
   /* Other members */
}
```

Using non-delegate-based asynchronous method calls is similar to using the
BeginInvoke( ) and EndInvoke( ) methods provided by a delegate class: you dispatch
the asynchronous operation using Begin<Operation>, and you can call End<Operation>
to block until completion, wait for the operation (or multiple operations) to complete, or use a callback method. However, there is no uniform requirement to call
End<Operation> on the original object that dispatched the Begin<Operation> call.
With some classes (such web service proxy classes or Stream-derived classes), you
can create a new object and call End<Operation> on it. Example 7-10 demonstrates
this technique when using a web service proxy class.

Example 7-10. Asynchronous web-service call with a completion callback

```
public class CalculatorWebServiceClient
{
   public void AsyncAdd( )
   {
      //Calculator is the WSDL.exe-generated proxy class
      Calculator calculator = new Calculator( );

      calculator.BeginAdd(2,3,OnMethodCompletion,null);
   }
   void OnMethodCompletion(IAsyncResult asyncResult)
   {
      //Calculator is the WSDL.exe-generated proxy class
```

```
    Calculator calculator = new Calculator( );

    int result;
    result = calculator.EndAdd(asyncResult);
    Trace.WriteLine("Operation returned " + result);
  }
}
```

> The web service proxy class generated by *WSDL.exe* offers another
> mechanism for asynchronous invocation, discussed in Chapter 8.
> When adding a web reference using Visual Studio 2005, it will only
> offer that other mechanism in the proxy class.

Asynchronous Error Handling

Output parameters and return values aren't the only elements unavailable at the time
an asynchronous call is dispatched: exceptions are missing as well. After calling
BeginInvoke( ), control returns to the client, but it may be some time before the asynchronous method encounters an error and throws an exception, and it may be some
time after that before the client actually calls EndInvoke( ). .NET must therefore provide some way for the client to know that an exception was thrown and be allowed
to handle it. The .NET solution is straightforward: when the asynchronous method
throws an exception, .NET catches it, and when the client calls EndInvoke( ) .NET
re-throws that exception object, letting the client handle the exception. If a callback
method is provided, .NET calls the callback method immediately after the exception
is thrown on the object side. For example, suppose the Calculator class has a
Divide( ) method, defined as:

```
    public class Calculator
    {
        public int Divide(int argument1,int argument2)
        {
            return argument1/argument2;
        }
        //Other methods
    }
```

Divide( ) throws a DivideByZeroException if the denominator (argument2) passed in is
zero. Example 7-11 demonstrates how you might handle this error.

Example 7-11. Asynchronous error handling

```
public class CalculatorClient
{
    public void AsyncDivide( )
    {
        Calculator calculator = new Calculator( );
        BinaryOperation oppDel = calculator.Divide;
        oppDel.BeginInvoke(2,0,OnMethodCompletion,null);
```

Example 7-11. Asynchronous error handling (continued)

```
    }
    void OnMethodCompletion(IAsyncResult asyncResult)
    {
        AsyncResult resultObj = (AsyncResult)asyncResult;
        Debug.Assert(resultObj.EndInvokeCalled == false);
        BinaryOperation oppDel  = (BinaryOperation)resultObj.AsyncDelegate;
        try
        {
            int result = 0;
            result = oppDel.EndInvoke(asyncResult);
            Trace.WriteLine("Operation returned " + result);
        }
        catch(DivideByZeroException exception)
        {
            Trace.WriteLine(exception.Message);
        }
    }
}
```

 When you use a completion callback method, you must provide for error handling in the callback. If the call to EndInvoke( ) results in an exception and no error handling is in place, the exception will terminate your application.

Asynchronous Events

The most common use for delegates in .NET is for event subscription and publishing. Example 7-12 contains a simple definition of an event publisher and subscriber.

Example 7-12. Event publisher and subscriber, using synchronous event publishing

```
using NumberChangedEventHandler = GenericEventHandler<int>;

public class MyPublisher
{
    public event NumberChangedEventHandler NumberChanged;
    public void FireEvent(int number)
    {
        if(NumberChanged != null)
        {
            NumberChanged(number);
        }
    }
}
public class MySubscriber
{
    public void OnNumberChanged(int number)
    {...}
}
```

Consider the following client code, which hooks subscribers to the publisher and fires the event:

```
MyPublisher  publisher   = new MyPublisher();
MySubscriber subscriber1 = new MySubscriber();
MySubscriber subscriber2 = new MySubscriber();

publisher.NumberChanged += subscriber1.OnNumberChanged;
publisher.NumberChanged += subscriber2.OnNumberChanged;
publisher.FireEvent(3);
```

When a publisher fires an event, it's blocked until all the subscribers have finished handling the event, and only then does control return to the publisher. Disciplined and well-behaved subscribers should not perform any lengthy operations in their event-handling method, because that prevents other subscribers from handling the event (not to mention blocking the publisher). The problem is, how does the publisher know if it's dealing with disciplined subscribers? The reality is, of course, that the publisher can't tell. The publisher must therefore defensively assume that all subscribers are undisciplined. I call this the *undisciplined subscriber* problem. The solution to it is to fire the events asynchronously.

One option is to implement an asynchronous event firing by publishing the event on a worker thread. The problem with using a worker thread is that although it allows for asynchronous publishing, the publishing is serialized, because the subscribers are notified one at a time. The proper solution is to use threads from a thread pool and try to publish to each subscriber on a different thread. This isolates the undisciplined subscribers and allows concurrent and asynchronous publishing. At this point, you may be wondering why you can't simply use the built-in support delegates have for asynchronous invocation using threads from the pool. For example, the publisher in Example 7-12 could add a new method called FireEventAsync() and use BeginInvoke() to publish asynchronously:

```
public void FireEventAsync(int number)
{
   if(NumberChanged != null)
   {
      //Likely to raise exception:
      NumberChanged.BeginInvoke(number,null,null);
   }
}
```

Unfortunately, you can't call BeginInvoke() on the event member directly, because BeginInvoke() can be invoked only if the delegate's internal list of target methods contains just one target. As stated earlier in this chapter, if the delegate has more than one target in its list, an exception of type ArgumentException will be thrown. The workaround is to iterate over the delegate's internal invocation list, calling BeginInvoke() on each target in the list. Chapter 6 demonstrated how to access that list using the delegate's GetInvocationList() method:

```
public virtual Delegate[] GetInvocationList();
```

GetInvocationList() returns a collection of delegates; each corresponds to a single target sink method, and therefore you can call BeginInvoke() on these delegates. Example 7-13 shows the implementation of the FireEventAsync() method. Note that you have to downcast the individual delegates to the actual delegate type. Note also that when you publish events asynchronously, the publisher has no use for return values or output from the event handlers. Therefore, EndInvoke() isn't used, and the publisher passes null for the last two parameters of BeginInvoke().

Example 7-13. Firing events asynchronously

```
using NumberChangedEventHandler = GenericEventHandler<int>;

public class MyPublisher
{
   public event NumberChangedEventHandler NumberChanged;

   public void FireEventAsync(int number)
   {
      if(NumberChanged == null)
      {
         return;
      }
      Delegate[] delegates = NumberChanged.GetInvocationList();
      foreach(Delegate del in delegates)
      {
         NumberChangedEventHandler sink = (NumberChangedEventHandler)del;
         sink.BeginInvoke(number,null,null);
      }
   }
}
```

There is a problem with the technique in Example 7-13, however: the code is coupled to the delegate type you invoke. You have to repeat such code in every case where you want to publish events asynchronously for every delegate type.

Asynchronous EventsHelper

Fortunately, you can compensate for the problem just described. Example 7-14 shows the FireAsync() method of the EventsHelper static class, which automates asynchronous defensive event publishing.

Example 7-14. Automating asynchronous event publishing with EventsHelper

```
public static class EventsHelper
{
   delegate void AsyncFire(Delegate del,object[] args);

   public static void FireAsync(Delegate del,params object[] args)
   {
      if(del == null)
```

Example 7-14. Automating asynchronous event publishing with EventsHelper (continued)

```
         {
            return;
         }
         Delegate[] delegates = del.GetInvocationList( );
         AsyncFire asyncFire = InvokeDelegate;
         foreach(Delegate sink in delegates)
         {
            asyncFire.BeginInvoke(sink,args,null,null);
         }
   }
   static void InvokeDelegate(Delegate del,object[] args)
   {
      del.DynamicInvoke(args);
   }
   //Synchronous publishing methods, discussed in Example 6-11
   public static void Fire(...)
   {...}
}
```

The technique shown in Example 7-14 is similar to that presented in Example 6-10: you use the params modifier to pass in any collection of arguments, as well as the delegate containing the subscriber list. The FireAsync( ) method iterates over the internal collection of the passed-in delegate. For each delegate in the list, it uses another delegate of type AsyncFire to asynchronously call the private helper method InvokeDelegate( ). InvokeDelegate( ) simply uses the DynamicInvoke( ) method of the Delegate type to invoke the delegate. Using EventHelper to publish events asynchronously is easy when compared to Example 7-13:

```
using NumberChangedEventHandler = GenericEventHandler<int>;

public class MyPublisher
{
   public event NumberChangedEventHandler NumberChanged;

   public void FireEventAsync(int number)
   {
      EventsHelper.FireAsync(NumberChanged,number);
   }
}
```

 When using EventsHelper from Visual Basic 2005, you need to use the matching compiler-generated member variable suffixed with Event, as shown in Chapter 6.

Type-safe asynchronous EventsHelper

As with Example 6-10, the problem with the AsyncFire( ) method of Example 7-14 is that it is not type-safe. AsyncFire( ) uses an array of objects, and any mismatch in the number and type of arguments will not be discovered at compile time. At runtime, the use of `BeginInvoke( )` on the helper method `InvokeDelegate( )` will suppress any error propagation, and you will not be aware of the problem. The solution is identical to the one used in the synchronous case: have `EventsHelper` combine `AsyncFire( )` with `GenericEventHandler`, and commit to using `GenericEventHandler` (which is a good idea in general). The compiler will correctly infer the delegate type to use and enforce type safety with the number and type of the arguments. The type-safe asynchronous version of `EventsHelper` is shown in Example 7-15.

Example 7-15. Type-safe asynchronous publishing with EventsHelper

```
public static class EventsHelper
{
   delegate void AsyncFire(Delegate del,object[] args);

   //Same as FireAsync( ) in Example 7-14
   public static void UnsafeFireAsync(Delegate del,params object[] args)
   {...}

   public static void FireAsync(GenericEventHandler del)
   {
      UnsafeFireAsync(del);
   }
   public static void FireAsync<T>(GenericEventHandler<T> del,T t)
   {
      UnsafeFireAsync(del,t);
   }
   public static void FireAsync<T,U>(GenericEventHandler<T,U> del,T t,U u)
   {
      UnsafeFireAsync(del,t,u);
   }
   public static void FireAsync<T,U,V>(GenericEventHandler<T,U,V> del,T t,U u,V v)
   {
      UnsafeFireAsync(del,t,u,v);
   }
   public static void FireAsync<T,U,V,W>(GenericEventHandler<T,U,V,W> del,
                                         T t,U u,V v,W w)
   {
      UnsafeFireAsync(del,t,u,v,w);
   }
   public static void FireAsync<T,U,V,W,X>(GenericEventHandler<T,U,V,W,X> del,
                                           T t,U u,V v,W w,X x)
   {
      UnsafeFireAsync(del,t,u,v,w,x);
   }
   public static void FireAsync<T,U,V,W,X,Y>(GenericEventHandler<T,U,V,W,X,Y> del,
                                             T t,U u,V v,W w,X x,Y y)
   {
      UnsafeFireAsync(del,t,u,v,w,x,y);
   }
   public static void FireAsync<T,U,V,W,X,Y,Z>(GenericEventHandler<T,U,V,W,X,Y,Z> del,
                                               T t,U u,V v,W w,X x,Y y,Z z)
```

Example 7-15. Type-safe asynchronous publishing with EventsHelper (continued)

```
    {
        UnsafeFireAsync(del,t,u,v,w,x,y,z);
    }
    public static void FireAsync(EventHandler del,object sender,EventArgs e)
    {
        UnsafeFireAsync(del,sender,e);
    }
    public static void FireAsync<E>(EventHandler<E> del,object sender,E e)
                                                        where E : EventArgs
    {
        UnsafeFireAsync(del,sender,e);
    }
    //Rest same as Example 7-14
}
```

If you can only commit to using `EventHandler`, Example 7-15 contains type-safe support for it as well. The non-type-safe method `UnsafeFireAsync( )` of `EventsHelper` is still available when you cannot use `GenericEventHandler` or `EventHandler`, and the lack of type safety with this approach is a small price to pay compared with the problem of Example 7-13.

.NET Queued Components

.NET's built-in support for asynchronous method invocation standardizes asynchronous calls and saves you writing a lot of error-prone plumbing code. Asynchronous calls in enterprise applications, however, often require additional support, such as for disconnected work, error handling, auto-retry mechanisms, and transaction support. For such cases, .NET provides an advanced asynchronous call mechanism called *queued components* as part of its .NET Enterprise Services (`System.EnterpriseServices` namespace). Queued components use the Microsoft Message Queue (MSMQ) to queue asynchronous calls and transport them to the target server component. A discussion of .NET queued components is beyond the scope of this book, but you can read about them in Chapters 8 and 10 of my book *COM and .NET Component Services* (O'Reilly).

Asynchronous Invocation Pitfalls

By now you have probably come to appreciate the elegance of .NET asynchronous calls, and the ease with which you can turn a synchronous component and its client code into an asynchronous implementation. However, no technology is without its pitfalls. Following is a rundown of the technical pitfalls you are likely to encounter when using .NET asynchronous calls. There is also a major conceptual consequence when dealing with asynchronous calls rather than synchronous calls, which merits a dedicated section of its own at the end of this chapter.

Threading Concurrency and Synchronization

In using asynchronous method calls, you must be aware of potential problems concerning thread concurrency, state corruption, and re-entrance. An asynchronous method is invoked on a thread from the .NET thread pool. When the call is made, the called object may already be servicing a normal call from a synchronous client on another thread, along with additional asynchronous calls on different threads. A completion callback method is also a potential pitfall, because it too is executed on a different thread and can have multiple threads calling it.

In general, you should invoke methods asynchronously only on thread-safe objects—that is, objects that allow multiple threads to safely access them concurrently. Even when using thread-safe objects, you must keep a watchful eye out for race conditions and deadlocks. In addition, the object whose method you invoke asynchronously must not have *thread affinity* (i.e., it must not rely on always running on the same thread) or use thread-specific resources such as thread local storage or thread-relative static variables.

Thread-Pool Exhaustion

.NET speeds up asynchronous calls by using threads from the thread pool. However, the pool isn't boundless. A pool with too many threads becomes a liability, because the operating system wastes a lot of cycles just on thread context switches. If you have too many pending asynchronous method calls in progress, you may reach the pool's upper limit. At that point, no further asynchronous calls will be dispatched, and all future asynchronous calls will in effect be serialized, waiting for worker threads to return to the pool. The default .NET thread pool is configured to use 25 threads per CPU. Avoid indiscriminate use of asynchronous calls or any long or blocking operations in the methods invoked asynchronously. Consider using your own worker threads for long-duration blocking operations.

Premature Access by Reference and Reference Types

If the asynchronous method signature contains value types passed by reference or reference types, even though these parameters will be part of the call to BeginInvoke( ), you shouldn't try to access them before calling EndInvoke( ). Code can be especially error-prone when you use reference types as both input and output parameters. Example 7-16 demonstrates this point. In the example, the values of the X and Y member variables of the MyPoint object change silently between the call to BeginInvoke( ) and the return of EndInvoke( ). The only safe way to access the object passed as an incoming and outgoing parameter to BeginInvoke( ) is to call EndInvoke( ) first.

Example 7-16. Reference types have correct values only after the call to EndInvoke()

```
public class MyPoint
{
```

```
    public int X;
    public int Y;
}

public delegate void MyDelegate(MyPoint obj);

public class MyClient
{
    public void Swap(MyPoint obj)
    {
        int temp = obj.X;
        obj.X = obj.Y;
        obj.Y = temp;
    }
    public void AsyncSwap( )
    {
        MyPoint point = new MyPoint ( );
        point.X = 3;
        point.Y = 4;

        MyDelegate swapDel = Swap;
        IAsyncResult asyncResult = swapDel.BeginInvoke(point,null,null);

        //BeginInvoke( ) does not change the values of reference types or value types
        //passed by reference. This may or may not assert:
        Debug.Assert(point.X == 3);
        Debug.Assert(point.Y == 4);

        swapDel.EndInvoke(asyncResult);

        Debug.Assert(point.X == 4);
        Debug.Assert(point.Y == 3);
    }
}
```

Lengthy Constructors

The asynchronous invocation mechanism described in this chapter can be used only on methods. In .NET, constructors are always synchronous. This can pose a problem if a component's constructor performs operations that take a long time to complete (such as opening a database connection). In such cases, you should use the *two-phase create* pattern. First put the trivial (and usually fast) code for initialization in the constructor, and then provide a separate method called Initialize( ) to perform the lengthy operations. This allows your clients to construct objects of your components asynchronously if they need to. A more advanced solution is to use a class factory and have the class factory expose methods such as Create( ) for synchronous instantiation and BeginCreate( ) and EndCreate( ) for asynchronous instantiation.

Cleaning Up After EndInvoke

Whenever calling `BeginInvoke( )`, the delegate will construct a new `AsyncResult` object and return it. That object will have a reference to a single `WaitHandle` object, accessible via the `AsyncWaitHandle` property. Calling `EndInvoke( )` on the delegate used to dispatch the call does not close the handle. Instead, that handle will be closed when the `AsyncResult` object is garbage-collected. As with any other case of using an unmanaged resource, you have to be mindful about your application deterministic finalization needs. It is possible (in theory at least), for the application to dispatch asynchronous calls faster than .NET's ability to collect those handles, resulting with a resource leak. To compensate, you can explicitly close that handle after calling `EndInvoke( )`. For example, using the same definitions as Example 7-7, you would write:

```
void OnMethodCompletion(IAsyncResult asyncResult)
{
   AsyncResult resultObj = (AsyncResult)asyncResult;
   BinaryOperation oppDel = (BinaryOperation)resultObj.AsyncDelegate;
   int result = oppDel.EndInvoke(asyncResult);

   asyncResult.AsyncWaitHandle.Close();

   //Rest of the implementation
}
```

In a similar manner you can fix up `EventsHelper.UnsafeFireAsync( )` to always close the handle after dispatching the event asynchronously by providing an anonymous method for a completion callback, and closing the handle in that method:

```
public static void UnsafeFireAsync(Delegate del,params object[] args)
{
   if(del == null)
   {
      return;
   }
   Delegate[] delegates = del.GetInvocationList( );
   AsyncFire asyncFire = InvokeDelegate;
   AsyncCallback cleanup = delegate(IAsyncResult asyncResult)
                           {
                               asyncResult.AsyncWaitHandle.Close( );
                           };
   foreach(Delgate sink in delegates)
   {
      asyncFire.BeginInvoke(sink,args,cleanUp,null);
   }
}
```

Synchronous Versus Asynchronous Processing

Although it's technically possible to call the same component synchronously and asynchronously, the likelihood that a component will be accessed both ways is low.

The reason is that using a set of components asynchronously requires drastic changes to the workflow of the client program, and as a result the client can't simply use the same execution sequence logic that it would for synchronous access. Consider, for example, an online store application. Let's suppose the client (a server-side object executing a customer request) accesses a Store object, where it places the customer's order details. The Store object uses three well-factored helper components to process the order: Order, Shipment, and Billing. In a synchronous scenario, the Store object calls the Order object to place the order. Only if the Order object succeeds in processing the order (i.e., if the item is available in the inventory) does the Store object call the Shipment object, and only if the Shipment object succeeds does the Store object access the Billing component to bill the customer. This sequence is shown in Figure 7-1.

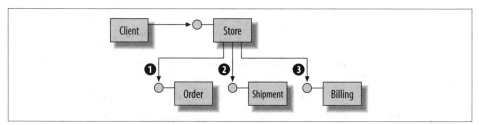

Figure 7-1. Synchronous processing of a client order

The down side to the pattern shown in Figure 7-1 is that the store must process orders synchronously and serially. On the surface, it might seem that if the Store component invoked its helper objects asynchronously, it could increase its throughput because it could process incoming orders as fast as the client submitted them. The problem in doing so is that it's possible for the calls to the Order, Shipment, and Billing objects to fail independently. Because their methods would be invoked in a nondeterministic order, depending on thread availability in the thread pool, overall system load, and so on, things could go wrong in many ways. For example, the Order object might discover there were no items in the inventory matching the customer request after the Billing object had already billed the customer for it.

Using asynchronous calls on a set of interacting components requires that you change your code and your workflow. To call the helper components asynchronously, the Store component should call only the Order object, which in turn should call the Shipment object only if the order processing was successful (see Figure 7-2), to avoid the potential inconsistencies just mentioned. Similarly, only in the case of successful shipment should the Shipment object asynchronously call the Billing object.

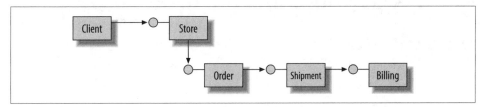

Figure 7-2. Revised workflow for asynchronous processing of a client order

In general, if you have more than one component in your asynchronous workflow, you should have each component invoke the next one in the logical execution sequence. Needless to say, such a programming model introduces tight coupling between components (they have to know about each other) and changes to their interfaces (you have to pass in additional parameters, which are required for the desired invocation of components downstream).

The conclusion from this simple example is that using asynchronous instead of synchronous invocation introduces major changes to the component interfaces and the client workflow. Asynchronous invocation on a component that was built for synchronous execution works only in isolated cases. When you're dealing with a set of interacting components, it's better to simply spin off a worker thread to call them and use the worker thread to provide asynchronous execution. This will preserve the component interfaces and the original client execution sequence. Of course, to do that, you need to understand .NET concurrency management and multithreading, the subjects of the next chapter.

CHAPTER 8

Multithreading and Concurrency Management

In a single-threaded application, all operations, regardless of type, duration, or priority, execute on a single thread. Such applications are simple to design and build. All operations are serialized; that is, the operations never run concurrently, but rather one at a time. However, there are many situations in which employing multiple threads of execution in your application will increase its performance, throughput, and scalability, as well as improving its responsiveness to users and clients. That said, multithreading is one of the most poorly understood and applied concepts of contemporary programming, and many developers tend to misuse the multithreading features and services available on their programming platforms.

This chapter begins with an explanation of .NET threads and shows you how to create and use them. You'll also learn how to spawn and manage multiple threads, develop thread-safe components, and avoid some of the common pitfalls of multithreaded programming. The chapter then moves on to discuss how to use .NET to synchronize the operations of multiple threads and manage concurrent attempts to access components. The chapter ends by describing several useful .NET multithreading services, including thread pool, timers, and thread local storage.

Threads and Multithreading

In modern computing terminology, a *thread* is simply a path of execution within a process. Every application runs on at least one thread, which is initialized when the process within which the application runs is started up. The threads of an application always execute within the context provided by the application process. Typically, you find two kinds of operations in any application: CPU-bound and I/O-bound operations. *CPU-bound* operations use the machine's central processing unit (CPU) to perform intensive or repetitious computations. *I/O-bound* operations are tied to an input or output device such as a user-interface peripheral (keyboard, screen, mouse, or printer), a hard drive (or any non-memory durable storage), a network or communication port, or any other hardware device.

It's often useful to create multiple threads within an application, so that operations that are different in nature can be performed in parallel and the machine's CPU (or CPUs) and devices can be used as efficiently as possible. An I/O-bound operation (such as disk access), for example, can take place concurrently with a CPU-bound operation (such as the processing of an image). As long as two I/O-bound operations don't use the same I/O device (such as disk access and network-socket access), having them run on two different threads will improve your application's ability to efficiently handle these I/O devices and increase the application's throughput and performance. In the case of CPU-bound operations, on a single-CPU machine there is no performance advantage to allocating two distinct threads to run separate CPU-bound operations. However, you should definitely consider doing so on a multi-CPU machine, because multithreading is the only way to use the extra processing power available through each additional CPU.

Almost all modern applications are multithreaded, and many of the features users take for granted would not be possible otherwise. For example, a responsive user interface implies multithreading. The application processes user requests (such as printing or connecting to a remote machine) on a different thread than the one employed for the user interface. If the same thread were being used, the user interface would appear to hang while the other requests were being processed. With multithreading, because the user interface is on a different thread, it remains responsive while the user's requests are being processed. Multiple threads are also useful in applications that require high throughput. When your application needs to process incoming client requests as fast as it can, it's often advantageous to spin off a number of worker threads to handle requests in parallel.

 Do not create multiple threads just for the sake of having them. You must examine your particular case carefully and evaluate all possible solutions. The decision to use multiple threads can open a Pandora's box of thread-synchronization and component-concurrency issues, as you'll see later in this chapter.

Components and Threads

A component-oriented application doesn't necessarily need to be multithreaded. The way in which an application is divided into components is unrelated to how many execution threads it uses. In any given application, you're as likely to have several components interacting with one another on a single thread of execution as you are to have multiple threads accessing a single component. What is special about component-oriented applications has to do with the intricate synchronization issues inherent in the nature of component development and deployment. You will see later in this chapter how .NET addresses these challenges.

Working with Threads

In .NET, a thread is the basic unit of execution. .NET threads are managed code representations of the underlying threads of the operating system. Under the current version of .NET on Windows, .NET threads map one-to-one to Win32 native threads. However, this mapping can be changed in other hosts. For example, SQL Server 2005 is a managed CLR host and is capable of using fibers for managed threads. Throughout this chapter, the underlying host is considered to be Windows unless otherwise specified. For each thread, the operating system allocates registers, a program counter, a stack, and a stack pointer, and assigns it a time slot and a priority. The operating system (presently) is the one responsible for thread scheduling and thread context switches, as well as thread-manipulation requests such as start and sleep. .NET exposes some of the native thread properties (such as priority). It also associates various managed-code properties with each thread, such as state, exception handlers, security principal (discussed in Chapter 12), name, unique ID, and culture (required for localization).

The .NET class `Thread`, defined in the `System.Threading` namespace, represents a managed thread. The `Thread` class provides various methods and properties to control the managed thread.

 Calling the methods of the `Thread` class (be they static or instance methods) is always done on the stack of the calling thread, not on the stack of the thread represented by the `Thread` object. The one exception to this rule occurs when the calling thread calls methods on a `Thread` object that represents itself.

You can get hold of the thread on which your code is currently running by using the `CurrentThread` read-only static property of the `Thread` class:

```
public sealed class Thread
{
   public static Thread CurrentThread {get;}
   //Other methods and properties
}
```

The `CurrentThread` property returns an instance of the `Thread` class. Each thread has a unique thread identification number, called a *thread ID*. You can access the thread ID via the `ManagedThreadId` property of the `Thread` class:

```
using System.Threading;

Thread currentThread = Thread.CurrentThread;
int threadID = currentThread.ManagedThreadId;
Trace.WriteLine("Thread ID is "+ threadID);
```

`Thread.ManagedThreadId` is guaranteed to return a value that is unique process-wide. It's worth mentioning that the thread ID obtained by `ManagedThreadId` isn't related to the native thread ID allocated by the underlying operating system. You can verify that by opening Visual Studio's Threads debug window (Debug → Windows) during a debugging session and examining the value in the ID column (see Figure 8-1). The ID column reflects the physical thread ID. The ManagedThreadId property simply returns a unique hash of the thread object. Having different IDs allows .NET threads in different hosting environments (such as Windows or SQL Server 2005) to map differently to the native operating support.

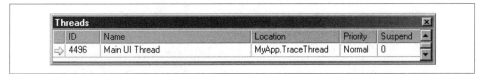

Figure 8-1. The Threads debug window

Another useful property of the Thread class is the Name string property. Name allows you to assign a human-readable name to a thread:

```
using System.Threading;

Thread currentThread = Thread.CurrentThread;
string threadName = "Main UI Thread";
currentThread.Name = threadName;
```

Only you as the developer can assign the thread name, and by default, a new .NET thread is nameless. You can only set the thread's name once. Although naming a thread is optional, I highly recommend doing so because it's an important productivity feature. Windows doesn't have the ability to assign a name to a thread. In the past, when you debugged native Windows code, you had to record the new thread ID in every debugging session (using the Threads debug window). These IDs were not only confusing (especially when multiple threads were involved) but also changed in each new debugging session. Visual Studio's Threads debug window (see Figure 8-1) displays the value of the Name property, thus easing the task of tracing and debugging multithreaded applications. You can even set a breakpoint filter, instructing the debugger to break only when a thread with a specific name hits the breakpoint. Name is a good example of a managed-code property that .NET adds to native threads.

 In Visual Studio 2005, breakpoint filters are disabled by default. To enable them, go to Tools → Options → Debugging → General and check the "Enable breakpoint filters" checkbox. Now, you can set a breakpoint filter by selecting Filter... from the breakpoint context menu.

Creating Threads

To spawn a new thread, you need to create a new Thread object and associate it with a method that is referred to as the *thread method*. The new Thread object executes the method on a separate thread. The thread terminates once the thread method returns. The thread method can be a static or an instance method, can be public or private, and can be called on your object or on another. The only requirement is that the thread method should have either one of these signatures:

```
void <MethodName>();
void <MethodName>(object argument);
```

depending on whether or not you want to pass in an argument.

If you want to use an argument-less thread method, you associate a Thread object with the thread method by using a dedicated delegate called ThreadStart, defined as:

```
public delegate void ThreadStart();
```

One of the Thread class constructors accepts as a single construction parameter an instance of the ThreadStart delegate, which targets the thread method:

```
public sealed class Thread
{
    public Thread(ThreadStart start);
    //Other methods and properties
}
```

Once you've created a new Thread object, you must explicitly call its Start() method to have it actually execute the thread method. Example 8-1 demonstrates creating and using a new thread.

Example 8-1. Spinning off a new thread

```
public class MyClass
{
    public void ShowMessage()
    {
        Thread currentThread = Thread.CurrentThread;
        string caption = "Thread ID = ";
        caption += currentThread.ManagedThreadId;
        MessageBox.Show("ShowMessage runs on a new thread",caption);
    }
}
MyClass obj = new MyClass();

ThreadStart threadStart = obj.ShowMessage;
Thread workerThread = new Thread(threadStart);
workerThread.Start();
```

Calling the Start() method is a non-blocking operation, meaning that control returns immediately to the client that started the thread, even though it may be some time before the new thread actually starts (depending on the operating system's internal threading management). As a result, after calling Start( ), don't make any assumptions in your code that the thread is actually running.

Although you should have only one thread method as a target for the ThreadStart delegate, you can associate it with multiple targets, in which case the new thread executes all methods in order, and the thread terminates once the last target method returns. However, there's little practical use for such a setting. In general, you should have only one target thread method. You can enforce that by passing the thread method name directly to the Thread constructor, instead of using a delegate variable:

```
Thread workerThread = new Thread(obj.ShowMessage);
```

Designing thread methods

A thread method can do whatever you want it to, but typically it will contain a loop of some sort. In each loop iteration, the thread performs a finite amount of work and then checks some condition, which lets it know whether to perform another iteration or to terminate:

```
public void MyThreadMethod( )
{
    while(<some condition>)
    {
        <Do some work>
    }
}
```

Threads and Exceptions

If the thread method completes its execution, .NET will shutdown the thread gracefully. However, any unhandled exception thrown on the call stack of the thread will terminate not just the thread but also will trigger shutdown of hosting process itself. The one exception to this rule is the ThreadAbortException (discussed later on), which will only terminate the aborted thread. This behavior is a breaking change introduced by .NET 2.0. In contract, .NET 1.1 will only terminate the thread that encountered the unhandled exception. When porting .NET 1.1 applications to .NET 2.0, make sure that your thread methods always catch and handle any exception, otherwise you risk unplanned application termination.

The condition is usually the result of some external event telling the thread that its work is done—it can be as simple as checking the value of a flag or waiting on a synchronization event. The condition is usually changed by another thread. Consequently, changing and verifying the condition must be done in a thread-safe manner, using threading synchronization objects, as explained later in this chapter.

Blocking Threads

The Thread class provides a number of methods you can use to block the execution of a thread, similar in their effect to the native mechanisms available to Windows programmers. These include suspending a thread, putting a thread to sleep, waiting for a thread to die. Developers often misuse these mechanisms without ever realizing they were doing anything wrong. This section outlines the various blocking options and discusses why it's a bad idea to use most of them.

Suspending and resuming a thread

The Thread class provides the Suspend( ) method, which suspends the execution of a thread, and the Resume( ) method, which resumes a suspended thread:

```
public sealed class Thread
{
   public void Resume( );
   public void Suspend( );
   //Other methods and properties
}
```

Anybody can call Suspend( ) on a Thread object, including objects running on that thread, and there is no harm in calling Suspend( ) on an already suspended thread. Obviously, only clients on other threads can resume a suspended thread. Suspend( ) is a non-blocking call, meaning that control returns immediately to the caller and the thread is suspended later, usually at the next safe point. A *safe point* is a point in the code where it's safe for garbage collection to take place. (Recall from Chapter 4 that when garbage collection occurs, .NET must suspend all running threads to compact the heap, move objects in memory, and patch client-side references.) The JIT compiler identifies those points in the code that are safe for suspending the thread (such as when returning from method calls or branching for another loop iteration). When Suspend( ) is called, the thread is suspended once it reaches the next safe point.

The bottom line is that suspending a thread isn't an instantaneous operation. The need to suspend and then resume a thread usually results from a need to synchronize the execution of that thread with other threads, but using Suspend( ) and Resume( ) for that purpose isn't recommended because there is no telling when these operations will take place. Consequently, .NET 2.0 applies the Obsolete attribute to Suspend( ) and Resume( ), warning you not to use them. If you need to suspend the execution of a thread and then resume it later, you should use the dedicated .NET synchronization objects (described later). The synchronization objects provide a deterministic way of blocking a thread or signaling it to continue executing. In general, you should avoid explicitly suspending and resuming threads.

Putting a thread to sleep

The Thread class provides two overloaded versions of the static Sleep( ) method, which puts a thread to sleep for a specified timeout:

```
public sealed class Thread
{
    public static void Sleep(int millisecondsTimeout);
    public static void Sleep(TimeSpan timeout);
    //Other methods and properties
}
```

Because Sleep( ) is a static method, you can put only your own thread to sleep:

```
Thread.Sleep(20);//Sleep for 20 milliseconds
```

Sleep( ) is a blocking call, meaning that control returns to the calling thread only after the sleep period has elapsed. Sleep( ) puts the thread in a special queue of threads waiting to be awakened by the operating system. Any thread that calls Sleep( ) willingly relinquishes the remainder of its allocated CPU time slot, even if the sleep timeout is less than the remainder of the time slot. Consequently, calling Sleep( ) with a timeout of zero is a way to force a thread context switch:

```
Thread.Sleep(0);//Forces a context switch
```

If no other thread with the same or higher priority is ready to run, control returns to the thread (thread priority is discussed later, in the section "Thread Priority and Scheduling").

You can also put a thread to sleep indefinitely, using the Infinite static constant of the Timeout class:

```
Thread.Sleep(Timeout.Infinite);
```

Of course, putting a thread to sleep indefinitely is an inefficient use of the system services; it's better to simply terminate the thread (by returning from the thread method). If you need to block a thread until some event takes place, use .NET synchronization objects. In fact, you should generally avoid putting a thread to sleep, unless you specifically want the thread to act as a kind of timer. Traditionally, you put threads to sleep to cope with race conditions, by explicitly removing some of the threads involved in the race condition. A *race condition* is a situation in which thread T1 needs to have another thread, T2, complete a task or reach a certain state. The race condition occurs when T1 proceeds as if T2 is ready, when in fact it may not be. Sometimes T1 has its own processing to do, and that (in a poorly designed system) usually keeps it busy long enough to avoid the race condition. Occasionally, however, T1 will complete before T2 is ready, and an error will occur. Using Sleep( ) to resolve a race condition is inappropriate, because it doesn't address the root cause of the race condition (usually, the lack of proper synchronization between the participating threads). Putting threads to sleep is at best a makeshift solution, because the race condition can still manifest itself in different ways; also, it isn't likely to work when more threads get involved. Avoid putting a thread to sleep, and use .NET synchronization objects instead.

A Minute for TimeSpan

Traditionally, most APIs in Windows that deal with time use some form of physical time measurement, such as seconds or milliseconds. You probably have no problem converting a minute or two to seconds. However, it's harder to convert 1 hour and 48 minutes into seconds, or 2 days. The TimeSpan struct addresses this issue by providing many methods for time conversion and representing time periods in a uniform manner. For example, if you need to represent 2 days, use the static method FromDays( ), which returns a TimeSpan value representing 2 days:

```
TimeSpan TimeSpan = TimeSpan.FromDays(2);
```

Many of the methods discussed in this chapter that deal with blocking a thread have versions that accept TimeSpan instead of physical time units.

Spinning while waiting

The Thread class provides another sleep-like operation, called SpinWait( ):

```
public static void SpinWait(int iterations);
```

When a thread calls SpinWait( ), the calling thread waits the number of iterations specified but is never added to the queue of waiting threads. As a result, the thread is effectively put to sleep without relinquishing the remainder of its CPU time slot. The .NET documentation doesn't define what an iteration is, but it's likely mapped to a predetermined number (probably just one) of no-operation (NOP) assembly instructions. Consequently, the following SpinWait( ) instruction will take a different amount of time to complete on machines with different CPU clock speeds:

```
int long Million = 1000000;
Thread.SpinWait(Million);
```

SpinWait( ) isn't intended to replace Sleep( ), but rather is available as an advanced optimization technique. If you know that some resource your thread is waiting for will become available in the immediate future, it's potentially more efficient to spin and wait than it would be to use either Sleep( ) or a synchronization object, because these force a thread context switch, which is one of the most expensive operations performed by the operating system. However, even in the esoteric cases for which SpinWait( ) was designed, using it amounts to an educated guess at best. SpinWait( ) gains you nothing if the resource isn't available at the end of the call, or if the operating system preempts your thread because its time slot has elapsed or because another thread with a higher priority is ready to run. In general, I recommend that you always use deterministic programming (synchronization objects, in this case) and avoid optimization techniques.

Joining a thread

The Thread class's Join( ) method allows one thread to wait for another thread to terminate. Any client that has a reference to a Thread object can call Join( ) and have the client thread blocked until the thread terminates:

```
static void WaitForThreadToDie(Thread thread)
{
    thread.Join( );
}
```

Join( ) returns regardless of the cause of death—either natural (the thread returns from the thread method) or unnatural (the thread encounters an exception).

Note that it is imperative to always check before calling Join( ) that you are not joining your own thread:

```
static void WaitForThreadToDie(Thread thread)
{
    Debug.Assert(Thread.CurrentThread.ManagedThreadId !=
                thread.ManagedThreadId);
    thread.Join( );
}
```

Doing so will prevent a deadlock of waiting for your own thread to die. Join( ) is useful when dealing with application shutdown; when an application starts its shutdown procedure, it typically signals all the worker threads to terminate and then waits for the threads to terminate before proceeding with the shutdown. The standard way of doing this is to call Join( ) on the worker threads. Calling Join( ) is similar to waiting on a thread handle in the Win32 world, and it's likely that the Join( ) method implementation does just that.

The Join( ) method has two overloaded versions, allowing you to specify a waiting timeout:

```
public sealed class Thread
{
    public void Join( );
    public bool Join(int millisecondsTimeout);
    public bool Join(TimeSpan timeout);
    //Other methods and properties
}
```

When you specify a timeout, Join( ) returns when the timeout has expired or when the thread is terminated, whichever happens first. The bool return value is set to false if the timeout has elapsed but the thread is still running, and to true if the thread is dead.

Interrupting a waiting thread

You can rudely awaken a sleeping or waiting thread by calling the Interrupt( ) method of the Thread class:

```
public void Interrupt( );
```

Calling Interrupt( ) unblocks a sleeping thread (or a waiting thread, such as a thread that called Join( ) on another thread) and throws an exception of type ThreadInterruptedException in the unblocked thread. If the code the thread executes doesn't catch that exception, the thread is terminated by the runtime.

If a call to Thread.Interrupt( ) is made on a thread that isn't sleeping or waiting, the next time the thread tries to go to sleep or wait .NET immediately throws an exception of type ThreadInterruptedException in its call stack. Note, however, that calling Interrupt( ) doesn't interrupt a thread that is executing unmanaged code via interop; nor does it interrupt a thread that is in the middle of a call to SpinWait( ), because as far as the operating system is concerned that thread is not actually waiting at all.

Again, you should avoid relying on drastic solutions such as throwing exceptions to unblock another thread. Use .NET synchronization objects instead, to gain the benefits of structured and deterministic code flow.

Aborting a Thread

The Thread class provides an Abort( ) method, which can forcefully try to terminate a .NET thread. Calling Abort( ) throws an exception of type ThreadAbortException in the thread being aborted. ThreadAbortException is a special kind of exception. Even if the thread method uses exception handling to catch exceptions, as in the following example code:

```
public void MyThreadMethod( )
{
   try
   {
      while(<some condition>)
      {
         <Do some work>
      }
   }
   catch
   {
      //Handle exceptions here
   }
}
```

after the catch statement is executed, .NET re-throws the ThreadAbortException to terminate the thread. This is done so that non-structured attempts that ignore the abort by jumping to the beginning of the thread method simply don't work:

```
//Code that doesn't work when ThreadAbortException is thrown
public void MyThreadMethod( )
{
   Resurrection:
   try
   {
```

```
        while(<some condition>)
        {
            <Do some work>
        }
    }
    catch
    {
        goto Resurrection;
    }
}
```

 Using non-structured goto instructions is strongly discouraged in any case. Never use goto, except to fall through in a C# switch statement.

The Abort( ) method has two overloaded versions:

```
public sealed class Thread
{
    public void Abort( );
    public void Abort(object stateInfo)
    //Other methods and properties
}
```

One version allows the party that calls Abort( ) to provide a generic parameter of type object called stateInfo. stateInfo can convey application-specific information to the aborted thread, such as why it's being aborted. The aborted thread can access the stateInfo object via the ExceptionState public property of the ThreadAbortException class, if the thread is using exception handling.

Example 8-2 demonstrates using Abort( ) to terminate a thread. The example creates a new thread, whose thread method simply traces an incrementing integer to the Output window. The thread method uses exception handling, and it traces to the Output window the information passed to it using the stateInfo parameter of Abort( ). Note that the thread that called Abort( ) uses Join( ) to wait for the thread to die. This is the recommended practice, because the thread can perform an open-ended number of operations in its catch and finally exception-handling statements.

Example 8-2. Terminating a thread using Abort( )

```
public class MyClass
{
    public void DoWork( )
    {
     try
     {
        int i = 0;
        while(true)
        {
            Trace.WriteLine(i++);
        }
```

Example 8-2. Terminating a thread using Abort( ) (continued)

```
        }
        catch(ThreadAbortException exception)
        {
            string cause;
            cause = (string)exception.ExceptionState;
            Trace.WriteLine(cause);
        }
    }
}
MyClass obj = new MyClass( );
Thread workerThread = new Thread(obj.DoWork);
workerThread.Start( );

/* Do some work, then: */

workerThread.Abort("Time to go");
workerThread.Join( );
```

If Abort( ) is called before the thread is started, .NET doesn't start the thread when
Thread.Start( ) is called. If Thread.Abort( ) is called while the thread is blocked
(either by calling Sleep( ) or Join( ), or if the thread is waiting on one of the .NET
synchronization objects), .NET unblocks the thread and throws a
ThreadAbortException in it. However, you can't call Abort( ) on a suspended thread.
Doing so results in an exception of type ThreadStateException on the calling side,
with the error message "Thread is suspended; attempting to abort." .NET then terminates the suspended thread without letting it handle the exception.

The Thread class also has an interesting counter-abort method—the static
ResetAbort( ) method:

```
    public static void ResetAbort( );
```

Calling Thread.ResetAbort( ) in a catch statement prevents .NET from re-throwing a
ThreadAbortException at the end of the catch statement:

```
    catch(ThreadAbortException exception)
    {
        Trace.WriteLine("Refusing to die");
        Thread.ResetAbort( );
        //Do more processing or even goto somewhere
    }
```

ResetAbort( ) requires the ControlThread security permission. Permissions are explained in Chapter 12.

Terminating a thread by calling Abort( ) isn't recommended, for a number of reasons. The first is that it forces the thread to perform an ungraceful exit. Often, the
thread needs to release resources it holds and perform some sort of cleanup before

terminating. You can, of course, handle exceptions and put the cleanup code in the finally method, but you typically want to handle unexpected errors that way and not use it as the standard way to terminate a thread. Second, nothing prevents the thread from abusing .NET and either performing as many operations as it likes in the catch statement, jumping to a label, or calling ResetAbort( ). If you want to terminate a thread, you should do so in a structured manner, using the .NET synchronization objects. You should signal the thread method to exit by using a member variable or event. Later, after a discussion of manual synchronization, this chapter presents a template for terminating threads using this technique, without resorting to Abort( ).

Calling Thread.Abort( ) has another liability: if the thread makes an interop call (using COM interop or P-Invoke), the interop call may take a while to complete. If Thread.Abort( ) is called during the interop call, .NET doesn't abort the thread; it lets the thread complete the interop call, only to abort it when it returns. This is another reason why Thread.Abort( ) isn't guaranteed to succeed (or succeed immediately).

Thread States

.NET manages a state machine for each thread and moves the threads between states. The ThreadState enum defines the set of states a .NET managed thread can be in:

```
[Flags]
public enum ThreadState
{
    Aborted          = 0x00000100,
    AbortRequested   = 0x00000080,
    Background       = 0x00000004,
    Running          = 0x00000000,
    Stopped          = 0x00000010,
    StopRequested    = 0x00000001,
    Suspended        = 0x00000040,
    SuspendRequested = 0x00000002,
    Unstarted        = 0x00000008,
    WaitSleepJoin    = 0x00000020
}
```

For example, if a thread is in the middle of a Sleep( ), Join( ), or wait call on one of the synchronization objects, the thread is in the ThreadState.WaitSleepJoin state. .NET throws an exception of type ThreadStateException when it tries to move the thread to an inconsistent state—for example, by calling Start( ) on a thread at the ThreadState.Running state or trying to abort a suspended thread (ThreadState.Suspended). The Thread class has a public read-only property called ThreadState that you can access to find the exact state of a thread:

```
public ThreadState ThreadState{get;}
```

The ThreadState enum values can be bit-masked together, so testing for a given state is typically done as follows:

```
Thread workerThread;
//Some code to initialize workerThread, then:
ThreadState state = workerThread.ThreadState;

if((state & ThreadState.Unstarted) == ThreadState.Unstarted)
{
    workerThread.Start();
}
```

However, by the time you retrieve the thread's state and decide to act upon it, the state may already have changed. I don't recommend ever designing your application so that you rely on the information provided by the ThreadState property; rather, you should design so that your code doesn't depend on the thread being in a particular state. If your thread transitions between logical states specific to your application, such as beginning or finishing tasks, use .NET synchronization objects to synchronize transitioning between those states.

The only time you might need to rely on state information is to check whether the thread is alive, which is required sometimes for diagnostics or control flow. Even then, you should use the Boolean read-only public property IsAlive instead of the ThreadState property:

```
public bool IsAlive { get; }
```

For example, there is little point in calling Join() on a thread if the thread isn't alive:

```
Thread workerThread;
//Some code to start workerThread, then:
if(workerThread.IsAlive)
{
    workerThread.Join();
}
Trace.WriteLine("Thread is dead");
```

Foreground and Background Threads

.NET defines two kinds of managed threads: *background* and *foreground*. The two thread types are exactly the same, except that .NET keeps the process alive as long as there is at least one foreground thread running, whereas a background thread doesn't keep the .NET process alive once all foreground threads have exited.

New threads are created as foreground threads by default. To mark a thread as a background thread, you need to set the Thread object's IsBackground property to true:

```
public bool IsBackground { get; set; }
```

When the last foreground thread in a .NET application (actually, in an application domain, discussed in the section "Synchronizing Threads") terminates, .NET shuts down the application. The .NET runtime then tries to terminate all the remaining background threads by throwing a ThreadAbortException in each. Background threads are a poor man's solution for application shutdown: instead of designing the application correctly to keep track of what threads it created (and which threads are still running and need to be terminated when the application shuts down), a quick and dirty solution is to let .NET try to terminate all the background threads for you. Normally, you shouldn't count on .NET to kill your background threads for you. You should have a deterministic, structured way of shutting down your application—in other words, you should do your own bookkeeping and explicitly control the lifecycles of each of your threads, taking steps to shut down all threads on exit.

Thread Priority and Scheduling

Each thread is allocated a fixed time slot to run on the CPU and assigned a priority. In addition, each thread is either ready to run or waiting for some event to occur, such as a synchronization object being signaled or a sleep timeout elapsing. The underlying operating system schedules for execution those threads that are ready to run based on the threads' priorities. Thread scheduling is *preemptive*, meaning that the thread with the highest priority always gets to run. If a thread T1 with priority P1 is running, and suddenly thread T2 with priority P2 is ready to run, and P2 is greater than P1, the operating system will preempt (pause) T1 and allow T2 to run. If multiple threads with the same (highest) priority are ready to run, the operating system will let each run for the duration of its CPU time slot and then preempt it in favor of another thread with the same priority, in a round-robin fashion.

The Thread class provides the Priority property of the enum type ThreadPriority, which allows you to retrieve or set the thread priority:

```
public ThreadPriority Priority { get; set; }
```

The enum ThreadPriority provides five priority levels:

```
public enum ThreadPriority
{
    Lowest,
    BelowNormal,
    Normal,
    AboveNormal,
    Highest
}
```

New .NET threads are created by default with a priority of ThreadPriority.Normal. Developers often abuse thread-priority settings as a way to control the flow of a multithreaded application, to work around race conditions. Tinkering with thread priorities generally isn't an appropriate solution, though, and it can lead to some adverse side effects and other race conditions. For example, say you have two threads that are involved in a race condition. By increasing one thread's priority in the hope that it will preempt the other and thus win the race, you often just decrease the probability of the race condition occurring (rather than eliminating it altogether), because the thread with the higher priority can still be switched out or blocked. In addition, you must consider whether it makes sense to always run that thread at a higher priority. Granting it a high priority could paralyze other aspects of your application, because it won't only preempt the thread with which you're trying to avoid the race condition. You could, of course, increase the priority only temporarily, but then you would address just that particular occurrence of the race condition and remain exposed to future occurrences.

You may be tempted to always keep that thread at a high priority and also increase the priorities of other affected threads, but this is also problematic. Often, increasing one thread's priority causes an inflation of thread priorities all around, because the normal balance and time-sharing governed by the operating system is disturbed. The result can be a set of threads, all with the highest priority, still involved in race conditions. The major adverse effect now is that .NET itself suffers, because many of its internal threads (such as threads used to manage memory, execute remote calls, and so on) are suddenly competing with your high-priority threads.

A further complication when manipulating priority settings is that preemptive operating systems (such as Windows) may dynamically change threads' priorities to resolve priority-inversion situations. A *priority inversion* occurs when a thread with a lower priority runs instead of a thread with a higher priority. Because .NET threads are currently mapped to the underlying Windows threads, these dynamic changes propagate to the managed threads as well. Consider, for example, three managed threads, T1, T2, and T3, with respective priorities of ThreadPriority.Lowest, ThreadPriority.Normal, and ThreadPriority.Highest. T3 is waiting for a resource held by T1. T1 is ready to run to release the resource, except that T2 is now running, preventing T1 from executing. As a result, T2 prevents T3 from running, and priority inversion takes place because T3 has a priority greater than that of T2.

To cope with priority inversions, the operating system not only keeps track of thread priorities but also maintains a scoreboard showing who got to run and how often. If a thread is denied the CPU for a long time (a few seconds), the operating system dynamically boosts that thread's priority to a higher priority, lets it run for a couple of time slots with the new priority, and then resets the priority back to its original value. In the previous scenario, this allows T1 to run, release the resource T3 is waiting for, and then regain its original priority. Once the resource is available, T3 will be ready to run and will preempt T2.

The point of this example and the earlier arguments is that you should avoid trying to control the application flow by setting thread priorities. Instead, use .NET synchronization objects to control and coordinate the flow of your application and to resolve race conditions. Set threads' priorities to values other than ThreadPriority. Normal only when the semantics of the application require it. For example, if you develop a screen saver, its threads should run at priority ThreadPriority.Lowest so that other background operations (such as compilation, network access, or number crunching) can take place without being affected by the screen saver.

Synchronizing Threads

For all its advantages, introducing multithreading into your application opens up a Pandora's box of synchronization and concurrency-management issues. With multithreading, you have to worry about threads deadlocking themselves while contesting for the same resources, you must take steps to synchronize access to objects by concurrent multiple threads, and you need to be prepared to handle method reentrancy.

When it comes to programming components that are likely to be used by you or by others in multithreaded applications, you must ensure they are *thread-safe*. A thread-safe component is one that is equipped with mechanisms to prevent multiple threads from simultaneously accessing its methods and corrupting its state. Imagine, for example, a linked list component that provides methods for adding and removing elements from a list. When the component adds or removes an element, the component keeps the list in a temporarily inconsistent state, while node references are updated and written to reflect the change. If a client asks to add an element to the list on one thread (T1), and that thread is preempted by another thread (T2) during the request, T1 can leave the list in an inconsistent state, and T2 can crash trying to access the list. To make the list thread-safe, you should make sure that only one thread can access it at a time and that all other threads are barred until the current thread has finished.

With multithreaded applications, you must also concern yourself with avoiding deadlocks. In its simplest form, a *deadlock* occurs when one thread (T1), which owns thread-safe resource R1, tries to access another thread-safe resource (R2) at the same time that a second thread (T2), which owns R2, tries to access R1 (see Figure 8-2).

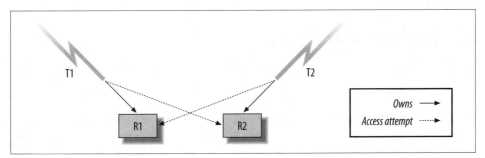

Figure 8-2. A deadlock between two threads

 There are many ways to create a deadlock, and some of them are complex, involving multiple threads with multiple resources and synchronization objects. There are some defensive programming techniques to reduce the likelihood of deadlocks (such as always acquiring and releasing the resources in the same order), but by far the best prevention is to simply avoid them by design in the first place. You must analyze the intended behavior of your application's threads well before coding your first thread.

Multithreading defects are notoriously hard to isolate, reproduce, and eliminate. They often involve rare race conditions, and fixing one problem often introduces another. Traditionally, writing robust, high-performance multithreaded code was no trivial matter; it required a great deal of skill and discipline. .NET tries to ease multithreaded application development by providing a rich infrastructure compared to native Windows. In particular, .NET tries to simplify component concurrency management.

 COM managed concurrency through the use of apartments, which were difficult to use and understand. .NET eliminates that awkward model.

By default, all .NET components execute in a multithreaded environment, and concurrent access to them by multiple threads is allowed. As a result, the state of the object can be corrupted if multiple threads access it at the same time. To avoid this problem, .NET provides two synchronization approaches: automatic and manual. *Automatic synchronization* allows you to simply decorate the component with an attribute and have .NET synchronize concurrent access to the object. *Manual synchronization* requires using .NET synchronization objects. In fact, .NET offers a range of options in the synchronization spectrum: you can synchronize access to a set of objects, an individual object, a particular method, or a critical code section, or you can just protect an individual class member. This range allows you to make trade-offs between ease of use and flexibility, and productivity and throughput.

The next two sections first describe .NET automatic synchronization for context-bound objects and then demonstrate the use of .NET locks provided for manual synchronization.

Automatic Synchronization

To understand the ways in which .NET can automatically synchronize access to components, you must first understand the relationship that .NET maintains between components, processes, application domains, and contexts. When a .NET application starts, the operating system launches an unmanaged process, which loads the .NET runtime. However, a .NET application can't execute directly in the unmanaged process. Instead, .NET provides a managed abstraction of the operating-system process in the form of an application domain, or *app domain*. Because app domains are a logical abstraction, a single unmanaged process can contain more than one app domain (see Figure 8-3). Chapter 10 discusses app domains in detail.

The app domain isn't the innermost execution scope of a .NET component. .NET provides a level of indirection between components and app domains, in the form of *contexts*. Contexts enable .NET to provide *component services* such as thread synchronization to a component. In fact, one definition of a context is that it's a logical grouping of components, all configured to use the same set of component services.

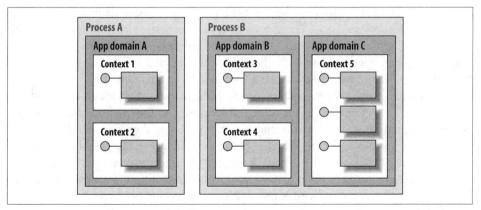

Figure 8-3. NET app domains and contexts

Every app domain starts with one context, called the *default context*, and .NET creates new contexts as required.

By default, .NET components aren't aware that contexts exist. When a client in the app domain creates an object, .NET gives back to the client a direct reference to the new object. Such objects always execute in the context of the calling client. However, in order to take advantage of .NET component services, components must be context-bound, meaning they must always execute in the same context. Such components must derive directly or indirectly from the class `ContextBoundObject`:

```
public class MyClass : ContextBoundObject
{...}
```

Clients never have a direct reference to a context-bound object; instead, they have a reference to a proxy. .NET provides its component services by intercepting the calls clients make into the context via the proxy and performing some pre- and post-call processing. Chapter 11 discusses contexts in depth. In the context of this chapter (no pun intended), all you need to know is that you can have .NET synchronize access to any context-bound component by decorating the component class definition with the Synchronization attribute, defined in the `System.Runtime.Remoting.Contexts` namespace:

```
using System.Runtime.Remoting.Contexts;

[Synchronization]
public class MyClass : ContextBoundObject
{
    public MyClass( )
    {}
    public void DoSomething( )
    {}
    //Other methods and data members
}
```

The Synchronization attribute, when applied on a ContextBoundObject-based class, instructs .NET to place the object in a context and associate the object with a lock. When a client on thread T1 attempts to access the object by calling a method on it (or accessing a public member variable), the client actually interacts with a proxy. .NET intercepts the client access and tries to acquire the lock associated with the object. If the lock isn't currently owned by another thread, .NET acquires the lock and proceeds to access the object on thread T1. When the call returns from the method, .NET releases the lock and returns control to the client. If the object is then accessed by another thread (T2), T1 is blocked until T2 releases the lock. In fact, while the object is being accessed by one thread, all other threads are placed in a queue and are granted access to the object one at a time, in order. The result of this context-bound synchronization is that .NET provides a *macro lock* for the object, meaning that object as a whole—even parts of the state that aren't being accessed by the client—is locked during access.

Synchronization Domains

.NET could have allocated one lock for each context-bound object, but that would be inefficient. If the components are all designed to participate in the same activity on behalf of a client and execute on the same thread, objects can share a lock. In such situations, allocating one lock per object would be a waste of resources and processing time, because .NET would have to perform additional locks and unlocks on every object access. Moreover, the noteworthy argument in favor of sharing locks among objects is that sharing locks reduces the likelihood of deadlocks. If two objects interact with each other and each has its own lock, it's possible for the two objects to be used by two different clients on different threads, so they will deadlock trying to access each other. However, if the objects share a lock, only one client thread is allowed to access them at a time.

In .NET, a set of context-bound objects that share a lock are said to be in a *synchronization domain*. Each synchronization domain has one lock, and within the same synchronization domain, concurrent calls from multiple threads aren't possible. When a thread accesses one object in a synchronization domain, that thread (and only that thread) can also access the rest of the objects in the synchronization domain. The synchronization domain locks all objects in the domain from access by other threads, even though the current thread accesses only one object at a time.

Synchronization Domains and Contexts

A synchronization domain is independent of contexts, and it can include objects from multiple contexts. However, the synchronization domain is limited to a single app domain, which means that objects from different app domains can't share a synchronization domain lock. A context can belong to at most one synchronization domain at any given time, and may not belong to one at all. If a context belongs to a synchronization domain, all objects in that context belong to that synchronization domain. The reason is that if objects differ in the way they are configured to use synchronization domains, .NET puts them in different contexts in the first place. The relationship between app domains, synchronization domains, contexts, and objects is shown in Figure 8-4.

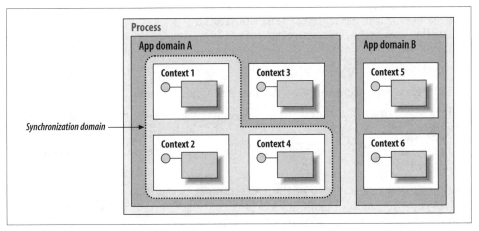

Figure 8-4. A synchronization domain

Configuring Synchronization Domains

It's up to you to decide how a component is associated with a synchronization-domain lock: you need to decide whether the object needs a lock at all, and if so whether it can share a lock with other objects or requires a new lock. The SynchronizationAttribute class provides a number of overloaded constructors:

```
public class SynchronizationAttribute : ContextAttribute, IContextAttribute
                                        //Other interfaces
{
    public static const int NOT_SUPPORTED = 1;
    public static const int SUPPORTED     = 2;
    public static const int REQUIRED      = 4;
    public static const int REQUIRES_NEW  = 8;

    // Constructors
    public SynchronizationAttribute( );
    public SynchronizationAttribute(int flag);
    public SynchronizationAttribute(int flag, bool reentrant);
    public SynchronizationAttribute(bool reentrant);
    //Other methods and properties
}
```

Four integer constants are defined: NOT_SUPPORTED, SUPPORTED, REQUIRED, and REQUIRES_NEW. These constants determine which synchronization domain the object will reside in relation to its creating client. For example:

```
[Synchronization(SynchronizationAttribute.REQUIRES_NEW)]
public class MyClass : ContextBoundObject
{}
```

The default constructor of the SynchronizationAttribute class uses REQUIRED, and so do the other constructors that don't require a value for the constant. As a result, these declarations are equivalent:

```
[Synchronization]
[Synchronization(SynchronizationAttribute.REQUIRED)]
[Synchronization(SynchronizationAttribute.REQUIRED,false)]
[Synchronization(false)]
```

An object can reside in any of these synchronization domains:

- In its creator's synchronization domain (the object shares a lock with its creator)
- In a new synchronization domain (the object has its own lock and starts a new synchronization domain)
- In no synchronization domain at all (there is no lock, so concurrent access is allowed)

An object's synchronization domain is determined at the time of its creation, based on the synchronization domain of its creator and the constant value provided to the Synchronization attribute. If the object is configured with synchronization NOT_SUPPORTED, it will never be part of a synchronization domain, regardless of whether or not its creator has a synchronization domain. If the object is configured with SUPPORTED and its creator has a synchronization domain, .NET places the object in its creator's synchronization domain. If the creating object doesn't have a synchronization domain, the newly created object will not have a synchronization domain. If the object is configured with synchronization support set to REQUIRED, .NET puts it in its creator's synchronization domain if the creating object has one. If the creating object doesn't have a synchronization domain and the object is configured to require synchronization, .NET creates a new synchronization domain for the object. Finally, if the object is configured with synchronization support set to REQUIRES_NEW, .NET creates a new synchronization domain for it, regardless of whether its creator has a synchronization domain or not. The .NET synchronization domain allocation decision matrix is summarized in Table 8-1.

Table 8-1. Synchronization domain (SD) allocation decision matrix

Object SD support	Creator has an SD	Object will take part in
NOT_SUPPORTED	No	No SD
SUPPORTED	No	No SD
REQUIRED	No	New SD
REQUIRES_NEW	No	New SD
NOT_SUPPORTED	Yes	No SD
SUPPORTED	Yes	Creator's SD
REQUIRED	Yes	Creator's SD
REQUIRES_NEW	Yes	New SD

Figure 8-5 shows an example of synchronization domain flow. In the figure, a client that doesn't have a synchronization domain creates an object configured with synchronization set to REQUIRED. Because the object requires a synchronization domain and its creator has none, .NET creates a new synchronization domain for it. The object then goes on to create four more objects. Two of them, configured with synchronization REQUIRED and SUPPORTED, are placed within the creating object's synchronization domain. The component configured with synchronization NOT_SUPPORTED has no synchronization domain. The last component is configured with synchronization set to REQUIRES_NEW, so .NET creates a new synchronization domain for it. You may be wondering why .NET partly bases the synchronization-domain decision on the object's creating client. The heuristic .NET uses is that the calling patterns, interactions, and synchronization needs between objects usually closely match their creation relationship. The question now is, when should you use the various Synchronization attribute construction values?

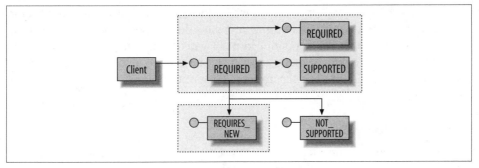

Figure 8-5. Synchronization domain flow

 The designer of the SynchronizationAttribute class didn't follow basic type-safety practices, and provided the synchronization value in the form of constants instead of an enumeration. As a result, this usage of SynchronizationAttribute:

```
[Synchronization(1234)]
public class MyClass : ContextBoundObject
{}
```

compiles but throws an ArgumentException at runtime. If an enum such as this:

```
public enum SynchronizationOption
{
    NotSupported,Supported,Required,RequiresNew
}
```

had been defined, the result would have been type-safe.

Synchronization NOT_SUPPORTED

An object set to NOT_SUPPORTED never participates in a synchronization domain. The object must provide its own synchronization mechanism. You should use this setting only if you expect concurrent access and you want to provide your own synchronization mechanisms. In general, avoid this setting. A context-bound object should take advantage of component-services support as much as possible.

Synchronization SUPPORTED

An object set to SUPPORTED will share its creator's synchronization domain if it has one and will have no synchronization domain of its own if the creator doesn't have one. This is the least useful setting, because the object must provide its own synchronization mechanism in case its creator doesn't have a synchronization domain, and you must make sure that the mechanism doesn't interfere with the synchronization domain when one is used. As a result, it's more difficult to develop the component. SUPPORTED is available for the rare case in which the component itself has no need for synchronization, yet downstream objects it creates do require it. By setting synchronization to SUPPORTED, the component can propagate the synchronization domain of its creating client to the downstream objects and have them all share one synchronization domain, instead of a few separate synchronization domains. This reduces the likelihood of deadlocks.

Synchronization REQUIRED

REQUIRED is by far the most common value for .NET context-bound objects, and hence it's also the default of the SynchronizationAttribute class. When an object is set to REQUIRED, all calls to the object will be synchronized; the only question is whether the object will have its own synchronization domain or share its creator's synchronization domain. If you don't care about the object having its own synchronization domain, always use this setting.

Synchronization REQUIRES_NEW

When an object is set to REQUIRES_NEW, the object must have a new synchronization domain, distinct from the creator's synchronization domain, and its own lock. The object will never share its context or the synchronization domain with its creator.

Choosing between REQUIRED and REQUIRES_NEW

Deciding that your object requires synchronization is usually straightforward. If you anticipate that multiple clients on multiple threads will try to access your object, and you don't want to write your own synchronization mechanism, you need synchronization. The more difficult question to answer is whether your object should require its own synchronization lock or whether you should configure it to use the lock of its creator. Try basing your decision on the pattern of calls to your object.

Consider the calling pattern in Figure 8-6. In this pattern, Object 2 is configured with synchronization set to REQUIRED and is placed in the same synchronization domain as its creator, Object 1. Although the two objects share a lock, they do not interact with each other. While Client A is accessing Object 1, Client B comes along on another thread, wanting to call methods on Object 2. Client B could safely access Object 2, because it doesn't violate the synchronization requirement for the creating object (Object 1). However, because it uses a different thread than Client A, it's blocked and forced to wait until Client A is finished.

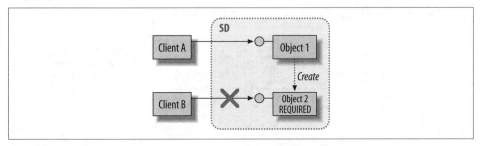

Figure 8-6. A calling pattern

If, on the other hand, you configure Object 2 to require its own synchronization domain using REQUIRES_NEW, the object will be able to process calls from other clients at the same time as Object 1 (see Figure 8-7). However, if the creator object (Object 1) does need to call Object 2, these calls will potentially block, and they will be more expensive because they must cross context boundaries and pay the overhead of trying to acquire the lock.

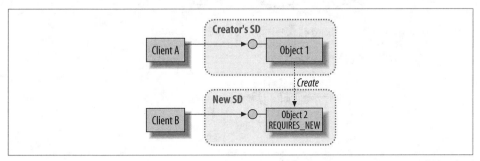

Figure 8-7. Having separate synchronization domains enables clients to be served more efficiently

A classic example of configuring components to require new synchronization domains is when class factories are used to create objects. Class factories usually require thread safety, because they service multiple clients. However, once the factory creates an object, it hands the object back to a client and has nothing more to do with it. You definitely don't want all the objects created by a class factory to share the same synchronization domain as the factory, because no one could use them while the factory creates new objects. In that case, configure the created objects to require new synchronization domains.

Synchronization-Domain Reentrancy

A synchronization domain allows only one thread to enter and locks all the objects in the domain. .NET releases the lock automatically when the thread winds its way back up the call chain, leaving the synchronization domain from the same object through which it entered. Figure 8-8 demonstrates this point: a thread enters a synchronization domain, acquires the lock, and releases it only when it returns from Object 1, leaving the synchronization domain. But what should .NET do if an object makes a call outside the synchronization domain while the call is still in progress inside the domain? This situation is shown in Figure 8-9.

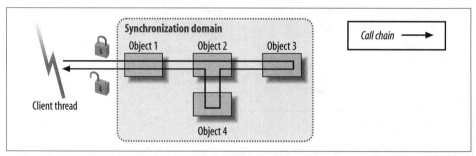

Figure 8-8. Releasing a lock when the call chain exits on the original entry object

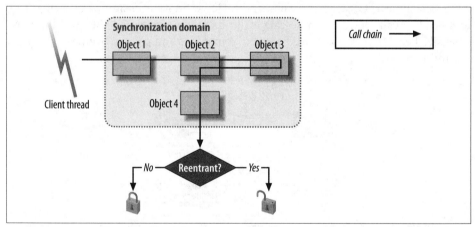

Figure 8-9. If reentrancy is set to true, NET releases the synchronization domain lock while the outgoing call is in progress

By default, .NET doesn't release the synchronization-domain lock when the thread exits the domain through a route other than the entry object, such as Object 4 in Figure 8-9. However, because the thread can spend an indefinite amount of time on the outgoing call, it can indefinitely deny other threads access to the synchronization-domain objects. If you want to allow other threads access to the synchronization-domain objects while the current thread makes a call outside the synchronization domain, you need to provide a true value for the reentrant parameter of the SynchronizationAttribute class constructors:

```
[Synchronization(true)]
public class MyClass : ContextBoundObject
{}
```

Be aware that synchronization-domain reentrancy isn't implemented. As a result, the mechanism behaves as if you always pass in false for reentrancy.

In Figure 8-9, if Object 4 is configured to allow reentrancy, when it makes a call outside the synchronization domain .NET releases the lock and allows other threads to enter the domain. Note that when the thread that made the outbound call tries to reenter the synchronization domain it must reacquire the lock, just like any other thread calling from outside the domain. Reentrancy introduces coupling between the objects in the synchronization domain, because the original entry object (Object 1 in Figure 8-9) must also be set for reentrancy, to release the lock when the call chain exits via it.

Allowing for reentrancy is an optimization technique that can increase your application performance and throughput, at the expense of thread safety. In general, I recommend not allowing for reentrancy unless you are convinced that the outgoing call leaves the synchronization domain in a consistent, thread-safe state—that is, that the outgoing thread has no more interactions with the objects in the synchronization domain (apart from returning and winding up the call chain) and that it will exit via the original entry object.

In general, it's a bad design decision to access objects outside your synchronization domain, regardless of whether you can still make things work using the reentrant parameter. If you need to access another object, by design, that object should be part of your synchronization domain. Only clients in non-synchronized contexts should make cross–synchronization domain calls.

Synchronization Domain Pros and Cons

Automatic synchronization for context-bound objects via synchronization domain is by far the easiest synchronization mechanism available to .NET developers. It's a modern synchronization technique that formally eliminates synchronization problems and your need to code around them and test your handcrafted solutions. The resulting productivity gain is substantial. Synchronization domains offer an additional major benefit, too. As explained in Chapter 1, component concurrency management is a core principle of component-oriented programming. A component vendor can't assume that multiple concurrent client threads will not access their components. As a result, unless the vendor states that its components aren't thread-safe, the vendor must provide thread-safe components. Without a way of sharing a lock with the clients, there would always be a synchronization boundary between the vendor server components and the client components. The result would impede performance, because incoming calls would have to negotiate both client-side and server-side locks. More importantly, it would also increase the probability of deadlocks, in the case of different client components competing to use different server components. The ability to share a lock between components developed by different parties is an important feature of .NET as a component technology, analogous to COM's apartments but without the cumbersome model and accompanying liabilities.

Unfortunately, no technology is perfect, and synchronization domains aren't without flaws:

- You can use them only with context-bound objects. For all other .NET types, you must still use manual synchronization objects.

- There is a penalty for accessing context-bound objects via proxies and interceptors. In some intense calling patterns, this can pose a problem.

- A synchronization domain doesn't protect static class members and static methods. For those, you must use manual synchronization objects.

- A synchronization domain isn't a throughput-oriented mechanism. The incoming thread locks a whole set of objects, even if it interacts with only one of them. That lock precludes other threads from accessing these objects, which can degrade your application throughput.

Caveats aside, I believe that relying on advanced component services (such as synchronization) is a necessity in almost any decent-sized application (or whenever productivity and quality are a top priority), and that the benefits automatic synchronization offers outweigh the drawbacks of using context-bound objects.

Manual Synchronization

.NET manual synchronization provides a rich set of *synchronization locks* familiar to any veteran Win32 programmer, such as monitors, events, mutexes, semaphores, and interlocks. .NET also introduces some language features that automate the use of locks, and a new lock type (the reader/writer lock). Manual synchronization is at the other end of the spectrum from automatic synchronization, on a number of dimensions. First, whereas a synchronization domain is in effect a mega-macro lock, manual synchronization offers fine-grained control over what is locked: you can control access to an object, its individual members, or even a single line of code. As a result, you can potentially improve overall application performance and throughput.

You can use manual synchronization on any .NET component, whether context-bound or not. Unlike with automatic synchronization, when you use manual synchronization, as the name implies, you explicitly manage the locking and unlocking of the lock. Consequently, with this approach the Pandora's box of synchronization is wide open, and unless you carefully design your manual-synchronization mechanism you can introduce deadlocks and other multithreading defects, such as object state corruption and hard-to-resolve race conditions. In this section, I will provide you (where appropriate) with design guidelines and rules of thumb that will allow you to apply manual synchronization productively.

The Monitor

A Monitor is a lock designed to work with .NET reference types only. The Monitor static class associates a lock with an object. While one thread owns the lock associated with that object, no other thread can acquire the lock. Monitor provides only static methods, accepting the target object as a parameter.

The two most commonly used methods of Monitor are Enter( ) and Exit( ):

```
public static class Monitor
{
    public static void Enter(object obj);
    public static void Exit(object obj);
    //Other methods
}
```

Enter( ) acquires a lock for an object and locks it; Exit( ) unlocks it. A client that wants to access a non-thread-safe object calls Enter( ), specifying the object. The client uses the object and then calls Exit( ) to allow other threads to access the object, as shown in Example 8-3.

Example 8-3. Using Monitor to control access to an object

```
public class MyClass
{
    public void DoSomething()
    {...}
    //Class members
}

MyClass obj;
//Some code to initialize obj;

//This section is now thread-safe:

Monitor.Enter(obj);
obj.DoSomething();
Monitor.Exit(obj);
```

Any object, from any thread, can call Enter( ) to try to access the object. If the monitor is owned by one thread, and a second thread tries to obtain that monitor, Enter( )
blocks the second thread until the first thread calls Exit( ). If there is more than one
pending thread, they are placed in a queue called the *lock queue* and served from the
queue in order. There is no harm in calling Enter( ) multiple times on the same
object, provided you make a matching number of calls to Exit( ) to release the lock.
However, only the thread that called Enter( ) can make the corresponding call to
Exit( ). Trying to call Exit( ) on a different thread results in an exception of type
SynchronizationLockException.

Monitor also provides the TryEnter( ) Boolean method, which allows a client thread
to try to acquire the lock without being blocked:

```
public static bool TryEnter(object obj);
```

If the lock is available, TryEnter( ) locks it and returns true. If the lock is owned by
another thread, TryEnter( ) returns immediately to its caller, with a return value of
false.

TryEnter( ) has two other overloaded methods that allow the client to specify a timeout to wait to acquire the lock if it's owned by another thread:

```
public static bool TryEnter(object obj,int millisecondsTimeout);
public static bool TryEnter(object obj,TimeSpan timeout);
```

TryEnter( ) is of little use, because the calling client itself should be able to deal with
an object that is unavailable. TryEnter( ) is provided for the advanced and esoteric
cases of high-throughput threads that can't afford to block on nice-to-have operations.

I also recommend avoiding TryEnter( ) because of a general design guideline when dealing with locks: always postpone acquiring a lock until the last possible moment, and release it as soon as possible. This reduces the likelihood of a deadlock and improves overall throughput. If you have something to do instead of acquiring a lock, do it and obtain the lock after that.

Protecting static members and methods

You can also use the Monitor class to provide thread-safe access to static class methods or properties by giving it the type to lock instead of a particular instance, as shown in Example 8-4.

Example 8-4. Using Monitor to control access to a static method

```
public class MyClass
{
    static public void DoSomething( )
    {...}
    //Static class members
}

//This section is now thread-safe:
Monitor.Enter(typeof(MyClass));
MyClass.DoSomething( );
Monitor.Exit(typeof(MyClass));
```

Error handling

You must call Exit( ) on the object you locked using Enter( ), even if an exception has been thrown; otherwise, the object will not be accessible by clients on other threads. Example 8-5 shows the same code as Example 8-3, this time with proper error handling. Placing the call to Exit( ) in the finally statement ensures that Exit( ) is called regardless of whether the try statement encounters an exception.

Example 8-5. Using Monitor with error handling

```
public class MyClass
{
    public void DoSomething( )
    {...}
    //Class members
}

MyClass obj;
//Some code to initialize obj;

Monitor.Enter(obj);
try
{
    obj.DoSomething( );
}
```

Example 8-5. Using Monitor with error handling (continued)

```
finally
{
    Monitor.Exit(obj);
}
```

To ease the task of using Monitor in conjunction with error handing, C# provides the lock statement, which causes the compiler to automatically generate calls to Enter( ) and Exit( ) in a try/finally statement. For example, when you write this code:

```
MyClass obj;
//Some code to initialize obj;

lock(obj)
{
    obj.DoSomething( );
}
```

the compiler replaces the lock statement with the code shown in Example 8-5 instead. Visual Basic 2005 offers similar compiler support via the SyncLock statement:

```
Public Class MyVBClass
    Sub DoSomething( )
        ...
    End Sub
    'Class members
End Class

Dim obj As MyVBClass
'Some code to initialize obj;

SyncLock (obj)
    obj.DoSomething( )
End SyncLock
```

As when using raw Monitor, you can use the lock statement to protect a static method or access to a static member by providing a type instead of an instance:

```
public class MyClass
{
    static public void DoSomething( )
    {...}
    //Static class members
}
lock(typeof(MyClass))
{
    MyClass.DoSomething( );
}
```

In cases where you need to lock multiple objects, avoid nesting or stacking multiple lock statements:

```
MyClass obj1 = new MyClass();
MyClass obj2 = new MyClass();
MyClass obj3 = new MyClass();

lock(obj1)
lock(obj2)
lock(obj3)
{
    //Use the objects
}
```

The compiler will allow you to stack the lock statements, but this is inherently dangerous—if another thread is also using multiple lock statements to acquire the same objects, but in a different order, you will end up with a deadlock. When multiple locking is required, use WaitHandle (described later).

Encapsulating Monitor

Using a Monitor object to protect an object from concurrent access, as shown in Example 8-5, is asking for trouble. The reason is simple: using Monitor is done at the discretion of the client developer. Nothing prevents a client from ignoring other threads and accessing an object directly, without using a lock. Of course, such an action will cause a conflict if another thread is currently accessing the object, even if that thread was disciplined enough to use a lock. To guard against undisciplined access, encapsulate the lock inside the component and use Monitor on every public method and property, passing this as the object to lock. Encapsulating the lock is the classic object-oriented solution for thread-safe objects. Example 8-6 demonstrates this solution.

Example 8-6. Encapsulating Monitor to promote loose coupling and thread safety

```
public class MyClass
{
    /* Class members */
    public void DoSomething()
    {
        lock(this)
        {
            //Do something
        }
    }
}
MyClass obj;
//Some code to initialize obj;
obj.DoSomething();
```

Encapsulating the lock inside the method promotes loose coupling between the clients and the object, because now the clients don't need to care about the object's synchronization needs. It also promotes thread safety, because the method (or property) access is safe by definition.

You can also encapsulate the lock statement for static methods or properties:

```
public class MyClass
{
    static public void DoSomething( )
    {
        lock(typeof(MyClass))
        {
            //Do something
        }
    }
    //Static member variables
}
```

> In general, exposing public class member variables directly is inadvisable, and it's doubly so when multithreading is involved because there is no way to encapsulate the lock. At the very least, you should use properties that call lock(this) to access member variables.

Note that when you use the lock statement in a method that returns a value (such as a property), there is no need to use a temporary variable, because the finally block executes after the return instruction:

```
public class MyClass
{
    int m_Number;
    public int Number
    {
        get
        {
            lock(this)
            {
                return m_Number;
            }
        }
    }
}
```

Thread-safe structures

You should also provide for thread-safe, encapsulated access to structures. The problem with structures is that they are value types, and therefore you cannot pass a structure itself to Monitor. To overcome this problem, add to your structure a do-nothing object member variable and use that as the reference type for the lock statement, as shown in Example 8-7.

Example 8-7. Encapsulated thread-safe access to a structure using a member object

```
public interface ICloneable<T>
{
   T Clone( );
}
public struct MyStruct : ICloneable<MyStruct>
{
   int m_Number;
   object m_Lock;

   public MyStruct(int number)
   {
      m_Number = number;
      m_Lock = new object( );
   }
   public int Number
   {
      set
      {
         Debug.Assert(m_Lock != null);
         lock(m_Lock)
         {
            m_Number = value;
         }
      }
      get
      {
         Debug.Assert(m_Lock != null);
         lock(m_Lock)
         {
            return m_Number;
         }
      }
   }
   public MyStruct Clone( )
   {
      MyStruct clone = new MyStruct(Number);
      return clone;
   }
}
MyStruct myStruct = new MyStruct(3);
//This is thread-safe and encapsulated access
myStruct.Number = 4;
```

A problem specific to this use of safe structures is that all copies of the structure will share the lock. In the following example, locking struct1 will also lock struct2:

```
MyStruct struct1 = new MyStruct(3);
MyStruct struct2 = struct1
```

To get around that, you need to make a deep copy of the structure when assigning it. Since you cannot overload the assignment operator, you can clone the structure instead:

```
MyStruct struct1 = new MyStruct(3);
MyStruct struct2 = struct1.Clone( );
```

This is why MyStruct in Example 8-7 implements the interface ICloneable<T>.

The next problem is that you can instantiate a struct using its default constructor, without going through the parameterized one that allocates the lock:

```
MyStruct myStruct = new MyStruct( );
```

To compensate for that, the properties assert that the lock is valid:

```
Debug.Assert(m_Lock != null);
```

Given the difficulties in providing problem-free thread-safe structures, I believe that structures should be used predominantly in a single-threaded environment, and that you should consider the use of classes instead of structures when confronted with these problems.

Monitor and generics

You can use a Monitor to provide for thread-safe access to members of a generic type parameter:

```
public class MyClass<T>
{
   T m_T;
   public void SomeMethod( )
   {
      lock(m_T)
      {
         //Use m_T
      }
   }
}
```

However, in general you should not use a Monitor on generic type parameters. Monitors can be used only with reference types, and when you use generic types the compiler cannot tell in advance whether you will provide a reference or a value type parameter. It will let you use the Monitor, but if you provide a value type as the type parameter, the Monitor.Enter( ) call will have no effect at runtime. The only times when you can safely lock the generic type parameter are when you can constrain it to be a reference type:

```
public class MyClass<T> where T : class
{...}
```

or to derive from a base class:

```
public class SomeClass
{...}
public class MyClass<T> where T : SomeClass
{...}
```

Consequently, when using generics it is much better to lock the entire object instead:

```
public class MyClass<T>
{
    T m_T;
    public void SomeMethod( )
    {
        lock(this)
        {...}
    }
}
```

This also has the benefit of reducing the likelihood of a deadlock in the event that you need to lock additional members—locking the whole object grants safe access to all members in one atomic operation.

Synchronized methods

When you use Monitor, you can protect individual code sections of a method and thus have a fine level of control over when you lock the object for access. You need to lock the object only when you access its member variables. All other code that uses local stack-allocated variables is thread-safe by definition:

```
public class MyClass
{
    int m_Number = 0;
    public void DoSomething( )
    {
        //This loop doesn't need to lock the object
        for(int i=0;i<10;i++)
        {
            Trace.WriteLine(i);
        }
        //Lock the object because state is being accessed
        lock(this)
        {
            Trace.WriteLine("Number is " + m_Number);
        }
    }
}
```

As a result, you can interweave locked code with unlocked code as required. This is called *fragmented locking*. However, fragmented locking is a serious liability, because it results in error-prone code. During code maintenance, someone might add access to a member variable (either directly or by using a method) in a non-synchronized code section, which can result in object state corruption. Consequently, you should avoid fragmented locking and opt instead for locking the object for the duration of the method:

```
public class MyClass
{
    int m_Number = 0;
    public void DoSomething()
    {
        lock(this)
        {
            for(int i=0;i<10;i++)
            {
                Trace.WriteLine(i);
            }
            Trace.WriteLine("Number is " + m_Number);
        }
    }
}
```

Because this programming model is so common, .NET has built-in compiler support for it, called *synchronized methods*. The MethodImpl method attribute, defined in the System.Runtime.CompilerServices namespace, accepts an enum of type MethodImplOptions. One of the enum values is MethodImplOptions.Synchronized. When the MethodImpl method attribute is applied on a method with that enum value, the compiler instructs the .NET runtime to lock the object on method entry and unlock it on exit. This is semantically equivalent to encasing the method code with a lock statement. For example, consider this method definition:

```
using System.Runtime.CompilerServices;

public class MyClass
{
    [MethodImpl(MethodImplOptions.Synchronized)]
    public void DoSomething()
    {
        /* Method code */
    }
    //Class members
}
```

This method is semantically identical to the following:

```
public class MyClass
{
    public void DoSomething()
    {
        lock(this)
        {
            /* Method code */
        }
    }
    //Class members
}
```

You can use the MethodImpl method attribute on static methods as well, and even on properties:

```
using System.Runtime.CompilerServices;

public class MyClass
{
    int m_Number = 0;
    int Number
    {
        [MethodImpl(MethodImplOptions.Synchronized)]
        get
        {
            return m_Number;
        }
        [MethodImpl(MethodImplOptions.Synchronized)]
        set
        {
            m_Number = value;
        }
    }
}
```

 The difference between synchronized methods and synchronization domains is that synchronized methods can lead to deadlocks. Imagine two objects, each servicing a client on a different thread and each having a reference to the other. If they try to access each other, as in Figure 8-2, the result is a deadlock. Had the two objects been part of a synchronization domain, the first thread to access one of the objects would have locked the other object as well, thereby avoiding a deadlock.

Waiting and signaling with Monitor

In some cases, after acquiring the lock associated with an object, you may want to release the lock and wait until another thread has accessed the object. Once the other thread is done with the object it can then signal your thread, at which point you want to reacquire the lock and continue executing.

To allow for this, the Monitor class provides the Wait( ) method:

```
public static bool Wait(object obj);
```

Wait( ) releases the lock and waits for another thread to call Monitor. You can call Wait( ) on an object only after you have locked it by calling Monitor.Enter( ) on it and only within that synchronized code section:

```
public void LockAndWait(object obj)
{
    lock(obj)
    {
        //Do some work, then wait for another thread to do its work
        Monitor.Wait(obj);
        /* This code is executed only after the
```

```
            signaling thread releases the lock */
        }
    }
```

While your thread is in the call to Wait( ), other threads can call Enter( ) on the object and then call Wait( ), so you can end up with multiple threads all waiting for a signal. All these pending threads are placed in a dedicated queue associated with the lock, called the *wait queue*. To unlock a waiting thread, a different thread must acquire the lock and then use the Pulse( ) or PulseAll( ) Monitor methods:

```
    public static void Pulse(object obj);
    public static void PulseAll(object obj);
```

You can call Pulse( ) on an object only if you own its monitor:

```
    public void LockAndPulse(object obj)
    {
        lock(obj)
        {
            //Do some work, then pulse one other thread to continue its work
            Monitor.Pulse(obj);
            /* This code is still the owner of the lock */
        }
    }
```

Pulse( ) removes the first thread from the wait queue and adds it to the end of the lock queue (the same queue that handles multiple concurrent calls to Enter( )). Only when the pulsing thread calls Exit( ) does the next thread from the lock queue get to run, and it may not necessarily be the thread that was pulsed out of the wait queue. If you want to pulse all the waiting threads out of the wait queue, you can use the PulseAll( ) method. When PulseAll( ) is called all waiting threads are moved to the lock queue, where they continue to execute in order.

The Wait( ) method blocks the calling thread indefinitely. However, there are four overloaded versions of the Wait( ) method that accept a timeout and return a Boolean value:

```
    public static bool Wait(object obj,int millisecondsTimeout);
    public static bool Wait(object obj,int millisecondsTimeout, bool exitContext);
    public static bool Wait(object obj,TimeSpan timeout);
    public static bool Wait(object obj,TimeSpan timeout, bool exitContext);
```

The Boolean value lets you know whether Wait( ) has returned because the specified timeout has expired (false) or because the lock has been reacquired (true). Note that the Wait( ) version that doesn't accept a timeout also returns a Boolean value, but that value will always be true (that version should have had a void return value).

The interesting parameter of the overloaded Wait( ) method is bool exitContext. If Wait( ) is called from inside a synchronization domain, and if you pass in true for exitContext, .NET exits the synchronization domain before blocking and waiting. This allows other threads to enter the synchronization domain. Once the Monitor object is signaled, the thread has to enter the domain and own the Monitor lock in order to run. The default behavior in the Wait( ) versions that don't use this parameter isn't to exit the synchronization domain.

Note that you can still block indefinitely using one of the overloaded methods that accepts a TimeSpan parameter, by passing the Infinite static constant of the Timeout class:

```
Monitor.Wait(obj,Timeout.Infinite);
```

 As explained earlier in this chapter, calling Thread.Interrupt( ) will unblock a thread from a Monitor call to Enter( ), TryEnter( ), or Wait( ) and throw an exception of type ThreadInterruptedException in the unblocked thread (see the section "Interrupting a waiting thread").

Waitable Handles

In Windows, you can synchronize access to data and objects using a *waitable handle* to a system-provided lock. You pass the handle to a set of Win32 API calls to block your thread or signal to other threads waiting on the handle. The class WaitHandle provides a managed-code representation of a native Win32 waitable handle. The WaitHandle class is defined as:

```
public abstract class WaitHandle : MarshalByRefObject,IDisposable
{
    public WaitHandle( );
    public static const int WaitTimeout;
    public SafeWaitHandle SafeWaitHandle{get; set;}
    public virtual void Close( );

    public static bool WaitAll(WaitHandle[] waitHandles);
    public static bool WaitAll(WaitHandle[] waitHandles,
                            int millisecondsTimeout, bool exitContext);
    public static bool WaitAll(WaitHandle[] waitHandles,
                            TimeSpan timeout, bool exitContext);

    public static int WaitAny(WaitHandle[] waitHandles);
    public static int WaitAny(WaitHandle[] waitHandles,
                            int millisecondsTimeout, bool exitContext);
    public static int WaitAny(WaitHandle[] waitHandles,
                            TimeSpan timeout, bool exitContext);

    public virtual bool WaitOne( );
    public virtual bool WaitOne(int millisecondsTimeout, bool exitContext);
    public virtual bool WaitOne(TimeSpan timeout, bool exitContext);

    public static bool SignalAndWait(WaitHandle toSignal, WaitHandle toWaitOn);
    public static bool SignalAndWait(WaitHandle toSignal, WaitHandle toWaitOn,
                                int millisecondsTimeout, bool exitContext);
    public static bool SignalAndWait(WaitHandle toSignal, WaitHandle toWaitOn,
                                TimeSpan timeout, bool exitContext);
}
```

WaitHandle either signals an event between one or more threads or protects a resource from concurrent access. WaitHandle is an abstract class, so you can't instantiate WaitHandle objects. Instead, you create a specific subclass of WaitHandle, such as a Mutex. This design provides a common base class for the different locks, so you can wait on a lock or a set of locks in a polymorphic manner, without caring about the actual types.

A WaitHandle object has two states: *signaled* and *non-signaled*. In the non-signaled state, any thread that tries to wait on the handle is blocked until the state of the handle changes to signaled. The waiting methods are defined in the WaitHandle base class, while the signaling operation is defined in the subclasses.

Finally, note that WaitHandle is derived from the class MarshalByRefObject. As you will see in Chapter 10, this allows you to pass WaitHandle objects as method parameters between app domains or even machines.

WaitHandle is used frequently in the .NET Framework, and some .NET types provide a WaitHandle object for you to wait on. For example, recall the IAsyncResult interface described in Chapter 7. IAsyncResult provides the AsyncWaitHandle property of type WaitHandle, which waits for one or more asynchronous method calls in progress.

Using WaitHandle

WaitHandle provides two types of pure waiting methods—single-handle wait and multiple-handles wait—and one combination of signaling and waiting. The single-handle wait allows you to wait on a single handle using one of the overloaded WaitOne( ) methods. You have to instantiate a particular subclass of WaitHandle and then call WaitOne( ) on it. The thread calling WaitOne( ) is blocked until some other thread uses a specific method on the subclass to signal it. You'll see some examples of this later. The parameter-less WaitOne( ) method blocks indefinitely, but you can use two of the overloaded versions to specify a timeout. If you do specify a timeout, and the timeout expires without the handle being signaled, WaitOne( ) returns false. You also can specify whether or not to exit a synchronization domain, as with the overloaded versions of the Wait( ) method of the Monitor class.

The WaitAll( ) and WaitAny( ) methods allow you to wait on a collection of WaitHandle objects. Both are static methods, so you need to separately create an array of waitable handle objects and then wait for all or any one of them to be signaled (using WaitAll( ) or WaitAny( ), respectively). Like WaitOne( ), the WaitAll( ) and WaitAny( ) methods by default wait indefinitely, unless you specify a timeout. Again, you can also specify whether or not you want to exit the synchronization domain. The WaitAll( ) version that accepts a timeout returns true if the handles were signaled before the timeout expired and false if the timeout expired without the handles being signaled. WaitAny( ) returns an integer index referencing the handle that was signaled. If the timeout expires before any of the handles WaitAny( ) is waiting for are signaled, WaitAny( ) returns WaitHandle.WaitTimeout.

WaitHandle also offers *signal-and-wait* methods, such as this one:

```
public static bool SignalAndWait(WaitHandle toSignal,WaitHandle toWaitOn);
```

These methods address the need of signaling one handle while waiting on another, and doing so in one atomic operation. Without these methods there would be no sure way of performing these two tasks at one point in time, because between the two calls there could be a context switch. SignalAndWait( ) is instrumental in programming two threads to rendezvous at a particular point in time, as demonstrated later.

Once you're done with the handle, you should call Close( ) on it to close the underlying Windows handle. If you fail to do so, the handle will be closed during garbage collection.

WaitHandle has one interesting property, called SafeWaitHandle, defined as:

```
public SafeWaitHandle SafeWaitHandle{get; set;}
```

You can use SafeWaitHandle to retrieve the underlying Windows handle associated with the lock object, find out if the handle is closed, and you can even force a handle value yourself. SafeWaitHandle is provided for advanced interoperability scenarios with legacy code, in which you need to use a specific handle value that's obtained by some propietary interoperation mechanism.

WaitHandle versus Monitor

There are two key differences between using a Monitor to wait for and signal an object and using a waitable handle. First, Monitor can be used only on a reference type, whereas a waitable handle can synchronize access to value types as well as reference types. The second difference is the ability WaitHandle provides to wait on multiple objects as one atomic operation. When you are trying to wait for multiple objects, it's important to dispatch the wait request to the operating system as one atomic operation. As mentioned earlier, if this is done on an individual lock basis there's a possibility of a deadlock occurring if a second thread tries to acquire the same set of locks, but in a different order.

 It's likely that the implementation of WaitOne( ) uses the Win32 API call WaitForSingleObject( ) and that the implementations of WaitAny( ) and WaitAll( ) use the Win32 API call WaitForMultipleObjects( ).

The Mutex

The Mutex is a WaitHandle-derived class that ensures mutual exclusion of threads from a resource or code section. The Mutex class is defined as:

```
public sealed class Mutex : WaitHandle
{
    public Mutex( );
    public Mutex(bool initiallyOwned);
```

```
        public Mutex(bool initiallyOwned, string name);
        public Mutex(bool initiallyOwned, string name,
                     out bool createdNew);
        public static Mutex OpenExisting(string name);

        public void ReleaseMutex( );

        //Security members
}
```

An instance of Mutex assigns one of two logical meanings to the handle state: *owned* or *unowned*. A mutex can be owned by exactly one thread at a time. To own a mutex, a thread must call one of the wait methods of its base class, WaitHandle. If the mutex instance is unowned, the thread gets ownership. If another thread owns the mutex, the thread is blocked until the mutex is released. Once the thread that owns the mutex is done with the resource, it calls the ReleaseMutex( ) method to set the mutex state to unowned, thus allowing other threads access to the resource associated with and protected by the mutex. Only the current owner of the mutex can call ReleaseMutex( ). If a different thread tries to release the mutex, .NET throws an exception of type ApplicationException (although the exception type SynchronizationLockException exception would probably have been a more consistent choice).

If more than one thread tries to acquire the mutex, the pending callers are placed in a queue and served one at a time, in order. If the thread that currently owns the mutex tries to acquire it by making additional waiting calls, it isn't blocked, but it should make a matching number of calls to ReleaseMutex( ). If the thread that owns the mutex terminates without releasing it, the mutex is considered *abandoned*, and .NET releases the mutex automatically. If another thread tries to wait for an abandoned mutex, .NET throws a MutexAbandoned exception.

To ensure that ReleaseMutex( ) is always called, place the call in a finally statement.

Using a mutex

The default constructor of the Mutex class creates the mutex in the unowned state. If the creating thread wants to own the mutex, the thread must wait for the mutex first. The three other parameterized, overloaded versions of the constructor accept the bool initiallyOwned flag, letting you explicitly set the initial state of the mutex. Setting initiallyOwned to true grants the creating thread ownership of the mutex.

Example 8-8 demonstrates using a mutex to provide a thread-safe string property. The mutex is created in the class constructor. The set and get accessors acquire the mutex before setting or reading the actual member variable and then release the mutex. Note the use of a temporary variable in the set, so you can release the mutex before returning. Also note the call to Close( ) in the Dispose( ) method.

Example 8-8. Using a mutex

```
public class MutexDemo : IDisposable
{
    Mutex m_Mutex;
    string m_MyString;

    public MutexDemo( )
    {
        m_Mutex = new Mutex( );
    }

    public string MyString
    {
        set
        {
            m_Mutex.WaitOne( );
            m_MyString = value;
            m_Mutex.ReleaseMutex( );
        }
        get
        {
            m_Mutex.WaitOne( );
            string temp = m_MyString;
            m_Mutex.ReleaseMutex( );
            return temp;
        }
    }
    public void Dispose( )
    {
        m_Mutex.Close( );
    }
}
```

 The Mutex is a secure resource—you can provide it with a list of authorized identities and control who has access to it. See the MSDN Library for more information.

Named mutexes

The Mutex parameterized constructors also allow you to specify a mutex name in the name parameter. The *mutex name* is any identifying string, such as "My Mutex". By default, a mutex has no name, and you can pass in a null value to create an explicitly nameless mutex. If you do provide a name, any thread on the machine, including threads in other app domains or processes, can try to access the named mutex. When you specify a name, the operating system will check whether somebody else has already created a mutex with that name, and if so will give the creating thread a local object representing the global mutex. A named mutex allows for cross-process and cross-app-domain communication. If you try to create a named mutex, you should pass false for initiallyOwned, because even if the mutex is already owned by another thread in a different process, .NET will not block your thread. The other option is to call the constructor version that accepts the out bool createdNew parameter, which will let you know whether you succeeded in owning the named mutex.

If you want to bind to an existing named mutex, instead of trying to create a new mutex with the same name (which may simply create a new mutex for you if no such global named mutex is available), you can use the OpenExisting() static method of the Mutex class:

```
public static Mutex OpenExisting(string name);
```

If any process on the machine has already created a mutex with the specified name, OpenExisting() returns a Mutex object referencing that named mutex. If there is no existing mutex with that name, OpenExisting() throws an exception of type WaitHandleCannotBeOpenedException.

A named mutex has a number of liabilities. First, it couples the applications using it, because they have to know the mutex name in advance. Second, in general it is a bad idea to have publicly exposed locks. If the mutex is supposed to protect some global resource, you should encapsulate the mutex in the resource. This decouples the client applications and is more robust, because you do not depend on the client applications being disciplined enough to try to acquire the mutex before accessing the resource. I consider named mutexes to be a thing of the past, a relic from Windows that you should use only when porting legacy code that took advantage of them to .NET. (This same reservation holds for named events and named semaphores, which are discussed later.)

There is, however, a surprisingly useful technique that relies on a named mutex, not necessarily to synchronize access to a system-wide resource, but rather as a crude but simple and easy-to-use cross-process communications mechanism that facilitates a singleton application. A *singleton application* is an application that has only a single instance of it running at any moment in time (similar to Microsoft Outlook), regardless of how many times the user tries to launch the application. Singleton applications are often rich-client Windows Forms applications, although you could have a middle-tier singleton (as discussed in Chapter 10). Example 8-9 shows the SingletonApp static class, which is used exactly as a normal, multi-instance Windows Forms Application class, except it makes sure the application is a singleton:

```
static class Program
{
    static void Main()
    {
        SingletonApp.Run(new MyForm());
    }
}
```

SingletonApp is defined in the class library *WinFormsEx.dll* and is available in the source code accompanying this book.

Example 8-9. The SingletonApp class

```
public static class SingletonApp
{
   static Mutex m_Mutex;

   public static void Run(Form mainForm)
   {
      bool first = IsFirstInstance();
      if(first)
      {
         Application.ApplicationExit += OnExit;
         Application.Run(mainForm);
      }
   }
   static bool IsFirstInstance()
   {
      Assembly assembly = Assembly.GetEntryAssembly();
      string name = assembly.FullName;

      m_Mutex = new Mutex(false,name);
      bool owned = false;
      owned = m_Mutex.WaitOne(TimeSpan.Zero,false);
      return owned ;
   }
   static void OnExit(object sender,EventArgs args)
   {
      m_Mutex.ReleaseMutex();
      m_Mutex.Close();
   }
   //Other overloaded versions of Run()
}
```

If no other instance of the application is running, the form MyForm is displayed. If there is another instance running, the application exits. The SingletonApp class provides the same Run( ) methods as the Application class.

Implementing a singleton application requires some sort of cross-process communications mechanism, because if the user launches a new instance of the application it will be in a new process, yet it must detect if another process hosting the same application is already running. To this end, the SingletonApp class uses the helper method IsFirstInstance( ):

```
static bool IsFirstInstance()
{
   Assembly assembly = Assembly.GetEntryAssembly();
   string name = assembly.FullName;

   m_Mutex = new Mutex(false,name);
   bool owned = false;
   owned = m_Mutex.WaitOne(TimeSpan.Zero,false);
   return owned ;
}
```

IsFirstInstance( ) creates a named mutex, and then proceeds to wait on it for a timeout of zero. The mutex must have a unique name, to avoid collisions with other named mutexes that might exist in the system. However, if SingletonApp were to use a hardcoded unique name (such as a GUID), two different applications that used SingletonApp on the same machine at the same time would collide with each other. The solution is to use the name of the EXE application assembly that loaded the class library containing SingletonApp. The entry assembly name should be unique enough, and if the entry assembly is signed, it will also contain a token of the public key to guarantee uniqueness.

If this is the only instance of the application running, the mutex is unowned, and the wait operation returns immediately, indicating ownership. If another instance is running, the wait operation returns false. Internally, SingletonApp uses a normal Application class. If it is the only instance running, it will delegate to that class the actual implementation of Run( ). Otherwise, it will simply ignore the request to run a new form. When the singleton application shuts down, it must release the mutex to allow a new instance to run. Fortunately, the Application class provides the ApplicationExit event, which signals that the application is shutting down. SingletonApp subscribes to it, and in its handling of the application exit event it releases the named mutex and closes it.

Waitable Events

The class EventWaitHandle derives from WaitHandle and is used to signal an event across threads. The EventWaitHandle class is defined as:

```
public class EventWaitHandle : WaitHandle
{
   public EventWaitHandle(bool initialState,EventResetMode mode);
   public EventWaitHandle(bool initialState,EventResetMode mode,string name);
   public EventWaitHandle(bool initialState,EventResetMode mode,string name,
                       ref bool createdNew);
   public static EventWaitHandle OpenExisting(string name);
   public bool Reset( );
   public bool Set( );
   //Security members
}
```

An EventWaitHandle object can be in two states: *signaled* and *non-signaled*. The Set( ) and Reset( ) methods set the state of the handle to signaled or non-signaled, respectively. The term *waitable event* is used because if the state of the handle is non-signaled, any thread that calls one of the wait methods of the base class WaitHandle is blocked until the handle becomes signaled. The constructors of EventWaitHandle all accept the initialState flag. Constructing an event with initialState set to true creates the event in a signaled state, while false constructs it in a non-signaled state.

A waitable event can be named or unnamed, similar to a mutex. A named event can be shared across processes and can be used in some legacy porting or cross-process communication scenarios. To construct a named event, you need to use one of the EventWaitHandle constructors that take the string name parameter. The name construction parameter functions in an identical manner to the corresponding parameter for specifying a mutex name. EventWaitHandle also offers the OpenExisting( ) method, which provides the same functionality discussed previously (see "Named mutexes").

EventWaitHandle comes in two flavors: *manual-reset* and *auto-reset*. You control which type you require by providing its constructor with an enum of type EventResetMode, defined as:

```
public enum EventResetMode
{
    AutoReset,
    ManualReset
}
```

To automate the selection, .NET provides two strongly typed subclasses of EventWaitHandle, whose entire definitions and implementations are as follows:

```
public class ManualResetEvent : EventWaitHandle
{
    public ManualResetEvent(bool initialState) :
                         base(initialState,EventResetMode.ManualReset)
    {}
}
public class AutoResetEvent : EventWaitHandle
{
    public AutoResetEvent(bool initialState) :
                         base(initialState,EventResetMode.AutoReset)
    {}
}
```

As you can see, all the ManualResetEvent and AutoResetEvent classes do is provide EventWaitHandle with the matching value of EventResetMode. The main difference between working with the strongly typed subclasses or with EventWaitHandle directly is that the subclasses do not offer a named version.

Manual-reset events

Using ManualResetEvent (or EventWaitHandle directly) is straightforward. First, you construct a new event object that multiple threads can access. When one thread needs to block until some event takes place, it calls one of ManualResetEvent's base class's (i.e., WaitHandle's) waiting methods. When another thread wants to signal the event, it calls the Set( ) method. Once the state of the ManualResetEvent object is signaled, it stays signaled until some thread explicitly calls the Reset( ) method. This is why it's called a manual-reset event. Note that while the event state is set to signaled, all waiting threads are unblocked. Example 8-10 demonstrates using a ManualResetEvent object.

Example 8-10. Using ManualResetEvent

```
public class EventDemo : IDisposable
{
    ManualResetEvent m_Event;

    public EventDemo( )
    {
        m_Event = new ManualResetEvent(false);//Created unsignaled

        Thread thread = new Thread(DoWork);
        thread.Start( );
    }
    void DoWork( )
    {
        int counter = 0;
        while(true)
        {
            m_Event.WaitOne( );
            counter++;
            Trace.WriteLine("Iteration # "+ counter);
        }
    }
    public void GoThread( )
    {
        m_Event.Set( );
        Trace.WriteLine("Go Thread!");
    }
    public void StopThread( )
    {
        m_Event.Reset( );
        Trace.WriteLine("Stop Thread!");
    }
    public void Dispose( )
    {
        m_Event.Close( );
    }
}
```

In this example, the class EventDemo creates a new thread whose thread method DoWork( ) traces a counter value in a loop to the Output window. However, DoWork( ) doesn't start tracing right away—before every loop iteration, it waits for the m_Event member of type ManualResetEvent to be signaled. Signaling is done by calling the GoThread( ) method, which simply calls the Set( ) method of the event. Once the event is signaled, DoWork( ) keeps tracing the counter until the StopThread( ) method is called. StopThread( ) blocks the thread by calling the Reset( ) method of the event. You can start and stop the thread execution as many times as you like using the event. A possible output of Example 8-10 might be:

```
Go Thread!
Iteration # 1
Iteration # 2
Iteration # 3
```

```
Stop Thread!
Go Thread!
Iteration # 4
Iteration # 5
Stop Thread!
```

Note that the class `EventDemo` closes the event object in its `Dispose()` method.
`Dispose()` should also signal the thread to terminate, as demonstrated later.

Auto-reset events

An auto-reset event is identical to a manual-reset event, with one important difference: once the state of the event is set to signaled, it remains so until a single thread
is released from its waiting call, at which point the state reverts automatically to non-
signaled. If multiple threads are waiting for the event, they are placed in a queue and
are taken out of that queue in order. If no threads are waiting when `Set()` is called,
the state of the event remains signaled.

Note that if multiple threads are waiting for the handle to become signaled, there is
no way to release just one of them using a manual-reset event. The reason for this is
that there could be a context switch between the call to `Set()` and `Reset()`, and multiple threads could be unblocked. The auto-reset event combines the `Set()` and
`Reset()` calls into a single atomic operation.

If the event in Example 8-10 were an auto-reset event instead of a manual-reset
event, a possible output might be:

```
Go Thread!
Iteration # 1
Go Thread!
Iteration # 2
Go Thread!
Iteration # 3
Go Thread!
Iteration # 4
```

The worker thread traces a single iteration at a time and blocks between iterations
until the next call to `GoThread()`. There would be no need to call `StopThread()`.

Waitable events versus monitors

Both `EventWaitHandle` and the `Monitor` class allow one thread to wait for an event and
another thread to signal (or pulse) the event. The main difference between the two
mechanisms is that after a monitor is pulsed, it has no recollection of the action.
Even if no thread is waiting for the monitor when it's pulsed, the next thread to wait
for the monitor will be blocked. Events, on the other hand, have "memory"; their
state remains signaled. A manual-reset event remains signaled until it is reset explicitly, and an auto-reset event remains signaled until a thread waits on it or until it is
reset explicitly.

Thread rendezvous example

The *rendezvous problem* is a classic problem of multithreaded applications: how can you safely have two threads execute some code, then have the threads wait for one another at some virtual meeting point, and then continue their execution simultaneously after the conjunction?

Example 8-11 lists the Rendezvous helper class.

Example 8-11. The Rendezvous helper class

```
public class Rendezvous
{
    AutoResetEvent m_First = new AutoResetEvent(true);
    AutoResetEvent m_Event1 = new AutoResetEvent(false);
    AutoResetEvent m_Event2 = new AutoResetEvent(false);

    public void Wait()
    {
        bool first = m_First.WaitOne(TimeSpan.Zero,false);
        if(first)
        {
            WaitHandle.SignalAndWait(m_Event1,m_Event2);
        }
        else
        {
            WaitHandle.SignalAndWait(m_Event2,m_Event1);
        }
    }
    public void Reset()
    {
        m_First.Set();
    }
}
```

Example 8-12 demonstrates using the Rendezvous class.

Example 8-12. Using the Rendezvous class

```
public class RendezvousDemo
{
    Rendezvous m_Rendezvous = new Rendezvous();

    public void ThreadMethod1()
    {
        //Do some work, then
        m_Rendezvous.Wait();
        //Continue executing
    }
    public void ThreadMethod2()
    {
        //Do some work, then
        m_Rendezvous.Wait();
        //Continue executing
```

Example 8-12. Using the Rendezvous class (continued)

```
    }
}
RendezvousDemo demo = new RendezvousDemo( );
Thread thread1 = new Thread(demo.ThreadMethod1);
thread1.Start( );

Thread thread2 = new Thread(demo.ThreadMethod2);
thread2.Start( );
```

The RendezvousDemo class in Example 8-12 has two methods, used as the thread methods for two different threads. When the two threads execute their respective thread methods, they do so concurrently. At some point, each thread calls the Wait( ) method of the Rendezvous class. Whichever thread calls Wait( ) first is blocked until the second thread calls Wait( ). Once the second thread calls Wait( ), both threads automatically resume execution.

Implementing Rendezvous relies on the SignalAndWait( ) method of the WaitHandle class. Internally, Rendezvous defines two auto-reset events: m_Event1 and m_Event2. When the Wait( ) method is called on one thread, it signals m_Event1 and waits for m_Event2 to become signaled. When the Wait( ) method is called on the other thread, it does the opposite: it signals m_Event2 and waits for m_Event1 to become signaled. Note that signaling and waiting is done as one atomic operation, thanks to SignalAndWait( ). This assures adherence with the rendezvous requirement that both threads wait for one another and then continue execution simultaneously. The only remaining question is how Rendezvous knows which thread is the first thread to call Wait( ). To address that issue Rendezvous has another auto-reset event, called m_First, which is initialized in the signaled state. The first thing Wait( ) does is verify the status of m_First, without blocking. It does this by waiting on it with a timeout of zero:

```
    bool first = m_First.WaitOne(TimeSpan.Zero,false);
```

The zero timeout assigns the returned value of WaitOne( ) the semantic of being the first to call it. Since m_First is an auto-reset event, you are guaranteed that only one thread can reach the conclusion that it is first—the WaitOne( ) call will atomically set its state to non-signaled, and the second thread to call it will get back false without blocking. Had m_First been a manual-reset event, Rendezvous would have been susceptible to a race condition of the first thread checking the status of m_First but being switched out before acting upon it, and having the second thread think that it is the first thread too. Once Wait( ) knows whether it is called on the first or second thread, it knows also the order in which to pass the events to SignalAndWait( ).

Rendezvous also offers the Reset( ) method—you must call Reset( ) before the two threads try to rendezvous again, in order to reset the value of m_First.

The Semaphore

Semaphore is another WaitHandle-derived class, introduced by .NET 2.0. The defini-tion of the Semaphore class is:

```
public sealed class Semaphore : WaitHandle
{
    public Semaphore(int initialCount, int maximumCount);
    public Semaphore(int initialCount, int maximumCount,string name);
    public Semaphore(int initialCount, int maximumCount,string name,
                                                        ref bool createdNew);
    public static Semaphore OpenExisting(string name);
    public int Release();
    public int Release(int releaseCount);
    //Security members
}
```

The Semaphore class assigns a signaled or non-signaled semantic to the state of the WaitHandle base class. You could use a semaphore to synchronize access to a resource, similar to using a mutex, but semaphores are actually designed for cases where you need to control the execution of threads in some countable manner—that is, where instead of signaling a thread to just execute or stop, you want it to perform a number of operations, such as retrieving the next three messages from a message queue. Internally, the semaphore maintains a counter. As long as the counter's value is a positive number, the handle is considered signaled, and therefore any thread that calls one of the wait methods of the Semaphore base class will not be blocked. When the counter is zero, the handle is considered non-signaled, and all threads will be blocked until the counter is incremented.

The Semaphore class's constructors all take two values. The initialCount argument indicates which value to initialize the counter to, and the maximumCount argument indicates the highest allowed value for the internal counter. initialCount can be zero or greater, and maximumCount must be one or greater. Of course, initialCount must be less than or equal to maximumCount, or an ArgumentException is raised. If the counter's value is a positive number and a thread calls one of the waiting methods, the thread is not blocked and the counter is decremented by one. When the counter reaches zero, all waiting threads are blocked. You can increment the value of the counter by one by calling the Release() method. You can also increment the counter by any value by calling the version of Release() that accepts an integer. If calling one of the Release() methods causes the counter's value to exceed the maximum counter value set during construction, Release() throws an exception of type SemaphoreFullException.

Like Mutex and EventWaitHandle, Semaphore offers constructor versions that accept a string name parameter, and these constructors function in a similar manner to those of Mutex and EventWaitHandle. Semaphore also supports the OpenExisting() static method, which offers the same functionality discussed previously (under "Named mutexes").

A semaphore with a maximum counter value of one is equivalent to a mutex. Mutexes are sometimes referred to as *binary semaphores*.

Example 8-13 demonstrates using a semaphore.

Example 8-13. Using a semaphore

```csharp
public class SemaphoreDemo : IDisposable
{
    Semaphore m_Semaphore;

    public SemaphoreDemo( )
    {
        //Create semaphore with initial counter of 0, max value of 5
        m_Semaphore = new Semaphore(0,5);
        Thread thread = new Thread(Run);
        thread.Start( );
    }
    void Run( )
    {
        int counter = 0;
        while(true)
        {
            m_Semaphore.WaitOne( );
            counter++;
            Trace.WriteLine("Iteration # " + counter);
        }
    }
    public void DoIterations(int iterations)
    {
        m_Semaphore.Release(iterations);
    }
    public void Dispose( )
    {
        m_Semaphore.Close( );
    }
}
```

The class SemaphoreDemo contains the m_Semaphore member variable. In this example, m_Semaphore is initialized with a value of zero and has a maximum allowed value of five. SemaphoreDemo launches a thread with the Run( ) method for a thread method. As long as the internal counter value of m_Semaphore is a positive number, Run( ) will trace to the Output window the number of iterations it performs. The DoIterations( ) method increments m_Semaphore by the specified number of iterations, which will enable Run( ) to trace just as many iterations. As a result, the following client-side code:

```csharp
SemaphoreDemo demo = new SemaphoreDemo( );
demo.DoIterations(3);
```

will result in this output:

```
Iteration # 1
Iteration # 2
Iteration # 3
```

The Interlocked

If all you want to do is increment or decrement a value, or exchange or compare values, there is a more efficient mechanism than using one or more mutexes: .NET provides the Interlocked class to address this need. Interlocked supports a set of static methods that access a variable in an atomic manner:

```
public static class Interlocked
{
    public static int Increment(ref int location);
    public static int Add(ref int location,int value);

    public static int Decrement(ref int location);

    public static int CompareExchange(ref int location,int value,int comparand);
    public static object CompareExchange(ref object location,object value,
                                                        object comparand);
    public static T CompareExchange<T>(ref T location1, T value, T comparand)
                                                            where T : class;
    public static object Exchange(ref object location, object value);
    public static int Exchange(ref int location, int value);
    public static T Exchange<T>(ref T location1, T value) where T : class;

    public static long Read(ref long location);
    //Additional methods for double, float, long, IntPtr
}
```

For example, here is how to use the Interlocked class for incrementing an integer as a thread-safe operation, returning the new value:

```
int i = 8;
int newValue = Interlocked.Increment(ref i);
Debug.Assert(i == 9);
Debug.Assert(newValue == 9);
```

Interlocked provides overloaded methods for more complex operations: Exchange( ) assigns a value from one variable to another, and CompareExchange( ) compares two variables and, if they are equal, assigns a new value to one of them. Like Increment( ) and Decrement( ), these two complex operations have overloaded methods for common primitive types, but also for generic type parameters and object variables. Interlocked is especially useful when both read and write operations are needed.

The Reader/Writer Lock

Consider a member variable or a property that is frequently read and written by multiple threads. Locking the whole object using a `Monitor` object is inefficient, because a macro lock will lock all member variables. Using a mutex dedicated to that member variable (as in Example 8-8) is also inefficient, because if no thread is writing a new value, multiple threads can concurrently read the current value. This common pattern is called *multiple readers/single writer*, because you can have many threads reading a value but only one thread writing to it at a time. While a write operation is in progress, no thread should be allowed to read. .NET provides a lock designed to address the multiple readers/single writer situation, called `ReaderWriterLock`. The `ReaderWriterLock` class is defined as:

```
public sealed class ReaderWriterLock
{
    public ReaderWriterLock();

    public bool IsReaderLockHeld{ get; }
    public bool IsWriterLockHeld{ get; }
    public int  WriterSeqNum{ get; }

    public void AcquireReaderLock(int millisecondsTimeout);
    public void AcquireReaderLock(TimeSpan timeout);
    public void AcquireWriterLock(int millisecondsTimeout);
    public void AcquireWriterLock(TimeSpan timeout);
    public bool AnyWritersSince(int seqNum);
    public void DowngradeFromWriterLock(ref LockCookie lockCookie);
    public LockCookie ReleaseLock();
    public void ReleaseReaderLock();
    public void ReleaseWriterLock();
    public void RestoreLock(ref LockCookie lockCookie);
    public LockCookie UpgradeToWriterLock(int millisecondsTimeout);
    public LockCookie UpgradeToWriterLock(TimeSpan timeout);
}
```

You use the `AcquireReaderLock()` method to acquire a lock for reading a value and `AcquireWriterLock()` to acquire a lock for writing a value. Once you are done reading or writing, you need to call `ReleaseReaderLock()` or `ReleaseWriterLock()`, respectively. The `ReaderWriterLock` keeps track of the threads owning it and applies the multiple readers/single writer semantics: if no thread calls `AcquireWriterLock()`, every thread that calls `AcquireReaderLock()` isn't blocked and is allowed to access the resource. If a thread calls `AcquireWriterLock()`, `ReaderWriterLock` blocks the caller until all the currently reading threads call `ReleaseReaderLock()`.`ReaderWriterLock` then blocks any further calls to `AcquireReaderLock()` and `AcquireWriterLock()`, and grants the writing thread access.

Pending writing threads are placed in a queue and are served in order, one by one. In effect, `ReaderWriterLock` serializes all writing threads, allowing access one at a time, but it allows concurrent reading accesses. As you can see, `ReaderWriterLock` is a throughput-oriented lock. `ReaderWriterLock` provides overloaded methods that accept a timeout for acquiring the lock, the `UpgradeToWriterLock()` method to upgrade a reader lock to a writer lock (e.g., for when, based on the information read, you may need to write something instead), and the `DowngradeFromWriterLock()` method to convert a write request in progress to a read request. `ReaderWriterLock` also automatically handles nested lock requests by readers and writers.

Example 8-14 demonstrates a typical case that uses `ReaderWriterLock` to provide multiple readers/single writer semantics to a property. The constructor creates a new instance of `ReaderWriterLock`. The get accessor calls `AcquireReaderLock()` before reading the member variable and `ReleaseReaderLock()` after reading it. The set accessor calls `AcquireWriterLock()` before assigning a new value to the member variable and `ReleaseWriterLock()` after updating the property with the new value.

Example 8-14. Using ReaderWriterLock

```
public class MyClass
{
   string m_MyString;
   ReaderWriterLock m_RWLock;
   public MyClass()
   {
      m_RWLock = new ReaderWriterLock();
   }

   public string MyString
   {
      set
      {
         m_RWLock.AcquireWriterLock(Timeout.Infinite);
         m_MyString = value;
         m_RWLock.ReleaseWriterLock();
      }
      get
      {
         m_RWLock.AcquireReaderLock(Timeout.Infinite);
         string temp = m_MyString;
         m_RWLock.ReleaseReaderLock();
         return temp;
      }
   }
}
```

 To ensure that the reader/writer lock will be released even if an exception is thrown, you must place the calls to `ReleaseReaderLock()` and `ReleaseWriterLock()` in a `finally` statement. Unfortunately, there is no built-in support via a lock-like statement.

The WorkerThread Wrapper Class

The source code accompanying this book contains the WorkerThread class, which is a high-level wrapper class around the basic .NET Thread class. WorkerThread is defined as:

```
public class WorkerThread : IDisposable
{
    public WorkerThread( );
    public WorkerThread(bool autoStart);
    public int ManagedThreadId{get;}
    public Thread Thread{get;}
    public WaitHandle Handle{get;}
    public void Start( );
    public void Dispose( );
    public void Kill( );
    public void Join( );
    public bool Join(int millisecondsTimeout);
    public bool Join(TimeSpan timeout);
    public string Name{get;set;}
    public bool IsAlive{get;}
    public void Dispose( );
}
```

WorkerThread provides easy thread-creation and other features, including a Kill( ) method for terminating threads (instead of using Abort( )). The potentially dangerous methods of the Thread class are not present in the interface of WorkerThread, but the good ones are maintained. WorkerThread also enforces the best practices of using .NET threads discussed so far. Example 8-15 shows the implementation of WorkerThread. Because the Thread class is sealed, I had to use containment rather than derivation when defining WorkerThread. WorkerThread has the m_ThreadObj member variable of type Thread, representing the underlying wrapped thread. You can access the underlying thread via the Thread property of WorkerThread, if you want to be able to do direct thread manipulation.

Example 8-15. The WorkerThread wrapper class

```
public class WorkerThread : IDisposable
{
    ManualResetEvent m_ThreadHandle;
    Thread m_ThreadObj;
    bool m_EndLoop;
    Mutex m_EndLoopMutex;

    public override int GetHashCode( )
    {
        return m_ThreadObj.GetHashCode( );
    }
    public override bool Equals(object obj)
    {
        return m_ThreadObj.Equals(obj);
    }
```

Example 8-15. The WorkerThread wrapper class (continued)

```
public int ManagedThreadId
{
   get
   {
      return m_ThreadObj.ManagedThreadId;
   }
}
public Thread Thread
{
   get
   {
      return m_ThreadObj;
   }
}
protected bool EndLoop
{
   set
   {
      m_EndLoopMutex.WaitOne( );
      m_EndLoop = value;
      m_EndLoopMutex.ReleaseMutex( );
   }
   get
   {
      bool result = false;
      m_EndLoopMutex.WaitOne( );
      result = m_EndLoop;
      m_EndLoopMutex.ReleaseMutex( );
      return result;
   }
}
public WorkerThread( )
{
   m_EndLoop = false;
   m_ThreadObj = null;
   m_EndLoopMutex = new Mutex( );
   m_ThreadHandle = new ManualResetEvent(false);
   m_ThreadObj = new Thread(Run);
   Name = "Worker Thread";
}
public WorkerThread(bool autoStart) : this( )
{
   if(autoStart)
   {
      Start( );
   }
}
public WaitHandle Handle
{
   get
   {
      return m_ThreadHandle;
```

Example 8-15. The WorkerThread wrapper class (continued)

```
      }
   }
   public void Start()
   {
      Debug.Assert(m_ThreadObj != null);
      Debug.Assert(m_ThreadObj.IsAlive == false);
      m_ThreadObj.Start();
   }
   public void Dispose()
   {
      Kill();
   }
   void Run()
   {
      try
      {
         int i = 0;
         while(EndLoop == false)
         {
            Trace.WriteLine("Thread is alive, Counter is " + i);
            i++;
         }
      }
      finally
      {
         m_ThreadHandle.Set();
      }
   }
   public void Kill()
   {
      //Kill() is called on client thread - must use cached Thread object
      Debug.Assert(m_ThreadObj != null);
      if(IsAlive == false)
      {
         return;
      }
      EndLoop = true;
      //Wait for thread to die
      Join();
      m_EndLoopMutex.Close();
      m_ThreadHandle.Close();
   }
   public void Join()
   {
      Join(Timeout.Infinite);
   }
   public bool Join(int millisecondsTimeout)
   {
      TimeSpan timeout = TimeSpan.FromMilliseconds(millisecondsTimeout);
      return Join(timeout);
   }
   public bool Join(TimeSpan timeout)
```

Example 8-15. The WorkerThread wrapper class (continued)

```
   {
      //Join( ) is called on client thread - must use cached Thread object
      Debug.Assert(m_ThreadObj != null);
      if(IsAlive == false)
      {
         return true;
      }
      Debug.Assert(Thread.CurrentThread.ManagedThreadId !=
                   m_ThreadObj.ManagedThreadId);
      return m_ThreadObj.Join(timeout);
   }
   public string Name
   {
      get
      {
         return m_ThreadObj.Name;
      }
      set
      {
         m_ThreadObj.Name = value;
      }
   }
   public bool IsAlive
   {
      get
      {
         Debug.Assert(m_ThreadObj != null);
         bool handleSignaled = m_ThreadHandle.WaitOne(0,true);
         while(handleSignaled == m_ThreadObj.IsAlive)
         {
            Thread.Sleep(0);
         }
         return m_ThreadObj.IsAlive;
      }
   }
}
```

Launching a New Worker Thread

WorkerThread provides for one-phase thread creation, because it can encapsulate the use of the ThreadStart delegate. Its constructor accepts a Boolean value called autoStart. If autoStart is true, the constructor will create a new thread and start it:

```
WorkerThread workerThread;
workerThread = new WorkerThread(true);//Auto-start the worker thread
```

If autoStart is false, or if you're using the default constructor, you need to call WorkerThread's Start( ) method, just like when using the raw Thread class:

```
WorkerThread workerThread = new WorkerThread( );
workerThread.Start( );
```

The thread method of WorkerThread is the private Run( ) method. In Example 8-15, all Run( ) is doing is tracing to the Output window the value of a counter. WorkerThread provides a default name for the underlying thread, but you should provide your own meaningful value for the thread name, using the Name property. Note that WorkerThread returns the ID of the underlying thread in its own implementation of ManagedThreadId.

Joining WorkerThread and the Thread Handle

WorkerThread provides a Join( ) method, which safely asserts that Join( ) is called on a different thread (i.e., not the underlying thread) to avoid a deadlock. Join( ) also verifies that the thread is alive before it is called on the wrapped thread. One of the shortcomings of the basic Thread class is that it does not provide a waitable handle of type WaitHandle for clients to wait for a thread to die. If all you need to wait for is for a single thread to terminate, Join( ) is adequate. However, there is no safe way to combine waiting for a thread to terminate with other waiting operations as a single atomic wait request, which creates the potential for a deadlock.

To address this problem WorkerThread exposes a property called Handle, of type WaitHandle, which is signaled when the thread terminates. To implement Handle, WorkerThread has a member variable of type ManualResetEvent, called m_ThreadHandle. The WorkerThread constructors instantiate m_ThreadHandle in a non-signaled state. When the Run( ) method returns, it signals the m_ThreadHandle handle. To ensure that the handle is signaled regardless of how the Run( ) method exits, the signaling is done in a finally statement. WorkerThread also provides the Boolean property IsAlive, which not only calls the underlying thread's IsAlive property but also verifies that m_ThreadHandle's state is consistent (meaning that if the underlying thread is alive the handle is not signaled, and vice versa). You can test whether a ManualResetEvent object is signaled by waiting on it with a timeout of zero and checking the value retuned by the Wait( ) method. There is, however, a potential race condition that IsAlive needs to cope with: if the Run( ) method has signaled the handle but has not yet returned, the underlying thread will still be in the alive state, even though the handle has been signaled. This is possible, of course, only for the briefest of moments. IsAlive therefore relinquishes control of the reminder of its CPU time quota using Thread.Sleep(0), allowing the underlying thread to be switched back in and terminated.

Terminating the Worker Thread

One of the most common synchronization challenges developers face is the task of killing worker threads, usually upon application shutdown. As mentioned previously, you should avoid calling Thread.Abort( ) to terminate your threads. Instead, in each iteration, the thread method should check a flag that signals it whether to do another iteration or to return from the method.

As shown in Example 8-15, the thread method Run( ) traces to the Output window the value of a counter in a loop:

```
int i = 0
while(EndLoop == false)
{
    Trace.WriteLine("Thread is alive, Counter is " + i);
    i++;
}
```

Before every loop iteration, Run( ) checks the Boolean property EndLoop. If EndLoop is set to false, Run( ) performs another iteration. The Kill( ) method provided by WorkerThread sets EndLoop to true, causing Run( ) to return and the thread to terminate. EndLoop actually gets and sets the value of the m_EndLoop member variable. Because Kill( ) is called on a client thread, you must provide thread-safe access to m_EndLoop. You can use any of the manual locks presented in this chapter: for example, you can lock the whole WorkerThread object using Monitor, or you can use ReaderWriterLock (although it's excessive for a property that will be written only once). I chose to use Mutex:

```
bool EndLoop
{
    set
    {
        m_EndLoopMutex.WaitOne( );
        m_EndLoop = value;
        m_EndLoopMutex.ReleaseMutex( );
    }
    get
    {
        bool result = false;
        m_EndLoopMutex.WaitOne( );
        result = m_EndLoop;
        m_EndLoopMutex.ReleaseMutex( );
        return result;
    }
}
```

Kill( ) should return only when the worker thread is dead. To that end, Kill( ) calls Join( ) on the worker thread, after verifying the thread is alive. However, because Kill( ) is called on the client thread, the WorkerThread object must store a Thread object referring to the worker thread as a member variable. Fortunately, there is already such a member—the m_ThreadObj member variable. You can only store the thread value in the thread method; you can't store it in the constructor, which executes on the creating client's thread. This is exactly what Run( ) does in this line:

```
m_ThreadObj = Thread.CurrentThread;
```

Note that calling Kill( ) multiple times is harmless. Also note that Kill( ) does the cleanup of closing the mutex and the thread handle. But what if the client never calls

Kill( )? To deal with that eventuality, the WorkerThread class implements IDisposable and a destructor, both of which call Kill( ):

```
public void ~WorkerThread( )
{
   Kill( );
}
public void Dispose( )
{
   Kill( );
}
```

It's important to understand that Kill( ) isn't the same as Dispose( ). Kill( ) handles execution flow, such as application shutdown or timely termination of threads, whereas Dispose( ) caters to memory and resource management and disposes of other resources the WorkerThread class might hold. Dispose( ) only calls Kill( ) as a contingency, in case the client developer forgets to do so.

Synchronizing Delegates

As stated in Chapter 6, in .NET when a delegate has no targets, its value is set to null. Consequently, you must always check that the delegate is not null before invoking it. Otherwise, .NET will raise a null reference exception:

```
public class MyPublisher
{
   public event EventHandler MyEvent;
   public void FireEvent( )
   {
      if(MyEvent != null)
         MyEvent(this,EventArgs.Empty);
   }
}
```

Unfortunately, such a check is insufficient in a multithreaded environment because of the potential for a race condition to develop with regard to accessing the delegate. Because .NET applications execute on top of a preemptive operating system, it is possible that a thread context switch may take place in between comparing the delegate to null and invoking it. If this occurs, the thread that was switched in can remove the invocation targets from the delegate, so that when your thread is switched back in it will access a null delegate and will crash. There are a number of solutions to this race condition. You can ensure that the internal invocation list always has at least one member by initializing it with a do-nothing anonymous method. Because no external party can have a reference to the anonymous method, no external party can remove the method, so the delegate will never be null:

```
public class MyPublisher
{
   public event EventHandler MyEvent = delegate{};
   public void FireEvent( )
```

```
    {
        MyEvent(this,EventArgs.Empty);
    }
}
```

However, I believe that initializing all delegates this way is impractical. Another option is to add event accessors and lock the object (or the delegate) in add and remove, as well as during invocation. The problem with this approach is that it may force you to maintain the lock for a long period of time, because the event publishing may be a lengthy operation. As long as you maintain the lock, nobody can add or remove subscriptions. Yet another solution is to copy the delegate to a temporary variable, and check and invoke that temporary variable instead of the original delegate:

```
public class MyPublisher
{
    public event EventHandler MyEvent;
    public void FireEvent()
    {
        EventHandler temp = MyEvent;
        if(temp != null)
            temp(this,EventArgs.Empty);
    }
}
```

Copying the delegate addresses the race condition, because delegates are immutable. Making any change to the state of the delegate (such as removing subscribers) creates a new delegate object on the heap and updates the reference to which the delegate points. By copying the delegate to a temporary variable, you keep a copy of the original state of the delegate, irrespective of any thread context switches. Unfortunately, however, the JIT compiler may optimize the code, eliminate the temporary variable, and use the original delegate directly. That puts you back where you started, susceptible to the race condition.

Instead of using a temporary variable, you could use a method that accepts the delegate as a parameter:

```
public class MyPublisher
{
    public event EventHandler MyEvent;
    public void FireEvent()
    {
        FireEvent(MyEvent);
    }
    void FireEvent(EventHandler handler)
    {
        if(handler != null)
            handler(this,EventArgs.Empty);
    }
}
```

Passing the delegate as a parameter copies the reference to the invocation list. However, the JIT compiler's optimizations may still subvert your attempt: the JIT compiler is within its rights to inline the use of the helper method and use the delegate directly, leaving you exposed to the race condition yet again. To prevent the JIT compiler from inlining the helper method, you can use the MethodImpl attribute with the MethodImplOptions.NoInlining flag to instruct the JIT compiler not to inline the method under any circumstance:

```
public class MyPublisher
{
    public event EventHandler MyEvent;
    public void FireEvent()
    {
        FireEvent(MyEvent);
    }
    [MethodImpl(MethodImplOptions.NoInlining)]
    void FireEvent(EventHandler handler)
    {
        if(handler != null)
            handler(this,EventArgs.Empty);
    }
}
```

Chapter 6 introduced the EventsHelper static utility class, used to defensively publish events, while Chapter 7 added defensive asynchronous event publishing to it. You can retrofit EventsHelper to address the race condition and deal with the JIT compiler's optimizations, as shown in Example 8-16.

Example 8-16. The thread-safe EventsHelper

```
public static class EventsHelper
{
    delegate void AsyncFire(Delegate del,object[] args);

    static void InvokeDelegate(Delegate del,object[] args)
    {
        del.DynamicInvoke(args);
    }
    [MethodImpl(MethodImplOptions.NoInlining)]
    public static void UnsafeFire(Delegate del,params object[] args)
    {
        if(del == null)
        {
            return;
        }
        Delegate[] delegates = del.GetInvocationList();
        foreach(Delegate sink in delegates)
        {
            try
            {
                InvokeDelegate(sink,args);
            }
            catch
```

Example 8-16. The thread-safe EventsHelper (continued)

```
      {}
   }
}
[MethodImpl(MethodImplOptions.NoInlining)]
public static void UnsafeFireAsync(Delegate del,params object[] args)
{
   if(del == null)
   {
      return;
   }
   Delegate[] delegates = del.GetInvocationList( );
   AsyncFire asyncFire = InvokeDelegate;
   AsyncCallback cleanUp = delegate(IAsyncResult asyncResult)
                           {
                              asyncResult.AsyncWaitHandle.Close();
                           };
   foreach(Delegate sink in delegates)
   {
      asyncFire.BeginInvoke(sink,args,cleanUp,null);
   }
}
//Rest is same as Example 7-15.
}
```

Note that when using `EventsHelper`, the race condition is hidden from the publishing component—as before, all the publisher has to do is use `EventsHelper` to publish the event in a defensive, thread-safe manner:

```
public class MyPublisher
{
   public event EventHandler MyEvent;
   public void FireEvent( )
   {
      EventsHelper.Fire(MyEvent,this,EventArgs.Empty);
   }
}
```

The Visual Basic 2005 `RaiseEvent` statement has been upgraded to include copying of the delegate to a temporary variable. However, due to the JIT optimization just described, this solution is insufficient. In Visual Basic 2005, it is imperative that you use `EventsHelper` instead.

Using .NET Multithreading Services

In addition to the basic multithreading features described at the beginning of this chapter, .NET offers a set of advanced services. Some of these features, such as thread local storage, timers, and the thread pool, are also available in a similar format to Windows developers. Some other features, such as thread-relative static variables, are .NET innovations or are specific aspects of .NET application frameworks. This section briefly describes these .NET multithreading services.

Thread-Relative Static Variables

By default, static variables are visible to all threads in an app domain. This is similar to classic C++ (or Windows), in which static variables are accessible to all threads in the same process. The problem with having all the threads in the app domain able to access the same static variables is the potential for corruption and the resulting need to synchronize access to those variables, which in turn increases the likelihood of deadlocks. Synchronizing access may be a necessary evil, if indeed the static variables need to be shared between multiple threads. However, for cases where such sharing isn't necessary, .NET supports *thread-relative* static variables: each thread in the app domain gets its own copy of the static variable. You use the ThreadStatic attribute to mark a static variable as thread-relative:

```
public class MyClass
{
    [ThreadStatic]
    static string m_MyString;
    public static string MyString
    {
        set{m_MyString = value;}
        get{return m_MyString;}
    }
}
```

You can apply the ThreadStatic attribute only to static member variables, not to static properties or static methods; however, you can still wrap the static member with a static property. Thread-relative static variables enforce thread safety and the need to protect the variables, because only a single thread can access them and because each thread gets its own copies of the static variables. Thread-relative static variables usually also imply thread affinity between objects and threads—the objects will expect to always run on the same thread, so they will have their own versions of the variables. When using thread-relative static variables, you should also be aware of the following pitfall: each thread must perform initialization of the thread-relative static variables, because the static constructor has no effect on thread-relative statics.

Thread-relative static variables are an interesting feature of the .NET runtime, but I find them to be of little practical use. You are more likely to want to share the static variables with other threads than to make them thread-relative, and because exposing a member variable directly is a bad idea in general, you are likely to use the static property to access the variable. As you saw in the previous section on manual synchronization, encapsulating the locking in the property is easy enough, and it seems to be worth the trouble to be able to share the variable between threads.

Thread Local Storage

Objects allocated off the global managed heap are all visible and accessible to all threads in the app domain. However, .NET also provides a thread-specific heap, called the *thread local storage* (TLS). The TLS is actually part of the thread's stack, and therefore only that thread can access it. You can use the TLS for anything you'd use the global heap for, but there is no need to synchronize access to objects allocated off the TLS because only one thread can access them. The downside to using the TLS is that components that wish to take advantage of it must have thread affinity, because they must execute on the same thread to access the same TLS.

Framework developers often use the TLS to store additional contextual information about the call as it winds its way between objects. The TLS provides *slots* in which you can store objects. The slot is an object of type `LocalDataStoreSlot`. A `LocalDataStoreSlot` object is nothing more than a type-safe key object, defined as:

```
public sealed class LocalDataStoreSlot
{}
```

You use the `LocalDataStoreSlot` object to identify the slot itself. There are two kinds of slots: *named* and *unnamed*. The garbage collector frees unnamed slots automatically, but you must free named slots explicitly. You allocate and use slots via static methods of the `Thread` class:

```
public sealed class Thread
{
    public static LocalDataStoreSlot AllocateDataSlot();
    public static LocalDataStoreSlot AllocateNamedDataSlot(string name);

    public static void FreeNamedDataSlot(string name);
    public static LocalDataStoreSlot GetNamedDataSlot(string name);

    public static void SetData(LocalDataStoreSlot slot, object data);
    public static object GetData(LocalDataStoreSlot slot);
}
```

Using a named slot

You can use the `AllocateNamedDataSlot()` method to allocate a named slot and get back a `LocalDataStoreSlot` object. You then use the `SetData()` method to store data in the slot:

```
int number = 8;
LocalDataStoreSlot dataSlot;
dataSlot = Thread.AllocateNamedDataSlot("My TLS Slot");

Thread.SetData(dataSlot,number);
```

Any object on the thread can use the `GetNamedDataSlot()` method to get back a `LocalDataStoreSlot` object and then call `GetData()` to retrieve the data stored:

```
object obj;

LocalDataStoreSlot dataSlot;
dataSlot = Thread.GetNamedDataSlot("My TLS Slot");
```

```
obj = Thread.GetData(dataSlot);
Thread.FreeNamedDataSlot("My TLS Slot");

int number = (int)obj;
Debug.Assert(number == 8);
```

Once you are done with the named slot, you must call `FreeNamedDataSlot( )` to deallocate it.

Using an unnamed slot

The method AllocateDataSlot( ) allocates a LocalDataStoreSlot object similar to the AllocateNamedDataSlot( ) method. The two main differences between named and unnamed slots are that all clients accessing the unnamed slot must share the LocalDataStoreSlot object (because there is no way to reference it by name) and that there is no need to free the unnamed slot object manually. Again, you use SetData( ) to store data in the slot and GetData( ) to retrieve the stored data:

```
//Storing:
int number = 8;
LocalDataStoreSlot dataSlot;
dataSlot = Thread.AllocateDataSlot( );
Thread.SetData(dataSlot,number);

//Retrieving:
object obj;
obj = Thread.GetData(dataSlot);
int number = (int)obj;
Debug.Assert(number == 8);
```

Physical Thread Affinity

When running under Windows, .NET threads are mapped one-to-one to operating-system threads. As a result, physical thread affinity is guaranteed. However, different hosting environments (such as SQL Server 2005) may choose a different, less direct mapping and occasionally assign different physical threads to your .NET managed thread. If your code is hosted in such an environment and you acquire an operating-system resource that inherently has physical thread affinity (such as any WaitHandle-derived class), your code will not function correctly if the host swaps physical threads underneath. In .NET 2.0, the Thread class provides the static methods BeginThreadAffinity( ) and EndThreadAffinity( ). Calling these methods enables you to signal to the hosting environment that you require physical thread affinity and that the host should not change the physical thread associated with your managed thread while executing the code inside the thread affinity–sensitive section.

The Thread Pool

Creating a worker thread and managing its lifecycle yourself gives you ultimate control over that thread. It also increases the overall complexity of your application. If all you need to do is dispatch a unit of work to a worker thread, instead of creating a thread, you can take advantage of a .NET-provided thread. In each process, .NET provides a pool of worker threads called the *thread pool*. The thread pool is managed by .NET, and it contains a set of threads ready to serve application requests. .NET makes extensive use of the thread pool itself. For example, it uses the thread pool for asynchronous calls (discussed in Chapter 7), remote calls (discussed in Chapter 10), and timers (discussed later in this chapter). You access the .NET thread pool via the public static methods of the ThreadPool static class. Using the thread pool is straightforward. First you create a delegate of type WaitCallback, targeting a method with a matching signature:

```
public delegate void WaitCallback(object state);
```

You then provide the delegate to one of the ThreadPool class's static methods (typically QueueUserWorkItem( )):

```
public static class ThreadPool
{
    public static bool QueueUserWorkItem(WaitCallback callBack);
    /* Other methods */
}
```

As the method name implies, dispatching a work unit to the thread pool is subject to pool limitations—that is, if there are no available threads in the pool, the work unit is queued and is served only when a worker thread returns to the pool. Pending requests are served in order.

Example 8-17 demonstrates using the thread pool. For diagnostic purposes, you can find out whether the thread your code runs on originated from the thread pool by using the IsThreadPoolThread property of the Thread class (as shown in this example).

Example 8-17. Posting a work unit to the thread pool

```
void ThreadPoolCallback(object state)
{
    Thread currentThread = Thread.CurrentThread;
    Debug.Assert(currentThread.IsThreadPoolThread);
    int threadID = currentThread.ManagedThreadId;
    Trace.WriteLine("Called on thread with ID :" + threadID);
}

ThreadPool.QueueUserWorkItem(ThreadPoolCallback);
```

A second overloaded version of QueueUserWorkItem( ) allows you to pass in a state object to the callback method, in the form of a generic object:

```
public static bool QueueUserWorkItem(WaitCallback callBack,object state);
```

If you don't provide such a parameter (as in Example 8-17), .NET passes in null. While you can use the state object to pass parameters to the callback method, another common use is to pass in an identifier. The identifier enables the same callback method to handle and distinguish between multiple posted requests.

The ThreadPool class also supports a number of other useful ways to queue a work unit. The RegisterWaitForSingleObject() method allows you to provide a waitable handle as a parameter. The thread from the thread pool waits for the handle and only calls the callback once the handle is signaled. You can also specify a waiting timeout. The GetAvailableThreads() method allows you to find out how many threads are available in the pool, and the GetMaxThreads() method returns the maximum size of the pool.

 The .NET thread pool isn't boundless. Avoid lengthy operations in the callback so that the thread returns to the pool as quickly as possible, to service other clients. If you require lengthy operations, create dedicated threads.

Configuring the thread pool

The thread pool actually has two types of threads in it: *worker threads* are used for tasks such as asynchronous execution or timers, and *completion port threads* are used in conjunction with server operations such as network-sockets processing. Most applications only interact (directly or indirectly) with the worker threads and do not care about the completion port threads.

The thread pool needs to maintain a balance between the overhead of a large number of active threads and the latency in responding to new client requests. If there are too many active threads servicing requests, the overhead of the thread context switches can have a serious detrimental effect. If, on the other hand, there are too few threads, client requests may have to spend too much time queuing up for service. Interestingly enough, many experiments and benchmarks have shown that regardless of the technology used, for an average application with an average load, the optimal pool size is one thread per application per CPU. As long as the work unit queued up is small enough, restricting the number of threads in the thread pool eliminates costly thread context switches. Recall from Chapter 7 that by default, the maximum number of worker threads in the pool is 25 per CPU per process. The reason for this limit is that there could potentially be multiple applications in the process using the thread pool. The default maximum number for completion port threads is 1,000.

The ThreadPool class provides methods for controlling the maximum numbers of threads in the thread pool:

```
public static class ThreadPool
{
    public static void GetMaxThreads(out int workerThreads,
                                     out int completionPortThreads);
```

```
    public static bool SetMaxThreads(int workerThreads,
                                      int completionPortThreads);
    /* Other methods */
}
```

You can only use `SetMaxThreads()` to provide a new maximum number of threads that is greater than the number of CPUs on the machine. Any other value will cause `SetMaxThreads()` to return `false` and ignore your request.

Typically, you'll want to set one maximum value without affecting the other. The `SetNewThreadPoolMax()` method below demonstrates a safe way of setting a new maximum value for the worker threads:

```
    public static void SetNewThreadPoolMax(int max)
    {
        Debug.Assert(max > Environment.ProcessorCount);

        int workerThreads,completionPortThreads;
        ThreadPool.GetMaxThreads(out workerThreads,
                                 out completionPortThreads);
        ThreadPool.SetMaxThreads(max,completionPortThreads);
    }
```

That said, I must again caution you against tinkering with the maximum number of threads in the thread pool, and especially increasing that number. Unless you have performed benchmarks and profiling that categorically prove that a specific number yields better throughput required for your application without any collateral damage, you are taking on the liability of either increasing the overhead of thread context switches and degrading performance or increasing request latency.

Another performance-related aspect of the thread pool is the question of how many threads the thread pool should keep when it is idle (that is, when there are no pending client requests). That idle-time count is called the thread pool *minimum size*. If the minimum size is too small, a spike in client requests will quickly exhaust the number of ready-to-run threads, and the thread pool will have to create new threads (up to the maximum number of threads) to deal with them. This will introduce latency and increase response time. If, on the other hand, the minimum number is too large, you will be paying needlessly for maintaining the threads.

By default, the thread pool maintains single worker and completion port threads and creates new threads as required. Excess threads are culled away periodically. You can control the minimum pool size using the `GetMinThreads()` and `SetMinThreads()` methods:

```
    public static class ThreadPool
    {
        public static void GetMinThreads(out int workerThreads,
                                         out int completionPortThreads);
        public static bool SetMinThreads(int workerThreads,int completionPortThreads);

        /* Other methods */
    }
```

Unlike the maximum pool size, there are no hard-and-fast rules as to the best minimum size. If the default values are inadequate, you will need to test your application under different load characteristics (uniform, erratic, spikes, etc.) to determine the optimal minimum values.

Custom Thread Pools

The .NET thread pool is a simple and efficient general-purpose thread pool. However, it does not support features such as canceling a queued request or separating the act of posting a request from executing it. If you require such functionality you will have to implement your own thread pool, in which case you may want to implement the interface IbackgroundTaskThreadMarshaller, found in the System.ComponentModel namespace:

```
public interface IBackgroundTaskThreadMarshaller : IDisposable
{
    object ActivateNewTask();
    void DeactivateTask(object id);
    void Post(Delegate d,object[] args);
}
```

IBackgroundTaskThreadMarshaller allows you to post a task to the custom thread pool in the form of a delegate and its arguments, and then explicitly instruct the custom thread pool manager to execute it via the ActivateNewTask() method. The custom thread pool manager will multiplex its threads on the activated requests. To cancel the task, simply call DeactivateTask(), using the ID returned from the activation call. Presently, no class in .NET implements IBackgroundTaskThreadMarshaller.

ISynchronizeInvoke

When a client on thread T1 calls a method on an object, that method is executed on the client's thread, T1. However, what should be done in cases where the object must always run on the same thread (say, T2)? Such situations are common when thread affinity is required. For example, .NET Windows Forms windows and controls must always process messages on the same thread that created them. To address such situations, .NET provides the ISynchronizeInvoke interface, in the System.ComponentModel namespace:

```
public interface ISynchronizeInvoke
{
    object Invoke(Delegate method,object[] args);
    IAsyncResult BeginInvoke(Delegate method,object[] args);
    object EndInvoke(IAsyncResult result);
    bool InvokeRequired {get;}
}
```

Using ISynchronizeInvoke

ISynchronizeInvoke provides a generic and standard mechanism for invoking methods on objects residing on other threads. For example, if the object implements ISynchronizeInvoke, the client on thread T1 can call ISynchronizeInvoke's Invoke( ) on the object. The implementation of Invoke( ) blocks the calling thread, marshals the call to T2, executes the call on T2, marshals any returned values to T1, and returns control to the calling client on T1. Invoke( ) accepts a delegate targeting the method to invoke on T2, and a generic array of objects as parameters.

Example 8-18 demonstrates the use of ISynchronizeInvoke. In the example, a Calculator class implements ISynchronizeInvoke and provides the Add( ) method for adding two numbers.

Example 8-18. Using ISynchronizeInvoke

```
public class Calculator : ISynchronizeInvoke
{
   public int Add(int argument1,int argument2)
   {
      int threadID = Thread.CurrentThread.ManagedThreadId;
      Trace.WriteLine("Calculator thread ID is " + threadID);
      return argument1 + argument2;
   }
   //ISynchronizeInvoke implementation
   public object Invoke(Delegate method,object[] args)
   {...}
   public IAsyncResult BeginInvoke(Delegate method,object[] args)
   {...}
   public object EndInvoke(IAsyncResult result)
   {...}
   public bool InvokeRequired
   {get{...}}
}
//Client-side code
public delegate int BinaryOperation(int argument1,int argument2);

int threadID = Thread.CurrentThread.ManagedThreadId;
Trace.WriteLine("Client thread ID is " + threadID);

Calculator  calculator = new Calculator( );

BinaryOperation addDelegate = calculator.Add;

object[] args = {3,4};
int sum = 0;
sum = (int)calculator.Invoke(addDelegate,args);
Debug.Assert(sum ==7);

/* Possible output:
Calculator thread ID is 29
Client thread ID is 30
*/
```

Because the call is marshaled to a different thread from that of the caller, you might want to invoke it asynchronously. This functionality is provided by the BeginInvoke( ) and EndInvoke( ) methods. These methods are used in accordance with the general asynchronous programming model described in Chapter 7. In addition, because ISynchronizeInvoke can be called on the same thread as the thread to which the caller is trying to redirect the call, the caller can check the InvokeRequired property. If it returns false, the caller can call the object methods directly.

 ISynchronizeInvoke methods aren't type-safe. In case of a mismatch, an exception is thrown at runtime instead of a compilation error. You cannot try to wrap it with a type-safe use of GenericEventHandler, because you cannot overload based on returned type. Pay extra attention when using ISynchronizeInvoke, because the compiler won't be there for you.

Windows Forms and ISynchronizeInvoke

Windows Forms base classes make extensive use of ISynchronizeInvoke. The Control class (and every class derived from Control) relies on the underlying Windows messages and a message-processing loop (the *message pump*) to process them. The message loop must have thread affinity, because messages to a window are delivered only to the thread that created that window. In general, you must use ISynchronizeInvoke to access a Windows Forms window from another thread. Unfortunately, that often results in a cumbersome programming model when accessing windows and controls from multiple threads. Consider the code in Example 8-19. If multiple threads need to update the text of the m_Label control, instead of merely setting the Text property, you are required to use a helper method (an anonymous method, in this example*) and a delegate dedicated to the task of setting the text of a label. Real-life examples will of course get much more complex and messy, with a high degree of internal coupling, because any changes to the user-interface layout, the controls on the forms, and the required behavior are likely to cause major changes to the code.

Example 8-19. Thread-safe access to a Windows Forms label

```
partial class MyForm : Form
{
   delegate void SetLabel(Label label,string str);

   Label m_Label = new Label( );

   //UpdateLabel is called by multiple threads
   void UpdateLabel(string text)
   {
```

---

* For more information on anonymous methods, see my May 2004 article in the *MSDN Magazine*, "Create Elegant Code with Anonymous Methods, Iterators, and Partial Classes."

Example 8-19. Thread-safe access to a Windows Forms label (continued)

```
    ISynchronizeInvoke synchronizer = m_Label;
    if(synchronizer.InvokeRequired == false)
    {
       m_Label.Text = text;
       return;
    }
    SetLabel del = delegate(Label label,string str)
                   {
                      label.Text = str;
                   };
    synchronizer.Invoke(del,new object[]{m_Label,text});
  }
  //Rest of the class
}
```

It is much better to encapsulate the interaction with ISynchronizeInvoke whenever possible, to simplify the overall programming model. Example 8-20 lists the code for SafeLabel, a Label-derived class that provides thread-safe access to its Text property.

Example 8-20. Encapsulating ISynchronizeInvoke

```
public class SafeLabel : Label
{
   delegate void SetString(string text);
   delegate string GetString();
   override public string Text
   {
      set
      {
         if(InvokeRequired)
         {
            SetString setTextDel = delegate(string text)
                                   {
                                      base.Text = text;
                                   };
            Invoke(setTextDel,new object[]{value});
         }
         else
            base.Text = value;
      }
      get
      {
         if(InvokeRequired)
         {
            GetString getTextDel = delegate()
                                   {
                                      return base.Text;
                                   };
            return (string)Invoke(getTextDel,null);
         }
         else
            return base.Text;
```

Example 8-20. Encapsulating ISynchronizeInvoke (continued)

```
    }
  }
}
```

SafeLabel overrides its base class's Text property and finds out if invoking is allowed on the calling threads. If it is not allowed, SafeLabel uses its base class's implementation of ISynchronizeInvoke to marshal the call to the correct thread. Using SafeLabel, the code in Example 8-19 is reduced to this:

```
partial class MyForm : Form
{
    Label m_Label = new SafeLabel();

    //UpdateLabel is called by multiple threads
    void UpdateLabel(string text)
    {
        m_Label.Text = text;
    }
    //Rest of the class
}
```

The source code accompanying this book contains in the assembly *WinFormsEX.dll* the code not only for SafeLabel but also for other commonly used controls, such as SafeButton, SafeListBox, and SafeTextBox.

Events and ISynchronizeInvoke

The fact that some subscribers may require you to invoke them on the correct thread poses an interesting challenge to event publishers. It is no longer good enough to simply invoke the delegate, because you might be calling some of the subscribers (especially in a Windows Forms application) on the wrong thread. You must manually iterate over the delegate's internal invocation list, and examine each delegate in that list. You can access the object the delegate points to via the Target property that every delegate inherits from the Delegate base class. Then you need to query the target for ISynchronizeInvoke and use it to invoke the target method. Instead of repeating this for every delegate invocation, you can extend EventsHelper to always publish the event to the correct thread, as shown in Example 8-21.

Example 8-21. Adding correct thread invocation to EventsHelper

```
public static class EventsHelper
{
    static void InvokeDelegate(Delegate del,object[] args)
    {
        ISynchronizeInvoke synchronizer;
        synchronizer = del.Target as ISynchronizeInvoke;
        if(synchronizer != null)//Requires thread affinity
        {
            if(synchronizer.InvokeRequired)
            {
                synchronizer.Invoke(del,args);
```

Example 8-21. Adding correct thread invocation to EventsHelper (continued)

```
            return;
         }
      }
      //Not requiring thread affinity or Invoke() is not required
      del.DynamicInvoke(args);
   }
   //Rest of EventsHelper is same as Example 8-16
}
```

In Example 8-21, instead of simply calling DynamicInvoke( ) on the delegate, as in Example 8-16, InvokeDelegate( ) first checks whether the target object supports ISynchronizeInvoke and whether Invoke( ) is required. Example 8-21 represents the final version of EventsHelper in this book.

Implementing ISynchronizeInvoke

In the abstract, when you implement ISynchronizeInvoke, you need to post the method delegate to the actual thread the object needs to run on, and you need to have it call DynamicInvoke( ) on the delegate in Invoke( ) and BeginInvoke( ). Implementing ISynchronizeInvoke is a nontrivial programming feat. The source files accompanying this book contain a helper class called Synchronizer, which is a generic implementation of ISynchronizeInvoke. You can use Synchronizer as-is, by either deriving from it or containing it as a member object and then delegating your implementation of ISynchronizeInvoke to it:

```
   public class Calculator : ISynchronizeInvoke
   {
      ISynchronizeInvoke m_Synchronizer = new Synchronizer();
      public int Add(int argument1,int argument2)
      {
         return argument1 + argument2;
      }
      public object Invoke(Delegate method, object[] args)
      {
         return m_Synchronizer.Invoke(method,args);
      }
      //Rest of the implementation of ISynchronizeInvoke via
      //delegation to m_Synchronizer
   }
```

Here are the key elements of implementing Synchronizer:

- Synchronizer uses a nested class called WorkerThread.

- WorkerThread has a queue of work items. WorkItem is a class containing the method delegate and the parameters.

- Both Invoke( ) and BeginInvoke( ) add to the work-item queue.

- WorkerThread creates a worker thread, which monitors the work-item queue. When the queue has items, the worker thread retrieves them and calls DynamicInvoke( ) on the method.

Windows Forms and Asynchronous Calls

Synchronizing multithreaded access to Windows Forms windows and controls is an issue with asynchronous calls as well. As explained in Chapter 7, using a completion callback method is the preferred option in an event-driven application such as a Windows Forms application. The problem is that both the asynchronous method and the completion callback execute on a thread from the thread pool, and therefore they cannot access the Windows Forms elements directly. This significantly complicates the programming model and precludes easy implementation of features that are important for a client application, such as progress reports and cancellation. To address this predicament, .NET 2.0 provides a component called BackgroundWorker that you can use in your Windows Forms applications to manage asynchronous operations safely and easily.

You can find BackgroundWorker in the Components tab of a Windows Forms project. If you drop it on a form, you can use BackgroundWorker to dispatch asynchronous work and to report progress and completion, all while encapsulating the interaction with ISynchronizeInvoke. Using this approach yields a much smoother and superior programming model. Example 8-22 shows the definition of BackgroundWorker and its supporting classes.

Example 8-22. Partial listing of BackgroundWorker

```
public class BackgroundWorker : Component
{
   public event DoWorkEventHandler DoWork;
   public event ProgressChangedEventHandler ProgressChanged;
   public event RunWorkerCompletedEventHandler RunWorkerCompleted;
   public bool CancellationPending{get;}
   public void RunWorkerAsync();
   public void RunWorkerAsync(object argument);
   public void ReportProgress(int percent);
   public void CancelAsync();
   //More members
}

public delegate void DoWorkEventHandler(object sender,DoWorkEventArgs e);
public delegate void ProgressChangedEventHandler(object sender,
                                         ProgressChangedEventArgs e);
public delegate void RunWorkerCompletedEventHandler(object sender,
                                         RunWorkerCompletedEventArgs e);
public class CancelEventArgs : EventArgs
{
   public bool Cancel{get;set;}
}
public class DoWorkEventArgs : CancelEventArgs
{
   public bool Result{get;set;}
   public object Argument{get;};
}
```

Example 8-22. Partial listing of BackgroundWorker (continued)

```
public class ProgressChangedEventArgs : EventArgs
{
   public int ProgressPercentage{get;}
}
public class AsyncCompletedEventArgs : EventArgs
{
   public object UserState{get;}
   public Exception Error{get;}
   public bool Cancelled{get;}
}
public class RunWorkerCompletedEventArgs : AsyncCompletedEventArgs
{
   public object Result{get;};
}
```

BackgroundWorker has a public delegate called DoWork, of type DoWorkEventHandler. To invoke a method asynchronously, wrap a method with a matching signature to DoWorkEventHandler and add it as a target to DoWork. Then call the RunWorkerAsync( ) method to invoke the method on a thread from the thread pool:

```
BackgroundWorker backgroundWorker;
backgroundWorker = new BackgroundWorker( );
backgroundWorker.DoWork += OnDoWork;
backgroundWorker.RunWorkerAsync( );

void OnDoWork(object sender,DoWorkEventArgs doWorkArgs)
{...}
```

Any party interested in being notified when the asynchronous method is completed should subscribe to the RunWorkerCompleted member delegate of BackgroundWorker. RunWorkerCompleted is a delegate of type RunWorkerCompletedEventHandler. The completion notification method accepts a parameter of type RunWorkerCompletedEventArgs, which contains the result of the method execution. You need to set the Result property of DoWorkEventArgs inside the asynchronous method, as well as any error and cancellation information.

BackgroundWorker cannot simply invoke the RunWorkerCompleted delegate when the asynchronous method execution is completed, because that invocation will be on the thread from the thread pool. Thus, any control or form that subscribed to RunWorkerCompleted cannot be called directly. Instead, BackgroundWorker checks whether each of the target objects in RunWorkerCompleted supports ISynchronizeInvoke, and if Invoke( ) is required. If so, it marshals the call to the owning thread of the target object.

To support progress reports, BackgroundWorker provides a member delegate called ProgressChanged, of type ProgressChangedEventHandler. Any party interested in progress notifications should subscribe to ProgressChanged. When the asynchronous method wishes to notify about a progress update, it calls BackgroundWorker's ReportProgress( ) method to correctly marshal the progress notification to any Windows Forms object.

To cancel a method, anybody from any thread can call BackgroundWorker's CancelAsync() method. Calling CancelAsync() results in the CancellationPending property of BackgroundWorker returning true. Inside the asynchronous method, you should periodically check the value of CancellationPending; if it is true, you should set the Cancel property of DoWorkEventArgs to true and return from the method. In the completion method, you can check the value of the Cancelled property of RunWorkerCompletedEventArgs to detect whether the method ran to its completion or was cancelled. You can also check the Error property for any exceptions that might have taken place.

 To ease the transition of applications from .NET 1.1 to .NET 2.0, the source code accompanying this book contains my implementation of BackgroundWorker, which you can use in your .NET 1.1–based solutions. The .NET 1.1 implementation of BackgroundWorker is polymorphic with that of .NET 2.0 and functions in an identical manner. The techniques used in the implementation of BackgroundWorker are similar to those used in the final version of EventsHelper (Example 8-21).

Web service proxy classes

Example 7-10 showed asynchronous invocation of a simple calculator web service:

```
public class Calculator
{
    [WebMethod]
    public int Add(int argument1,int argument2)
    {
        return argument1 + argument2;
    }
    //Other methods
}
```

When the client uses *WSDL.exe* to create a proxy class targeting the Calculator web service, the web service proxy class contains methods such as BeginAdd( ) and EndAdd( ), used for asynchronous invocation. Although not delegate-based, these methods comply with the programming model presented in Chapter 7: the asynchronous call is delegated to a thread from the thread pool, and that thread calls back on a callback method to notify about completion. However, if the web service client is a Windows Forms object, the callback method cannot call back on the thread from the thread pool—you have to marshal the callback to the correct owning thread. One solution would be to use the BackgroundWorker component, as shown in Example 8-23.

Example 8-23. Using BackgroundWorker for safe asynchronous web service invocation by a Windows Forms client

```
partial class CalculatorWebServiceClient : Form
{
    public void AsyncAdd( )
    {
        //Calculator is the auto-generated proxy class
```

```
    Calculator calculator = new Calculator( );

    BackgroundWorker worker = new BackgroundWorker( );
    worker.DoWork += OnDoWork;
    worker.RunWorkerCompleted += OnCompleted;
    worker.RunWorkerAsync(calculator);
}
//Executes on thread from thread pool
void OnDoWork(object sender,DoWorkEventArgs e)
{
    Calculator calculator = e.Argument as Calculator;
    e.Result = calculator.Add(2,3);
}
//Executes on correct Windows Forms thread
void OnCompleted(object sender,RunWorkerCompletedEventArgs e)
{
    if(e.Error != null)
    {
        throw e.Error;
    }
    MessageBox.Show("Add returned " + e.Result);
}
}
```

However, `BackgroundWorker` is overkill—once dispatched, there is no way to cancel the web service call, and there are no progress reports (a key feature of `BackgroundWorker`). As a result, both the *WSDL.exe*-generated web service proxy class and the proxy class generated when adding a web reference using Visual Studio 2005 supports yet another asynchronous method invocation pattern (on top of the `BeginAdd( )` and `EndAdd( )` methods, which non–Windows Forms clients can still use). The `Calculator` web service proxy class contains the following members and supporting types:

```
public partial class Calculator : SoapHttpClientProtocol
{
    public event AddCompletedEventHandler AddCompleted;
    public void AddAsync(int argument1,int argument2);
    public void AddAsync(int argument1,int argument2,object userState);
    public new void CancelAsync(object userState);
    //Additional members
}
public delegate void AddCompletedEventHandler(object sender,
                                  AddCompletedEventArgs args);

//AsyncCompletedEventArgs is defined in Example 8-22
public class AddCompletedEventArgs : AsyncCompletedEventArgs
{
    public int Result{get;}
}
```

For each web method, the proxy class will contain two methods of the form:

```
public void <Method Name>Async(<parameters>);
public void <Method Name>Async(<parameters>,object userState);
```

To dispatch the asynchronous web method, you call one of two versions of the `AddAsync( )` method.

The `AddAsync( )` method is dispatched on a thread from the thread pool. When the method completes, the proxy class raises an event. The web service proxy class provides an event member for each web method. The events take the form of:

```
public delegate void <Method Name>CompletedEventHandler(object sender,
                               <Method Name>CompletedEventArgs args);
```

In the case of the `Add( )` method, that event is the `AddCompleted` event. You can add to that event any callback method with a matching signature: the first parameter is an `object` and the second is a strongly typed `AsyncCompletedEventArgs`-derived class. The completion event argument class contains a property called `Result`, which matches the web service method's returned value. If the web service method has no returned value, the proxy class uses `AsyncCompletedEventArgs` as the event argument. `AsyncCompletedEventArgs` also contains the `Error` property, of type `Exception`, which contains any error information about the asynchronous call.

You can use the same completion callback method to handle multiple asynchronous invocations—simply provide `<Method Name>Async( )` with an identifier or state specific for that invocation as the last parameter of type `object`. Inside the completion callback, you can access the state object via the `UserState` property of `AsyncCompletedEventArgs`. You can even cancel an asynchronous method execution in progress, by passing a unique identifier as a state object and using that identifier to call the `CancelAsync( )` method:

```
Calculator calculator = new Calculator( );
calculator.AddCompleted += OnCompleted;
Guid ID = Guid.NewGuid( );
calculator.AddAsync(2,3,ID);
//To cancel:
calculator.CancelAsync(ID);
public void OnCompleted(object sender,AddCompletedEventArgs args)
{...}
```

When the method is canceled, the completion event is raised immediately and the `Cancelled` property of `AsyncCompletedEventArgs` is set to true.

Normally, the completion event will be invoked on the thread from the thread pool. However, if the thread that dispatched the asynchronous call is processing Windows messages, the event will be processed on the message-processing thread. This is accomplished by sending a special message to that thread that makes it invoke the completion delegate as the message processing. Example 8-24 demonstrates the same client code as Example 8-23, except it uses the alternative mechanism just described.

Several classes support a similar pattern for safe asynchronous invocation. For example, the PictureBox control offers it for asynchronous image loading, and the SoundPlayer class offers it for asynchronous media loading. Another example of a class that includes such support is the Ping class that offers a SendAsync( ) method.

Example 8-24. Safe asynchronous web service invocation by a Windows Forms client

```
partial class CalculatorWebServiceClient : Form
{
   public void AsyncAdd( )
   {
      //Calculator is the auto-generated proxy class
      Calculator calculator = new Calculator( );
      calculator.AddCompleted += OnCompleted;
      calculator.AddAsync(2,3);
   }
   public void OnCompleted(object sender,AddCompletedEventArgs args)
   {
      if(args.Error != null)
      {
         throw args.Error;
      }
      if(args.Cancelled)
      {
         MessageBox.Show("Web service call cancelled");
         return;
      }
      MessageBox.Show("Add returned " + args.Result);
   }
}
```

The mechanism just described is a particular implementation of a complex design pattern called *synchronization contexts*. Synchronization contexts are unrelated to synchronization domains and .NET contexts. The Windows Forms implementation of the asynchronous operation is done via WindowsFormsOperationSynchronizationContext, which posts the message whose handling invokes the completion callback on the owning thread. For more information on synchronization contexts, see the MSDN Library.

Timers

Applications often need a certain task to occur at regular time intervals. Such services are implemented by timers. A *timer* is an object that repeatedly calls back into the application at set intervals. For example, you can use a timer to update the user interface with anything from stock quotes to available disk space. You can also use a timer to implement a *watchdog*, which periodically checks the status of various components or devices in your application. For example, you can poll communication ports or check the status of job queues. Many decent-sized applications use timers, for a wide range of purposes. In the past, developers were left to their own devices when implementing timers. They usually did so by creating a worker thread whose thread method executed the following logic in pseudo-code:

```
public class Timer
{
    public void ThreadMethod()
    {
        while(true)
        {
            Tick();
            Thread.Sleep(Interval);
        }
    }
    public int Interval
    {get;set;}
    void Tick()
    {
        /* Call back into the application */
    }
}
```

However, such solutions had disadvantages: you had to write code to start and stop the timer, manage the worker thread, change the interval, and hook the timer to the application's callback function. Furthermore, if you took advantage of timers made available by the operating system (such as the CreateWaitableTimer() function of the Win32 API) you coupled your application to that mechanism, and switching to a different implementation wasn't trivial.

.NET comes out of the box with not one, but three complementary timer mechanisms you can use in your applications. All three mechanisms comply with the same set of generic requirements, allowing the application using the timer to:

- Start and stop the timer repeatedly
- Change the timer interval
- Use the same callback method to service multiple timers and be able to distinguish among the different timers

This section discusses and contrasts .NET's timer mechanisms and recommends where and when to use each of them.

System.Timers.Timer

The System.Timers namespace contains a Timer class, defined as follows:

```
public class System.Timers.Timer : Component,ISupportInitialize
{
    public Timer();
    public Timer(double interval);
```

```
      public bool AutoReset{get; set; }
      public bool Enabled{get; set; }
      public double Interval{get; set;}
      public ISynchronizeInvoke SynchronizingObject { get; set; }

      public event ElapsedEventHandler Elapsed;

      public void Close();
      public void Start();
      public void Stop();

      /* Other members */
   }
```

The System.Timers.Timer class has an event member called Elapsed, a delegate of type ElapsedEventHandler, which is defined as:

```
   public delegate void ElapsedEventHandler(object sender,ElapsedEventArgs e);
```

You provide Elapsed with timer-handling methods with a matching signature:

```
   void OnTick(object sender,ElapsedEventArgs e)
   {...}
```

The System.Timers.Timer class calls into these methods at specified timer intervals, using a thread from the thread pool. You specify an interval using the Interval property. The sender argument to the timer-handling method identifies the timer object. As a result, the same timer method can be called by multiple timers, and you can use the sender argument to distinguish among them. To hook up the timer to more than one timer-handling method, simply add more targets to the Elapsed event. The ElapsedEventArgs class provides the time the method was called. It is defined as:

```
   public class ElapsedEventArgs : EventArgs
   {
       public DateTime SignalTime{get;}
   }
```

To start or stop the timer notifications, simply call the Start( ) or Stop( ) methods. The Enabled property allows you to silence the timer by not raising the event. Consequently, Enabled and the Start( ) and Stop( ) methods are equivalent. Finally, when the application shuts down, call the Close( ) method of the timer to dispose of the system resources it used. Example 8-25 demonstrates using System.Timers.Timer.

Example 8-25. Using System.Timers.Timer

```
using System.Timers;

class SystemTimerClient
{
   System.Timers.Timer m_Timer;

   int m_Counter;
   public int Counter
   {
```

Example 8-25. Using System.Timers.Timer (continued)

```
        get
        {
            lock(this)
            {
                return m_Counter;
            }
        }
        set
        {
            lock(this)
            {
                m_Counter = value;
            }
        }
    }
    public SystemTimerClient()
    {
        m_Counter = 0;
        m_Timer = new System.Timers.Timer();
        m_Timer.Interval = 1000;//One second
        m_Timer.Elapsed += OnTick;
        m_Timer.Start();
        //Can block this thread because the timer uses
        //a thread from the thread pool
        Thread.Sleep(4000);
        m_Timer.Stop();
        m_Timer.Close();
    }
    void OnTick(object source,ElapsedEventArgs e)
    {
        string tickTime = e.SignalTime.ToLongTimeString();
        m_Counter++;
        Trace.WriteLine(m_Counter + " " + tickTime);
    }
}

SystemTimerClient obj = new SystemTimerClient();

//Output:
1 4:20:48 PM
2 4:20:49 PM
3 4:20:50 PM
```

 Because the timer-handling method is called on a different thread, make sure you synchronize access to the object members. This prevents state corruption.

Of particular interest is the SynchronizingObject property of System.Timers.Timer, which allows you to specify an object implementing ISynchronizeInvoke to be used by the timer to call back into the application (instead of calling directly, using the thread pool). For example, here is the code required to use System.Timers.Timer in a Windows Forms Form-derived class:

```
partial class SystemTimerClient : Form
{
    System.Timers.Timer m_Timer;
    int m_Counter;

    public SystemTimerClient()
    {
        m_Counter = 0;
        m_Timer = new System.Timers.Timer();
        m_Timer.Interval = 1000;//One second
        m_Timer.Elapsed += OnTick;
        m_Timer.SynchronizingObject = this;//Form implements ISynchronizeInvoke
        m_Timer.Start();
    }
    void OnTick(object source,ElapsedEventArgs e)
    {
        //Called on the main UI thread, not on a thread from the pool
    }
}
```

By default, SynchronizingObject is set to null, so the timer uses threads from the pool directly.

System.Threading.Timer

The System.Threading namespace contains another Timer class, defined as:

```
public sealed class System.Threading.Timer : MarshalByRefObject,IDisposable
{
    public Timer(TimerCallback callback,object state,long dueTime,long period);
    /* More overloaded constructors */

    public bool Change(int dueTime, int period);
    /* More overloaded Change() */

    public void Dispose();
}
```

System.Threading.Timer is similar to System.Timers.Timer: it too uses the thread pool. The main difference is that it provides fine-grained and advanced control; you can set its due time (that is, when it should start ticking), and you can pass any generic information to the callback tick method. To use System.Threading.Timer, you need to provide its constructor with a delegate of type TimerCallback, defined as:

```
public delegate void TimerCallback(object state);
```

The delegate targets a timer callback method, invoked on each timer tick. The state object is typically the object that created the timer, so you can use the same callback method to handle ticks from multiple senders, but you can of course pass in any other argument you like. The other parameter the timer constructor accepts is the timer period (i.e., the timer interval). To change the timer period, simply call the Change( ) method, which accepts the new due time and period. System.Threading. Timer doesn't provide an easy way to start or stop the timer. It starts ticking immediately after the constructor (actually, after the due time has elapsed), and to stop it you must call its Dispose( ) method. If you want to restart it, you must create a new timer object. Example 8-26 demonstrates the use of System.Threading.Timer.

Example 8-26. Using System.Threading.Timer

```
using System.Threading;

class ThreadingTimerClient
{
    System.Threading.Timer m_Timer;
    int m_Counter;
    public ThreadingTimerClient( )
    {
        m_Counter = 0;
        Start( );
        //Can block this thread because the timer uses a thread from the thread pool
        Thread.Sleep(4000);
        Stop( );
    }
    void Start( )
    {
        m_Timer = new System.Threading.Timer(OnTick,null,0,1000);
    }
    void Stop( )
    {
        m_Timer.Dispose( );
        m_Timer = null;
    }
    void OnTick(object state)
    {
        m_Counter++;
        Trace.WriteLine(m_Counter);
    }
}
ThreadingTimerClient obj = new ThreadingTimerClient( );

//Output:
1
2
3
```

System.Windows.Forms.Timer

The System.Windows.Forms namespace contains a third Timer class, defined as:

```
public class System.Windows.Forms.Timer : Component
{
    public Timer( );
    public Timer(IContainer container);
```

```
        public virtual bool Enabled{get; set;}
        public int Interval {get; set; }
        public event EventHandler Tick;
        public void Start( );
        public void Stop( );
    }
```

Although the `System.Windows.Forms.Timer` methods look like those of `System.Timers.Timer`, `System.Windows.Forms.Timer` doesn't use the thread pool to call back into the Windows Forms application. Instead, it's based on the good old `WM_TIMER` Windows message. Instead of using a thread, the timer posts a `WM_TIMER` message to the message queue of its current thread, at the specified interval. Using `System.Windows.Forms.Timer` is like using `System.Timers.Timer`, except the timer-handling method is of the canonical signature defined by the `EventHandler` delegate. The fact that virtually the same set of methods can use drastically different underlying mechanisms is a testimony to the degree of decoupling from the ticking mechanisms that timers provide to the applications using them.

 Visual Studio has built-in Designer support for the Windows Forms timer. Simply drag-and-drop a timer from the Windows Forms toolbox control to the form. The Designer then displays the timer icon underneath the form and allows you to set its properties.

Because all the callbacks are dispatched on the main UI thread, there is no need to manage concurrency when using Windows Forms timers. However, this may be a problem if the processing is long, because the user interface will not be responsive during the processing.

Choosing a timer

If you are developing a Windows Forms application, you should use `System.Windows.Forms.Timer`. In all other cases, I recommend using `System.Timers.Timer`. Its methods are easy to use, while `System.Threading.Timer`'s methods are cumbersome and offer no substantial advantage.

Volatile Fields

To optimize access to object fields, the compiler may cache a member variable's value in a local temporary variable after the first time it is read. If the variable is read repeatedly without an attempted write, the subsequent reads can access the temporary variable instead of the actual object:

```
class MyClass
{
    public int Number;
}
MyClass obj = new MyClass( );
int number1 = obj.Number;
int number2 = obj.Number; //Compiler may use cached value here
```

This may yield better performance, especially in tight loops:

```
while(<some condition>)
{
    int number = obj.Number;
    /* Using number */
}
```

The problem is that if a thread context switch takes place after the assignment to number1 but before the assignment to number2, and the new thread changes the value of the field, number2 will still be assigned the old cached value. Of course, it's a bad idea to expose member variables directly in public—you should always access them via properties. However, in the rare case that you do want to expose public fields without synchronizing access to them, the C# compiler supports *volatile fields*. A volatile field is a field defined using the volatile reserved word:

```
class MyClass
{
    public volatile int Number;
}
```

When a field is marked as volatile, the compiler doesn't cache its value and always reads the field value. Similarly, the compiler writes assigned values to volatile fields immediately, even if no read operation takes place in between. The Thread class offers multiple versions of the VolatileRead( ) and VolatileWrite( ) static methods:

```
public sealed class Thread
{
    public static int VolatileRead(ref int address);
    public static object VolatileRead(ref object address);
    public static void VolatileWrite(ref int address,int value);
    public static void VolatileWrite(ref object address,object value);
    //Additional versions of VolatileRead( ) and VolatileWrite( )
}
```

VolatileRead( ) reads the latest version of a memory address, and VolatileWrite( ) writes to the address, making the address available to all threads. Using both VolatileRead( ) and VolatileWrite( ) consistently on a member variable has the same effect as marking it as volatile.

Visual Basic 2005 has no equivalent to the C# volatile keyword, so its developers can only use VolatileRead( ) and VolatileWrite( ).

 Avoid volatile fields—instead, lock your object or fields to guarantee deterministic and thread-safe access.

.NET and COM's Apartments

.NET doesn't have an equivalent to COM's apartments. As you have seen throughout this chapter, every .NET component resides in a multithreaded environment, and it's up to you to provide proper synchronization. The question is, what threading model should .NET components present to COM when interoperating with COM components as clients?

The Thread class provides three methods for managing its apartment state: GetApartmentState( ), SetApartmentState( ), and TrySetApartmentState( ). The methods are defined as follows:

```
public enum ApartmentState
{
    STA,
    MTA,
    Unknown
}
public sealed class Thread
{
    public ApartmentState GetApartmentState( );
    public void SetApartmentState(ApartmentState state);
    public bool TrySetApartmentState(ApartmentState state);
    //Other methods and properties
}
```

These methods accept or return the enum ApartmentState.

ApartmentState.STA stands for single-threaded apartment; ApartmentState.MTA stands for multithreaded apartment. The semantic of ApartmentState.Unknown is the same as that of ApartmentState.MTA.

By default, the Thread apartment state is set to ApartmentState.Unknown, resulting in the MTA apartment state.

 Threads from the thread pool use the MTA apartment state.

You can programmatically instruct .NET as to what apartment state to present to COM by calling SetApartmentState( ) and providing either ApartmentState.STA or ApartmentState.MTA (but not ApartmentState.Unknown):

```
Thread workerThread = new Thread(ThreadMethod);
workerThread.SetApartmentState(ApartmentState.STA);
workerThread.Start( );
```

If the apartment state of the managed thread matches that of the COM object on which it tries to invoke a method, COM will run the object on that thread. If the threading model is incompatible, COM will marshal the call to the COM object's apartment, according to the COM rules. Obviously, a match in apartment model will result in better performance.

You can only set the threading model before the thread starts to run. If you try to set the apartment model of an already executing thread, an exception of type

InvalidOperation will be raised. If you are unsure as to whether the thread is already running or not, you can use the TrySetApartmentState( ) method, which returns true if setting the thread's apartment state was successful (because the thread was not started yet) or false if it failed. (Obviously, it is better to always know deterministically the state of your thread, so you don't have to rely on half-measures like TrySetApartmentState( ).) Finally, you can always retrieve the apartment state of your thread using the GetApartmentState( ) method.

You can also use either the STAThread or the MTAThread method attribute to declaratively set the apartment state. Although the compiler doesn't enforce this rule, you should apply these attributes only to the Main( ) method and use programmatic settings for your worker threads:

```
[STAThread]
static void Main( )
{...}
```

Note that you can set the apartment model only once, regardless of whether you do it declaratively or programmatically. Future attempts to change it, even if the thread is not running, will result in an InvalidOperation exception.

 The Windows Forms application wizard automatically applies the STAThread attribute to the Main( ) method of a Windows Forms application. This is done for two reasons. The first is in case the application hosts ActiveX controls, which are STA objects by definition. The second is in case the Windows Forms application interacts with the Clipboard, which still uses COM interop. With the STAThread attribute, the underlying physical thread uses OleInitialize( ) instead of CoInitializeEx( ) to set up the apartment model. OleInitialize( ) automatically does the additional initialization required for enabling drag-and-drop.

There is one side effect to selecting an apartment threading model: you can't call WaitHandle.WaitAll( ) with multiple handles from a thread whose apartment state is set to ApartmentState.STA. If you do, .NET throws an exception of type NotSupportedException. This is probably because the underlying implementation of WaitHandle.WaitAll( ) uses the Win32 call WaitForMultipleObjects( ), and that call blocks the STA thread from pumping COM calls in the form of messages to the COM objects. Note that when a managed thread makes a call outside managed code for the first time, .NET calls CoInitializeEx( ) with the appropriate apartment state, even if the thread doesn't intend to interact with COM objects directly.

CHAPTER 9
Serialization and Persistence

In a component-oriented application, the component instances (the objects) maintain their *state* (the object's member variables) in memory and apply business logic on that state. But how is this state initially generated, and what happens to it when the application shuts down or when the user selects Save? In almost every application, object states aren't created out of thin air when the application starts. An application typically loads some file containing data and converts the information in the file into live objects. Similarly, when the application shuts down, the object state is saved (or, *persisted*) to a file. Traditionally, this is referred to as *serialization* and *deserialization*. These terms were originally coined to describe a simple binary dump of an object's state to a file and its subsequent recovery. In such cases, the application wrote the state of the object serially, one bit at a time. When the application later read the information, it processed the information serially in exactly the same order into a memory location and associated that location with an object.

Classic object-oriented programming didn't offer much in the way of implementing serialization. Consequently, not only did developers spend much of their valuable time on mundane serialization code instead of adding business value to their applications, but the resulting solutions were proprietary and singular. There was no generic way for two applications to share serialization files, because each used its own format, even if both applications ran on the same platform and used the same language, memory layout, word size, and so on.

With component-oriented applications, serialization is a critical issue. If an application contains several components from various vendors, how can it persist its objects into a single file without the individual components overwriting and destroying the information persisted there by other components?

.NET provides a standard, straightforward way to serialize and deserialize objects. Even though the .NET solution is trivial to use (in most cases, you aren't required to provide any explicit serialization code), it's also extensible, and you can provide your own serialization formats and implementations. .NET serialization is used not only to implement object persistence but also to facilitate the marshaling of objects and object references to remote clients.

This chapter describes the .NET types and tools for implementing serialization on both the server and client sides; shows how to provide custom serialization; and suggests solutions for dealing with special cases, such as the serialization of class hierarchies.

Automatic Serialization

.NET implements the automatic serialization of objects by means of *reflection*, a simple and elegant technique that uses metadata exposed by every .NET component. Reflection is discussed in detail in Appendix C. .NET can capture the value of every one of an object's fields and serialize it to memory, to a file, or to a network connection. .NET also supports automatic deserialization: .NET can create a new object, read its persisted field values, and, using reflection, set the values of its fields. Because reflection can access private fields, including base-class fields, .NET can take a complete snapshot of the state of an object during serialization and perfectly reconstruct that state during deserialization. Another advantage of reflection-based serialization is that the code used by .NET is completely general-purpose—the state of every .NET type can be read or set using reflection.

.NET serializes the object state into a stream. A *stream* is a logical sequence of bytes, independent of any particular medium (file, memory, communication port, or other resource). This extra level of indirection means that you can use the same serialization infrastructure with any medium, simply by selecting an appropriate stream type. The various stream types provided by .NET all derive from the abstract class Stream, defined in the System.IO namespace. Although you need a Stream instance to serialize and deserialize an object, there is usually no need to interact explicitly with the methods and properties of the Stream itself.

 .NET serialization is object-based. As a result, only instance fields are serialized. Static fields are excluded from serialization.

The Serializable Attribute

By default, user-defined types (classes and structs) aren't serializable. The reason is that .NET has no way of knowing whether a reflection-based dump of the object state to a stream makes sense. Perhaps the object members have some transient value or state (such as an open database connection or communication port). If .NET simply serialized the state of such an object, when you constructed a new object by deserializing it from the stream you would end up with a defective object. Consequently, serialization can be performed only with the developer's consent.

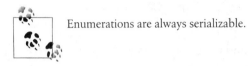 Enumerations are always serializable.

To indicate to .NET that instances of your class are serializable, you can add the Serializable attribute to your class definition. For example:

```
[Serializable]
public class MyClass
{
    public string SomeString;
    public int SomePublicNumber;
    int m_SomePrivateNumber;
    /* Methods and properties */
}
```

In most cases, decorating a user-defined type definition with the Serializable attribute is all you need to do. If the class has member variables that are complex types themselves, .NET automatically serializes and deserializes these members as well:

```
[Serializable]
public class MyOtherClass
{...}

[Serializable]
public class MyClass
{
    MyOtherClass m_Obj;
    /* Methods and properties */
}
```

The result is recursive iteration over an object and all its contained objects. The object can be the root of a huge graph of interconnected objects, as shown in Figure 9-1.

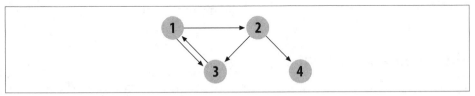

Figure 9-1. .NET serialization traverses the entire object graph

Regardless of its depth, .NET captures the entire state of any graph and serializes it. The recursive traversal algorithm used by .NET is smart enough to detect cyclic references in the graph, tagging objects it has already visited and thereby avoiding processing the same object twice. This approach allows .NET to serialize complex data structures such as doubly linked lists.

Non-Serializable Members

When a class is serializable, .NET insists that all its member variables be serializable as well. If it discovers a non-serializable member, it throws an exception of type SerializationException during serialization. However, what if the class or a struct has a member that can't be serialized? That type will not have the Serializable attribute and will preclude the containing type from being serialized. Commonly, that non-serializable member is a reference type that requires some special initialization. The solution to this problem requires marking such a member as non-serializable and taking a custom step to initialize it during deserialization.

To allow a serializable type to contain a non-serializable type as a member variable, you need to mark the member with the NonSerialized field attribute:

```
public class MyOtherClass
{...}

[Serializable]
public class MyClass
{
    [NonSerialized]
    MyOtherClass m_Obj;
    /* Methods and properties */
}
```

When .NET serializes a member variable, it first reflects it to see whether it has the NonSerialized attribute. If so, .NET ignores that variable and simply skips over it. This allows you to preclude from serialization even serializable types:

```
[Serializable]
public class MyClass
{
    [NonSerialized]
    int m_Number;
}
```

However, when .NET deserializes the object, it initializes each non-serializable member variable to the default value for that type (null for all reference types). It's then up to you to provide code to initialize the variables to their correct values. To that end, the object needs to know when it's being deserialized. The notification takes place by implementing the interface IDeserializationCallback, defined in the System.Runtime.Serialization namespace:

```
public interface IDeserializationCallback
{
    void OnDeserialization(object sender);
}
```

IDeserializationCallback's single method, OnDeserialization( ), is called after .NET has deserialized the object, allowing it to perform the required custom initialization steps. The sender parameter is ignored and is always set to null by .NET.

Example 9-1 demonstrates how you can implement IDeserializationCallback. In the example, the class MyClass has a database connection as a member variable. The connection object (SqlConnection) isn't a serializable type and so is marked with the NonSerialized attribute. MyClass creates a new connection object in its implementation of OnDeserialization( ), because after deserialization the connection member is set to its default value of null. MyClass then initializes the connection object by providing it with a connection string and opens it.

Example 9-1. Deserialized event using IDeserializationCallback

```
using System.Runtime.Serialization;

[Serializable]
public class MyClass : IDeserializationCallback
{
   [NonSerialized]
   IDbConnection m_Connection;
   string m_ConnectionString;

   public void OnDeserialization(object sender)
   {
      Debug.Assert(m_Connection == null);
      m_Connection = new SqlConnection( );
      m_Connection.ConnectionString = m_ConnectionString;
      m_Connection.Open( );
   }
   /* Other members */
}
```

 You can't initialize class members marked with the readonly directive in OnDeserialization( )—such members can only be initialized in a constructor. If you need to initialize read-only members, you have to use custom serialization, described later in this chapter.

On non-sealed classes, it is important to use either implicit interface implementation of IDeserializationCallback and have the base class mark its OnDeserialization( ) method as virtual to allow subclasses to override it, or to use the technique shown in Chapter 3 for explicit interface implementation by a class hierarchy. When class hierarchies are involved, you need to call your base-class implementation of OnDeserialization( ), and that requires a non-private implementation:

```
[Serializable]
public class MyBaseClass : IDeserializationCallback
{
   public virtual void OnDeserialization(object sender)
   {...}
}
[Serializable]
public class MySubClass : MyBaseClass
{
```

```
    public override void OnDeserialization(object sender)
    {
        //Perform custom steps, then:
        base.OnDeserialization(sender);
    }
}
```

Delegates and serialization

All delegate definitions are compiled into serializable classes. This means that when you serialize an object that has a delegate member variable, the internal invocation list of the delegate is serialized too. I believe that this renders delegates inherently non-serializable. There are no guarantees that the target objects in the internal list are serializable, so sometimes the serialization will work and sometimes it will throw a serialization exception. In addition, the object containing the delegate typically does not know or care about the actual state of the delegate. This is especially true when the delegate is used to manage event subscriptions, because the exact number and identities of the subscribers are often transient values that should not be persisted between application sessions.

You should mark delegate member variables as non-serializable, using the NonSerialized attribute:

```
[Serializable]
public class MyClass
{
    [NonSerialized]
    EventHandler m_MyEvent;
}
```

In the case of events, you must also add the field attribute qualifier when applying the NonSerialized attribute:

```
[Serializable]
public class MyPublisher
{
    [field:NonSerialized]
    public event EventHandler MyEvent;
}
```

Serialization Formatters

It's up to the client to decide which stream type to use for serialization and in which format the data should be represented. A *formatter* is an object that implements the IFormatter interface, defined in the System.Runtime.Serialization namespace:

```
public interface IFormatter
{
    object Deserialize(Stream serializationStream);
    void Serialize(Stream serializationStream, object graph);
    /* Other methods */
}
```

`IFormatter`'s significant methods are `Serialize()` and `Deserialize()`, which perform the actual serialization and deserialization. .NET ships with two formatters: a binary formatter and a Simple Object Access Protocol (SOAP) formatter. The binary formatter generates a compact binary representation of the object's state. It's relatively fast to serialize an object into binary format and to deserialize an object from binary format. The SOAP formatter, as the name implies, persists the object's state using a text-based XML format. Naturally, the SOAP formatter is considerably slower than the binary formatter, because serialization requires composing a SOAP envelope and deserialization requires SOAP parsing. In addition, the resulting serialization data (i.e., the file size or memory footprint) is bigger. The only advantage of using the SOAP formatter is that it's platform-neutral: you can provide the serialization information (via network stream or file access) to applications running on non-Windows-based platforms, and they can deserialize equivalent objects on their side or serialize their objects back to the .NET side. In general, unless cross-platform interoperability is required, you should always use the binary formatter.

The Binary Formatter

The binary formatter is the class `BinaryFormatter`, defined in the `System.Runtime.Serialization.Formatters.Binary` namespace. To serialize an object with the binary formatter, create a stream object (such as a file stream) and call the `Serialize()` method of the formatter, providing the formatter with the object to serialize and the stream to serialize it to. When you are done with the stream, remember to dispose of it. Example 9-2 shows how to serialize an object of type `MyClass` to a file stream.

Example 9-2. Binary serialization using a file stream

```
using System.Runtime.Serialization.Formatters.Binary;

MyClass obj = new MyClass();

IFormatter formatter = new BinaryFormatter();

//Creating a stream
Stream stream;
stream = new FileStream(@"C:\temp\obj.bin",FileMode.Create,FileAccess.Write);

using(stream)
{
   formatter.Serialize(stream,obj);
}
```

To deserialize an object, you need to open the appropriate stream (matching the type of stream used for serialization) and call the `Deserialize()` method of the formatter, as shown in Example 9-3. You will receive back an object reference.

Example 9-3. Binary deserialization using a file stream

```
using System.Runtime.Serialization.Formatters.Binary;

MyClass obj; //No new!

IFormatter formatter = new BinaryFormatter();

//Opening a stream
Stream stream;
stream = new FileStream(@"C:\temp\obj.bin",FileMode.Open,FileAccess.Read);

using(stream)
{
   obj = (MyClass)formatter.Deserialize(stream);
}
```

There are a few things worth mentioning regarding deserialization. First, make sure to open a stream on an existing medium, instead of creating a new one and destroying the existing serialized information. Second, note that there is no need to create an object explicitly using new. The Deserialize() method creates a new object and returns a reference to it. In fact, during deserialization, no constructor is ever called. Third, Deserialize() returns an amorphous object reference, so you need to downcast it to the correct object type being deserialized. If the downcast type is different from the type that was serialized, an exception is thrown. Finally, be sure to dispose of the stream when you are finished.

The SOAP Formatter

The SoapFormatter class, defined in the System.Runtime.Serialization.Formatters. Soap namespace, is used exactly like the BinaryFormatter class. The only difference is that it serializes using a SOAP format instead of binary format. Example 9-4 demonstrates serialization into a file stream using the SOAP formatter.

Example 9-4. SOAP serialization using a file stream

```
using System.Runtime.Serialization.Formatters.Soap;

//In the MyClassLibrary assembly:
namespace MyNamespace
{
   [Serializable]
   public class MyClass
   {
      public int Number1;
      public int Number2;
   }
}

//In the client's assembly:
MyClass obj = new MyClass();
obj.Number1 = 123;
```

Example 9-4. SOAP serialization using a file stream (continued)

```
obj.Number2 = 456;

IFormatter formatter = new SoapFormatter( );

Stream stream;
stream = new FileStream(@"C:\temp\obj.xml",FileMode.Create,FileAccess.Write);
using(stream)
{
   formatter.Serialize(stream,obj);
}
```

Example 9-5 shows the resulting file content. The deserialization using a SOAP formatter is exactly like that in Example 9-3, except it uses the SOAP formatter instead of the binary one.

Example 9-5. The SOAP format serialization output of Example 9-9

```
<SOAP-ENV:Envelope
    xmlns:xsi="http://www.w3.org/2001/XMLSchema-instance"
    xmlns:xsd="http://www.w3.org/2001/XMLSchema"
    xmlns:SOAP-ENC="http://schemas.xmlsoap.org/soap/encoding/"
    xmlns:SOAP-ENV="http://schemas.xmlsoap.org/soap/envelope/"
    xmlns:clr="http://schemas.microsoft.com/soap/encoding/clr/1.0"
    SOAP-ENV:encodingStyle="http://schemas.xmlsoap.org/soap/encoding/">
    <SOAP-ENV:Body>
        <a1:MyClass
            id="ref-1"
             xmlns:a1="http://schemas.microsoft.com/clr/nsassem/
                     MyNamespace/MyClassLibrary%2C%20
                     Version%3D1.0.898.27976%2C%20
                     Culture%3Dneutral%2C%20
                     PublicKeyToken%3Dnull">
            <Number1>123</Number1>
            <Number2>456</Number2>
        </a1:MyClass>
    /SOAP-ENV:Body>
</SOAP-ENV:Envelope>
```

Generic Formatters

The IFormatter interface was defined before generics were available in .NET, but with the introduction of generics in .NET 2.0 you can improve on the available implementations of IFormatter by providing generic and type-safe wrappers around them. You can define the IGenericFormatter interface that provides similar methods to IFormatter, except it uses generic methods:

```
public interface IGenericFormatter
{
    T Deserialize<T>(Stream serializationStream);
    void Serialize<T>(Stream serializationStream,T graph);
}
```

Using generic methods is preferable to making the whole interface generic, because it allows you to use the same formatter instance but change the type parameter being serialized or deserialized in every call. You can simply implement IGenericFormatter by encapsulating a non-generic formatter, and delegate the calls to it. Example 9-6 shows the generic class GenericFormatter<F>, which implements IGenericFormatter.

Example 9-6. Implementing IGenericFormatter

```
public class GenericFormatter<F> : IGenericFormatter where F : IFormatter,new( )
{
   IFormatter m_Formatter = new F( );

   public T Deserialize<T>(Stream serializationStream)
   {
      return (T)m_Formatter.Deserialize(serializationStream);
   }
   public void Serialize<T>(Stream serializationStream,T graph)
   {
      m_Formatter.Serialize(serializationStream,graph);
   }
}

public class GenericBinaryFormatter : GenericFormatter<BinaryFormatter>
{}

public class GenericSoapFormatter : GenericFormatter<SoapFormatter>
{}
```

GenericFormatter<F> is defined using the generic type parameter F. F is constrained to implement IFormatter and provide a default constructor. Then, GenericFormatter<F> declares a member of type IFormatter and assigns into it a new F object:

```
IFormatter m_Formatter = new F( );
```

Example 9-6 also defines two subclasses of GenericFormatter<F>: GenericBinaryFormatter and GenericSoapFormatter. All they do is provide the binary or the SOAP formatter, respectively, as a type parameter to GenericFormatter<F>. You could define GenericBinaryFormatter and GenericSoapFormatter with the using statement, like this:

```
using GenericBinaryFormatter = GenericFormatter<BinaryFormatter>;
using GenericSoapFormatter   = GenericFormatter<SoapFormatter>;
```

but that would have file scope only. In this case, inheritance is good for strong typing and shorthand across files and assemblies.

Example 9-7 demonstrates the use of the generic, type-safe formatters.

Example 9-7. Using the generic formatters

```
[Serializable]
public class MyClass
{...}

MyClass obj1 = new MyClass();
MyClass obj2;

IGenericFormatter formatter = new GenericBinaryFormatter();
Stream stream;
stream = new FileStream(@"C:\temp\obj.bin",FileMode.Create,FileAccess.ReadWrite);
using(stream)
{
   formatter.Serialize(stream,obj1);
   stream.Seek(0,SeekOrigin.Begin);
   obj2 = formatter.Deserialize<MyClass>(stream);
}
```

 The next version of the serialization infrastructure (a part of Indigo) will contain a generic version of IFormatter similar to IGenericFormatter.

Serialization of Generic Type Parameters

.NET allows you to have serializable generic types:

```
[Serializable]
public class MyClass<T>
{...}
```

If the serializable type is generic, the metadata captured by the formatter contains information about the specific type parameters used. Consequently, each permutation of a generic type with a specific parameter type is considered a unique type. For example, you cannot serialize an object of type MyClass<int> and then deserialize it into an object of type MyClass<string>. Serializing an instance of a generic type is no different from serializing a non-generic type. However, when you deserialize that type, you need to declare a variable with the matching specific type parameter, and you must specify these types again when you call `Deserialize()`. Example 9-8 demonstrates serialization and deserialization of a generic type.

Example 9-8. Client-side serialization of a generic type

```
[Serializable]
public class MyClass<T>
{...}

MyClass<int> obj1 = new MyClass<int>();
MyClass<int> obj2;

IGenericFormatter formatter = new GenericBinaryFormatter();
Stream stream;
stream = new FileStream(@"C:\temp\obj.bin",FileMode.Create,FileAccess.ReadWrite);
using(stream)
{
   formatter.Serialize(stream,obj1);
   stream.Seek(0,SeekOrigin.Begin);
   obj2 = formatter.Deserialize<MyClass<int>>(stream);
}
```

 You cannot use the SOAP formatter to serialize generic types.

Serialization Events

.NET 2.0 introduces support for serialization events. .NET calls designated methods on your class when serialization and deserialization take place. Four serialization and deserialization events are defined. The *serializing event* is raised just before serialization takes place, and the *serialized event* is raised just after serialization. Similarly, the *deserializing event* is raised just before deserialization, and the *deserialized event* is raised after deserialization. Both classes and structures can take advantage of serialization events. You designate methods as serialization event handlers using method attributes, as shown in Example 9-9.

Example 9-9. Applying the serialization event attributes

```
[Serializable]
public class MyClass
{
   [OnSerializing]
   void OnSerializing(StreamingContext context)
   {...}
   [OnSerialized]
   void OnSerialized(StreamingContext context)
   {...}
   [OnDeserializing]
```

Example 9-9. Applying the serialization event attributes (continued)

```
    void OnDeserializing(StreamingContext context)
    {...}
    [OnDeserialized]
    void OnDeserialized(StreamingContext context)
    {...}
}
```

Note that the class itself must still be marked for serialization. Each serialization event-handling method must have the following signature:

```
    void <Method Name>(StreamingContext context);
```

This is required because internally .NET still uses delegates to subscribe and invoke the event-handling methods. If the attributes are applied on methods with incompatible signatures, .NET will throw a SerializationException.

StreamingContext is a structure informing the object why it is being serialized. The StreamingContext structure provides the State property of the enum type StreamingContextStates. Possible reasons for serialization include remoting (across app domain or process), persisting to a file, and so on. The context parameter is largely ignored; it is used only in advanced esoteric scenarios in which the serialization and deserialization actions are context-sensitive.

The event attributes are defined in the System.Runtime.Serialization namespace.

As the attribute names imply, the OnSerializing attribute designates a method handling the serializing event, and the OnSerialized attribute designates a method handling the serialized event. Similarly, the OnDeserializing attribute designates a method handling the deserializing event, and the OnDeserialized attribute designates a method handling the deserialized event. Figure 9-2 is a UML activity diagram depicting the order in which events are raised during serialization.

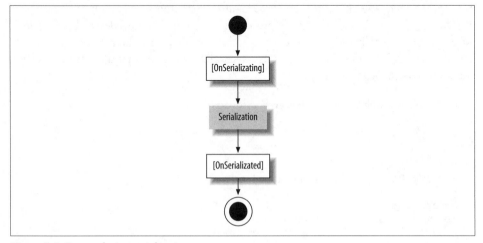

Figure 9-2. Events during serialization

.NET first raises the serializing event, thus invoking the corresponding event handlers (there can be more than one, as you will see shortly). Next, .NET serializes the object, and finally the serialized event is raised and its event handlers are invoked.

Figure 9-3 is a UML activity diagram depicting the order in which deserialization events are raised.

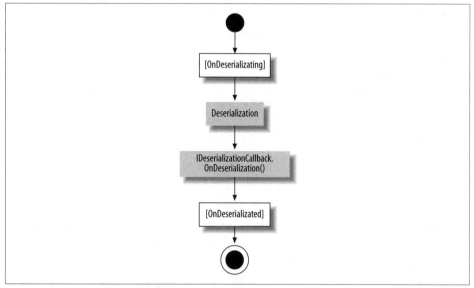

Figure 9-3. Events during deserialization

Unlike with the serialization events, with deserialization .NET has to accommodate the use of IDeserializationCallback. .NET first raises the deserializing event and then performs the deserialization. If the class implements IDeserializationCallback, .NET then calls the OnDeserialization( ) method and finally raises the deserialized event. Note that in order to call the deserializing event-handling methods .NET has to first construct an object—however, it does so without ever calling your class's default constructor.

> The next version of the serialization infrastructure (a part of Indigo) will provide a compatible programming model that supports an analogous set of serialization events.

Applying the Event Attributes

.NET allows you to apply the same serialization event attributes on multiple methods of the class. For example:

```
[OnSerializing]
void OnSerializing1(StreamingContext context)
{...}
[OnSerializing]
void OnSerializing2(StreamingContext context)
{...}
```

The canonical example for applying the same serialization event attribute on multiple methods is when dealing with partial classes:

```
[Serializable]
public partial class MyClass
{
    [OnSerializing]
    void OnSerializing1(StreamingContext context)
    {...}
}

public partial class MyClass
{
    [OnSerializing]
    void OnSerializing2(StreamingContext context)
    {...}
}
```

This decoupled the various parts of the partial class, because it enables each part of the class to deal with the class members it is responsible for, and have a dedicated serialization event handling method for them.

While you can also apply multiple attributes on the same event-handling method, as follows:

```
[OnSerializing]
[OnSerialized]
void OnSerialization(StreamingContext context)
{...}
```

the usefulness of doing so is questionable. The method will be called once per attribute, and there is no easy way to detect which event is raised inside the method.

Serialization Events and Class Hierarchies

A significant advantage of using attributes for event-handler identification (as opposed to interfaces) is that the event mechanism is decoupled from the class hierarchy. When using attributes, the event-handling methods are called for each level in a class hierarchy. There is no need to call your base class's event-handling methods, and there is no problem if those base methods are private. The events are raised according to the order of the hierarchy, and the event attributes are not inherited. For example, when serializing an object of type MySubClass, defined as:

```
[Serializable]
public class MyBaseClass
{
```

```
    [OnSerializing]
    void OnSerializing1(StreamingContext context)
    {...}
}
[Serializable]
public class MySubClass : MyBaseClass
{
    [OnSerializing]
    void OnSerializing2(StreamingContext context)
    {...}
}
```

the OnSerializing1( ) method is called first, followed by a call to OnSerializing2( ). The situation could therefore get messy when virtual methods are involved and the subclass overrides its base class's handling of a serialization event, and even calls it. To deal with this problem, the serialization infrastructure throws an exception of type SerializationException if any of the event attributes are applied on a virtual or abstract method or on an overriding method.

 The serialization event attributes throw a SerializationException when applied on a class method that implements an interface method and are ignored when applied to a method in the interface definition.

Use of the new inheritance qualifier is still allowed in conjunction with serialization events. Since no other party besides .NET should call a serialization event-handling method, I recommend always designating such methods as private.

Using the deserializing event

Since no constructor calls are ever made during deserialization, the deserializing event-handling method is logically your deserialization constructor. It is intended for performing some custom pre-deserialization steps—typically, initialization of non-serializable members. Any value settings done on the serializable members will be in vain, because the formatter will set those members again during deserialization, using values from the serialization stream. The main difference between IDeserializationCallback and the deserializing event is that IDeserializationCallback's OnDeserialization( ) method is called after deserialization is complete, while the deserializing event is called before deserialization starts. You should only place in the deserializing event-handling method any initialization steps that are independent of the values saved in the serialization stream. In contrast, in OnDeserialization( ) you can take advantage of already deserialized members (such as a database connection string, as in Example 9-1). Other steps you can take in the deserializing event-handling method are setting specific environment variables (such as thread local storage), performing diagnostics, or signaling some global synchronization events.

Using the deserialized event

Taking advantage of the deserialized event makes the use of IDeserializationCallback redundant, as the two are logically equivalent—both let your class respond to the post-deserialization event and initialize or reclaim non-serializable members, while using already deserialized values. Example 9-10 demonstrates this point. It performs exactly the same task as Example 9-1, except it relies on the deserialized event rather than IDeserializationCallback.

Example 9-10. Initializing non-serializable resources using the deserialized event

```
[Serializable]
public class MyClass
{
   [NonSerialized]
   IDbConnection m_Connection;
   string m_ConnectionString;

   [OnDeserialized]
   void OnDeserialized(StreamingContext context)
   {
      m_Connection = new SqlConnection();
      m_Connection.ConnectionString = m_ConnectionString;
      m_Connection.Open();
   }
}
```

Serialization and Versioning

An application may wish to serialize the state of multiple objects of multiple types to the same stream. Consequently, a simple dump of object state will not do—the formatter must also capture each object's type information. During deserialization, the formatter needs to read the type's metadata and initialize a new object according to the information serialized, populating the corresponding fields. The easiest way to capture the type information is to record the type's name and reference in its assembly. For each object serialized, the formatter persists the state of the object (the values of the various fields) and the version and full name of its assembly, including a token of the assembly's public key (if a strong name is used). This can be seen in Example 9-5. When the formatter deserializes the object, it loads its assembly and reflects the type's metadata.

The formatters by default comply with .NET's general version-binding and resolving policy, described in Chapter 5. If the serialized type's assembly does not have a strong name, the formatters try to load a private assembly and completely ignore any version incompatibility between the version captured during serialization and the version of the assembly found. If the serialized type's assembly has a strong name, .NET insists on using a compatible assembly. If such an assembly is not found, .NET raises an exception of type FileLoadException.

Both the binary and SOAP formatters also provide a way to record only the friendly name of the assembly, without any version or public-key token, even if the assembly has a strong name. The formatters provide a public property called `AssemblyFormat`, of the enum type `FormatterAssemblyStyle`, defined in the `System.Runtime.Serialization.Formatters` namespace:

```
public enum FormatterAssemblyStyle
{
   Full,
   Simple
}
public sealed class BinaryFormatter : IFormatter,...
{
   public FormatterAssemblyStyle AssemblyFormat{get; set;}
   //Other members, including implementation of IFormatter
}
public sealed class SoapFormatter : IFormatter,...
{
   public FormatterAssemblyStyle AssemblyFormat{get; set;}
   //Other members, including implementation of IFormatter
}
```

Note that the `AssemblyFormat` property is not part of the `IFormatter` interface. The default value of `AssemblyFormat` is `FormatterAssemblyStyle.Full`. If you set it to `FormatterAssemblyStyle.Simple`, no version-compatibility checks will take place during deserialization. For example, consider this SOAP serialization code:

```
MyClass obj = new MyClass();
obj.Number1 = 123;
obj.Number2 = 456;

SoapFormatter formatter = new SoapFormatter();
formatter.AssemblyFormat = FormatterAssemblyStyle.Simple;

Stream stream;
stream = new FileStream(@"C:\temp\obj.xml",FileMode.Create,FileAccess.Write);
using(stream)
{
   formatter.Serialize(stream,obj);
}
```

This code results in the following SOAP envelope body:

```
<SOAP-ENV:Body>
   <a1:MyClass id="ref-1"
      xmlns:a1="http://schemas.microsoft.com/clr/nsassem/
      MyNamespace/MyClassLibrary">
      <Number1>123</Number1>
      <Number2>456</Number2>
   </a1:MyClass>
</SOAP-ENV:Body>
```

Although this option exists, I strongly discourage you from circumventing version serialization and type verification. At best, a potential incompatibility will result in an exception of type SerializationException. At worst, your application may later crash unexpectedly because the incompatible type required some custom initialization steps.

Type-Version Tolerance

In .NET 1.1, there had to be absolute compatibility between the metadata used to serialize a type and the metadata used to deserialize a type. This meant that if your application had clients with the serialized state of your types, your type members' metadata had to be immutable, or you would break those clients.

In .NET 2.0, the formatters acquired some version-tolerance capabilities. The tolerance is with respect to changes in the type metadata, not changes to the assembly version itself. Imagine a class-library vendor that provides a serializable component. The various client applications are responsible for managing the serialization medium (typically a file). Suppose the vendor changes the component definition, by adding a member variable. Such a change does not necessitate a version change, because binary compatibility is maintained. New client applications can serialize the new component properly. However, the serialization information captured by the old applications is now incompatible, and will result in a SerializationException if used in .NET 1.1. The vendor can, of course, increment the assembly version number, but doing so will prevent the old clients from taking advantage of the new functionality. The formatters in .NET 2.0 were redesigned to handle such predicaments.

In the case of removing an unused member variable, the binary formatter will simply ignore the additional information found in the stream. For example, suppose you use this class (but not a struct) definition and serialize it using a binary formatter:

```
//Version 1.0
[Serializable]
public class MyClass
{
    public int Number1;
    public int Number2;
}
```

Without changing the assembly version, remove one of the member variables:

```
//Version 2.0
[Serializable]
public class MyClass
{
    public int Number1;
}
```

You can then rebuild, redeploy, and deserialize instances of version 2.0 of MyClass with the serialization information captured using version 1.0 of MyClass.

The real challenge in type-version tolerance is dealing with new members, because the old serialization information does not contain any information about them. By default, the formatters are not tolerant toward the new members and will throw an exception when they encounter them.

.NET 2.0 addresses this problem by providing a field attribute called `OptionalField`—a simple attribute with a single public property of type int, called `VersionAdded`:

```
[AttributeUsage(AttributeTargets.Field,Inherited = false)]
public sealed class OptionalFieldAttribute : Attribute
{
    public int VersionAdded(get;set);
}
```

Applying the `OptionalField` attribute has no effect during serialization, and fields marked with it will be serialized into the stream. This is because `OptionalField` is meant to be applied on new fields of your type, and it causes the formatters to ignore the new members during deserialization:

```
//Version 1.0
[Serializable]
public class MyClass
{
    public int Number1;
}
//Version 2.0
[Serializable]
public class MyClass
{
    public int Number1;
    [OptionalField]
    public int Number2;
}
```

That said, if the new member variable has a good-enough default value, such as the application's default directory or user preferences, you can use values provided by the new clients to synthesize values for the old clients. You will need to provide these values in your handling of the deserializing event. If you do so before deserialization and the stream does contain serialized values, the serialized values are preferable to the synthesized ones, and the deserialization process will override the values you set in the handling of the deserializing event.

Consider, for example, this class version:

```
//Version 1.0
[Serializable]
public class MyClass
{
    public int Number1;
}
```

Suppose you want to add a new class member called `Number2`, while using the old serialization information. You need to provide handling to the deserializing event, and in it initialize `Number2`:

```
[Serializable]
public class MyClass
{
```

```
      public int Number1;
      [OptionalField]
      public int Number2;

      [OnDeserializing]
      void OnDeserializing(StreamingContext context)
      {
         Number2 = 123;
      }
}
```

But what if the values you synthesize are somehow dependent on the version of the class in which they are added? You can store version information in the OptionalField attribute, using its VersionAdded member:

```
[OptionalField(VersionAdded = 1)]
public int Number2;
```

In the deserializing event handler you will need to use reflection to read the value of the VersionAdded field and act accordingly, as shown in Example 9-11. This example uses the helper method OptionalFieldVersion( ) of the SerializationUtil static helper class. OptionalFieldVersion( ) accepts the type and the member variable name to reflect, returning the value of the VersionAdded field:

```
public static string OptionalFieldVersion(Type type,string member);
```

Example 9-11. Relying on VersionAdded

```
[Serializable]
public class MyClass
{
   public int Number1;

   [OptionalField(VersionAdded = 1)]
   public int Number2;

   [OnDeserializing]
   void OnDeserializing(StreamingContext context)
   {
      int versionAdded;
      versionAdded = SerializationUtil.OptionalFieldVersion(typeof(MyClass),
                                                    "Number2");

      if(versionAdded == 1)
         Number2 = 123;
      if(versionAdded == 2)
         Number2 = 456;
   }
}

public static class SerializationUtil
{
   public static int OptionalFieldVersion(Type type,string member)
   {
      Debug.Assert(type.IsSerializable);
```

Example 9-11. Relying on VersionAdded (continued)

```
        MemberInfo[] members = type.GetMember(member,BindingFlags.Instance |
                                                     BindingFlags.NonPublic|
                                                     BindingFlags.Public   |
                                                     BindingFlags.DeclaredOnly);
        Debug.Assert(members.Length == 1);
        object[] attributes =
    members[0].GetCustomAttributes(typeof(OptionalFieldAttribute),false);
        Debug.Assert(attributes.Length == 1);//Exactly one attribute is expected

        OptionalFieldAttribute attribute;
        attribute = attributes[0] as OptionalFieldAttribute;
        return attribute.VersionAdded;
    }
}
```

 The next version of the serialization infrastructure (a part of Indigo) will provide a formatter that is version-tolerant, as well as support for version-added information for the optional fields.

Serialization and Streams

Using a file stream isn't mandatory—you can serialize an object's state into any type of stream, such as a network or memory stream. Example 9-12 demonstrates how to serialize and deserialize an object to and from a memory stream, using the same definitions as in Example 9-4.

Example 9-12. Serialization and deserialization using a memory stream

```
MyClass obj = new MyClass();
obj.Number1 = 123;

IGenericFormatter formatter = new GenericBinaryFormatter();

//Create a memory stream
Stream stream = new MemoryStream();
using(stream)
{
    formatter.Serialize(stream,obj);

    obj = null;
    stream.Position = 0; //Seek to the start of the memory stream

    obj = formatter.Deserialize<MyClass>(stream);
}

Debug.Assert(obj.Number1 == 123);
```

.NET remoting uses a memory stream when marshaling an object by value across app domains. Marshaling by value is covered in Chapter 10.

You can actually use a memory stream to clone a serializable object, too. Example 9-13 shows the static Clone( ) method of the SerializationUtil static helper class.

Example 9-13. Cloning a serializable object

```
public static class SerializationUtil
{
   static public T Clone<T>(T source)
   {
      Debug.Assert(typeof(T).IsSerializable);

      IGenericFormatter formatter = new GenericBinaryFormatter( );
      Stream stream = new MemoryStream( );
      using(stream)
      {
         formatter.Serialize(stream,source);
         stream.Seek(0,SeekOrigin.Begin);

         T clone = formatter.Deserialize<T>(stream);
         return clone;
      }
   }
   //Rest of SerializationUtil
}
```

The Clone( ) method first verifies that the object passed in for cloning is serializable, by obtaining the type of the source object. The type Type provides a Boolean read-only property called IsSerializable, which returns true if the type has the Serializable attribute. Clone( ) then uses the GenericBinaryFormatter helper class to serialize and deserialize the object into and out of the memory stream. Clone( ) returns the deserialized object (in essence, a deep copy of the source object). Using Clone( ) is straightforward:

```
[Serializable]
public class MyClass
{...}

MyClass obj1 = new MyClass( );
MyClass obj2 = SerializationUtil.Clone(obj1);
```

> You can use SerializationUtil.Clone( ) as an easy way to implement
> the ICloneable interface:
>
> ```
> [Serializable]
> public class MyClass : ICloneable
> {
>     public object Clone( )
>     {
>         return SerializationUtil.Clone(this);
>     }
> }
> ```

Serializing Multiple Objects

A noteworthy aspect of using streams in serialization is that there are no limits to the
number of objects or types you can serialize into a stream. It all depends on the way
you manage the stream and the sequence in which you write and read the information. For example, to serialize additional objects into the same stream, all you need
to do is continue to write to the stream with the formatter. Of course, you have to
deserialize the objects in exactly the same order in which you serialized them, as
shown in Example 9-14. You can use the same formatter object or create a new one.

Example 9-14. Serializing multiple objects to the same stream

```
[Serializable]
public class MyClass
{...}
[Serializable]
public class MyOtherClass
{...}

MyClass obj1 = new MyClass( );
MyClass obj2 = new MyClass( );
MyOtherClass obj3 = new MyOtherClass( );

IGenericFormatter formatter = new GenericBinaryFormatter( );

Stream stream;
stream = new FileStream(@"C:\temp\obj.bin",FileMode.Create,FileAccess.Write);

using(stream)
{
   formatter.Serialize(stream,obj1);
   formatter.Serialize(stream,obj2);
   formatter.Serialize(stream,obj3);
}

obj1 = obj2 = null;
obj3 = null;
```

Example 9-14. Serializing multiple objects to the same stream (continued)

```
//Later on:
stream = new FileStream(@"C:\temp\obj.bin",FileMode.Open,FileAccess.Read);
using(stream)
{
   obj1 = formatter.Deserialize<MyClass>(stream);
   obj2 = formatter.Deserialize<MyClass>(stream);
   obj3 = formatter.Deserialize<MyOtherClass>(stream);
}
```

You can achieve a similar effect with memory streams, too, as long as the memory stream automatically allocates additional memory.

Another option is to append the state of additional objects to an existing storage. In the case of a file stream, open the file in append mode:

```
MyClass obj1 = new MyClass();
MyClass obj2 = new MyClass();

IGenericFormatter formatter = new GenericBinaryFormatter();

//Create a new file
Stream stream;
stream = new FileStream(@"C:\temp\obj.bin",FileMode.Create,FileAccess.Write);
using(stream)
{
   formatter.Serialize(stream,obj1);
}

//Append another object
stream = new FileStream(@"C:\temp\obj.bin",FileMode.Append,FileAccess.Write);
using(stream)
{
   formatter.Serialize(stream,obj2);
}
```

Custom Serialization

Sometimes, the default automatic serialization provided by the Serializable attribute is insufficient. Perhaps the object state contains sensitive information, such as a credit card number. In that case, you may want to encrypt the state instead of using a plain by-value serialization. Some other examples that might require custom serialization solutions are if you have some internal knowledge of how to serialize the event subscribers, if which members get serialized depends on the state of the object, or if you want to perform additional proprietary initialization steps during deserialization.

The ISerializable Interface

.NET provides an easy-to-use mechanism for custom serialization that extends the serialization infrastructure. To provide custom serialization and deserialization behavior, you need to implement the ISerializable interface, defined in the System.Runtime.Serialization namespace:

```
public interface ISerializable
{
    void GetObjectData(SerializationInfo info,StreamingContext context);
}
```

Every time a client serializes an object, .NET reflects the object's metadata to see whether the serializable object implements ISerializable. If it does, .NET calls GetObjectData( ) to retrieve the object's state. At this point, it's up to the object to provide the state information in whichever way it wants. You will see an example of implementing ISerializable shortly.

To support the matching custom deserialization, the object must provide a special parameterized *custom deserialization constructor* with this signature:

```
<Class Name>(SerializationInfo info,StreamingContext context);
```

.NET calls this constructor during deserialization. The constructor can (and should) be defined as protected to prevent normal clients from calling it. .NET uses reflection to invoke the custom deserialization constructor and thus isn't impeded by the constructor being protected. If the class implements the ISerializable interface but doesn't provide a custom deserialization constructor, the compiler doesn't warn you. Instead, during deserialization, .NET throws an exception of type SerializationException.

In .NET, interfaces aren't allowed to have any implementation details and therefore can't define constructors. The design decision the architects of .NET serialization took was to force a runtime check for the custom deserialization constructor, instead of a compile-time check. However, I believe a better design decision would have been to provide a SetObjectData( ) method on ISerializable and, during deserialization, to use reflection to set the fields of a new object.

Note that the client isn't required to treat an object that implements ISerializable any differently from an object that uses automatic serialization. Custom serialization is purely a component-side facility. The client uses the formatters and streams, as with automatic serialization.

Implementing ISerializable

Both GetObjectData( ) and the custom deserialization constructor accept a parameter of type SerializationInfo called info. SerializationInfo provides methods for getting or adding field values. Each field is identified by a string. Because SerializationInfo was defined before generics were available, SerializationInfo has type-safe methods for most of the CLR-defined types, such as int and string. For each such type, SerializationInfo provides two methods in this form:

```
void AddValue(string name, <Type> value);
<Type> Get<Type>(string name);
```

Here's an example:

```
public sealed class SerializationInfo
{
    public void AddValue(string name, short value);
    public void AddValue(string name, int value);
    //Other AddValue( ) methods

    public int    GetInt32(string name);
    public string GetString(string name);
    //Other Get<Type>( ) methods

    //Other methods and properties
}
```

For all other field types, SerializationInfo provides methods like these to add or get an object:

```
public void AddValue(string name, object value);
public object GetValue(string name, Type type);
```

The second parameter that both GetObjectData( ) and the custom deserialization constructor accept is the context parameter, of type StreamingContext. Example 9-15 demonstrates both ISerializable and the custom deserialization constructor. The way the class in Example 9-15 implements custom serialization has no advantage over automatic serialization; it simply shows how to provide custom serialization. It's up to you to provide the required custom steps.

Example 9-15. Implementing ISerializable

```
[Serializable]
public class MyClass : ISerializable
{
    int m_Number;
    string m_SomeString;
    public virtual void GetObjectData(SerializationInfo info,
                                      StreamingContext context)
    {
        info.AddValue("m_Number",m_Number);
        info.AddValue("m_SomeString",m_SomeString);
    }
    protected MyClass(SerializationInfo info,StreamingContext context)
    {
        m_Number = info.GetInt32("m_Number");
        m_SomeString = info.GetString("m_SomeString");
    }
```

Example 9-15. Implementing ISerializable (continued)

```
    public MyClass()
    {}
}
```

 When you implement ISerializable, the type must still be decorated with the Serializable attribute. Otherwise, .NET considers the type non-serializable and ignores ISerializable.

If the serialized class is a generic class, you need to use the AddValue( ) and GetValue( ) methods that accept an object while specifying the type, as shown in Example 9-16.

Example 9-16. Custom serialization of a generic class

```
[Serializable]
public class MyClass<T> : ISerializable
{
   T m_T;
   public MyClass()
   {}
   public void GetObjectData(SerializationInfo info,StreamingContext ctx)
   {
      info.AddValue("m_T",m_T,typeof(T));
   }
   protected MyClass(SerializationInfo info,StreamingContext context)
   {
      m_T = (T)info.GetValue("m_T",typeof(T));
   }
}
```

GenericSerializationInfo

The introduction of generics in .NET 2.0 allows you to improve on the available SerializationInfo and shield the client code from the type retrieval and explicit casting.

Example 9-17 presents the GenericSerializationInfo utility class, which exposes generic AddValue( ) and GetValue( ) methods. GenericSerializationInfo encapsulates a regular SerializationInfo object, passed to it as a construction parameter.

Example 9-17. The GenericSerializationInfo utility class

```
public class GenericSerializationInfo
{
   SerializationInfo m_SerializationInfo;
   public GenericSerializationInfo(SerializationInfo info)
   {
      m_SerializationInfo = info;
   }
   public void AddValue<T>(string name,T value)
   {
      m_SerializationInfo.AddValue(name,value,value.GetType());
```

Example 9-17. The GenericSerializationInfo utility class (continued)

```
    }
    public T GetValue<T>(string name)
    {
        object obj = m_SerializationInfo.GetValue(name,typeof(T));
        return (T)obj;
    }
}
```

Example 9-18 shows the same custom serialization code as Example 9-16, except it uses `GenericSerializationInfo`. Note the use of type inference in the call to `AddValue( )`.

Example 9-18. Using GenericSerializationInfo

```
[Serializable]
public class MyClass<T> : ISerializable
{
    T m_T;
    public MyClass( )
    {}
    public void GetObjectData(SerializationInfo info,StreamingContext ctx)
    {
        GenericSerializationInfo genericInfo = new GenericSerializationInfo(info);
        genericInfo.AddValue("m_T",m_T); //Using type inference
    }
    protected MyClass(SerializationInfo info,StreamingContext context)
    {
        GenericSerializationInfo genericInfo = new GenericSerializationInfo(info);
        m_T = genericInfo.GetValue<T>("m_T");
    }
}
```

`GenericSerializationInfo` is a cleaner way of using custom serialization, even on non-generic-type class members. For example, using `GenericSerializationInfo` in the class `MyClass` from Example 9-15, you could write:

```
    genericInfo.AddValue("m_SomeString",m_SomeString);
```

and:

```
    m_SomeString = genericInfo.GetValue<string>("m_SomeString");
```

Custom serialization and IDeserializationCallback

Implementing `IDeserializationCallback` allows a type to be notified after deserialization takes place and to perform additional, custom deserialization steps. You can implement both `IDeserializationCallback` and `ISerializable`, but when you implement `ISerializable` there is really no need for `IDeserializationCallback`, because you can place the custom steps in the custom deserialization constructor.

Custom serialization and serialization events

It is technically possible to use the serializing and deserializing events for custom serialization and avoid implementing ISerializable; however, this will come at a high price in programming model and code readability and maintainability. You will need to have a separate set of member variables, all marked as non-serializable. The type itself will use those members, and the serialization events will perform the custom steps (such as encryption or decryption) on the non-serializable members and then copy them to the set of serializable member variables, whose sole purpose will be to be serialized and deserialized. Needless to say, such an approach is cumbersome and error-prone. It is better to stick with the dedicated ISerializable standard mechanism.

Constraining Serialization

A generic class that has generic type parameters as members can still be marked for serialization:

```
[Serializable]
public class MyClass<T>
{
    T m_T;
}
```

However, in such cases the generic class is serializable only if the generic type parameter specified is serializable. Consider this code:

```
public class SomeClass
{}
MyClass<SomeClass> obj;
```

obj is not serializable, because the type parameter SomeClass is not serializable. Consequently, MyClass<T> may or may not be serializable, depending on the generic type parameter used. This may result in a run-time loss of data or system corruption, because the client application may not be able to persist the state of the object.

To make things even worse, the type parameter itself might be a generic type, whose own type parameters might not be serializable, and so on:

```
[Serializable]
public class MyClass<T>
{
    T m_T;
}
[Serializable]
public class SomeClass<T>
{}
public class SomeOtherClass
{}
//Will not work:
MyClass<SomeClass<SomeOtherClass>> obj;
```

Presently, .NET does not provide a mechanism for constraining a generic type parameter to be serializable. However, there are three workarounds to guarantee deterministic serialization behavior. The first is to mark all member variables of the generic type parameter as non-serializable:

```
[Serializable]
public class MyClass<T>
{
   [NonSerialized]
   T m_T;
}
```

Of course, this may seriously damage the generic class MyClass<T>'s ability to function properly, in the case where you do need to serialize the state of members of a generic type. The second workaround is to place a constraint on the generic type parameter to implement ISerializable:

```
[Serializable]
public class MyClass<T> where T : ISerializable
{
   T m_T;
}
```

This ensures that all instances of MyClass<T>, regardless of the type parameter, are serializable, but it places the burden of implementing custom serialization on all generic type parameters used. The third and best solution is to perform a single runtime check before any use of the type MyClass<T> and abort the use immediately, before any damage can take place. The trick is to place the runtime verification in the C# static constructor. Example 9-19 demonstrates this technique.

Example 9-19. Runtime enforcement of generic type parameter serialization

```
[Serializable]
class MyClass<T>
{
   T m_T;
   static MyClass()
   {
      SerializationUtil.ConstrainType(typeof(T));
   }
}
public static class SerializationUtil
{
   public static void ConstrainType(Type type)
   {
      bool serializable = type.IsSerializable;
      if(serializable == false)
      {
         string message = "The type " + type + " is not serializable";
         throw new SerializationException(message);
      }
      bool genericType = type.IsGenericType;
```

Example 9-19. Runtime enforcement of generic type parameter serialization (continued)

```
      if(genericType)
      {
         Type[] typeArguments = type.GetGenericArguments();
         Debug.Assert(typeArguments.Length >= 1);
         Array.ForEach(typeArguments,ConstrainType);
      }
   }
   //Rest of SerializationUtil
}
```

The C# static constructor is invoked exactly once per type per app domain, upon the first attempt to instantiate an object of that type. In Example 9-19, the static constructor calls the static helper method `ConstrainType()` of `SerializationUtil`. `ConstrainType()` then verifies that the specified type is serializable by checking the `IsSerializable` property of the type. If the type is not serializable, `ConstrainType()` throws a `SerializationException`, thus aborting any attempt to use the type.

To deal with the issue of having generic types as type parameters, `ConstrainType` checks if the type in question is a generic type. If so, it obtains an array of all its type parameters, and recursively calls itself verifying that each type parameter down the declaration chain is serializable.

> Performing the constraint verification in the static constructor is a technique applicable to any constraint that you cannot enforce at compile time yet have some programmatic way of determining and enforcing at runtime.

Serialization and Class Hierarchies

When you apply the `Serializable` attribute to a class, it affects only that class—it doesn't make any derived classes serializable, because the `Inherited` property of the `AttributeUsage` attribute applied on the `Serializable` attribute is set to `false`. For example, if you derive `MyClass` from `MyBaseClass`, `MyClass` isn't serializable:

```
[Serializable]
public class MyBaseClass
{}
public class MyClass : MyBaseClass
{}
```

At first glance this may appear awkward, but it does make design sense: `MyBaseClass` has no way of knowing whether its subclasses will have non-serializable members, so it would be wrong for them to automatically inherit the serializable status. If you design a class hierarchy and you want to support serialization of any type in the hierarchy, be sure to mark each level with the `Serializable` attribute:

```
[Serializable]
public class MyBaseClass
```

```
{}
[Serializable]
public class MyClass : MyBaseClass
{}
[Serializable]
public class MyOtherClass : MyClass
{}
```

Custom Serialization and Base Classes

If any of the classes in the hierarchy implements ISerializable, there are a few design guidelines you have to follow to allow subclasses to provide their own custom serialization and to correctly manage the custom serialization of the base classes:

- Only the topmost base class that uses custom serialization needs to derive from ISerializable.

- When using implicit interface implementation, a base class must define its GetObjectData( ) method as virtual to allow subclasses to override it. When using explicit interface implementation, follow the technique shown in Chapter 3 for combining explicit interface implementation and a class hierarchy.

- In a subclass implementation of GetObjectData( ), after serializing its own state, the subclass must call its base class's implementation of GetObjectData( ).

- In its implementation of the deserializing constructor, the subclass must call its base class's deserializing constructor.

- The deserializing constructor should be protected, to allow a subclass to call its base class's deserializing constructor.

Example 9-20 demonstrates how to implement these points; you can use it as a template for combining custom serialization and class hierarchies.

Example 9-20. Combining custom serialization with a class hierarchy

```
[Serializable]
public class MyBaseClass : ISerializable
{
   public MyBaseClass( )
   {}
   int m_BaseNumber;
   public virtual void GetObjectData(SerializationInfo info,
                                     StreamingContext context)
   {
     //Add MyBaseClass members
     GenericSerializationInfo genericInfo = new GenericSerializationInfo(info);
     genericInfo.AddValue("m_BaseNumber",m_BaseNumber);
   }
   protected MyBaseClass(SerializationInfo info,StreamingContext context)
   {
     //Read MyBaseClass members and initialize them
     GenericSerializationInfo genericInfo = new GenericSerializationInfo(info);
```

Example 9-20. Combining custom serialization with a class hierarchy (continued)

```
        m_BaseNumber = genericInfo.GetValue<int>("m_BaseNumber");
   }
}

[Serializable]
public class MySubClass : MyBaseClass
{
   public MySubClass()
   {}
   int m_SubNumber;
   public override void GetObjectData(SerializationInfo info,
                                      StreamingContext context)
   {
      //Add MySubClass members
      GenericSerializationInfo genericInfo = new GenericSerializationInfo(info);
      genericInfo.AddValue("m_SubNumber",m_SubNumber);
      base.GetObjectData(info,context);
   }
   protected MySubClass(SerializationInfo info,StreamingContext context):
                                                     base(info,context)
   {
      //Read MySubClass members and initialize them
      GenericSerializationInfo genericInfo = new GenericSerializationInfo(info);
      m_SubNumber = genericInfo.GetValue<int>("m_SubNumber");
   }
}
```

 If a base class provides custom serialization, all subclasses derived from it can use only custom serialization.

Manual Base-Class Serialization

Combining class hierarchies and serialization, whether fully automatic or custom, is straightforward: all classes either use only the Serializable attribute, or use the attribute and also implement ISerializable. However, the picture isn't so clear when it comes to deriving a serializable class from a class not marked with the Serializable attribute, as in this case:

```
public class MyBaseClass
{}
[Serializable]
public class MySubClass : MyBaseClass
{}
```

In fact, in such a case, .NET can't serialize objects of type MySubClass at all, because it can't serialize their base classes. Trying to serialize an object of type MySubClass results in an exception of type SerializationException. Such a situation may occur when deriving from a class in a third-party assembly where the vendor neglected to mark its class as serializable.

The good news is that there is a workaround for such a case. The solution presented here isn't a sure cure, because it assumes that none of the base classes require custom serialization steps. It merely compensates for the oversight of not marking the base class as serializable.

The workaround is simple: the subclass can implement ISerializable, use reflection to read and serialize the base classes' fields, and use reflection again to set these fields during deserialization. The static SerializationUtil helper class provides the two static methods SerializeBaseType( ) and DeserializeBaseType( ), defined as:

```
public static class SerializationUtil
{
    public static void SerializeBaseType(object obj,
                                SerializationInfo info,
                                StreamingContext context);
    public static void DeserializeBaseType(object obj,
                                SerializationInfo info,
                                StreamingContext context);

    //Rest of SerializationUtil
}
```

All the subclass needs to do is implement ISerializable and use SerializationUtil to serialize and deserialize its base classes:

```
public class MyBaseClass
{}
[Serializable]
public class MySubClass : MyBaseClass,ISerializable
{
    public MySubClass( )
    {}
    public void GetObjectData(SerializationInfo info,StreamingContext context)
    {
        SerializationUtil.SerializeBaseType(this,info,context);
    }
    protected MySubClass(SerializationInfo info,StreamingContext context)
    {
        SerializationUtil.DeserializeBaseType(this,info,context);
    }
}
```

If the subclass itself has no need for custom serialization and only implements ISerializable to serialize its base class, you can use SerializationUtil to serialize the subclass as well. SerializationUtil provides these overloaded versions of SerializeBaseType( ) and DeserializeBaseType( ):

```
public static void SerializeBaseType(object obj,bool serializeSelf,
                                SerializationInfo info,
                                StreamingContext context);
public static void DeserializeBaseType(object obj,bool deserializeSelf,
                                SerializationInfo info,
                                StreamingContext context);
```

These versions accept a flag instructing them whether to start serialization with the type itself instead of its base class:

```
public void GetObjectData(SerializationInfo info,StreamingContext context)
{
   //Serializing this type and its base classes
   SerializationUtil.SerializeBaseType(this,true,info,context);
}
protected MyClass(SerializationInfo info,StreamingContext context)
{
   //Deserializing this type and its base classes
   SerializationUtil.DeserializeBaseType(this,true,info,context);
}
```

 SerializationUtil is also useful in cases where a class needs to provide custom serialization, even though simple use of the Serializable attribute would have sufficed for that class. This may occur because, as mentioned previously, if any class in a class hierarchy provides custom serialization, all its subclasses must do so as well. It can also occur when a type is constrained to implement Iserializable, to be used as a generic type parameter in a generic class.

Example 9-21 demonstrates the implementations of SerializeBaseType and DeserializeBaseType.

Example 9-21. Implementing SerializeBaseType and DeserializeBaseType

```
public static class SerializationUtil
{
   public static void SerializeBaseType(object obj,
                              SerializationInfo info,StreamingContext context)
   {
      Type baseType = obj.GetType( ).BaseType;
      SerializeBaseType(obj,baseType,info,context);
   }
   static void SerializeBaseType(object obj,Type type,SerializationInfo info,
                                              StreamingContext context)
   {
      if(type == typeof(object))
      {
         return;
      }
      BindingFlags flags = BindingFlags.Instance|BindingFlags.DeclaredOnly|
                     BindingFlags.NonPublic|BindingFlags.Public;
      FieldInfo[] fields = type.GetFields(flags);
      foreach(FieldInfo field in fields)
      {
         if(field.IsNotSerialized)
         {
            continue;
         }
         string fieldName = type.Name + "+" + field.Name;
```

Example 9-21. Implementing SerializeBaseType and DeserializeBaseType (continued)

```
            info.AddValue(fieldName,field.GetValue(obj));
        }
        SerializeBaseType(obj,type.BaseType,info,context);
    }
    public static void DeserializeBaseType(object obj,SerializationInfo info,
                                                    StreamingContext context)
    {
        Type baseType = obj.GetType( ).BaseType;
        DeserializeBaseType(obj,baseType,info,context);
    }
    static void DeserializeBaseType(object obj,Type type,SerializationInfo info,
                                                    StreamingContext context)

    {
        if(type == typeof(object))
        {
            return;
        }
        BindingFlags flags = BindingFlags.Instance|BindingFlags.DeclaredOnly|
                            BindingFlags.NonPublic|BindingFlags.Public;
        FieldInfo[] fields = type.GetFields(flags);
        foreach(FieldInfo field in fields)
        {
            if(field.IsNotSerialized)
            {
                continue;
            }
            string fieldName = type.Name + "+" + field.Name;
            object fieldValue = info.GetValue(fieldName,field.FieldType);
            field.SetValue(obj,fieldValue);
        }
        DeserializeBaseType(obj,type.BaseType,info,context);
    }
    //Rest of SerializationUtil
}
```

When `SerializationUtil` serializes an object's base class, it needs to serialize all the base classes leading to that base class as well. You can access the base-class type using the BaseType property of Type:

```
Type baseType = obj.GetType( ).BaseType;
```

With the `GetFields( )` method of Type, you can get all the fields (private and public) declared by the type, as well as any public or protected fields available via its own base classes. This isn't good enough for serialization, though, because you need to capture all the private fields available from all levels of the class hierarchy, including ones with the same name. The solution is to serialize each level of the class hierarchy separately and thus access each level's private fields. `SerializeBaseType( )` calls a private helper method, also called `SerializeBaseType( )`, providing it with the level of the class hierarchy to serialize:

```
SerializeBaseType(obj,baseType,info,context);
```

The private SerializeBaseType( ) serializes that level and then calls itself recursively, serializing the next level up the hierarchy:

```
SerializeBaseType(obj,type.BaseType,info,context);
```

The recursion stops once it reaches the System.Object level:

```
static void SerializeBaseType(object obj,Type type,SerializationInfo info,
                        StreamingContext context)
{
    if(type == typeof(object))
    {
        return;
    }
    /* Rest of the implementation */
}
```

To serialize a particular level, the private SerializeBaseType( ) calls GetFields( ) with a binding flags mask (BindingFlags.DeclaredOnly), which instructs it to return all fields defined by this type only and not its base types. This ensures that as it visits the next levels up the hierarchy, it doesn't end up serializing fields more than once. It also binds to instance and not static fields, because static fields are never serialized:

```
BindingFlags flags = BindingFlags.Instance|BindingFlags.DeclaredOnly|
                    BindingFlags.NonPublic|BindingFlags.Public;
```

The private SerializeBaseType( ) then calls GetFields( ) and stores the result in an array of FieldInfo objects:

```
FieldInfo[] fields = type.GetFields(flags);
```

This solution needs to deal with a class hierarchy in which some levels actually use the Serializable attribute, such as class A in this example:

```
[Serializable]
class A
{}
class B : A
{}
[Serializable]
class C : B,ISerializable
{...}
```

Because class A may contain some fields marked with the NonSerialized attribute, the solution needs to check that the fields are serializable. This is easy to do via the IsNotSerialized Boolean property of FieldInfo:

```
foreach(FieldInfo field in fields)
{
    if(field.IsNotSerialized)
    {
        continue;
    }
    //Rest of the iteration loop
}
```

Since different levels can declare private fields with the same names in the same class hierarchy, the private SerializeBaseType( ) prefixes each field name with its declaring type separated by a +:

```
string fieldName = type.Name + "+" + field.Name;
```

The value of a field is obtained via the GetValue( ) method of FieldInfo and is then added to the info parameter:

```
info.AddValue(fieldName,field.GetValue(obj));
```

Deserialization of the base class (or classes) is similar to serialization and is also done recursively until the System.Object level is reached. The public DeserializeBaseType( ) method accesses the base type and calls the private helper method DeserializeBaseType( ). At each level in the class hierarchy, the private DeserializeBaseType( ) retrieves the collection of fields for that type. For each field, it creates a name by appending the name of the current level to the name of the field, gets the value from info, and sets the value of the corresponding field, using the SetValue( ) method of the FieldInfo class:

```
string fieldName = type.Name + "+" + field.Name;
object fieldValue =
info.GetValue(fieldName,field.FieldType);field.SetValue(obj,fieldValue);
```

CHAPTER 10

Remoting

Modern applications are no longer isolated, standalone entities limited to a single process or machine. Distributed applications allow you to put components in close proximity to the resources they use, let multiple users access the application, improve scalability and throughput, and increase overall availability and fault isolation. It's difficult to imagine a modern distributed application without components. Component-oriented programming is especially geared toward distribution, because it's all about breaking the application into a set of interacting components that you can then distribute to different locations.

This chapter shows how to access remote .NET components using a technology called *.NET remoting*. Remoting is related to .NET as DCOM is to COM in its ability to connect to components on remote machines, and like DCOM, .NET remoting can also access components in other processes (similar to COM's local servers). .NET remoting is a vast topic. Although each facet of remoting is simple enough, there are a multitude of terms and details to master before you can build even a simple distributed application. Nevertheless, this richness offers a highly flexible programming model.

This chapter begins by explaining the fundamental concepts of remoting and the key elements of the .NET remoting architecture. You will then see how to apply .NET remoting, in a set of comprehensive code samples. Like most things in .NET, there are many ways to achieve the same result. The emphasis in this chapter is on understanding the basic concepts, the trade-offs you face in using them, and the practical aspects of using remoting. Without going into every nook and cranny, but armed with an understanding of the basics of remoting you can go after the more esoteric features if the need ever arises.

The main advantage of remoting is that it is an extensible open architecture, as opposed to technologies like DCOM. You will see some very useful examples of this extensibility in the next chapter. If you do not need the extensibility, you should consider using Enterprise Services for intranet connectivity or web services for opening your application as a service to the Internet, instead of remoting.

Application Domains

All .NET components and applications require a managed environment to run in. However, the underlying operating system knows nothing about managed code; it provides processes only. Processes are also unaware that .NET exists; they provide raw elements such as memory, handle tables, and so on. Managed code therefore can't execute directly in the native operating system process—there is a need for a bridge between managed code and unmanaged code. The bridging link is a concept called an *application domain*, or *app domain*. You can think of the app domain as the .NET equivalent of a process, with one important difference: an app domain is built on top of the unmanaged process, and there is no requirement for one-to-one mapping between app domains and operating system processes. As a result, a single physical process can actually host multiple app domains (see Figure 10-1).

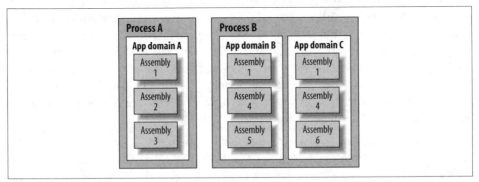

Figure 10-1. Processes, app domains, and assemblies

App Domains Versus Physical Processes

App domains are better perceived as *logical* processes, instead of real processes. The fact that a single physical process can host multiple app domains yields important benefits. The main reason why developers resorted to multiple processes in the past was to provide fault isolation. If all the components of an application and their clients are in the same process and a component has a fatal error that crashes the process, it brings down the entire application, including the clients. Similarly, if the client has a fatal error, the components go down with it. By distributing the clients and servers of an application to separate processes, an application achieves fault isolation—in the event of a fault only the culprit process goes down, allowing you to handle the error or perform a graceful exit.

Another reason for distributing the components of an application across processes is security. Server objects are often called on to authenticate incoming client calls or to perform access control and authorization before allowing a given call to access a component. Having separate processes allows for separate security identifiers for each process and for the enforcement of authentication on cross-process calls. Unfortunately, however, there are significant penalties to using multiple processes:

- Creating a new process is time-consuming, as is the disposal of an existing process.

- Keeping a process running is expensive, both in terms of memory and of the resources the operating system allocates to each process. Having too many processes running can significantly degrade system performance.

- Making a cross-process call involves a call penalty, because crossing a process boundary is very expensive compared to making a direct call. Cross-process calls rely on special mechanisms such as named pipes, sockets, and LPC/RPC.

- Coding is more complex—the client's code for making a direct local call on an object is very different from that of making the same call on the object in a different process.

Compared with traditional unmanaged processes, .NET app domains can provide single-process performance with lower overhead. They can also provide the isolation and other benefits of multiple processes, even if they share the same physical process. You can start and shut down app domains independently of their hosting processes, and you can even debug them separately. For example, all ASP.NET web applications share the same physical worker process by default, but each web application is put in its own dedicated app domain. The time it takes to create or destroy an app domain is a fraction of that required for a physical process, and keeping an app domain alive is considerably cheaper. Furthermore, cross–app domain calls in the same process are faster than cross-process calls. .NET also maintains a strict security boundary between app domains, so objects in one app domain can't interfere with the objects (or data) in another, unless the objects agree to cooperate using .NET remoting.

 In unmanaged C++, static variables are visible to all clients in the same process. In C#, each app domain gets its own separate set of static variables.

In the interest of fault isolation and security, each app domain loads and maintains its own set of assemblies. Consider, for example, the app domains in Figure 10-1. Because App Domain B and App Domain C require the class library *Assembly 1*, on Windows .NET loads *Assembly 1* twice and gives each app domain its own copy. This allows clients in each app domain to interact with *Assembly 1* independently of other clients in other app domains.

App Domains and the .NET Platform

The .NET runtime itself is a set of Windows DLLs, implemented in unmanaged C++. These DLLs provide the managed heap, garbage collector, JIT compiler, assembly resolver and loader, and all the other elements that make managed code possible. The app domain merely enables the assemblies it loads to access these services (see Figure 10-2)—in effect, this is how the app domain bridges the unmanaged world and the managed world. However, it's important to note that all app domains in the same process share the same managed heap.

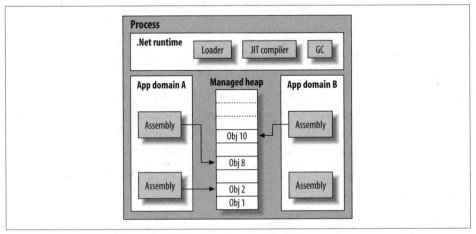

Figure 10-2. App domains provide their assemblies with access to the .NET runtime services

 Sharing the same heap has security implications, which are addressed in Chapter 12.

App domains and threads

.NET managed threads have no app domain affinity, meaning that a thread can enter and exit any app domain that runs in the same underlying process. Typically, when you create a thread in your app domain, that thread executes a thread method and accesses only local objects. However, nothing prevents you from having threads created in one app domain access objects in another app domain in the same process. There is one detail you need to be aware of, though: when an app domain shuts down (i.e., when `AppDomain.Unload( )` is called), it terminates all the threads that happen to be calling objects in it by calling `Thread.Abort( )` on each of them.

App Domains and Remoting

Like traditional cross-process calls, you make cross–app domain calls using *remoting*, a programmatic act that accesses an object outside its hosting app domain. .NET uses exactly the same remote-call architecture for all cases, whether the cross–app domain call is between two app domains in the same process, between app domains in two different processes on the same machine, or between app domains on two separate machines (see Figure 10-3).

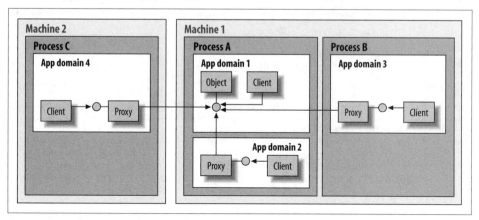

Figure 10-3. All cross–app domain calls use remoting

 Accessing an object outside its context in the same app domain is a special case of remoting and is discussed in Chapter 11.

Clients in the same app domain as the called object can each have a direct reference to the object (see Figure 10-3). Clients in a different app domain use a proxy to connect to the object. A *proxy* is an object that provides exactly the same interfaces, public methods, properties, and members as the real object. .NET generates the proxy on the fly, based on the object's metadata. Even though the proxy has the same public entry points as the object, it can't serve the clients because the object's actual code and state reside only where the object is. All the proxy knows is how to bind to the object and forward the calls made on the proxy to the object. Forwarding a call to an object is called *marshaling*. Marshaling is a nontrivial feat: its end goal is to provide the client with the illusion that it's calling a local object and to provide the server with the illusion that it's servicing a local client. Neither the server nor the client explicitly uses remote mechanisms such as pipes, RPC, or sockets, because these details are encapsulated in the proxy. .NET does require, however, that if an object is accessed by proxy, the object's class must derive directly or indirectly from the abstract class `MarshalByRefObject`. You will learn more about marshaling and how it relates to the .NET remoting architecture later in this chapter.

The AppDomain Class

.NET represents app domains with the AppDomain class, which provides numerous methods for loading assemblies, creating objects from those assemblies, and configuring app domain security. You can get hold of an object representing the app domain within which your component code is currently running by accessing the static property CurrentDomain of the AppDomain class:

```
AppDomain currentAppDomain;
currentAppDomain = AppDomain.CurrentDomain;
```

Alternatively, you can call the GetDomain( ) static method of the Thread class, which also returns an AppDomain object representing the current domain:

```
AppDomain currentAppDomain;
currentAppDomain = Thread.GetDomain( );
```

Every app domain has a readable name. Use the FriendlyName read-only property of the AppDomain class to obtain the name of the app domain:

```
AppDomain currentAppDomain;
currentAppDomain = AppDomain.CurrentDomain;

Trace.WriteLine(currentAppDomain.FriendlyName);
```

The default app domain

Every unmanaged process hosting .NET components is created by launching a .NET EXE assembly, such as a console application, a Windows Forms application, or a Windows Service application. Each such EXE has a Main( ) method, which is the entry point to the new app domain in the process. When the EXE is launched, .NET creates a new app domain called the *default app domain*. The name of the default app domain is that of the hosting EXE assembly (such as *MyApp.exe*). The default app domain cannot be unloaded, and it remains running throughout the life of the hosting process. For diagnostic purposes, you can verify whether your code executes in the default app domain using the IsDefaultAppDomain( ) method of the AppDomain class:

```
AppDomain currentAppDomain;
currentAppDomain = AppDomain.CurrentDomain;
Debug.Assert(currentAppDomain.IsDefaultAppDomain( ));
```

 As mentioned in Chapter 2, when debugging inside Visual Studio 2005, the EXE assembly is actually loaded in the VSHost process. Consequently, in a debug session of the *MyApp.exe* assembly, the default app domain's name will be *MyApp.vshost.exe*.

Creating objects in app domains

The AppDomain class offers a few permutations of a CreateInstance( ) method that allows you to explicitly create a new instance of any type in the app domain. For example, one of the versions of CreateInstance( ) is called CreateInstanceAndUnwrap( ), defined as:

```
public object CreateInstanceAndUnwrap(string assemblyName, string typeName);
```

CreateInstanceAndUnwrap( ) accepts an assembly filename and a fully qualified type name. CreateInstanceAndUnwrap( ) then creates an instance of the type and returns an object representing it. Example 10-1 demonstrates CreateInstanceAndUnwrap( ).

 When you specify an assembly name to any of the methods of AppDomain, the calling assembly must reference the assembly being specified.

Example 10-1. Explicitly creating an object in the current app domain

```
//In the MyClassLibrary.dll assembly:
namespace MyNamespace
{
    public class MyClass
    {
        public void TraceAppDomain( )
        {
            AppDomain currentAppDomain;
            currentAppDomain = AppDomain.CurrentDomain;

            Console.WriteLine(currentAppDomain.FriendlyName);
        }
    }
}

//In the MyApp.exe assembly:
using MyNamespace;

public class MyClient
{
    static void Main( )
    {
        AppDomain currentAppDomain;
        currentAppDomain = AppDomain.CurrentDomain;
        Console.WriteLine(currentAppDomain.FriendlyName);

        MyClass obj;
        obj = (MyClass)currentAppDomain.CreateInstanceAndUnwrap("MyClassLibrary",
                                                    "MyNamespace.MyClass");
        obj.TraceAppDomain( );
    }
}
//Output:
MyApp.exe //Traces MyApp.vshost.exe when running in the debugger
```

In this example, a class called MyClass is defined in the MyNamespace namespace in the *MyClassLibrary.dll* class library assembly. MyClass provides the TraceAppDomain( ) method, which traces the name of its current app domain to the Console window. The client is in a separate EXE assembly called *MyApp.exe*. The client obtains its current AppDomain object and traces its name. When running outside the debugger, the trace yields MyApp.exe—the name of the default app domain. Next, instead of creating an instance of MyClass directly using new, the client calls CreateInstanceAndUnwrap( ), providing the assembly name and the fully qualified type name. When the client calls the TraceAppDomain( ) method on the new MyClass object, the object traces MyApp.exe to the Console window because it shares the app domain of the client (the default app domain, in this example).

The client can use CreateInstanceAndUnwrap( ) to create types defined in its own assembly, by providing its own assembly name. Note that CreateInstanceAndUnwrap( ) uses the default constructor of the object. To provide construction parameters you need to use another version of CreateInstanceAndUnwrap( ), which accepts an array of construction parameters:

```
public object CreateInstanceAndUnwrap(string assemblyName, string typeName,
                                      object[] activationAttributes);
```

The client can also specify explicitly how to bind to the server assembly, using yet another overloaded version of CreateInstanceAndUnwrap( ).

 Interacting with app domains is usually required by framework vendors who want to explicitly create new app domains and load assemblies and types into them. I find that during conventional development I need to interact with app domains only to configure security policies or for advanced security purposes. For example, Chapter 12 uses the current AppDomain object to set an authorization policy to take advantage of .NET role-based security, and Appendix B uses the AppDomain object to change the default security principal.

Creating a new app domain

You typically create new app domains for the same reasons you create processes in traditional Windows development: to provide fault isolation and security isolation. The AppDomain class provides the static CreateDomain( ) method, which allows you to create new app domains:

```
public static AppDomain CreateDomain(string friendlyName);
```

CreateDomain( ) creates a new app domain in the same process and returns an AppDomain object representing the new app domain. The new app domain must be given a new name when you call CreateDomain( ).

The AppDomain type is derived from MarshalByRefObject. Deriving from MarshalByRefObject allows .NET to pass a reference to the AppDomain object outside its app domain boundaries. When you create a new app domain using the CreateDomain( ) method, .NET creates a new app domain, retrieves a reference to the AppDomain object, and marshals it back to your current domain.

Example 10-2 demonstrates how to create a new app domain and then instantiate a new object in the new app domain.

Example 10-2. Creating a new app domain and a new object in it

```
//In the MyClassLibrary.dll assembly:

namespace MyNamespace
{
    public class MyClass : MarshalByRefObject
    {
        public void TraceAppDomain( )
        {
            AppDomain currentAppDomain;
            currentAppDomain = AppDomain.CurrentDomain;

            Console.WriteLine(currentAppDomain.FriendlyName);
        }
    }
}


//In the MyApp.exe assembly:
using MyNamespace;

public class MyClient
{
    static void Main( )
    {
        AppDomain currentAppDomain;
        currentAppDomain = AppDomain.CurrentDomain;
        Console.WriteLine(currentAppDomain.FriendlyName);

        AppDomain newAppDomain;
        newAppDomain = AppDomain.CreateDomain("My new AppDomain");
        MyClass obj;
        obj = (MyClass)newAppDomain.CreateInstanceAndUnwrap("MyClassLibrary",
                                                "MyNamespace.MyClass");
        obj.TraceAppDomain( );
    }
}
//Output:
MyApp.exe //Or MyApp.vshost.exe when running in the debugger
My new AppDomain
```

Example 10-2 is similar to Example 10-1, with a few notable exceptions. The class MyClass is derived from MarshalByRefObject, so you can access it across app domains. The client traces its own app domain name (MyApp.exe) and then creates a new app domain using the CreateDomain( ) static method. As in Example 10-1, the client creates a new object of type MyClass in the new app domain and asks it to trace its app domain. When the program is executed, the name My new AppDomain is displayed in the console, confirming that the object is in the newly created app domain.

Unwrapping remote objects

You're probably wondering why the word Unwrap is appended to the CreateInstanceAndUnwrap( ) method. As already mentioned, accessing a remote object is done through a proxy. For optimization purposes, .NET separates the act of creating an object from the act of setting up a proxy on the client side. This allows you to create a remote object and set up the proxy later. The AppDomain class provides a set of CreateInstance( ) methods that create a new object but return a handle to the remote object in the form of ObjectHandle:

```
public virtual ObjectHandle CreateInstance(string assemblyName, string typeName);
```

ObjectHandle is defined in the System.Runtime.Remoting namespace. It implements the IObjectHandle interface:

```
public interface IObjectHandle
{
   object Unwrap( );
}
public class ObjectHandle : MarshalByRefObject,IObjectHandle
{
    public ObjectHandle(object obj);
    public virtual object Unwrap( );
}
```

The Unwrap( ) method sets up the proxy on the client side. You can actually unwrap a handle multiple times, either by the same client or by different clients. Using the same object definitions as Example 10-2, here is how to unwrap an object handle:

```
AppDomain newAppDomain;
IObjectHandle  handle;
MyClass obj;

newAppDomain = AppDomain.CreateDomain("My new AppDomain");
handle = newAppDomain.CreateInstance("MyClassLibrary","MyNamespace.MyClass");

//Only now a proxy is set up:
obj = (MyClass)handle.Unwrap( );
obj.TraceAppDomain( );
```

Typically, there is no need to manually unwrap object handles. .NET provides the option for the advanced case in which you want to pass the handle between clients in different app domains, instead of the object itself. As a result, the client can defer loading the assembly containing the object metadata (a required step when setting up a proxy) until the client actually needs to use the object.

The Host App Domain

.NET calls the app domain that contains the server object the *host* app domain. The host app domain can be in the same process as the client app domain, in a different process on the same machine, or on a different machine altogether. To qualify as a host, the app domain must register itself as such with .NET, letting .NET know which objects the host is willing to accept remote calls on, and in what manner. Because .NET is aware of the host only after registration, the host must be running before remote calls are issued. The available hosting options are discussed later in this chapter.

 COM differed from .NET in that if calls were made to a hosting process that was not running, COM would launch it and let it host objects. New COM activation requests would then be redirected to the already running process. COM could do that because the Registry held the registration information regarding which process to launch and because once the process was running, it registered the objects it was hosting programmatically. .NET doesn't use the Registry (hence the limitation).

Both the client and the host app domains require access to the server assembly. The client app domain needs the server metadata to compile against, and at runtime .NET requires the server assembly on the client side so it can reflect its metadata and build a proxy. The IL code in the assembly isn't required at compile time or at runtime on the client's side. The host app domain requires the server assembly at runtime to create the hosted components and for call-marshaling purposes. If the host is doing programmatic registration (discussed later in this chapter), that host must have access to the server assembly at compile time as well.

Unless you explicitly create a new app domain in your own process (as in Example 10-2), the host app domain will be in a different process, in the form of an EXE assembly. You could put the server code in the same EXE as the host and have the client application add a reference to the host directly. However, that would make it more complicated for the client to use the same remote type when other hosts are hosting that type. The common solution to this problem is to separate the host, the server, and the client to different assemblies: the host resides in an EXE assembly, the server in a class library assembly, and the client application in a different class library or EXE assembly. That way, the client can use the metadata in the server class library at compile time and redirect the remote calls to any host that loads the same server class library. At runtime, the client loads the class library only to use its metadata; again, it has no need for the code in it. The host assembly uses the server assembly's metadata at compile time if it uses programmatic object registration; at runtime, the host uses both the metadata and the code in the server assembly to host the class library objects. Figure 10-4 depicts what the client and the host require of the server class library assembly at compile time and at runtime.

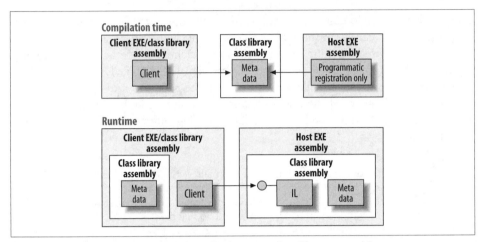

Figure 10-4. Client and host requirements for the server class library assembly

 Making a class library DLL available to remote clients by hosting it in an EXE host is analogous to providing a surrogate process to a COM in-process DLL. In fact, the canonical COM surrogate process is called *dllhost.exe*.

Remote Object Types

If the referenced object is in the same app domain as the client, usually no proxies are involved, and the client will hold a direct reference to the object. The question is, what happens when you try to call methods on a remote object in another app domain? By default, objects are not accessible from outside their own app domains, even if the call is made from another app domain in the same process. The rationale behind this decision is that .NET must first enforce app domain isolation and security. If you intend your objects to be accessed from outside their app domains, you must allow this explicitly in your design and class definition. .NET provides two options for accessing an object across an app domain boundary: *by value* or *by reference*. Accessing an object by value means that when a client in App Domain 2 calls a method on an object in App Domain 1, the object is first copied to App Domain 2, so the client gets its own cloned copy of the object. Once a copy is transferred to the remote client, the two objects are distinct and can change state independently. Any change made to the object's state in App Domain 2 applies only to that local copy, which is completely separate from the original object. This is often referred to as *marshaling by value* and is similar to the analogous behavior in COM. The second way to access a remote object is by reference. In this case, the remote clients hold only a reference to the object, in the form of a proxy. Access by reference is often referred to as *marshaling by reference* (which was the standard behavior provided by COM).

Marshaling by Value

When an object is marshaled by value, .NET must make a copy of the object's state, transfer the state to the calling app domain, and build up a new object based on that state. There are some difficulties, however. .NET needs to know which parts of the object's state can be marshaled by value and which parts can't. .NET has to obtain the state of an existing object and then build a new object based on that state. And what if the object also wants to provide some custom marshaling-by-value mechanism? Luckily, .NET already has the infrastructure to handle such issues: serialization. The requirements for marshaling by value and for generic serialization are identical. To marshal an object by value, all .NET has to do is serialize the object to a stream and deserialize the object in the remote app domain. As a result, to enable marshaling by value, the component must be serializable. As explained in Chapter 9, serializable components can either use the Serializable attribute or implement the ISerializable interface for custom serialization. For example, consider the following class definition:

```
[Serializable]
public class MyClass
{
    public int Number;
}
```

Suppose an instance of this class has 3 as the value of the Number member and is accessed across an app domain boundary by a remote client. .NET marshals the object by value and gives the remote client a copy of the object. Immediately after marshaling, the cloned object has 3 as the value of the Number member (see Figure 10-5). When the remote client in App Domain 3 assigns the value 4 to Number, this assignment affects only its own new and distinct copy. Marshaling by value works across any app domain boundary, be it in the same process or across machines.

The primary use for marshaling by value is when you want to pass a structure as a method parameter. Typically, structures are used as data containers and have no logic associated with them. Structures are very useful as method parameters, but unless a struct is serializable, you can't use it as a parameter to a remote call.

When you marshal a struct by value to a remote object, you actually get the same semantics as with a local object because value types are, by default, passed in by value:

```
[Serializable]
public struct MyPoint
{
```

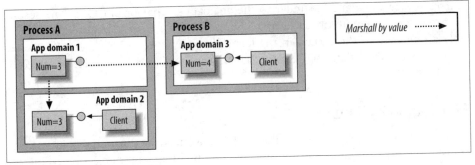

Figure 10-5. Marshaling by value

```
    public int X;
    public int Y;
}

public class RemoteClass : MarshalByRefObject
{
    public void MyMethod(MyPoint point)
    {
        point.X++;
    }
}
```

Changes made to the structure on the server side don't affect the structure on the client side:

```
//Remote client:
MyPoint point;
point.X = 1;

RemoteClass obj = new RemoteClass();
obj.MyMethod(point);
Debug.Assert(point.X == 1);
```

However, if you pass the structure by reference using the out or ref parameter modifiers, changes made on the remote server side will affect the client's copy of the structure:

```
public class RemoteClass : MarshalByRefObject
{
    public void MyMethod(ref MyPoint point)
    {
        point.X++;
    }
}
//Remote client:
MyPoint point;
point.X = 1;

RemoteClass obj = new RemoteClass();
obj.MyMethod(ref point);
Debug.Assert(point.X == 2);
```

This is the same as when you pass a structure by reference in the local case.

The usefulness of marshaling a class instance by value is marginal, because the classic client/server model doesn't fit well with marshaling by value. Marshaling by value for reference types is provided for when the client needs to make frequent calls of short duration to the object, and paying the penalty for marshaling the object state to the client is more efficient than paying the penalty multiple times for marshaling the call to the object and back. Imagine, for example, a distributed image-capturing and processing system. You want the machine capturing the images to do so as fast as it can, and you want the processing to be done on a separate machine. The capturing machine can create an image object, then have the processing client access the object (that would make it copy the image) and process it locally. That said, there is usually a better design solution, such as transferring the image data explicitly as a method parameter. In general, it's often a lot easier to simply marshal a reference to the object to the client and have the client invoke calls on the object via a proxy, as described next.

Marshaling by Reference

The second remoting option is marshal by reference, and it's by far the more common way to access objects across app domains. As explained previously, when marshaling by reference is employed, the client accesses the remote object using a proxy (see Figure 10-3). The proxy forwards calls made on it to the actual object. To designate a component for marshaling by reference, the class must derive directly (or have one of its base classes derive) from the class MarshalByRefObject, defined in the System namespace. Objects derived from MarshalByRefObject are bound for life to the app domain in which they were created and can never leave it.

Examine Example 10-2 again. The client has a reference to a proxy, which forwards the call to TraceAppDomain( ) to the new app domain; this is why it traces the remote app domain's name. If the remote object is serializable in addition to being derived from MarshalByRefObject, you can use serialization to persist the object's state, but the object is still accessed by reference. Any static method or member variable on a marshaled-by-reference class is always accessed directly; no proxy is involved, because statics aren't associated with any particular object.

.NET does allow the client app domain and the host app domain to be the same app domain. In that case, the client can still interact with the marshaled-by-reference object using a proxy, even though both share the same app domain. Clients may want to do that in order to activate the object in different ways. However, short-circuiting remoting this way is an esoteric case. In the vast majority of cases, deriving from MarshalByRefObject has no bearing on intra–app domain calls, and clients in the same app domains get direct references to the object.

Marshaling-by-Reference Activation Modes

.NET supports two kinds of marshal-by-reference objects: *client-activated* and *server-activated*. The two kinds map to three activation modes: *client-activated object*, *server-activated single-call*, and *server-activated singleton*. The different activation modes control object state management, object sharing, the object lifecycle, and the way in which the client binds to an object. The client decides whether to use client-activated or server-activated objects. If the client chooses client-activated objects, just one activation mode is available. If the client chooses server-activated objects, it's up to the hosting app domain to decide whether the client will get a server-activated single-call object or a server-activated singleton object. These objects are called server-activated because it's up to the host to activate the object on behalf of the client and bind it to the client. The hosting app domain indicates to .NET which activation modes it supports, using server registration. The host can support both client- and server-activated objects, or just one of these types; it's completely at the discretion of the host. If it decides to support a server-activated mode, the host must register its objects either as single-call objects or as singleton objects, but not both. This will all become clearer later in this chapter, when you see the actual registration code. The next sections explain the different activation modes.

Client-Activated Object

Client-activated object mode is the classic client/server activation mode: when a client creates a new object, the client gets a new object. That object is dedicated to the client, and it's independent of all other instances of the same class. Different clients in different app domains get different objects when they create new objects on the host (see Figure 10-6). There are no limitations on constructing client-activated objects, and you can use either parameterized constructors or the default constructor. The constructor is called exactly once, when the client creates the new remote object; if parameterized constructors are used, .NET marshals the construction parameters to the new object. Clients can choose to share their objects with other clients, either in their own app domains or in other app domains. Like local objects, client-activated objects can maintain state in memory. To make sure the remote object isn't disconnected from the remoting infrastructure and collected by its local garbage collector, client-activated objects require leasing when they make cross-process calls, to keep the objects alive for as long as the clients are using them. Leasing, discussed later in this chapter, provides a timestamp extending the life of the object.

Client-activated object mode is similar to the default DCOM activation model, with one important difference: the host app domain must register itself as a host willing to accept client-activated calls before remote calls are issued. As mentioned earlier, this means the process containing the host app domain must be running before such calls are made.

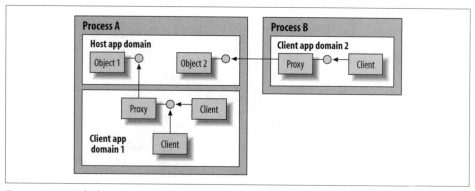

Figure 10-6. With client-activated objects, each client gets an independent object to use

Server-Activated Single Call

The fundamental problem with the client-activated object mode is that it doesn't scale well. The server object may hold expensive or scarce resources, such as database connections, communication ports, or files. Imagine an application that has to serve many clients. Typically, these clients create the remote objects they need when the client application starts and dispose of them when the client application shuts down. What impedes scalability with client-activated objects is that the client applications can hold onto objects for long periods of time, while actually using the objects for only a fraction of that time. If your design calls for allocating an object for each client, you will tie up such crucial limited resources for long periods and will eventually run out of resources. A better activation model is to allocate an object for a client only while a call is in progress from the client to the object. That way, you have to create and maintain in memory only as many objects as there are concurrent calls, not as many objects as there are clients. This is exactly what the single-call activation mode is about: when the client uses a server-activated single-call object, for each method call .NET creates a new object, lets it service the call, and then discards it. Between calls, the client holds a reference to a proxy that doesn't have an actual object at the end of the wire. The following list shows how single-call activation works; its steps are illustrated in Figure 10-7.

1. The object executes a method call on behalf of a remote client.
2. When the method call returns, if the object implements IDisposable, .NET calls IDisposable.Dispose( ) on it. .NET then releases all references it has to the object, making it a candidate for garbage collection. Meanwhile, the client continues to hold a reference to a proxy and doesn't know that its object is gone.
3. The client makes another call on the proxy.
4. The proxy forwards the call to the remote domain.
5. .NET creates an object and calls the method on it.

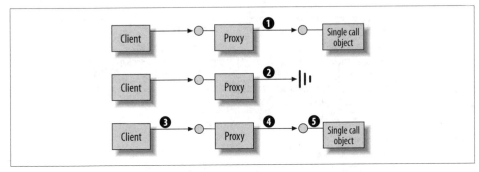

Figure 10-7. Single-call activation mode

Benefits of single-call objects

The obvious benefit of using single-call objects is the fact that you can dispose of the expensive resources the objects occupy long before the clients dispose of the objects. By the same token, acquiring the resources is postponed until they are actually needed by a client. Keep in mind that creating and destroying the object repeatedly on the object side without tearing down the connection to the client (with its client-side proxy) is a lot cheaper than creating and disposing of the object altogether. Another benefit is that even if the client isn't disciplined enough to explicitly discard the object, this has no effect on scalability, because the object is discarded automatically.

If the client does call `IDisposable.Dispose( )` on the object, it has the detrimental effect of recreating the object just so the client can call `Dispose( )` on it. This is followed by a second call to `Dispose( )` by the remoting infrastructure.

Designing a single-call object

Although in theory you can use single-call activation on any component type, in practice, you need to design the component and its interfaces to support the single-call activation mode from the ground up. The main problem is that the client doesn't know it's getting a new object each time it makes a call. Single-call components must be *state-aware*; that is, they must proactively manage their state, giving the client the illusion of a continuous session. A state-aware object isn't the same as a stateless object. In fact, if the single-call object were truly stateless, there would be no need for single-call activation in the first place. A single-call object is created just before every method call and deactivated immediately after each call. Therefore, at the beginning of each call, the object should initialize its state from values saved in some storage, and at the end of the call, it should return its state to the storage. Such storage is typically either a database or the filesystem. However, not all of an object's state can be saved as-is. For example, if the state contains a database connection, the object must reacquire the connection at the beginning of every call and dispose of the connection at the end of the call, or in its implementation of `IDisposable.Dispose( )`.

Using single-call activation mode has one important implication for method design: every method call must include a parameter to identify the object whose state needs to be retrieved. The object uses that parameter to gets its state from the storage and not the state of another instance of the same type. Examples of such identifying parameters are the account number for bank account objects, the order number for objects processing orders, and so on. Example 10-3 shows a template for implementing a single-call class. The class provides the MyMethod( ) method, which accepts a parameter of type Param (a pseudo-type invented for this example) that identifies the object.

Example 10-3. Implementing a single-call component

```
public class Param
{...}

public class MySingleCallComponent : MarshalByRefObject,IDisposable
{
   public MySingleCallComponent( )
   {}
   public void MyMethod(Param objectIdentifier)
   {
      GetState(objectIdentifier);
      DoWork( );
      SaveState(objectIdentifier);
   }
   void GetState(Param objectIdentifier)
   {...}
   void DoWork( )
   {...}
   void SaveState(Param objectIdentifier)
   {...}

   public void Dispose( )
   {...}
   /* Class members/state */
}
```

The object then uses the identifier to retrieve its state and to save the state back at the end of the method call.

Another design constraint when dealing with single-call objects has to do with constructors. Because .NET re-creates the object automatically for each method call, it doesn't know how to use parameterized constructors, or which parameters to provide to them. As a result, a single-call object can't have parameterized constructors. In addition, because the object is constructed only when a method call takes place, the actual construction call on the client side is never forwarded to the objects:

```
MySingleCallComponent obj;
obj = new MySingleCallComponent( ); //No constructor call is made

obj.MyMethod( );//Constructor executes
obj.MyMethod( );//Constructor executes
```

Single-call activation clearly involves a trade-off between performance (the overhead of reconstructing the object's state on each method call) and scalability (holding on to the state and the resources it ties up). There are no hard-and-fast rules as to when and to what extent you should trade performance for scalability. You may need to profile your system and ultimately redesign some objects to use single-call activation and others not to use it.

Applying the single-call mode

The single-call activation mode (see Example 10-3) works well when the amount of work to be done in each method call is finite, and there are no more activities to complete in the background once a method returns. You should not spin off background threads or dispatch asynchronous calls back into the object, because the object will be disposed of once the method returns. Because the single-call object retrieves its state from some storage on every method call, single-call objects work very well in conjunction with a load-balancing machine, as long as the state repository is some global resource accessible to all machines. The load balancer can redirect calls to different machines at will, knowing that each single-call object can service the call after retrieving its state.

Enterprise Services JITA

.NET Enterprise Services offer a set of smart instance-management techniques for .NET serviced components. One of those services is *just-in-time activation* (JITA), which works much like single-call objects. JITA has a few advantages over single-call objects, mainly the ability to combine it with other Enterprise Services instance-management techniques (such as object pooling). Other advantages are JITA's integration with distributed transactions and its ability to manage local as well as remote objects. JITA is described in Chapters 3 and 10 of my book *COM and .NET Component Services* (O'Reilly).

Server-Activated Singleton

The server-activated singleton activation mode provides a single, well-known object to all clients. Because the clients connect to a single, well-known object, .NET ignores the client calls to new, even if the singleton object has not yet been created (the .NET runtime in the client app domain has no way of knowing what goes on in the host app domain anyway). The singleton is created when the first client tries to access it. Subsequent client calls to create new objects and subsequent access attempts are all channeled to the same singleton object (see Figure 10-8). Example 10-4 demonstrates these points: you can see from the trace output that the constructor is called only once, on the first access attempt, and that obj2 is wired to the same object as obj1.

Example 10-4. A singleton object is created when first accessed, then used by all clients

```csharp
public class MySingleton : MarshalByRefObject
{
   int m_Counter = 0;

   public MySingleton()
   {
      Trace.WriteLine("MySingleton.MySingleton()");
   }
   public void TraceCounter()
   {
      m_Counter++;
      Trace.WriteLine(m_Counter);
   }

}
//Client-side code:
MySingleton obj1;
MySingleton obj2;

Trace.WriteLine("Before calling obj1 constructor");
obj1 = new MySingleton();
Trace.WriteLine("After  calling obj1 constructor");

obj1.TraceCounter(); //Constructor will be called here
obj1.TraceCounter();

Trace.WriteLine("Before calling obj2 constructor");
obj2 = new MySingleton();
Trace.WriteLine("After  calling obj2 constructor");

obj2.TraceCounter();
obj2.TraceCounter();

//Output:
Before calling obj1 constructor
After  calling obj1 constructor
MySingleton.MySingleton()
1
2
Before calling obj2 constructor
After  calling obj2 constructor
3
4
```

Because the singleton constructor is only called implicitly by .NET under the covers, a singleton object can't have parameterized constructors. Parameterized constructors are also banned because of an important semantic characteristic of the singleton activation mode: at any given point in time, all clients share the same state of the singleton object (see Figure 10-8). If parameterized constructors were allowed, different clients could call them with different parameters, which would result in a different

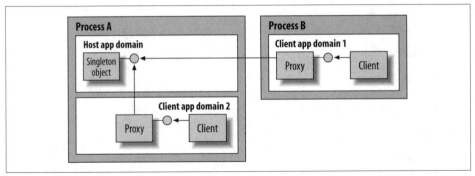

Figure 10-8. With a server-activated singleton object, all clients share the same well-known object

state for each client. If you try to create a singleton object using a parameterized constructor, .NET throws an exception of type `RemotingException`.

 COM also supported singletons by allowing you to provide a special class factory that always returned the same object. The COM singleton behaved much like a .NET singleton. Using ATL, designating a class as a singleton was done by replacing the default class factory macro with the singleton macro. The main difference between a COM singleton and a .NET singleton is that with .NET, the object becomes a singleton because the host registers it as such. Other hosts can register the same component type as a single-call or client-activated object. With COM, the singleton was always a singleton.

Using singleton objects

Singleton objects are the sworn enemy of scalability, because a single object can sustain only so many concurrent client calls. Take care before deciding to use a singleton object. Make sure that the singleton will not be a hotspot for scalability and that your design will benefit from sharing the singleton's object state. In general, you should use a singleton object only if it maps well to a true singleton in the application logic, such as a logbook to which all components should log their activities. Other examples are a single communication port or a single mechanical motor. Avoid using a singleton if there is even the slightest chance that the business logic will allow more than one such object in the future (e.g., if a second communication port or another motor may be added). The reason is clear: if your clients all depend on implicitly being connected to the well-known object, and more than one object is available, the clients will suddenly need to have a way to bind to the correct object. This can have severe implications for the application's programming model. Because of these limitations, I recommend that you generally avoid singletons and instead find ways to share the state of the singleton, instead of the singleton object itself. That said, there are cases when using a singleton is a good idea; for example, class factories are usually implemented as singletons.

Singleton object lifecycle

Once a singleton object is created, it should live forever. That presents a problem to the .NET garbage-collection mechanism, because even if no client presently has a reference to the singleton object, the semantics of the singleton activation mode stipulate that the singleton be kept alive so that future clients can connect to it and its state. .NET uses leasing to keep an object in a different process alive, but once the lease expires, .NET disconnects the singleton object from the remoting infrastructure and eventually garbage-collects it. Thus, you need to explicitly provide the singleton with a long enough (or even infinite) lease. The "Leasing and Sponsorship" section in this chapter addresses this issue.

A singleton object shouldn't provide a deterministic mechanism to finalize its state, such as implementing IDisposable. If it's possible to deterministically dispose of a singleton object, it will present you with a problem: once disposed of, the singleton object becomes useless. Furthermore, subsequent client attempts to access or create a new singleton will be channeled to the disposed object. A singleton by its very nature implies that it's acceptable to keep the object alive in memory for a long period of time, and therefore there is no need for deterministic finalization. A singleton object should use only a Finalize( ) method (the C# destructor).

It's important to emphasize again that, in principle, you don't need to cross app domains when using the different activation modes. As long as a proxy is present between the client and the marshal-by-reference object, the client can activate the object as single-call or singleton, even if it's in the same app domain. In practice, however, you're likely to use the server-activated single-call and singleton modes only on remote objects.

Activation Modes and Synchronization

In a distributed application, the hosting domain registers the objects it's willing to expose, and their activation modes, with .NET. Each incoming client call into the host is serviced on a separate thread from the thread pool. That allows the host to serve remote client calls concurrently and maximize throughput. The question is, what effect does this have on the objects' synchronization requirements?

You can use synchronization domains to synchronize access to remote objects, but bear in mind that synchronization domains can't flow across app domains. If a client creates a remote object that requires synchronization, the object will have a new synchronization domain, even if the remote client was already part of a synchronization domain.

Client-activated objects and synchronization

Client-activated objects are no different from classic client/server objects with respect to synchronization. If multiple clients share a reference to an object, and the clients can issue calls on multiple threads at the same time, you must provide for synchronization to avoid corrupting the state of the object. As explained in Chapter 8, it would be best if the locking were encapsulated in the component itself, by using either synchronization domains or manual synchronization. The reason is clear: any client-side locking (e.g., via the lock statement) locks only the proxy, not the object itself. Another noteworthy point has to do with thread affinity: because each incoming call can be on a different thread, the client-activated object should not make any assumptions about the thread it's running on and should avoid mechanisms such as thread-relative static members or thread local storage. This is true even if it's always the same client accessing the object and that client always runs on the same thread.

Single-call objects and synchronization

In the case of a single-call object, object-state synchronization isn't a problem, because the object's state in memory exists only for the duration of that call and can't be corrupted by other clients. However, synchronization is required when the objects store state between method calls. If you use a database, you have to either explicitly lock the tables or use transactions with the appropriate isolation levels to lock the data. If you use the filesystem, you need to prevent sharing of the files you access while a call is in progress.

Singleton objects and synchronization

Unlike client-activated objects, the clients of a singleton object may not even be aware they are actually sharing the same object. As a result, synchronization of a singleton object should be enforced on the object side. You can use either a synchronization domain or manual synchronization, as explained in Chapter 8. Like a client-activated object, a singleton object must avoid thread affinity.

The .NET Remoting Architecture

The .NET remoting architecture is a modular and extensible architecture. As shown in Figure 10-9, the basic building blocks on the client side are proxies, formatters, and transport channels. On the host side, the building blocks are transport channels, formatters, and call dispatchers. In addition, .NET provides a way to uniquely locate and identify remote objects. This section provides an overview of the remoting architecture's building blocks and how they interact with each other.

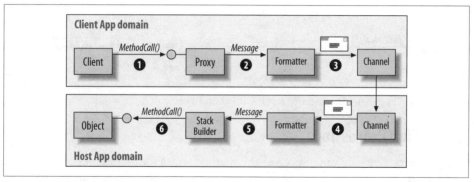

Figure 10-9. .NET remoting architecture

Client-Side Processing

The client never interacts with a remote object directly. Instead, it interacts with a proxy, which provides the exact same public entry points as the remote object. It's the proxy's job to allow the client to make a method call or access a property on it, and then to marshal that call to the actual object. Every proxy is bound to at most one object, although multiple proxies can access a single object. The proxy also knows where the object is. When the client makes a call on the proxy (Step 1 in Figure 10-9), the proxy takes the parameters to the call (the stack frame), creates a message object, and asks a formatter object to process the message (Step 2 in Figure 10-9). The formatter serializes the message object and passes it to a channel object, to transport to the remote object (Step 3 in Figure 10-9). While all this is happening, the proxy blocks the client, waiting for the call to return. Once the call returns from the channel, the formatter deserializes the returned message and returns it to the proxy. The proxy places the output parameters and the returned value on the client's call stack (just like the real object does for a direct call), and finally returns control to the client.

The proxy has actually two parts to it (see Figure 10-10). The first is called a *transparent proxy*. The transparent proxy, implemented by the sealed private class TransparentProxy, exposes the same entry points (as well as base type and interfaces) as the actual object. The transparent proxy converts the stack frame to a message and then passes the message to the real proxy. The *real proxy* knows how to connect to the remote object and forward the message to it. The real proxy is a class derived from the RealProxy abstract class; it has nothing to do with the actual remote object type. By default, .NET provides a concrete subclass (the internal class RemotingProxy). The advantage of breaking the proxy into two parts is that it allows you to use the .NET-provided transparent proxy while providing your own custom real proxy.

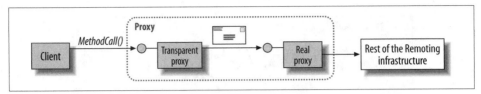

Figure 10-10. The proxy has two parts: a transparent and a real proxy

Server-Side Processing

Once the server-side channel receives the method, it forwards the message to a *formatter* (Step 4 in Figure 10-9). The formatter deserializes the message and passes it to the *stack builder* (Step 5 in Figure 10-9). The stack builder reads the message and calls the object based on the method and its parameters in the message (Step 6 in Figure 10-9). The object itself is never aware that a remote client is accessing it, because as far as it's concerned, the client is the stack builder. Once the call returns to the stack builder, it returns a reply message to the server-side formatter. The formatter serializes the message and returns it to the channel to transport to the client.

Formatters

Because the proxy and the stack builder serialize and deserialize messages, all they need to do is take advantage of the serialization mechanism described in Chapter 9. Out of the box, .NET provides a SOAP formatter and a binary formatter. The binary formatter requires much less processing time to serialize and deserialize than the SOAP formatter, so in intense calling patterns the binary formatter gets better performance. This is because it takes more time to compose and parse a SOAP message, as opposed to the binary format, which is practically used as-is. In addition, the message in binary format has a smaller payload and reduces overall network latency. However, SOAP is the format of choice for going through a firewall when HTTP is used as the transport protocol (although you can use a binary format, too). If there is no interoperability need, or no firewall is present between the host and the client, you should use a binary format for performance reasons.

Transport Channels

Once the message (either from the proxy to the stack builder or vice versa) is serialized, what protocol transports the message to the other side? Out of the box, .NET provides three transport protocols for remote calls: TCP, HTTP, and IPC. These are called *transport channels*. TCP and HTTP were available with .NET 1.0, and .NET 2. 0 introduced the IPC channel. IPC stands for *Inter-Process Communication* and is based on named pipes. The main advantage of IPC is that because you can use it only for cross-process calls on the same machine, hosts that expose only IPC channels are inherently more secure than hosts that expose TCP or HTTP channels.

It's important to state that the question of what transport protocol to use is independent of the question of what format is used to serialize the message. You can use the SOAP or binary formats over either TCP, HTTP, or IPC. However, if you choose the default transport channel configuration, when you select TCP or IPC, .NET uses a binary format; when you select HTTP, .NET uses the SOAP format. This policy makes sense, because if there is no firewall between the client and the host, a binary protocol (TCP or IPC) with a binary format yields the best performance. If a firewall is present, a text-based protocol (HTTP) with the SOAP format is required to go through the firewall.

Both the host and the client app domains need to indicate to .NET which channels they intend to use. This is called *channel registration*. The host app domain needs to register the channels through which it's willing to accept calls from remote clients. It can register any one channel, or all of them. The client needs to register the channels on which it wishes to accept callbacks (discussed later). The client can register one channel or multiple channels. If you have access to other custom channels, you can use them on both sides.

Remoting Versus Web Services

At first glance, .NET remoting over HTTP using SOAP sounds just like a web service. Although web services also use HTTP and SOAP, web services and remoting serve different purposes. Remoting can be used only when both the client and the server are implemented using .NET. Web services, on the other hand, are platform-agnostic and can connect any platform to any other. The trade-off is, of course, in type expressiveness and activation models. With remoting, you can use any serializable or marshal by reference–derived class. With web services, you are limited to types that can be expressed with SOAP and WSDL, and there is no easy way to pass an object reference. Another difference is that you use web services over the Internet, whereas you use remoting when both ends are in the same protected and secure LAN. In addition, you can use remoting with TCP or other channels, but web services are usually limited to HTTP.

In the case of a remote call across two app domains in the same physical process, .NET uses the same architecture as with a call across processes or across machines. However, .NET doesn't use the network-oriented channels or IPC, because doing so would be a waste of resources and would incur a performance penalty. Instead, for this case .NET automatically (as in Example 10-2) uses a dedicated channel called CrossAppDomainChannel. This channel is internal to the remoting infrastructure assembly and isn't available to you. Because both client and server share the same physical process, the CrossAppDomainChannel channel uses the client's thread to invoke the call on the object, and the thread pool isn't involved.

Object Locations and Identity

Every remote object is associated with a *uniform resource locator* (URL). The URL provides the location of the remote object, and it must be mapped to an actual location in which a host app domain is listening for remote activation requests. The URL has the following structure:

```
<protocol>://<host identifier>:<port number>
```

The URL tells .NET where and how to connect with a remote object; that is, what protocol to use to transport the call, to what host (which typically means which machine), and, in the case of TCP and HTTP, on which port of the host machine to try to connect. For example, here is a possible URL:

```
tcp://localhost:8005
```

This URL instructs .NET to connect to a host on the local machine on port 8005, and to use TCP for the transport protocol.

The following URL instructs .NET to use HTTP for the transport protocol and to try to connect to port 8006 on the local machine:

```
http://localhost:8006
```

When using IPC, there is no need to specify a port number. All the URL needs to contain is the pipe's name:

```
ipc://MyHost
```

A URL can also optionally contain an application name section:

```
<protocol>://<machine name>:<port number>[/<application name>]
```

For example:

```
http://localhost:8006/MyApp
```

If a client wants to use a client-activated remote object, the information in the URL is sufficient for .NET to connect to the remote host, create an object on the remote machine, and marshal a reference back to the client. As a result, a URL is all that is required to identify a remote client-activated object.

The situation is different for server-activated objects. When the client tries to connect to a server-activated object, it must provide the server with additional information identifying which well-known object it wants to activate. For example, the host could have a number of singleton objects of the same type, servicing different clients. That additional identification information is in the form of a *uniform resource identifier* (URI). The URI is appended to the activation URL, like so:

```
<URL>/<URI>
```

Here are a few examples:

```
tcp://localhost:8005/MyRemoteServer
http://localhost:8006/MyRemoteServer
ipc://MyHost/MyRemoteServer
```

The URI can be any string, as long as it's unique in the scope of the host app domain. The host is responsible for registering with .NET the well-known objects it's willing to export, and the URIs have to match to those supplied by the clients. Note that the client supplies the URI, but it's the host who decides whether the client gets a well-known singleton object identified by the URI or a single-call object, which is actually not a well-known instance at all (nonetheless, both server-activation types are called *well-known objects*).

Whenever you marshal a remote object reference across an app domain boundary, the reference carries with it the location of the object (in the form of a URL). This is required so that .NET will know where to hook up the proxy. The URL also enables .NET to correctly resolve object references when clients pass them around. Imagine a client in App Domain A that has a proxy referencing an object in App Domain B. When that client passes a reference to the proxy to another client in App Domain C, the client in App Domain C gets a reference to the object in App Domain B, and its proxy will point directly at the object, not at the proxy in App Domain A.

Error Handling

When a client has a direct reference to an object, exceptions thrown by the object wind their way up the call stack. The client can then catch the exceptions and handle them, or let them propagate up the call chain. With remote objects, the client has a direct reference only to a proxy, and the object is called on a different stack frame. If a remote object throws an exception, .NET catches that exception, serializes it, and sends it back to the proxy. The proxy then re-throws the exception on the client's side. The resulting programming model, as far as the client is concerned, is very similar to that of handling errors with local objects in the same app domain as the client.

Advanced .NET Remoting

Almost every point in the .NET remoting architecture is extensible, and you can replace core building blocks with your own or intercept the remote calls in various stages. .NET lets you provide custom formatters and transport channels as well as your own implementation of proxies, which allows you to intervene in proxy creation, marshaling, and object binding. You can provide special hooks to monitor the system behavior or add security or proprietary logging, and you can do all that without having the client or the server do anything different. Advanced .NET remoting is beyond the scope of this book, but you can read about it in *Advanced .NET Remoting*, by Ingo Rammer (Apress).

Building a Distributed Application

Finally, after so many definitions and abstractions, it's time to put it all to use and see how to build a server, a host app domain to host the server object, and a client application to consume the remote object. Both the host and the client application need to indicate to .NET how they intend to use remoting. The host needs to register with .NET the channels and formats on which it's willing to accept remote calls, the remote types it's willing to export, their activation modes, and their URIs (if applicable). The client application needs to register with .NET the types it wants to access remotely, and any channels to be used for callbacks. There are two ways to achieve all this: programmatically and administratively. If you use programmatic configuration, you gain maximum flexibility because at any time you can change the activation modes, object locations, and channels used. Both the client and the host can use programmatic configuration. If you use administrative configuration, you save your remoting settings in a configuration file. Both the client and the server can use administrative configuration. You can also mix and match (i.e., have some settings in the configuration files and programmatically configure others), although normally you use one or the other of these methods, not both at the same time. Administrative configuration lets you change the settings and affect the way your distributed application behaves, even after deployment; it's the preferred way to handle remoting in most cases. This section demonstrates both techniques using the same sample application. I will explain programmatic configuration first and, armed with the understanding of the basic steps, will then examine the administrative configuration settings.

Programmatic Channel Registration

A remoting *channel* is any component that implements the IChannel interface, defined in the System.Runtime.Remoting.Channels namespace. You rarely need to interact with a channel object directly—all you have to do is register them. Out of the box, .NET provides three implementations of the IChannel interface: the TcpChannel, HttpChannel, and IpcChannel classes, defined in the System.Runtime.Remoting. Channels.Tcp, System.Runtime.Remoting.Channels.Http, and System.Runtime. Remoting.Channels.Ipc namespaces, respectively. The host application needs to register which channels it wishes to use, using the static method RegisterChannel() of the ChannelServices class:

```
public sealed class ChannelServices
{
    public static void RegisterChannel(IChannel channel);
    //Other methods
}
```

Typically, the host will put the channel registration code in its Main() method, but it can register the channels anywhere else, as long as the registration takes place before remote calls are issued. Note that you can register the same channel type only once per app domain, unless you explicitly assign it a different name, as described later.

Host channel registration

The host must register at least one channel if it wants to export objects. To register a TCP or HTTP channel, the host first creates a new channel object, providing as a construction parameter the port number associated with this channel. Next, the host registers the new channel. For example:

```
using System.Runtime.Remoting.Channels;
using System.Runtime.Remoting.Channels.Tcp;

//Registering TCP channel
IChannel channel = new TcpChannel(8005);
ChannelServices.RegisterChannel(channel);
```

When a new remote call is accepted, the channel grabs a thread from the thread pool and lets it execute the call, while the channel continues to monitor the port. This way, .NET can serve incoming calls as soon as they come off the channel. Note that the number of concurrent calls .NET remoting can service is subject to the thread-pool limitation. Once the pool is exhausted, new requests are queued until requests in progress are complete.

To register an IPC channel, the host provides the IpcChannel constructor with the pipe's name:

```
using System.Runtime.Remoting.Channels;
using System.Runtime.Remoting.Channels.Ipc;

//Registering IPC channel
IChannel ipcChannel = new IpcChannel("MyHost");
ChannelServices.RegisterChannel(ipcChannel);
```

The named pipe is a global resource on the host machine, and therefore it must be unique machine-wide. No other host on the same machine can open a named pipe with the same name; doing so will yield a RemotingException.

The host can register multiple channels, like so:

```
using System.Runtime.Remoting.Channels;
using System.Runtime.Remoting.Channels.Tcp;
using System.Runtime.Remoting.Channels.Http;
using System.Runtime.Remoting.Channels.Ipc;

//Registering TCP channel
IChannel tcpChannel = new TcpChannel(8005);
ChannelServices.RegisterChannel(tcpChannel);

//Registering http channel
IChannel httpChannel = new HttpChannel(8006);
ChannelServices.RegisterChannel (httpChannel);

//Registering IPC channel
IChannel ipcChannel = new IpcChannel("MyHost");
ChannelServices.RegisterChannel(ipcChannel);
```

When the host instantiates a channel, .NET creates a background thread to open a socket and listen to activation requests on the port. As a result, you can run blocking operations after creating and registering a channel, because you won't affect the thread monitoring the channel. For example, this is valid host-side registration code:

```
static void Main( )
{
   //Registering TCP channel
   IChannel channel = new TcpChannel(8005);
   ChannelServices.RegisterChannel(channel);

   Thread.Sleep(Timeout.Infinite);
}
```

An inherent limitation of network programming is that on a given machine you can open a given port only once. Consequently, you can't open multiple channels on the same port on a given machine. For example, you can't register channels this way:

```
//You can't register multiple channels on the same port
IChannel tcpChannel = new TcpChannel(8005);
ChannelServices.RegisterChannel(tcpChannel);

IChannel httpChannel = new HttpChannel(8005);
ChannelServices.RegisterChannel(httpChannel);
```

Registering multiple channels targeting the same port number causes an exception to be thrown at runtime. In addition, you can register a channel type only once, even if you use different ports:

```
//You can only register a channel once, so this will not work:

IChannel tcpChannel1 = new TcpChannel(8005);
ChannelServices.RegisterChannel(tcpChannel1);

IChannel tcpChannel2 = new TcpChannel(8007);
ChannelServices.RegisterChannel(tcpChannel2);//Throws RemotingException
```

The same is true for the IPC channel—the host can register only a single IPC channel per app domain.

When the host application shuts down, .NET automatically frees the port (or the named pipe) so other hosts on the machine can use it. However, it's customary that as soon as you no longer need the channels, you unregister them explicitly using the static method UnregisterChannel( ) of the ChannelServices class:

```
IChannel channel = new TcpChannel(8005);
ChannelServices.RegisterChannel(channel);

/* Accept remote calls here */

//When done—unregister channel(s):
ChannelServices.UnregisterChannel(channel);
```

Channels and formats

The default constructors shown so far automatically select the appropriate default formatter. By default, the `TcpChannel` and `IpcChannel` classes use the binary formatter to format messages between the client and the host. The `HttpChannel` class uses the SOAP formatter by default. However, as stated previously, you can combine any channel with any format. The channel classes provide the following constructors:

```
public class TcpChannel : <base types>
{
    public TcpChannel(IDictionary properties,
                      IClientChannelSinkProvider clientSinkProvider,
                      IServerChannelSinkProvider serverSinkProvider);
    /* Other constructors and methods  */
}

public class HttpChannel : <base types>
{
    public HttpChannel(IDictionary properties,
                       IClientChannelSinkProvider clientSinkProvider,
                       IServerChannelSinkProvider serverSinkProvider);
    /* Other constructors and methods  */
}
public class IpcChannel : <base types>
{
    public IpcChannel(IDictionary properties,
                      IClientChannelSinkProvider clientSinkProvider,
                      IServerChannelSinkProvider serverSinkProvider);
    /* Other constructors and methods  */
}
```

These constructors accept a collection of key/value pairs and two sink interfaces. The collection is a dictionary of predetermined channel-configuration properties, such as the new channel's name and the port number. The two sink interfaces are where you can provide a formatter instead of accepting the default. The `clientSinkProvider` parameter registers a channel on the client's side (when client-side registration takes place for callbacks); the `serverSinkProvider` parameter registers a channel on the host's side. The available formatters for the host are `SoapServerFormatterSinkProvider` and `BinaryServerFormatterSinkProvider`, implementing the `IServerChannelSinkProvider` interface. The available formatters are `SoapClientFormatterSinkProvider` and `BinaryClientFormatterSinkProvider`, implementing the `IClientChannelSinkProvider` interface. The details of these interfaces and format-providing classes are immaterial; the important thing is that you can use one to explicitly force a message format.

 Refer to the MSDN Library for more information on the configuration parameters and the way they affect the channels.

Here is how to register a SOAP formatter using a TCP channel on the host side:

```
IServerChannelSinkProvider formatter;
formatter = new SoapServerFormatterSinkProvider();

IDictionary channelProperties = new Hashtable();
channelProperties["name"] = "MyServerTCPChannel";
channelProperties["port"] = 8005;

IChannel channel = new TcpChannel(channelProperties,null,formatter);
ChannelServices.RegisterChannel(channel);
```

Note that the second construction parameter is ignored. When doing the same on the client side, you need not provide a port number, and you provide the formatter as the second (instead of the third) parameter:

```
IClientChannelSinkProvider formatter;
formatter = new SoapClientFormatterSinkProvider();

IDictionary channelProperties = new Hashtable();
channelProperties["name"] = "MyClientTCPChannel";

IChannel channel = new TcpChannel(channelProperties,formatter,null);
ChannelServices.RegisterChannel(channel);
```

Programmatic Type Registration

The host must indicate to .NET which objects it's willing to expose as client-activated objects and which to expose as server-activated objects (and in what mode). The client can also indicate to .NET which objects it wants to access remotely. Both host and client register these types using the static methods of the RemotingConfiguration class. Configuration can be done only once per app domain, for both the host and the client.

Host type registration

To register the instances of the MyClass type as well-known server-activated objects, the host uses the static method RegisterWellKnownServiceType() of the RemotingConfiguration class:

```
public static void RegisterWellKnownServiceType(Type type,
                                                string objectUri,
                                                WellKnownObjectMode mode);
```

The host needs to provide the server type, a URI, and the desired server-activation mode: singleton or single-call. The mode parameter is of the enum type WellKnownObjectMode, defined as:

```
public enum WellKnownObjectMode {SingleCall,Singleton}
```

For example, to register the type MyClass, defined as:

```
public class MyClass : MarshalByRefObject
{...}
```

as a single-call object, the host writes:

```
Type serverType = typeof(MyClass);

RemotingConfiguration.RegisterWellKnownServiceType(serverType,
                                        "MyRemoteServer",
                                        WellKnownObjectMode.SingleCall);
```

The host can also register generic remote classes. The host is required to provide a specific type parameter, such as:

```
public class MyClass<T> : MarshalByRefObject
{...}
Type serverType = typeof(MyClass<int>);

RemotingConfiguration.RegisterWellKnownServiceType(serverType,
                                        "MyRemoteServer",
                                        WellKnownObjectMode.SingleCall);
```

Note that the specific type parameter used must be a marshalable type—that is, either serializable or derived from MarshalByRefObject. Consequently, a generic remote type will typically place a derivation constraint from MarshalByRefObject on its generic type parameters when expecting reference type parameters:

```
public class MyClass<T> : MarshalByRefObject where T : MarshalByRefObject
{...}
```

If the object's URL contains an application name section, the host can prefix the URI with the application name:

```
RemotingConfiguration.RegisterWellKnownServiceType(serverType,
                                        "MyApp/MyRemoteServer",
                                        WellKnownObjectMode.SingleCall);
```

The host can't associate multiple URIs with the same type, even it uses different activation modes for each URI, because the more recent registration overrides the previous one:

```
RemotingConfiguration.RegisterWellKnownServiceType(serverType,
                                        "MyRemoteServer1",
                                        WellKnownObjectMode.SingleCall);

//Last registration wins
RemotingConfiguration.RegisterWellKnownServiceType(serverType,
                                        "MyRemoteServer2",
                                        WellKnownObjectMode.Singleton);
```

However, the host can use the same URI with multiple types:

```
Type serverType1 = typeof(MyClass);
Type serverType2 = typeof(MyOtherClass);

RemotingConfiguration.RegisterWellKnownServiceType(serverType1,
                                        "MyRemoteServer",
                                        WellKnownObjectMode.SingleCall);
```

```
RemotingConfiguration.RegisterWellKnownServiceType(serverType2,
                                                   "MyRemoteServer",
                                                   WellKnownObjectMode.SingleCall);
```

When registering a type on the host's side as a client-activated object, there is no need to provide a URI. Registering a type as a client-activated object is done using the static method `RegisterActivatedServiceType( )`:

```
Type serverType = typeof(MyClass);

RemotingConfiguration.RegisterActivatedServiceType(serverType);
```

If the client-activated object's URL contains an application name part, the host must register an application name via the `ApplicationName` static property:

```
RemotingConfiguration.ApplicationName = "MyApp";
```

If the object's URL doesn't contain an application name, setting the `ApplicationName` property has no effect on client-activated objects. Setting the `ApplicationName` property always affects server-activated objects, making it mandatory to use the application name as part of these URLs.

Client-side type registration

.NET provides clients with a number of ways to activate remote objects. One of them is the same as for local objects—using new. Another is by using the static methods of the `Activator` class, `GetObject( )`, and `CreateInstance( )`. The `Activator` class (discussed later in this chapter) provides quite a few overloaded versions for each method. If you use new or some version of the `CreateInstance( )` method, you need to register the object on the client side as a remote object. In essence, client-side registration associates a type with a URL and URI, so that when the client tries to create an instance of that type, .NET knows it should create the object at the location specified, rather than as a local object. If you use the `GetObject( )` method, you need not register the type on the client side, because the parameters to `GetObject( )` contain the object's URI and URL. However, you can only use `GetObject( )` for server-activated objects, so in general, type registration is a required step on the client side as well.

To register a type as a client-activated object, the client uses the `RegisterActivatedClientType( )` method, providing the type and the URL:

```
Type serverType = typeof(MyClass);
string url = "tcp://localhost:8005";

RemotingConfiguration.RegisterActivatedClientType(serverType,url);
```

When using IPC, the URL needs to contain only the pipe's name:

```
string url = "ipc://MyHost";
```

To register a type as a server-activated object, the client uses the `RegisterWellKnownClientType( )` method, providing the type, the URL, and the well-known object's URI:

```
Type serverType = typeof(MyClass);
string url = "tcp://localhost:8005/MyRemoteServer";

RemotingConfiguration.RegisterWellKnownClientType(serverType,url);
```

When using IPC, simply append the URI to the URL:

```
string url = "ipc://MyHost/MyRemoteServer";
```

Remember that the client decides whether it wants a client- or a server-activated object, and the host decides which kind of server-activated object to serve the client. This is why the client doesn't need to specify the activation mode in the call to RegisterWellKnownClientType( ).

Once registration is done on the client side, any new activation requests in the client app domain are redirected to the remote host:

```
using RemoteServer;

MyClass obj = new MyClass ();
obj.SomeMethod( );
```

Programmatic Configuration Example

Instead of fragmented code samples, it's now time for a more comprehensive example showing how the different steps required for programmatic configuration fit together, on both the client and the host side. As mentioned previously, since both the host and the client require the server's metadata, it's best if the server is in a class library. This section walks you through Example 10-5—a fully functional distributed application. The source code accompanying this book contains the Remoting-Demo (Programmatic) solution, with three projects: the *ServerAssembly* class library, the *RemoteServerHost* EXE assembly, and the *Client* EXE assembly. Both EXE assemblies are Windows Forms applications that allow you to select channels and activation modes. The class MyClass provides a parameter-less constructor to be used in all activation modes. The constructor brings up a message box so that you can tell when a new object is created, which is especially useful when experimenting with single-call or singleton objects. The single public method of MyClass is Count( ), which pops up a message box showing the incremented value of a counter. The counter indicates the state lifecycle in the different activation modes. The message boxes have as their captions the name of the current app domain. The *RemoteServerHost* application is a dialog-based application. Its Main( ) method registers TCP, IPC, and HTTP channels and then displays the dialog shown in Figure 10-11.

Displaying a form by calling Application.Run( ) is a blocking operation, and control returns to the Main( ) method only when the dialog is closed. This, of course, has no effect on the channels registered, because worker threads are used to monitor the channels. When the dialog is closed, the Main( ) method unregisters the channels and exits. The Server Host dialog lets you check how the host registers the MyClass type it exports: as client-activated, server-activated, or both. If you select Server Activated, you

Figure 10-11. Server Host lets you programmatically decide which activation modes to register

need to choose between Single Call and Singleton, using the radio buttons. When you click the Register Object button, the OnRegister() method is called (see Example 10-5). OnRegister() simply registers the object based on the user-interface selections. Note that you can register the object both as client- and server-activated.

The *Client* application displays the dialog shown in Figure 10-12. You can select either Client Activated or Server Activated (but not both), and then register the type with the OnRegister() method. The interesting part of the client application is the way it constructs the activation URL for the object registration. The helper method GetActivationURL() constructs a URL based on the channel selected (starts with tcp://, http://, or ipc://) and appends the URI only if Server Activated mode is selected. OnRegister() calls GetActivationURL() and then registers the type accordingly. When you click "new" in the Client of Remote Object dialog, it simply uses new to create a new instance of MyClass and calls Count() twice, either remotely (if you registered) or locally (if no registration took place).

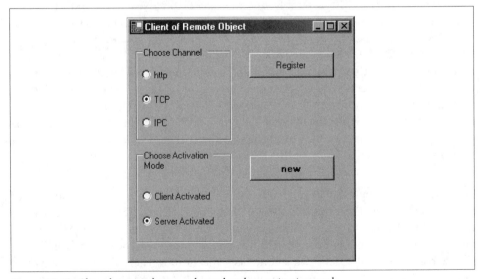

Figure 10-12. Client lets you choose a channel and an activation mode

Revisiting SingletonApp

Chapter 8 introduced the class SingletonApp, used to produce a singleton Windows Forms application. While the code shown in Example 8-9 works fine, it does lack a feature—if the singleton application is minimized and the user tries to launch a new instance, it would have been nice to restore the minimized app to the normal state. You can achieve that easily using an IPC channel. The first time the application is launched, in addition to creating the named mutex, it will do the following:

- Save a copy of the activated form in a static variable
- Register an IPC channel
- Register a single-call object that monitors activation requests

The second time the application is launched, after detecting that there is already a running instance, it will connect to the first instance over the IPC channel and ask it to activate its main window. The first instance will check if the main window is available and is minimized, and if so will restore it (or just bring it to the foreground). When the singleton application shuts down, it unregisters the IPC channel. The source code available with this book contains this revised version of SingletonApp.

Example 10-5. Programmatic remoting configuration

```
/////////////////////   ServerAssembly class library   /////////////////////////
namespace RemoteServer
{
   public class MyClass : MarshalByRefObject
   {
      int m_Counter = 0;
      public MyClass( )
      {
         string appName = AppDomain.CurrentDomain.FriendlyName;
         MessageBox.Show("Constructor",appName);
      }
      public void Count( )
      {
         m_Counter++;
         string appName = AppDomain.CurrentDomain.FriendlyName;
         MessageBox.Show("Counter value is " + m_Counter,appName);
      }
   }
}
/////////////////////   RemoteServerHost EXE assembly   /////////////////////////
using RemoteServer;

partial class ServerHostDialog : Form
{
   Button RegisterButton;
   RadioButton m_SingletonRadio;
   RadioButton m_SingleCallRadio;
   CheckBox m_ClientActivatedCheckBox;
```

Example 10-5. Programmatic remoting configuration (continued)

```
CheckBox m_ServerActivatedCheckBox;
GroupBox m_GroupActivationMode;

public ServerHostDialog()
{
   InitializeComponent();
}
void InitializeComponent()
{...}

static void Main()
{
   //Registering TCP channel
   IChannel tcpChannel = new TcpChannel(8005);
   ChannelServices.RegisterChannel(tcpChannel);

   //Registering http channel
   IChannel httpChannel = new HttpChannel(8006);
   ChannelServices.RegisterChannel(httpChannel);

   //Registering IPC channel
   IChannel ipcChannel = new IpcChannel("MyHost");
   ChannelServices.RegisterChannel(ipcChannel);

   Application.Run(new ServerHostDialog());

   //Do not have to, but cleaner:
   ChannelServices.UnregisterChannel(tcpChannel);
   ChannelServices.UnregisterChannel(httpChannel);
   ChannelServices.UnregisterChannel(ipcChannel);
}
void OnRegister(object sender,EventArgs e)
{
   Type serverType = typeof(MyClass);

   //if the client activated checkbox is checked:
   if(m_ClientActivatedCheckBox.Checked)
   {
      RemotingConfiguration.RegisterActivatedServiceType(serverType);
   }

   //if the server activated checkbox is checked:
   if(m_ServerActivatedCheckBox.Checked)
   {
      if(m_SingleCallRadio.Checked)
      {
         //Allow Server activation, single call mode:
         RemotingConfiguration.RegisterWellKnownServiceType(serverType,
                                          "MyRemoteServer",
                               WellKnownObjectMode.SingleCall);
      }
      else
```

Example 10-5. Programmatic remoting configuration (continued)

```
            {
                //Allow Server activation, singleton mode:
                RemotingConfiguration.RegisterWellKnownServiceType(serverType,
                                                    "MyRemoteServer",
                                    WellKnownObjectMode.Singleton);
            }
        }
    }
}
}
///////////////////////// Client EXE assembly /////////////////////////////
using RemoteServer;

partial class ClientForm : Form
{
    RadioButton m_HttpRadio;
    RadioButton m_TCPRadio;
    RadioButton m_ServerRadio;
    RadioButton m_ClientRadio;
    GroupBox m_ChannelGroup;
    GroupBox m_ActivationGroup;
    Button m_NewButton;
    Button m_RegisterButton;

    public ClientForm()
    {
        InitializeComponent();
    }
    void InitializeComponent()
    {...}
    static void Main()
    {
        Application.Run(new ClientForm());
    }
    string GetActivationURL()
    {
        if(m_TCPRadio.Checked)
        {
            if(m_ServerRadio.Checked)
            {
                //Server activation over TCP. Note object URI
                return "tcp://localhost:8005/MyRemoteServer";
            }
            else
            {
                //Client activation over TCP
                return "tcp://localhost:8005";
            }
        }
        if(m_HttpRadio.Checked)//http channel
        {
            if(m_ServerRadio.Checked)
```

Example 10-5. Programmatic remoting configuration (continued)

```
        {
            //Server activation over http. Note object URI
            return "http://localhost:8006/MyRemoteServer";
        }
        else
        {
            //Client activation over http
            return "http://localhost:8006";
        }
    }
    else//IPC channel
    {
        if(m_ServerRadio.Checked)
        {
            //Server activation over IPC. Note object URI
            return "ipc://MyHost/MyRemoteServer";
        }
        else
        {
            //Client activation over IPC
            return "ipc://MyHost";
        }
    }
}
void OnRegister(object sender,EventArgs e)
{
    Type serverType = typeof(MyClass);
    string url = GetActivationURL();

    if(m_ServerRadio.Checked)
    {
        RemotingConfiguration.RegisterWellKnownClientType(serverType,url);
    }
    else //Client activation mode
    {
        //Register just once:
        RemotingConfiguration.RegisterActivatedClientType(serverType,url);
    }
}
void OnNew(object sender,EventArgs e)
{
    MyClass obj;
    obj = new MyClass();
    obj.Count();
    obj.Count();
}
}
```

Administrative Configuration

Both client and host applications can take advantage of a configuration file to specify their remoting settings instead of making programmatic calls. Although you can use whatever name you want for the configuration file, the convention is to give it the same name as the application, but suffixed with *.config*, like so: *<app name>.exe. config*. For example, if the host assembly is called *RemoteServerHost.exe*, the configuration file will be called *RemoteServerHost.exe.config*. The configuration file is an XML file, and it can be the same configuration file that captures custom version-binding policies, as discussed in Chapter 5. You'll find the remoting configuration section in the `<application>` tag, under the `<system.runtime.remoting>` tag:

```
<?xml version="1.0" encoding="utf-8"?>
<configuration>
   <system.runtime.remoting>
      <application>
         <!--Remoting configuration setting goes here -->
      </application>
   </system.runtime.remoting>
</configuration>
```

Both the client and the host load the configuration file using the static `Configure()` method of the `RemotingConfiguration` class, providing the name of the configuration file:

```
public static void Configure(string filename);
```

Based on the instructions in the configuration file, .NET programmatically registers the channels and the objects, so that you don't need to write appropriate code. If at runtime .NET can't locate the specified file, an exception of type `RemotingException` is thrown. Typically, both the client and the host application call the `Configure()` method in their `Main()` methods, but you can call it anywhere else, as long as you call it before making any remote calls:

```
static void Main()
{
   RemotingConfiguration.Configure("RemoteServerHost.exe.config");
   //Rest of Main()
}
```

 All the design directives and limitations described in the context of programmatic configuration also apply to administrative configuration.

Visual Studio 2005 and configuration files

Visual Studio 2005 can automatically generate a configuration file prefixed with your application name. Bring up the Add New Item dialog, and select the Application Configuration File template, as shown in Figure 10-13. Name the file *App.config*. The name of the file does matter—it must be exactly *App.config*.

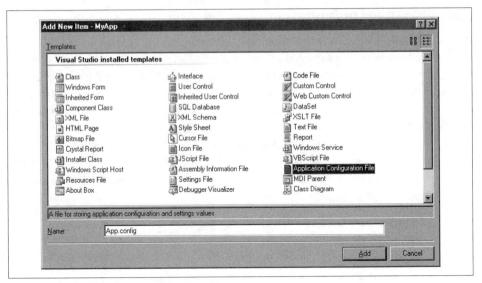

Figure 10-13. Adding the App.config file

Visual Studio 2005 will add the *App.config* file to the project (with a build action set to None). Open the file and add the remoting settings to it. After every successful build, Visual Studio 2005 will copy the *App.config* file to the project output folder and rename it *<app name>.exe.config*. The old copy of the config file is erased.

If you already have a configuration file in the format of *<app name>. exe.config*, but not the *App.config* file, Visual Studio 2005 will erase it (not substitute it) and you will lose your settings.

If you adopt the convention of always naming your configuration files in the format of *<app name>.exe.config*, and you always place the file in the application directory, you can improve on RemotingConfiguration.Configure( ). Example 10-6 shows the static helper class RemotingConfigurationEx, with a parameter-less Configure( ) method.

Example 10-6. The RemotingConfigurationEx helper class

```
public static class RemotingConfigurationEx
{
    public static void Configure()
    {
        string fileName = AppDomain.CurrentDomain.FriendlyName + ".config";
        RemotingConfiguration.Configure(fileName);
    }
}

static void Main()
{
    RemotingConfigurationEx.Configure(); //Automatically loads
```

Example 10-6. The RemotingConfigurationEx helper class (continued)

```
                                            //the correct file
    //Rest of Main( )
}
```

Recall that the Main( ) method runs in the default app domain, whose name matches that of the application EXE assembly. RemotingConfigurationEx retrieves the friendly name of the app domain, appends *.config* to it, and passes that as the filename for RemotingConfiguration.Configure( ). In most cases, using RemotingConfiguration. Configure( ) avoids hardcoding the configuration filename.

Administrative Channel Registration

The machine-wide configuration file *Machine.config* contains global channel definitions and configurations, under the <system.runtime.remoting> tag. In particular, it contains definitions for the HTTP, TCP, and IPC channels and points to where the types implementing them reside. You can take advantage of these definitions and reference them in your configuration file.

Host channels registration

The host needs to add a <channel> tag for each channel it wishes to register. The channels are added under the <channels> tag. For example, to register a TCP channel on port 8005, you would write:

```
<?xml version="1.0" encoding="utf-8"?>
<configuration>
   <system.runtime.remoting>
      <application>
         <channels>
            <channel ref="tcp"  port="8005"/>
         </channels>
      </application>
   </system.runtime.remoting>
</configuration>
```

The host uses the ref attribute to refer to the predefined tcp channel. You can register different channels this way, as long as they use different ports:

```
<channels>
   <channel ref="tcp"  port="8005"/>
   <channel ref="http" port="8006"/>
   <channel ref="ipc"  portName="MyHost"/>
</channels>
```

If you want to register custom channels, you can either add their definitions to the *Machine.Config* file and simply reference them, or include the type name and the assembly identity (including strong name) in the <channel> tag. See the MSDN Library for more information on using custom channels.

Channels and formats

When the host configures a channel as just shown, .NET uses the default formatters associated with each transport protocol. However, you can configure it to use a different formatter, using the <clientProviders> tag. For example, here are the settings required to configure the HTTP channel to use the binary formatter:

```
<configuration>
    <system.runtime.remoting>
        <application>
            <channels>
                <channel ref="http">
                    <clientProviders>
                        <formatter ref="binary"/>
                    </clientProviders>
                </channel>
            </channels>
        </application>
    </system.runtime.remoting>
</configuration>
```

Administrative Type Registration

As with programmatic type registration, the host configuration file can contain a list of the objects it's willing to expose, either as client-activated objects or as server-activated objects, and in what mode. The client configuration file can contain a list of the types it wants to access remotely and their URLs and URIs, if required. When the client or host references a type, it must specify a fully qualified name (type name and its namespace) as well as the type's assembly. Any misspellings or namespaces incompatibilities will be discovered only at runtime.

Host type registration

The host uses the <service> tag to contain a list of the types it exposes. Each type has an entry indicating its activation mode and URI, if required. For example, here is how the host registers the type MyClass from the RemoteServer namespace in the *ServerAssembly* assembly as a client-activated object:

```
<application>
    <service>
        <activated  type="RemoteServer.MyClass,ServerAssembly"/>
    </service>
</application>
```

The host can also expose the type MyClass as a server-activated object and specify the activation mode and the URI:

```
<application>
    <service>
        <activated  type="RemoteServer.MyClass,ServerAssembly"/>
        <wellknown  type="RemoteServer.MyClass,ServerAssembly"
                    mode="SingleCall" objectUri="MyRemoteServer"/>
    </service>
</application>
```

With administrative configuration, the host is subjected to the same URI constraints as with programmatic configuration. The host can also specify an application name with the same semantics as assigning a name programmatically:

```
<application name="MyApp">
    ...
</application>
```

To register a generic type, provide the type parameter in double square brackets. For example, to register the class MyClass<T> with an integer, you should write:

```
<service>
    <wellknown type="RemoteServer.MyClass[[System.Int32]],ServerAssembly"
               mode="SingleCall" objectUri="MyRemoteServer"/>
</service>
```

The double square brackets are required in case you need to specify multiple generic type parameters, in which case each type parameter would be encased in a separate pair of brackets, separated by a comma. For example, to register the class MyClass<T,U> with an integer and a string, you would write:

```
<service>
    <wellknown type="RemoteServer.MyClass[[System.Int32],[System.String]],
                     ServerAssembly" mode="SingleCall" objectUri="MyRemoteServer"/>
</service>
```

Client-side type registration

The client uses the <client> tag to contain a list of the types it wants to consume remotely. It must provide the objects' URLs and URIs, if required. The client can register a given type only once, just as when registering programmatically.

To register a type as a client-activated object, the client uses the <activated> tag, providing the type's name and assembly:

```
<application>
    <client url="tcp://localhost:8005">
        <activated  type="RemoteServer.MyClass,ServerAssembly"/>
    </client>
</application>
```

The object's URL is provided as an attribute of the <client> tag. To register a type as a server-activated object, the client uses the <wellknown> tag:

```
<application>
    <client>
        <wellknown type="RemoteServer.MyClass,ServerAssembly"
                   url="tcp://localhost:8005/MyRemoteServer"/>
    </client>
</application>
```

Note that when you use the <wellknown> tag, the URL and URI are specified as attributes of the <wellknown> tag, rather than as attributes of the <client> tag.

If you need to register multiple remote types on the client's side, you need to use multiple <client> tags:

```
<application>
    <client url="tcp://localhost:8005">
        <activated   type="RemoteServer.MyClass,ServerAssembly"/>
    </client>
    <client>
        <wellknown  type="RemoteServer.MyOtherClass,ServerAssembly"
        url="tcp://localhost:8005/MyRemoteServer"/>
    </client>
</application>
```

To register remote generic types on the client side, use the same syntax for describing the type parameters as the host.

> The .NET Configuration tool has what looks like visual administrative support for managing the remoting part of an application configuration file. Unfortunately, that support leaves much to be desired: the tool doesn't generate a blank configuration file, and its ability to edit existing files with existing remoting attributes is partial at best.

Administrative Configuration Example

Example 10-7 demonstrates a host and client using a configuration file to provide remote access to the same object as in Example 10-5. The source code accompanying this book contains the RemotingDemo (Administrative) solution, with three projects: the *ServerAssembly* class library, the *RemoteServerHost* EXE assembly, and the *Client* EXE assembly. Both EXE assemblies are Windows Forms applications, but this time there are no settings to select because they are all defined in the configuration file. The *ServerAssembly* class library is the same class library from Example 10-5, providing the class MyClass. The host configuration file exposes the MyClass type both as a client-activated object and as a single-call object, and it registers both TCP and HTTP as transport channels. The host calls RemotingConfigurationEx.Configure() in its Main() method and then displays a blank dialog. The client configuration file registers the type MyClass as a client-activated object (the client can associate the type with only a single activation mode).

The client configuration file provides the type's URL, using TCP as the transport channel. The client application calls RemotingConfigurationEx.Configure( ) in its Main( ) method and then displays the client dialog. The client dialog has a single button on it, allowing you to create new remote objects.

Example 10-7. Administrative remoting configuration using configuration files

```
//////////////  RemoteServerHost.exe.config : the host configuration file  ////////
<?xml version="1.0" encoding="utf-8"?>
<configuration>
   <system.runtime.remoting>
      <application>
         <service>
            <activated  type="RemoteServer.MyClass,ServerAssembly"/>
            <wellknown  type="RemoteServer.MyClass,ServerAssembly"
                        mode="SingleCall" objectUri="MyRemoteServer"/>
         </service>
         <channels>
            <channel ref="tcp"  port="8005"/>
            <channel ref="http" port="8006"/>
         </channels>
      </application>
   </system.runtime.remoting>
</configuration>
/////////////////////  RemoteServerHost EXE assembly  ///////////////////////////
partial class ServerHostDialog : Form
{
   public ServerHostDialog( )
   {
      InitializeComponent( );
   }
   void InitializeComponent( )
   {...}

   static void Main( )
   {
      RemotingConfigurationEx.Configure( );
      Application.Run(new ServerHostDialog( ));
   }
}
//////////////  Client.exe.config: the client configuration file  //////////////
<?xml version="1.0" encoding="utf-8"?>
<configuration>
   <system.runtime.remoting>
      <application>
         <client url="tcp://localhost:8005">
            <activated  type="RemoteServer.MyClass,ServerAssembly"/>
         </client>
      </application>
   </system.runtime.remoting>
</configuration>
/////////////////////////  Client EXE assembly  ////////////////////////////////
using RemoteServer;
```

```
partial class ClientForm : Form
{
   Button m_NewButton;

   public ClientForm( )
   {
      InitializeComponent( );
   }

   void InitializeComponent( )
   {...}

   static void Main( )
   {
      RemotingConfigurationEx.Configure( );
      Application.Run(new ClientForm( ));
   }
   void OnNew(object sender,EventArgs e)
   {
      MyClass obj;
      obj = new MyClass( );
      obj.Count( );
      obj.Count( );
   }
}
```

Creating Remote Objects

If the client has registered a type as a remote type (either programmatically or administratively), the client can use the plain new operator to create any kind of remote type, be it client- or server-activated. However, as mentioned already, .NET provides clients with several ways to connect to remote objects. These options differ in their need for pre-registration of the type and in their ability to connect to client-activated objects.

RemotingServices.Connect( )

The client can choose to connect explicitly to a remote object using the static method Connect( ) of the RemotingServices class:

```
public static object Connect(Type classToProxy, string url);
```

Calling Connect( ) explicitly creates a proxy to the remote object on the client side. You can use Connect( ) only to connect to server-activated objects, and you can use only the default constructor. Using the same definitions as in Example 10-5, here is how to create a remote server-activated object using Connect( ):

```
Type serverType = typeof(MyClass);
string url = "tcp://localhost:8005/MyRemoteServer";
```

```
MyClass obj;

obj = (MyClass)RemotingServices.Connect(serverType,url);
obj.Count( );
```

Connect( ) doesn't affect other attempts of the client to create instances of the type, meaning that if no type registration takes place, after a call to Connect( ), calls to new create the type locally in the client's app domain. In fact, you can even register the type, associate it with one location, and then have Connect( ) activate an instance at another location.

Activator.GetObject( )

The Activator class provides the static method GetObject( ):

```
public static object GetObject(Type type,string url);
```

GetObject( ) works like RemotingServices.Connect( ) does, allowing the client to connect to a server-activated object:

```
Type serverType = typeof(MyClass);
string url = "tcp://localhost:8005/MyRemoteServer";

MyClass obj;

obj = (MyClass)Activator.GetObject(serverType,url);
obj.Count( );
```

GetObject( ) doesn't require type registration on the client side, and it doesn't affect registration of the type.

Activator.CreateInstance( )

The Activator class provides many overloaded versions of the static method CreateInstance( ). CreateInstance( ) lets you create any object type (client- or server-activated) and lets you have fine-grained control over the creation process. Some of the versions require type registration before invocation. This version:

```
public static object CreateInstance(Type type);
```

is no different from new and creates the instance at the remote location registered:

```
Type serverType = typeof(MyClass);
MyClass obj;

obj = (MyClass)Activator.CreateInstance(serverType);
obj.Count( );
```

CreateInstance( ) also offers a generic version:

```
public static T CreateInstance<T>( );
```

The generic version is, of course, superior to the object-based version, as it is type-safe:

```
MyClass obj = Activator.CreateInstance<MyClass>( );
obj.Count( );
```

The following version allows you to pass in construction parameters for client-activated objects in the form of an array of objects:

```
public static object CreateInstance(Type type, object[] args);
```

CreateInstance( ) chooses the best-fitting constructor, similarly to how the compiler chooses a constructor. If you want to create a remote instance without registering the type beforehand, use a version that accepts an array of activation attributes:

```
public static object CreateInstance(Type type,object[] args,
                                              object[] activationAttributes);
```

You can pass in as an activation attribute an instance of UrlAttribute, defined in the System.Runtime.Remoting.Activation namespace:

```
using System.Runtime.Remoting.Activation;
using RemoteServer;

object[] attArray = {new UrlAttribute("tcp://localhost:8005")};
Type serverType = typeof(MyClass);

//No registration is required:
MyClass obj = (MyClass)Activator.CreateInstance(serverType,null,attArray);
obj.Count( );
```

CreateInstance( ) is available for advanced creation scenarios. This version:

```
public static ObjectHandle CreateInstance(string assemblyName,string typeName);
```

creates an instance of the specified type and delays setting up a proxy and loading the server assembly until the object handle is unwrapped:

```
using RemoteServer;

ObjectHandle handle;
handle = Activator.CreateInstance("ServerAssembly","RemoteServer.MyClass");

//Proxy is only set up here, and assembly is loaded locally
MyClass obj = (MyClass)handle.Unwrap( );
obj.Count( );
```

Note that you have to specify the fully qualified type name. Other versions of CreateInstance( ) allow you to specify locale and security information.

Table 10-1 compares the various options available when creating or activating remote objects.

Table 10-1. Creating and activating remote object options

Creating option	Requires registration	Client-activated objects	Server-activated objects
new	Yes	Yes	Yes
RemotingServices.Connect( )	No	No	Yes
Activator.GetObject( )	No	No	Yes
Activator.CreateInstance( )	Depends	Yes	Yes

Creating remote generic objects

You can use the `Activator` class to create instances of generic remote objects, such as this one:

```
public class MyServer<T> : MarshalByRefObject
{...}
```

You need to provide the specific type parameters to use, and you must provide the specific types when explicitly casting the returned object:

```
string url = "tcp://localhost:8005/MyRemoteServer";
Type serverType = typeof(MyServer<int>);
MyServer<int>obj;
obj = (MyServer<int>)Activator.GetObject(serverType,url);
```

You can, of course, also use the generic `CreateInstance( )` method to create generic types:

```
MyServer<int> obj;
obj = Activator.CreateInstance<MyServer<int>>( );
```

 It would have been useful if `GetObject( )` were to offer a generic version, like this:

```
        public static T GetObject<T>(string url);
```

Remote Callbacks

Callbacks are just as useful in distributed applications as they are in local applications. A client can pass in as a method parameter a reference to a client-side marshal-by-reference object to be used by a remote object. A client can also provide a remote server with a delegate targeting a client-side method, so that the remote server can raise an event or simply call the client-side method. The difference in the case of remote callbacks is that the roles are reversed: the remote server object becomes the client, and the client (or client-side object) becomes the server. In fact, as far as the server is concerned, the client (or the target object) is essentially a client-activated object, because the server has no URI associated with the target object and cannot treat it as a well-known object.

To receive a remote callback, the client needs to register a port and a channel and have .NET listen on that port for remote callbacks. The problem is, how does the remote server know about that port? And for that matter, how does the remote server object know what URL to use to connect to the client? The answer is built into the remoting architecture. As mentioned already, whenever a reference to an object is marshaled across an app domain boundary, the object reference contains information about the location of the remote object and the channels the host has registered. The object reference is part of the proxy. When the server calls the proxy, the proxy knows where to marshal the call and which channel and port to use. In essence, this is also how delegates work across remoting. The client can create a delegate that targets a method on an object on the client's side and then add that delegate to a public delegate or an event maintained by the server object. Recall from Chapter 7 that every delegate definition is actually compiled to a class. The delegate class is a serializable class and is marshaled by value, which includes a serialization of the internal invocation list of the delegate. Each delegate in the list has a reference to its target object (available via the Target property of the delegate). If the target object is derived from MarshalByRefObject, the serialized delegate will contain only a proxy to the target object.

Registering callback channels

The client must register the channels on which it would like to receive remote callbacks. The client provides a port number to the channel constructor, just like the host application does:

```
//Registering a channel with a specific port number on the client side,
//to enable callbacks:
IChannel channel = new TcpChannel(9005);
ChannelServices.RegisterChannel(channel);
```

When the client invokes a call on the server, the client needs to know in advance which ports the host is listening on. This isn't the case when the server makes a callback to the client, because the proxy on the server side already knows the client-side port number. Consequently, the client doesn't really have to use a pre-designated port for the callback; any available port will do. To instruct .NET to select an available port automatically and listen on that port for callbacks, the client simply needs to register the channels with port 0:

```
//Instructing .NET to select any available port on the client side
IChannel channel = new TcpChannel(0);
ChannelServices.RegisterChannel(channel);
```

Or, if you're using a configuration file:

```
<channels>
    <channel ref="tcp"  port="0"/>
</channels>
```

The client can also register an IPC channel for the callbacks:

```
//Registering an IPC callback channel
IChannel ipcChannel = new IpcChannel("MyCallback");
ChannelServices.RegisterChannel(ipcChannel);
```

An interesting scenario is when the client registers multiple channels for callbacks. The client can assign a priority to each channel, using a named property called priority as part of a collection of named properties provided to the channel constructor (similar to explicitly specifying a formatter). The client can also assign priorities to channels in the configuration file:

```
<application>
    <channels>
```

```
            <channel ref="tcp"    port="0"  priority="1"/>
            <channel ref="http"   port="0"  priority="2"/>
        </channels>
    </application>
```

The channels' priority information is captured by the object reference. The remote server tries to use the channels according to their priority levels. If the client registers multiple channels but doesn't assign priorities, the host selects a channel for the call.

Remote callbacks and type filtering

Every remoting channel has a filter associated with it. The filter controls the kinds of types the channel is willing to serialize across. In a distributed application the server is inherently more susceptible to attacks than the client, and it is particularly susceptible to being handed a harmful callback object by a malicious client. To protect against such attacks, the default level of the filter is set to *Low*. *Low-level* type filtering allows only a limited set of types to be passed in as parameters to remote methods as callback objects. Types allowed under low type filtering include remoting infrastructure types and simple compositions of reference types out of primitive types. *Full* type filtering allows all marshalable types to be passed in as callback objects. Setting the filter level to Full does not eliminate the security threat; it just makes it your explicit decision to take the risk, rather than Microsoft's decision.

To enable callbacks, the host must set its type-filtering level to Full. In most practical scenarios the client must elevate its type filtering to Full as well, unless only very simple callback objects are involved. Changing the type filtering is done on a per-formatter-per-channel basis. You can set the type filtering to Full both programmatically and administratively. To set it programmatically, supply a set of properties to the channel, and set the TypeFilterLevel property of the channel formatter to Full. TypeFilterLevel is of the enum type TypeFilterLevel, defined as:

```
public enum TypeFilterLevel
{
    Full,
    Low
}
```

For example, here is how you programmatically set the type filtering of the binary formatter using a TCP channel on the host side:

```
BinaryServerFormatterSinkProvider formatter;
formatter = new BinaryServerFormatterSinkProvider();
formatter.TypeFilterLevel = TypeFilterLevel.Full;

IDictionary channelProperties = new Hashtable();
channelProperties["name"] = "FullHostTCPChannel";
channelProperties["port"] = 8005;

IChannel channel = new TcpChannel(channelProperties,null,formatter);
ChannelServices.RegisterChannel(channel);
```

When using an IPC callback channel, instead of port number you will need to provide the pipe's name in the portName property:

```
channelProperties["portName"] = "MyClientCallback";
```

To set the filter level administratively, use the serverProviders tag under each channel, and set the filter level for each formatter. For example, to set type filtering to Full for a TCP channel on the host side, provide this configuration file:

```
<channels>
   <channel ref="tcp" port="8005">
      <serverProviders>
         <formatter ref="soap"   typeFilterLevel="Full"/>
         <formatter ref="binary" typeFilterLevel="Full"/>
      </serverProviders>
   </channel>
</channels>
```

Here is the matching client-side configuration file:

```
<channels>
   <channel ref="tcp" port="0">
      <serverProviders>
         <formatter ref="soap"   typeFilterLevel="Full"/>
         <formatter ref="binary" typeFilterLevel="Full"/>
      </serverProviders>
   </channel>
</channels>
```

Note the use of port 0 on the client side, which tells .NET to automatically select any available port for the incoming callback.

Remote callbacks and metadata

Another side effect of reversing the roles of the client and server when dealing with remote callbacks has to do with the client's metadata. At runtime, the host must be able to build a proxy to the client-side object, and therefore the host needs to have access to the object's metadata. As a result, you typically need to package the client-side callback objects (or event subscribers) in class libraries and have the host reference those assemblies. You can use the technique shown in Chapter 6 for sinking interfaces with remote event subscribers. The host needs to have access only to the metadata describing the interface, not to the actual subscribers.

Remote callbacks and error handling

On top of the usual things that can go wrong when invoking a callback, with remote callbacks there is also the potential for network problems and other wire-related issues. This is a particular concern in the case of remote event publishers, since they have to try to reach every subscriber and may have to wait a considerable amount of time for each because of network latency. However, because a publisher/subscriber relationship is by its very nature a looser relationship than that of a client and server, often the publisher doesn't need to concern itself with whether the subscriber managed to process the event successfully, or even if the event was delivered at all. If that is the case with your application, it's better if you don't publish events simply by calling the delegate. Instead, publish the events using the asynchronous event-publishing technique that uses the EventsHelper class, introduced in Chapter 7 and refined in Chapter 8.

There is something you can do on the subscriber's side to make the life of the remote publisher easier. The OneWay attribute, defined in the System.Runtime.Remoting. Messaging, makes any remote method call a fire-and-forget asynchronous call. If you designate a subscriber's event-handling method as a one-way method, the remoting infrastructure only dispatches the callback and doesn't wait for a reply or for completion. As a result, even if you publish an event by calling a delegate directly, the event publishing will be asynchronous and concurrent: it's asynchronous because the publisher doesn't wait for the subscribers to process the event, and it's concurrent because every remote subscriber is served on an impendent worker thread (remote calls use threads from the thread pool). In addition, any errors on the subscriber's side don't propagate to the publisher's side, so the publisher doesn't need to program to catch and handle exceptions raised by the event subscribers.

 Because static members and methods aren't remotable (no object reference is possible), you can't subscribe to a remote static event, and you can't provide a static method as a target for a remote publisher. You can only pass a remote object a delegate targeting an instance method on the client side. If you pass a remote publisher a delegate targeting a static method, the event is delivered to a static method on the remote host side.

Remote callback example

Example 10-8 shows a publisher firing events on a remote subscriber. The source code accompanying this book contains the Remote Events solution, with three projects: the *ServerAssembly* class library, the *RemoteServerHost* EXE assembly, and the *Client* EXE assembly. These projects are a variation of the projects presented in Example 10-7. The host is identical to the one in Example 10-7; the only changes are in the host configuration file. The host exposes the type RemoteServer.MyPublisher as a client-activated object and as a server-activated object. The host also elevates type filtering to Full on its channels. The *ServerAssembly* class library contains both the subscriber and the publisher classes. Recall that this is required so that both the client and the host can gain access to these types' metadata. Note that both the publisher and the subscriber are derived from MarshalByRefObject. The publisher uses GenericEventHandler by aliasing it to NumberChangedEventHandler:

```
using NumberChangedEventHandler = GenericEventHandler<int>;
```

The publisher publishes to the subscribers in the FireEvent( ) method using EventsHelper. The subscriber is the MySubscriber class. The subscriber's event-handling method is OnNumberChanged( ), which pops up a message box with the value of the event's argument:

```
[OneWay]
public void OnNumberChanged(int number)
{
    MessageBox.Show("New Value: " + number);
}
```

The interesting part of OnNumberChanged( ) is that it's decorated with the OneWay attribute. As a result, the publisher's FireEvent( ) method actually fires the event asynchronously and concurrently to the various subscribers. The client configuration file is the same as in Example 10-7, except this time the client registers the port 0 with the channel, which allows the client to receive remote callbacks. Interestingly enough, the subscriber is simple enough to pass on the client channel even with client-side type filtering set to Low. The client configuration file registers the publisher as a remote object. The client creates a local instance of the subscriber and a remote instance of the publisher, and saves them as class members. The client is a Windows Forms dialog. The dialog allows the user to subscribe to or unsubscribe from the publisher, and to fire the event. The dialog reflects the event's argument in a text box. Subscribing to and unsubscribing from the event are done using the conventional += and -= operators, as in the local case.

Example 10-8. Remote events

```
/////////////  RemoteServerHost.exe.config : the host configuration file  ////////
<?xml version="1.0" encoding="utf-8"?>
<configuration>
  <system.runtime.remoting>
    <application>
      <service>
        <activated   type="RemoteServer.MyPublisher,ServerAssembly"/>
        <wellknown   type="RemoteServer.MyPublisher,ServerAssembly"
                     mode="SingleCall" objectUri="MyRemotePublisher"/>
      </service>
      <channels>
        <channel ref="tcp" port="8005">
          <serverProviders>
            <formatter ref="soap"   typeFilterLevel="Full"/>
            <formatter ref="binary" typeFilterLevel="Full"/>
          </serverProviders>
        </channel>
        <channel ref="http" port="8006">
          <serverProviders>
            <formatter ref="soap"   typeFilterLevel="Full"/>
            <formatter ref="binary" typeFilterLevel="Full"/>
          </serverProviders>
        </channel>
      </channels>
```

Example 10-8. Remote events (continued)

```
    </application>
  </system.runtime.remoting>
</configuration>
///////////////////////   ServerAssembly class library  ///////////////////////////
using NumberChangedEventHandler = GenericEventHandler<int>;

namespace RemoteServer
{
   public class MyPublisher : MarshalByRefObject
   {
      public event NumberChangedEventHandler NumberChanged;
      public void FireEvent(int number)
      {
         EventsHelper(NumberChanged,number);
      }
   }
   public class MySubscriber : MarshalByRefObject
   {
      [OneWay]
      public void OnNumberChanged(int number)
      {
         MessageBox.Show("New Value: " + number);
      }
   }
}
////////////////   Client.exe.config: the client configuration file  ///////////////
<?xml version="1.0" encoding="utf-8"?>
<configuration>
   <system.runtime.remoting>
      <application>
         <client url="tcp://localhost:8005">
            <activated   type="RemoteServer.MyPublisher,ServerAssembly"/>
         </client>
         <channels>
            <channel ref="tcp"  port="0"/>
         </channels>
      </application>
   </system.runtime.remoting>
</configuration>
////////////////////////////   Client EXE assembly  /////////////////////////////////
using RemoteServer;


partial class SubscriberForm : Form
{
   Button m_FireButton;
   Button m_SubscribeButton;
   Button m_UnsubscribeButton;
   TextBox m_NumberValue;

   MyPublisher  m_Publisher;
   MySubscriber m_Subscriber;
```

Example 10-8. Remote events (continued)

```
    public SubscriberForm( )
    {
       InitializeComponent( );

       m_Publisher  = new MyPublisher( );
       m_Subscriber = new MySubscriber( );
    }
    void InitializeComponent( )
    {...}

    static void Main( )
    {
       RemotingConfigurationEx.Configure( );

       Application.Run(new SubscriberForm( ));
    }
    void OnFire(object sender,EventArgs e)
    {
       int number = Convert.ToInt32(m_NumberValue.Text);
       m_Publisher.FireEvent(number);
    }
    void OnUnsubscribe(object sender,EventArgs e)
    {
       m_Publisher.NumberChanged -= m_Subscriber.OnNumberChanged;
    }
    void OnSubscribe(object sender,EventArgs e)
    {
       m_Publisher.NumberChanged += m_Subscriber.OnNumberChanged;
    }
}
```

Separating the Server Code from its Metadata

As explained previously, both the client and the host require the server assembly.
The client requires the server's metadata to compile against and to build a proxy at
runtime. At runtime, the host requires the server's IL to host the components and the
metadata for call-marshaling purposes. If the host is doing programmatic registration, the host requires the metadata at compile time as well.

You can reduce the client application's dependency on the server class library by
allowing access to the server objects via interfaces only and by splitting the server
into two class libraries: one with the interface definitions only and one with the
actual interface implementation. You can then deploy on the client's side only the
interfaces assembly, not the assembly with the actual code, which remains on the
server. The only issue now is how the client will instantiate the types that support the
interfaces. In fact, there are a number of options:

- Name the interfaces and implementation assemblies the same, including the strong name. Make sure both have the same version number. Add to the interfaces assembly the definitions of the classes implementing them, with stubbed-out implementation; this allows the client to compile. Using type registration, redirect the types to the host.

- Use a class factory to instantiate the objects and have the factory return interfaces only. The class factory will be in a separate class library assembly altogether. The factory assembly will require access to the assembly implementing the interfaces, but no other clients will need that assembly.

- If the remote object is server-activated, use `Activator.GetObject()` or `RemotingServices.Connect()` to create an instance of the interface. This works because the host instantiates the type behind the interface and returns only the interface. This technique doesn't work with new because it won't compile, and `Activator.CreateInstance()` will fail at runtime.

To avoid deploying assemblies with code on the client's side, you can use the *SoapSuds.exe* command-line utility. *SoapSuds.exe* extracts the metadata of the types in a server assembly and generates wrapper classes that point to the server assembly's remote location. For each public class that derives from `MarshalByRefObject`, *SoapSuds.exe* generates a class with a matching name that derives from the abstract class `RemotingClientProxy`.

Use command-line switches to provide the input assembly and the remote host URL:

```
soapsuds -inputassemblyfile:ServerAssembly
        -outputassemblyfile:ClientProxy.dll
        -serviceendpoint:http://localhost:8006/MyRemoteServer
```

Next, add a reference in the client's assembly to the wrapper classes assembly instead of the actual server assembly. In that respect, the wrapper classes act as a proxy to the real proxy.

The main advantage of *SoapSuds.exe* is that you can use it to generate wrapper classes even if the server assembly is an EXE assembly (i.e., the host and the server are the same assembly) and avoid adding a reference to the host directly. However, *SoapSuds.exe* has a number of limitations:

- It hardcodes the channel and host location into the wrapper classes. If you want the client to use them to connect to other hosts, you have to programmatically set the `Url` property of the wrapper class.

- The wrapper classes work only if the host is listening on HTTP channels and using the SOAP format.

- You can use the wrapper classes to connect only to server-activated objects.

- It's cumbersome to create wrapper classes if the host uses multiple URIs associated with the types in the input assembly.

Providing a Host as a System Service

Implementing a host requires only a few lines of code, as shown in Example 10-7. The downside isn't the amount of work required to provide a host; it's that the host has to be running before remote calls are issued. As a result, you are likely to provide your host in the form of a system service. .NET makes implementing a service straightforward, as shown in Example 10-9. Add to an EXE assembly a class derived from ServiceBase, which is found in the System.ServiceProcess namespace. In the Main( ) method of the assembly, run the service. Override the OnStart( ) method of ServiceBase, and either register channels and objects or load a configuration file. You will also need to include in the assembly a class derived from Installer (defined in the System.Configuration.Install namespace) to install the EXE as a system service. The Installer-derived class captures various service parameters, such as the startup mode and the account under which to run the service. Next, you need to install the service using the *InstallUtil.exe* command-line utility. Visual Studio 2005 can automate many of these phases, including the installer class, and it can even generate a service setup project to install the service. Please refer to the MSDN documentation for additional information on developing system services.

Example 10-9. Providing a host as a system service

```
using System.ComponentModel;
using System.ServiceProcess;
using System.Configuration.Install;

public class MyHostService : ServiceBase
{
   static void Main( )
   {
      ServiceBase.Run(new MyHostService( ));
   }
   protected override void OnStart(string[] args)
   {
      RemotingConfigurationEx.Configure( );
   }
}

[RunInstaller(true)]
public class HostInstaller : Installer
{
   ServiceProcessInstaller m_ServiceProcessInstaller;
   ServiceInstaller m_ServiceInstaller;

   public HostInstaller( )
   {
      InitializeComponent( );
   }
   void InitializeComponent( )
   {
      m_ServiceProcessInstaller = new ServiceProcessInstaller( );
```

Example 10-9. Providing a host as a system service (continued)

```
        m_ServiceInstaller = new ServiceInstaller( );

        m_ServiceProcessInstaller.Account = ServiceAccount.LocalSystem;
        m_ServiceProcessInstaller.Password = null;
        m_ServiceProcessInstaller.Username = null;

        m_ServiceInstaller.DisplayName = "MyHostService";
        m_ServiceInstaller.ServiceName = "MyHostService";
        m_ServiceInstaller.StartType   = ServiceStartMode.Automatic;

        Installer[]installers = {m_ServiceProcessInstaller,m_ServiceInstaller};
        Installers.AddRange(installers);
    }
}
```

Hosting with IIS

Instead of providing your own service, you can host your remote components in the worker process that the Internet Information Server (IIS) uses to host web applications. There are a few reasons why you might want to host your components with IIS. The first is that the worker process is a service, so it will always be running when client requests are sent. The second reason is security: you can take advantage of IIS's built-in security to provide call authentication. The third is that your remote objects will also be available as web services. To host with IIS, follow these guidelines:

- Create a new virtual root under IIS.
- The server assembly must be in a known location. You can put it either in the GAC, or in a \bin folder under the root.
- Server-activated objects' URIs must end with either .rem or .soap, such as MyServer.rem.
- Avoid registering channels. IIS requires you to use HTTP, over port 80 by default. If you need a different port, configure it using the IIS snap-in. The only reason to register a channel would be to use the binary format instead of the default SOAP.
- Don't register an application name. IIS will use the virtual root as the app name.
- If you use a configuration file:
  - Place it in the root.
  - The configuration filename must be *web.config*.

You can host both client- and server-activated objects in IIS.

Leasing and Sponsorship

.NET manages the lifecycle of objects using garbage collection. .NET keeps track of memory allocation and objects accessed by all the clients in the app domain. When an object becomes unreachable by its clients, the garbage collector eventually collects it. If the objects are in the same app domain as the clients, garbage collection functions fine. In fact, even in the case of a client in one app domain accessing an object in a different app domain in the same process, garbage collection still works, because all app domains in the same process share the same managed heap. In the case of remote objects accessed across processes and machines, however, the strategy breaks down because the object may not have any local clients. In this case, if garbage collection were to take place, the garbage collector would not find any references to the object and would deem it garbage, even though there are remote clients (on other machines, or even in separate processes on the same machine) who wish to use the object. The rest of this section addresses this challenge.

In the following discussion, a "remote object" is an object in a different process. The core piece of the .NET remoting architecture designed to address this problem is called *leasing and sponsorship*. The idea behind leasing is simple: each server object accessed by remote clients is associated with a lease object. The *lease object* literally gives the server object a lease on life. When a client creates a remote server object (that is, actually creates it, rather than connects to an existing instance), .NET creates a lease object and associates it with the server object. A special entity in .NET remoting called the *lease manager* keeps track of the server objects and their lease objects. Each lease object has an initial lease time. The clock starts ticking as soon as the first reference to the server object is marshaled across the app domain boundary, and the lease time is decremented as time goes by. As long as the lease time doesn't expire, .NET considers the server object as being used by its clients. The lease manager keeps a reference to the server object, which prevents the server object from being collected in case garbage collection is triggered. When the lease expires, .NET assumes that the server object has no remaining remote clients. .NET then disconnects the server object from the remoting infrastructure. The server object becomes a candidate for garbage collection and is eventually destroyed. After the object is disconnected, any client attempt to access it results in an exception of type `RemotingException`, letting the client know the object has been disconnected. This may appear strange at first, because the object may very well still be alive. .NET behaves this way because otherwise, the client's interaction with the remote object will be nondeterministic. If .NET allowed remote clients to access objects past their lease time, it would work some of the time but would fail in those cases in which garbage collection had already taken place.

If the remote object is disconnected because the lease has expired, the client can't call any method on it, including `IDisposable.Dispose()`. This may have serious scalability consequences. When the object contains expensive resources, make sure to use single-call objects—these don't require leasing, and .NET calls `IDisposable.Dispose()` on them automatically.

But what about those cases where there are still some remote clients who would like to keep the server object alive after its lease expires? The smart thing to do is to contact such clients and ask them to extend the lease, or, in .NET terminology, to *sponsor* the lease. Clients that wish .NET to contact them when a server object's lease expires need to provide .NET with a special *sponsor object*. When the time comes, .NET will contact the sponsor object, giving it a chance to extend the lease. This interaction is illustrated in Figure 10-14.

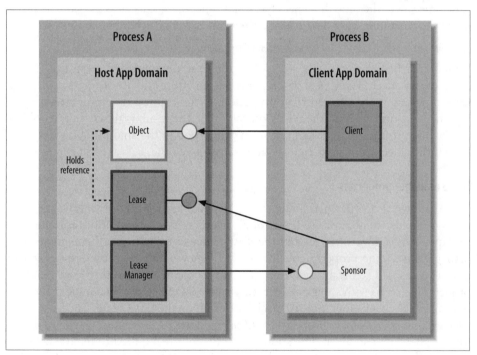

Figure 10-14. Leasing and sponsorship

The sponsor can extend the lease or refuse to do so. A given server object can have multiple sponsors associated with its lease. The lease manager keeps a list of all the sponsors associated with each lease, and when the lease expires the lease manager starts traversing the sponsor list, looking for a sponsor willing to extend the lease. If such a sponsor is found, the lease manager extends the lease. Otherwise, the lease manager disconnects the server object.

Lease Properties

Every lease has a number of properties associated with it. These properties control the manner in which the lease manager interacts with the remote object's lease. .NET assigns some global default values to these properties, but you can instruct .NET to use other default values. You can even override the default lease properties for individual objects. The *expired time* is the time that has expired since the beginning of the lease. A lease has a *lease time* property. By default, if you don't configure it differently, each lease's *lease time* property is initially set to five minutes. .NET could simply disconnect the object when the expired time is equal to the lease time, but what should it do if clients continue to call the object? This clearly indicates that the object is still useful. Every lease has a *renew on call time* property; if the lease is about to expire, .NET automatically extends the lease on every call by the value set in the call time renewal property. The default call time renewal is two minutes. The *current lease time* value (the time the object has to live unless the lease is extended) is a product of the remaining lease time and the renew on call time, according to this formula:

```
current lease time = MAX(lease time–expired time,renew on call time)
```

If the renew on call time value is less than the lease time minus the expired time, it will have no effect. The renew on call time has an effect only if it is greater than the lease time minus the expired time. In that case, the expired time property is reset, and the lease time is set to the renew on call time. The result is that even if an object is very busy, its lease time doesn't grow in proportion to the amount of traffic it has. Even if the object has a spike in load, after some quiet time, its lease will expire.

Lease manager properties

There are two properties pertaining to the lease manager itself. Obviously, the lease manager needs to monitor the leases of all remote server objects in its app domain. The question is, how often should the lease manager examine the leases? The lease manager's *poll time* property governs the frequency with which the lease manager polls the leases. The default poll time is set to 10 seconds. The other lease manager property has to do with sponsors. The lease sponsors can reside on remote machines, or it may take them a long time to reach a decision on the lease's fate. The lease manager's *sponsorship timeout* property controls how long the lease manager should wait for a reply from a sponsor. The sponsorship timeout is required to handle network failures, or even the case of a sponsor machine being down. If the lease manager tries to reach a sponsor and the sponsor doesn't reply within the sponsorship timeout period, the lease manager removes that sponsor from the sponsor list associated with the lease.

Configuring global default properties

If you don't like the default values of the various lease and lease manager properties, you can provide your own. You can do so both programmatically and administratively, using the application configuration file. To configure global defaults program-matically, use the static properties of the LifetimeServices class, defined in the System.Runtime.Remoting.Lifetime namespace:

```
public sealed class LifetimeServices
{
   public static TimeSpan LeaseManagerPollTime { get; set; }
   public static TimeSpan LeaseTime           { get; set; }
   public static TimeSpan RenewOnCallTime     { get; set; }
   public static TimeSpan SponsorshipTimeout  { get; set; }
}
```

You typically use these properties in the Main( ) method of your host:

```
static void Main( )
{
   LifetimeServices.LeaseTime      = TimeSpan.FromMinutes(10);
   LifetimeServices.RenewOnCallTime = TimeSpan.FromMinutes(15);

   /* Register types or load configuration file */
}
```

Note that you must set the global leasing defaults before you register types (program-matically or using the configuration file). The host can start servicing remote calls immediately after registration, and if you haven't already set the new defaults, these initial calls will not use them.

To provide the new global default values in the host configuration file, use the <lifetime> element:

```
<configuration>
   <system.runtime.remoting>
     <application>
       <lifetime
         leaseTime = "10M"
         sponsorshipTimeOut = "1M"
         renewOnCallTime = "15M"
         LeaseManagePollTime = "8s"
       />
     </application>
   </system.runtime.remoting>
</configuration>
```

Configuring a Lease

Every lease object implements the ILease interface, defined in the System.Runtime.Remoting.Lifetime namespace:

```
public interface ILease
{
   TimeSpan CurrentLeaseTime   {get;}
   LeaseState CurrentState     {get;}
   TimeSpan InitialLeaseTime   {get;set;}
   TimeSpan RenewOnCallTime    {get;set;}
   TimeSpan SponsorshipTimeout {get;set;}
```

```
      void Register(ISponsor obj);
      void Register(ISponsor obj,TimeSpan renewalTime);
      TimeSpan Renew(TimeSpan renewalTime);
      void Unregister(ISponsor obj);
   }
```

The ILease interface allows you to control and configure the lease properties for an individual object, as well as to manage sponsors for that lease. Both the object and its clients can obtain the ILease interface. An individual lease can be in one of a number of states; the most important are *initial*, *active*, and *expired*. You can obtain the state of the lease by accessing the CurrentState read-only property of the ILease interface. CurrentState is of the enum type LeaseState:

```
      public enum LeaseState
      {
         Active,
         Expired,
         Initial,
         Null,
         Renewing
      }
```

A remote class can provide its own values to the lease's properties, giving the object control over its lifetime. To do so, override the InitializeLifetimeService( ) method defined in MarshalByRefObject and return a lease object. .NET calls InitializeLifetimeService( ) immediately after the remote object's constructor, but before a reference to the object is marshaled back to the client. InitializeLifetimeService( ) is never called if a local client creates the object. Although you can return from InitializeLifetimeService( ) any object that implements the ILease interface, in practice you need to obtain the lease already associated with your object and modify its properties. You do that by calling your base class's InitializeLifetimeService( ) method and modifying the lease properties, as shown in Example 10-10. You can set the lease properties only if the lease is in the LeaseState.Initial state, and this is asserted in the example.

Example 10-10. Providing new lease properties for an object

```
public class MyServer : MarshalByRefObject
{
   public override object InitializeLifetimeService( )
   {
      ILease lease = (ILease)base.InitializeLifetimeService( );
      Debug.Assert(lease.CurrentState == LeaseState.Initial);

      //Set lease properties
      lease.InitialLeaseTime     = TimeSpan.FromMinutes(30);
      lease.RenewOnCallTime      = TimeSpan.FromMinutes(10);
      lease.SponsorshipTimeout   = TimeSpan.FromMinutes(2);
      return lease;
   }
}
```

Renewing a Lease

Both the object and its clients can extend the lease explicitly by obtaining the object's lease and calling the ILease.Renew( ) method, providing a new lease time. Renewing a lease explicitly affects the current lease time according to this formula:

```
current lease time = MAX(lease time-expired time,renewal time)
```

This means that the renewal time will have an effect only if the renewal time is greater than the lease time minus the expired time. In that case, the expired time is reset, and the lease time becomes the renewal time. Consequently, if different clients all try to explicitly renew a lease, the lease will not grow to the value of their combined renewal sum; this ensures that the object remains connected only when clients require it. Both the client and the object obtain the lease associated with the object using the static method GetLifetimeService( ) of the RemotingServices class:

```
public static object GetLifetimeService(MarshalByRefObject obj);
```

You can renew a lease only if it's in the LeaseState.Active state. For example, here is how a client renews a lease:

```
MyClass obj;
obj = new MyClass( );

ILease lease = (ILease)RemotingServices.GetLifetimeService(obj);
Debug.Assert(lease.CurrentState == LeaseState.Active);
lease.Renew(TimeSpan.FromMinutes(30));
```

If the object wants to renew its own lease, it simply calls GetLifetimeService( ), providing itself as the parameter:

```
public class MyServer : MarshalByRefObject
{
   public void SomeMethod( )
   {
      ILease lease = (ILease)RemotingServices.GetLifetimeService(this);
      Debug.Assert(lease.CurrentState == LeaseState.Active);

      lease.Renew(TimeSpan.FromMinutes(30));
      //Do some work
   }
}
```

Providing a Sponsor

As mentioned already, a sponsor is a third party whom .NET consults when a lease expires, giving that party an opportunity to renew the lease. The sponsor must implement the ISponsor interface, defined as:

```
public interface ISponsor
{
   TimeSpan Renewal(ILease lease);
}
```

The lease manager calls ISponsor's single method, Renewal( ), when the lease expires, asking for new lease time. To add a sponsor to a lease object, simply obtain the lease object by using GetLifetimeService( ) and call the ILease. Register( ) method:

```
public class MySponsor : MarshalByRefObject,ISponsor
{
    public TimeSpan Renewal(ILease lease)
    {
        Debug.Assert(lease.CurrentState == LeaseState.Active);
        //Renew lease by 5 minutes
        return TimeSpan.FromMinutes(5);
    }
}
ISponsor sponsor = new MySponsor( );
MyClass obj = new MyClass( );

//Register the sponsor
ILease lease = (ILease)RemotingServices.GetLifetimeService(obj);
lease.Register(sponsor);
```

If the sponsor doesn't want to renew the lease, it can return TimeSpan.Zero:

```
public TimeSpan Renewal(ILease lease)
{
    Debug.Assert(lease.CurrentState == LeaseState.Active);
    //Refuse to renew lease:
    return TimeSpan.Zero;
}
```

However, it probably makes more sense to unregister the sponsor instead. Because the sponsor is called across an app domain boundary, the sponsor must be a remotable object, meaning it must be marshaled either by value or by reference. If you derive the sponsor from MarshalByRefObject, the sponsor will reside on the client's side, and it can base its decision about the renewal time on client-side events or properties that it's monitoring. That raises an interesting question: if the lease keeps the remote server object alive, and the sponsor keeps the lease alive, who keeps the sponsor alive? The answer is that somebody on the client side must keep a reference to the sponsor, typically as a class member variable. Doing so also allows the client to remove the sponsor from the lease when the client shuts down, by calling the ILease.Unregister( ) method (the client can also unregister the sponsor in its implementation of IDisposable.Dispose( )). Unregistering sponsors improves overall performance, because the lease manager doesn't spend time trying to reach sponsors that aren't available.

If you mark only the sponsor as serializable, when you register the sponsor it's marshaled by value to the host's side and will reside there. This eliminates the marshaling overhead of contacting the sponsor, but it also disconnects the sponsor from the client. A marshaled-by-value sponsor can only base its decisions about renewing leases on information available on the host's side.

Sponsors and remoting

When the sponsor is a marshaled-by-reference object, the client application must register a port with its channels to allow the remote lease manager to call back to the sponsor, and it must set the type filtering to Full. The client generally doesn't care which port is used for the callbacks, so it can register port number 0 to instruct .NET to automatically select an available port. The channel, port number, and sponsor object location are captured when the reference to the sponsor object is marshaled to the remote host.

Client and leases

A single lease can have multiple sponsors, and multiple clients can all share the same sponsor. In addition, a single sponsor can be registered with multiple remote leases. Typically, a client application will have one sponsor for all its remote objects. As a result, a remote object will typically have as many sponsors to its lease as it has distinct client applications using it. When a client application shuts down, it unregisters its sponsor from all the remote leases it sponsors.

Leasing and Remote Activation Modes

Server-activated single-call objects don't need leasing, because such objects are disconnected immediately after each call. This isn't the case for server-activated singleton objects and client-activated objects, though.

Leasing a singleton object

The singleton design pattern semantics mandate that once it's created, the singleton object lives forever. Thus, the default lease time of five minutes doesn't make sense for singleton objects. If you don't change this default and no client accesses the singleton object for more than five minutes after it's created (or just two minutes after the first five minutes), .NET deactivates the singleton. Future calls from the clients are silently routed to a new singleton object. .NET supports infinite lease time. When you design a singleton object, override InitializeLifetimeService() and return a null object as the new lease, indicating to .NET that this lease never expires:

```
public class MySingleton : MarshalByRefObject
{
    public override object InitializeLifetimeService()
    {
        return null;
    }
}
```

Returning an infinite lease relieves you of managing global lease defaults or dealing with sponsors. In fact, you can use an infinite lease with any object activation mode, but it makes sense only in the case of a singleton.

Leasing a client-activated object

Client-activated objects are the most affected by the leasing mechanism. The only safe way to manage client-activated objects is to use sponsors. All other options, such as setting global lease properties or configuring individual objects' leases, are guesses or heuristics at best. Ultimately, only the client knows when it no longer requires an object. The sponsor should renew each object's lease with an amount of time that on the one hand balances network traffic and load on the lease manager, and on the other hand is granular enough to manage the resources the object may hold. If the sponsor provides too short a renewed lease the lease manager will have to query it frequently to renew the lease, which may result in unnecessary traffic. If the sponsored lease is too long, the lease manager may end up keeping the remote object alive when the client no longer needs it. Every case is unique, and when throughput and performance are a concern, you will have to investigate and profile the system with various sponsorship renewal times. I can, however, offer the following rule of thumb: in general, the sponsorship time should be the same as the initial lease time. The reason is that if the initial lease time is good enough for your case—that is, it doesn't generate too much traffic and isn't too coarse—it's likely to be just as suitable for the sponsors on subsequent lease-extension requests.

Example 10-11 demonstrates a client using a client-activated object whose lifetime is controlled by a sponsor. You can use this code as a template or a starting point for your remote client-activated objects. The source code accompanying this book contains Example 10-11 in the Leasing solution. The solution has three projects: the *ServerAssembly* class library, the *RemoteServerHost* EXE assembly, and the *Client* EXE assembly. These projects are very similar to those presented in Example 10-7. The host is identical to the one in Example 10-7; the only difference is in the configuration file. The host registers the MyCAO type as a client-activated object. Because the sponsor is provided to the host in the form of a remote callback object, the host must set its channel's type-filtering level to Full. The rest of the host is omitted from Example 10-11. The *ServerAssembly* class library contains the MyCAO definition, so both the client and the host can access its metadata. The client assembly contains the MySponsor class, because there is no need to put the sponsor in a class library; all the host needs is the metadata for the ISponsor interface, which is already part of the .NET class libraries. The MySponsor implementation of Renewal( ) simply extends the lease by the initial lease time. The client configuration file designates the MyCAO type as a remote client-activated object, and it registers the port 0 with the channel, as well as elevating type filtering to Full to allow calls back to the sponsor. The client's class (ClientForm) has as member variables both the remote client-activated object and the sponsor. In its constructor, the client creates new instances of the server and the sponsor and registers the sponsor with the lease of the client-activated object. The client is a Windows Forms dialog, with a single button. When clicked, the button simply calls the client-activated object. When the user closes the dialog, the client unregisters the sponsors.

Example 10-11. Sponsoring a client-activated object

```
/////////////   RemoteServerHost.exe.config : the host configuration file  ////////
<?xml version="1.0" encoding="utf-8"?>
<configuration>
   <system.runtime.remoting>
      <application>
         <service>
            <activated  type="RemoteServer.MyCAO,ServerAssembly"/>
         </service>
         <channels>
            <channel ref="tcp" port="8005">
               <serverProviders>
                  <formatter ref="soap"   typeFilterLevel="Full"/>
                  <formatter ref="binary" typeFilterLevel="Full"/>
               </serverProviders>
            </channel>
         </channels>
      </application>
   </system.runtime.remoting>
</configuration>
////////////////////   ServerAssembly class library  /////////////////////////////
namespace RemoteServer
{
   public class MyCAO : MarshalByRefObject
   {
      int m_Counter = 0;
      public void Count( )
      {
         m_Counter++;
         string appName = AppDomain.CurrentDomain.FriendlyName;
         MessageBox.Show("Counter value is " + m_Counter,appName);
      }
   }
}
////////////////   Client.exe.config: the client configuration file  //////////////
<?xml version="1.0" encoding="utf-8"?>
<configuration>
   <system.runtime.remoting>
      <application>
         <client url="tcp://localhost:8005">
            <activated  type="RemoteServer.MyCAO,ServerAssembly"/>
         </client>
         <channels>
            <channel ref="tcp" port="0">
              <serverProviders>
                  <formatter ref="soap" typeFilterLevel="Full"/>
                  <formatter ref="binary" typeFilterLevel="Full"/>
               </serverProviders>
            </channel>
         </channels>
      </application>
   </system.runtime.remoting>
</configuration>
```

Example 10-11. Sponsoring a client-activated object (continued)

```
////////////////////////// Client EXE assembly //////////////////////////////
using System.Runtime.Remoting.Lifetime;

public class MySponsor : MarshalByRefObject,ISponsor
{
   public TimeSpan Renewal(ILease lease)
   {
      Debug.Assert(lease.CurrentState == LeaseState.Active);

      return lease.InitialLeaseTime;
   }
}

using RemoteServer;

partial class ClientForm : Form
{
   Button m_CallButton;

   ISponsor m_Sponsor;
   MyCAO m_MyCAO;

   public ClientForm( )
   {
      InitializeComponent( );

      m_Sponsor = new MySponsor( );
      m_MyCAO = new MyCAO( );

      //Register the sponsor
      ILease lease = (ILease)RemotingServices.GetLifetimeService(m_MyCAO);
      lease.Register(m_Sponsor);
   }
   void InitializeComponent( )
   {...}

   static void Main( )
   {
      RemotingConfigurationEx.Configure( );

      Application.Run(new ClientForm( ));
   }
   void OnCall(object sender,EventArgs e)
   {
      m_MyCAO.Count( );
   }
   void OnClosed(object sender,EventArgs e)
   {
      //Unegister the sponsor
      ILease lease = (ILease)RemotingServices.GetLifetimeService(m_MyCAO);
      lease.Unregister(m_Sponsor);
```

Example 10-11. Sponsoring a client-activated object (continued)

```
   }
}
```

Sponsorship Management

The sponsor in Example 10-11 is a completely general-purpose sponsor that simply returns the initial lease time (whatever that may be) on every renewal request. The problem with the code shown in Example 10-11 is that the client has to keep track of its remote objects and manually unregister each remote lease's sponsor when the application shuts down. However, you can automate this by providing a client-side sponsorship manager, in the form of the SponsorshipManager[*] helper class:

```
public class SponsorshipManager : MarshalByRefObject,
                                  ISponsor,
                                  IDisposable,
                                  IEnumerable<ILease>

{
   public void Dispose( );
   public TimeSpan Renewal(ILease lease);
   public IEnumerator<ILease> GetEnumerator( );

   public void Register(MarshalByRefObject obj);
   public void Unregister(MarshalByRefObject obj);
   public void UnregisterAll( );
   public void OnExit(object sender,EventArgs e);
}
```

Example 10-12 shows the implementation of SponsorshipManager, which is available with the source code of this book.

Example 10-12. The SponsorshipManager helper class

```
public class SponsorshipManager : MarshalByRefObject,
                                  ISponsor,
                                  IDisposable,
                                  IEnumerable<ILease>
{
  IList<ILease> m_LeaseList = new List<ILease>( );

  ~SponsorshipManager( )
  {
    UnregisterAll( );
  }
  void IDisposable.Dispose( )
  {
```

---

[*] I first presented SponsorshipManager in the December 2003 issue of *MSDN Magazine*.

Example 10-12. The SponsorshipManager helper class (continued)

```
    UnregisterAll();
}
TimeSpan ISponsor.Renewal(ILease lease)
{
    Debug.Assert(lease.CurrentState == LeaseState.Active);
    return lease.InitialLeaseTime;
}
IEnumerator<ILease> IEnumerable<ILease>.GetEnumerator()
{
    foreach(ILease lease in m_LeaseList)
    {
        yield return lease;
    }
}
IEnumerator IEnumerable.GetEnumerator()
{
    IEnumerable<ILease> enumerable = this;
    return enumerable.GetEnumerator()
}
public void OnExit(object sender,EventArgs e)
{
    UnregisterAll();
}
public void Register(MarshalByRefObject obj)
{
    ILease lease = (ILease)RemotingServices.GetLifetimeService(obj);
    Debug.Assert(lease.CurrentState == LeaseState.Active);

    lease.Register(this);
    lock(this)
    {
        m_LeaseList.Add(lease);
    }
}
public void Unregister(MarshalByRefObject obj)
{
    ILease lease = (ILease)RemotingServices.GetLifetimeService(obj);
    Debug.Assert(lease.CurrentState == LeaseState.Active);

    lease.Unregister(this);
    lock(this)
    {
        m_LeaseList.Remove(lease);
    }
}
public void UnregisterAll()
{
    lock(this)
    {
        while(m_LeaseList.Count>0)
        {
            ILease lease = m_LeaseList[0];
```

Example 10-12. The SponsorshipManager helper class (continued)

```
                lease.Unregister(this);
                m_LeaseList.RemoveAt(0);
            }
        }
    }
}
```

The ClientSponsor Class

.NET provides a class for sponsorship management called ClientSponsor, defined as:

```
    public class ClientSponsor : MarshalByRefObject,ISponsor
    {
        public ClientSponsor();
        public ClientSponsor(TimeSpan renewalTime);
        public TimeSpan RenewalTime{get;set;}
        public void Close();
        public bool Register(MarshalByRefObject obj);
        public virtual TimeSpan Renewal(ILease lease);
        public void Unregister(MarshalByRefObject obj);
    }
```

ClientSponsor is similar in its design and use to SponsorshipManager, but unlike with SponsorshipManager, which returns the initial lease timeout for each lease, with ClientSponsor the client must explicitly set a single fixed lease renewal timeout for all sponsored leases. Because of this behavior, I recommend that you use SponsorshipManager instead of ClientSponsor.

SponsorshipManager implements ISponsor by returning the initial lease time of the provided lease. In addition, it maintains in a member variable called m_LeaseList a generic linked list of all the leases it sponsors. SponsorshipManager provides the Register( ) method:

```
    public void Register(MarshalByRefObject obj);
```

Register( ) accepts a remote object, extracts the lease from it, registers SponsorshipManager as the sponsor, and adds the lease to the internal list. The Unregister( ) method of the SponsorshipManager class is defined as:

```
    public void Unregister(MarshalByRefObject obj);
```

This method removes the lease associated with the specified object from the list and unregisters SponsorshipManager as a sponsor. SponsorshipManager also provides the UnregisterAll( ) method:

```
    public void UnregisterAll( );
```

This method unregisters SponsorshipManager from all the lease objects in the list. Note that the list access is done in a thread-safe manner by locking the

SponsorshipManager on every access. Thread safety is required because multiple clients on multiple threads can use the same SponsorshipManager instance to manage their remote leases. However, the clients should not bother themselves with calling Unregister( ) or UnregisterAll( )—SponsorshipManager provides an event-handling method called OnExit( ):

```
public void OnExit(object sender,EventArgs e);
```

OnExit( ) calls UnregisterAll( ) as a response to the client application shutting down. Example 10-13 shows how to use SponsorshipManager by a Windows Forms client.

Example 10-13. Using SponsorshipManager

```
partial class ClientForm : Form
{
   Button m_CallButton;
   SponsorshipManager m_SponsorshipManager;
   MyCAO m_MyCAO; //The remote CAO

   public ClientForm( )
   {
      InitializeComponent( );

      m_SponsorshipManager = new SponsorshipManager( );
      m_MyCAO = new MyCAO( );

      m_SponsorshipManager.Register(m_MyCAO);
      Application.ApplicationExit += m_SponsorshipManager.OnExit;
   }
   void InitializeComponent( )
   {...}

   static void Main( )
   {
      RemotingConfigurationEx.Configure( );
      Application.Run(new ClientForm( ));
   }
   void OnCall(object sender,EventArgs e)
   {
      m_MyCAO.Count( );
   }
}
```

The client in Example 10-13 maintains as member variables a remote object of type MyCAO (defined in Example 10-11) and a SponsorshipManager object. The client registers the remote object with SponsorshipManager and hooks up the application OnExit event with the SponsorshipManager OnExit( ) event-handling method. SponsorshipManager does the rest—it registers itself as the sponsor, and it unregisters all the remote leases it sponsors automatically when the client shuts down. Finally, note the use of C# 2.0 iterators* in implementing the IEnumerable<ILease> interface.

The interface allows clients to iterate over the list of managed sponsors, if the need ever arises:

```
SponsorshipManager sponsorshipManager = new SponsorshipManager();
//Some code to initialize sponsorshipManager, then:
foreach(ILease lease in sponsorshipManager)
{...}
```

.NET and Location Transparency

As explained in Chapter 1, a core principle of component-oriented programming is location transparency. Location transparency means that the same client-side code can interact both with local objects and with remote objects, and ideally, the same component can be used either locally or remotely (see Figure 10-3). Put differently, if a component works locally, it should work remotely, and if a client can use a component locally, it should be able to use the component remotely. There should be nothing in the client code pertaining to location. DCOM supported location transparency—as long as the Registry contained the right settings, location transparency was a reality in DCOM. Thus, after dozens of pages analyzing .NET remoting, it's time to ask: does .NET support location transparency, and if so, to what degree?

This section examines location transparency with regard to marshal-by-reference objects only. Both DCOM and .NET allow marshal-by-value objects (although not with the same ease), but marshal-by-value objects clearly don't comply with location transparency in DCOM or in .NET. I also don't think that the location transparency principle on the component side is relevant to singleton or single-call objects. These server-activated components are different by design: a single-call object must manage its state, and a singleton object is bound to a particular single resource. However, the client of a server-activated object can still benefit from location transparency.

As you've seen, there are many ways to achieve the same result in .NET remoting, and the differences are usually a trade-off between flexibility and ease of use. To maximize compliance with location transparency, the host and the client should use configuration files and always load them, even if they don't contain a remoting section. This allows you to modify the component locations and make changes only in the configuration files, similar to making changes in the Registry to modify the locations of DCOM components. The client and the host should avoid explicit channel and object registration, and the client should use new to create remote objects. The result on both the client side and the host side is a single line of code (loading the configuration file):

---

* If you are unfamiliar with C# 2.0 iterators, see my article "Create Elegant Code with Anonymous Methods, Iterators, and Partial Classes" in the May 2004 issue of *MSDN Magazine*.

```
RemotingConfigurationEx.Configure( );
```

However, even if the host and the client use configuration files, there are still unavoidable deviations from full compliance with location transparency:

- The remote component must derive from MarshalByRefObject. In .NET (unlike in DCOM), you can't take any component the client uses and access it remotely.
- The remote host must be running before the clients try to connect to it. DCOM, on the other hand, could launch the remote process automatically.
- The client has to provide a sponsor for client-activated objects. DCOM used reference counting instead.

With these constraints in mind, if I were to grade it, I'd give .NET a C in absolute terms on compliance with location transparency.

CHAPTER 11

Context and Interception

One of the most important aspects of .NET as a component technology is its use of contexts to facilitate component services. The core design pattern is *interception*: intercepting a call from a client to an object, performing some pre-call processing, forwarding the call to the object, and doing some post-call processing before returning control back to the client. Objects indicate to .NET which component services they need, and using interception, .NET makes sure the objects get the required runtime environment. .NET component services are mostly the result of integrating COM+ into .NET. In addition, .NET allows you to provide your own custom component services. This chapter starts by providing a brief introduction to interception-based component services. You will then learn how .NET components can use such services and what the underlying architecture is that enables them. The chapter concludes by demonstrating how you can extend .NET by providing your own custom component services.

.NET Component Services

.NET provides component services via call interception. To intercept a call, .NET must insert a proxy between the client and the object and do some pre- and post-call processing. Call interception is the key to valuable, productivity-oriented component services. For example, interception can provide thread safety by trying to acquire a lock before accessing the object and then proceeding to call the object. While the call is in progress, calls coming in from other clients are intercepted as well, and those calls will be blocked when they try to access the lock. When the call returns from the object to the proxy, it unlocks the lock to allow other clients to use the object. Another example of an interception-based component service is *call authorization*: the proxy can verify that the caller has appropriate credentials (such as being a member of a specified role) to call the object, and deny access if it does not. The problem with call interception is that an app domain is too coarse an execution scope; even though cross–app domain calls always go through a proxy, some app domain calls use direct references. To address this problem, app domains are further subdivided into contexts, and objects execute in contexts rather than app domains (see Figure 11-1).

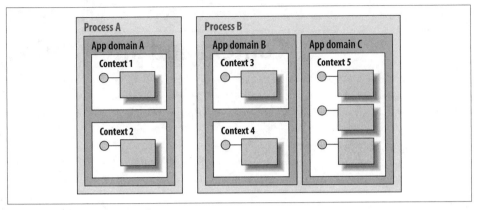

Figure 11-1. App domains and contexts

In .NET, the *context* is the innermost execution scope of an object. Components indicate to .NET which services they require using special context attributes. All objects in the same context are compatible in terms of their component services requirements, and .NET doesn't need to perform pre- and post-call processing when these objects access one another. You can, therefore, define a context as a logical grouping of objects that rely on the same set of services. Calls into the context are intercepted to ensure that the objects always get the appropriate runtime environment they require to operate.

Contexts and Object Types

What if a component doesn't require any services? Why should it pay the interception penalty for cross-context access? To address this point, .NET objects are classified into two categories: those that care about component services and want to use them, and those that don't. By default, objects are context-agnostic and have no context affinity, which means they always execute in the contexts of their calling clients. Because such context-agnostic objects "jump" from one context to the next, they are referred to as *context-agile objects*. The clients of a context-agile object each have a direct reference to it, and no proxies are involved when making intra–app domain calls. Note that objects that derive from MarshalByRefObject are accessed via a proxy across app domains but are agile inside an app domain. Marshal-by-value objects are also context-agile.

The other type of object is called a *context-bound object*. Context-bound objects always execute in the same context. The designation and affinity of a context-bound object to a context is decided when the object is created and is fixed for the life of the object. To qualify as a context-bound object, the object must derive directly (or have one of its base classes derive) from the abstract class ContextBoundObject:

```
public class MyClass : ContextBoundObject
{...}
```

The client of a context-bound object never has a direct reference to it. Instead, the client always interacts with a context-bound object via a proxy. Because ContextBoundObject is derived from MarshalByRefObject, every context-bound object is also marshaled by reference across app domain boundaries. This makes perfect sense, because the context-bound object can't leave its context, let alone its app domain.

Component Services Types

.NET provides two kinds of component services: context-bound services and Enterprise Services. The *context-bound services* are available to any context-bound object. .NET offers only one such service: the synchronization domain, described in Chapter 8. Using the Synchronization context attribute, a context-bound component gains automatic synchronization and lock sharing:

```
[Synchronization]
public class MyClass : ContextBoundObject
{
    public MyClass()
    {}
    public void DoSomething()
    {}
}
```

When you add the Synchronization attribute, .NET ensures that only one thread at a time is allowed to access the object, without requiring you to spend the effort implementing this functionality yourself, and you don't have to worry about deadlocks. Clients of such objects don't need to worry about synchronization either. Although this is the only context-bound service provided out-of-the-box, the .NET context is an extensible mechanism, and you can define your own custom context attributes for custom services and extensions. The rest of this chapter examines the .NET context and context-bound objects in detail, and demonstrates how to develop custom context-bound services and attributes.

The second kind of component services are *.NET Enterprise Services* (see the sidebar ".NET Enterprise Services"). Enterprise Services offer more than 20 component services covering an impressive array of domains, from transactions to loosely coupled events to web services. Enterprise Services are available only to classes derived from the class ServicedComponent. ServicedComponent is in turn derived from ContextBoundObject, so you can say that Enterprise Services are a specialization of context-bound services. If you develop a serviced component, you normally indicate which services the component relies on by using dedicated attributes.

Enterprise Services attributes aren't .NET context attributes, but rather COM+ context attributes.

.NET Enterprise Services

.NET Enterprise Services are a set of component services designed to ease the development of Enterprise applications. .NET Enterprise Services are the result of integrating COM+ into .NET, and they offer the same range of services essential to any Enterprise application. For the most part, the semantics of the services, the algorithms behind them, the benefits, and the implied programming models remain exactly the same as they were for COM components. .NET components that take advantage of Enterprise Services are called *serviced components* because they derive from the class ServicedComponent, defined in the System.EnterpriseServices namespace. You can configure the services by using context attributes in your code. For example, if you want .NET to maintain a pool of your objects, and you want there to be at least 3 but no more than 10 objects in the pool, use the ObjectPooling attribute:

```
using System.EnterpriseServices;

[ObjectPooling(MinPoolSize = 3,MaxPoolSize = 10)]
public class MyComponent : ServicedComponent
{...}
```

If you also want transaction support, use the Transaction attribute:

```
using System.EnterpriseServices;

[Transaction]
[ObjectPooling(MinPoolSize = 3,MaxPoolSize = 10)]
public class MyComponent : ServicedComponent
{...}
```

You can also configure the pool parameters (and any other services) after deployment by using the COM+ Component Services Explorer. However, due to .NET's ability to persist the attributes in the assembly metadata, there is often no need to use the Component Services Explorer for services configuration. You can read about .NET Enterprise Services in my book *COM and .NET Component Services* (O'Reilly).

The .NET Context

Every new app domain starts with a single context, called the *default context*. The default context provides no component services at all. The main reason why it exists is to help maintain a consistent programming model. The first object created in the new app domain is placed in the default context, even if it isn't a context-bound object. This maintains the design principle that all objects execute in a context, even if they don't care about component services. An app domain can contain multiple contexts, and .NET creates new contexts as needed. There is no limit to the number of contexts an app domain can contain. A given context belongs to exactly one app domain and can host multiple context-bound objects (see Figure 11-1). Every context has a unique ID (an integer) called the *context ID*. The context ID is guaranteed to be unique in the scope of an app domain. Every .NET context has a *context object* associated with it. The context object is an instance of the class Context, defined in the System.Runtime.Remoting.Contexts namespace. You typically don't need to interact with the context object. However, for diagnostics and tracing purposes, it's sometimes useful to retrieve the context ID, using the ContextID read-only property of the context object:

```
public class Context
{
   public virtual int ContextID{get;}
   //Other members
}
```

Every object can access the context object of the context it's executing by using the CurrentContext static read-only property of the Thread class:

```
public sealed class Thread
{
   public static Context CurrentContext{ get; }
   /* Other members  */
}
```

For example, here is how an object can trace its context ID:

```
int contextID = Thread.CurrentContext.ContextID;
Trace.WriteLine("Context ID is " + contextID);
```

Note that threads can enter and exit contexts, and in general, they have no affinity to any particular context.

Assigning Objects to Contexts

As presented earlier, there are two kinds of .NET types: context-agile and context-bound. Both always execute in a context, and the main difference is in their affinity to that context. The context-agile behavior is the .NET default. Any class that doesn't derive from ContextBoundObject is context-agile. Context-agile objects have no interest in component services; they can execute in the contexts of their calling clients because .NET doesn't need to intercept incoming calls to them. When a client creates a context-agile object, the object executes in the context of its creating client. The client gets a direct reference to the object, and no proxies are involved. The client can pass the object reference to a different client in the same context or in a different context. When the other client uses the object, the object executes in the context of that client. The context-agile model is shown in Figure 11-2. Note that it's incorrect to state that a context-agile object has no context. It does have one—the context of the client making the call. If the context-agile object retrieves its context object and queries the value of the context ID, it gets the same context ID as its calling client.

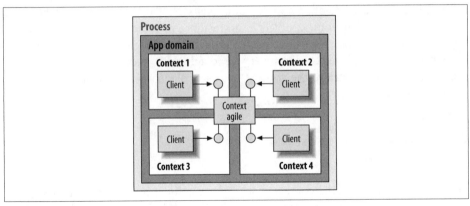

Figure 11-2. A context-agile object

COM+ also had the notion of context-agile objects, in the form of objects that aggregated the free-threaded marshaler (FTM). The FTM introduced some nasty side effects in cases in which the object had other COM+ objects as members, though, and was therefore a technique to avoid.

The picture is drastically different when it comes to context-bound objects. A context-bound object is bound to a particular context for life. The decision regarding which context the object resides in takes place when the object is created and is based on the services the object requires and the context of its creating client. If the creating client's context is "good enough" for the object's needs—i.e., the context has adequate properties, and the client and the object use a compatible set of component services—the object is placed in its creating client's context. If, on the other hand, the object requires some other service that the creating client's context doesn't support, .NET creates a new context and places the new object in it. Note that .NET doesn't try to find out if there is already another appropriate context for the object in that app domain. The algorithm is simple: the object either shares its creator's context or gets a new context. This algorithm intentionally trades memory and context-management overhead for speed in allocating the new object to a context. The other alternative would be to examine each of a potentially long list of existing contexts, but that search might take a long time to complete and impede performance. If the object is placed in a different context from that of its creating client, the client gets back from .NET a reference to a proxy instead of a direct reference (see Figure 11-3). The proxy intercepts the calls the client makes on the object and performs some pre- and post-call processing to provide the object with the services it requires.

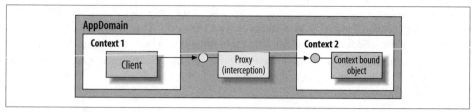

Figure 11-3. Clients of a context-bound object access it via a proxy

 The .NET policy for allocating context-bound objects to contexts is very similar to the COM+ context activation policy.

The Call Interception Architecture

The cross-context interception architecture is similar to the one used across app domain boundaries. Recall from Chapter 10 that in .NET, the proxy has two parts: a transparent proxy and a real proxy. The transparent proxy exposes the same public entry points as the object. When the client calls the transparent proxy, it converts the stack frame to a message and passes the message to the real proxy. The message is an object implementing the IMessage interface:

```
public interface IMessage
{
    IDictionary Properties{ get; }
}
```

The message is a collection of properties, such as the method's name and its arguments. The real proxy knows where the actual object resides. In the case of a call across app domains, the real proxy needs to serialize the message using a formatter and pass it to the channel. In the case of a cross-context call, the real proxy needs to apply interception steps before forwarding the call to the object. An elegant design solution allows .NET to use the same real proxy in both cases. The real proxy doesn't know about formatters, channels, or context interceptors; it simply passes the message to a message sink. A message sink is an object that implements the IMessageSink interface, defined in the System.Runtime.Remoting.Messaging namespace:

```
public interface IMessageSink
{
    IMessageSink NextSink{ get; }
    IMessageCtrl AsyncProcessMessage(IMessage msg,IMessageSink replySink);
    IMessage SyncProcessMessage(IMessage msg);
}
```

.NET strings together message sinks in a linked list. Each message sink knows about the next sink in the list (you can also get the next sink via the NextSink property). The real proxy calls the SyncProcessMessage( ) method of the first sink, allowing it to

process the message. After processing the message, the first sink calls
`SyncProcessMessage()` on the next sink. In the case of cross–app domain calls, the
first sink on the client's side is the message formatter (look at Figure 10-9 again).
After formatting the message, the formatter sink passes it to the next sink—the transport channel. When the `SyncProcessMessage()` method returns to the proxy, it
returns the returned message from the object.

 The `IMessageSink` interface also provides the `AsyncProcessMessage()`
method, which intercepts asynchronous calls (a topic that's beyond
the scope of this book).

Cross-context sinks

In the case of a cross-context call, there is no need for a formatter; .NET uses an
internal channel called `CrossContextChannel`, which is also a message sink. However,
there is a difference in component services configuration between the client and the
object, and it's up to the sinks to compensate for these differences. .NET installs as
many message sinks as required between the client's context and the object (see
Figure 11-4).

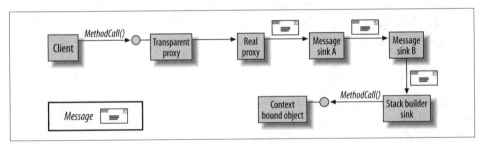

Figure 11-4. A cross-context call to a context-bound object

The .NET context interception architecture is similar to the Decorator design pattern[*] and is a private case of aspect-oriented programming (discussed later, in the
sidebar "Contexts, AOP, and Indigo"). A typical message sink does both pre- and
post-call processing. The canonical example is again thread synchronization. The
sink needs to acquire a lock before proceeding to call the object, and it must release
the lock after the method returns. The next sink down the call chain may enforce
security, and so on.

It's best to use an example to demystify the way sinks work. Example 11-1 shows a
generic sink implementation. The sink constructor accepts the next sink in the chain.
When the `SyncProcessMessage()` method is called, the sink performs some pre-call

---

[*] See *Design Patterns: Elements of Reusable Object-Oriented Software*, by E. Gamma, R. Helm, R. Johnson,
and J. Vlissides (Addison-Wesley).

processing and then calls SyncProcessMessage( ) on the next sink. The call advances down the sink chain until it reaches a *stack-builder sink*, the last sink. The stack builder converts the message to a stack frame and calls the object. When the call returns to the stack builder, it constructs a return message with the method results and returns that message to the sink that called it. That sink then does its post-call processing and returns control to the sink that called it, and so on. Eventually, the call returns to the generic sink. The generic sink now has a chance to examine the returned message and do some post-call processing before returning control to the sink that called it. The first sink in the chain returns control to the real proxy, providing it with the returned message from the object. The real proxy returns the message to the transparent proxy, which places it back on the calling client's stack.

Example 11-1. Generic implementation of a message sink

```
public class GenericSink : IMessageSink
{
    IMessageSink m_NextSink;

    public GenericSink(IMessageSink nextSink)
    {
        m_NextSink = nextSink;
    }

    public IMessageSink NextSink
    {
        get
        {
            return m_NextSink;
        }
    }
    public IMessage SyncProcessMessage(IMessage msg)
    {
        PreCallProcessing(msg);

        //This calls the object:
        IMessage returnedMessage = m_NextSink.SyncProcessMessage(msg);

        PostCallProcessing(returnedMessage);

        return returnedMessage;
    }
    void PreCallProcessing(IMessage msg)
    {
        /* Do some pre-call processing */
    }
    void PostCallProcessing(IMessage msg)
    {
        /* Do some post-call processing */
    }
    public IMessageCtrl AsyncProcessMessage(IMessage msg,IMessageSink replySink)
    {
```

Example 11-1. Generic implementation of a message sink (continued)

```
    /* Handle the asynchronous call, then: */
    return m_NextSink.AsyncProcessMessage(msg,replySink);
  }
}
```

Message sink types

Call interception can take place in two places. First, sinks can intercept calls coming into the context and do some pre- and post-call processing, such as locking and unlocking a thread lock. Such sinks are called *server-side sinks*. Second, sinks can intercept calls going out of the context and do some pre- and post-call processing. Such sinks are called *client-side sinks*. For example, using a client-side sink, the Synchronization attribute can optionally track calls outside the synchronization domain and unlock locks to allow other threads access. This is done using a client-side sink. You will see later how to install sinks.

Server-side sinks intercepting all calls into the context are called *server context sinks*. Server-side sinks intercepting calls to a particular object are called *server object sinks*. The server is responsible for installing server-side sinks. Client-side sinks installed by the client are called *client context sinks*, and they affect all calls going out of the context. Client-side sinks installed by the object are called *envoy sinks*. An envoy sink intercepts calls only to the particular object with which it's associated. The last sink on the client's side and the first sink on the server's side are instances of the type CrossContextChannel. The resulting sink chain is comprised of segments, each of which is a different type of sink, as shown in Figure 11-5. Because there must be a stack builder at the end of the sink chain to convert messages, .NET installs a terminator at the end of each segment. A *terminator* is a sink of the segment's type; it does the final processing for that segment and forwards the message to the next segment. For example, the last message sink in the server context sink segment is called the ServerContextTerminatorSink. The terminators behave like true dead ends: if you call IMessageSink.NextSink on a terminator, you get back a null reference. The actual next sink (the first sink in the next segment) is a private member of the terminator. As a result, there is no way to iterate using IMessageSink.NextSink on the entire length of the interception chain.

 There is another type of sink, called a *dynamic sink*, that lets you add a sink programmatically at runtime, without using attributes. Dynamic sinks are beyond the scope of this book.

Same-Context Calls

A context-bound object must always be accessed via a proxy across a context boundary, so that the various sinks can be in place to intercept the calls. The question now is, what happens if a client in the same context as the object passes a reference to the

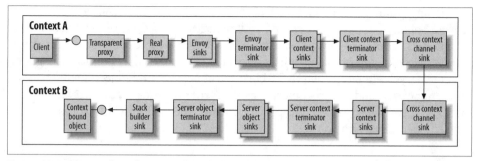

Figure 11-5. Client-side and server-side sink chains

object to a client in a different context (for example, by setting the value of some static variable)? If the same-context client has a direct reference to the object, how can .NET detect that and introduce a proxy between the object and the new client? .NET solves the problem by always having the object accessed via a proxy, even by clients in the same context (see Figure 11-6). Because the client and the object share the same context, there is no need for message sinks to perform any pre- or post-call processing. The interception layer consists of the transparent and real proxy, and a single message sink—the stack builder. When the same-context client passes its reference to the transparent proxy to clients in other contexts, .NET detects that and sets up the correct interception chain between the new clients and the object.

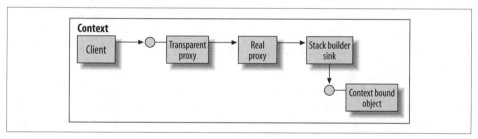

Figure 11-6. Even in the same context, clients access a context-bound object using a proxy

In the COM+ world, same-context clients had direct references to the objects. As a result, developers had to manually marshal those references—that is, they had to manually set up the proxy, and the two clients had to coordinate on the marshaling protocol. This was often done using the Global Interface Table (GIT).

Context-Bound Objects and Remoting

Context-bound objects are a special case of .NET remoting (in particular, of client-activated objects). In many respects .NET treats them just like remote objects, but it does optimize some elements of its remoting architecture for context-bound objects—for example, as mentioned previously, the channel used for cross-context calls is an optimized channel called CrossContextChannel. For truly remote client-activated objects, .NET creates a lease and manages the lifecycle of the object via the lease and its sponsors. However, because the client of a context-bound object shares with it the same app domain, .NET can still use garbage collection to manage the object's lifecycle. In fact, when .NET creates a context-bound object it still creates a lease for it, and the object can even override MarshalByRefObject.InitializeLifetimeService() and provide its own lease. However, the lease doesn't control the lifetime of the object.

 With truly remote objects, when the TCP or HTTP channels marshal a reference across a process boundary, these channels set up the lease. With cross-context or cross–app domain objects, the CrossContextChannel and CrossAppDomainChannel channels ignore the lease and let the remote objects be managed via garbage collection.

Custom Component Services

The ability to install custom component services in .NET is a major advancement for software engineering and component-oriented programming. Custom component services allow you to fine-tune and optimize the way .NET services your particular application and business logic. Custom component services decouple clients from objects, because they don't need to coordinate the execution of the custom service; you can focus on implementing the business logic, rather than the service. Examples of custom services include application logging and tracing, performance counters, custom thread management, filtering of method calls, parameter checks, event subscriptions, and so on.

Custom component services are provided in the form of *custom context attributes*. Ordinary custom attributes (such as the ones discussed in Appendix C) have no use unless you provide the reflection code to look for these attributes, interpret their values, and act upon them. .NET is indifferent to such custom attributes. Unlike generic custom attributes, .NET is very much aware of custom context attributes when they are used on context-bound objects. Context attributes must derive from the class ContextAttribute, defined in the System.Runtime.Remoting.Contexts namespace. When creating a new context-bound object, .NET reflects the object's metadata and places it in the appropriate context based on the behavior of the attributes. Custom context attributes can affect the context in which the object is activated and can be used to install all four types of message sink interceptors. The next two sections demonstrate how to build custom context attributes and component services. First, you will see how to develop a custom context attribute and how it affects the activation context; then you'll look at how to install custom message sinks. Finally, you'll walk though the development of two real-life, useful custom component services.

Custom context attributes and custom message sinks are undocumented features of .NET. Microsoft is committed to supporting contexts in future versions of .NET, but not to extending the infrastructure and adding features.

Building a Custom Context Attribute

Each context has a set of properties associated with it. The properties are the component services the context supports. A context-bound object shares a context with its client only if the client's context has all the services the component requires—in other words, if the context has the required properties. If the client's context doesn't have one or more of the properties the object requires, .NET creates a new context and puts the object in it. In addition, a context property may require a new context regardless of the properties of the client's context. You use context attributes to specify the required services. The context attributes are those that decide whether or not the client's context is sufficient.

To understand how context attributes affect context activation, consider a custom context attribute that adds a color property to a context. The color is an enum of the type ColorOption:

```
public enum ColorOption{Red,Green,Blue};
```

You use ColorAttribute as a class attribute on a class derived from ContextBoundObject:

```
[Color(ColorOption.Blue)]
public class MyClass: ContextBoundObject
{...}
```

Obviously, a color property isn't much of a service, but it's a good example. .NET creates objects of the class MyClass in the client's context only if the creating client's context has a color property and if its value is set to ColorOption.Blue. Otherwise, .NET creates a new context, lets the attribute set its color property to ColorOption.Blue, and places the new object in the new context. ColorAttribute also has a default constructor, setting the context color to ColorOption.Red:

```
[Color]//Default is ColorOption.Red
public class MyClass: ContextBoundObject
{...}
```

Example 11-2 shows the implementation of the ColorAttribute custom context attribute.

Example 11-2. The ColorAttribute custom context attribute

```
using System.Runtime.Remoting.Contexts;
using System.Runtime.Remoting.Activation;

public enum ColorOption {Red,Green,Blue};
```

Example 11-2. The ColorAttribute custom context attribute (continued)

```csharp
[AttributeUsage(AttributeTargets.Class)]
public class ColorAttribute : ContextAttribute
{
   ColorOption m_Color;

   public ColorAttribute() : this(ColorOption.Red)//Default color is red
   {}

   public ColorAttribute(ColorOption color) : base("ColorAttribute")
   {
      m_Color = color;
   }
   //Add a new color property to the new context
   public override void GetPropertiesForNewContext(IConstructionCallMessage ctor)
   {
      IContextProperty colorProperty = new ColorProperty(m_Color);
      ctor.ContextProperties.Add(colorProperty);
   }
   //ctx is the creating client's context
   public override bool IsContextOK(Context ctx,IConstructionCallMessage ctorMsg)
   {
      ColorProperty contextColorProperty = null;
      //Find out if the creating context has a color property. If not, reject it
      contextColorProperty = ctx.GetProperty("Color") as ColorProperty;
      if(contextColorProperty == null)
      {
         return false;
      }
      //It does have a color property. Verify color match
      return (m_Color == contextColorProperty.Color);
   }
}

//The ColorProperty is added to the context properties collection by the
//ColorAttribute class
public class ColorProperty : IContextProperty
{
   ColorOption m_Color;

   public ColorProperty(ColorOption ContextColor)
   {
      Color = ContextColor;
   }
   public string Name
   {
      get
      {
         return "Color";
      }
   }
   //IsNewContextOK called by the runtime in the new context
   public bool IsNewContextOK(Context ctx)
```

Example 11-2. The ColorAttribute custom context attribute (continued)

```
{
   ColorProperty newContextColorProperty = null;
   //Find out if the new context has a color property. If not, reject it
   newContextColorProperty = ctx.GetProperty("Color") as ColorProperty;
   if(newContextColorProperty == null)
   {
      return false;
   }
   //It does have color property. Verify color match
   return (Color == newContextColorProperty.Color);
}

public void Freeze(Context ctx)
{}
//Color needs to be public so that the attribute class can access it
public ColorOption Color
{
   get
   {
      return m_Color;
   }
   set
   {
      m_Color = value;
   }
}
}
```

ColorAttribute has a member called m_Color that contains the required context color. The color is specified during the attribute construction, either explicitly or by using the default constructor. As a custom context attribute, it derives from ContextAttribute. The single constructor of ContextAttribute requires a string naming the new context attribute. This is provided by a call to the ContextAttribute constructor in the ColorAttribute constructor:

```
public ColorAttribute(ColorOption color) : base("ColorAttribute")
{...}
```

ContextAttribute derives from and provides a virtual implementation of the IContextAttribute interface, defined as:

```
public interface IContextAttribute
{
   void GetPropertiesForNewContext(IConstructionCallMessage msg);
   bool IsContextOK(Context ctx,IConstructionCallMessage msg);
}
```

The IsContextOK( ) method lets the context attribute examine the creating client's context, which is provided in the ctx parameter. If the client's context is adequate, no further action is required, and .NET activates the new object in the creating client's context. If the context attribute returns false from IsContextOK( ), .NET creates a new context and calls GetPropertiesForNewContext( ), letting the context attribute add new properties to the new context. Because a single object can have more than one context attribute, .NET can optimize its queries of the attributes. .NET starts iterating over the attribute list, calling IsContextOK( ) on each one. As soon as it finds an attribute in the list that returns false, .NET aborts the iteration and creates a new context. It then calls GetPropertiesForNewContext( ) on each context attribute, letting it add its properties to the new context. ColorAttribute needs to override both methods of IContextAttribute and manage its single context property. Context properties are objects that implement the IContextProperty interface:

```
public interface IContextProperty
{
    string Name{ get; }
    void Freeze(Context newContext);
    bool IsNewContextOK(Context newCtx);
}
```

Each context property is identified by name via the Name property of IContextProperty. ColorAttribute uses a helper class called ColorProperty to implement IContextProperty. ColorProperty names itself as "Color". ColorProperty also provides the Color public property of type ColorOption. This allows for type-safe checking of the color value.

In its implementation of IsContextOK( ), ColorAttribute checks whether the client's context has a property called "Color". If it doesn't, IsContextOK( ) returns false. If the client's context has a color property, ColorAttribute verifies that there is a color match by comparing the value of the color property with its own color.

The implementation of GetPropertiesForNewContext( ) is straightforward as well: the single parameter is an object of type IConstructionCallMessage, providing a collection of properties for the new context via the ContextProperties property. ColorAttribute creates an object of type ColorProperty, initializes it with the required color, and adds it to the collection of properties for the new context.

Because a single context-bound object can have multiple context attributes, it's possible that some will conflict with others. To handle such an eventuality, after adding all the properties to the new context, .NET calls IsNewContextOK( ) on each property. If a property returns false, .NET aborts creating the new object and throws an exception of type RemotingException. In IsNewContextOK( ), ColorAttribute simply verifies that the new context has the correct color. The Freeze( ) method lets a context property know that the final location of the context is established and available for advanced use only.

Figure 11-7 is a UML activity diagram summarizing the process flow when using a custom context attribute and a context property. The diagram shows the order in which the various methods take place and the resulting activation logic.

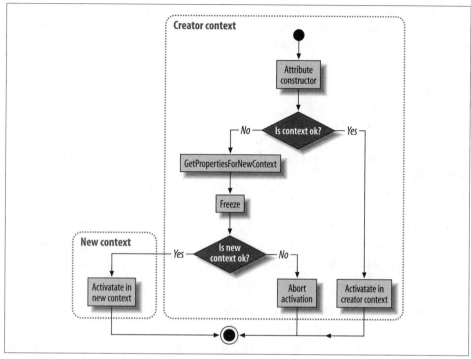

Figure 11-7. *Custom context attribute and property activity diagram*

Installing a Custom Message Sink

To provide a useful component service, the custom context attribute must install at least one custom message sink. The message sink can be either a server context sink, a client context sink, an envoy sink, or a server object sink. Commonly, a custom context attribute installs only a server context sink. The other sinks are intended for advanced cases, but you can install one if the need arises. For each type of custom sink you wish to contribute to the interception chain, the custom context property must implement a matching interface.

Providing a server context sink

To contribute a server context sink, the custom context property needs to implement the IContributeServerContextSink interface, defined as:

```
public interface IContributeServerContextSink
{
    IMessageSink GetServerContextSink(IMessageSink nextSink);
}
```

In its implementation of GetServerContextSink( ), the context property creates a sink object and concatenates it to the next sink in the chain, which is provided as the method parameter. GetServerContextSink( ) should return the new sink it created so that .NET can add it to the interception chain. For example, here is how to install GenericSink (presented in Example 11-2) as a server context sink:

```
public IMessageSink GetServerContextSink(IMessageSink nextSink)
{
    IMessageSink sink = new GenericSink(nextSink);
    return sink;
}
```

The server context sink intercepts all calls coming into the context. .NET calls GetServerContextSink( ) after its call to IContextProperty.IsNewContextOK( ) and before creating the object, allowing the context property to provide the sink. A server context sink can intercept construction calls.

Providing a client context sink

To install a client context sink, the context property needs to implement the IcontributeClientContextSink interface, defined as:

```
public interface IContributeClientContextSink
{
    IMessageSink GetClientContextSink(IMessageSink nextSink);
}
```

A client context sink affects the context-bound object only when it's the client of another object outside the context; it intercepts all calls exiting the context. .NET calls GetClientContextSink( ) only when the object makes its first call outside the context. The information in the message object passed to the sink pertains to the target object, not the client.

Providing an envoy sink

The context property can also implement the IContributeEnvoySink interface, defined as:

```
public interface IContributeEnvoySink
{
    IMessageSink GetEnvoySink(MarshalByRefObject obj,IMessageSink nextSink);
}
```

In this case, when a proxy to an object on the client's side is set up, the proxy has an envoy sink as part of the interception chain leading to that object. The envoy sink intercepts all calls going from the client to the object. Other objects accessed by the client aren't affected. Every time a new client in a different context connects to the object, .NET installs an envoy sink in that client's context. .NET calls GetEnvoySink( ) after creating the new object but before returning control to the client. You can't intercept construction calls with an envoy sink.

Providing an object sink

To install a server object sink, the context property needs to implement the IContributeObjectSink interface, defined as:

```
public interface IContributeObjectSink
{
    IMessageSink GetObjectSink(MarshalByRefObject obj,IMessageSink nextSink);
}
```

The object sink is installed on an object-by-object basis, which means it intercepts calls only to the object whose reference is provided in the GetObjectSink() call. Other calls into the context aren't affected. .NET calls GetObjectSink() before the first method call is forwarded to the object. As a result, you can't intercept construction calls with an object sink.

Processing messages

The IMessage interface presented previously is a collection of information about the method being intercepted. Although you can retrieve that information from the dictionary, there is a better way. When you intercept an incoming call, the different message objects (used for synchronous methods, asynchronous methods, and constructor calls) all support the IMethodMessage interface, defined as:

```
public interface IMethodMessage : IMessage
{
    int ArgCount{ get; }
    object[] Args{ get; }
    bool HasVarArgs{ get; }
    LogicalCallContext LogicalCallContext { get; }
    MethodBase MethodBase { get; }
    string MethodName{ get; }
    object MethodSignature{ get; }
    string TypeName{ get; }
    string Uri{ get; }
    object GetArg(int argNum);
    string GetArgName(int index);
}
```

IMethodMessage provides information about the method name, its arguments, the type on which the method was called, and the object's location. You can use that information in your pre-call message-processing logic. After the last sink—the stack builder—invokes the call on the object, it returns a different message object. Again, there are several types of returned method objects, but they are all polymorphic with the IMethodReturnMessage interface, defined as:

```
public interface IMethodReturnMessage : IMethodMessage
{
    Exception Exception { get; }
    int OutArgCount { get; }
    object[] OutArgs { get; }
    object ReturnValue { get; }
```

```
    object GetOutArg(int argNum);
    string GetOutArgName(int index);
}
```

`IMethodReturnMessage` derives from `IMethodMessage` and provides additional informa-tion about the method's returned value, the values of any outgoing parameters, and any exceptions. The fact that exception information is captured is of particular inter-est. If the object throws an exception, the stack-builder sink silently catches it and saves it in the returned message object. This allows all the sinks up the call chain to examine the exception object. When control returns to the proxy, if exception infor-mation is present, the proxy re-throws it on the calling client's side.

The Logbook Service

It's time to put all the knowledge and intricacies described so far to good use, with a comprehensive and useful real-life example. One of the most beneficial steps you can take to achieve a robust application and faster time to market is to add a logging capability to your application. This section presents you with the logbook—a simple custom component service that allows you to automatically log method calls and exceptions. The logbook is your product's flight recorder, and in a distributed envi-ronment, it's worth its weight in gold; with it, you can analyze why something didn't work the way it was supposed to. Examining the logbook entries, you can analyze what took place across machines and applications, and the source of the problem is usually almost immediately evident. The logbook is also useful for troubleshooting customer problems in post-deployment scenarios. The logbook intercepts incoming calls to your context-bound objects and logs most of the information in the mes-sages. As you will see shortly, you can use the same logbook to record method invo-cations from multiple machines and have the various entries interleaved in order.

Each logbook entry contains the following information, captured automatically by the logbook:

- The location where the method was invoked: machine name, app domain name, thread ID and name, and context ID
- The caller's identity (username)
- Information about the target object: its assembly, its type, and the member being accessed (constructor, method, property, indexer, or event)
- The invocation date and time
- Error information, if an exception was thrown: the type of the exception and the exception message

Using the logbook

A key requirement in designing the logbook was that it should require no explicit participation on behalf of the object. The object should focus on implementing its business logic, and the logbook should do the logging. To add logging support for a

Contexts, AOP, and Indigo

The next generation of Microsoft distributed application technology is code named Indigo. Indigo unifies the three remote-call technologies available in .NET: Enterprise Services, remoting, and web services. This new technology is designed to connect publicly exposed services. A *service* in Indigo terminology is something that exposes logical functionality across boundaries (e.g., machine or technology boundaries). Inside an Indigo service, you will still use conventional .NET programming. Indigo provides Enterprise Services–like services to the services it connects, such as propagation of transactions and security call contexts, thread synchronization, event publishing and subscription, and so on. Indigo is based on the exchange of messages. Indigo services are implemented using message interception and pre- or post-call processing. Indigo has its own notion of contexts, and it also provides for interception-based custom services.

Although .NET contexts will not be able to map into Indigo contexts, using them today has the potential of benefiting your Indigo applications in the future. The reason is that the programming model itself is reusable. Using interception-based component services takes the weight of developing the plumbing and infrastructure off the developers' shoulders and lets them be more productive by focusing on the business logic. This is, of course, the idea behind aspect-oriented programming (AOP): allowing you to add aspects to the business logic and leave the logic free of plumbing.

While AOP as a generic mechanism is impossible to implement due to the aspect-ordering problem, the ability to add a custom service to your application is very valuable indeed. When you implement a service in an aspect-oriented application, there are two things you need to do: you need to implement the decorating aspect, and you need to apply it. The aspect implementation is always specific to the technology used and is not trivial to port—it is tied to the particulars of your supporting technology. For example, the context sink interceptor implementation is not reusable and does not easily transfer to other technologies. You will have to reinvest in implementing your aspects and services in Indigo. However, aspects provide you with a valuable programming model on the using side by extracting from the application the code used for security, logging, and so on. This programming model is transferable across technologies—that is, if you use a .NET context attribute for logging, and the component code itself does not contain any logging logic, this programming model will be transferable to Indigo. Simply replace the context logging attribute with the equivalent Indigo logging attribute, and you get Indigo-based logging, without affecting the component code. Because there can be many components using any given .NET context-based service, the cost of implementing the service is amortized over many components; the real savings is in maintaining the programming model and its benefits on the component side.

context-bound object, add the `LogbookAttribute` custom context attribute, defined in the `ContextLogger` namespace:

```
using ContextLogger;
```

```
[Logbook]
```

```
public class MyClass : ContextBoundObject
{...}
```

The logbook service allows you to choose what information to log. Sometimes, it's necessary to record everything that takes place (method calls and errors). In other situations, it's sufficient to log only errors and exceptions. To that end, the logbook provides the enum LogOption, defined as:

```
public enum LogOption
{
   MethodCalls,
   Errors
}
```

You can provide the constructor of LogbookAttribute with the appropriate enum value. For example, to log only unhandled exceptions, write:

```
[Logbook(LogOption.Errors)]
public class MyClass : ContextBoundObject
{...}
```

The parameter-less constructor of LogbookAttribute defaults to LogOption. MethodCalls, so these two declarations are equivalent and can log both method calls and errors:

```
[Logbook]
[Logbook(LogOption.MethodCalls)]
```

The logbook service architecture

When you apply LogbookAttribute to a context-bound class, it requires private contexts for each instance to support logging of all calls coming into the object. If it were possible for two objects using the LogbookAttribute to share a context, cross-context calls would be logged, but intra-context calls made on one another wouldn't. The LogbookAttribute adds to the new context a property called LogContextProperty, which contributes a server-context sink called LogSink. LogSink intercepts all calls to the object but doesn't log them itself; instead, it uses the Logbook component, which encapsulates the actual logging mechanism. The implementation provided here logs to a SQL Server database, but you can replace that with any other repository. The Logbook is a remote singleton residing in an EXE host. As a result, all objects using the logbook service actually log to the same repository, in order. This is a key feature that allows you to trace the execution of a distributed application, because the host can be on a dedicated machine used by all other machines.

Figure 11-8 depicts the logbook architecture. In addition, a logbook viewer application is provided; it displays in a grid control the content of the logbook database entries table. The logbook viewer allows you to filter the grid to display methods and errors, or just errors. The application has another feature, too: you can export the logbook entries to a logfile, as well as display the content of an existing logfile. The logbook viewer doesn't connect to the database directly. Instead, it too connects to the singleton Logbook. The viewer doesn't directly connect to the database for two reasons. The first is that if it did, you would couple the viewer to the repository used and would have to modify the viewer each time you switched repositories. The Logbook provides the necessary indirection. Second, to avoid database synchronization issues, the Logbook is the single data access component, and it provides the synchronization.

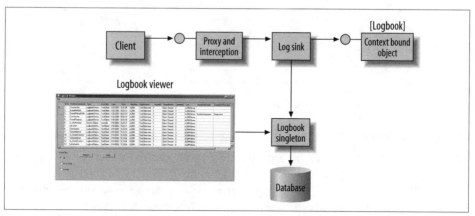

Figure 11-8. The logbook service architecture supports logging in a distributed environment

The source files accompanying this book include the Logbook solution. The solution comprises the following projects. The *ContextLogger* class library contains the LogbookAttribute, the LogContextProperty, the LogSink, and the Logbook component itself. Logbook is an ADO.NET component that can access an SQL Server database. (You will need to create a database called *Logbook* with an *Entries* table by running the included *Logbook.sql* script file.) The *LogbookHost* project is a simple Windows Forms EXE that hosts Logbook. The *LogbookHost* configuration file exposes the Logbook type as a server-activated singleton object. The *TestClient* project is a Windows Forms application that has a test class and the test client. The test class is a context-bound class that uses the LogbookAttribute. The test client is a form that is able to exercise various calls on the test object. The configuration file of the *TestClient* application registers the Logbook component as a remote server-activated object whose URL connects to the *LogbookHost* application. The *LogbookViewer* project contains the logbook viewer, which lets you browse the logbook entries or clear the table (see Figure 11-9). The *LogbookViewer* application registers the Logbook component as a remote server as well.

You can extend and modify the logbook to suit your particular needs: you can log parameter types and values, and you can use other repositories besides SQL Server.

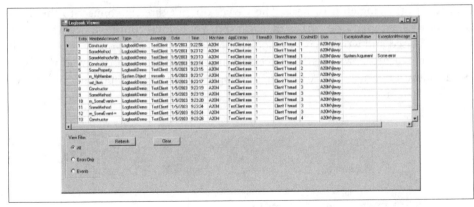

Figure 11-9. The logbook viewer application

Implementing the logbook

The `LogbookAttribute` class isn't that different from the `ColorAttribute` class presented in Example 11-2. It refuses the client's context in its `IsContextOK( )` method and installs the `LogContextProperty` property in its `GetPropertiesForNewContext( )` method. Example 11-3 shows the implementation of `LogbookAttribute`.

Example 11-3. Implementation of the LogbookAttribute class

```
[AttributeUsage(AttributeTargets.Class)]
public class LogbookAttribute : ContextAttribute
{
   LogOption m_LogOption;

   public LogbookAttribute( ): this(LogOption.MethodCalls)
   {}

   public LogbookAttribute(LogOption logOption) : base("LogbookAttribute")
   {
      m_LogOption = logOption;
   }
   /// Add a new logbook property to the new context
   public override void GetPropertiesForNewContext(IConstructionCallMessage ctor)
   {
      IContextProperty logProperty = new LogContextProperty(m_LogOption);
      ctor.ContextProperties.Add(logProperty);
   }

   //Called by the runtime in the creating client's context
   public override bool IsContextOK(Context ctx,IConstructionCallMessage ctorMsg)
   {
      return false;
   }
}
```

LogContextProperty implements the IContributeServerContextSink interface, installing the LogSink server context sink:

```
public class LogContextProperty : IContextProperty,IContributeServerContextSink
{
    LogOption m_LogOption;

    public IMessageSink GetServerContextSink(IMessageSink nextSink)
    {
        IMessageSink logSink = new LogSink(nextSink,m_LogOption);
        return logSink;
    }
    /* Rest of the implementation  */
}
```

The interesting part of the logbook service is the LogSink class. LogSink implements the IMessageSink interface. In its implementation of IMessageSink, LogSink processes the message object and constructs an instance of the LogbookEntry structure, providing it with the information extracted from the message. LogbookEntry stores the information provided as construction parameters and captures additional information such as the object's location and execution scope. LogSink then passes the LogbookEntry object to the Logbook component. Because the logbook is accessed as a remote component, LogbookEntry is marshaled by value using the Serializable attribute. Example 11-4 contains the code for LogbookEntry.

Example 11-4. The LogbookEntry structure

```
[Serializable]
public struct LogbookEntry
{
    public LogbookEntry(string assemblyName,string typeName,string methodName,
                                                string eventDescription):
                this(assemblyName,typeName,methodName,String.Empty,String.Empty)
    {
        Event = eventDescription;
    }
    public LogbookEntry(string assemblyName,string typeName,string methodName):
                this(assemblyName,typeName,methodName,String.Empty,String.Empty)
    {}
    public LogbookEntry(string assemblyName,string typeName,string methodName,
                                string exceptionName,string exceptionMessage)
    {
        AssemblyName     = assemblyName;
        TypeName         = typeName;
        MemberAccessed   = methodName;
        ExceptionName    = exceptionName;
        ExceptionMessage = exceptionMessage;
        Event = String.Empty;

        MachineName   = Environment.MachineName;
        AppDomainName = AppDomain.CurrentDomain.FriendlyName;
        ThreadID      = Thread.CurrentThread.ManagedThreadId();
```

Example 11-4. The LogbookEntry structure (continued)

```
        ThreadName     = Thread.CurrentThread.Name;
        ContextID      = Thread.CurrentContext.ContextID;
        Date = DateTime.Now.ToShortDateString();
        Time = DateTime.Now.ToLongTimeString();
        if(Thread.CurrentPrincipal.Identity.IsAuthenticated)
        {
            UserName = Thread.CurrentPrincipal.Identity.Name;
        }
        else
        {
            UserName = "Unauthenticated";
        }
    }
    //Location
    public readonly string MachineName;
    public readonly string AppDomainName;
    public readonly int    ThreadID;
    public readonly string ThreadName;
    public readonly int    ContextID;
    //Identity
    public readonly string UserName;
    //Object info
    public readonly string AssemblyName;
    public readonly string TypeName;
    public readonly string MemberAccessed;
    public readonly string Date;
    public readonly string Time;
    //Exception
    public readonly string ExceptionName;
    public readonly string ExceptionMessage;
    //Event
    public readonly string Event;
}
```

Example 11-5 contains most of the implementation of LogSink. The constructor saves the logging filer (methods or errors), as well as the next message sink in the chain, and creates a new Logbook object (a proxy to the remote singleton). In SyncProcessMessage(), LogSink downcasts the message object to IMethodMessage and passes it to a few helper parsing methods. LogSink then forwards the call to the next sink down the chain, to eventually call the object. When the call returns, LogSink downcasts the returned message to IMethodReturnMessage and uses other helper methods to get the exception information (if an exception took place). When the processing is done, LogSink constructs a LogbookEntry object and adds it to the logbook using the Logbook object.

Example 11-5. The LogSink class

```
public class LogSink : IMessageSink
{
    IMessageSink m_NextSink;
```

Example 11-5. The LogSink class (continued)

```
LogOption m_LogOption;
Logbook m_Logbook;

public LogSink(IMessageSink nextSink,LogOption logOption)
{
   m_LogOption = logOption;
   m_NextSink = nextSink;
   m_Logbook = new Logbook( );
}
public IMessageSink NextSink
{
   get {return m_NextSink;}
}
public IMessage SyncProcessMessage(IMessage msg)
{
   IMethodMessage methodMessage = msg as IMethodMessage;
   Debug.Assert(methodMessage != null);
   string assemblyName = GetAssemblyName(methodMessage);
   string typeName      = GetTypeName(methodMessage);
   string methodName    = GetMethodName(methodMessage);

   IMethodReturnMessage returnedMessage;
   returnedMessage = m_NextSink.SyncProcessMessage(msg) as IMethodReturnMessage;
   Debug.Assert(returnedMessage != null);

   string exceptionName     = GetExceptionName(returnedMessage);
   string exceptionMessage  = GetExceptionMessage(returnedMessage);

   LogbookEntry logbookEntry = new LogbookEntry(assemblyName,
                                          typeName,methodName,
                                          exceptionName,exceptionMessage);

   DoLogging(logbookEntry);

   return returnedMessage;
}
public IMessageCtrl AsyncProcessMessage(IMessage msg,IMessageSink replySink)
{
   /* Processing of the message, similar to SyncProcessMessage( )  */
}

void DoLogging(LogbookEntry logbookEntry)
{
   if(m_LogOption == LogOption.MethodCalls)
   {
      LogCall(logbookEntry);
   }
   if(m_LogOption == LogOption.Errors)
   {
      if(logbookEntry.ExceptionName != String.Empty)
      {
         LogCall(logbookEntry);
```

Example 11-5. The LogSink class (continued)

```
        }
     }
  }
  void LogCall(LogbookEntry logbookEntry)
  {
     m_Logbook.AddEntry(logbookEntry);
  }
  static string GetMethodName(IMethodMessage methodMessage)
  {
     /* Processes methodMessage.MethodName  */
  }
  static string GetTypeName(IMethodMessage methodMessage)
  {
     /* Processes methodMessage.TypeName   */
  }
  static string GetAssemblyName(IMethodMessage methodMessage)
  {
     /* Processes methodMessage.TypeName   */
  }
  static string GetExceptionName(IMethodReturnMessage returnedMessage)
  {
     /* Processes returnedMessage.Exception */
  }

  static string GetExceptionMessage(IMethodReturnMessage returnedMessage)
  {
     /* Processes returnedMessage.Exception.Message */
  }
}
```

The Logbook component derives from the Component class, defined in the System. ComponentModel namespace. Deriving from Component allows you to use Visual Studio 2005 to generate much of the ADO.NET data connectivity classes and code. However, Logbook must be available for remoting. Fortunately, Component derives from MarshalByRefObject. The Logbook component overrides InitializeLifetimeService( ) and provides a null lease. This is required to maintain the singleton semantics:

```
public class Logbook : Component
{
   //Logbook should be used as a singleton
   public override object InitializeLifetimeService( )
   {
      return null;
   }
   /* Rest of the implementation */
}
```

The Logbook component uses ADO.NET to connect to the *Logbook* database and store or retrieve the entries using a DataSet. Logbook is a thread-safe component that locks itself in every method call to synchronize concurrent access.

Although this functionality is unrelated to contexts and interception, I thought it would be handy if any object (even a non-context-bound object using the service) could explicitly log information to the logbook. This is done using the static method AddEvent( ) of Logbook:

```
public class MyClass
{
    public void SomeMethod()
    {
        Logbook.AddEvent("Some event took place");
    }
}
```

The AddEvent( ) implementation captures the same information as LogSink, and it uses the same LogbookEntry struct. The big difference is that AddEvent( ) doesn't use interception. Instead, it uses the StackFrame class, defined in the System.Diagnostics namespace:

```
public static void AddEvent(string description)
{
    StackFrame frame = new StackFrame(1);//Get the frame of the caller

    string typeName     = frame.GetMethod().DeclaringType.ToString();
    string methodName   = frame.GetMethod().Name;
    string assemblyName = Assembly.GetCallingAssembly().GetName().Name;

    LogbookEntry logbookEntry = new LogbookEntry(assemblyName,
                                         typeName,methodName,description);

    Logbook logbook = new Logbook();
    logbook.AddEntry(logbookEntry);
}
```

StackFrame provides access to information on every caller up the call chain. In this case, AddEvent( ) simply extracts the information on the method that called it.

The Transaction Management Service

.NET 2.0 introduces an innovative transaction management service in the System. Transactions namespace. A transaction managed by System.Transactions is stored in the thread local storage and is called the *ambient transaction*. System.Transactions-enabled resource managers (such as SQL Server 2005) detect the ambient transaction and automatically enlist in the transaction, similar to the auto-enlistment of Enterprise Services resource managers. This for the most part eliminates the need to manage the transaction yourself. The main feature of System.Transactions is its ability to automatically promote the transaction across transaction managers, from the *lightweight transaction manager* (LTM) used with a single object and a single durable resource to the *OleTx transaction manager* used to manage a distributed transaction. For more information about System.Transactions, see my whitepaper "Introducing System. Transactions in the Microsoft .NET Framework Version 2" (MSDN, April 2005).

When not using Enterprise Services (and until the release of Indigo), System. Transactions supports only an explicit programming model. You typically interact with an object of type TransactionScope, defined as:

```
public class TransactionScope : IDisposable
{
    public TransactionScope( );
    public TransactionScope(TransactionScopeOption scopeOptions);
    //Additional constructors

    public void Complete( );
    public void Dispose( );
}
```

As the name implies, the TransactionScope class is used to scope a code section with a transaction, as demonstrated in Example 11-6. Internally in its constructor, the TransactionScope object creates a transaction (an LTM transaction, by default) and assigns it as the ambient transaction. TransactionScope is a disposable object—the transaction will end once the Dispose( ) method is called (the end of the using statement in Example 11-6).

Example 11-6. Using the TransactionScope class

```
TransactionScope scope = new TransactionScope( );
using(scope)
{
    /* Perform transactional work here */

    //No errors - commit transaction
    scope.Complete( );
}
```

The TransactionScope object has no way of knowing whether the transaction should commit or abort. To address this, TransactionScope internally maintains a consistency bit, which is set by default to false. You can set the consistency bit to true by calling the Complete( ) method. If the consistency bit is set to false when the transaction ends, the transaction will abort; otherwise, it will try to commit. Note that once you call Complete( ), there is no way to set the consistency bit back to false.

Transaction flow management

Transaction scopes can nest both directly and indirectly. A *direct scope nesting* is simply one scope nested inside another. An *indirect scope nesting* occurs when you call a method that uses a TransactionScope object from within a method that uses its own scope. You can also have multiple scope nesting, involving both direct and indirect nesting. The topmost scope is referred to as the *root scope*. The question is, of course, what is the relation between the root scope and all the nested scopes? How will nesting a scope affect the ambient transaction? To address these questions, the TransactionScope class provides several overloaded constructors that accept an enum of the type TransactionScopeOption, defined as:

```
public enum TransactionScopeOption
{
   Required,
   RequiresNew,
   Suppress
}
```

The value of TransactionScopeOption lets you control whether the scope takes part in a transaction, and, if so, whether it will join the ambient transaction or be the root scope of a new transaction. For example, here is how you specify the value of the TransactionScopeOption in the scope's constructor:

```
TransactionScope scope;
scope = new TransactionScope(TransactionScopeOption.Required);
using(scope)
{...}
```

The default value for the scope option is TransactionScopeOption.Required. The TransactionScope object determines which transaction to belong to when it is constructed. Once determined, the scope will always belong to that transaction. TransactionScope bases its decision on two factors: whether an ambient transaction is present and the value of the TransactionScopeOption parameter.

A TransactionScope object has three options:

- Join the ambient transaction.
- Be a new scope root; that is, start a new transaction and have that transaction be the new ambient transaction inside its own scope.
- Not take part in a transaction at all.

If the scope is configured with TransactionScopeOption.Suppress, it will never be part of a transaction, regardless of whether an ambient transaction is present.

If the scope is configured with TransactionScopeOption.Required, and an ambient transaction is present, the scope will join that transaction. If, on the other hand, there is no ambient transaction, the scope will create a new transaction and become the root scope.

If the scope is configured with TransactionScopeOption.RequiresNew, it will always be the root scope. It will start a new transaction, and its transaction will be the new ambient transaction inside the scope.

The way the values of TransactionScopeOption affect the flow of the transaction is analogous to the way the integer constants provided to the Synchronization attribute control the flow of the synchronization domain, as discussed in Chapter 8.

Declarative transaction support

You can use context-bound objects and call interception to provide declarative support for System.Transactions. You will need to install a server context sink that wraps the call to the next sink down the chain in a TransactionScope. Example 11-7 shows the TransactionAttribute class. Obviously, you will also need a context attribute that adds a context property that installs the sink. These two classes (TransactionAttribute and TransactionalProperty, respectively) are very similar to LogbookAttribute and LogContextProperty. The TransactionAttribute's constructor accepts an enum of the type TransactionScopeOption, indicating how the transaction should flow through this context-bound object. The default constructor uses TransactionScopeOption.Required.

Example 11-7. The TransactionAttribute class

```
using System.Transactions;

[AttributeUsage(AttributeTargets.Class)]
public class TransactionAttribute : ContextAttribute
{
   TransactionScopeOption m_TransactionOption;

   public TransactionAttribute() : this(TransactionScopeOption.Required)
   {}

   public TransactionAttribute(TransactionScopeOption transactionOption) :
                                          base("TransactionAttribute")
   {
      m_TransactionOption = transactionOption;
   }
   //Add a new transaction property to the new context
   public override void GetPropertiesForNewContext(IConstructionCallMessage ctor)
   {
      IContextProperty transactional;
      transactional = new TransactionalProperty(m_TransactionOption);
      ctor.ContextProperties.Add(transactional);
   }
   //Provides a private context
   public override bool IsContextOK(Context ctx,
                              IConstructionCallMessage ctorMsg)
   {
      return false;
   }
}
```

The TransactionalProperty class installs the TransactionSink class as a server context sink, providing it with the transaction scope option:

```
   public class TransactionalProperty: IContextProperty,
                              IContributeServerContextSink
   {
      TransactionScopeOption m_TransactionOption;
```

```
    public IMessageSink GetServerContextSink(IMessageSink nextSink)
    {
       IMessageSink transactionSink;
       transactionSink = new TransactionSink(nextSink,m_TransactionOption);
       return transactionSink;
    }
    //Rest of the implementation
}
```

The interesting work, of course, is done by TransactionSink, shown in Example 11-8.

Example 11-8. The TransactionSink class provides a transactional context

```
public class TransactionSink : IMessageSink
{
   IMessageSink m_NextSink;
   TransactionScopeOption m_TransactionOption;

   public TransactionSink(IMessageSink nextSink,
                          TransactionScopeOption transactionOption)
   {
      m_TransactionOption = transactionOption;
      m_NextSink = nextSink;
   }

   public IMessageSink NextSink
   {
      get
      {
         return m_NextSink;
      }
   }
   public IMessage SyncProcessMessage(IMessage msg)
   {
      IMethodReturnMessage returnedMessage = null;

      Exception exception;
      TransactionScope scope = new TransactionScope(m_TransactionOption);
      using(scope)
      {
         try
         {
            returnedMessage = (IMethodReturnMessage)m_NextSink.
                                                     SyncProcessMessage(msg);
            exception = returnedMessage.Exception;
         }
         catch(Exception sinkException)
         {
            exception = sinkException;
         }
         if(exception == null)
         {
            scope.Complete( );
         }
```

Example 11-8. The TransactionSink class provides a transactional context (continued)

```
        return returnedMessage;
    }
}
    public IMessageCtrl AsyncProcessMessage(IMessage msg,IMessageSink replySink)
    {
        string message = "Transactional calls must be synchronous"
        throw new InvalidOperationException(message);
    }
}
```

In SyncProcessMessage( ), TransactionSink constructs a new TransactionScope object, passing its constructor the original value of the TransactionScopeOption enum passed to the Transaction attribute. A using statement with the scope object wraps the call to SyncProcessMessage() on the next sink down the chain. If no exception has occurred, SyncProcessMessage() calls Complete() on the scope and returns.

Example 11-9 demonstrates the use of the Transaction attribute.

Example 11-9. Using the Transaction attribute

```
[Transaction]
public class RootClass : ContextBoundObject
{
    public void CreateObjects()
    {
        Class1 obj1 = new Class1();
        Class2 obj2 = new Class2();
        Class3 obj3 = new Class3();
    }
}

[Transaction]
public class Class1 : ContextBoundObject
{}

[Transaction(TransactionScopeOption.Suppress)]
public class Class2 : ContextBoundObject
{}

[Transaction(TransactionScopeOption.RequiresNew)]
public class Class3 : ContextBoundObject
{}
```

Figure 11-10 depicts the resulting transactions after executing this TransactionDemo() method:

```
    //Non-transactional client
    class MyClient
    {
        public void TransactionDemo()
        {
            RootClass root = new RootClass();
```

```
      root.CreateObjects( );
   }
}
```

The `RootClass` class is configured to require a transaction. Since it is being called by a non-transactional client (`MyClient` is not even context-bound), there is no ambient transaction. `RootClass` therefore starts a new transaction and becomes its root. When the client calls `CreateObjects( )` on the `RootClass` object, the object creates three other context-bound objects, each configured with a different `TransactionScopeOption` value. `Class1` is configured to require a transaction, so it will join the transaction of the `RootClass` object. `Class2` suppresses any transaction flow, so it will execute without an ambient transaction. `Class3` requires a new transaction, so it will be placed in a new transaction.

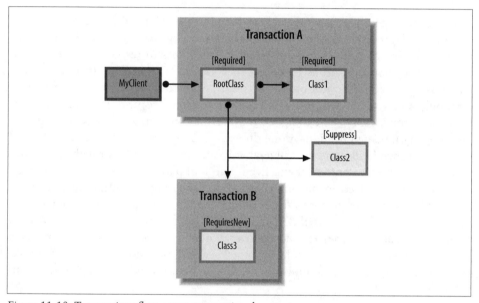

Figure 11-10. Transactions flow across transactional contexts

You can add granularity to the `Transaction` attribute and, instead of being object-based (that is, all calls are transactional), make it method-based. Define a method-level attribute and apply it to the methods you wish to be called transitionally. Have `SyncProcessMessage( )` reflect the target method to see if it has the attribute, and if so, wrap the method call with a `TransactionScope`.

CHAPTER 12

Security

In traditional operating systems such as Windows or Unix, the security model is user-oriented. Processes execute under a certain security identity—usually that of the launching user—and the operating system grants access to resources or permission to perform certain operations based on that identity. Typically, either the user is omnipotent (an administrator or root account), or the user is restricted and can perform only a narrow set of operations. The user-oriented security model has a number of shortcomings. For one thing, even powerful users can make mistakes, such as installing harmful applications from dubious sources or simply launching email viruses. In general, all users are vulnerable to attacks, and only through experience do users learn how to prevent them. Even if no foul play is involved, users are often required to be involved in making runtime decisions about the nature of components, such as whether or not to trust content coming from a particular source. Furthermore, restricted users often don't get to work in an environment that is tailored to their needs and preferences, and the overall quality of their sessions suffers. New breeds of threats such as worms, luring attacks, and Trojan horses target such weaknesses and can wait for an administrator to log on before striking—long after the initial security breach.

In today's component-oriented environment, there is a need for a component-oriented security model. A component-oriented operating system (such as the CLR) needs to examine not only what the user is allowed to do, but also what operations a given piece of code is allowed to do and what evidence that code provides to establish its identity and authenticity. This is exactly what the .NET security model is all about. .NET component-oriented security complements Windows user-based security, providing system administrators and developers granular control and flexibility without compromising overall security. This results in a productivity gain because, for the most part, you don't need to bother with programmatic security; it also improves the trustworthiness of applications built with .NET. This chapter describes the component- and user-oriented security facilities available to .NET developers.

.NET application frameworks such as ASP.NET and Web Services provide their own security infrastructures to authenticate and authorize callers. Such application-specific security is subjected to the security infrastructure described in this chapter.

The .NET Security Architecture

.NET component-oriented security is based on an elegant concept: using an administration tool, the system administrator grants assemblies certain permissions to perform operations with external entities such as the filesystem, the Registry, the user interface, and so on. .NET provides the system administrator with multiple ways to identify which assembly gets granted what permission and what evidence the assembly needs to provide in order to establish its identity. At runtime, whenever an assembly tries to perform a privileged operation or access a resource, .NET verifies that the assembly and its calling assemblies have permission to perform that operation. Although the idea is intuitive enough, there are a substantial number of new terms and concepts to understand before configuring .NET security for your own applications. The rest of this section describes the elements of the .NET security architecture. The next sections describe how to administratively configure security and take programmatic control over security.

Permissions

A *permission* is a grant to perform a specific operation. Permissions have both a *type* and a *scope*. A file I/O permission is different from a user-interface permission in type because they control access to different types of resources. Similarly, a reflection permission is different from an unmanaged code access permission because they control the execution of different types of operations. In scope, a permission can be very narrow, wide, or unrestricted. For example, a file I/O permission can allow reading from a particular file, while writing to the same file may be represented by a different file I/O permission (narrow scope). Alternatively, a file I/O permission may grant access to an entire directory (or a drive), or grant unrestricted access to the filesystem. .NET defines 25 types of permissions that govern all operations and resources an application is likely to use (see Table 12-1).

Of particular interest is the Security permission type, which controls both sensitive operations and security configuration. The list of privileged operations includes execution, invocation of unmanaged code, creating and controlling app domains, serialization, thread manipulation, and remoting configuration. The security configuration aspect includes permission to assert granted permissions; skip assembly verification; control security policies, evidences, and principals; and extend the security infrastructure. These facets are described later.

.NET permissions are subject to the underlying Windows or resource security permissions. For example, if the filesystem is NTFS, it can still deny an application access to a file if the identity under which the application is running isn't granted access to that file. Other examples are when accessing user-specific environment variables and when accessing a SQL server that has its own security policy.

Table 12-1. Security permission types

Permission type	Grants permission to	Example
ASP.NET Hosting	Host ASP.NET objects. Defines several levels.	Minimal level permission is required for using the ASP.NET authentication and authorization classes.
Data Protection	Use the `ProtectedData` class to protect or unprotect data and memory.	Encrypt a memory block using `ProtectedData.Protect( )`.
Directory Services	Access Active Directory. Allows browsing a path or writing to it.	Browse all content under *LDAP://*.
Distributed Transactions	Create a new distributed transaction.	Unrestricted use of distributed transactions.
DNS	Domain-name servers. Permission is required to resolve URLs at runtime.	Deny access to or grant unrestricted access to DNS.
Environment Variables	Read or write the value of specific environment variables.	Write the `PATH` environment variable.
Event Log	Write, browse, or audit an event log on a specified machine. Can also deny access to event log.	Browse the event log on *localhost*.
File Dialog	Display the common dialogs used to open or save files, or deny permission to display the dialogs.	Display the File Save dialog.
File I/O	Read, write, or append data to a file, or all files in a directory. Grants path-discovery permission as well.	Write to *c:\temp\Myfile.txt*.
Isolated Storage	Allow or disallow administration; configure isolation policy and disk quotas.	Allow administration of isolated storage by the user of the assembly and allocate a disk quota of at most 10 KB.
Key Container	Create and delete key containers; export and import keys; sign, open, or encrypt containers.	Import an existing key from a container.
Message Queue	Browse, peek, send, or receive messages from a specified message queue. Allow queue administration as well.	Grant unrestricted access to all message queues.
OLE DB	Access specified OLE DB providers. Can specify whether a blank password is permitted for all providers.	Grant access to the Microsoft OLE DB provider for SQL Server.
Performance Counter	Browse or instrument specified performance counters on designated machines.	Instrument the thread performance counter on the current machine.
Printing	Print (either in safe mode, default mode, or all modes).	Allow all printing operations to all accessible printers.

Table 12-1. Security permission types (continued)

Permission type	Grants permission to	Example
Reflection	Discover member and type information about other assemblies using reflection. Emit code at runtime.	Allow reflection of both type and member information on other assemblies but deny emission of new code at runtime.
Registry	Read, write, or create Registry keys.	Read the values stored under `HKEY_LOCAL_MACHINE\SOFTWARE\`.
Security	Control various security aspects.	Allow unmanaged code access.
Service Controller	Control or browse services on specified machines.	Control (start and stop) the fax service on the local machine.
Socket Access	Accept connections on or connect to specific ports on specified machines using either TCP or UDP (or both).	Allow connecting and accepting calls on port 8005 using TCP on the local machine.
SQL Client	Access SQL servers using ADO.NET, and specify whether a blank password is permitted.	Allow unrestricted access to all SQL servers available on the intranet.
Store	Create and delete certificate stores, enumerate existing stores, enumerate certificates in a store, add or remove a certificate from a store.	Permission to add a certificate to a store.
User Interface	Interact with the user using all top-level windows and events, safe top-level windows, safe subwindows, or no windows at all. Control access to the clipboard.	Allow displaying all windows but disallow clipboard access.
Web Access	Allow connecting to or accepting requests from specified web hosts.	Allow invoking a particular web service.
Web Browser	Render content in the web browser Windows Forms control. Can be unrestricted or restricted to rendering only simple HTML (that is, without ActiveX, HTML scripts, Java applets, or other potentially unsafe operations).	Allow restricted use of the web browser control.

Permission Sets

Individual permissions are just that—individual. To function properly, a given assembly often requires a set of permissions of particular scope and type. .NET allows system administrators to use *permission sets*, or collections of individual permissions. A permission set can contain as many individual permissions as required. Administrators can construct custom permission sets, or they can use pre-existing, well-known permission sets. .NET provides seven predefined permission sets, also known as *named permission sets*: Nothing, Execution, Internet, LocalIntranet, Everything, FullTrust, and SkipVerification. Table 12-2 presents the individual permissions granted by each named permission set.

Table 12-2. The named permission sets

Permissions	Nothing	Execution	Internet	LocalIntranet	Everything	FullTrust	SkipVerification
ASP.NET Hosting						Unrestricted	
Data Protection					Unrestricted	Unrestricted	
Directory Services						Unrestricted	
Distributed Transactions						Unrestricted	
DNS				Unrestricted	Unrestricted	Unrestricted	
Environment Variables				Read USERNAME	Unrestricted	Unrestricted	
Event Log					Unrestricted	Unrestricted	
File Dialog			File Open	Unrestricted	Unrestricted	Unrestricted	
File IO					Unrestricted	Unrestricted	
Isolated Storage			Domain isolation by user with 10 KB disk quota	Assembly isolation by user, unrestricted disk quota	Unrestricted	Unrestricted	
Key Container					Unrestricted	Unrestricted	
Message Queue						Unrestricted	
OLE DB					Unrestricted	Unrestricted	

Table 12-2. The named permission sets (continued)

Permissions	Nothing	Execution	Internet	LocalIntranet	Everything	FullTrust	SkipVerification
Performance Counter					Unrestricted	Unrestricted	
Printing			Safe printing	Default	Unrestricted	Unrestricted	
Reflection				Emit	Unrestricted	Unrestricted	
Registry					Unrestricted	Unrestricted	
Security		Execution	Execution	Execution and assertion	All, except skip verification	Unrestricted	Skip code-safety verification
Service Controller						Unrestricted	
Socket Access					Unrestricted	Unrestricted	
SQL Client					Unrestricted	Unrestricted	
Store					Unrestricted	Unrestricted	
User Interface			Safe top-level windows, clipboard ownership	Unrestricted	Unrestricted	Unrestricted	
Web Access					Unrestricted	Unrestricted	
Web Browser			Restricted	Restricted	Unrestricted	Unrestricted	

The named permission sets offer a spectrum of trust:

The Nothing permission set

Grants nothing. Code that has only the Nothing permission set can't execute, and .NET will refuse to load it. The Nothing permission set is used when there is a need to prevent assemblies from running, typically because the code origin is known to be untrustworthy and dangerous. For example, the default .NET security policy associates any code coming from the list of untrusted sites (maintained by Internet Explorer) with the Nothing permission set, effectively preventing such code from causing any harm.

The Execution permission set

Allows code to load and run, but doesn't permit interaction with any kind of external resource and doesn't perform any privileged operations. When an assembly is assigned the Execution permission set (but nothing else), the assembly can perform operations such as numerical calculations, but it can't save the results. By default, .NET does not use the Execution permission set.

The Internet permission set

Gives code some ability to execute and display a user interface, so should be used carefully. Generally, you shouldn't trust code coming from the Internet unless the site of origin is explicitly trusted. Note that the default .NET security policy grants the Internet permission set to all code coming from the Internet. Administrators can change that and explicitly assign the Internet permission set to only selected trusted sites.

The LocalIntranet permission set

Code coming from the local intranet is, of course, more trustworthy than code coming from the Internet. As a result, the LocalIntranet permission set grants code wide permissions. .NET's default associates the LocalIntranet permission set with code originating from the local intranet.

The Everything permission set

Grants code most permissions except for directory services, distributed transactions, message queue, service control, ASP.NET hosting, and permission to skip verification. The lack of permission to skip security verification means that the code must be verifiable. *Verifiable code* is code that can be verified in a formal manner as type-safe. CLR-compliant compilers can emit unverifiable code, such as unsafe code in C#. You can use the Everything permission set to ensure that the managed code invoked has all the permissions required for normal operation and yet it doesn't use techniques such as pointer arithmetic to access restricted memory areas or areas owned by other app domains (more on that at the end of the chapter). By default, .NET doesn't use the Everything permission set.

The FullTrust permission set

Allows unimpeded access to all resources. .NET trusts such code implicitly and allows it to perform all operations. Only the most trustworthy code should be granted this permission, because there are no safeguards. By default, all code executing from the local machine is granted full.

The SkipVerification permission set

Grants a single permission—permission to skip code-safety verification. You can use the SkipVerification permission set to explicitly allow unverifiable code, without risking it touching any external resources or performing sensitive operations. For example, imagine porting legacy C or C++ code to C#, when the legacy code uses complex pointer arithmetic. In that case, it may be easier to keep that pointer arithmetic in place using unsafe code than to fully rewrite safer C#. It's overkill to grant that code FullTrust permissions; instead, grant it the SkipVerification permission set and any other specific permissions it may require. Granting assemblies only the minimum permissions they require is a good guideline, because it reduces the chances of damage caused by a malicious party luring a benign assembly to do dirty work on its behalf.

Assemblies and Code Origin

Component-based security obviously has a lot to do with *code origin*—that is, where the code is coming from. Code origin has nothing to do with remote calls, because the remote object executes locally on the remote machine. Code origin is relevant only when loading an assembly from a remote location. You can load a remote assembly in a number of ways. First, you can have the application indicate in its code-binding policy that it requires an assembly from another machine (by specifying the machine name), or perhaps that the assembly is coming from a network-mapped drive. Applications can also programmatically load an assembly at runtime from a remote location using the static method LoadFrom( ) of the Assembly class:

```
public static Assembly LoadFrom(string assemblyFile);
```

For example:

```
Assembly assembly;
assembly = Assembly.LoadFrom("\\SomeMachine\MyAssembly.dll");
```

That said, by far the most common case of loading an assembly from a remote location is using ClickOnce deployment. As you will see later on in this chapter, a few features of the security infrastructure and Visual Studio 2005 are dedicated for the use of ClickOnce applications.

Security Evidence

System administrators grant permissions to assemblies based on the assembly's identity. The question is, what sort of evidence should an assembly present to .NET in order to establish its identity? A *security evidence* is some form of proof that an assembly can provide to substantiate its identity. Evidences are vital for .NET security, because without them rogue assemblies can pretend to be something they aren't and gain unauthorized access to resources or operations. There are two types of evidences: origin-based and content-based evidences. An *origin-based evidence* simply examines where the assembly is coming from and is independent of the actual content of the assembly. The standard origin-based evidences are Application Directory, GAC, Site, URL, and Zone. A *content-based evidence* examines the content of the assembly, looking for a specific match with specified criteria. The standard content-based evidences are Strong Name, Publisher, and Hash. There is no relationship between permission sets and evidences. A single assembly can be granted multiple permission sets and satisfy a different evidence for each permission set, or it can satisfy the same evidence associated with multiple permission sets. .NET also defines a wildcard—the All Code evidence. Here is a description of the available evidences and how to select an appropriate security evidence.

The All Code evidence

The All Code evidence is satisfied by all assemblies.

The Application Directory evidence

The Application Directory evidence is satisfied by all assemblies coming from the same directory as or a child directory of the running application. Typically, this evidence allows an application to trust code deployed together with it but distrust other code on the same machine or anywhere else.

The GAC evidence

The GAC evidence is satisfied by all assemblies originating from the GAC. Because only an administrator can install assemblies in the GAC, the GAC evidence is used to implicitly demand that whoever installed the evaluated assembly was an administrator. Assemblies that satisfy the GAC evidence are somewhat more trustworthy than assemblies installed by non-administrators, but to what degree is a question of judgment.

The Site evidence

The Site evidence is satisfied by all assemblies coming from a specified site, such as *http://www.somesite.com* or *ftp://www.somesite.com*. The protocol (and port number, if specified) is ignored, and only the top-level domain portion is used. .NET also ignores any subsite specifications, such as the */myfolder* in *http://www.somesite.com/ myfolder*, and extracts the domain name only. Sites can also point to a specific machine, as in *tcp://somemachine/myfolder*.

The URL evidence

The URL evidence is satisfied by all assemblies coming from a specified URL. The URL evidence is more specific than the Site evidence, because .NET takes into account protocol, port number, and subfolders. For example, the following are considered different URL evidences but identical Site evidences:

http://www.somesite.com
ftp://www.somesite.com
http://www.somesite.com/myfolder
tcp://somesite.com

You can use an asterisk at the end of a URL to indicate that the URL evidence applies to all code coming from a sub-URL as well:

http://www.somesite.com/*

The Zone evidence

The Zone evidence is satisfied by all assemblies coming from the specified zone. .NET defines five zones:

The My Computer zone
Identifies code coming from the local machine.

The Local Intranet zone
Identifies code coming from machines on the same LAN. The local intranet is any location identified by a universal name convention (UNC), usually in the form of *<machinename>**<further scope>* (e.g., *\\Somemachine\SomeShared-Folder*). You can also identify a location as part of the Local Intranet zone using a URL, as long as the URL doesn't contain dots (e.g., *http://Somemachine\SomeSharedFolder* or *tcp://Somemachine\SomeSharedFolder*). Note that even if you specify your own local machine name (e.g., *\\MyMachine* or *http://localhost*), it will be considered part of the Local Intranet zone, not the My Computer zone. Network-mapped drives are also considered part of the Local Intranet zone.

The Internet zone
Identifies code coming from the Internet. The Internet is considered as any location identified by a dotted or numeric IP address, such as *http://www.somesite.com* or *http://66.129.71.238*. Note that by default, even if the URL points to a location on the LAN (including the local machine), such as *http://127.0.0.1*, it's still considered part of the Internet zone.

 If you wish to include local intranet sites as part of the local intranet but refer to them using a generic Internet dotted or numeric URL, you need to add those sites explicitly to the intranet site list. To do so, open Internet Explorer and display the Security tab on the Internet Options dialog. Select the Local Intranet icon, and click the Sites button (see Figure 12-1). In the Local Intranet dialog, click Advanced, and add web sites to this zone. You can add even non-intranet web sites to the Local Intranet zone.

The Trusted Sites zone

Identifies code coming from a list of trusted Internet sites. You can add sites to and remove sites from the Trusted Sites list using Internet Explorer—go to the Security tab on the Internet Options dialog, select the Trusted Sites icon, and click Sites (see Figure 12-1) to display the Trusted Sites dialog.

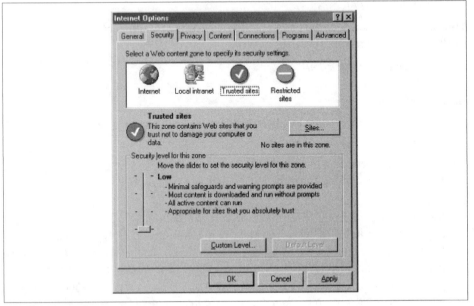

Figure 12-1. Managing zones using Internet Explorer

The Untrusted Sites zone

Identifies code coming from a list of untrusted Internet sites. You can add sites to and remove sites from the Untrusted Sites list using Internet Explorer, similarly to adding sites to and removing sites from the Trusted Sites list.

 When you add sites to the lists of trusted and untrusted sites using Internet Explorer, the lists are maintained per user, not per machine. There is no easy documented way to add sites to a machine-wide list.

The Strong Name evidence

The Strong Name evidence is satisfied by all assemblies whose public keys match a specified key value. The Strong Name evidence is an excellent way to trust all code coming from a particular vendor, assuming the vendor uses the same public key to sign all its assemblies. The Strong Name evidence can optionally contain the assembly names and/or version numbers. As a result, the system administrator can opt to trust only a particular version of a specific assembly coming from a particular vendor identified by a public key. That said, the name and version typically are not supplied—

doing so implies that a vendor can be trusted with only that particular assembly or version, which is conceptually inconsistent with the notion of a trustworthy vendor.

The Hash evidence

The Hash evidence grants the permission set associated with it to the single assembly whose computational hash matches a specified hash. The assembly in question need not have a strong name. As a result, the Hash evidence is useful only for uniquely identifying an assembly with a friendly name and granting permissions only to that trusted assembly. The Hash evidence is the most stringent form of evidence, but it is also the most maintenance-intensive—you need to update it on every revision of the assembly. The Hash evidence can be used to detect changes to an assembly, even if the new assembly has the same strong name and version number. System administrators can configure which cryptographic hashing algorithm to use: either SHA1 (the default) or MD5.

The Publisher evidence

The Publisher evidence is satisfied by all assemblies that are digitally signed with a specified certificate, such as AuthentiCode. To digitally sign an assembly with a certificate, first build it, and then use the *SignTool.exe* command-line utility, specifying the assembly to sign and the file containing the digital certificate. *SignTool.exe* can optionally launch a wizard to guide you through the signing process.

Selecting a security evidence

Choosing a security level to apply always involves a trade-off between risks and usability. In general, you should prefer content- to origin-based evidence, because content-based evidence is more accurate. For example, the Strong Name evidence safely and consistently identifies an assembly. With origin-based evidence such as the Site evidence, the same assembly may be trusted if it comes from one site but not trusted if it comes from a different site. In addition, origin-based evidence is more susceptible to subversion than content-based evidence. It's next to impossible to fake a strong name, but it's possible to fool your machine into thinking that a certain IP address maps to a trusted site by subverting the DNS server. Another breach of origin-based evidence is compromising the proxy server on the local network so that instead of returning an assembly from a trusted site, it returns a different assembly but makes it look like it came from a trusted site. You should do a careful threat analysis, and trust origin-based evidences only as far as the DNS and other network facilities can be trusted. Origin-based evidences let you interact with much wider sets of assemblies than content-based evidences, which require individual configuration. Origin-based evidences also let you apply a generic security blanket, without having intimate knowledge of the assemblies on the client machine; content-based evidences, on the other hand, require you to be intimately aware of the making of the assemblies. Consequently, origin-based evidences are often used by framework developers (such as Microsoft), while application developers favor content-based evidences.

Code Groups and Security Policies

.NET uses code groups to classify assemblies when it decides on the security permissions granted for each assembly. A *code group* is a binding of a single permission set with a particular evidence (see Figure 12-2).

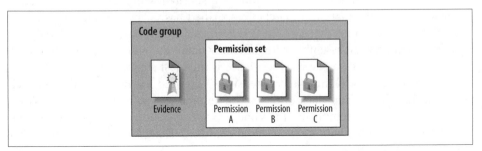

Figure 12-2. A code group is a binding of a single permission set and a single evidence

To be granted the permissions in the permission set associated with the code group, an assembly must first satisfy the evidence of that code group. However, a meaningful security policy needs to be much more granular than what a single code group with a single evidence and permission set can express. A .NET *security policy* is a collection of code groups. Code groups in a policy are independent of one another in every respect. They can all use the same evidence, different evidences, or a mix. Similarly, different code groups can use different or identical permission sets. The permissions granted by a policy to a given assembly is the union of all the individual permissions granted by the evaluated code groups in that policy whose evidence the assembly satisfies. For example, consider the security policy in Figure 12-3. In this figure, the assembly satisfies the evidences of code groups A, B, and C, but not the evidences required by code groups D and E. As a result, the assembly will be granted only the union of the permissions granted by code groups A, B, and C.

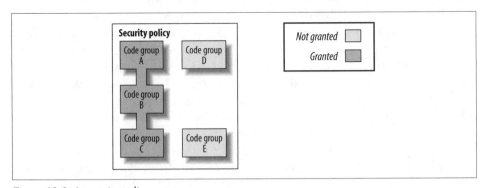

Figure 12-3. A security policy

Combining policies

.NET allows administrators to provide multiple security policies. The benefit of having multiple security policies is that it enables policies to have different scopes. Some policies can be restrictive and should be applied only in specific cases, such as with individual users or machines with limited privileges. Some policies can be more permissive and apply to all machines and users in an organization. Therefore, it's quite possible that an assembly is granted some permissions by one policy but is denied the same permissions by another policy. Because all the policies must concur on the allowed permissions, the actual permissions granted to an assembly are the intersection of all the permissions granted by *all* the security policies (see Figure 12-4).

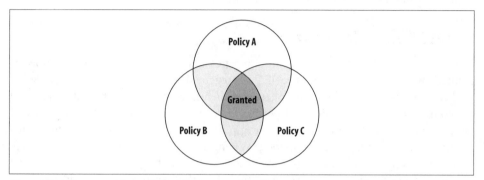

Figure 12-4. An assembly is allowed the intersection of permissions granted by the various polices

Policy levels

In actuality, there are only four types (or levels) of security policies, and .NET is aware of these four levels. Although technically administrators can configure these policy levels in any way, the convention is to use them according to their intent. The *Enterprise policy* should define a policy that affects all machines in the enterprise. Each machine should have a *Machine policy* defining a policy specific to that machine, and the *User policy* should define a policy for each individual user. The system administrator configures these three policy levels. The last policy level is the *Application Domain policy*, which applies only to code running in a specific application domain. You can only configure the Application Domain policy programmatically, by calling the SetAppDomainPolicy() method of the AppDomain class. Customizing the Application Domain policy is primarily for advanced cases—for example, for creating an app domain with deliberately low permissions so that you can load untrusted code into that domain. The default Application Domain policy grants all code full trust. Tool vendors can also take advantage of the App Domain policy. For example, Visual Studio 2005 supports partial-trust debugging, as described later in this chapter. Partial-trust debugging relies on installing a custom App Domain security policy. (App Domain security policies are beyond the scope of this chapter. For additional information, see the MSDN Library.)

System administrators typically take advantage of the hierarchical nature of the policy levels, placing policies that are more restrictive downstream and the more liberal policies upstream. This allows overall flexibility with granular security policies, tight in some places and looser in others. For example, the Enterprise policy is likely to contain only the known, must-be-blocked web sites or vendors. Other than that, the Enterprise policy can be very liberal, permitting all other operations and zones. Individual machines can be restricted if necessary, via the Machine policy. For instance, a development machine can have more permissions than a public machine in a reception area. Similarly, some users (such as system administrators) can have liberal, if not unrestricted, User policies, while non-technical staff can have very restricted User policies, even if they all share the same machine.

How It All Works Together

When .NET loads an assembly, it computes the permissions that assembly is granted: for each security policy, .NET aggregates the permissions from the evaluated code groups satisfied in that policy, and then .NET intersects the policies to find the combined overall collection of permissions the assembly is granted. That set of permissions is calculated only once (per app domain), and it persists in memory for as long as the assembly remains loaded. Whenever an assembly invokes calls on one of the .NET Framework classes (or any other class, including your own, as explained later), that class may demand from .NET that the assembly calling it have the required security permissions to access it. For example, the file I/O classes demand appropriate file I/O permissions, and Windows Forms applications demand user interface permissions. If the assembly doesn't have the appropriate security permissions, a security exception is thrown. However, it isn't sufficient that the assembly that called the demanding class has the requested permissions—if .NET were to check for permissions only on the assembly immediately up the call chain, that could constitute a security breach. Imagine a malicious assembly that doesn't have the required permissions to access a class such as FileStream. That assembly could work around the lack of permissions by calling instead a benign assembly that has the permissions to do its dirty work for it. Therefore, whenever a class demands security permission checks, .NET traverses the entire call stack, making sure that every assembly up the call chain has the required permissions. This is known as the security permission *stack walk*. When the first assembly without permissions is found during the stack walk, .NET aborts the stack walk and throws an exception at the point where the original security demand took place.

If an exception is raised because of lack of a security permission, you can find which permission is missing by examining the PermissionType property of the SecurityException object. Other useful properties of SecurityException include which method demanded the security permission (the Method property), the assembly that failed the call (the FailedAssemblyInfo property), and the origin of that assembly (the Zone and Url properties).

Configuring Permissions

Now it's time to learn how to configure the various policies, code groups, permissions, and evidences. .NET provides two ways for system administrators to configure code access security policies: the first is to use a command-line utility called *caspol.exe*; the second is to use the .NET Configuration tool. Both methods are comparable in features and capabilities. You typically use the .NET Configuration tool to configure security and export the security policies to deploy on other machines. You can use *caspol.exe* during installation to make dynamic changes. This chapter demonstrates the .NET Configuration tool. Please refer to the MSDN Library to learn about the equivalent command-line switches for *caspol.exe*.

The .NET Configuration tool has a folder called *Runtime Security Policy*, which contains an item for each of the three policies that system administrators can use to mange code access security: Enterprise, Machine, and User. Each policy item has subfolders containing its code groups, permissions sets, and custom policy assemblies (see Figure 12-5).

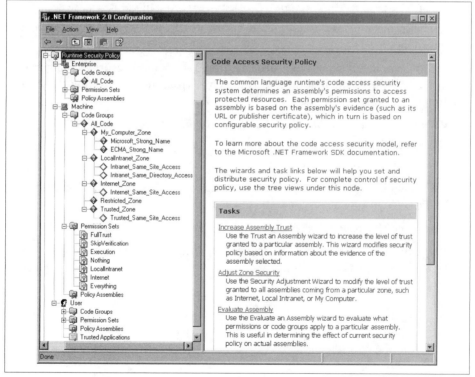

Figure 12-5. Runtime Security Policy configuration using the .NET Configuration tool

The .NET Configuration tool lets system administrators nest code groups. If the parent code group's evidence is met, .NET will not continue to evaluate child code groups. Only if the parent's evidence is not met will .NET continue to examine child code groups and aggregate their permissions (if their evidence requirements are met). In the Properties page on the General tab of each parent code group, an administrator can specify what to do when the evidence associated with this code group is satisfied. The first instruction, called *Exclusive*, instructs .NET to include only permissions from this code group in the policy. Multiple code groups can claim to be exclusive. However, if a policy has at least a single exclusive code group, all the code groups must be mutually exclusive, meaning that the evaluated assembly can meet the membership condition of at most one code group. It's considered an error if the assembly meets more than one code group's membership condition when one of the matches is an exclusive group. The added degree of code-group coupling and restriction when using exclusive code groups makes this a setting to avoid.

The second instruction is called *Level Final*. It instructs .NET to stop evaluating lower-level policies. The policy hierarchy is Enterprise, Machine, and User. Setting Level Final at the User policy has no effect (unless app domain–specific policies are employed), while setting it at the Enterprise policy level will render the Machine and User policies meaningless. If it is used at all, Level Final should be used at the Machine policy level only.

Each security policy is stored in a dedicated XML-formatted security configuration file, and the .NET Configuration tool is merely a visual tool for editing those files. The Enterprise policy file resides at:

> *<Windows Directory>\Microsoft.NET\Framework\<Version>\config\\
> enterprisesec.config*

The Machine policy file resides at:

> *<Windows Directory>\Microsoft.NET\Framework\<Version>\config\ security.\\
> config*

The User policy file resides at:

> *<Documents and Settings>\<User Name>\Application Data\Microsoft\CLR\\
> Security Config\<Version>\security.config*

In principle, only a system administrator should modify the security policy configuration files. On an NTFS system, be sure to allow only administrators the right to modify these files. A non-NTFS system has a potential security breach, because any user can modify the security policy configuration files using a text editor. A truly secure .NET system must rely on a properly configured NTFS filesystem. In addition, various NTFS crackers allow even non-administrators to modify the files when booting from DOS. To get around this problem, I recommend that you encrypt the User policy files. Bring up the User policy file's Properties page, and select Advanced from the General tab. Next, check the "Encrypt content to secure data" checkbox. You need to encrypt every User policy file used on the machine this way.

.NET Default Configuration

All three policies contain in their *Permission Sets* folders the same set of named permission sets, although none of the policies uses all its permission sets. The reason why the policies are deployed with all the named sets is so that system administrators can use these predefined sets in their own custom code groups. In addition, system administrators can change the default code groups to use other permission sets (you will see how shortly). The default Microsoft naming convention is to name code groups after the evidence they use. I find this to be a flawed convention, because it is confusing: code groups in different policies often use the same evidence but grant different permissions. Fortunately, this is only a convention, and you can name (or rename) code groups as you like.

The Enterprise and User policies

Both the Enterprise and the User policies contain by default a single code group called All_Code. The All_Code code group (as its name implies) uses the All Code evidence with the FullTrust permission set, which means that by default, as far as the Enterprise and User policies are concerned, all assemblies are unrestricted. As a result, by default, neither the Enterprise nor the User policies have any effect on restricting code access, because their intersection with the third policy—the Machine policy—yields the Machine policy intact. Administrators can add custom child code groups to both the Enterprise and User policies' All_Code code groups, thus customizing these policies. In that case, make sure to change the default permission grant, because it will mask out any child code groups.

The Machine policy

The Machine policy is where the default .NET code access security takes place. The Machine policy has a single root code group called All_Code. All_Code uses the All Code evidence with the Nothing permission set. As a result, by itself it grants nothing, and instead it relies on the following nested code groups to grant permissions:

- The My_Computer_Zone code group uses the Zone evidence, with the zone set to My Computer (see Figure 12-6).

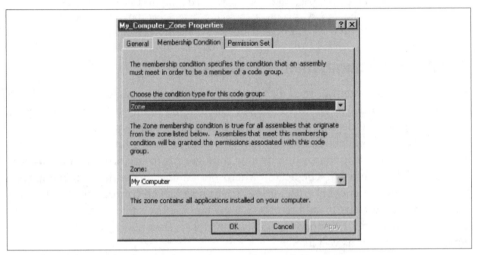

Figure 12-6. The Membership Condition tab on a code group's Properties page

This code group grants the FullTrust permission set. Consequently, by default, all code coming from the local computer gets full trust. The My_Computer_ Zone code group has two nested child code groups, called Microsoft_Strong_ Name and ECMA_Strong_Name (see Figure 12-5). These nested code groups use the Strong Name evidence, in which the value is set to the Microsoft public key and the ECMA public key, respectively. The permission set granted by both of these nested code groups is FullTrust. As a result, by default, any assembly originating from Microsoft or ECMA is granted unrestricted access regardless of its zone, even if other code groups restrict that zone. This is because when calculating a policy, .NET unites all permissions of the evaluated code groups under that policy.

- The LocalIntranet_Zone code group uses the Zone evidence, with the zone set to Local Intranet. The permission set is LocalIntranet. A potential problem with this code group is that the LocalIntranet permission set doesn't grant any file I/O or web access permissions (see Figure 12-7).

This may prevent an assembly originating in the intranet from functioning properly because it requires access to its original install directory or its original site.

Figure 12-7. The Permission Set tab on a code group's Properties page

There is really no harm in allowing access to these two locations, because whoever deployed the assembly there must have trusted it over there. To compensate for these two limitations, the LocalIntranet_Zone code group contains two nested code groups (see Figure 12-5). The Intranet_Same_Site_Access code group allows code to access its site of origin, and the Intranet_Same_Directory_ Access code group allows code to access its original install directory. These custom code groups can't be edited using the .NET Configuration tool; they use special custom permissions. See the MSDN Library for information about custom permissions.

- The Internet_Zone code group uses the Zone evidence, with the zone set to Internet. The permission set used is Internet. This code group has a child code group called Internet_Same_Site_Access (see Figure 12-5). Because the Internet permission doesn't grant web access, the Internet_Same_Site_Access code group uses a custom permission that allows code coming from a site to connect to its site of origin.

- The Restricted_Zone code group uses the Zone evidence, with the zone set to Untrusted Sites. Not surprisingly, the permission set used is Nothing.

- The Trusted_Zone code group uses the Zone evidence, with the zone set to Trusted Sites. The permission set used is the Internet permission set. This code group has a child code group called Trusted_Same_Site_Access (see Figure 12-5). Because the Internet permission doesn't grant web access, the Trusted_Same_Site_Access code group uses a custom permission that allows code coming from a trusted site to connect to its site of origin. This is the same custom permission used by the Internet_Same_Site_Access code group.

Table 12-3 summarizes the default permissions granted by the Machine policy (same as the overall default policy).

Table 12-3. The default Machine policy

Code group	Evidence	Permission set granted
All_Code	All Code	Nothing
My_Computer_Zone	My Computer zone	FullTrust
Microsoft_Strong_Name	Microsoft public key	FullTrust
ECMA_Strong_Name	ECMA public key	FullTrust
LocalIntranet_Zone	Local Intranet zone	LocalIntranet
Intranet_Same_Site_Access	Local Intranet zone	Access site of origin
Intranet_Same_Directory_Access	Local Intranet zone	Access directory of origin
Internet_Zone	Internet zone	Internet
Internet_Same_Site_Access	Internet zone	Access site of origin
Restricted_Zone	Untrusted Sites zone	Nothing
Trusted_Zone	Trusted Sites zone	Internet
Trusted_Same_Site_Access	Trusted site	Access site of origin

Custom Permission Sets

System administrators can apply the predefined named permission sets in the contexts indicated by their names. However, you can't directly modify a named permission set—instead, you must duplicate it and modify the copy. System administrators can define custom permission sets (either from copies of existing sets or from scratch) and compose very granular permissions suitable for their particular needs. The only requirement is that a custom permission set must not have the same name as one of the existing permission sets, because permission sets must be given unique names.

 You can directly modify the Everything permission set, because it isn't considered one of the standard .NET predefined named permission sets. It was likely just an addition by the developers of the .NET Configuration tool.

To duplicate a named permission set (or any other custom permission set), go to the *Permission Sets* folder, select the desired permission set, and then right-click it and select Duplicate from the pop-up context menu. The .NET Configuration tool then creates a new permission set in the policy, named *Copy of <original name>*.

To create a new permission set from scratch, right-click the *Permission Sets* folder and select New from the context menu. This brings up the Create Permission Set wizard. The first dialog box lets you name the new permission set and provide a description (see Figure 12-8).

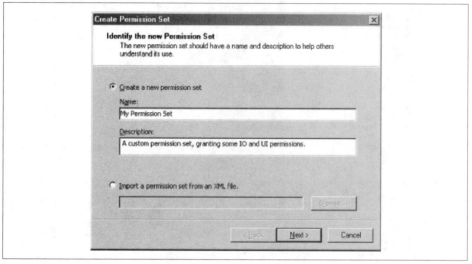

Figure 12-8. Identifying a new permission set

Once you've created a new permission set, its description will be displayed in the right-hand pane of the .NET Configuration tool when that permission set is selected. The first dialog box in the wizard also lets you provide an XML file containing definitions of custom permissions (such as permission not available via the tool itself). In most cases, however, you are likely to simply select permissions from the existing permission types. Click Next to move to the next dialog box in the wizard, which allows you to assign individual permissions to the new permission set (see Figure 12-9).

When you add a permission type from the left-hand pane, it brings up a dedicated dialog for that type, allowing you to add individual permissions of that type. For example, suppose the new permission set is required to grant file I/O and user interface (UI) permissions. For file I/O, the permissions required are read permission for the C drive, and full access to *C:\temp*. For UI, the permissions required are access to all windows and events, but no access to the clipboard. To configure the file I/O permissions, select File IO in the left hand pane of the dialog, and click Add. This brings up the File IO Permission Settings dialog, shown in Figure 12-10.

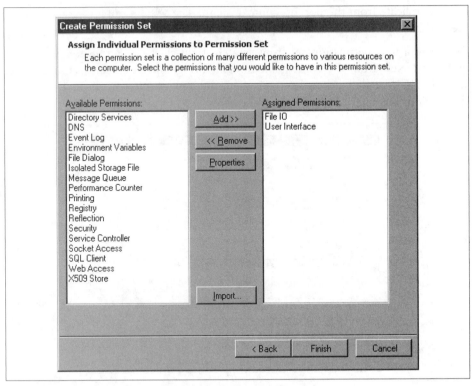

Figure 12-9. Selecting individual permissions for the permission set

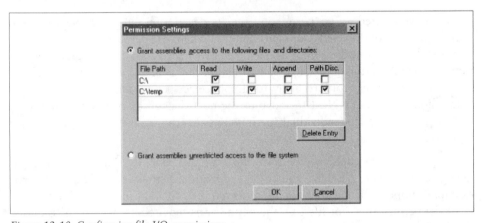

Figure 12-10. Configuring file I/O permissions

The dialog has a grid in which each line corresponds to a single file I/O permission. You can also grant unrestricted access to the filesystem. Configure the required settings, then click OK to return to the previous dialog. To configure the UI permissions, select User Interface in the left-hand pane and click Add. This brings up the UI

Permission Settings dialog, shown in Figure 12-11. Grant access to all windows and events, and deny access to the clipboard. Click OK to return to the previous dialog, then click Finish to complete configuring the new permission set. You can now use this permission set with any code group in the policy.

 You can't share permission sets between policies. If you want the same custom permission set in a different policy, copy the custom permission set by dragging and dropping it to the other policy's *Permission Sets* node.

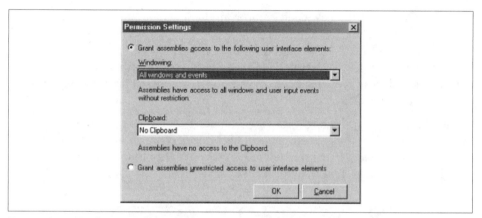

Figure 12-11. Configuring UI permissions

Once you have created a custom permission set (either from scratch or by duplicating an existing permission set), you can change it by selecting Change Permissions from its context menu. This brings up the Create Permission Set dialog shown in Figure 12-9, which lets you modify the permission set.

 To operate, the Microsoft-provided CLR assemblies demand the Full-Trust permission set. This demand is satisfied by the default policy configuration, because code coming from the local machine is granted full trust. Whenever you change the default policy (e.g., when granting a particular user specific permissions), make sure that the new policy grants the CLR assemblies full trust. The easiest way to do that is to copy the Microsoft_Strong_Name code group from the Machine policy and add it to the Enterprise and User policies.

Custom Code Groups

With custom code groups, unlike with predefined permission sets, you can change every detail. You can change the permission sets or the evidence required via the code group's Properties page. You can delete any existing code group, and you can duplicate an existing code group (with all its nested code groups), rename it, and modify its composition. With the .NET Configuration tool, you can even drag-and-drop code groups across policies. The .NET Configuration tool also allows you to create new code groups, but only as a child code group of an existing code group. Once created, you can move the new code group anywhere under the policy code group tree by dragging and dropping it to a new location.

For example, suppose you want to create a new code group that grants all assemblies signed with your organization's public key the Everything permission set. This can be very handy when different teams use each other's assemblies across the local intranet.

The logical place for the new code group is in the Machine policy, as another child code group under the My_Computer_Zone code group, a sibling to the Microsoft_Strong_Name and ECMA_Strong_Name code groups. Note that if your organization is using Enterprise or User policies that are different from the default (of granting all code full trust), you will have to place the new code group in those policies as well, because .NET intersects policies.

In the Machine policy, highlight the My_Computer_Zone code group, right-click it, and select New from the context menu. This brings up the Create Code Group wizard. In the first dialog, name the new code group My Applications, provide a short description (see Figure 12-12), and click Next.

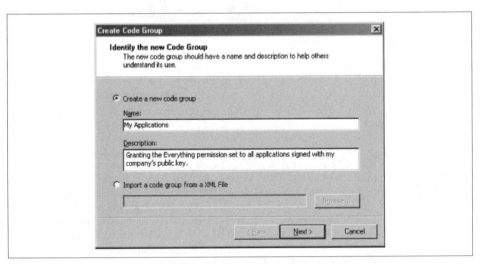

Figure 12-12. Creating a new code group

On the "Choose a condition type" dialog, you need to select the evidence type to be used by this code group, and its value. Select Strong Name from the condition type drop-down combo box (see Figure 12-13). The lower part of the dialog will change to reflect the value of the requested strong key. The easiest way to provide the public key value is to import it from an already-signed assembly. Click the Import button to bring up a file-browsing dialog. Browse to a signed assembly (either an EXE or a DLL), and select it. The wizard then reads the public key from the assembly's manifest and populates the "Public key" text box.

Figure 12-13. Choosing an evidence type and value for a code group

Click Next to proceed to the next dialog, where you need to assign a permission set to the new code group. You can use any existing permission set in the policy (see Figure 12-14), by selecting it from the drop-down combo box. Select Everything, click Next, and click Finish on the next dialog. The new code group is now part of the policy.

 .NET provides the class SecurityManager, which lets you programmatically configure the security policy. SecurityManager offers no advantage over using *caspol.exe* or the .NET Configuration tool. In fact, these two administration tools actually use SecurityManager under the covers.

Non-administrative permissions

Most of the permissions in Table 12-1 can be administered using the .NET Configuration tool. However, there is no easy granular administrative support for the ASP.NET Hosting, Data Protection, Distributed Transactions, Key Container, and Web Browser permissions. The less-than-desirable approach to granting these permissions is to grant the application full trust. This is undesirable because letting an application run with more permissions than it actually requires leaves you susceptible to luring attacks (i.e., when an application is lured into doing something on behalf of a less privileged party).

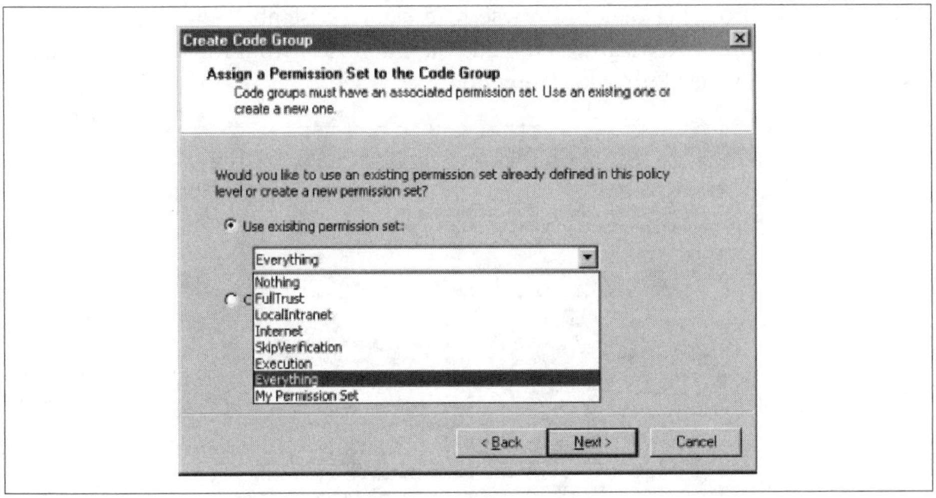

Figure 12-14. Assigning a permission set to a code group

The solution involves adding a custom permission set and a dedicated code group. For example, suppose you have a client application that uses transactions that can be promoted to distributed transactions. In addition, the application needs the following permissions: permission to execute and permission to display a user interface. You can achieve that using two code groups that use the same evidence (such as the application's strong name): the first code group, called MyAppAdmin, grants all the permissions you can grant administratively (execution and user interface), and the second code group, called MyAppCustom, grants the custom permission set—a single unrestricted DistributedTransaction permission, in this example. You will need a custom permission set represented by an XML file. For the unrestricted DistributedTransaction permission, create a text file called *DistributedTransactionUnrestricted.xml* with the following text inside:

```
<PermissionSet class="System.Security.PermissionSet" version="1">
    <IPermission class="System.Transactions.DistributedTransactionPermission,
                  System.Transactions,
                  Version=2.0.0.0, Culture=neutral,
                  PublicKeyToken=b77a5c561934e089"
                  version="1"
                  Unrestricted="True"/>
</PermissionSet>
```

As you can see, the custom permission set schema is straightforward: it lists the fully qualified name of the permission type, its assembly, and the permission itself (unrestricted, in this example). Next, right-click on the *Permission Sets* folder in the Machine policy, and select New from the pop-up context menu. Select the "Import a permission set from an XML file" option, browse to the *DistributedTransactionUnrestricted.xml* file, and click Finish. This will add a new permission set called CustomPermissionSet0 to the *Permission Sets* folder. Rename it DistributedTransactionUnrestricted. In the *Code*

Groups folder, add a new code group called MyAppCustom that uses the same evidence as MyAppAdmin, but grants the DistributedTransactionUnrestricted permission set.

Administrating Security for ClickOnce Applications

While ClickOnce applications are completely subject to code access security, you administer such applications in a different manner from that of other kinds of .NET applications. Each ClickOnce application has an *application manifest*. You associate your ClickOnce application with a certificate using the Signing pane of the project properties. The manifest has a version number and is digitally signed using a publisher certificate. The individual assemblies comprising the ClickOnce application may all come from different vendors, or they may not even have strong names at all. The application manifest lists the assemblies comprising the ClickOnce application, using a hash and a strong name token (if present). You can think of it as an application-level manifest that describes a collection of collectively deployed individual assemblies and their supporting files. The separation of the manifest's digital signature from the assemblies' strong names enables system administrators to trust individual applications rather than the original component vendors. Most importantly, each ClickOnce application manifest lists the security permissions required as a bare minimum for that application to function properly.

When the user for the first time clicks the link which downloads the ClickOnce application, the user is then prompted with a Security Warning dialog, asking permission to install the ClickOnce application. The dialog identifies the publisher of the ClickOnce application, using the name in the certificate. If the user approves the installation, the application's files are not just downloaded and installed, but the application is also granted all the permissions listed in its manifest. When executing, the application will be granted only the permissions listed in its manifest. After the first time the user installs the application (and approves the installation in the subsequent Security Warning dialog), the user is not prompted again when clicking the installation link.

You can use the .NET Administration tool to see which permissions were granted to a ClickOnce application.

The User policy contains a node called *Trusted Applications* (see Figure 12-5). This node contains a list of all the already installed ClickOnce applications. If you remove an entry from the Trusted Applications list, next time the user tries to install that application, the user will be prompted using the Security Warning dialog, as if the application was never installed.

You can view the permissions granted to a particular ClickOnce application: Right-click on the matching entry in the Trusted Applications node and display its properties (see Figure 12-15).

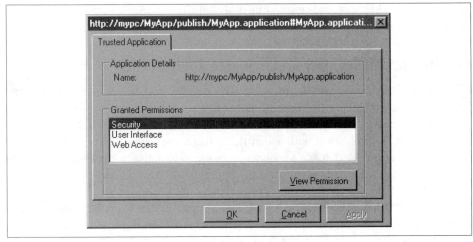

Figure 12-15. Permissions granted to a trusted ClickOnce application

 In addition to adding an entry in the Trusted Applications list, when installing a ClickOnce application, the certificate used to sign the application is added to the user's personal certificates store.

ClickOnce versioning and security

Every version of a ClickOnce application gets its own entry in the Trusted Applications list. Different versions of the same application can request different permissions. When trying to install a new version of a previously installed application, .NET may or may not prompt the user to approve the installation. If the new version of the application contains in its application manifest permissions that are not a subset of a previously installed version, the user is prompted again using the Security Warning dialog. However, if the new version contains the same permissions (or a subset of the permissions demanded by a previously installed version), then the user is not prompted.

Trusting ClickOnce application publishers

By default, every time a new ClickOnce application is deployed, even if that application is published by a publisher that the user has already approved other applications from, the user is still going to get the Security Warning dialog prompt.

In a dynamic environment, with multiple ClickOnce applications, this approach could get quickly out of hand.

To address that, .NET enables trusting not only specific ClickOnce applications but application publishers. Administrators can add a publisher certificate to the Trusted Publishers list on the client machines. When the user launches a ClickOnce application whose application manifest is signed by a trusted publisher, the user will not be prompted, and the application will be granted the permissions specified in the application manifest. If the administrator added the certificate to the Trusted Publishers store at the machine level, it affects all users on that machine. If the administrator added the certificate to the Trusted Publishers store of a particular user, then only that user is not prompted.

In addition, .NET makes a distinction between verified certificates and unverified certificates. A *verified certificate* is any certificate issued by a known authority such as VeriSign or Thawte. Verified certificates are stored in the Trusted Root Certification Authorities certificate container. An *unverified certificate* is any other certificate, such as the test certificates that you can generate using Visual Studio 2005 in the application's properties Signing pane.

Certificate Management

You can add and remove certificates to a store using the certificate manager application. Type certmgr.exe in a command prompt to bring up the Certificates dialog. The dialog lists the available stores and allows the user to manage them. Alternatively, for batch installations you can use the certmgr.exe in command-line mode, for example:

```
certmgr –add MyCompany.cer –s TrustedPublisher
```

You can also add certificates to a store using Visual Studio 2005. This is especially useful when using a test certificate. First, you need to sign the ClickOnce application manifest using the project properties Signing pane. Click the Create Test Certificate... button and provide a password for the certificate. Next, Click the More Details... button, to bring up the Certificate dialog. On the General tab, click the Install Certificate... button to bring up the Certificate Import wizard, and click Next. Select the "Place all certificates in the following store" radio button, and click the Browse... button. Select the certificate store (such as Trusted Publishers) and finish the wizard. When working with unverified certificates (such as test certificates) and desiring suppressed security warning prompt, you will need to use the Certificate Import wizard twice—once to add the certificate to the Trusted Publishers store, and once to add the certificate to the Trusted Root Certification Authorities store.

If the publisher certificate used to sign the ClickOnce application is unverified, then the user will be prompted even if the certificate was added to the Trusted Publishers list. To suppress the prompt when using a private, or a third party unverified certificate, simply add that certificate to the Root Certification Authorities certificate container.

Administrators can block all ClickOnce applications from a particular publisher by adding that publisher's certificate to the Untrusted Certificates list on the client machine. In such a case, the user will not be prompted and will not be allowed to make the trust decision—the application will simply not be allowed to be installed and run.

Custom Security Policies

Knowing how to configure both custom permission sets and custom code groups is actually the last step in deploying a custom security policy. The real question is, what is a good security policy? While the exact optimized answer may vary between different applications, vendors, and customers, there are a few general recommendations. First, I believe the default .NET security policy is inadequate. Any users can copy potentially malicious assemblies to their computers, where the default policy will grant them full trust. Furthermore, the rest of the code groups in the default policy all use origin-based evidence, which is inherently only as secure as your resolution service. If someone subverts your resolution service, malicious assemblies coming from malicious sites could be trusted. The default policy uses origin-based evidences because it is better to have some security blanket than none at all, and it does not need to know anything about the content of your assemblies in order to provide for content-based evidence. On the other hand, you are in charge of the content of your assemblies, and you can use content-based evidences (such as the Strong Name evidence). It is also very important to emphasize again that *any* custom policy you deploy must grant all assemblies signed with the Microsoft or ECMA strong names full trust. Granting full trust to Microsoft assemblies is required because .NET must trust itself in order to run. In fact, the .NET Configuration tool will warn you if the custom policy you configure does not grant Microsoft assemblies full trust. Although it's an undocumented requirement, you must also grant ECMA assemblies full trust in order for your applications and assemblies to work. The .NET Configuration tool will not warn you if you do not, but your applications will not even load. This is probably because the assembly used to verify user types relies on the ECMA strong name, as part of the standardization of extending the CLR type system. In addition, I believe that in a distributed enterprise environment you actually need two security policies: one for the application servers, and one for the client machines.

Custom server-side policy

A server machine in an enterprise environment is typically dedicated to the set of applications developed by a single team or company. Because of that, you can deploy the following security policy: keep a single root code group that grants nothing to all code. This will force .NET to always evaluate the nested code groups. Add the following three code groups to the policy under the root:

- Grant Microsoft assemblies full trust.
- Grant ECMA assemblies full trust.
- Grant all assemblies signed with your own strong name full trust.

Next, remove all other code groups from the policy, as shown in Figure 12-16. Name the new code group after the authority (e.g., the team or company) that issued the strong name. Remove all entries from the Trust Applications node in the User policy. This server-side policy will enable only your applications to run on the server. If you need to add other applications from other vendors to the server, after careful evaluation of the trustworthiness of the vendors, identify those using a strong name.

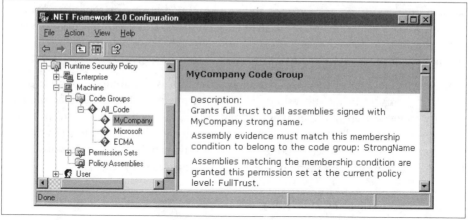

Figure 12-16. Recommended server-side security policy

Custom client-side policy

Typically, a client machine in an enterprise environment is used for a variety of applications from multiple vendors. It is impractical to assume that you could own or lock down those machines solely for the purpose of using your applications. You cannot remove all code groups from the client machine, because that could potentially preclude the execution of other applications. Not only that, but there are no guarantees that the client machines would actually grant your applications permission to execute or call to the server. On a client machine, you can either rely on the ClickOnce deployment mechanism (if your client application is deployed using ClickOnce) or use traditional code groups and permission sets (for conventional client applications). For a traditional client application, I recommend that you deploy a single code group under the root of the policy. Name the new code group after the product it enables. The code group will identify your assemblies using a strong name, and should grant them only the bare permissions required to function. Typically, these are:

- Permission to execute
- Permission to display a user interface
- Permission to call to the server

It is better to grant your client assemblies only these permissions rather than full trust, because granting your assemblies more permissions than they actually require will make them potentially susceptible to luring attacks, where they are lured into doing things they should not do on behalf of a less-privileged party.

Similarly, a ClickOnce application should request the same permissions in its application manifest.

Security Administration Utilities

The .NET Configuration tool provides a number of utilities and services to manage security at a level above code groups and policies. In addition, the tool provides ways to reset policies, examine or trust individual assemblies, and deploy security policies.

Resetting policies

One essential feature of the .NET Configuration tool is the ability to reset a policy (or all of them) to the default values. This is instrumental when experimenting with security configuration. To reset an individual policy, simply select Reset from its context menu. You can also undo the last change made by selecting Undo from the policy's context menu. To reset all policies at once to their default configurations, select Reset All from the context menu of the *Runtime Security Policy* folder.

Reseting the User policy (or all the policies) does not affect the Trusted Applications list.

Managing policy files

You can create new security policy files by selecting New from the context menu of the *Runtime Security Policy* folder. The New Security Policy dialog lets you specify the level of policy file to create—Enterprise, Machine, or User—and a name for the new file. The new file will have as a starting point the default settings for that policy level. You can modify the policy and then assign this new file on the same machine or anywhere else.

First, select Open from the context menu of the *Runtime Security Policy* folder. This brings up the Open Security Policy dialog, which lets you specify which policy level to apply to the configuration file. You can open the default configuration file for that level or assign a specific configuration file (see Figure 12-17).

Adjusting security

The .NET Configuration tool provides a simple, coarse way for system administrators to manage code groups, without bothering with permission sets, evidences, and the like. Selecting Adjust Security from the context menu of the *Runtime Security Policy* folder brings up the Security Adjustment wizard. The first dialog box lets you decide whether the adjustments should apply to the machine or the current user level only; there is no Enterprise level. The next dialog box presents the five zones (My Computer, Local Intranet, Internet, Trusted Sites, and Untrusted Sites) and a track bar (see Figure 12-18).

Adjusting the track-bar position assigns a different permission set to the selected zone. Even though the description of the positions of the track bar to the right don't state so,

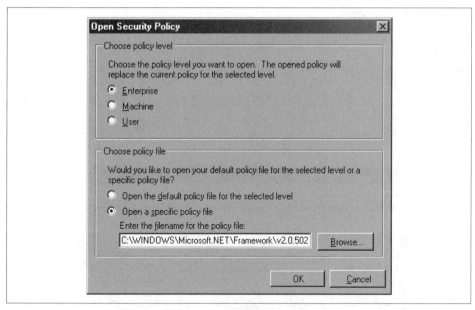

Figure 12-17. Opening and assigning a new security policy file

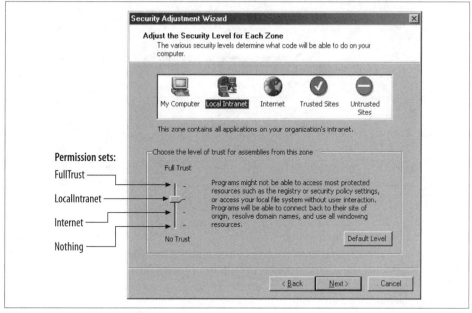

Figure 12-18. Adjusting zone security using the adjustment wizard

the positions map to the FullTrust, LocalIntranet, Internet, and Nothing permission sets, as shown in Figure 12-18. When you click Next, the last dialog box of the adjustment wizard presents a summary of the new security setting for the five zones.

Evaluating an assembly

Sometimes it isn't easy to find out why a particular assembly isn't granted the expected security permissions. The .NET Configuration tool lets you evaluate an assembly to find out which code group grants permissions to that assembly, and which permissions are granted. Selecting Evaluate Assembly from the context menu of the *Runtime Security Policy* folder brings up the Evaluate an Assembly wizard. You need to specify the filename and location of the assembly to evaluate, and what to evaluate (see Figure 12-19).

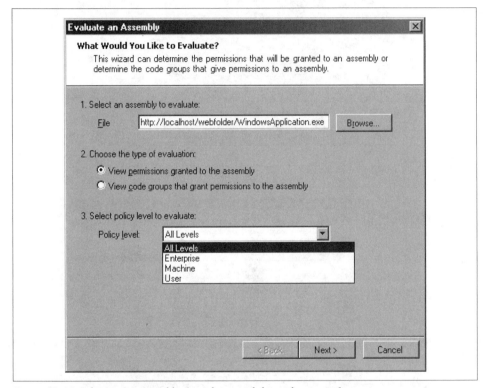

Figure 12-19. Selecting an assembly to evaluate and the evaluation information

If you need to verify which evidences the assembly meets, you can have the wizard list all the code groups that grant permissions to the assembly. Alternatively, you can have the wizard list the actual permissions granted to see what the assembly ends up with. You also need to select the evaluation level; you can select a specific policy level or all levels. Once you select that information, click Next to see the evaluation report. Depending on your selections in the previous dialog, you are either presented with a hierarchical list of code groups (as in Figure 12-20) or a list of permission sets. If you chose to view the permissions, you can examine each permission type to see the value of individual permissions it grants.

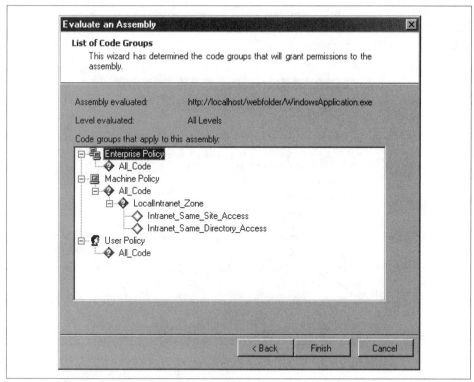

Figure 12-20. Code group membership evaluation report

Trusting an assembly

Sometimes, the system administrator may have explicit knowledge that a particular assembly is trustworthy even though it doesn't satisfy enough code groups to operate. In that case, the administrator can simply add a new code group identifying that assembly with a Hash evidence (or a strong name and version) and grant it the desired permission sets. This is especially handy when it comes to making exceptions to a custom server-side policy (such as the one described previously). The .NET Configuration tool supports an automated way to reach the same end result. Select Trust Assembly from the context menu of the *Runtime Security Policy* folder to bring up the Trust an Assembly wizard. In the first dialog box, you need to decide whether to make the changes apply machine-wide or just to the current user. The next dialog lets you browse to where the assembly in question resides. Once you've provided a path or URL to the assembly, if the assembly does not have a strong name, the wizard presents a track bar that lets you select the minimum level of security permission for the assembly (see Figure 12-21). The different positions of the track bar assign the FullTrust, LocalIntranet, Internet, and Nothing permission sets, as shown in Figure 12-18. The next dialog of the wizard presents a summary of changes made. When you finish the wizard, a new code group is added to the policy specified on the first dialog. The new code group is called *Wizard_<N-1>*, where *N* stands for the number of times the wizard has been asked to trust a different assembly (or the same assembly with different evidences).

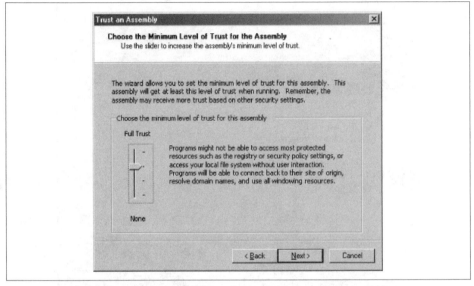

Figure 12-21. Trusting a particular assembly and assigning it an explicit permission set

The wizard will also add custom code groups to allow the assembly to call to its site and directory of origin, when applicable. If you don't like the permission set assigned by the wizard, you can change it to another permission set defined in the policy.

What evidence the wizard-generated code group uses depends on the assembly. If the assembly does not have a strong name or a certificate, the code group will use the Hash evidence to assign the selected permission set. If the assembly has a strong name or even a certificate, the wizard will present another dialog box asking the user for further guidance on whom to trust (see Figure 12-22).

If you choose "This one assembly," the wizard will use the assembly's friendly name, strong name, and version number as evidence. If the assembly has a certificate, you can choose to trust all assemblies from the same publisher. You can also choose to trust all assemblies with the same strong name or strong name and version number.

Exporting security policies

Once the system administrator has finished configuring security on a master machine, you need to replicate that configuration. This chapter has already hinted at a number of manual ways to deploy security configuration by manipulating the actual configuration files. The .NET Configuration tool provides an automated way. Select Create Deployment Package from the context menu of the *Runtime Security*

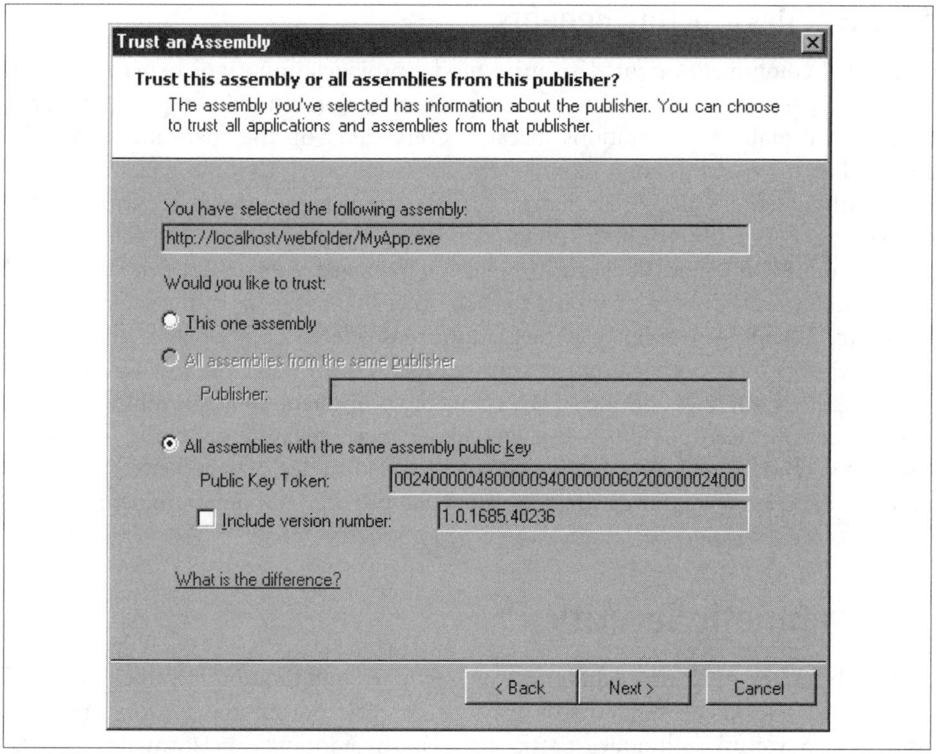

Trust an Assembly

Trust this assembly or all assemblies from this publisher?

The assembly you've selected has information about the publisher. You can choose to trust all applications and assemblies from that publisher.

You have selected the following assembly:

`http://localhost/webfolder/MyApp.exe`

Would you like to trust:

○ This one assembly

○ All assemblies from the same publisher

    Publisher:

⊙ All assemblies with the same assembly public key

    Public Key Token: `0024000004800000940000000602000000024000`

    ☐ Include version number: `1.0.1685.40236`

What is the difference?

[< Back]   [Next >]   [Cancel]

Figure 12-22. Trusting a strongly named assembly and its publisher

Policy folder to bring up the Deployment Package wizard. In the dialog, you need to select which policy level you wish to export into an MSI file, and specify the MSI file name. You can now incorporate the MSI file into your application's installation files, or send it to other machines. When activated, the exported MSI file overrides the existing policy and installs the exported policy instead.

It's easy to restrict permission sets and code groups to a point at which .NET is completely paralyzed (when the CLR assemblies aren't granted full trust) and even the .NET Configuration tool can't function. When this happens, you can't undo your changes. When experimenting with .NET security, I recommend making a copy of the default policy configuration files so that you can manually restore security and functionality to a known state. You can either copy the files directly or use the .NET Configuration tool to replicate the default configuration files. Another recovery strategy is to generate deployment packages of the policies and use them to restore the old policies. You can also use the command-line utility *caspol.exe* to reset all policies:

```
caspol.exe -a -reset
```

Security Infrastructure Benefits

The .NET component-oriented security model provides important benefits to both component vendors and consumers. Component vendors can rely on not being lured to carry out malicious operations, because every caller up the chain must have the required security permissions. Component consumers can rely on the fact that malicious components won't cause harm, because the evidence-based security mechanism grants permissions only to known, trusted components. This is all achieved in a loosely coupled manner: the security policy is managed outside both the client and server code, and they aren't coupled to each other by the details of the security infrastructure. Changes in security policies don't cascade to components, and system administrators have both a great deal of granular control and the freedom to exercise it, because there is nothing in the client or component code pertaining to security. The end user gets a consistent experience, regardless of the operation performed, and no real-time involvement is required to decide whether to trust content coming from a vendor or site. Finally, .NET provides administrators with a centralized place to administer and deploy security policies.

Programmatic Security

Although for the most part administrative security configuration is sufficient, .NET also provides various programmatic ways to control and enforce security. You can use these powerful techniques to tighten security, optimize performance, handle unknown security policies, and deal with questionable components. In addition, programmatic security can configure security at the component level (unlike administrative security configuration, which is only as granular as a single assembly). All the permission types have corresponding classes and attributes available to you. In fact, administrative configuration uses these classes indirectly; the security configuration files are just a list of classes to use when providing the configurable permissions.

Although system administrators can grant assemblies permissions by using administrative configuration, there is no programmatic way to grant permissions. The reason is clear: if that were possible, a rogue assembly could grant itself permissions and go about causing harm. Programmatic security can deny security permissions or demand that some permission be granted. You can use the permission classes dynamically during runtime or apply them as class or assembly attributes, indicating which security action to take and when.

The Permission Classes

The permission types listed in Table 12-1 all have corresponding permission classes, such as the FileIOPermission class or the UIPermission class. Most permission classes are defined in the System.Security.Permissions namespace, but some are spread all over the .NET Framework. All permission classes implement a set of interfaces, including IPermission, which is defined as:

```
public interface IPermission : ISecurityEncodable
{
    IPermission Copy( );
    void Demand( );
    IPermission Intersect(IPermission target);
    bool IsSubsetOf(IPermission target);
    IPermission Union(IPermission target);
}
```

IPermission is defined in the System.Security namespace. The base interface ISecurityEncodable, used mostly when constructing and persisting custom permissions, provides methods to convert the permissions to and from XML security elements.

Permission demand

The most useful method of IPermission is Demand( ), which triggers a stack walk demanding the permission of all the callers up the stack. For example, here is the code required to trigger a stack walk; it verifies that all the callers up the stack have permission to write to the *C:\Temp* directory:

```
IPermission permission;
string path = @"C:\Temp\";
permission = new FileIOPermission(FileIOPermissionAccess.Write,path);
permission.Demand( ); //Trigger stack walk
```

If during the stack walk .NET discovers a caller coming from an assembly without the demanded permission, it aborts the stack walk, and the call to Demand( ) throws an exception of type SecurityException.

Using Demand( ) is how the various .NET application frameworks classes require that whoever calls them have the required security permissions. For example, the file I/O class FileStream demands permission to perform the appropriate operations (such as opening or creating files) in its constructors. You can take advantage of Demand( ) to tighten security and optimize performance as well.

For example, demanding permissions is recommended when a component uses a resource on behalf of a client. Consider the StreamWriter class. It demands file I/O permission when it's constructed with a path parameter, but subsequent calls on its methods cause no demands. The reason the designer of the StreamWriter class decided not to demand the file I/O permission in every call is because it would have rendered the class useless for performing intense file I/O operations. For example, if the client writes the entire Encyclopedia Britannica to the disk one character at a time in a tight loop, demanding the permission every time would kill the application. Not demanding the permission may be fine if a component creates a StreamWriter object and never uses it on behalf of external clients, even indirectly. But in reality, the reason a component creates a resource is to use it to service its clients. Thus, if the permission is demanded only when a component is constructed, a malicious and untrusted client could simply wait for a trusted client to successfully create the component and its resources, and then call its resource–accessing methods.

Unlike the designer of the StreamWriter class, however, you are intimately aware of the particular context in which the StreamWriter class is used. If the file I/O operations performed are not extreme, the component can compensate by explicitly demanding the appropriate permissions, as shown in Example 12-1.

Example 12-1. Protecting a resource by demanding access permission

```
using System.IO;
using System.Security;
using System.Security.Permissions;

public class MyClass
{
   StreamWriter m_Stream;
   string m_FileName = @"C:\Temp\MyFile.txt";
   public MyClass()
   {
      //The StreamWriter demands permissions here only:
      m_Stream = new StreamWriter(m_FileName);
   }
   public void Save(string text)
   {
      //Must demand permission here:
      IPermission permission;
      permission = new FileIOPermission(FileIOPermissionAccess.Write,m_FileName);
      permission.Demand();
      m_Stream.WriteLine(text);
   }
}
```

Another example is an object that is about to perform a lengthy, intensive calculation and then save it to the disk. Ultimately, if the callers up the stack don't have the required permission, the file I/O classes throw an exception when trying to open the file. Instead of wasting time and resources performing a calculation that can't eventually be saved, the object can first demand the permission and then proceed with the calculation only if it's certain it can persist the results. Example 12-2 demonstrates this technique.

Example 12-2. Optimizing by demanding permission before performing the operation

```
class MyClass
{
   public void Calclulate(string resultsFileName)
   {
      IPermission permission;
      permission = new FileIOPermission(FileIOPermissionAccess.Write,
                                                    resultsFileName);
```

Example 12-2. Optimizing by demanding permission before performing the operation (continued)

```
      try
      {
          permission.Demand( );
      }
      catch(SecurityException exception)
      {
          string message = exception.Message;
          message += ": Caller does not have permission to save results";
          MessageBox.Show(message);
          return;
      }
      // Perform calculation here and save results
      DoWork( );
      SaveResults(resultsFileName);
   }
   //Helper methods:
   void DoWork( )
   {...}
   void SaveResults(string resultsFileName)
   {...}
}
```

Note that calling Demand( ) verifies only that the callers up the call chain have the requested security permission. If the object calling Demand( ) itself doesn't have permission, when it tries to access the resource or perform the operation, the resource (or operation) may still throw a security exception.

Permission interactions

Some permissions imply other permissions. For example, file I/O access permission to a folder implies access permission to individual files in the same folder. The IPermission interface provides a number of methods that examine how two different permissions relate to each other. The IsSubsetOf( ) method returns true if a specified permission is a subset of the current permission object:

```
IPermission  permission1;
IPermission  permission2;
string path1 = @"C:\temp\";
string path2 = @"C:\temp\MyFile.txt";

permission1 = new FileIOPermission(FileIOPermissionAccess.AllAccess,path1);
permission2 = new FileIOPermission(FileIOPermissionAccess.Write,path2);

Debug.Assert(permission2.IsSubsetOf(permission1));
```

The Intersect( ) method of IPermission returns a new permission object that is the intersection of the original permission object and the specified permission object, and the Union( ) method returns a new permission object equivalent to the union of the two. .NET uses these methods when calculating the union of permissions granted by the evaluated code groups in a policy and when calculating the intersection of the policies.

Custom Permission

In the rare case of components using a resource type (such as a hardware item) not protected by any of the built-in permissions, you can provide custom permission classes. The custom permission typically grants access to the resource only, instead of to a communication mechanism (such as a communication port or the filesystem) that can access other resources. All .NET permission classes derive from the abstract class CodeAccessPermission, which provides the implementation of the stack walk. You can start creating a custom permission by deriving from CodeAccessPermission. Custom permission classes can be used both programmatically and administratively (via custom XML representation). The assembly containing the custom permissions must be strongly named and deployed in the GAC. In addition, it must be granted full trust, and .NET must be aware of it. To register the assembly with .NET, use the .NET Configuration tool. Each policy has a folder called *Policy Assemblies* (see Figure 12-5). Select Add from the folder's context menu, then select the custom permission assembly from the list of assemblies in the GAC. Note that you must deploy the custom permission assembly and register it on every machine that has applications using it.

Stack-Walk Modifiers

An object can modify the behavior of the stack walk as it passes through it. Each permission class implements the IStackWalk interface, defined as:

```
public interface IStackWalk
{
   void Assert( );
   void Demand( );
   void Deny( );
   void PermitOnly( );
}
```

The Demand( ) method of IStackWalk triggers a stack walk, and the permission classes channel the implementation to that of IPermission.Demand( ). The other three methods, Assert( ), Deny( ), and PermitOnly( ), each install a *stack-walk modifier*—an instruction modifying the behavior of the walk. At any given stack frame (i.e., the scope of a method), there can be only a single stack-walk modifier. Trying to install a second modifier results in an exception of type SecurityException. The stack modifier removes itself automatically once the method returns or when a call to a static reversion method of CodeAccessPermission is called, such as RevertDeny( ), RevertAssert( ), RevertPermitOnly( ), or RevertAll( ). Stack-walk modifiers are very useful for optimizing and tightening the current security policy, serving as a programmatic override to the configuration set by the administrator.

Denying and permitting permissions

In general, a component vendor can't assume that its components will always be deployed in a properly configured and secure environment. Sometimes you should be able to override the administrative security policy and programmatically enforce stricter policies—for example, when the global security policy is turned off, too liberal for your sensitive needs, or simply unknown. Other cases may involve dealing with components from questionable origin. Calling IStackWalk.Deny() denies the permission represented by the underlying permission class and aborts the stack walk, even if the global security policy configuration grants the calling assembly that permission. Example 12-3 demonstrates denying write permission to all the drives on the machine before invoking a method on a questionable component.

Example 12-3. Explicitly denying permissions

```
public void SomeMethod()
{
   string[] drives = Environment.GetLogicalDrives();

   IStackWalk stackWalker;
   stackWalker = new FileIOPermission(FileIOPermissionAccess.Write,drives);

   stackWalker.Deny();

   QuestionableComponent obj = new QuestionableComponent();
   obj.DoSomething();

   CodeAccessPermission.RevertDeny();

   /* Do more work */
}
```

In this example, SomeMethod() constructs a new FileIOPermission object, targeting all the drives on the machine. Using the IStackWalk interface, SomeMethod() denies all write access to these drives. Any attempt by the questionable component to write to these drives results in an exception of type SecurityException. The permission denial remains in effect until the method that called Deny() returns. If you want to revert the denial in the scope of the calling method (for example, to do some file I/O yourself), you need to call the static method RevertDeny() of the CodeAccessPermission class, as shown in Example 12-3.

Sometimes it's simpler to just list what you permit, using the PermitOnly() method of IStackWalk. When a stack walk reaches a method that called PermitOnly(), only that permission is presented, even if other permissions are granted administratively. Example 12-4 demonstrates permitting access only to the *C:\temp* directory, but nothing else.

Example 12-4. Permitting a particular permission only

```
public void SomeMethod( )
{
    string path = @"C:\temp";
    IStackWalk stackWalker;
    stackWalker = new FileIOPermission(FileIOPermissionAccess.AllAccess,path);

    stackWalker.PermitOnly( );

    QuestionableComponent obj = new QuestionableComponent( );
    obj.DoSomething( );

    CodeAccessPermission.RevertPermitOnly( );

    /* Do more work */
}
```

Like Deny( ), PermitOnly( ) remains in effect until the calling method returns or until the method calls the static method RevertPermitOnly( ) of CodeAccessPermission.

 When using a delegate to fire an event at unknown subscribers you can explicitly deny or permit only some permissions, which reduces the risk of calling a delegate that may have lured you into calling it.

Asserting permissions

A stack walk to verify security permissions is a powerful and elegant idea, but it doesn't come without a cost. A stack walk is expensive, and in intense calling patterns or when the call stack is long, it results in a performance and throughput penalty. Consider the following code:

```
void SaveString(string text,string fileName)
{
    StreamWriter stream = new StreamWriter(fileName,true);//append text
    using(stream)
    {
        stream.WriteLine(text);
    }
}

string[] array = new string[9];

array[0] = "Every";
array[1] = "string";
array[2] = "in";
array[3] = "this";
array[4] = "array";
array[5] = "causes";
array[6] = "a";
array[7] = "stack";
array[8] = "walk";
```

```
string fileName = @"C:\Temp\MyStrings.txt";

foreach(string item in array)
{
    SaveString(item,fileName);
}
```

Every time the code writes to the file, it triggers a walk all the way up the stack. After the first stack walk, all the subsequent stack walks are redundant, because the call chain doesn't change between loop iterations. To efficiently handle such cases, use the Assert( ) method of IStackWalk:

```
string fileName = @"C:\Temp\MyStrings.txt";

IStackWalk stackWalker;
stackWalker = new FileIOPermission(FileIOPermissionAccess.Write,fileName);
stackWalker.Assert( );

foreach(string itemin array)
{
    SaveString(item,fileName);
}
CodeAccessPermission.RevertAssert( );
```

When asserting security permission, stack walks demanding it stop in the current stack frame and don't proceed up. The assertion remains in effect until the method returns or until the static method RevertAssert( ) is called. Note that you can assert a single permission only in the same method scope (unless RevertAssert( ) or RevertAll( ) is called).

Because the stack walk stops at the level that asserts the permission, it's quite possible that callers further up the call chain that initiated the call don't have the permission to do the operations carried out by the downstream objects. It looks as if the ability to assert permissions may look like a technique that circumvents .NET's code access security policy—that is, a malicious assembly can assert whatever security permission it wants and then start roaming on the machine. Fortunately, there are two safeguards. First, if the asserting assembly isn't granted the permission it tries to assert, the assertion has no effect. When code down the call chain demands the asserted permission, it triggers a stack walk. When the stack walk reaches the assertion stack-walk modifier, it also verifies that the asserting assembly has that permission. If it doesn't, the stack walk is aborted, and the call demanding permission throws a security exception. The second safeguard is that not all code can assert permissions. Only code granted the Security permission, with the right to assert permissions, can call Assert( ). If the permission to assert isn't granted, a security exception is thrown on the assertion attempt. .NET doesn't use a stack walk to verify that permission to assert is granted. Instead, it verifies that the asserting assembly has that permission at link time, as described later in this chapter.

Only the most trustworthy code should be granted the right to assert, because of the level of risk involved in not completing stack walks.

Another important point regarding permission assertion is that it doesn't always guarantee stopping the stack walk, because the asserted permission may be only a subset of the permission demand that triggered the stack walk. In that case, the assert instruction only stops the stack walk for its particular type and value. The stack walk may proceed up the call stack looking for other permission grants.

Asserting unmanaged code access permission

Performance penalties aside, the more significant side effect of the stack walk is that it can prevent code that should run from operating. Nowhere is this more evident than when it comes to unmanaged code access.

A potential security loophole opens when you call outside the managed-code environment using the interoperation (*interop*) layer. The interop layer allows managed code to invoke calls on COM components, or simply call DLL entry points using the platform-specific invocation mechanism (*P-Invoke*). Unmanaged code is completely exempt from .NET code access policies because it executes directly against the operating system. Using interop, a malicious managed component can have the unmanaged code do its dirty work on its behalf. Naturally, only the most trustworthy assemblies should be granted unmanaged code permission. Accordingly, the managed side of the interop layer demands that all code accessing it have the Security permission with the right to access unmanaged code.

The problem is, all .NET Framework classes that rely on the underlying services of the operating system require the interop layer. Consider the case of the FileStream class. To call it, code requires only file I/O permission, which is a more liberal and less powerful permission than the unmanaged code access permission. However, because the FileStream class uses P-Invoke to call the Win32 API on behalf of the caller, any attempt to use the FileStream class triggers a demand for unmanaged code access permission by the interop layer. To shield the caller, the FileStream class asserts the unmanaged code access permission, so it doesn't propagate the demand for that permission to its clients. Without the assertion, only the most trusted components could have used FileStream. Because it's signed with the Microsoft public key, the FileStream class is granted the FullTrust permission set, and its assertion of unmanaged code access succeeds. Instead of unmanaged code access demand, the FileStream class demands only file I/O permission.

The next question is, how should you handle your own interop calls to the unmanaged world? For example, consider the following code that uses P-Invoke to import the definition of the MessageBoxA Win32 API call, which displays a message box to the user:

```
using System.Runtime.InteropServices;

public class MsgBox
{
   [DllImport("user32",EntryPoint="MessageBoxA")]
   public static extern int Show(HandleRef handle,string text,string caption,
                                                          int msgType);
}
//Client side:
HandleRef handle = new HandleRef(null,IntPtr.Zero);
MsgBox.Show(handle,"Called using P-Invoke","Some Caption",0);
```

Every time the Show( ) method is called, it triggers a demand for unmanaged code access permission. This has the detrimental effect of both a performance penalty and a functionality impasse if the caller doesn't have generic unmanaged code access permission but is trusted to carry out the specific imported unmanaged call. There are a few solutions. The first is to mimic the behavior of the .NET Framework classes and assert the unmanaged code access permission, using a managed wrapping method around the imported unmanaged call. Example 12-5 demonstrates this technique.

Example 12-5. Asserting unmanaged code access permission around an interop method

```
using System.Runtime.InteropServices;
using System.Security;
using System.Security.Permissions;

public class MsgBox
{
   [DllImport("user32",EntryPoint="MessageBoxA")]
   private static extern int Show(HandleRef handle,string text,string caption,
                                                           int msgType);
   public static void Show(string text,string caption)
   {
      IStackWalk stackWalker;
      stackWalker = new SecurityPermission(SecurityPermissionFlag.UnmanagedCode);
      stackWalker.Assert( );

      HandleRef handle = new HandleRef(null,IntPtr.Zero);
      Show(handle,text,caption,0);
   }
}
//Client side:
MsgBox.Show("Called using P-Invoke","Some Caption");
```

To assert the unmanaged code access permission, you assert the SecurityPermission permission, constructed with the SecurityPermissionFlag.UnmanagedCode enum value. The recommended practice, however, is never to assert one permission without demanding another permission in its place, as shown in Example 12-6.

Example 12-6. Asserting unmanaged code permission and demanding UI permission

```
public static void Show(string text,string caption)
{
    IStackWalk stackWalker;
    stackWalker = new SecurityPermission(SecurityPermissionFlag.UnmanagedCode);
    stackWalker.Assert();

    IPermission permission;
    permission = new UIPermission(UIPermissionWindow.SafeSubWindows);
    permission.Demand();

    HandleRef handle = new HandleRef(null,IntPtr.Zero);
    Show(handle,text,caption,0);
}
```

Note that the code in Example 12-6 installs what amounts to a *stack-walk filter*. As the stack walk makes its way through the stack frame, the filter allows only the user-interface part of the unmanaged code demand to go up the call stack. The assertion converts a generic demand to a more specific demand. This is perfectly safe, because you know that the client is not going to use the Show( ) method for all the things unmanaged code enables—the caller will use it only for user-interface purposes.

The second solution is to suppress the interop layer's demand for unmanaged code access permission altogether. .NET provides a special attribute called SuppressUnmanagedCodeSecurityAttribute, defined in the System.Security namespace:

```
[AttributeUsage(AttributeTargets.Class|AttributeTargets.Method|
                AttributeTargets.Interface|AttributeTargets.Delegate,
                AllowMultiple = true,Inherited = false)]
public sealed class SuppressUnmanagedCodeSecurityAttribute : Attribute
{
    public SuppressUnmanagedCodeSecurityAttribute();
}
```

You can apply the SuppressUnmanagedCodeSecurity attribute only to an interop method, to a class that contains interop methods, to a delegate used to invoke an interop method, or to an interface that the class implements. It is ignored in all other cases. The following example shows how to apply the attribute to an interop method:

```
[SuppressUnmanagedCodeSecurity]
[DllImport("user32",EntryPoint="MessageBoxA")]
public static extern int Show(HandleRef handle,string text,string caption,
                                                          int msgType);
```

The interop layer now will not demand that unmanaged code access permission be granted when the Show( ) method is invoked. The only safeguard is that at runtime, during the link phase to the interop method, .NET will demand unmanaged code access permission from the immediate caller up the stack (you will see how to demand permission at link time later). This allows callers up the call chain without unmanaged code access permission to call other clients with that permission and actually invoke the interop method.

A similar issue arises when importing COM objects to .NET, and you can also suppress demands for unmanaged code access permission by the imported COM objects. The *TlbImp* command-line utility provides the /unsafe switch:

```
tlbimp <COM TLB or DLL name> /out:<interop assembly name> /unsafe
```

When you use this switch, the Runtime Callable Wrapper (RCW)—the managed code wrapped around the COM object—will only perform link-time demands for the unmanaged code access permission, instead of doing stack walks on every call. Needless to say, you should use SuppressUnmanagedCodeSecurityAttribute and /unsafe with extreme caution, and only when you know that the call chain to the interop method is secure.

> Since you should never assert a permission without demanding a different permission instead, in the case of using the /unsafe switch with imported COM objects, you should build a wrapper around the RCW and have it demand the specific required permissions.

The third solution is to use security permission attributes. The next section examines this option.

Permission Attributes

All security permission classes have equivalent attribute classes. You can apply the security attributes instead of programmatically creating a permission class and demanding a stack walk or installing a stack-walk modifier. Using the permission attributes is called *declarative security*. All the attributes are used in a similar manner. Their constructor accepts an enum of type SecurityAction, indicating what security action to take:

```
public enum SecurityAction
{
    Assert,
    Demand,
    DemandChoice
    Deny,
    InheritanceDemand,
    InheritanceDemandChoice
    LinkDemand,
    LinkDemandChoice
    PermitOnly,
    RequestMinimum,
    RequestOptional,
    RequestRefuse
}
```

In addition, you need to set public properties of the attributes, instructing .NET what permission values to take upon the security action. Example 12-7 is similar to Example 12-2, except it uses declarative security to demand file I/O permission for a specific predetermined file before proceeding to perform the calculation.

Example 12-7. Declaratively demanding permission before performing an operation

```
class MyClass
{
    [FileIOPermission(SecurityAction.Demand,Write = @"C:\Results.txt")]
    public void Calclulate()
    {
        //Perform calculation here and save results
        DoWork();
        SaveResults();
    }
    //Helper methods:
    void DoWork()
    {...}
    void SaveResults()
    {...}
}
```

In Example 12-7, .NET demands file I/O permission in every call to the method. If you need to repeat the same security actions in all the methods of a class, you can apply the security attribute on the class itself:

```
[FileIOPermission(SecurityAction.Demand,Write = @"C:\Results.txt")]
class MyClass
{...}
```

The main difference between declarative security and programmatic security is evident when you compare Example 12-7 to Example 12-2. With programmatic security, the value of the permission (such as a filename, call time, parameter values, machine name, and so on) can be decided at runtime. With declarative security, the value is static and has to be known at compile time. In general, whenever the permission value is known at compile time, you should use declarative instead of programmatic security. Example 12-8 is functionally identical to Example 12-6, but it's much simpler because it uses declarative security.

Example 12-8. Declaratively asserting unmanaged code access permission and demanding UI permission

```
[SecurityPermission(SecurityAction.Assert,UnmanagedCode = true)]
[UIPermission(SecurityAction.Demand,
                        Window = UIPermissionWindow.SafeSubWindows)]
public static void Show(string text,string caption)
{
    HandleRef handle = new HandleRef(null,IntPtr.Zero);
    Show(handle,text,caption,0);
}
```

You can also apply declarative security directly on the interop method, instead of the wrapper method.

When you apply a security attribute to the scope of a class, it affects all members of the class.

Choice actions

.NET 2.0 added the choice options to the SecurityAction enum, allowing you to combine permissions in a logical OR, instead of AND. Consider the following security demands on the method SomeMethod( ):

```
[UIPermission(SecurityAction.Demand,Unrestricted = true)]
[FileIOPermission(SecurityAction.Demand,Unrestricted = true)]
void SomeMethod( )
{...}
```

Because SomeMethod( ) has two security permission demands on it, both permissions have to be granted for the method to be used. If you want instead to demand that either one of the permissions has to be granted, use the SecurityAction.DemandChoice value:

```
[UIPermission(SecurityAction.DemandChoice,Unrestricted = true)]
[FileIOPermission(SecurityAction.DemandChoice,Unrestricted = true)]
void SomeMethod( )
{...}
```

Now at least one of the permissions has to be granted, but not necessarily both. This sort of demand is called a *demand choice*.

Link-time demands

Declarative security offers capabilities not available with programmatic security demands. You can request that the permission be demanded at link time, during JIT compilation, instead of at call time. Link-time demands are specified using the SecurityAction.LinkDemand value for the security action. For example:

```
[UIPermission(SecurityAction.LinkDemand,
              Window = UIPermissionWindow.SafeTopLevelWindows)]
public void DisplaySomeUI( )
{}
```

When the security action is set to the SecurityAction.LinkDemand value, .NET demands permission only of the caller immediately up the call chain linking to the method. Subsequent calls to the method aren't verified to have the permission. If the client doesn't have the demanded permission, a security exception is raised as early as possible—usually when the client first tries to link to the method, instead of at a later point in time. You can still demand the security permission on every call using programmatic security, but if you don't demand permission on every call, you eliminate the stack-walk penalty. The downside to this approach is that malicious clients can use a middleman component with the required permissions to link against the demanding component and then call the middleman, without being subjected to the stack walk. Use SecurityAction.LinkDemand without a per-call demand only if you know that the call chain leading to the object will remain static and is secure.

Link-time demands are especially useful in conjunction with the attribute StrongNameIdentityPermissionAttribute, defined as:

```
[AttributeUsage(AttributeTargets.Assembly|AttributeTargets.Class|
                AttributeTargets.Struct|AttributeTargets.Constructor|
                AttributeTargets.Method,AllowMultiple = true,Inherited = false)]
public sealed class StrongNameIdentityPermissionAttribute :
                                             CodeAccessSecurityAttribute
{
   public StrongNameIdentityPermissionAttribute(SecurityAction action);
   public string Name{get;set;}
   public string PublicKey{get;set;}
   public string Version { get; set; }
}
```

This attribute lets you insist that the assembly linking into your code is signed with a specified public key:

```
public static class PublicKeys
{
   public const string MyCompany = "1234567890...ABCDEF";
}

[StrongNameIdentityPermission(SecurityAction.LinkDemand,
                                    PublicKey = PublicKeys.MyCompany)]
public void MyMethod( )
{...}
```

You can apply the attribute StrongNameIdentityPermission on any user type. You can even insist on a particular version number and assembly name. The canonical use of StrongNameIdentityPermission is when you are forced to use a public class or a public method because of design considerations, so that you can call it from other assemblies you provide. Logically, however, these public types or methods are for your application's internal private use; you do not want other assemblies from other vendors to use your own application-internal types. In that case, all you need to do is demand your own public key so that no other party can use these public types or methods.

There is a pitfall associated with demanding StrongNameIdentityPermission: you cannot demand multiple keys, because an assembly can have only a single strong name. If you have multiple vendors to whom you want to allow access, use the LinkDemandChoice value instead:

```
[StrongNameIdentityPermission(SecurityAction.LinkDemandChoice,
                                   PublicKey = PublicKeys.Vendor1)]
[StrongNameIdentityPermission(SecurityAction.LinkDemandChoice,
                                   PublicKey = PublicKeys.Vendor2)]
public void MyMethod( )
{...}
```

To use `StrongNameIdentityPermissionAttribute`, you need a string representing a public key. You can use the .NET Configuration tool to extract the public key from an assembly by constructing a code group that uses the Strong Name evidence (see Figure 12-13) and simply copying and pasting the value from the "Public key" text box. Another solution is to use the *sn.exe* command-line utility. The *-e* switch extracts the public key from an assembly, and the *-tp* switch converts the key to a string representation.

Inheritance demand

A malicious party can derive from a class, override demanding methods, and then provide its own implementation that does not demand the permission, yet uses much of the functionality at the base-class level. In addition, the subclass can use protected members and helper methods for its own purposes. Component library vendors can use declarative security to prevent malicious parties from abusing their components via inheritance. The component vendor can apply the required security permissions using the `SecurityAction.InheritanceDemand` value, indicating to .NET to demand the permission of the subclasses. For example, here's how the `BaseClass` class can demand that its subclasses have been granted unrestricted access to the filesystem:

```
[FileIOPermission(SecurityAction.InheritanceDemand,Unrestricted=true)]
public class BaseClass
{}
```

When an inheritance demand is applied to a method, it verifies that the overriding subclass has the requested permission. Inheritance demand takes place during load time, and no stack walks are involved.

Neither programmatic nor declarative security can protect against untrusted code accessing public fields, because no stack calls are involved. Never provide public fields, and always use properties.

As with link-time demand and regular demands, SecurityAction also provides the InheritanceDemandChoice value. InheritanceDemandChoice allows you to specify a number of permission attributes and demand that subclasses be granted at least one of them.

The WebBrowser Control and Code-Access Security

When using the WebBrowser control it is not enough to have WebBrowser permission, because the control demands also the safe top level windows permission (a part of UserInterface permission). This is because the WebBrowser control can cause new windows to be popped up. In addition, the WebBrowser control also demands the following: a link-time demand and inheritance demand for FullTrust, and a FullTrust demand on its constructor:

```
[PermissionSet(SecurityAction.LinkDemand,Name="FullTrust")]
[PermissionSet(SecurityAction.InheritanceDemand,
                                    Name="FullTrust")]
public class WebBrowser : WebBrowserBase
{
   [PermissionSet(SecurityAction.Demand,Name="FullTrust")]
   public WebBrowser();
   //Rest of the members
}
```

This renders the control mostly useless for partially trusted clients, because such clients tend to link against the control directly, create it and use it, and thus require FullTrust themselves. The inclusion of the WebBrowser permission in the LocalIntranet, Internet and Everything named permission set is therefore mostly of little use if at all.

Permission Set Classes

Instead of constructing individual permissions and demanding them, or using a permission to modify a stack walk, you can programmatically construct permission sets. In fact, the main reason for using a permission set is to install a stack-walk modifier that combines multiple permissions (remember that you can install only a single stack-walk modifier). Creating a permission set programmatically is similar to composing a new permission set using the .NET Configuration tool—you create individual permission objects and aggregate them in a permission set object. Using a permission set is an easy way to install a stack-walk modifier that denies, permits, or asserts multiple permissions. Example 12-9 demonstrates composing a permission set with file I/O and UI permissions and denying it before accessing a questionable component.

Example 12-9. Creating and denying a permission set

```
public void SomeMethod( )
{
    PermissionSet permissionSet;
    //Create an empty permission set
    permissionSet = new PermissionSet(PermissionState.None);

    IPermission  filePermision;
    string path = @"C:\";
    filePermision = new FileIOPermission(FileIOPermissionAccess.AllAccess,path);

    permissionSet.AddPermission(filePermision);

    IPermission UIPerm;
    UIPerm = new UIPermission(PermissionState.Unrestricted);

    permissionSet.AddPermission(UIPerm);

    IStackWalk stackWalker = permissionSet;

    stackWalker.Deny( );

    QuestionableComponent obj = new QuestionableComponent( );
    obj.DoSomething( );

    CodeAccessPermission.RevertDeny( );
}
```

You can explicitly revert a stalk-walk modifier set by a permission set using the static methods of CodeAccessPermission, or you can wait for the method to return, as with an individual permission modifier.

Permission set collection

Using individual permissions, as in Example 12-1, you can demand that all callers up the stack have a particular permission. If you have multiple permissions to demand, you can build a permission set (as in Example 12-9) and demand that the callers are granted all the permissions in the permission set:

```
PermissionSet permissionSet = new PermissionSet(PermissionState.None);
permissionSet.AddPermission(...);
permissionSet.AddPermission(...);
permissionSet.Demand( );
```

.NET 2.0 introduces an interesting use of permission sets: the ability to demand that the callers up the stack are granted at least one of any number of permissions sets specified. The class PermissionSetCollection is defined as:

```
public sealed class PermissionSetCollection : ICollection,IEnumerable
{
    public PermissionSetCollection( );
    public void Add(PermissionSet permSet);
```

```
    public void Demand( );
    //Rest of the members
}
```

This is a simple collection of permission sets. You can add new permission sets using the Add( ) method. When you call the Demand( ) method, it performs a stack walk, demanding that every caller up the stack satisfies at least one of the permission sets in the collection (that is, satisfies all the permissions in at least one of the permission sets in the collection). This is akin to performing a programmatic (instead of declarative) demand choice for the permission sets in the collection. Since a permission set can contain a single permission, effectively you can use PermissionSetCollection to generate a demand choice for individual permissions (this is the only way in .NET to perform a programmatic demand choice for individual permissions). For example, consider the code in Example 12-1. You could relax the strict demand for file I/O permission by demanding that the callers up the stack either have file I/O permissions or were installed in the GAC. As mentioned at the beginning of this chapter, because only an administrator can install assemblies in the GAC, such assemblies are somewhat more trustworthy than assemblies installed by non-administrators. You can demand GAC installation using the GacIdentityPermission class.

Example 12-10 demonstrates the use of PermissionSetCollection with the modified Save( ) method from Example 12-1. It defines the static helper class SecurityUtil, with the DemandChoice( ) method. DemandChoice( ) accepts an array of IPermission objects. For each permission object in the array, DemandChoice( ) creates a PermissionSet object and adds it to a PermissionSetCollection object. DemandChoice( ) then demands the permission set collection, thus triggering a demand choice. The use of the params array qualifier in DemandChoice( ) makes it easy to call it with any number of permissions.

Example 12-10. Using PermissionSetCollection

```
public static class SecurityUtil
{
    public static void DemandChoice(params IPermission[] permissions)
    {
        PermissionSetCollection collection = new PermissionSetCollection( );
        foreach(IPermission permission in permissions)
        {
            PermissionSet permisssionSet = new PermissionSet(PermissionState.None);
            permisssionSet.AddPermission(permission);
            collection.Add(permisssionSet);
        }
        collection.Demand( );
    }
}
//Replaces the Save( ) method of Example 12-1
public void Save(string text)
{
    IPermission permission1;
    permission1 = new FileIOPermission(FileIOPermissionAccess.Write,m_FileName);
```

Example 12-10. Using PermissionSetCollection (continued)

```
    IPermission permission2;
    permission2 = new GacIdentityPermission( );
    SecurityUtil.DemandChoice(permission1,permission2);
    m_Stream.WriteLine(text);
}
```

Permission Set Attributes

You can declaratively instruct .NET to take a security action, such as demanding or asserting a permission set, using the `PermissionSetAttribute` class, defined as:

```
public sealed class PermissionSetAttribute : CodeAccessSecurityAttribute
{
    public PermissionSetAttribute(SecurityAction action);
    public SecurityAction Action{get;set;}
    public string File{get;set;}
    public string Name{get;set;}
    public string XML {get;set;}
    //Rest of the definition
}
```

Unlike with the programmatic composition of a permission set, when you use the `Name` property of the `PermissionSetAttribute` class, you are restricted to using only the predefined named permission sets, as in the following example:

```
[PermissionSet(SecurityAction.Demand,Name = "LocalIntranet")]
public void SomeMethod( )
{}
```

Note that you cannot use the Everything permission set (probably because it's specific to the .NET Configuration tool).

If you want to use a custom permission set declaratively, you need to provide the attribute with an XML representation of that set. You can assign the name of a file containing that XML to the `File` property of the attribute. Using a file gives you the option of changing the permission set you demand or assert after deployment. However, a file can be tempered with (unless you apply NTFS protections to it), and besides, declarative security attributes are better used in a static security context. With a custom permission set, I recommend that you use the `XML` property of `PermissionSetAttribute`. Whether you use the `File` property or the `XML` property, you will need to prepare the XML representation of your custom permission set. The easiest way to do that is to write a short program that constructs the permission set programmatically and then calls its `ToString( )` method. The `ToString( )` method of the `PermissionSet` class returns the XML encoding of the permission set. Next, either save that string to a file (for use with the `File` property), or hardcode it in the assembly for use with the `XML` property, as shown in Example 12-11.

Example 12-11. Defining and using a custom permission set

```
//Step 1: Construct a custom permission set programmatically and
//encode into XML

IPermission permission1 = new UIPermission(PermissionState.Unrestricted);
IPermission permission2 = new FileIOPermission(PermissionState.Unrestricted);
PermissionSet permisssionSet = new PermissionSet(PermissionState.None);
permisssionSet.AddPermission(permission1);
permisssionSet.AddPermission(permission2);
//Copy the resulting string from the trace:
Trace.WriteLine(permisssionSet.ToString( ));

//Step 2: Build a constant representing the custom permission set
public static class CustomPermissions
{
   public const string MyPermissionSet = @"
<PermissionSet class = ""System.Security.PermissionSet"" version=""1"">
   <IPermission class = ""System.Security.Permissions.UIPermission,
                                    mscorlib,
                                    Version=2.0.0.0,Culture=neutral,
                                    PublicKeyToken=b77a5c561934e089""
                                    version=""1""
                                    Unrestricted=""true""/>
   <IPermission class = ""System.Security.Permissions.FileIOPermission,
                                    mscorlib,
                                    Version=2.0.0.0,Culture=neutral,
                                    PublicKeyToken=b77a5c561934e089""
                                    version=""1""
                                    Unrestricted=""true""/>
</PermissionSet>";}

//Step 3: Use the custom permission set
[PermissionSet(SecurityAction.Demand,XML = CustomPermissions.MyPermissionSet)]
public void SomeMethod( )
{}
```

You can even combine your custom permission set with the named permission sets in a demand or demand-choice manner. If you use demand choice, only one of the demanded permission sets has to be satisfied:

```
[PermissionSet(SecurityAction.DemandChoice,
                                    XML = CustomPermissions.MyPermissionSet)]
[PermissionSet(SecurityAction.DemandChoice,
                                    Name = "LocalIntranet")]
public void SomeMethod( )
{}
```

Assembly-Wide Permissions

Instead of type-based or even method-based security configuration, you can declaratively apply security permission attributes to an entire assembly, affecting every component in the assembly. All the permission attributes can be applied at the assembly level as well, although the semantics of the security action taken are different from those for a type or method. In fact, you can't apply the values of the SecurityAction enum shown so far on an assembly, and the compiler enforces that. The SecurityAction enum provides three specific values that can be applied only at the assembly scope, again enforced by the compiler:

```
public enum SecurityAction
{
    //Assembly values:
    RequestMinimum,
    RequestOptional,
    RequestRefuse
    //More type and method values
}
```

 Even though the compiler provides the required degree of type safety for the SecurityAction enum, it would have been cleaner to factor it into two enums: SecurityActionType and SecurityActionAssembly.

You can use these security action values with an individual permission, such as a request for full access to the *C:\Temp* directory:

```
[assembly : FileIOPermission(SecurityAction.RequestMinimum,
                ViewAndModify= @"C:\temp")]
```

You can even use these values with a named permission set:

```
[assembly : PermissionSet(SecurityAction.RequestMinimum,Name = "Internet")]
```

You can apply an assembly permission attribute multiple times:

```
[assembly : FileIOPermission(SecurityAction.RequestMinimum,
                ViewAndModify= @"C:\temp")]
[assembly : FileIOPermission(SecurityAction.RequestMinimum,
                ViewAndModify= @"D:\temp")]
```

The SecurityAction.RequestMinimum value indicates to .NET that this assembly requires the specified permission or permission set to operate. Without it, there is no point in loading the assembly or trying to create the types in it. The SecurityAction. RequestRefuse value is useful when all the types in an assembly require denying a particular permission or permission set, or when you explicitly want to reduce the permissions granted to the assembly—when .NET computes the permissions granted to the assembly, it subtracts the refused permissions from the administratively granted permissions. The SecurityAction.RequestOptional value indicates to .NET what permissions this assembly wants in addition to the minimum permissions requested. Optional permissions also indicate that the assembly can operate without them and that no other permissions are required. Specifying optional and refused permissions can prevent the assembly from being granted permissions it doesn't require. Although not technically necessary, it's always better to refuse any permissions that an assembly is granted but doesn't require. Doing so reduces the chance of abuse by malicious clients and counters luring attacks. The final permissions granted must therefore take into account the assembly attributes and the configured policy.

If no assembly attributes are present, .NET grants the assembly the administratively configured permissions according to the security policies. However, if assembly security attributes are present, .NET follows the following algorithm. First, .NET retrieves the permissions granted by the .NET administrators. It then verifies that the requested minimum set of permissions is a subset of the granted policies. If so, .NET computes the union of the minimum and optional permissions, and intersects the result with the administratively granted permissions. Finally, .NET subtracts the refused permissions from the intersection. Figure 12-23 summarizes this algorithm by using formal notations.

$$\text{If } M \subseteq P:$$
$$G = P \cap (O \cup M) - R$$

Granted permissions	G
Minimum permissions	M
Optional permissions	O
Policies permissions	P
Refused permissions	R

Figure 12-23. Computing assembly permissions when assembly permission attributes are provided

Visual Studio 2005 and Security

Visual Studio 2005 has a few features that cater to code access security. First, it allows developers of ClickOnce applications to specify the permissions required for their ClickOnce applications. Visual Studio 2005 can also estimate the security permissions required by an application. Most importantly, Visual Studio supports partial-trust debugging, thus significantly streamlining the process of developing secure yet usable modern applications.

ClickOnce Permissions

Application assemblies (Console and Windows Forms applications) contain a Security tab in the project properties (see Figure 12-24). After checking the "Enable Click-Once Security Settings" checkbox, you can configure the security permissions required by the application if it is to be deployed as a ClickOnce application. Two modes are available: full trust and partial trust. If you select "This is a full trust application", the ClickOnce application manifest will demand the FullTrust permission set. If you select the "This is a partial trust application" radio button, you can also select three possible zones (or rather, permission sets) to associate with your Click-Once application: Internet, Local Intranet, and Custom. ClickOnce security settings are actually enabled automatically the first time you publish an application as a ClickOnce application, and they default to full trust. The dialog lists almost all of the .NET security permissions.

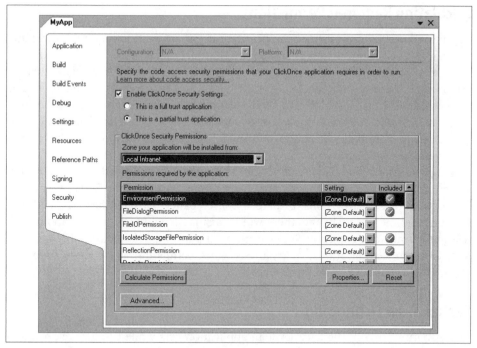

Figure 12-24. Visual Studio 2005 project Security pane

If you select the partial-trust radio button, once you've specified the zone, Visual Studio 2005 will automatically set each permission type to its default, according to the zone selected (Internet, Local Intranet, or Local Computer) If you select Custom for the zone, you must configure each permission type individually, and the default merely grants security execution permission. Even when not using Custom, you can still configure each individual permission type to a different value. You can explicitly exclude or include each permission type. When explicitly including a permission type, click the Properties button to display the Permission Settings dialog (the same dialog used by the .NET Configuration tool). You can then specifically configure that permission type. You can also click the Reset button to reset all permissions to the zone's defaults. The next time you publish the ClickOnce application, Visual Studio 2005 will capture the permissions you have configured in the application manifest. When installed on the client machine, the *Trust Applications* node in the User policy will include an entry matching the permissions you configured (see Figure 12-15 for an example).

You can also grant your ClickOnce application single web-access permission, allowing the application to connect back to its site of origin (where it was published from). In the project properties' Security pane, click the Advanced… button (see Figure 12-24) to bring up the Advanced Security Setting (see Figure 12-25), and check the "Grant the application access to its site of origin" checkbox.

Calculating Required Permissions

Visual Studio 2005 can estimate the permissions an application requires to operate. When you click the Calculate Permissions button, Visual Studio 2005 performs a static analysis of the current application and referenced assemblies. The analysis traverses all method calls, declarative attributes, and programmatic demands, and aggregates them into the calculated set of required permissions. To expedite the analysis, Visual Studio 2005 uses cached results for the .NET assemblies. The static analysis is only an estimate—it may overestimate the required permissions, because it analyzes all possible code paths (even those that are never used). It may also underestimate permissions, because it will not detect dynamically bounded calls made using reflection. After calculating the required permissions, Visual Studio 2005 updates the listbox with those permissions. If there is a discrepancy between the calculated permissions and the selected zone, there will be a small icon informing you about each relevant permission. You can use this feature with any application assembly (not just with ClickOnce applications) to try to see what permissions your application will require from your custom security policy.

Partial-Trust Debugging

The disparity between the trust level an application gets while being developed and when it is deployed may cause many previously unforeseen problems. After deployment, some operations will not be successful, resulting in nondeterministic behavior or even data corruption, and security exceptions may be thrown in places that simply sailed through during debugging. If you anticipate that your application will be deployed in a partial-trust environment, you must debug the application under partial trust as well. If you click the Advanced... button on the Security tab, it will bring up the Advanced Security Settings dialog (see Figure 12-25).

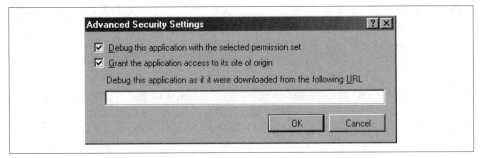

Figure 12-25. Enabling partial-trust debugging

This dialog lets you instruct Visual Studio 2005 to debug the application under the permission set configured in the Security tab. In fact, if you enable ClickOnce security settings on the Security tab, partial-trust debugging is turned on by default (though you can turn it off). In addition, you can grant the application permission to access its site of origin. You can also instruct Visual Studio 2005 to debug the application as if it were downloaded from a specified URL. To support partial-trust debugging, Visual Studio 2005 uses an App Domain policy, granting only the permissions configured for the application in the Security tab. Recall that the App Domain policy is the fourth policy intersected along with the Enterprise, Machine, and User policies. Even if all the other policies grant full trust (which they do by default), the presence of the App Domain policy restricts the granted permissions, yielding partial-trust debugging. Since the restricted App Domain policy is merely a debugging feature, it cannot persist into the built assembly. The solution is to use a host application that will load the application (as if it were a class library) into the restricted app domain. This is exactly what the *<application name>.vshost.exe* process does. Supporting partial-trust debugging is the main reason why Visual Studio 2005 resorts to *vshost.exe*.

Useful as it is, there is an interesting and important limitation to partial-trust debugging that may cause your application to behave differently under partial-trust debugging than under real deployment. Consider an application assembly called *MyApp* that uses a class library called *MyLibrary*. Now suppose that *MyLibrary* is granted full trust, and that it asserts some permissions that it does not want demanded of its client. If you deploy *MyApp* in a partial-trust environment (e.g., using the Internet permission set) that does not grant *MyApp* the asserted permission, the application should still function properly, because *MyLibrary* executes with full trust and hence can assert its permissions. However, if you debug *MyApp* under partial trust and choose the Internet zone, Visual Studio 2005 will install a matching App Domain policy that will restrict all assemblies in the app domain, including *MyLibrary*. The conclusion is that even though partial-trust debugging is a handy feature, there is no substitute for exhaustive system testing under the same security policy as in deployment.

Visual Basic 2005 and Security

When partial-trust debugging is enabled in a Visual Basic 2005 project, and the permissions are set for anything other than full trust, IntelliSense will provide a listing of the permissions required by that member on top of the usual member information, as shown in Figure 12-26.

Figure 12-26. Security-aware IntelliSense in Visual Basic 2005

This can be handy for letting you know which permissions the application will require as you develop it. However, IntelliSense does not always pick up all the permissions required by a given method or type, so you should not rely exclusively on the list it generates.

Principal-Based Security

As stated at the beginning of this chapter, .NET component-based security isn't a cure-all. There is still a need to verify that the user (or the account) under which the code executes has permission to perform the operation. In .NET, the user is referred to as the *security principal*. It's impractical to program access permissions for each individual user (although it's technically possible); instead, it is better to grant permissions to roles users play in the application domain. A *role* is a symbolic category of users who share the same security privileges. When you assign a role to an application resource, you are granting access to that resource to whomever is a member of that role. Discovering the roles users play in your business domain is part of your application-requirement analysis and design, as is factoring components and interfaces. By interacting with roles instead of particular users, you isolate your application from changes made in real life, such as adding new users, moving existing users between positions, promoting users, or users leaving their jobs. .NET allows you to apply role-based security both declaratively and programmatically, if the need to verify role membership is based on a dynamic decision.

Declarative Role-Based Security

Apply declarative role-based security using the attribute PrincipalPermissionAttribute, defined in the System.Security.Permissions namespace:

```
[AttributeUsage(AttributeTargets.Class|AttributeTargets.Method
                AllowMultiple = true,Inherited = false)]
public sealed class PrincipalPermissionAttribute : CodeAccessSecurityAttribute
{
   public PrincipalPermissionAttribute(SecurityAction action);
   public bool Authenticated{get;set;}
   public string Name{get;set;}
   public string Role{get;set;}
}
```

You apply the attribute to either classes or methods, specifying the security action to take and the role name. By default, a security role in .NET is a Windows user group. The examples in this chapter all use Windows user groups, but .NET allows you to provide your own custom role definitions, as demonstrated in Appendix B. When you specify a Windows user group as a role, you must prefix it with the domain name or the local machine name (if the role is defined locally only). For example, the following declaration grants access to MyMethod( ) only for code running under the identity of a user belonging to the Managers user group:

```
public class MyClass
{
    [PrincipalPermission(SecurityAction.Demand,Role=@"<domain>\Managers")]
    public void MyMethod( )
    {...}
}
```

If the user isn't a member of that role, .NET throws an exception of type
SecurityException. If multiple roles are allowed to access the method, you can apply
the attribute multiple times:

```
[PrincipalPermission(SecurityAction.Demand,Role=@"<domain>\Managers")]
[PrincipalPermission(SecurityAction.Demand,Role=@"<domain>\Customers")]
public void MyMethod( )
{...}
```

When multiple roles are applied to a method, the user is granted access if the user is
a member of at least one role. If you want to verify that the user is a member of both
roles, you need to use programmatic role-membership checks, discussed later.

> When it comes to PrincipalPermissionAttribute, SecurityAction.
> Demand behaves like SecurityAction.DemandChoice. You cannot com-
> bine SecurityAction.DemandChoice with PrincipalPermissionAttribute.
> This inconsistency originated with .NET 1.1, which did not have the
> SecurityAction.DemandChoice value.

You can apply the PrincipalPermissionAttribute at the class level as well:

```
[PrincipalPermission(SecurityAction.Demand,Role=@"<domain>\Managers")]
public class MyClass
{
    public void MyMethod( )
    {...}
}
```

When the attribute is applied at the class level, only clients belonging to the specified role can create an object of this type. This is the only way to enforce role-based
security on constructors, because you can't apply PrincipalPermissionAttribute on
class constructors.

By setting the Name property of PrincipalPermissionAttribute, you can even insist on
granting access to a particular user:

```
[PrincipalPermission(SecurityAction.Demand,Name = "Bill")]
```

You can also insist on a particular user and insist that the user be a member of a specific role:

```
[PrincipalPermission(SecurityAction.Demand,Name="Bill",Role=@"<domain>\Managers")]
```

This practice is inadvisable, however, because hardcoding usernames is fragile.

Enabling role-based security

Every app domain has a flag that instructs .NET which principal policy to use. The *principal policy* is the authorization mechanism that looks up role membership. You set the principal policy by calling the SetPrincipalPolicy( ) method of the AppDomain class:

```
public void SetPrincipalPolicy(PrincipalPolicy policy);
```

The available policies are represented by the values of the PrincipalPolicy enum:

```
public enum PrincipalPolicy
{
    NoPrincipal,
    UnauthenticatedPrincipal,
    WindowsPrincipal
}
```

By default, every .NET application (be it Windows Forms or ASP.NET) has PrincipalPolicy.UnauthenticatedPrincipal specified for its security policy. If you simply apply PrincipalPermissionAttribute (or use programmatic role-membership verification), all calls will be denied access, even if the caller is a member of the specified role.

To use role-based security in ASP.NET, the caller must be authenticated. With authenticated callers in ASP.NET, there is no need to call SetPrincipalPolicy( ), although it doesn't cause harm.

To enable role-based security in a Windows application, you must set the role-based security policy to PrincipalPolicy.WindowsPrincipal. It is a good idea to use this value even if you install a custom role-based security mechanism, as in Appendix B. This is because PrincipalPolicy.WindowsPrincipal enables the use of Windows accounts, and you have no idea if other components will try to do that. You need to set the principal policy in every app domain that uses role-based security. Typically, you place that code in the Main( ) method of an application assembly:

```
static public void Main( )
{
    AppDomain currentDomain = AppDomain.CurrentDomain;
    currentDomain.SetPrincipalPolicy(PrincipalPolicy.WindowsPrincipal);
}
```

If you create new app domains programmatically, you also need to set the principal policies in them.

 When you experiment with Windows role-based security, you often add users to or remove users from user groups. Because Windows caches user-group information at login time, the changes you make aren't reflected until the next login.

Role-based security and authentication

Role-based security controls user *authorization*—that is, what users are allowed to access. However, authorization is meaningless without *authentication*, or verification that the user is indeed who the user claims to be. In a Windows application, users have to log in and are therefore authenticated. Internet applications (such as ASP. NET applications or web services), on the other hand, sometimes grant anonymous access to users. It's therefore prudent to verify that users are authenticated when applying role-based authorization, in case your components are used in a non-authenticating environment. You can demand authentication by setting the `Authenticated` property of the `PrincipalPermissionAttribute` to true:

```
[PrincipalPermission(SecurityAction.Demand, Authenticated = true,
                                    Role=@"<domain>\Managers")]
```

 Declarative role-based security hardcodes the role name. If your application is deployed in international markets and you use Windows groups as roles, it's likely that the role names will not match. In that case, you have to use programmatic role verification and have some logic that maps the logical design-time roles to the local roles.

Programmatic Role-Based Security

As handy as declarative role-based security is, sometimes you need to programmatically verify role membership. Usually, you need to do that when the decision as to whether to grant access depends both on role membership and on some other values known only during call time. Another case in which programmatic role-membership verification is needed is when dealing with localized user groups.

Principal and identity

A *principal object* in .NET is an object that implements the `IPrincipal` interface, defined in the `System.Security.Principal` namespace as:

```
public interface IPrincipal
{
   IIdentity Identity{get;}
   bool IsInRole(string role);
}
```

The `IsInRole()` method returns true if the identity associated with this principal is a member of the specified role, and false otherwise. The `Identity` read-only property provides access to read-only information about the identity, in the form of an object implementing the `IIdentity` interface:

```
public interface IIdentity
{
   string AuthenticationType{get;}
   bool IsAuthenticated{get;}
   string Name{get;}
}
```

Every .NET thread has a principal object associated with it, obtained via the CurrentPrincipal static property of the Thread class:

```
public static IPrincipal CurrentPrincipal{get;set;}
```

For example, here is how to obtain the username from the principal object:

```
void GreetUser( )
{
   IPrincipal principal = Thread.CurrentPrincipal;
   IIdentity identity  = principal.Identity;
   string greeting = "Hello " + identity.Name;
   MessageBox.Show(greeting);
}
```

Verifying role membership

Imagine a banking application that lets users transfer sums of money between two specified accounts. Only customers and tellers are allowed to call this method, with the following business rule: if the amount transferred is greater than 5,000, only tellers are allowed to do the transfer. Declarative role-based security can verify that the caller is a teller or a customer, but it can't enforce the additional business rule. For that, you need to use the IsInRole( ) method of IPrincipal, as shown in Example 12-12.

Example 12-12. Programmatic role membership verification

```
using System.Security.Permissions;
using System.Security.Principal;
using System.Threading;

public class Bank
{
   const int MaxSum = 5000;

   [PrincipalPermission(SecurityAction.Demand,Role =@"<domain>\Customers")]
   [PrincipalPermission(SecurityAction.Demand,Role =@"<domain>\Tellers")]
   public void TransferMoney(double sum,long sourceAccount,long destinationAccount)
   {
      IPrincipal  principal;
      principal = Thread.CurrentPrincipal;
      Debug.Assert(principal.Identity.IsAuthenticated);

      bool isCustomer = false;
      bool isTeller   = false;
      isCustomer = principal.IsInRole(@"<domain>\Customers");
      isTeller   = principal.IsInRole(@"<domain>\Tellers");
      if(isCustomer && ! isTeller)//The caller is a customer not teller
      {
         if(sum > MaxSum)
         {
         string message = "Caller does not have sufficient authority to" +
                           "transfer this sum";
            throw new UnauthorizedAccessException(message);
```

Example 12-12. Programmatic role membership verification (continued)

```
        }
    }
    DoTransfer(sum,sourceAccount,destinationAccount);
    }
    //Helper method
    void DoTransfer(double sum,long sourceAccount,long destinationAccount)
    {...}
}
```

Example 12-12 demonstrates a number of points. First, even though it uses programmatic role-membership verification with the value of the sum argument, it still uses declarative role-based security as the first line of defense, allowing access only to users who are members of the Customers or Tellers roles. Second, you can programmatically assert that the caller is authenticated using the IsAuthenticated property of IIdentity. Finally, in case of unauthorized access, you can throw an exception of type UnauthorizedAccessException.

Windows Security Principal

In a Windows application, the principal object associated with a .NET thread is of type WindowsPrincipal:

```
    public class WindowsPrincipal : IPrincipal
    {
        public WindowsPrincipal(WindowsIdentity ntIdentity);

        //IPrincipal implementation
        public virtual IIdentity Identity{ get;}
        public virtual bool IsInRole(string role);
        //Additional methods:
        public virtual bool IsInRole(int rid);
        public virtual bool IsInRole(WindowsBuiltInRole role);
        public virtual bool IsInRole(SecurityIdentifier sid);
    }
```

WindowsPrincipal provides two additional IsInRole( ) methods that are intended to ease the task of localizing roles (i.e., Windows user groups). The first version takes an enum of type WindowsBuiltInRole matching the built-in Windows roles, such as WindowsBuiltInRole.Administrator or WindowsBuiltInRole.User. The other version of IsInRole( ) accepts an integer indexing specific roles. For example, a role index of 512 maps to the Administrators group. The MSDN Library contains a list of both the predefined indexes and ways to provide your own aliases and indexes to user groups. The default identity associated with the WindowsPrincipal object is an object of type WindowsIdentity that provides a number of methods beyond the implementation of IIdentity, including helper methods for verifying major user-group membership and impersonation. When asked to verify role membership, WindowsPrincipal retrieves the username from its identity object and looks it up in the Windows (or domain) user-group repository.

Custom Security Principal

There is a complete disconnection between declarative role-based security and the actual principal object type. When the PrincipalPermission attribute is asked to verify role membership, it simply gets hold of its thread's current principal object (in the form of IPrincipal) and calls its IsInRole( ) method. This disconnection is also true of programmatic role-membership verification that uses only IPrincipal, as shown in Example 12-13. The separation of the IPrincipal interface from its implementation is the key to providing role-based security mechanisms other than Windows user groups—all you need to do is provide an object that implements IPrincipal and set your current thread's CurrentPrincipal property to that object. In addition, code that installs a custom security principal must be granted permission to control security principals. Example 12-13 demonstrates installing a custom role-based security mechanism using a trivial custom principal.

Example 12-13. Implementing and installing a custom principal

```
public class MyCustomPrincipal : IPrincipal
{
   IIdentity m_OldIdentity;
   public MyCustomPrincipal( )
   {
      m_OldIdentity = Thread.CurrentPrincipal.Identity;
   }
   public IIdentity Identity
   {
      get {return m_OldIdentity;}
   }
   public bool IsInRole(string role)
   {
      switch(role)
      {
         case "Authors":
         {
            if (m_OldIdentity.Name == "Juval")
               return true;
            else
               return false;
         }
         default:
            return false;
      }
   }
}
//Installing the custom principal:
IPrincipal customPrincipal = new MyCustomPrincipal( );
Thread.CurrentPrincipal = customPrincipal;
```

In this example, the custom principal caches the current identity because it doesn't want to provide a new identity. The custom principal returns true from IsInRole( )

only if the role specified is "Authors" and the username is "Juval". Of course, a real-life custom principal also does some actual role-membership verification, such as accessing a dedicated table in a database. For example, Appendix B uses the ASP.NET custom principal in the context of a Windows Forms application, and that custom principal uses an SQL Server for storing roles and users. Fundamentally, however, the custom principal in Appendix B isn't much different from the custom principal in Example 12-13.

You have to install the custom security principal in every thread in your application that uses role-based security (either declaratively or programmatically), because by default .NET attaches the Windows principal to every new thread. Alternatively, you can provide .NET with a new default principal object to attach to new threads. To provide a new default principal, use the static method `SetThreadPrincipal()` of the AppDomain class. For example:

```
IPrincipal customPrincipal = new MyCustomPrincipal();
AppDomain currentDomain = AppDomain.CurrentDomain;
currentDomain.SetThreadPrincipal(customPrincipal);
```

Note that the new default is app domain–wide, and that you can't call `SetThreadPrincipal()` more than once per app domain. If you call it more than once, .NET throws an exception of type `PolicyException`.

> Some applications can't use Windows user groups as roles and have no need for an elaborate custom principal. For such simple cases, you can use the `GenericPrincipal` class. Its constructor accepts the identity object to use and a collection of roles the identity is a member of. `GenericPrincipal`'s implementation of `IsInRole()` simply scans that collection looking for a match.

Addressing Other Security Issues

This final section discusses a number of security issues, encompassing most of the security infrastructure discussed in this chapter. For the most part you only need to be aware of the issues, but in some cases you need to take specific actions to ensure proper secure execution of your applications.

Link-Time Demand and Reflection

When you demand a security permission at link time using the `SecurityAction.LinkDemand` value for the security action, the demand applies only to early-bound code—that is, code that uses the compile time (or actually, the JIT compilation-time) linker. Malicious code can use reflection with late-binding invocation to avoid the link-time demand. To close this potential security hole, when a method is invoked using late binding the .NET reflection libraries reflect the method, looking for security permission attributes with link-time demands. If any such attributes are found, the reflection libraries programmatically demand these permissions, triggering a stack walk that verifies whether a caller has circumvented the demand for the permissions. As a result, code that works with a certain call chain that uses early binding may not work when one of the callers uses late binding. This is because the reflection libraries convert a link-time demand (which affects only the immediate caller) to a full stack walk that affects all callers. This behavior is yet another reason to avoid late-binding invocation.

Link-Time Demand and Inheritance

Consider a subclass that uses a link-time security demand while overriding a base-class method. The subclass demand is security-tight only if the base class demands the same permission at link time. If you develop a class hierarchy that requires security, it's best to define an interface that the class hierarchy implements and demand link-time permission checks at the interface level. This provides the demand for every level in the class hierarchy.

Strongly Named Assemblies and Full Trust

A strongly named assembly can easily be shared by multiple applications whose components come from potentially untrusted origins. Imagine a component library vendor that produces an assembly and installs it in the GAC. That assembly is now available for use by any unknown, malicious client. To prevent even the potential for abuse, by default a .NET strongly named assembly can be used only by client assemblies granted the FullTrust permission set. This ensures that partially trusted clients can't use assemblies that are not properly secured. .NET enforces this default by placing a link-time demand for the FullTrust permission set on every public or protected method on every public class in the assembly. The JIT compiler does this automatically when it detects that the assembly has a strong name. For example, if a strong name is specified, the JIT compiler converts this method definition:

```
public void SomeMethod( )
{}
```

to this:

```
[PermissionSet(SecurityAction.LinkDemand,Name = "FullTrust")]
public void SomeMethod( )
{}
```

 A partially trusted assembly can still implement interfaces defined in a strongly named assembly, because interfaces have no implementations to protect and the compiler doesn't change their definitions.

This extra precaution can be a liability, especially if you intend for your assembly to be used by semi-trusted assemblies or to run in a partially trusted environment. For example, if the client assembly is a partially trusted ClickOnce application or if the client is coming from the local intranet, it won't be able to access your code. If you want to allow partially trusted callers to use your assembly, you can apply the attribute `AllowPartiallyTrustedCallersAttribute` to the assembly:

```
[assembly:AllowPartiallyTrustedCallers]
```

This instructs the compiler not to add the link-time demand for full trust to the public entry points.

Unsafe Code

C# (and potentially future .NET languages) allows you to use unsafe code to directly manipulate memory using pointers. Such C# code is called *unsafe* because it lets go of most of the safety of .NET memory management, such as bound-safe arrays. However, unsafe code is still managed code, because it runs in the CLR and it manipulates the managed heap. This can present a security breach, because objects from multiple assemblies (with potentially different security permissions) share the same heap. A malicious assembly may not have permission to access assemblies that are more privileged, but it can potentially use unsafe code to traverse the managed heap and read or modify the state of objects. Worse yet, even if you try to isolate questionable assemblies in one app domain and put trusted assemblies in another, it will be to no avail. Examine Figure 10-2 again. Because all app domains in the same physical process share the same managed heap, a malicious component could use unsafe code to access the other app domains. Clearly, only trusted assemblies should be granted permission to use unsafe code. .NET doesn't have an unsafe code permission, but it does have a security permission with the right to skip verification. Because unsafe code is unverifiable, you can use this permission to grant, in effect, permission for unsafe code. Note that the FullTrust permission set grants that permission, as does the dedicated SkipVerification permission set.

Security and Remote Calls

As long as the client and the object share the same physical process, .NET can enforce code access permission checks using stack walks, even when the call is made across app domains. This is possible because the cross–app domain remoting channel uses the original client thread to invoke the call, so the stack walk can detect callers without the required permissions. However, in a distributed application that spans processes and machines, multiple physical threads are involved every time the call flows to another location. Because each thread has its own stack, the stack-walk strategy as a mechanism for enforcing access permissions doesn't work when crossing the process boundary. Link-time permission demands are of no use either, because the component is linked against the trusted host, not the remote client. In addition, each machine may well have a different code access policy, and what is allowed on one machine may be forbidden on another.

Serialization

Imagine a class containing sensitive information that needs to interact with partially trusted clients. If a malicious client could provide its own serialization formatters, it would be able to gain access to the sensitive information or deserialize the class with bogus state. To prevent abuse by such serialization clients, a class can demand at link time that its clients have the security permission to provide a serialization formatter that uses the attribute SecurityPermissionAttribute with the SecurityPermissionFlag. SerializationFormatter flag:

```
[SecurityPermission(SecurityAction.LinkDemand,
                    Flags = SecurityPermissionFlag.SerializationFormatter)]
[Serializable]
public class MyClass
{...}
```

Of course, as discussed in Chapter 9, if the class has sensitive state information, you may want to consider using custom serialization to encrypt and decrypt the state during serialization and deserialization. The problem with demanding the serialization formatter permission at the class level is that it precludes clients that don't have that permission and don't even need to serialize the class from using the class at all. In such cases, it's better to provide custom serialization and demand the permission only on the deserialization constructor and GetObjectData( ):

```
[Serializable]
public class MyClass : ISerializable
{
    public MyClass( )
    {}

    [SecurityPermission(SecurityAction.LinkDemand,
                        Flags = SecurityPermissionFlag.SerializationFormatter)]
    public void GetObjectData(SerializationInfo info,StreamingContext context)
```

```
        {...}

    [SecurityPermission(SecurityAction.LinkDemand,
                        Flags = SecurityPermissionFlag.SerializationFormatter)]
    protected MyClass(SerializationInfo info,StreamingContext context)
    {...}
}
```

You can use the `SerializationUtil` helper class presented in Chapter 9 to automate the implementation of custom serialization.

If all you need are the standard .NET formatters, there is a different solution altogether to the problem of malicious serialization clients. Use the attribute `StrongNameIdentityPermissionAttribute` to demand at link time that only Microsoft-provided assemblies serialize and deserialize your class:

```
public static class PublicKeys
{
    public const string Microsoft = "002400000480000094000000060200000024000000"+
                                    "525341310004000001000100007D1FA57C4AED9F0"+
                                    "A32E84AA0FAEFD0DE9E8FD6AEC8F87FB03766C83"+
                                    "4C99921EB23BE79AD9D5DCC1DD9AD23613210290"+
                                    "0B723CF980957FC4E177108FC607774F29E8320E"+
                                    "92EA05ECE4E821C0A5EFE8F1645C4C0C93C1AB99"+
                                    "285D622CAA652C1DFAD63D745D6F2DE5F17E5EAF"+
                                    "0FC4963D261C8A12436518206DC093344D5AD293";
}

[Serializable]
public class MyClass : ISerializable
{
    public MyClass()
    {}

    [StrongNameIdentityPermission(SecurityAction.LinkDemand,
                        PublicKey = PublicKeys.Microsoft)]
    public void GetObjectData(SerializationInfo info,StreamingContext context)
    {...}

    [StrongNameIdentityPermission(SecurityAction.LinkDemand,
                        PublicKey = PublicKeys.Microsoft)]
    protected MyClass(SerializationInfo info,StreamingContext context)
    {...}
}
```

If you wish to allow either Microsoft or clients with the serialization formatter permission to serialize your class, use a link-time demand choice on both permissions:

```
[StrongNameIdentityPermission(SecurityAction.LinkDemandChoice,
                    PublicKey = PublicKeys.Microsoft)]
[SecurityPermission(SecurityAction.LinkDemandChoice,
                    Flags = SecurityPermissionFlag.SerializationFormatter)]
public void GetObjectData(SerializationInfo info,StreamingContext context)
{...}
```

```
[StrongNameIdentityPermission(SecurityAction.LinkDemandChoice,
                    PublicKey = PublicKeys.Microsoft)]
[SecurityPermission(SecurityAction.LinkDemandChoice,
                    Flags = SecurityPermissionFlag.SerializationFormatter)]
protected MyClass(SerializationInfo info,StreamingContext context)
{...}
```

Transactions

An application that uses transactions managed by the Light-Weight Transaction Manager (LTM) can consume resources from at most a single durable recourse such as SQL Server 2005. This, however, is not the case with a distributed transaction, which can interact with multiple resources, potentially across the network. This opens the way for both denial-of-service attacks by malicious code, or even just accidental excessive use of such resources. To prevent that, the System.Transactions namespace defines the DistributedTransaction security permission. Whenever a transaction is promoted from an LTM to OleTx transaction, the code that triggered the promotion will be verified to have the DistributedTransaction permission. Verification of the security permission is done like any other code-access security verification, using a stack walk, demanding from every caller up the stack the DistributedTransaction permission. Note again that the security demand will affect the code that triggered the promotion, not necessarily the code that created the LTM transaction in the first place (although that can certainly be the case if they are on the same call stack).

This permission demand is of particular importance for Smart Client applications deployed in a partial trust environment, such as the LocalInternet zone, that want to perform transactional work against multiple resources. None of the predefined partial trust zones grant the DistributedTransaction permission. You will have to grant that permission using a custom code group, or manually list that permission in the application's ClickOnce deployment manifest. Another solution altogether is to introduce a middle tier between the client application and the resources, and have the middle tier encapsulate accessing these resources transitionally.

Interface-Based Web Services

Web services are a great mechanism for business-to-business interaction, or for any crossing of boundaries such as technological, trust and security, deployment topology, organizational, geographical, or other boundaries. At the heart of web services is the ability to develop such services and invoke their methods with the same ease as with conventional components. The web services standard even provides for defining interfaces or logical abstract services. As explained in Chapter 1 and demonstrated throughout this book, separation of interface from implementation is a core principle of component-oriented programming and is essential for application extensibility and reuse. This appendix presents a set of simple steps for developing interface-based web services using Visual Studio 2005. The source code accompanying this book contains the code presented here and the complete CalculationServices solution that uses it.

.NET Web Services Support

Consider the SimpleCalculator web service, shown in Example A-1, which provides the four basic arithmetic operations.

Example A-1. The SimpleCalculator web service

```
using System.Web.Services;

[WebService(Namespace="http://CalculationServices",
            Description = "The SimpleCalculator Web Service provides the
                           four basic arithmetic operations for integers.")]
public class SimpleCalculator
{
   [WebMethod]
   public int Add(int argument1,int argument2)
   {
      return argument1 + argument2;
   }
   [WebMethod]
```

Example A-1. The SimpleCalculator web service (continued)

```
   public int Subtract(int argument1,int argument2)
   {
      return argument1 - argument2;
   }
   [WebMethod]
   public int Divide(int argument1,int argument2)
   {
      return argument1 / argument2;
   }
   [WebMethod]
   public int Multiply(int argument1,int argument2)
   {
      return argument1 * argument2;
   }
}
```

Using .NET, all you have to do to develop a web service is add the WebMethod attribute to the methods you wish to expose as web services—.NET will do the rest. The WebServiceAttribute attribute is optional, but you should use it. The attribute is defined as:

```
   [AttributeUsage(AttributeTargets.Class|AttributeTargets.Interface)]
   public sealed class WebServiceAttribute : Attribute
   {
      public WebServiceAttribute( );
      public string Description{get; set;}
      public string Name{get; set;}
      public string Namespace{get; set;}
   }
```

WebServiceAttribute lets you specify a web service namespace that contains your service, used like a normal .NET namespace to reduce collisions. If you don't specify a namespace, Visual Studio 2005 uses *http://tempuri.org/* as a default. A published service uses a specific URI as its namespace. WebServiceAttribute also allows you to provide a free-text description of the service. The description appears in the auto-generated browser page used by the service consumers and testers during development.

Producing client code for a web service is equally trivial. Select Add Web Reference from the client's project in Visual Studio 2005 and point the wizard at the site containing the web service *.aspx* file (you can also select a web service from your solution or from your machine). Once the wizard presents the available web services, select the desired web service and click Add Reference. This causes Visual Studio 2005 to generate a proxy class that the client uses to invoke the web service. Example A-2 shows the proxy class for the service presented in Example A-1, with some of the code removed for clarity.

Example A-2. The SimpleCalculator web service proxy class

```
public partial class SimpleCalculator : SoapHttpClientProtocol
{
```

Example A-2. The SimpleCalculator web service proxy class (continued)

```
    public SimpleCalculator( )
    {
       Url = Settings.Default.<App name>_<Reference name>_SimpleCalculator;
    }
    [SoapDocumentMethod("http://CalculationServices/Add")]
    public int Add(int argument1,int argument2)
    {
       object[] results = Invoke("Add",new object[]{argument1, argument2});
       return (int)(results[0]);
    }
    //Other methods and properties
}
```

The SimpleCalculator proxy class contains a public method for each of the methods exposed as web methods by the original web service. The proxy class (sometimes called a *web service wrapper class*) completely encapsulates the complex interaction with the remote service.

The proxy class provides the Url property, used to set and get the service's address. When adding a web reference in Visual Studio 2005, it will also add to Project's Settings class a property named according to this format:

```
    <App name>_<reference name>_<Service name>
```

and bind it to a matching entry in the application's configuration file, which contains the service's address. In addition, Visual Studio 2005 will decorate the property with the DefaultSettingValue attribute. The DefaultSettingValue attribute will contain the default address of the web service, in case the entry in the application configuration file is missing. The default address will simply be the originally referenced web address.

The client code can use the proxy class as if the SimpleCalculator object were a normal local object:

```
    SimpleCalculator calculator;
    calculator = new SimpleCalculator( );
    int result = calculator.Add(2,3);
    Debug.Assert(result == 5);
```

Problem Statement

With the programming model that was just presented, the client ends up programming directly against the service provider (SimpleCalculator, in this case), instead of against a generic abstraction of the service. A better approach is for the SimpleCalculator web service to be polymorphic with a service abstraction—that is, an interface. Programming against an interface rather than a particular service implementation enables the client to switch between different providers, with minimal or no changes. This way, the client becomes indifferent to changes in the service provider. For example, imagine the client wants to switch from SimpleCalculator to a different calculator web service, called ScientificCalculator, that supports the same interface as SimpleCalculator but is perhaps more accurate, faster, or cheaper. Ideally, either the client or the service providers would agree to define an abstract calculator interface, the ICalculator interface:

```
[WebInterface]//Imaginary attribute. Does not exist in .NET.
public interface ICalculator
{
    int Add(int argument1,int argument2);
    int Subtract(int argument1,int argument2);
    int Divide(int argument1,int argument2);
    int Multiply(int argument1,int argument2);
}
```

If such a web interface were available, the client could code against the interface definition, not a particular implementation, as shown in Example A-3.

Example A-3. Web services client-side interface-based programming model

```
ICalculator calculator = new ScientificCalculator();
//or
ICalculator calculator = new SimpleCalculator();

//This part of the client code is polymorphic with any provider of the service:
int result = calculator.Add(2,3);
Debug.Assert(result == 5);
```

 The next generation of Microsoft distributed application technology, code named Indigo, connects logical services using multiple transports, including web services. Indigo enforces the separation of interface from implementation by using the notion of an abstract contract definition, manifested by .NET interfaces.

The only thing that changes in the client's code when it switches between service providers is the line that decides on the exact interface implementation to use. You can even put that decision in a different assembly from that of the main client's logic and pass only interfaces between the two assemblies. The client can also use a class factory to create the object and get back an interface. There are other benefits to interface-based web services, too; for example, the client can publish the interface definition, making it easier for different service vendors to implement the client's requirements.

Solution

The technique presented next requires both the web service provider and the client to write their code in a slightly different way, in order to make use of interface-based web services. To create an interface-based web service, first expose the web service interface definition. For simplicity's sake, assume the service provider is responsible for both defining and implementing the interface. There is an easy way for the client or any other third party to expose the web service interface definition and have anybody implement it, but that requires one or two additional steps (described later).

Service-Side Steps

In Visual Studio 2005, select File → New → Web Site... to bring up the New Web Site dialog box. Select ASP.NET Web Service and name it CalculationServices. Visual Studio 2005 will create a skeletal web service called Service. You have no use for it, so remove the file *Service.asmx* from the root of the project and remove *Service.cs* from the *App_Code* folder. To add the web service interface, right-click on the project, then select Add New Item... from the context menu to bring up the Add New Item dialog. Select Web Service in the dialog, and name it ICalculator. Make sure that the "Place code in separate file" checkbox is checked, and click Add.

Open the *ICalculator.cs* file in the *App_Code* folder and change the ICalculator type definition from class to interface. Remove the constructor and the HelloWorld( ) method and the derivation from WebService. You can also remove the public interface accessibility modifier. Change the WebServiceBinding attribute to read:

```
[WebServiceBinding (Name = "ICalculator")]
```

Next, add the Add( ), Subtract( ), Divide( ), and Multiply( ) interface methods. Apply the WebMethod attribute to every method on the interface. The interface should now look like this:

```
[WebServiceBinding (Name = ICalculator)]
interface ICalculator
{
    [WebMethod(Description = "Adds two integers and returns the sum")]
    int Add(int argument1,int argument2);

    [WebMethod(Description = "Subtracts two integers and returns the result")]
    int Subtract(int argument1,int argument2);

    [WebMethod(Description = "Divides two integers and returns the result")]
    int Divide(int argument1,int argument2);

    [WebMethod(Description = "Multiplies two integers and returns the result")]
    int Multiply(int argument1,int argument2);
}
```

The WebServiceBinding attribute designates the ICalculator interface as an interface that defines a web service contract, but does not expose it as a web service. Other classes that have access to the ICalculator metadata definition can now implement (or *bind* to) the service contract definition.

Next, implement the ICalculator interface on the web service classes. Doing so is like implementing any other interface in .NET: the class should derive from the interface and provide the implementation for its methods. For example, use the Add New Item dialog to add two web services, called SimpleCalculator and ScientificCalculator. Clean up the wizard-generated code as described earlier. Add to the classes a derivation from the ICalculator interface, and implement it.

Add the WebService attribute for specifying the namespace and the description. Example A-4 shows the two implementations of ICalculator. Note that the compiler insists that the service provider implement all the methods defined by the interface.

Example A-4. Two different web services' implementations of the ICalculator interface

```
[WebService(Namespace="http://CalculationServices",
            Description = "The SimpleCalculator web service implements ICalculator.
                           It provides the four basic arithmetic operations.")]
class SimpleCalculator : ICalculator
{
   public int Add(int argument1,int argument2)
   {
      return argument1 + argument2;
   }
   //Other ICalculator methods
}


[WebService(Namespace="http://CalculationServices",
            Description = "The ScientificCalculator web service implements
            ICalculator. It provides the four basic arithmetic operations.")]
class ScientificCalculator : ICalculator
{
   public int Add(int argument1,int argument2)
   {
      return argument1 + argument2;
   }
   //Other ICalculator methods
}
```

 A class can implement multiple interfaces decorated with the WebServiceBinding attribute, each corresponding to a different service contract.

Now you need to expose the interface as a web interface. However, you cannot expose an interface as a web service. To overcome this hurdle, you need to provide an *interface shim*—an abstract class that exposes to the world what looks like a pure interface definition. Add to the web service project a class called ICalculatorShim, and place it in the file *ICalculatorShim.cs*. Define the class as abstract, and have it derive from ICalculator. Provide only abstract methods as interface implementation:

```
[WebService(Name = "ICalculator",Namespace="http://CalculationServices",
            Description = "This web service is only the definition of the
                        interface. You cannot invoke method calls on it.")]
abstract class ICalculatorShim : ICalculator
{
    public abstract int Add(int argument1,int argument2);
    public abstract int Subtract(int argument1,int argument2);
    public abstract int Divide(int argument1,int argument2);
    public abstract int Multiply(int argument1,int argument2);
}
```

Because it derives from ICalculator, the compiler enforces that the shim class exposes all the methods defined by the interface. Use the WebServiceAttribute attribute to provide the namespace and a description. Most importantly, set the Name property of WebServiceAttribute to ICalculator. Doing so exposes the service definition as ICalculator instead of ICalculatorShim.

Finally, modify the *ICalculator.asmx* file so that it will load the ICalculatorShim class from the correct file:

```
<%@ WebService Language="C#" CodeBehind="~/Code/ICalculatorShim.cs"
    Class="ICalculatorShim"%>
```

To verify that all is well so far, set the *ICalculator.asmx* file as the start page and run the project. The auto-generated browser test page presents the ICalculator interface definition (see Figure A-1).

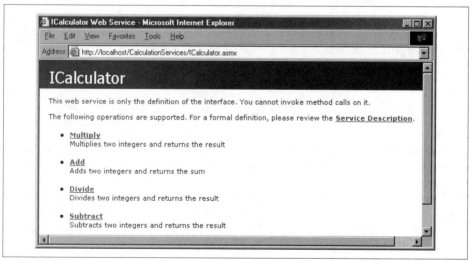

Figure A-1. The ICalculator auto-generated test page

If you try to invoke any of the methods you will get an error, because there is no implementation behind the service.

Client-Side Steps

The client needs to have the interface definition so that it can program against it. The client can obtain that definition in two ways. The first uses the *WSDL.exe* command-line utility. Using the /serverInterface switch, you can instruct *WSDL.exe* to generate an interface definition matching that of the web service contract. Assuming the interface definition resides at *http://localhost/CalculationServices.com/ICalculator.asmx*, run the utility with this command line:

```
WSDL.exe /serverInterface http://localhost/CalculationServices.com/ICalculator.asmx
         /out:ICalculator.cs
```

WSDL.exe will generate a file called *ICalculator.cs* containing the definition of an interface called IICalculator:

```
[WebServiceBinding (Name = "ICalculator",
                    Namespace="http://CalculationServices/")]
public partial interface IICalculator
{
    [WebMethod]
    [SoapDocumentMethod("http://CalculationServices/Add",...)]
    int Add(int argument1,int argument2);
    //Other IICalculatorSoap methods
}
```

Add the *ICalculator.cs* source file to the client project. The IICalculator definition in *ICalculator.cs* is oriented toward the interface implementer, not the service consumer. As such, it contains service-side attributes, such as WebService and WebMethod. You can safely remove these attributes, or you can keep them—they make no difference on the client side. Rename IICalculatorSoap to ICalculator.

 Using the *WSDL.exe* command-line utility with the /serverInterface switch is how a service provider imports an interface defined by another party.

The second way a client can import the interface definition is by adding a web reference to the ICalculator web service. After adding the reference, the client manually extracts the interface methods from the proxy class. To do so, point the Add Web Reference wizard to the site containing the interface definition. This generates a proxy class called ICalculator, which exposes the original ICalculator's methods as well as the methods used for asynchronous method invocation, as described in Chapter 8. Each of these methods is implemented to forward calls to the web service. Of course, for an interface definition, you need only method definitions. Remove all the interface method bodies and the other methods completely, including the constructor. Remove the SoapHttpClientProtocol base class and the public modifier on the methods, and then remove all class and method attributes. Finally, change the ICalculator definition from class to interface. The client side should now have the original interface definition.

Regardless of how the client imports the interface definition, it will need to consume the web services that actually implement the interface. Bring up the Add Web Reference wizard and point the wizard to where the implementations reside. Visual Studio 2005 will generate proxy classes for the interface implementations (SimpleCalculator and ScientificCalculator, in this case). These machine-generated proxy classes are the default proxy classes; they will look just like Example A-2 and will not refer to ICalculator. It's up to the client to provide polymorphism with ICalculator by adding a derivation from the interface:

```
public partial class ScientificCalculator : ICalculator
{}
public partial class SimpleCalculator : ICalculator
{}
```

Because the proxy classes are marked as partial classes, you can even add the interface derivation in a separate file and keep updating the proxy class files as needed.

Finally, the client can write interface-based web-services-polymorphic code, as in Example A-3. Note that the only difference between the two proxy classes is in the URL of the web service implementing the ICalculator interface. This leads to an interesting observation: in the web services world, from the client's perspective, the location of the service (i.e., the URL) is the object's type.

Note also that the technique described in this appendix works with other web service protocols besides SOAP—namely, HTTP-POST. Using the *WSDL.exe* utility, you can generate proxy classes that use these protocols and add the derivation from the web service interface.

Unifying Windows Forms and ASP.NET Security

By default, .NET role-based security uses Windows user groups for roles and Windows accounts for security identities. There are several drawbacks to this default policy. The security policy is only as granular as the user groups in the hosting domain. Often, you don't have control over your end customer's IT department. If you deploy your application in an environment in which the user groups are coarse or do not map well to actual roles users play in your application, or if the group names are slightly different, .NET's basic role-based security will be of little use to you. Role localization presents yet another set of challenges, because role names will differ between customer sites in different locales. Moreover, using Windows accounts for security identity means role-based security can work only if the users have accounts on the hosting domain or have a trust relationship with the domain that manages the user accounts. Consequently, Intranet applications often resort to storing their user credentials in a database, even when they're deployed in a homogenous Windows environment. Such applications should use a Windows Forms frontend, and they can be deployed using ClickOnce.

ASP.NET applications accessed over the Internet using a browser hardly ever use Windows accounts and groups. .NET 2.0 provides out-of-the-box custom credential management for ASP.NET applications. In ASP.NET 2.0, you can easily authenticate and authorize users without ever resorting to Windows accounts. In addition, the credentials store is well-designed, using the latest best practices for credential management (password salting, secure stored procedures, and so on). This infrastructure provides a high-quality, secure solution and helps productivity, saving ASP. NET developers valuable time and effort.

This appendix presents a set of interacting helper classes that enable a Windows Forms–based Intranet application to use the ASP.NET credential-management infrastructure with the same ease as if it were an ASP.NET application. Doing so provides Windows Forms–based Intranet applications with the same productivity benefits as those enjoyed by ASP.NET applications, and it offers a unified credentials store regardless of the application user interface.

One of the hallmarks of a well-designed middle tier is that it can be accessed uniformly by any frontend, such as a browser, a web service, or a Windows Forms application. Providing a unified solution decouples your business logic components from your presentation tier, so you can switch frontends at will. You will also see that providing a custom credential-management solution requires a holistic approach that takes into account the application deployment and code access security needs, as well as scalability, extensibility, design-time integration, and reuse contexts. This appendix also makes use of some little-known yet very useful .NET programming techniques as well as best practices mentioned throughout this book.

ASP.NET Security Infrastructure

Before you learn how to take advantage of ASP.NET's credential-management and security with non-ASP.NET applications, you need to learn a bit about the ASP.NET user credential management infrastructure. Out of the box, ASP.NET applications can store their custom user credentials in either SQL Server or SQL Server Express, or in Active Directory. That said, the credential-management architecture is that of a provider model, and you can easily add other storage options (such as an Access database). .NET 2.0 installs web site administration pages under \Inetpub\wwwroot\aspnet_webadmin\<version number>.

ASP.NET developers can configure their application directly from within Visual Studio 2005. When selecting ASP.NET Configuration from the Web Site menu, Visual Studio 2005 will browse to the ASP.NET administration pages and allow you to configure various parameters, including security configuration (see Figure B-1). You can configure the following aspects for your application:

- Select which store to use, such as an SQL Server or SQL Server Express. The information stored is credentials (username and password) and role-membership. You can even choose to use one repository for credentials and another for role membership.

- Create new users and delete existing ones.

- Create new roles and delete existing ones.

- Allocate users to roles.

- Additional features not relevant to this appendix.

Note that the same database tables are used to store the user information from multiple ASP.NET applications. As a result, each user or role record is also associated with a particular application name.

To use the SQL Server provider, run the setup file *aspnet_regsql.exe*, found under *\WINDOWS\Microsoft.NET\Framework\<Version>*. The setup program will create a new database called *aspnetdb*, containing the tables and stored procedures required to manage the credentials.

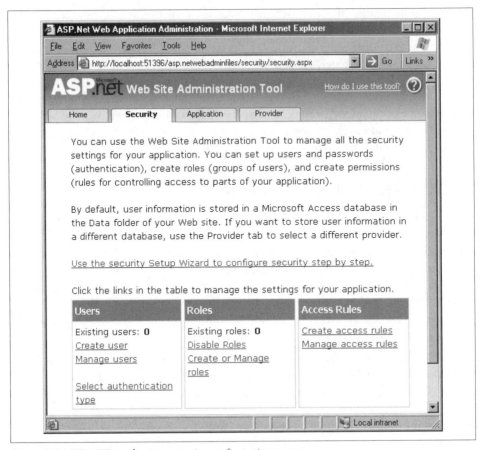

Figure B-1. ASP.NET application security configuration pages

ASP.NET Custom Authentication and Authorization

At runtime, ASP.NET can authenticate the callers using the credentials in the database. The easiest way to add that functionality to your web application is to drag-and-drop a Login control from the Security tab of the Visual Studio 2005 Toolbox onto a web form. The Login control collects a username and password from the user and authenticates the user using a class called MembershipProvider, defined as:

```
public abstract class MembershipProvider : ProviderBase
{
    public abstract string ApplicationName{get;set;}
    public abstract bool ValidateUser(string name,string password);
    //Additional members
}
```

`MembershipProvider`'s goal in the ASP.NET provider model is to encapsulate the actual provider used and the details of the actual data access. `MembershipProvider` makes it possible to change the membership provider without affecting the application. Depending on the configured security provider, the `Login` control uses a concrete data access class like `SqlMembershipProvider` when using SQL Server or SQL Server Express:

```
public class SqlMembershipProvider : MembershipProvider
{...}
```

However, the `Login` control interacts only with `MembershipProvider`'s base functionality. The `Login` control obtains the required membership provider by accessing the `Provider` static property of the `Membership` class, defined as:

```
public static class Membership
{
    public static string ApplicationName{get;set;}
    public static MembershipProvider Provider{get;}
    public static bool ValidateUser(string userName,string password);
    //Additional members
}
```

`Membership` offers many members, which support every aspect of user management. `Membership.Provider` retrieves the type of the configured provider from the web application configuration file.

 Because all membership providers derive from the abstract class `MembershipProvider`, if you write your own custom credential provider you need to derive from `MembershipProvider` as well.

The only two members of `Membership` that are relevant to this appendix are the `ApplicationName` property, used to set and retrieve the application name, and the `ValidateUser()` method, which authenticates the specified credentials against the store, returning `true` if they match and `false` otherwise. `Membership.ValidateUser` is shorthand for retrieving and using the configured provider.

You can also apply role-based security to authorize operations or access to resources. The *aspnetdb* database contains allocations of users to roles. Once a user is authenticated, ASP.NET will set the `User` property of the HTTP context and of the page to a custom security principal object called `RolePrincipal`:

```
public sealed class RolePrincipal : IPrincipal
{...}
```

`RolePrincipal` uses the abstract class `RoleProvider`:

```
public abstract class RoleProvider : ProviderBase
{
    public abstract string ApplicationName{get;set;}
    public abstract bool IsUserInRole(string username,string roleName);
    public abstract string[] GetRolesForUser(string userName);
    //Additional members
}
```

The `ApplicationName` property of `RoleProvider` binds the role provider to the particular application. The `IsUserInRole( )` method verifies the user's role membership. The `GetRolesForUser( )` method returns all the roles a specified user is a member of.

Just as membership providers must derive from `MembershipProvider`, all role providers (including custom role providers) must derive from `RoleProvider`. Depending on the configured security provider, `RolePrincipal` uses a corresponding data access class such as `SqlRoleProvider` to authorize the caller:

```
public class SqlRoleProvider : RoleProvider
{...}
```

You can obtain the required role provider by accessing the `Provider` static property of the `Roles` class, defined as:

```
public static class Roles
{
    public static string ApplicationName{get;set;}
    public static string[] GetRolesForUser(string username);
    public static bool IsUserInRole(string username,string roleName);
    public static RoleProvider Provider{get;}
    //Additional members
}
```

Both `Roles.GetRolesForUser( )` and `Roles.IsUserInRole( )` are shorthand, and they use the `Roles.Provider` property internally. `Roles.Provider` retrieves the type of the configured provider from the web application configuration file.

Solution Architecture

While my primary goal in this appendix is to show you how to unify Windows Forms and ASP.NET 2.0 security, I also want to provide a general-purpose custom authentication and authorization infrastructure for Windows Forms. Such an infrastructure should not necessarily be coupled to ASP.NET 2.0 and should easily use any custom credentials store, such as an Access or LDAP database. The first step is to decouple the infrastructure from the actual credentials store by defining the `IUserManager` interface:

```
public interface IUserManager
{
    bool Authenticate(string applicationName,string userName,string password);
    bool IsInRole(string applicationName,string userName,string role);
    string[] GetRoles(string applicationName,string userName);
}
```

The `Authenticate( )` method is used to authenticate the specified user credentials against the credentials store. `IsInRole( )` is used to authorize the user when using role-based security. `IUserManager` also provides the `GetRoles( )` method, which returns all the roles a specified user is a member of. `GetRoles( )` is useful when caching role membership, discussed later.

Authenticate( ) is used by an abstract Windows Forms custom control called
LoginControl. LoginControl is used similarly to its ASP.NET cousin—you add it (or
rather, a subclass of it) to your Windows Forms application, and the LoginControl
authenticates the caller. LoginControl obtains an implementation of IUserManager
and authenticates using the Authenticate( ) method. If the user specified valid credentials, LoginControl creates an implementation of IPrincipal called
CustomPrincipal. LoginControl provides CustomPrincipal with the implementation of
IUserManager and attaches CustomPrincipal to the current thread. The
CustomPrincipal class can use the IsInRole( ) or GetRoles( ) methods of IUserManager
to authorize the user. This architecture is shown in Figure B-2.

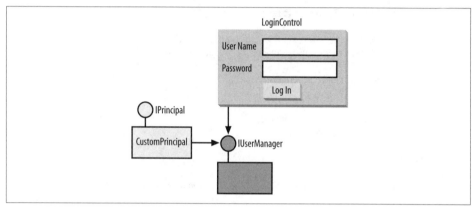

Figure B-2. The LoginControl architecture

Both LoginControl and CustomPrincipal are defined in the *WinFormsEx.dll* class
library assembly available with this book.

Note that CustomPrincipal never authenticates the user—it implicitly trusts
LoginControl to do so. This means that you should not allow CustomPrincipal to be
attached to a thread without going through valid authentication. To enforce that, the
CustomPrincipal class is an internal class, called only by LoginControl.

Implementing IPrincipal

The sole purpose of CustomPrincipal is to replace the Windows security principal
and service the PrincipalPermissionAttribute and PrincipalPermission classes.
CustomPrincipal should be installed only after successful authentication. To further
enforce and automate this design decision, CustomPrincipal doesn't have a public
constructor, so its clients have no direct way to instantiate it. Instead, the clients use
the Attach( ) public static method. Attach( ) first verifies that the identity provided is
that of an authenticated user:

```
Debug.Assert(user.IsAuthenticated);
```

If the user is authenticated, Attach( ) creates an object of type CustomPrincipal, providing it with the security identity and the implementation of IUserManager to use, as well as with the role-caching policy (see Example B-1).

Example B-1. The CustomPrincipal class

```
internal class CustomPrincipal : IPrincipal
{
    IIdentity m_User;
    IPrincipal m_OldPrincipal;
    IUserManager m_UserManager;
    string m_ApplicationName;
    string[] m_Roles;
    static bool m_ThreadPolicySet = false;

    CustomPrincipal(IIdentity user,string applicationName,
                    IUserManager userManager,bool cacheRoles)
    {
        m_OldPrincipal = Thread.CurrentPrincipal;

        m_User = user;
        m_ApplicationName = applicationName;
        m_UserManager = userManager;

        if(cacheRoles)
        {
            m_Roles = m_UserManager.GetRoles(m_ApplicationName,m_User.Name);
        }
        //Make this object the principal for this thread
        Thread.CurrentPrincipal = this;
    }
    static public void Attach(IIdentity user,string applicationName,
                              IUserManager userManager)
    {
        Attach(user,applicationName,userManager,false);
    }
    static public void Attach(IIdentity user,string applicationName,
                              IUserManager userManager,bool cacheRoles)
    {
        Debug.Assert(user.IsAuthenticated);

        IPrincipal customPrincipal = new CustomPrincipal(user,applicationName,
                                                  userManager,cacheRoles);

        AppDomain currentDomain = AppDomain.CurrentDomain;
        currentDomain.SetPrincipalPolicy(PrincipalPolicy.WindowsPrincipal);

        //Make sure all future threads in this app domain use this principal
        //but because default principal cannot be set twice:
        if(m_ThreadPolicySet == false)
        {
            currentDomain.SetThreadPrincipal(customPrincipal);
            m_ThreadPolicySet = true;
```

```
        }
    }
    public void Detach( )
    {
        Thread.CurrentPrincipal = m_OldPrincipal;
    }
    public IIdentity Identity
    {
        get
        {
            return m_User;
        }
    }
    public bool IsInRole(string role)
    {
        if(m_Roles != null)
        {
            Predicate<string> exists = delegate(string roleToMatch)
                                        {
                                            return roleToMatch == role;
                                        };
            return Array.Exists(m_Roles,exists);
        }
        else
        {
            return m_UserManager.IsInRole(m_ApplicationName,m_User.Name,role);
        }
    }
}
```

The constructor of CustomPrincipal saves the identity provided, as well as a reference to the previous principal associated with that thread. Most importantly, the constructor replaces the default principal by setting the CurrentPrincipal property of the current thread to itself:

```
    Thread.CurrentPrincipal = this;
```

To support logout semantics, CustomPrincipal provides the Detach( ) method for detaching itself from the thread and restoring the old principal saved during construction.

In addition, Attach( ) sets the default thread principal object to CustomPrincipal, so that it will be attached to new threads automatically. However, since you can set the thread principal object only once for each app domain, Attach( ) first verifies that this has not already been done (it is possible to attach and detach the principal), using the static flag m_ThreadPolicySet:

```
    if(m_ThreadPolicySet == false)
    {
        m_ThreadPolicySet = true;
        currentDomain.SetThreadPrincipal(customPrincipal);
    }
```

While authentication is a one-off cost, authorization can be a frequent operation. Since verifying role membership may be an expensive operation (e.g., by querying a database or calling a web service), CustomPrincipal can cache all the roles the user is a member of by saving the roles in the m_Roles member array. The constructor of CustomPrincipal takes a Boolean parameter called cacheRoles. If cacheRoles is true, the constructor will initialize m_Roles by calling the GetRoles() method of the provided user manager. While this will enable almost instant role-membership verifications, there is a drawback: if you cache roles, CustomPrincipal will not detect changes to the roles repository, such as when a user is removed from a particular role. This is why the Attach() version that does not take a cacheRoles parameter defaults to no caching. You should use caching with caution, only when the allocation of users to roles is a relatively infrequent event and when the performance and scalability goals mandate it.

As I mentioned in Chapter 12, you should set the app domain principal policy for each app domain where role-based security is employed to PrincipalPolicy. WindowsPrincipal. To save the developer the need for doing so, Attach() sets the principal policy as well:

```
AppDomain currentDomain = AppDomain.CurrentDomain;
currentDomain.SetPrincipalPolicy(PrincipalPolicy.WindowsPrincipal);
```

Implementing IPrincipal is straightforward: in its implementation of the Identity property, CustomPrincipal returns the saved identity. To implement IsInRole(), CustomPrincipal checks if there are any cached roles. If so, it searches the roles array using the static Exists() method of the Array type. Exists() takes a delegate of type Predicate, defined as:

```
public delegate bool Predicate<T>(T t);
```

Exists() evaluates the method targeted by the predicate for each item in the array and returns true if a match is found. IsInRole() initializes the predicate with an anonymous method that compares the role specified in the call to IsInRole() with the role passed in as a parameter. If there are no cached roles, IsInRole() delegates the query to the provided implementation of IUserManager.

The LoginControl Class

LoginControl provides two text boxes for capturing the username and password (see Figure B-3).

In addition, the control uses the ErrorProvider component to validate the user input. LoginControl will authenticate only if the user provides both a username and a password, and the error provider will alert the user of any missing input. Authentication takes place in the Click event-handling method for the Log In button. Example B-2 shows a partial listing of LoginControl, with some of the mundane code omitted in the interest of space.

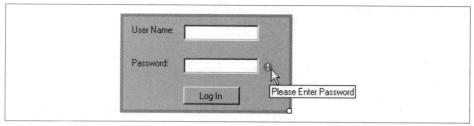

Figure B-3. The LoginControl

Example B-2. Partial listing of LoginControl

```
using LoginEventHandler = GenericEventHandler<LoginControl,LoginEventArgs>;

public class LoginEventArgs : EventArgs
{
   public LoginEventArgs(bool authenticated);
   public bool Authenticated{get;internal set;}
}

[DefaultEvent("LoginEvent")]
[ToolboxBitmap(typeof(LoginControl),"LoginControl.bmp")]
public abstract partial class LoginControl : UserControl
{
   string m_ApplicationName = String.Empty;
   bool m_CacheRoles = false;
   public event LoginEventHandler LoginEvent;

   [Category("Credentials")]
   public bool CacheRoles //Gets and sets m_CacheRoles
   {...}

   [Category("Credentials")]
   public string ApplicationName //Gets and sets m_ ApplicationName
   {...}

   string GetAppName()
   {
      if(ApplicationName != String.Empty)
      {
         return ApplicationName;
      }
      Assembly clientAssembly = Assembly.GetEntryAssembly();
      AssemblyName assemblyName = clientAssembly.GetName();
      return assemblyName.Name;
   }
   static public void Logout()
   {
      CustomPrincipal customPrincipal = Thread.CurrentPrincipal as CustomPrincipal;
      if(customPrincipal != null)
      {
         customPrincipal.Detach();
      }
```

Example B-2. Partial listing of LoginControl (continued)

```
   }
   static public bool IsLoggedIn
   {
      get
      {
         return Thread.CurrentPrincipal is CustomPrincipal;
      }
   }
   protected virtual void OnLogin(object sender,EventArgs e)
   {
      string userName = m_UserNameBox.Text;
      string password = m_PasswordBox.Text;

      /* Validation of userName and password using the error provider */

      string applicationName = GetAppName( );
      IUserManager userManager = GetUserManager( );

      bool authenticated;
      authenticated = userManager.Authenticate(applicationName,userName,password);
      if(authenticated)
      {
         IIdentity identity = new GenericIdentity(userName);
         CustomPrincipal.Attach(identity,applicationName,userManager,CacheRoles);
      }
      LoginEventArgs loginEventArgs = new LoginEventArgs(authenticated);
      EventsHelper.Fire(LoginEvent,this,loginEventArgs);
   }
   protected abstract IUserManager GetUserManager( );
}
```

Providing input to LoginControl

When using LoginControl, you need to provide it with the following information:

- Which credentials provider to use
- The application name
- The role-caching policy

Subclasses of LoginControl are responsible for specifying the credentials provider. The subclasses need to override GetUserManager( ) and return an implementation of IUserManager.

For the second and third items, LoginControl provides the properties ApplicationName and CacheRoles. Because LoginControl derives from UserControl, it natively integrates with the Windows Forms Designer. These two properties are available for visual editing during the design time of a form or a window that uses LoginControl. To enrich the Designer support, the properties are decorated with the Category attribute:

```
[Category("Credentials")]
```

When you select the Categories view of the control properties in the Designer, these properties will be grouped together under the Credentials category. Subclasses of LoginControl can add their own properties to this category, too.

LoginControl cannot be used on its own—it must be contained in another form or dialog, which can in turn be used by different applications with different application names. You have two options for supplying the application name: you can use the ApplicationName property to specify the name, or, if you do not know that name in advance (i.e., if you're developing a general-purpose container), LoginControl can retrieve the application name from the Windows Forms entry application assembly used to launch the control. During authentication, if no value is set in the ApplicationName property, LoginControl will use the friendly name of the entry assembly as the application name. This logic is encapsulated in the private helper method GetAppName( ).

The CacheRoles property can be set to true or false; LoginControl simply passes it as-is to CustomPrincipal.Attach( ). Unaltered, CacheRoles defaults to false.

Authenticating the user

The OnLogin( ) method is called when the user clicks the Log In button. After validating the username and password, OnLogin( ) calls GetAppName( ) to retrieve the application name. It then calls GetUserManager( ) to obtain an implementation of IUserManager. Authentication itself is done simply by calling the Authenticate( ) method of the user manager. If authentication was successful, OnLogin( ) wraps a generic identity object around the username and attaches the custom principal. Note that OnLogin( ) never interacts directly with the custom principal—all OnLogin( ) does is provide it with the IIdentity object, the application name, the caching policy, and the implementation of IUserManager to use.

The question now is what LoginControl should do after authentication. The control has no knowledge of the required behavior of its hosting container. If authentication fails, perhaps it should present a message box, or perhaps it should throw an exception. If authentication succeeds, perhaps it should close the hosting dialog, or move to the next screen in a wizard, or do something else. Since only the hosting application knows what to do after both successful and failed authentication, all LoginControl can do is inform it of whether the authentication succeeded by firing an event. To this end, LoginControl declares the delegate LoginEvent of the type GenericEventHandler<LoginControl,LoginEventArgs>. LoginEventArgs contains a Boolean property called Authenticated, which indicates the outcome of the authentication. To fire the login event to all interested subscribers, LoginControl uses defensive event publishing via EventsHelper.

LoginControl also provides two handy helpers. The static Boolean property IsLoggedIn allows the caller to query whether or not a user is logged in. LoginControl retrieves the current principal and checks if it is of the type CustomPrincipal. If the user is logged in, this of course will be the principal used. The static method Logout( ) allows the user to log out. Logout( ) retrieves the current principal and, if it is of the type CustomPrincipal, detaches it from the current thread. As explained previously, calling Detach( ) on CustomPrincipal will also restore the previous principal. Note that if multiple threads are involved, you will need to log out on each one of them.

The AspNetLoginControl

Example B-3 shows the definition of AspNetLoginControl.

Example B-3. The AspNetLoginControl class
```
public partial class AspNetLoginControl : LoginControl
{
   protected override IUserManager GetUserManager( )
   {
      return new AspNetUserManager( );
   }
}
```

AspNetLoginControl derives from LoginControl, and in its overriding of GetUserManager( ) it returns the AspNetUserManager implementation of IUserManager, which uses the ASP.NET providers directly (see Figure B-4).

AspNetUserManager is capable of using any valid ASP.NET 2.0 provider (hence its name). To use AspNetLoginControl, you will need to add to the application's configuration file the same values you would have placed in a web application configuration file, indicating which provider to choose as well as any provider-specific values and settings.

For example, to use the SQL Server provider (which is the default provider), add the settings shown in Example B-4 to the application configuration file. The connection string value shown in Figure B-4 is used to connect to the *aspnetdb* database on the local machine after default installation. Note the use of the enabled attribute of the roleManager tag to enable authorization.

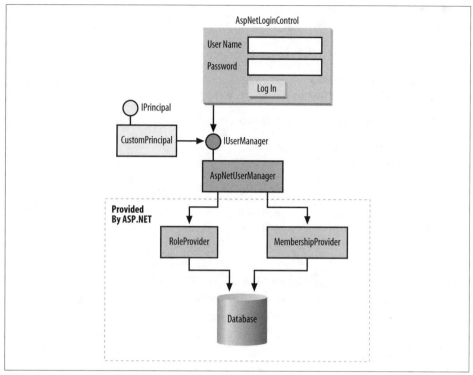

Figure B-4. The AspNetLoginControl control

Example B-4. Settings for AspNetLoginControl

```xml
<?xml version="1.0"?>
<configuration>
    <system.web>
        <roleManager enabled="true"/>
    </system.web>
    <connectionStrings>
        <remove name="LocalSqlServer"/>
        <add name="LocalSqlServer" connectionString="
            data source=(local);Integrated Security=SSPI;
            Initial Catalog=aspnetdb"/>
    </connectionStrings>
</configuration>
```

Implementing IUserManager

AspNetUserManager contains as member variables instances of the ASP.NET membership and role providers. All the functionality of IUserManager is accomplished by delegating to the ASP.NET providers (see Example B-5).

Example B-5. The AspNetUserManager class

```
class AspNetUserManager : IUserManager
{
    public bool Authenticate(string applicationName,string userName,string password)
    {
        Membership.ApplicationName = applicationName;
        return Membership.ValidateUser(userName,password);
    }
    public bool IsInRole(string applicationName,string userName,string role)
    {
        Roles.ApplicationName = applicationName;
        return Roles.IsUserInRole(userName,role);
    }
    public string[] GetRoles(string applicationName,string userName)
    {
        Roles.ApplicationName = applicationName;
        return Roles.GetRolesForUser(userName);
    }
}
```

To implement `Authenticate`, `AspNetUserManager` calls the `ValidateUser( )` method of `Membership`. To implement `IsInRole` and `GetRoles`, `AspNetUserManager` calls the `IsUserInRole( )` and `GetRolesForUser( )` methods of `Roles`.

> By default, NTFS security enforces access permission security to the application configuration file, so that only application administrators can modify the provider's settings.

AspNetLoginControl and Code Access Security

`AspNetLoginControl` works well, and you can certainly use it. However, it does have one important shortcoming you should be aware of. The ASP.NET providers were designed to be used on the server, and they require a few nontrivial permissions: unmanaged code access permission, unrestricted SQL Client access permission, and minimal ASP.NET Hosting permission. Typically, server-side applications run in an elevated trust environment (see Chapter 12 for a recommended server-side policy), potentially even full-trust, and will have no problem obtaining those permissions and executing properly.

`AspNetLoginControl`, on the other hand, is going to be used by Windows Forms applications. It is quite likely that such applications will be executing in a partial-trust environment, perhaps as ClickOnce applications. The client environment may very well not grant the applications using `AspNetLoginControl` the permissions they require to operate.

Table B-1 lists the permissions required for `AspNetLoginControl` and who demands them. These permissions are the product of both the control itself and the components it uses: `CustomPrincipal` and `AspNetUserManager`.

Table B-1. Security permissions required by AspNetLoginControl

Permission type	Specific permission value	Demanded by
Security	Execution	Any managed application, in order to run
Security	Unmanaged code access	The ASP.NET providers
ASP.NET Hosting	Minimal	The ASP.NET providers
SQL Client	Unrestricted	The ASP.NET providers, for accessing the database
Reflection	Unrestricted	EventsHelper, when using dynamic invocation of the login event
User Interface	Safe sub-windows	LoginControl, in order to display itself
Security	Control principal	CustomPrincipal, in order to set the principal policy and attach itself

You have a number of options in choosing how to deal with these permission demands. You can grant full trust to the *WinFormsEx.dll* assembly and all its clients, but that is unadvised, as discussed in Chapter 12.

Alternately, using the .NET Configuration tool, you can grant most of these permissions both to the *WinFormsEx.dll* assembly and to every client application that wants to use it. You can also list these permissions in the ClickOnce application manifest. To ease the task of granting the permissions, the source files accompanying this book contain the *WinFormsEx.xml* file—it's a custom permission set file that you can add to the .NET Configuration tool to grant the necessary permissions.

However, the best solution is to avoid the permissions demanded by the ASP.NET providers altogether and use a different implementation of IUserManager—one that does not demand server-side permissions in a client environment. This option is presented next.

The UserManager Web Service

The solution to the partial-trust problem is to wrap the ASP.NET providers with a web service. When using a web service, none of the security permission demands made by the providers will ever make their way back to the client.

Using a web service also has the advantage of better scalability, since only the web service will be using the connection to the database, rather than each individual client application. Another benefit of a web service is that it avoids potential security issues with clients authenticating themselves against SQL Server and secure connection string management on the client side. There are, however, a few considerations to bear in mind when using a web service:

Privacy

You should secure the communication between the clients and the web service, because the clients will be sending credentials over the wire. This can easily be done using HTTPS.

Additional call latency

This should be resolved using role caching.

Authenticating against the web service itself

This may not be an issue in your Intranet environment if you can sustain anonymous access to the web service.

Authorizing the web service calls

The web service allows callers to retrieve role information about a user. Role-membership information may be sensitive information on its own right—this can be dealt with by adding role-based security to the web service and authorizing the callers. Note that authorization requires authentication.

Using the technique described in Appendix A, you can expose IUserManager and its implementation as web services, as shown in Example B-6.

Example B-6. Implementing IUserManager by a web service

```
[WebServiceBinding (Name = "IUserManager")]
public interface IUserManager
{
    [WebMethod(Description = "Authenticates the user.")]
    bool Authenticate(string applicationName,string userName,string password);

    [WebMethod(Description = "Verifies user role's membership.")]
    bool IsInRole(string applicationName,string userName,string role);

    [WebMethod(Description = "Returns all roles the user is a member of.")]
    string[] GetRoles(string applicationName,string userName);
}

[WebService(Namespace = "http://SecurityServices",
            Description = "Wraps with a web service the ASP.NET providers.
                        This web service should be accessed over https.")]
class UserManager : IUserManager
{
    public bool Authenticate(string applicationName,string userName,string password)
    {
        if(HttpContext.Current.Request.IsSecureConnection == false)
        {
            HttpContext.Current.Trace.Warn("You should use HTTPS to avoid
                                        sending passwords in clear text");
        }
        Membership.ApplicationName = applicationName;
        return Membership.ValidateUser(userName,password);
    }
    public bool IsInRole(string applicationName,string userName,string role)
    {
        Roles.ApplicationName = applicationName;
        return Roles.IsUserInRole(userName,role);
    }
    public string[] GetRoles(string applicationName,string userName)
    {
```

Example B-6. Implementing IUserManager by a web service (continued)

```
    Roles.ApplicationName = applicationName;
    return Roles.GetRolesForUser(userName);
    }
}
```

The UserManager class in Example B-6 uses both Membership and Roles to obtain the configured providers from the web service configuration file. Note that each web method of UserManager also accepts the application name to use, so that a single web service can support multiple Windows Forms applications.

The WSLoginControl

WinFormsEx.dll contains the definition of WSLoginControl, shown in Example B-7.

Example B-7. The WSLoginControl class

```
public partial class WSLoginControl : LoginControl
{
    protected override IUserManager GetUserManager()
    {
        return new UserManager();
    }
}
```

WSLoginControl derives from LoginControl, and in its overriding of GetUserManager() it returns UserManager, a client-side web service proxy class used to invoke the UserManager web service. WSLoginControl can use any web service that manages user credentials, as long as it supports the IUserManager interface (hence its name). To generate the proxy class, add a web reference to the UserManager web service. Add to the machine-generated UserManager web service proxy class derivation from IUserManager. Since the proxy class is a partial class and is machine-generated, add that code, preferably in a separate file:

```
partial class UserManager : IUserManager
{}
```

WinFormsEx.dll already contains the definition of the UserManager web service proxy class. The code in the proxy class looks up the web service address from the application configuration file. Under the appSettings section, add to the application configuration file a key called UserManager, whose value is the web service address:

```
<?xml version="1.0"?>
<configuration>
   <appSettings>
      <add key="UserManager"
           value="http://localhost/SecurityServices/UserManager.asmx"/>
   </appSettings>
</configuration>
```

Figure B-5 shows WSLoginControl and CustomPrincipal, and their interaction with the UserManager web service.

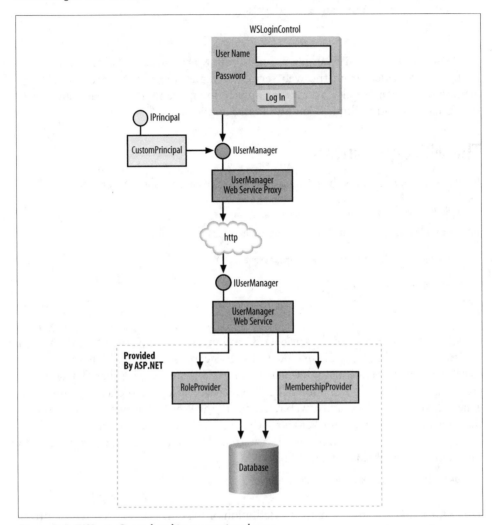

Figure B-5. WSLoginControl and its supporting classes

WSLoginControl and Code Access Security

Using a web service keeps the ASP.NET providers' permission demands on the server. The trade-off is that you will need instead to grant the clients web access permission to connect to the UserManager web service. You will also need to grant the rest of the permissions required by LoginControl and CustomPrincipal. Table B-2 lists the reduced permissions required when using a credential-management web service.

Table B-2. Security permissions required by WSLoginControl

Permission type	Specific permission value	Demanded by
Security	Execution	Any managed application, in order to run
Web Access	Connect to the UserManager web service	The UserManager proxy class, to be able to use the web service
Reflection	Unrestricted	EventsHelper, when using dynamic invocation of the login event
User Interface	Safe sub-windows	LoginControl, in order to display itself
Security	Control principal	CustomPrincipal, in order to set the principal policy and attach itself

Using the .NET Configuration tool, you can grant the permissions from Table B-2 both to the *WinFormsEx.dll* assembly and to every client application that wants to use it. You can also use Visual Studio 2005 to list these permissions in the Click-Once application manifest. In Visual Studio 2005, go to the Security tab in the project settings of a ClickOnce application that uses WSLoginControl. Check the "Enable ClickOnce Security Settings" checkbox and select the "This is a partial trust application" radio box. Under "Zone your application will be installed from", select (Custom). This will remove all permissions except execution permission. Next, select SecurityPermission, and under Settings select Include.

Click Properties... to bring up the Permission Settings dialog shown in Figure B-6.

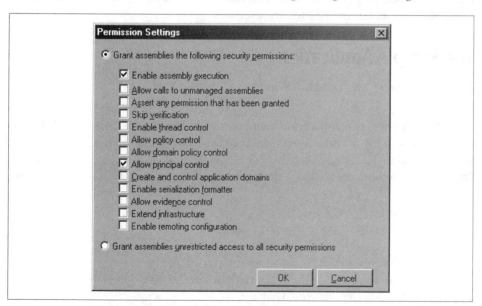

Figure B-6. Granting execution and principal control permissions

Select the assembly execution and principal control permissions, and click OK. To grant permission to call the web service, include the Web Access permission; in its properties, specify the UserManager's URL and allow the application to connect to it (see Figure B-7).

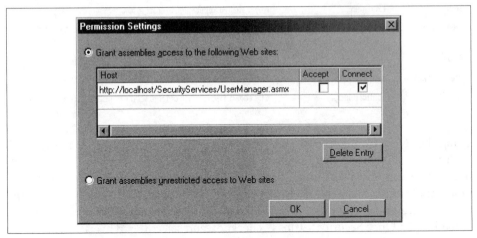

Figure B-7. Granting web service invocation permission

In a similar manner, grant the rest of the permissions from Table B-2 (User Interface and Reflection). When you publish your ClickOnce application, its application manifest will include these permissions. You can even use Visual Studio 2005 to debug the application under these partial-trust settings.

The Sample Application

Figure B-8 shows a sample Windows Forms MDI application that uses WSLoginControl.

In its Security tab, the application requests the permissions listed in Table B-2. It requires users to log in and authenticate themselves before creating a new document window. When the user selects the File → New menu item, it is handled by the OnFileNew( ) method. OnFileNew( ) demands that the user be a member of the Manager role:

```
[PrincipalPermission(SecurityAction.Demand,Role = "Manager")]
void OnFileNew(object sender,EventArgs args)
{...}
```

Before using the application, you will need to create the users and roles in the database. You can and should use the support Visual Studio 2005 offers for managing the credentials stored in the *aspnetdb* database.

Create a new ASP.NET web site. When using SQL Server, add to the web site configuration file the SQL Server connection string. Select ASP.NET Configuration from the Website menu to bring up the Web Site Administration pages (see Figure B-1).

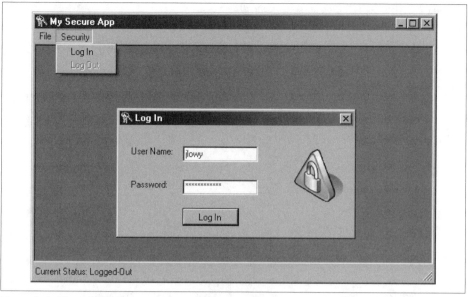

Figure B-8. The sample application

Select the Provider tab, then click the "Select a single provider for all site management data" link. Under the Provider list, click AspNetSqlProvider. Next, click the Security tab. Under Users, click "Select authentication type" and on the next page click "From the Internet". Then go back to the Security tab.

Under Roles, select "Enable roles" followed by "Create roles". Add a new role called Manager, and go back to the Security tab. Under Users, click "Create user" and provide the username and password as well as the other requested information. Make sure to check the Manager checkbox under Roles to make the new user a member of the Manager role. Click the Create User button, and you can now close Visual Studio 2005 (unless you would like to add more users and roles). Visual Studio 2005 uses a forward slash ("/") for the application name by default.

The LoginDialog Class

The sample application provides the Security menu item. When the user selects Security → Log In, the application brings up the LoginDialog dialog. LoginDialog is listed in Example B-8.

Example B-8. The LoginDialog class

```
partial class LoginDialog : Form
{
   LoginControl m_LogInControl;
   bool m_Authenticated;
   public LoginDialog( )
```

Example B-8. The LoginDialog class (continued)

```
{
    Authenticated = false;
    InitializeComponent();
}
public bool Authenticated
{
    get
    {
        return m_Authenticated;
    }
    protected set
    {
        m_Authenticated = value;
    }
}
void OnLogin(LoginControl sender,LoginEventArgs args)
{
    bool successful = args.Authenticated;
    if(successful == false)
    {
        MessageBox.Show("Invalid user name or password. Please try again",
                        "Log In",MessageBoxButtons.OK,MessageBoxIcon.Hand);
    }
    else
    {
        Authenticated = true;
        Close();
    }
}
static public void Logout()
{
    LoginControl.Logout();
}
static public bool IsLoggedIn
{
    get
    {
        return LoginControl.IsLoggedIn;
    }
}
}
```

 You can add the WSLoginControl to your Windows Forms toolbox and drop it on your dialogs. For the control's icon, I used the same icon as the ASP.NET Login control. All rights to icons used in this appendix belong to Microsoft.

LoginDialog is a simple dialog that contains the WSLoginControl. When you open LoginDialog in the Windows Forms Designer, you can set the WSLoginControl properties. LoginDialog sets the ApplicationName property to "/" and CacheRoles to False.

The application configuration files set the UserManager web service address to *http://localhost/SecurityServices/UserManager.asmx*.

The OnLogin() method of LoginDialog subscribes to the LoginEvent event of LoginControl. In the OnLogin() event-handling method, LoginDialog alerts the user with a message box if the login attempt failed. If the login was successful, LoginDialog sets a public property called Authenticated to true, and closes itself. Authenticated is used by the client of LoginDialog to find out the authentication outcome. Authenticated will be false if the user closed LoginDialog without logging in. Note that Authenticated uses public get and protected set accessors, to allow clients to retrieve the value but not set it.

The Security menu of the sample application also contains a Log Out option. The implementation calls the Logout() static method of LoginDialog, which delegates to LoginControl.Logout(), thereby detaching CustomPrincipal from the current thread. The sample application also uses a timer to update its status bar, which constantly informs the user of the login status. To find out whether or not the user is logged in, on every timer tick event the application checks the value of the LoginDialog. IsLoggedIn static property and updates the status bar accordingly. LoginDialog. IsLoggedIn simply delegates to LoginControl.IsLoggedIn.

APPENDIX C

Reflection and Attributes

Reflection is the programmatic act of reading the metadata associated with a type. You can read the metadata to learn what the type is and what is it made of (i.e., methods, properties, base classes). Reflection services are defined in the System. Reflection namespace. Reflection is most useful in conjunction with attributes, which are a way of adding information to a type and affecting the type's behavior. Reflection also has another esoteric feature not covered in this appendix: it allows you to define new types during runtime and emit the corresponding IL code and metadata (using the services found in the System.Reflection.Emit namespace). This appendix starts by reviewing some key .NET reflection techniques and then focuses on using and defining attributes.

System.Type

The abstract class Type, defined in the System namespace, is an abstraction of a .NET CLR type. Every .NET type, be it a .NET-provided type (from value types such as integers and enums to classes and interfaces) or a developer-defined type, has a corresponding unique Type value.

 The ability to uniquely identify a type by means of a Type object is analogous to the COM idea of identifying the type of a component by means of its unique CLSID.

The canonical base class of any .NET type is System.Object. Object (or just object in C#) has built-in support for retrieving the Type associated with any object by calling its GetType( ) method:

```
public class Object
{
    public Type GetType( );
    //Other methods
}
```

Having GetType( ) present in object allows you to call it on any .NET object:

```
public class MyClass
{...}

int number = 0;
MyClass obj = new MyClass( );

Type type1 = number.GetType( );
Type type2 = obj.GetType( );
```

Different instances of the same type must return the same Type value:

```
int number1 = 1;
int number2 = 2;

Type type1 = number1.GetType( );
Type type2 = number2.GetType( );

Debug.Assert(type1 == type2);
```

The typeof operator allows you to retrieve the Type associated with a type directly, without instantiating an object of that type:

```
Type type1 = typeof(int);
Type type2 = typeof(MyClass);
```

Type is your gateway to obtaining the metadata associated with a given type. To start, Type.ToString( ) returns the type's name:

```
Type type = typeof(MyClass);
string name = type.ToString( );
Debug.Assert(name == "MyClass");
```

But Type has a lot more to offer. It has more than 100 methods and properties that you can use to obtain metadata about the type. For example, the GetMethods( ) method returns an array of MethodInfo objects describing all the public methods of the type. GetMethods( ) is defined as:

```
public MethodInfo[] GetMethods( );
```

Example C-1 demonstrates using GetMethods( ) to trace to the output window all the public methods of the class MyClass.

Example C-1. Using Type.GetMethods() to reflect a type's public methods

```
using System.Reflection;

public class MyClass
{
    public MyClass( )
    {}
    public void Method1( )
    {}
    public static void Method2( )
    {}
```

Example C-1. Using Type.GetMethods() to reflect a type's public methods (continued)

```
   protected void Method3()
   {}
   private void Method4()
   {}
}
//Client code:
Type type = typeof(MyClass);

MethodInfo[] methodInfoArray = type.GetMethods();

//Trace all the public methods
foreach(MethodInfo methodInfo in methodInfoArray)
{
   Trace.WriteLine(methodInfo.Name);
}
//Output:
GetHashCode
Equals
ToString
Method1
Method2
GetType
```

This example demonstrates a few other key points. GetMethods() returns all the public methods of a type (instance or static), including those defined in its base class(es). In its output, Example C-1 lists four public methods of object that are not part of the MyClass definition.

GetMethods() doesn't return constructors. If you aren't satisfied with this behavior, you can use another version of GetMethods() that accepts a parameter telling it how to bind to the type:

```
public abstract MethodInfo[] GetMethods(BindingFlags bindingAttr);
```

The BindingFlags enumeration is a bit-mask enumeration that lets you specify whether to return only instance methods, only static methods, only nonpublic methods, methods defined only in this type (i.e., not inherited), and so on. Once you have obtained a MethodInfo object about a method, you can invoke it, even if it's a protected or private method. Example C-2 demonstrates how to invoke all the private methods of the MyClass class using the late-binding Invoke() method of the MethodInfo object. The Invoke() method is defined as:

```
public object Invoke(object obj, object[] parameters);
```

Late-binding invocation breaks every rule of encapsulation and type safety, because the compiler lets you invoke private methods and pass in as parameters anything you want. Late binding is available for esoteric cases and for tool developers. In general, avoid reflection-based late-binding invocation.

Example C-2 starts by obtaining a Type object from an instance (unlike Example C-1, which uses the class itself). Then it calls GetMethods( ), requesting back only nonpublic instance methods. Note that to invoke only private methods, further filtering is required after calling GetMethods( ), because GetMethods( ) returns both protected and private methods. The additional filtering is done by checking the IsPrivate property of the MethodInfo object. In Example C-2, only Method4( ) is invoked. Invoke( ) accepts the object to invoke the method on, and an array of objects as parameters for the method to invoke. In this example, Method4( ) has no parameters, so a null is passed in to Invoke( ).

Example C-2. Invoking only the private methods of an object using reflection

```csharp
using System.Reflection;

public class MyClass
{
    public MyClass( )
    {...}
    public void Method1( )
    {...}
    public void Method2( )
    {...}
    public static void Method5( )
    {...}
    protected void Method3( )
    {...}
    private void Method4( )
    {...}
}
//Client code
MyClass obj = new MyClass( );
Type type = typeof(MyClass);

MethodInfo[] methodInfoArray;
methodInfoArray = type.GetMethods(BindingFlags.NonPublic|BindingFlags.Instance);

//Invoke private methods only
foreach(MethodInfo methodInfo in methodInfoArray)
{
    if(methodInfo.IsPrivate)
    {
        methodInfo.Invoke(obj,null);
    }
}
```

 Use of the late-binding Invoke( ) method is similar to the old COM automation way of using IDispatch::Invoke( ) to invoke calls on objects.

Type offers numerous other methods in addition to GetMethods(). GetMethod() returns a MethodInfo object about one particular method. GetConstructors() and GetConstructor() return ConstructorInfo objects about the type's constructors. GetMember() and GetMembers() return information about the type's members. GetEvent() and GetEvents() return information about the events the type supports, and so on. The general form of retrieving the reflection information is Get<Element Name>. Type also offers many properties dealing with what kind of type is reflected: if it's a class or an interface, what its base class type is, and so on. For example:

```
Type type = typeof(MyClass);
Debug.Assert(type.IsClass);
```

See the MSDN Library for a complete listing of the Type members.

Attributes

The ability to reflect methods and type information is a nice and intriguing technology, but reflection really shines and demonstrates its value when you use it in conjunction with .NET attributes. The idea behind attributes is simple: instead of coding functionality and features into your objects, you can add them by decorating your objects with attributes. The information in the attributes is added to the metadata about the objects that the compiler generates (its methods, base classes, etc.). .NET (or your custom tools) can read the metadata, look for the attributes, and then perform the functionality and add the features the attributes specify without the object's or its developer's involvement. For example, when you want to combine enums in a binary masking value, you can use the Flags attribute:

```
[Flags]
public enum WeekDay
{
    Monday,
    Tuesday,
    Wednesday,
    Thursday,
    Friday,
    Saturday,
    Sunday,
}
```

When the compiler sees the Flags attribute, it allows you to combine enum values with the | (OR) operator, as if they were integer powers of 2. For example:

```
const WeekDay Weekend = WeekDay.Saturday|WeekDay.Sunday;
```

Another example is the Conditional attribute, defined in the System.Diagnostics namespace. This attribute directs the compiler to exclude from a build calls to any method it decorates if a specified condition isn't defined:

```
#define MySpecialCondition //usually DEBUG
```

```
public class MyClass
{
    public MyClass( )
    {}
    [Conditional("MySpecialCondition")]
    public void MyMethod( )
    {...}
}
//Client side code
MyClass obj = new MyClass( );
//This line is conditional
obj.MyMethod( );
```

Having the compiler do the method-call exclusion automatically is, of course, a major improvement over C++ or classic VB. In the past, when developers did code exclusion manually and then wanted to reinstate the method calls, they sometimes forgot to do so somewhere and thus caused defects in the code.

Attributes are used in every aspect of .NET programming: in asynchronous calls, in object persistence and serialization, in concurrency management, in remote calls, in security, in interoperability with COM and Windows, and in Enterprise Services.

Using Attributes

An attribute is actually a class in its own right. The attribute class should have the suffix Attribute in its name, and it must derive (directly or indirectly) from the class Attribute:

```
public class FlagsAttribute : Attribute
{...}
```

When you use attributes, you use square brackets [ ] (or angle brackets < > in Visual Basic 2005) around their names. However, the C# and Visual Basic 2005 compilers support a shorthand when using an attribute. If the attribute name ends with Attribute, the compiler lets you omit the Attribute suffix:

```
[Flags] //same as [FlagsAttribute]
public enum Color
{
    Red,Green,Blue,Purple = Red | Blue
}
```

You can stack as many attributes as you like on a type or a type member, as long as the attributes don't contradict each other. However, you can't apply any attribute to any type or type member. Each attribute has an attribute of type AttributeUsage associated with it that dictates which types (class, interface, enum, etc.), and which syntactic elements (constructor, method, parameter, returned value, etc.) the attribute is applicable to. AttributeUsage also dictates whether the attribute can be used multiple times on the same target. (You will learn more about AttributeUsage in the next section.) Attributes can also have a default constructor and can accept construction parameters. If a default constructor is available, you can use the attribute with or without parentheses:

```
[MyAttribute()] //same as [MyAttribute]
```

Attributes can accept construction parameters and have public properties that you can set. If you have both parameterized constructors and properties, you must specify the parameters to the constructor before setting the properties. There are limitations on the types of parameters the attribute constructors and properties can accept; for instance, they can't accept a class or struct as a parameter. The only permissible reference types are array, Type, and object.

Kinds of Attributes

There are three kinds of attributes in .NET. First, there are *standard attributes*, such as Flags and Conditional. Standard attributes are available in .NET out of the box. The .NET compilers and runtime know about these attributes and obey their directions. The second kind of attributes are *custom attributes*, which are attributes you provide. These go completely unnoticed by .NET, except that the compiler adds them as part of the metadata. As discussed in the next section, you have to write the reflection code to make sense of the custom attributes. Such attributes usually have domain-specific semantics. The third kind of attributes are *custom context attributes*. Both .NET and you can provide custom context attributes. .NET is fully aware of them and will comply with their directions and influence the decorated objects accordingly. Chapter 11 discusses context attributes at length.

Implementing Custom Attributes

Implementing a custom attribute (and the accompanying reflection code to make use of it) is easy and straightforward. For example, suppose you want to provide a custom attribute that adds a color option to your classes and interfaces. The color is an enum defined as:

```
public enum ColorOption {Red,Green,Blue};
```

The color attribute should also have:

- A default constructor that assigns ColorOption.Red to the target class or interface
- A parameterized constructor that accepts the color to assign to the target class or interface
- A property that accepts the color to assign to the target class or interface

Example C-3 shows the implementation of the ColorAttribute class.

Example C-3. Implementing a custom attribute

```
public enum ColorOption {Red,Green,Blue};

[AttributeUsage(AttributeTargets.Class|AttributeTargets.Interface)]
public class ColorAttribute : Attribute
{
    ColorOption m_Color;
    public ColorOption Color
    {
        get
        {
            return m_Color;
        }
        set
        {
            m_Color = value;
        }
    }
    public ColorAttribute( )
    {
        Color = ColorOption.Red;
    }
    public ColorAttribute(ColorOption color)
    {
        this.Color = color;
    }
}
```

Before walking though Example C-3, here are a few examples that use the
ColorAttribute custom attribute:

- Using the default constructor:
  ```
  [Color]
  public class MyClass1
  {}
  ```
- Using the parameterized constructor:
  ```
  [Color(ColorOption.Green)]
  public class MyClass2
  {}
  ```
- Using the property:
  ```
  [Color(Color = ColorOption.Blue)]
  public class MyClass3
  {}
  ```
- Using it on an interface:
  ```
  [Color]
  public interface IMyInterface
  {}
  ```

As you can see in Example C-3, there isn't much to implementing a custom attribute.
The ColorAttribute class derives from the Attribute class and defines the public

Color property to access the m_Color member variable. The AttributeUsage attribute indicates that the Color attribute can be applied only to classes or interfaces:

```
[AttributeUsage(AttributeTargets.Class|AttributeTargets.Interface)]
public class ColorAttribute : Attribute
{...}
```

As a result, trying to use the Color attribute on any other target (such as a method) doesn't compile:

```
public class MyClass
{
    [Color]//This will not compile
    public void MyMethd( )
    {}
}
```

The definition of AttributeUsageAttribute is:

```
public sealed class AttributeUsageAttribute : Attribute
{
    public AttributeUsageAttribute(AttributeTargets validOn);
    public bool AllowMultiple { get; set; }
    /* Other members */
}
```

Its constructor accepts an enum of type AttributeTargets, letting it know on which types this attribute is valid. The AttributeTargets enum offers a number of values, such as AttributeTargets.Method, AttributeTargets.Assembly, and so on.

The other interesting property of AttributeUsage is AllowMultiple. By default, AllowMultiple is set to false, so you can apply the Color attribute only once per class or interface. As a result, this usage doesn't compile:

```
[Color(ColorOption.Green)]
[Color]
public class MyClass
{}
```

However, if you explicitly set AllowMultiple to true, you can use the Color attribute multiple times on the same target:

```
[AttributeUsage(AttributeTargets.Class|AttributeTargets.Interface,
                                                AllowMultiple = true)]
public class ColorAttribute : Attribute
{...}
```

Reflecting Custom Attributes

When you write code to reflect attributes, it's often better to do so in the form of a static helper method that accepts an object or a type to reflect and returns the information, as shown in Example C-4. That way, other parties in your application can use the method, without bothering with instantiating an object first.

Example C-4. Reflecting a custom attribute

```
public static ColorOption GetColor(object obj)
{
   Type objType = obj.GetType( );
   Debug.Assert(objType.IsClass || objType.IsInterface);

   Type attribType = typeof(ColorAttribute);

   object[] attributeArray = objType.GetCustomAttributes(attribType,true);

   //Only one color attribute at the most
   Debug.Assert(attributeArray.Length == 0 || attributeArray.Length == 1);

   if(attributeArray.Length == 0)
   {
      return ColorOption.Red;
   }

   ColorAttribute colorAttribute = (ColorAttribute)attributeArray[0];
   return colorAttribute.Color;
}
```

The `GetColor( )` method in Example C-4 accepts an object as a parameter and constructs a `Type` representing the type of the parameter, verifying that it got either a class or an interface:

```
Debug.Assert(objType.IsClass || objType.IsInterface);
```

It then calls the `GetCustomAttributes( )` method of `Type` to get an array of all the attributes of the specified attribute type. Note that `GetCustomAttributes( )` returns all the attributes associated with the type, not just the custom attributes. A better name for it would be simply `GetAttributes( )`. After retrieving the array of attributes of type `ColorAttribute`, the `GetColor( )` method verifies that the size of the array is either 0 or 1, because there can be at most one color attribute associated with the object. If no attribute is associated with the object, the method returns `ColorOption. Red`. However, if one such attribute is present, the method returns its `Color` value.

What you choose to do with the knowledge of the color of the object is entirely domain-specific. All .NET provides is an easy-to-use and extensible mechanism for associating a custom attribute with a type and reflecting it.

Generics and Reflection

In .NET 2.0, reflection is extended to support generic type parameters. The type `Type` can represent generic types with specific type parameters (called *bounded* types), or unspecified (*unbounded*) types. As in C# 1.1, you can obtain the `Type` of any type by using the `typeof` operator or by calling the `GetType( )` method that every type supports. Regardless of the way you choose, both yield the same Type. For example, in the following code sample, type1 is identical to type2:

```
LinkedList<int,string> list = new LinkedList<int,string>();

Type type1 = typeof(LinkedList<int,string>);
Type type2 = list.GetType();
Debug.Assert(type1 == type2);
```

Both typeof and GetType() can operate on naked generic type parameters:

```
public class MyClass<T>
{
   public void SomeMethod(T t)
   {
      Type type = typeof(T);
      Debug.Assert(type == t.GetType());
   }
}
```

In addition, the typeof operator can operate on *unbounded generic types* (generic types that do not yet have specific type parameters). For example:

```
public class MyClass<T>
{}
Type unboundedType = typeof(MyClass<>);

Trace.WriteLine(unboundedType.ToString());
//Writes: MyClass`1[T]
```

The number 1 being traced is the number of generic type parameters of the type used. Note the use of the empty <>. To operate on an unbounded generic type with multiple type parameters, use a , in the empty <>:

```
public class LinkedList<K,T>
{...}
Type unboundedList = typeof(LinkedList<,>);
Trace.WriteLine(unboundedList.ToString());
//Writes: LinkedList`2[K,T]
```

To support generics, Type has special methods and properties designed to provide reflection information about the generic aspects of the types. Example C-5 shows these members.

Example C-5. Type's generic reflection members

```
public abstract class Type : //Base types
{
   public virtual bool ContainsGenericParameters{get;}
   public virtual Type[] GetGenericParameterConstraints();
   public virtual GenericParameterAttributes GenericParameterAttributes{get;}
   public virtual int GenericParameterPosition{get;}
   public virtual bool IsGenericParameter{get;}
   public virtual bool IsGenericType{get;}
   public virtual bool IsGenericTypeDefinition{get;}
```

Example C-5. Type's generic reflection members (continued)

```
    public virtual Type[] GetGenericArguments( );
    public virtual Type GetGenericTypeDefinition( );
    public virtual Type MakeGenericType(params Type[] typeArguments);
    //Rest of the members
}
```

The most useful of these new members are the IsGenericType property and the GetGenericArguments( ) and GetGenericTypeDefinition( ) methods. The rest of Type's generic-related members are for advanced and somewhat esoteric scenarios beyond the scope of this appendix. As its name indicates, IsGenericType is set to true if the type represented by the Type object uses generic type parameters. GetGenericArguments( ) returns an array of types corresponding to the bounded types used. GetGenericTypeDefinition( ) returns a Type representing the generic form of the underlying type.

Example C-6 demonstrates using these generic-handling Type members to obtain generic reflection information on a generic linked list.

Example C-6. Using Type for generic reflection

```
public class LinkedList<K,T>
{...}

LinkedList<int,string> list = new LinkedList<int,string>( );

Type boundedType = list.GetType( );
Debug.Assert(boundedType.IsGenericType);
Trace.WriteLine(boundedType.ToString( ));
//Writes: LinkedList`2[System.Int32,System.String]

Type[] parameters = boundedType.GetGenericArguments( );
Debug.Assert(parameters.Length == 2);
Debug.Assert(parameters[0] == typeof(int));
Debug.Assert(parameters[1] == typeof(string));

Type unboundedType = boundedType.GetGenericTypeDefinition( );
Debug.Assert(unboundedType.IsGenericTypeDefinition);
Trace.WriteLine(unboundedType.ToString( ));
//Writes: LinkedList`2[K,T]
```

As shown in Example C-6, a Type can refer to a generic type with bounded parameters (boundedType in this example) or to a generic type with unbounded parameters (unboundedType in this example).

Like Type, MethodInfo and its base class MethodBase also have members that reflect generic method information.

As in the non-generic case, you can use MethodInfo (as well as a number of other options) for late-binding invocation. However, the type of the parameters you pass for the late binding must match the bounded types used, instead of the generic type parameters (if any):

```
LinkedList<int,string> list = new LinkedList<int,string>();
Type type = list.GetType();
MethodInfo methodInfo = type.GetMethod("AddHead");
object[] args = {1,"AAA"};
methodInfo.Invoke(list,args);
```

Attributes and Generics

When defining an attribute, you can instruct the compiler that the attribute should target generic type parameters by using the GenericParameter value of the enum AttributeTargets:

```
[AttributeUsage(AttributeTargets.GenericParameter)]
public class SomeAttribute : Attribute
{...}
```

Note that C# 2.0 does not allow you to define generic attributes:

```
//Does not compile:
public class SomeAttribute<T> : Attribute
{...}
```

Yet internally, an attribute class can take advantage of generics by using generic types, or, like any other type, can define helper generic methods:

```
public class SomeAttribute : Attribute
{
   void SomeMethod<T>(T t)
   {...}
   LinkedList<int,string> m_List = new LinkedList<int,string>();
}
```

Generics

Generics[*] are some of the most powerful and useful features of .NET 2.0. Generics allow you to define a type-safe data structure or a utility helper class, without committing to the actual data types used. This results in a significant performance boost and higher-quality code, because you get to reuse data-processing algorithms without duplicating type-specific code. In concept, generics are similar to C++ templates, but they are drastically different in their implementation and capabilities. This appendix discusses the problems that generics address, how they are implemented and applied, and the benefits of the programming model.

Generics Problem Statement

Consider an everyday data structure such as a stack, providing the classic Push( ) and Pop( ) methods. When you develop a general-purpose stack, you would probably like to use it to store instances of various types. Under C# 1.1, you have to use an object-based stack, meaning that the internal data type used in the stack is an amorphous object, and the stack methods interact with objects:

```
public class Stack
{
    object[] m_Items;
    public void Push(object item)
    {...}
    public object Pop( )
    {...}
}
```

Example D-1 shows the full implementation of the object-based stack.

---

[*] This appendix contains excerpts from the white paper "An Introduction to C# Generics," by Juval Lowy, *MSDN Magazine*, November 2003, updated January 2005.

Example D-1. An object-based stack

```
public class Stack
{
    const int DefaultSize = 100;
    readonly int m_Size;
    int m_StackPointer = 0;
    object[] m_Items;

    public Stack() : this(DefaultSize)
    {}
    public Stack(int size)
    {
        m_Size = size;
        m_Items = new object[m_Size];
    }
    public void Push(object item)
    {
        if(m_StackPointer >= m_Size)
        {
            throw new StackOverflowException();
        }
        m_Items[m_StackPointer] = item;
        m_StackPointer++;
    }
    public object Pop()
    {
        m_StackPointer--;
        if(m_StackPointer >= 0)
        {
            return m_Items[m_StackPointer];
        }
        else
        {
            m_StackPointer = 0;
            throw new InvalidOperationException("Cannot pop an empty stack");
        }
    }
}
```

Because object is the canonical .NET base type, you can use the object-based stack to hold any type of items, such as integers:

```
Stack stack = new Stack();
stack.Push(1);
stack.Push(2);
int number = (int)stack.Pop();
```

However, there are two problems with object-based solutions. The first issue is performance. When you use value types, you have to box them in order to push and store them, and you must unbox the value types when popping them off the stack. Boxing and unboxing incurs a significant performance penalty in its own right, but it also increases the pressure on the managed heap, resulting in more garbage collections, which is not great for performance either. Even if you use reference types instead of value types, there is still a performance penalty because you have to cast from an object to the actual type you interact with and incur the casting cost:

```
Stack stack = new Stack( );
stack.Push("1");
string number = (string)stack.Pop( );
```

The second (and often more severe) problem with the object-based solution is type safety. Because the compiler lets you cast anything to and from object, you lose compile-time type safety. For example, the following code compiles fine but raises an invalid cast exception at runtime:

```
Stack stack = new Stack( );
stack.Push(1);
//This compiles, but is not type safe, and will throw an exception:
string number = (string)stack.Pop( );
```

You can overcome these two problems by providing a type-specific (and hence type-safe) performance stack. For integers, you can implement and use the IntStack:

```
public class IntStack
{
    int[] m_Items;
    public void Push(int item)
    {...}
    public int Pop( )
    {...}
}
IntStack stack = new IntStack( );
stack.Push(1);
int number = stack.Pop( );
```

For strings, you would implement the StringStack:

```
public class StringStack
{
    string[] m_Items;
    public void Push(string item)
    {...}
    public string Pop( )
    {...}
}
StringStack stack = new StringStack( );
stack.Push("1");
string number = stack.Pop( );
```

And so on. Unfortunately, solving the performance and type-safety problems this way introduces a third, and just as serious, problem: productivity impact. Writing a type-specific data structure is a tedious, repetitive, and error-prone task. When you fix a defect in the data structure, you have to fix it not just in one place, but in as many places as there are type-specific duplicates of what is essentially the same data structure. In addition, there is no way to foresee the use of unknown or as-yet-undefined future types, so you have to keep an object-based data structure as well. As a result, most developers find type-specific data structures to be impractical and opt for using object-based data structures, in spite of their deficiencies.

What Are Generics?

Generics allow you to define type-safe classes without compromising type safety, performance, or productivity. You implement the server only once as a generic server, while at the same time you can declare and use it with any type. To do that, use the < and > brackets, enclosing a generic type parameter. For example, here is how you define and use a generic stack:

```
public class Stack<T>
{
    T[] m_Items;
    public void Push(T item)
    {...}
    public T Pop()
    {...}
}
Stack<int> stack = new Stack<int>();
stack.Push(1);
stack.Push(2);
int number = stack.Pop();
```

Example D-2 shows the full implementation of the generic stack.

Example D-2. The generic stack

```
public class Stack<T>
{
    const int DefaultSize = 100;
    readonly int m_Size;
    int m_StackPointer = 0;
    T[] m_Items;

    public Stack() : this(DefaultSize)
    {}
    public Stack(int size)
    {
        m_Size = size;
        m_Items = new T[m_Size];
    }
    public void Push(T item)
    {
        if(m_StackPointer >= m_Size)
        {
            throw new StackOverflowException();
        }
        m_Items[m_StackPointer] = item;
        m_StackPointer++;
    }
```

Example D-2. The generic stack (continued)

```
public T Pop( )
{
   m_StackPointer--;
   if(m_StackPointer >= 0)
   {
      return m_Items[m_StackPointer];
   }
   else
   {
      m_StackPointer = 0;
      throw new InvalidOperationException("Cannot pop an empty stack");
   }
}
}
```

Example D-2 is the same as Example D-1, except that in Example D-2 every use of object has been replaced with T, and the Stack is defined using the generic type parameter T:

```
public class Stack<T>
{...}
```

When you use the generic stack, you have to instruct the compiler which type to use instead of the generic type parameter T, both when you declare the variable and when you instantiate it:

```
Stack<int> stack = new Stack<int>( );
```

The compiler and the runtime do the rest. All the methods (or properties) that accept or return a T will instead use the specified type (such as an integer).

> T is the *generic type parameter* (or type parameter), while the *generic type* is Stack<T>.

The advantage of this programming model is that the internal algorithms and data manipulation remain the same, while the actual data type can change based on the way the client uses your server code.

Generics Implementation

On the surface C# generics look syntactically similar to C++ templates, but there are important differences in the way they are implemented and supported by the compiler. This has significant implications for how you use generics.

Compared to C++ templates, C# generics can provide enhanced safety but are also somewhat limited in capabilities. In some C++ compilers, until you use a template class with a specific type, the compiler does not even compile the template code.

When you do specify a type, the compiler inserts the code inline, replacing every occurrence of the generic type parameter with the specified type. In addition, every time you use a specific type, the compiler inserts the type-specific code, regardless of whether you have already specified that type for the template class somewhere else in the application. It is up to the C++ linker to resolve this, and it is not always possible to do so. This may result in code bloating, increasing both the load time and the memory footprint.

In .NET 2.0, generics have native support in the IL and the CLR itself. When you compile generic C# server-side code, the compiler compiles it into IL, just like it would any other type. However, the IL only contains parameters or placeholders for the actual specific types. In addition, the metadata of the generic server contains generic information.

The client-side compiler uses that generic metadata to support type safety. When the client provides a specific type instead of a generic type parameter, the client's compiler substitutes the generic type parameter in the server metadata with the specified type. This provides the client's compiler with a type-specific definition of the server, as if generics were never involved. This way, the client compiler can enforce correct method parameters, type-safety checks, and even type-specific IntelliSense.

The interesting question is how .NET compiles the generic IL of the server to machine code. It turns out that the actual machine code produced depends on whether the specified types are value or reference types. If the client specifies a value type, the JIT compiler replaces the generic type parameters in the IL with the specified value type and compiles the IL into native code. However, the JIT compiler keeps track of type-specific server code it has already generated. Thus, if the JIT compiler is asked to compile the generic server with a value type it has already compiled to machine code, it simply returns a reference to that server code. Because the JIT compiler uses the same value-type-specific server code in all further encounters, there is no code bloating.

If the client specifies a reference type, the JIT compiler replaces the generic parameters in the server IL with object and compiles it into native code. That code will be used in any further requests for a reference type instead of a generic type parameter. Note that this way the JIT compiler only reuses actual code. Instances are still allocated off the managed heap according to their size, and there is no casting.

Generics in .NET let you reuse code and the effort you put into implementing it. The types and internal data can change without causing code bloat, regardless of whether you are using value or reference types. You can develop, test, and deploy your code once and then reuse it with any type, including future types, all with full compiler support and type safety. Because the generic code does not force the boxing and unboxing of value types, or the downcasting of reference types, performance is greatly improved. With value types there is typically a 200% performance gain, and with reference types you can expect up to a 100% performance gain in accessing the type (of course, the application as a whole may or may not experience any performance improvements).

Applying Generics

Because of the native support for generics in the IL and the CLR, all CLR 2.0–compliant languages can take advantage of generic types. For example, here is some Visual Basic 2005 code that uses the generic stack of Example D-2:

```
Dim stack As Stack(Of Integer)
stack = new Stack(Of Integer)
stack.Push(3)
Dim number As Integer
number = stack.Pop( )
```

You can use generics in classes and in structs. Here is a useful generic Point struct:

```
public struct Point<T>
{
    public T X;
    public T Y;
}
```

You can use the generic Point for integer coordinates:

```
Point<int> point;
point.X = 1;
point.Y = 2;
```

or for charting coordinates that require floating-point precision:

```
Point<double> point;
point.X = 1.2;
point.Y = 3.4;
```

Multiple Generic Types

A single type can define multiple generic type parameters. For example, consider the generic linked list shown in Example D-3.

Example D-3. A generic linked list

```
class Node<K,T>
{
    public K Key;
    public T Item;
    public Node<K,T> NextNode;

    public Node( )
    {
        Key      = default(K);
        Item     = default(T);
        NextNode = null;
    }
    public Node(K key,T item,Node<K,T> nextNode)
    {
        Key      = key;
```

Example D-3. A generic linked list (continued)

```
      Item    = item;
      NextNode = nextNode;
   }
}

public class LinkedList<K,T>
{
   Node<K,T> m_Head;

   public LinkedList( )
   {
      m_Head = new Node<K,T>( );
   }
   public void AddHead(K key,T item)
   {
      Node<K,T> newNode = new Node<K,T>(key,item,m_Head.NextNode);
      m_Head.NextNode = newNode;
   }
}
```

The linked list stores nodes:

```
   class Node<K,T>
   {...}
```

Each node contains a key (of the generic type parameter K) and a value (of the generic type parameter T). Each node also has a reference to the next node in the list. The linked list itself is defined in terms of the generic type parameters K and T:

```
   public class LinkedList<K,T>
   {...}
```

This allows the list to expose generic methods such as AddHead( ):

```
   public void AddHead(K key,T item);
```

Whenever you declare a variable of a type that uses generics, you must specify the types to use. However, the specified types can themselves be generic types. For example, the linked list has a member variable called m_Head of type Node<K,T>, used for referencing the first item in the list. m_Head is declared using the list's own generic type parameters K and T:

```
   Node<K,T> m_Head;
```

You need to provide specific types when instantiating a node, and again, you can use the linked list's own generic type parameters:

```
   public void AddHead(K key,T item)
   {
      Node<K,T> newNode = new Node<K,T>(key,item,m_Head.NextNode);
      m_Head.NextNode = newNode;
   }
```

Note that it is purely for readability purposes that the list uses the same names as the node for the generic type parameters. It could have used other names, such as:

```
public class LinkedList<U,V>
{...}
```

or:

```
public class LinkedList<KeyType,DataType>
{...}
```

In which case, m_Head would have been declared as:

```
Node<KeyType,DataType> m_Head;
```

When the client uses the linked list, it has to provide specific types. The client can choose integers as keys and strings as data items:

```
LinkedList<int,string> list = new LinkedList<int,string>();
list.AddHead(123,"AAA");
```

However, it can also choose any other combination, such as a timestamp for keys:

```
LinkedList<DateTime,string> list = new LinkedList<DateTime,string>();
list.AddHead(DateTime.Now,"AAA");
```

Generic Constraints

With C# generics, the compiler compiles the generic code into IL independent of any specific types the client will use. As a result, the generic code could try to use methods, properties, or members of the generic type parameters that are incompatible with the specific types the client uses. This is unacceptable, because it amounts to a lack of type safety. In C#, you need to instruct the compiler which constraints the client-specified types must obey in order for them to be used instead of the generic type parameters. There are three types of constraints, which the following sections will explore in detail:

Derivation constraint
> Indicates to the compiler that the generic type parameter derives from a base type such as an interface or a particular base class

Default constructor constraint
> Indicates to the compiler that the generic type parameter exposes a default public constructor (a public constructor with no parameters)

Value/reference type constraint
> Constrains the generic type parameter to be a value or a reference type

A generic type can employ multiple constraints, and you even get IntelliSense reflecting the constraints when using the generic type parameter (e.g., suggesting methods or members from the base type).

Note that although constraints are optional, they are often essential when developing a generic type. Without them, the compiler takes the more conservative, type-safe approach and allows access only to object-level functionality in your generic type parameters. Constraints are part of the generic type metadata, so the client-side compiler can take advantage of them as well. The client-side compiler allows the client developer to use only types that comply with the constraints, thus enforcing type safety.

An example will go a long way toward explaining the need for and use of constraints. Suppose you would like to add indexing or searching by key abilities to the linked list of Example D-3:

```
public class LinkedList<K,T>
{
   T Find(K key)
   {...}
   public T this[K key]
   {
      get
      {
         return Find(key);
      }
   }
}
```

This allows the client to write the following code:

```
LinkedList<int,string> list = new LinkedList<int,string>();

list.AddHead(123,"AAA");
list.AddHead(456,"BBB");
string item = list[456];
Debug.Assert(item == "BBB");
```

To implement the search, you need to scan the list, compare each node's key with the key you're looking for, and return the item of the node whose key matches. The problem is that the following implementation of Find( ) does not compile:

```
T Find(K key)
{
   Node<K,T> current = m_Head;
   while(current.NextNode != null)
   {
      if(current.Key == key) //Will not compile
      {
         break;
      }
      else

      {
         current = current.NextNode;
      }
   }
   return current.Item;
}
```

The compiler will refuse to compile this line:

```
if(current.Key == key)
```

because the compiler does not know whether K (or the actual type supplied by the client) supports the == operator. For example, structs do not provide such an implementation by default. You could try to overcome the == operator limitation by using the IComparable interface:

```
public interface IComparable
{
    int CompareTo(object obj);
}
```

CompareTo() returns 0 if the object you compare to is equal to the object implementing the interface, so the Find() method could use it as follows:

```
if(current.Key.CompareTo(key) == 0)
```

Unfortunately, however, this does not compile either, because the compiler has no way of knowing whether K (or the actual type supplied by the client) is derived from IComparable.

You could explicitly cast to IComparable to force the compiler to compile the comparing line, but you would do so at the expense of type safety:

```
if(((IComparable)(current.Key)).CompareTo(key) == 0)
```

If the type the client uses does not derive from IComparable, this will result in a runtime exception. In addition, when the key type used is a value type instead of the key type parameter, you force a boxing of the key, and that may have some performance implications.

Derivation Constraint

In C# 2.0, you use the where reserved keyword to define a constraint. Use the where keyword on the generic type parameter, followed by a derivation colon to indicate to the compiler that the generic type parameter implements a particular interface. For example, here is the derivation constraint required to implement the Find() method of LinkedList:

```
public class LinkedList<K,T> where K : IComparable
{
    T Find(K key)
    {
        Node<K,T> current = m_Head;
        while(current.NextNode != null)
        {
            if(current.Key.CompareTo(key) == 0)

            {
                break;
            }
```

```
        else
        {
            current = current.NextNode;
        }
    }
    return current.Item;
}
//Rest of the implementation
}
```

Note that even though the constraint allows you to use IComparable, it does not eliminate the boxing penalty when the key used is a value type, such as an integer. To
overcome this, the System namespace defines the generic interface IComparable<T>:

```
public interface IComparable<T>
{
    int CompareTo(T other);
}
```

You can constrain the key type parameter to support IComparable<T> with the key's
type as the type parameter, and by doing so you not only gain type safety but also
eliminate the boxing of value types when used as keys:

```
public class LinkedList<K,T> where K : IComparable<K>
{...}
```

In fact, all the types that supported IComparable in .NET 1.1 support IComparable<T>
in .NET 2.0. This enables you to use common types for keys, such as int, string,
Guid, DateTime, and so on. While IComparabl<T> is designed for sorting and ordering,
.NET also defines the IEquatable<T> that you can use just for comparing:

```
public interface IEquatable<T>
{
    bool Equals(T other);
}
```

In C# 2.0, all constraints must appear after the actual derivation list of the generic
class. For example, if LinkedList derives from the IEnumerable<T> interface (for itera-
tor support), you would put the where keyword immediately after it:

```
public class LinkedList<K,T> : IEnumerable<T> where K : IComparable<K>
{...}
```

When the client declares a variable of type LinkedList, providing a concrete type for
the list's key, the client-side compiler will insist that the key type is derived from
IComparable<T> (with the key's type as the type parameter) and will refuse to build
the client code otherwise.

You can constrain multiple interfaces on the same generic type parameter, separated
by a comma. For example:

```
public class LinkedList<K,T> where K : IComparable<K>,IConvertible
{...}
```

You can provide constraints for every generic type parameter your class uses:

```
public class LinkedList<K,T> where K : IComparable<K>
                             where T : ICloneable
{...}
```

You can also have a base-class constraint, stipulating that the generic type parameter is derived from a particular base class:

```
public class MyBaseClass
{...}
public class LinkedList<K,T> where K : MyBaseClass
{...}
```

However, you can only use at most one base class in a constraint, because C# does not support multiple inheritance of implementation. Obviously, the base class you constrain cannot be a sealed class, and the compiler enforces that. In addition, you cannot constrain System.Delegate or System.Array as a base class.

You can constrain both a base class and one or more interfaces, but the base class must appear first in the derivation constraint list:

```
public class LinkedList<K,T> where K : MyBaseClass, IComparable<K>
{...}
```

C# does allow you to specify a naked generic type parameter as a constraint:

```
public class LinkedList<T,U> where T : U
{...}
```

You can also use another generic type as a constraint:

```
public interface ISomeInterface<T>
{...}
public class LinkedList<K,T> where K : ISomeInterface<int>
{...}
```

When constraining another generic type as a base type, you can keep that type generic by specifying the generic type parameters of your own type parameter. For example, in the case of a generic base-class constraint:

```
public class MySubClass<T> where T : MyBaseClass<T>
{...}
```

Finally, note that when you provide a derivation constraint, the base type (interface or base class) you constrain must have consistent visibility with that of the generic type parameter you define. For instance, the following constraint is valid, because internal types can use public types:

```
public class MyBaseClass
{}
internal class MySubClass<T> where T : MyBaseClass
{}
```

However, if the visibility of the two classes were reversed, such as:

```
internal class MyBaseClass
{}
public class MySubClass<T> where T : MyBaseClass
{}
```

the compiler would issue an error—no client from outside the assembly will ever be able to use the generic type MySubClass, rendering MySubClass in effect an internal rather than a public type. (Outside clients cannot use MySubClass because to declare a variable of type MySubClass, they need to make use of a type that derives from the internal type MyBaseClass).

Constructor Constraint

Suppose you want to instantiate a new generic object inside a generic class. The problem is that the C# compiler does not know whether the specific type the client will use has a matching constructor, so it will refuse to compile the instantiation line. To address this problem, C# allows you to constrain a generic type parameter such that it must support a public default constructor. This is done using the new( ) constraint. For example, here is a different way of implementing the default constructor of the generic Node<K,T> from Example D-3:

```
class Node<K,T> where K : new( )
                where T : new( )
{
   public K Key;
   public T Item;
   public Node<K,T> NextNode;

   public Node( )
   {
      Key      = new K( );
      Item     = new T( );
      NextNode = null;
   }
   //Rest of the implementation
}
```

You can combine the constructor constraint with a derivation constraint, provided the constructor constraint appears last in the constraint list:

```
public class LinkedList<K,T> where K : IComparable<K>,new( )
                             where T : new( )
{...}
```

Class/Struct Type Constraint

You can constrain a generic type parameter to be a value type (such as an int, a bool, an enum, or any custom structure using the struct constraint):

```
public class MyClass<T> where T : struct
{...}
```

Similarly, you can constrain a generic type parameter to be a reference type (a class) using the class constraint:

```
public class MyClass<T> where T : class
{...}
```

The class/struct constraint cannot be used with base class constraint, because a base class constraint implies a class. Similarly, you cannot use the struct and the default constructor constraint, because default constructor constraint too implies a class. Though you can use the class and the default constructor constraint, it adds no value. You can combine the class/struct constraint with an interface constraint, as long as the class/struct type constraint appears first in the constraint list.

C# Coding Standard

A comprehensive coding standard is essential for a successful product delivery. The standard helps in enforcing best practices and avoiding pitfalls, and makes knowledge dissemination across the team easier. Traditionally, coding standards are thick, laborious documents, spanning hundreds of pages and detailing the rationale behind every directive. While these are still better than no standard at all, such efforts are usually indigestible by the average developer. In contrast, the C# coding standard presented in this appendix is very thin on the "why" and very detailed on the "what" and the "how." I believe that while fully *understanding* every insight that goes into a particular programming decision may require reading books such as this and even years of experience, applying the standard should not. When absorbing a new developer into your team, you should be able to simply point him or her at the standard and say: "Read this first." Being able to comply with a good standard should come before fully understanding and appreciating it—that should come over time, with experience. The coding standard presented next is based on this book, and it captures its best practices, dos and don'ts, helper classes, pitfalls, guidelines, and recommendations, as well as naming conventions and styles, project settings and structure, and framework-specific guidelines. Since I published this standard, it has become the de facto industry standard for C# and .NET development.

Naming Conventions and Styles

1. Use Pascal casing for type and method names and constants:

   ```
   public class SomeClass
   {
      const int DefaultSize = 100;
      public SomeMethod( )
      {}
   }
   ```

2. Use camel casing for local variable names and method arguments:

   ```
   int number;
   void MyMethod(int someNumber)
   {}
   ```

3. Prefix interface names with I:

```
interface IMyInterface
{..}
```

4. Prefix private member variables with m_.

5. Suffix custom attribute classes with Attribute.

6. Suffix custom exception classes with Exception.

7. Name methods using verb/object pairs, such as ShowDialog( ).

8. Methods with return values should have names describing the values returned, such as GetObjectState( ).

9. Use descriptive variable names.

    a. Avoid single-character variable names, such as i or t. Use index or temp instead.

    b. Avoid using Hungarian notation for public or protected members.

    c. Avoid abbreviating words (such as num instead of number).

10. Always use C# predefined types, rather than the aliases in the System namespace. For example:

```
object NOT Object
string NOT String
int    NOT Int32
```

11. With generics, use capital letters for types. Reserve suffixing Type for when dealing with the .NET type Type:

```
//Correct:
public class LinkedList<K,T>
{...}
//Avoid:
public class LinkedList<KeyType,DataType>
{...}
```

12. Use meaningful namespace names, such as the product name or the company name.

13. Avoid fully qualified type names. Use the using statement instead.

14. Avoid putting a using statement inside a namespace.

15. Group all framework namespaces together and put custom or third-party namespaces underneath:

```
using System;
using System.Collections.Generic;
using System.ComponentModel;
using System.Data;
using MyCompany;
using MyControls;
```

16. Use delegate inference instead of explicit delegate instantiation:
```
delegate void SomeDelegate();
public void SomeMethod()
{...}
SomeDelegate someDelegate = SomeMethod;
```
17. Maintain strict indentation. Do not use tabs or nonstandard indentation, such as one space. Recommended values are three or four spaces.
18. Indent comments at the same level of indentation as the code that you are documenting.
19. All comments should pass spellchecking. Misspelled comments indicate sloppy development.
20. All member variables should be declared at the top, with one line separating them from the properties or methods:
```
public class MyClass
{
    int m_Number;
    string m_Name;

    public void SomeMethod1()
    {}
    public void SomeMethod2()
    {}
}
```
21. Declare a local variable as close as possible to its first use.
22. A filename should reflect the class it contains.
23. When using partial types and allocating a part per file, name each file after the logical part that part plays. For example:
```
//In MyClass.cs
public partial class MyClass
{...}
//In MyClass.Designer.cs
public partial class MyClass
{...}
```
24. Always place an open curly brace ({) in a new line.
25. With anonymous methods, mimic the code layout of a regular method, aligned with the anonymous delegate declaration (this complies with placing an open curly brace in a new line):
```
delegate void SomeDelegate(string someString);
//Correct:
public void InvokeMethod()
{
    SomeDelegate someDelegate = delegate(string name)
                                {
                                    MessageBox.Show(name);
                                };
    someDelegate("Juval");
```

```
    }
    //Avoid
    public void InvokeMethod()
    {
        SomeDelegate someDelegate = delegate(string name){MessageBox.Show(name);};
        someDelegate("Juval");
    }
```

26. Use empty parentheses on parameter-less anonymous methods. Omit the parentheses only if the anonymous method could have been used on any delegate:

```
    delegate void SomeDelegate();
    //Correct
    SomeDelegate someDelegate1 = delegate()
                                {
                                    MessageBox.Show("Hello");
                                };
    //Avoid
    SomeDelegate someDelegate1 = delegate
                                {
                                    MessageBox.Show("Hello");
                                };
```

Coding Practices

1. Avoid putting multiple classes in a single file.

2. A single file should contribute types to only a single namespace. Avoid having multiple namespaces in the same file.

3. Avoid files with more than 500 lines (excluding machine-generated code).

4. Avoid methods with more than 25 lines.

5. Avoid methods with more than five arguments. Use structures for passing multiple arguments.

6. Lines should not exceed 80 characters.

7. Do not manually edit any machine-generated code.

   a. If modifying machine-generated code, modify the format and style to match this coding standard.

   b. Use partial classes whenever possible to factor out the maintained portions.

8. Avoid comments that explain the obvious. Code should be self-explanatory. Good code with readable variable and method names should not require comments.

9. Document only operational assumptions, algorithm insights, and so on.

10. Avoid method-level documentation.

    a. Use extensive external documentation for API documentation.

    b. Use method-level comments only as tool tips for other developers.

11. With the exception of zero and one, never hardcode a numeric value; always declare a constant instead.

12. Use the const directive only on natural constants, such as the number of days of the week.

13. Avoid using const on read-only variables. For that, use the readonly directive:

```
public class MyClass
{
   public const int DaysInWeek = 7;
   public readonly int Number;
   public MyClass(int someValue)
   {
      Number = someValue;
   }
}
```

14. Assert every assumption. On average, every fifth line is an assertion:

```
using System.Diagnostics;

object GetObject()
{...}

object someObject = GetObject();
Debug.Assert(someObject != null);
```

15. Every line of code should be walked through in a "white box" testing manner.

16. Catch only exceptions for which you have explicit handling.

17. In a catch statement that throws an exception, always throw the original exception (or another exception constructed from the original exception) to maintain the stack location of the original error:

```
catch(Exception exception)
{
   MessageBox.Show(exception.Message);
   throw; //Same as throw exception;
}
```

18. Avoid error code as method return values.

19. Avoid defining custom exception classes.

20. When defining custom exceptions:

    a. Derive the custom exception from Exception.

    b. Provide custom serialization.

21. Avoid multiple Main( ) methods in a single assembly.

22. Make only the most necessary types public; mark others as internal.

23. Avoid friend assemblies, as they increase interassembly coupling.

24. Avoid code that relies on an assembly running from a particular location.

25. Minimize code in application assemblies (i.e., EXE client assemblies). Use class libraries instead to contain business logic.

26. Avoid providing explicit values for enums:

```
//Correct
public enum Color
{
    Red,Green,Blue
}
//Avoid
public enum Color
{
    Red = 1,Green = 2,Blue = 3
}
```

27. Avoid specifying a type for an enum:

```
//Avoid
public enum Color : long
{
    Red,Green,Blue
}
```

28. Always use a curly brace scope in an if statement, even if it contains a single statement.

29. Avoid using the trinary conditional operator.

30. Avoid function calls in Boolean conditional statements. Assign into local variables and check on them:

```
bool IsEverythingOK( )
{...}
//Avoid:
if(IsEverythingOK( ))
{...}
//Correct:
bool ok = IsEverythingOK( );
if(ok)
{...}
```

31. Always use zero-based arrays.

32. Always explicitly initialize an array of reference types:

```
public class MyClass
{}
const int ArrraySize = 100;
MyClass[] array = new MyClass[ArrraySize];
for(int index = 0; index < array.Length; index++)
{
    array[index] = new MyClass();
}
```

33. Do not provide public or protected member variables. Use properties instead.

34. Avoid using the new inheritance qualifier. Use override instead.

35. Always mark public and protected methods as virtual in a non-sealed class.

36. Never use unsafe code, except when using interop.

37. Avoid explicit casting. Use the as operator to defensively cast to a type:

```
Dog dog = new GermanShepherd();
GermanShepherd shepherd = dog as GermanShepherd;
if(shepherd != null)
{...}
```

38. Always check a delegate for `null` before invoking it.

39. Do not provide public event member variables. Use event accessors instead.

40. Avoid defining event-handling delegates. Use `GenericEventHandler` instead.

41. Avoid raising events explicitly. Use `EventsHelper` to publish events defensively.

42. Always use interfaces.

43. Classes and interfaces should have at least a 2:1 ratio of methods to properties.

44. Avoid interfaces with one member.

45. Strive to have three to five members per interface.

46. Do not have more than 20 members per interface. The practical limit is probably 12.

47. Avoid events as interface members.

48. When using abstract classes, offer an interface as well.

49. Expose interfaces on class hierarchies.

50. Prefer using explicit interface implementation.

51. Never assume a type supports an interface. Defensively query for that interface:
```
SomeType obj1;
IMyInterface obj2;

/* Some code to initialize obj1, then: */
obj2 = obj1 as IMyInterface;
if(obj2 != null)
{
    obj2.Method1();
}
else
{
    //Handle error in expected interface
}
```

52. Never hardcode strings that will be presented to end users. Use resources instead.

53. Never hardcode strings that might change based on deployment, such as connection strings.

54. Use `String.Empty` instead of `""`:
```
//Avoid
string name = "";

//Correct
string name = String.Empty;
```

55. When building a long string, use `StringBuilder`, not string.

56. Avoid providing methods on structures.

    a. Parameterized constructors are encouraged.

    b. You can overload operators.

57. Always provide a static constructor when providing static member variables.

58. Do not use late-binding invocation when early binding is possible.

59. Use application logging and tracing.

60. Never use goto, except in a switch statement fall-through.

61. Always have a default case in a switch statement that asserts:

```
int number = SomeMethod();
switch(number)
{
    case 1:
        Trace.WriteLine("Case 1:");
        break;
    case 2:
        Trace.WriteLine("Case 2:");
        break;
    default:
        Debug.Assert(false);
        break;
}
```

62. Do not use the this reference unless invoking another constructor from within a constructor:

```
//Example of proper use of 'this'
public class MyClass
{
    public MyClass(string message)
    {}
    public MyClass() : this("Hello")
    {}
}
```

63. Do not use the base word to access base class members unless you wish to resolve a conflict with a subclass member of the same name or when invoking a base class constructor:

```
//Example of proper use of 'base'
public class Dog
{
    public Dog(string name)
    {}
    virtual public void Bark(int howLong)
    {}
}
public class GermanShepherd : Dog
{
    public GermanShepherd(string name) : base(name)
    {}
    override public void Bark(int howLong)
```

```
    {
        base.Bark(howLong);
    }
}
```

64. Do not use GC.AddMemoryPressure( ).

65. Do not rely on HandleCollector.

66. Implement Dispose( ) and Finalize( ) methods based on the template in Chapter 4.

67. Always run code unchecked by default (for the sake of performance), but explicitly in checked mode for overflow- or underflow-prone operations:

```
int CalcPower(int number,int power)
{
    int result = 1;
    for(int count = 1;count <= power;count++)
    {
        checked
        {
            result *= number;
        }
    }
    return result;
}
```

68. Avoid explicit code exclusion of method calls (#if...#endif). Use conditional methods instead:

```
public class MyClass
{
    [Conditional("MySpecialCondition")]
    public void MyMethod( )
    {}
}
```

69. Avoid casting to and from System.Object in code that uses generics. Use constraints or the as operator instead:

```
class SomeClass
{}
//Avoid:
class MyClass<T>
{
    void SomeMethod(T t)
    {
        object temp = t;
        SomeClass obj = (SomeClass)temp;
    }
}
//Correct:
class MyClass<T> where T : SomeClass
{
    void SomeMethod(T t)
    {
        SomeClass obj = t;
```

```
    }
}
```

70. Do not define constraints in generic interfaces. Interface-level constraints can often be replaced by strong typing:

```
public class Customer
{...}
//Avoid:
public interface IList<T> where T : Customer
{...}
//Correct:
public interface ICustomerList : IList<Customer>
{...}
```

71. Do not define method-specific constraints in interfaces.

72. If a class or a method offers both generic and non-generic flavors, always prefer using the generics flavor.

73. When implementing a generic interface that derived from an equivalent non-generic interface (such as IEnumerable<T>), use explicit interface implementation on all methods, and implement the non-generic methods by delegating to the generic ones:

```
class MyCollection<T> : IEnumerable<T>
{
    IEnumerator<T> IEnumerable<T>.GetEnumerator()
    {...}
    IEnumerator IEnumerable.GetEnumerator()
    {
        IEnumerable<T> enumerable = this;
        return enumerable.GetEnumerator();
    }
}
```

Project Settings and Project Structure

1. Always build your projects with Warning Level 4 (see Figure E-1).

2. Treat warnings as errors in the Release build (note that this is not the default of Visual Studio). Although it is optional, this standard recommends treating warnings as errors in Debug builds as well.

3. Avoid suppressing specific compiler warnings.

4. Always explicitly state your supported runtime versions in the application configuration file:

```
<?xml version="1.0"?>
<configuration>
   <startup>
      <supportedRuntime version="v2.0.5500.0"/>
      <supportedRuntime version="v1.1.5000.0"/>
   </startup>
</configuration>
```

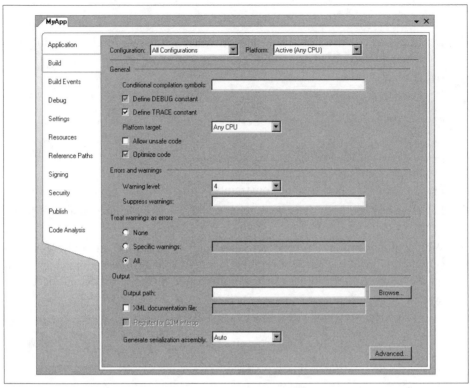

Figure E-1. The project Build pane

5. Avoid explicit custom version redirection and binding to CLR assemblies.

6. Avoid explicit preprocessor definitions (#define). Use the project settings for defining conditional compilation constants.

7. Do not put any logic inside *AssemblyInfo.cs*.

8. Do not put any assembly attributes in any file other than *AssemblyInfo.cs*.

9. Populate all fields in *AssemblyInfo.cs*, such as company name, description, and copyright notice.

10. All assembly references should use relative paths.

11. Disallow cyclic references between assemblies.

12. Avoid multi-module assemblies.

13. Avoid tampering with exception handling using the Exception window (Debug → Exceptions).

14. Strive to use uniform version numbers on all assemblies and clients in the same logical application (typically, a solution). Use the *SolutionInfo.cs* technique from Chapter 5 to automate.

15. Name your Visual Studio 2005 application configuration file *App.config*, and include it in the project.

16. Modify the Visual Studio 2005 default project structure to your project's standard layout, and apply a uniform structure for project folders and files.

17. A release build should contain debug symbols (see Figure E-2).

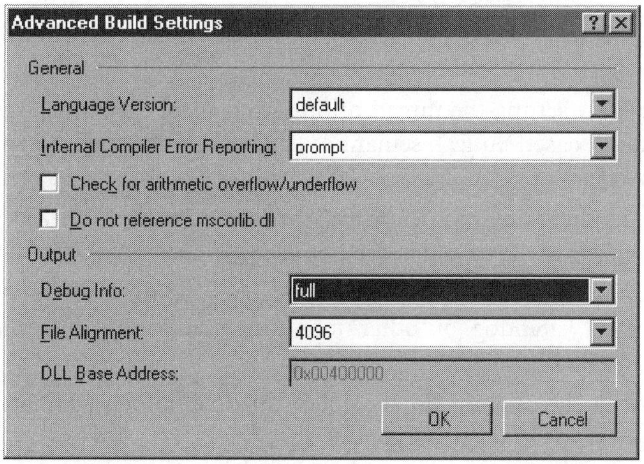

Figure E-2. The Advanced Build Settings dialog

18. Always sign your assemblies, including the client applications.

19. Use password-protected keys.

Framework-Specific Guidelines

Multithreading

1. Use synchronization domains. Avoid manual synchronization, because that often leads to deadlocks and race conditions.

2. Never call outside your synchronization domain.

3. Manage asynchronous call completion on a callback method. Do not wait, poll, or block for completion.

4. Always name your threads:

```
Thread currentThread = Thread.CurrentThread;
string threadName = "Main UI Thread";
currentThread.Name = threadName;
```

The name is traced in the debugger Threads window, making debug sessions more productive.

5. Do not call Suspend( ) or Resume( ) on a thread.

6. Do not call Thread.Sleep( ), except in the following conditions:

   a. Thread.Sleep(0) is an acceptable optimization technique to force a context switch.

   b. Thread.Sleep( ) is acceptable in testing or simulation code.

7. Do not call Thread.SpinWait( ).

8. Do not call Thread.Abort( ) to terminate threads. Use a synchronization object instead to signal the thread to terminate.

9. Avoid explicitly setting the thread priority to control execution. You can set the thread priority based on task semantics (such as ThreadPriority.BelowNormal for a screensaver).

10. Do not read the value of the ThreadState property. Use Thread.IsAlive( ) to determine whether the thread is dead or alive.

11. Do not rely on setting the thread type to background thread for application shutdown. Use a watchdog or other monitoring entity to deterministically kill threads.

12. Do not use the thread local storage unless thread affinity is guaranteed.

13. Do not call Thread.MemoryBarrier( ).

14. Never call Thread.Join( ) without checking that you are not joining your own thread:

```
void WaitForThreadToDie(Thread thread)
{
    Debug.Assert(Thread.CurrentThread.ManagedThreadId != thread.ManagedThreadId);
    thread.Join( );
}
```

15. Always use the lock( ) statement rather than explicit Monitor manipulation.

16. Always encapsulate the lock( ) statement inside the object it protects:

```
public class MyClass
{
    public void DoSomething( )
    {
        lock(this)
        {...}
    }
}
```

17. You can use synchronized methods instead of writing the lock( ) statement yourself.

18. Avoid fragmented locking.

19. Avoid using a Monitor to wait or pulse objects. Use manual or auto-reset events instead.

20. Do not use volatile variables. Lock your object or fields instead to guarantee deterministic and thread-safe access. Do not use `Thread.VolatileRead()`, `Thread.VolatileWrite()`, or the volatile modifier.

21. Avoid increasing the maximum number of threads in the thread pool.

22. Never stack `lock()` statements, because that does not provide atomic locking:

```
MyClass obj1 = new MyClass();
MyClass obj2 = new MyClass();
MyClass obj3 = new MyClass();

//Do not stack lock statements
lock(obj1)
lock(obj2)
lock(obj3)
{
    obj1.DoSomething();
    obj2.DoSomething();
    obj3.DoSomething();
}
```
Use `WaitHandle.WaitAll()` instead.

Serialization

1. Prefer the binary formatter.
2. Mark serialization event-handling methods as private.
3. Use the generic `IGenericFormatter` interface.
4. Always mark non-sealed classes as serializable.
5. When implementing `IDeserializationCallback` on a non-sealed class, make sure to do so in a way that allows subclasses to call the base class implementation of `OnDeserialization()`.
6. Always mark unserializable member variables as non-serializable.
7. Always mark delegates on a serialized class as non-serializable fields:

```
[Serializable]
public class MyClass
{
    [field:NonSerialized]
    public event EventHandler MyEvent;
}
```

Remoting

1. Prefer administrative configuration to programmatic configuration.
2. Always implement `IDisposable` on single-call objects.
3. Always prefer a TCP channel and a binary format when using remoting, unless a firewall is present.

4. Always provide a null lease for a singleton object:

```
public class MySingleton : MarshalByRefObject
{
   public override object InitializeLifetimeService()
   {
      return null;
   }
}
```

5. Always provide a sponsor for a client-activated object. The sponsor should return the initial lease time.

6. Always unregister the sponsor on client application shutdown.

7. Always put remote objects in class libraries.

8. Avoid using *SoapSuds.exe*.

9. Avoid hosting in IIS.

10. Avoid using uni-directional channels.

11. Always load a remoting configuration file in Main( ), even if the file is empty and the application does not use remoting:

```
static void Main()
{
   RemotingConfigurationEx.Configure();
   /* Rest of Main()  */
}
```

12. Avoid using Activator.GetObject( ) and Activator.CreateInstance( ) for remote object activation. Use new instead.

13. Always register port 0 on the client side, to allow callbacks.

14. Always elevate type filtering to Full on both client and host, to allow callbacks.

Security

1. Always demand your own strong name on assemblies and components that are private to the application, but are public (so that only you can use them):

```
public class PublicKeys
{
   public const string MyCompany = "1234567894800000940000000602000000240000"+
                                    "52534131000400000100010007D1FA57C4AED9F0"+
                                    "A32E84AA0FAEFD0DE9E8FD6AEC8F87FB03766C83"+
                                    "4C99921EB23BE79AD9D5DCC1DD9AD23613210290"+
                                    "0B723CF980957FC4E177108FC607774F29E8320E"+
                                    "92EA05ECE4E821C0A5EFE8F1645C4C0C93C1AB99"+
                                    "285D622CAA652C1DFAD63D745D6F2DE5F17E5EAF"+
                                    "0FC4963D261C8A12436518206DC093344D5AD293";
}
[StrongNameIdentityPermission(SecurityAction.LinkDemand,
                    PublicKey = PublicKeys.MyCompany)]
public class MyClass
{...}
```

2. Apply encryption and security protection on application configuration files.

3. When importing an interop method, assert unmanaged code permission and demand appropriate permission instead:

```
[DllImport("user32",EntryPoint="MessageBoxA")]
private static extern int Show(IntPtr handle,string text,string caption,
                                                        int msgType);
[SecurityPermission(SecurityAction.Assert,UnmanagedCode = true)]
[UIPermission(SecurityAction.Demand,
                        Window = UIPermissionWindow.SafeTopLevelWindows)]
public static void Show(string text,string caption)
{
    Show(IntPtr.Zero,text,caption,0);
}
```

4. Do not suppress unmanaged code access via the SuppressUnmanagedCodeSecurity attribute.

5. Do not use the /unsafe switch of *TlbImp.exe*. Wrap the RCW in managed code so that you can assert and demand permissions declaratively on the wrapper.

6. On server machines, deploy a code access security policy that grants only Microsoft, ECMA, and self (identified by a strong name) full trust. Code originating from anywhere else is implicitly granted nothing.

7. On client machines, deploy a security policy that grants client application only the permissions to execute, to call back the server, and to potentially display user interface. When not using ClickOnce, client application should be identified by a strong name in the code groups.

8. To counter a luring attack, always refuse at the assembly level all permissions not required to perform the task at hand:

```
[assembly:UIPermission(SecurityAction.RequestRefuse,
                    Window=UIPermissionWindow.AllWindows)]
```

9. Always set the principal policy in every Main( ) method to Windows:

```
public class MyClass
{
    static void Main( )
    {
        AppDomain currentDomain = AppDomain.CurrentDomain;
        currentDomain.SetPrincipalPolicy(PrincipalPolicy.WindowsPrincipal);
    }
    //other methods
}
```

10. Never assert a permission without demanding a different permission in its place.

Index

We'd like to hear your suggestions for improving our indexes. Send email to *index@oreilly.com*.

589

execution contexts
  default context for app domains, 402
  marshaling calls across, 37
  (see also contexts)
Execution permission set, 437, 440
execution scope, contexts and, 399
execution states of a thread
        (ThreadState), 197
Exit( ) (Monitor), 224
expired time (leases), 384
explicit casts, 53
  as operator, using, 55
  defining and using multiple interfaces, 54
  IDisposable interface, 95
explicit garbage collection, 86
explicit interface implementation, 50–52
  combining with class hierarchy, 63
  generic interfaces, 66
exporting security policies, 470
expression evaluation, design-time, 34
extending component-oriented
        applications, 5
extracting an interface
  from class implementation, 79
  from the definition of another, 81

F

factoring interfaces, 73–75
  metrics, 75–77
fault isolation, multiple processes and, 320
FieldInfo class
  GetValue( ), 318
  IsNotSerialized property, 317
  SetValue( ), 318
fields
  serialization, capturing from all levels of
        class hierarchy, 316
  volatile, 276
File Explorer, adding/removing assemblies in
        GAC, 114
file I/O permissions, 455
  demanding permission, 473–475
  denying/permitting with stack walk
        modifiers, 477
  LocalIntranet permission set, lacking
        in, 452
file stream
  appending state of additional objects
        to, 304
  binary serialization of, 286
  serialization with SOAP formatter, 287
FileIOPermission class, 472

FileLoadException class, 296
FileStream class, 480
FileStreamClient class (example),
        asynchronous read, 170
finalization, object, 86–90
  deterministic, 90–101
    Dispose( ) pattern, 91
    Dispose( ), with error handling, 93–97
    IDisposable pattern, 92
    open/close pattern, 91
  Dispose( ) and Finalize( ), using, 97–101
  explicit garbage collection, 86
  Finalize( ), implementation, 88–90
finalization queue, 86
Finalize( ), 86
  implementation of, 88–90
  singleton objects, use with, 341
  using with Dispose( ), 97–101
Fire( ) (EventsHelper), 144
  type safety, 146
fire-and-forget methods
  designating with OneWay attribute, 375
FireAsync( ) (EventsHelper), 175, 176
FireEvent( ), 153
firewalls, transport channels and serialization
        formats, 345
firing an event, 130, 174
  asynchronously, 175
  example, 131
  in Visual Basic 2005, 135
Flags attribute, 152, 548
foreground threads, 198
FormatterAssemblyStyle class, 297
formatters, 285–291, 344
  binary formatter, 286
  channels and, 351, 364
  defined, 285
  generic formatter, 288–290
  message serialization, 405
  security and, 508–510
  serialization and versioning, 296–298
  SOAP formatter, 287
  transport channels and, 345
  XML serialization, 289
  (see also serialization)
forms
  displaying with Application.Run( ), 355
  (see also Windows Forms)
fragmented locking, 221
FreeNamedDataSlot( ) (Thread), 255
free-threaded marshaler (FTM), 404
Freeze( ), 414

P

packaging
  client code, 2
  DLLs and COM components, 22
  .NET assemblies as basic unit, 23
parameter of type object, 138
params modifier, 145, 176
partial types, 26
  interfaces and, 57
partially trusted callers, adding to
       assemblies, 507
partial-trust debugging, 33, 494, 496
paths (references added to
       assemblies), 29–31
performance
  explicit garbage collection, costs of, 86
  JIT compilation and, 17
  multiple processes, overhead of, 321
  native image compilation and, 18
  transport channels and serialization
       formats, 345
permission classes, 472–475
  CodeAccessPermission class, derivation
       from, 476
  custom, 476
  demand for permission, 473–475
  interactions among permissions, 475
  IPermission interface, implementation
       of, 473
  ISecurityEncodable interface and, 473
  IStackWalk interface, implementation
       of, 476
permission sets, 449
  assigning different to a zone, 466
  attributes, 491
  binding with a particular evidence, 446
  classes, 488–491
  configuring for custom code groups, 459
  creating, 455
  custom, 454–457
  FullTrust, 451
  LocalIntranet, 452
  Nothing, 453
permissions, 435–437, 448
  AspNetLoginControl, 534
  assembly-wide, 494
  asserting with stack walk modifier, 478
    unmanaged code access
       permissions, 480–483

attributes, 483
  choice actions, 485
  inheritance demand, 487
  link-time demands, 485
ClickOnce applications, 494
for code, 14
configuring, 449–472
  ClickOnce applications, 461–463
  custom code groups, 457
  custom permission sets, 454–457
  custom security policies, 464–465
  .NET default configuration, 451–454
  security administration
       utilities, 466–471
  security infrastructure benefits, 472
custom, MSDN information on, 453
denying/permitting with stack walk
       modifier, 477
DistributedTransaction, 510
evaluating for an assembly, 468
identity, 487
.NET programming languages, CLR
       and, 18
permission sets, 437–441
permission types, listed, 436
required
  calculating, 496
  listing by IntelliSense, 497
security permission type, 435
trusted assemblies, 469
type and scope, 435
underlying Windows or resource security
       permissions, 436
to use unsafe code, 507
WSLoginControl, 538
PermissionSetAttribute class, 491
PermissionSetCollection class, 489
  using (example), 490
PermissionType property
       (SecurityException), 448
PermitOnly( ) (IStackWalk), 476, 477
persistence (see serialization)
.pfx (Personal Information Exchange)
       files, 110
physical thread affinity, 255
P-Invoke (platform-specific invocation
       mechanism), 480
platforms, portability of .NET on, 17
pointers, 507
Policy Assemblies folders, 476
policy levels (security), 447

PolicyException class, 505
poll time property (lease manager), 384
polling for asynchronous method
  completion, 165
polymorphism, 3
 class hierarchies and interfaces, 60
pooling objects in .NET component
  services, 402
ports
 channels and, 350
 registering for sponsors, 389
 for remote callbacks, 371
 URL information on, 346
preemptive thread scheduling, 199
principal object, 501
principal policy, 500
principal-based security, 498–505
 authentication and, 501
 custom security principal, 504
 declarative, 498–501
 enabling, 500
 GenericPrincipal class, 505
 programmatic, 501–503
 WindowsPrincipal class, 503
PrincipalPermissionAttribute class, 498–499
PrincipalPolicy enum type, 500
priority inversion (threads), 200
priority, thread, 199–200
 tinkering with, problems caused by, 199
private assemblies, 105
 avoiding mixing with shared, 106
 shared assemblies vs., 107
 strong names, 112
private class members, xvi
private fields, capturing for serialization, 316
private keys, 107
 handling for large organizations, 110
 protecting with password, 110
processes, 320
 penalties for using multiple, 321
 physical, app domains vs., 320–321
programmatic security
 declarative security vs., 484
 identity permissions, 487
 public fields and, 488
 role-based, 501–503
  verifying role membership, 502
 (see also security, programmatic)
programming languages
 CLR (Common Language
  Runtime), 15–21
 .NET, 13, 17

ProgressChanged delegate, 266
projects (C#), 581–583
properties
 interface, 56
  ration of methods to, 76
 lease, 384–385
 lease manager, 384
 managed-code, associated with
  threads, 186
 ThreadState, 197
protected internal access modifier, 36
proxies
 client access to context-bound
  object, 404
 client-side processing, use in, 343
 context and object types, 400
 defined, 323
 exceptions, throwing, 347
 ICalculator implementations, 519
 marshaling, use in, 38
 remote object access, 328
 same-context calls, 408
 SimpleCalculator class (example), 513
 transparent and real, 405
proxy classes, web service, 267–270
public access modifier, interfaces, 48
public class member variables, exposing
  directly, 218
public components, 36
public fields, security and, 488
public keys, 107
 delay signing, 110
public member variables and properties, xvi
publisher certificates (Trusted Publishers
  list), 462
Publisher evidence, 445
PublisherIdentityPermission class, 487
publishers (event), 130
 generic handling of subscriber
  connections, 152–154
 hooking to subscribers, 148
 loose coupling with subscribers, 136
 remote callback example, 375
 unhandled exceptions propagated from
  subscriber, 143
 using asynchronous event publishing, 174
 using synchronous event publishing, 173
publishing events defensively, 143–148
Pulse( ) (Monitor), 224
PulseAll( ) (Monitor), 224

user-oriented security model, 434
using statements, xvii, 93–97
  aliasing particular combination of specific
     names, 143
  generics and, 96
  interfaces and, 94–96

V

verifiable code, 440
verification of code, skipping, 441
verified certificates, 463
Version class, 105
version control, 14
version numbers, solution-wide, 111
VersionAdded field, 300
versioning, 10, 102–128
  assemblies as basic unit, 23
  assembly deployment models, 105
  assembly manifests and, 39
  assembly version numbers, 102–105
  class library components, 41
  ClickOnce applications, security and, 462
  CLR, 125–128
    side-by-side execution, 125
    specifying CLR version, 127–128
    version unification, 126
  custom version policy, 119–125
    application custom policies, 120–124
    global custom policies, 124
  DLL Hell and, 11
  DLLs, 22
  serialization and, 296–298
  serialization events and
    type-version tolerance, 298
  strong assembly names, 107–117
    friend assemblies, 113
    installing shared assembly, 114–117
    private assemblies, 112
    signing your assembly, 108–112
  Visual Studio 2005, 117–119
visibility modifiers
  component, 35
  interfaces, 48
Visual Basic
  choosing between C# and, 19
  My object, 19
Visual Basic 2005
  events, 135
  interface (reserved word), 46
Visual Basic.NET, 16
Visual C# 2005 (see C#)
Visual Studio 2005, 13

assemblies and, 25–34
assembly host, 33
assembly information files, 39
assembly version number, automating
    parts, 104
automating system service
    development, 380
breakpoint filters, 187
built-in Designer support for Windows
    Forms Timer, 276
Class Library project, 25
CLR version 2.0, 128
CLR-compliant languages, 16, 19
configuration files, 361
interface-based web service,
    creating, 515–517
interfaces, 77–81
  refactoring, 79–81
metadata, uses of, 38
multi-module assemblies, 23
security, 494–498
  calculating required permissions, 496
  ClickOnce permissions, 494
  partial-trust debugging, 496
versioning, 117–119
  specific reference version, 118
void return type
  for event delegates, 137
volatile fields, 276
VolatileRead( ) (Thread), 277
VolatileWrite( ) (Thread), 277

W

Wait( )
  Monitor class, 223, 224
  Rendezvous class, 237
  WorkerThread class, 247
wait queue, 224
waitable events, 232–237
  monitors vs., 235
WaitAll( ) (WaitHandle), 166, 226
WaitAny( ) (WaitHandle), 166, 226
WaitCallback delegate, 256
WaitForMultipleObjects( ), 279
WaitHandle class, 164, 225–227
  apartment threading models and, 279
  ManualResetEvent class, 232
  Monitor vs., 227
  Mutex class derived from, 227
  Semaphore class derived from, 238
  SignalAndWait( ), 237
  signal-and-wait methods, 227

About the Author

Juval Löwy is a software architect and the principal of IDesign, a company specializing in .NET architecture consulting and advanced .NET training. He is Microsoft's Regional Director for the Silicon Valley, working with Microsoft to help the industry adopt .NET. Juval participates in the Microsoft internal design review for future versions of .NET and related technologies. He has published numerous articles on almost every aspect of .NET development and is a frequent presenter at development conferences. Microsoft recognized Juval as a Software Legend—one of the world's top .NET experts and industry leaders. You can contact him at *www.idesign.net*.

Colophon

Our look is the result of reader comments, our own experimentation, and feedback from distribution channels. Distinctive covers complement our distinctive approach to technical topics, breathing personality and life into potentially dry subjects.

The animal on the cover of *Programming .NET Components*, Second Edition, is a land hermit crab (*Coenobita clypeatus*). Land hermit crabs are found in tropical areas of the Indo-region, the western Atlantic, and the western Caribbean. They live close to the shoreline and must have access to land and water.

The front half of a hermit crab is covered with a hard exoskeleton. The long abdomen has a softer exoskeleton that can adjust to fit into a spiraled shell. The large left claw is used for defense, for holding onto tree limbs, and for balance. The smaller right claw and the next pair of appendages are used for collecting and passing food and water to the mouth. Hermit crabs have stalked eyes with acute vision and two pairs of antennae. The longer pair of antennae is used for feeling, the shorter for smelling and tasting.

The land hermit crab doesn't have a hard shell of its own; it uses old empty shells to protect its soft body. As it grows in size, the hermit crab must find a larger shell. When danger threatens, it hides in the shell and closes the entrance with its hard claw. Hermit crabs are omnivores and scavengers. They eat worms, plankton, and organic debris.

Although land-based, these crabs must return to the sea to breed. Both males and females partially emerge from their shells to mate. The female lays her hundreds of eggs inside the borrowed shell. These eggs are safe and damp in the shell but, when they hatch, they must be released in the sea. The young are in danger until they find a shell of their own. When they reach adulthood, the crabs migrate to begin their terrestrial life. Land hermit crabs live about 10 years.

Sarah Sherman was the production editor for *Programming .NET Components*, Second Edition. Rachel Wheeler was the copyeditor, and Sada Preisch proofread the book. Jamie Peppard and Mary Anne Weeks Mayo provided quality control. Abby Fox provided production assistance. Ellen Troutman Zaig wrote the index.

Ellie Volckhausen designed the cover of this book, based on a series design by Edie Freedman. The cover image is a 19th-century engraving from the Dover Pictorial Archive. Karen Montgomery produced the cover layout with Adobe InDesign CS using Adobe's ITC Garamond font.

David Futato designed the interior layout. This book was converted by Keith Fahlgren to FrameMaker 5.5.6 with a format conversion tool created by Erik Ray, Jason McIntosh, Neil Walls, and Mike Sierra that uses Perl and XML technologies. The text font is Linotype Birka; the heading font is Adobe Myriad Condensed; and the code font is LucasFont's TheSans Mono Condensed. The illustrations that appear in the book were produced by Robert Romano, Jessamyn Read, and Lesley Borash using Macromedia FreeHand MX and Adobe Photoshop CS. The tip and warning icons were drawn by Christopher Bing. This colophon was compiled by Mary Anne Weeks Mayo.

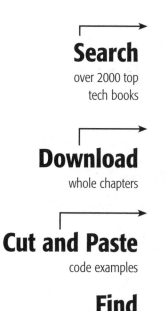
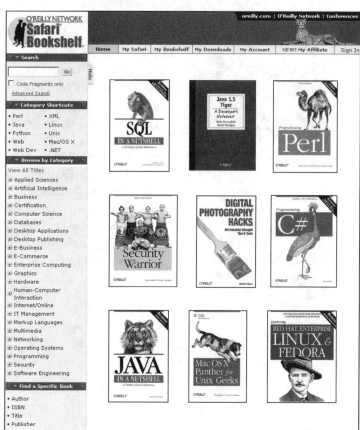

Related Titles Available from O'Reilly

O'REILLY®

Our books are available at most retail and online bookstores.
To order direct: 1-800-998-9938 • *order@oreilly.com* • *www.oreilly.com*
Online editions of most O'Reilly titles are available by subscription at *safari.oreilly.com*

Keep in touch with O'Reilly

1. Download examples from our books

To find example files for a book, go to:

www.oreilly.com/catalog

select the book, and follow the "Examples" link.

2. Register your O'Reilly books

Register your book at *register.oreilly.com*

Why register your books?
Once you've registered your O'Reilly books you can:

- Win O'Reilly books, T-shirts or discount coupons in our monthly drawing.
- Get special offers available only to registered O'Reilly customers.
- Get catalogs announcing new books (US and UK only).
- Get email notification of new editions of the O'Reilly books you own.

3. Join our email lists

Sign up to get topic-specific email announcements of new books and conferences, special offers, and O'Reilly Network technology newsletters at:

elists.oreilly.com

It's easy to customize your free elists subscription so you'll get exactly the O'Reilly news you want.

4. Get the latest news, tips, and tools

www.oreilly.com

- "Top 100 Sites on the Web"—PC Magazine
- CIO Magazine's Web Business 50 Awards

Our web site contains a library of comprehensive product information (including book excerpts and tables of contents), downloadable software, background articles, interviews with technology leaders, links to relevant sites, book cover art, and more.

5. Work for O'Reilly

Check out our web site for current employment opportunities:

jobs.oreilly.com

6. Contact us

O'Reilly Media
1005 Gravenstein Hwy North
Sebastopol, CA 95472 USA

TEL: 707-827-7000 or 800-998-9938
(6am to 5pm PST)

FAX: 707-829-0104

order@oreilly.com
For answers to problems regarding your order or our products. To place a book order online, visit:

www.oreilly.com/order_new

catalog@oreilly.com
To request a copy of our latest catalog.

booktech@oreilly.com
For book content technical questions or corrections.

corporate@oreilly.com
For educational, library, government, and corporate sales.

proposals@oreilly.com
To submit new book proposals to our editors and product managers.

international@oreilly.com
For information about our international distributors or translation queries. For a list of our distributors outside of North America check out:

international.oreilly.com/distributors.html

adoption@oreilly.com
For information about academic use of O'Reilly books, visit:

academic.oreilly.com

O'REILLY®

Our books are available at most retail and online bookstores.
To order direct: 1-800-998-9938 • *order@oreilly.com* • *www.oreilly.com*
Online editions of most O'Reilly titles are available by subscription at *safari.oreilly.com*